TEXT BOOK

An Introduction to
Literary Language

SECOND EDITION

TEXT BOOK

An Introduction to Literary Language

SECOND EDITION

Robert Scholes
Brown University

Nancy R. Comley
Queens College, CUNY

Gregory L. Ulmer
University of Florida

St. Martin's Press
New York

Editor: Nancy Lyman
Development editor: Edward Hutchinson
Managing editor: Patricia Mansfield-Phelan
Project editor: Nicholas Webb
Production supervisor: Joe Ford
Art director: Sheree Goodman
Cover design: Rod Hernandez

Library of Congress Catalog Card Number: 94-65189

Manufactured in the United States of America.

9 8 7 6 5
f e d c b a

For information, write:
St. Martin's Press, Inc.
175 Fifth Avenue
New York, NY 10010

ISBN: 0-312-04837-8

Acknowledgments
Acknowledgments and copyrights can be found at the back of the book on pages 308–11, which constitute an extension of the copyright page.

Preface to the New and Improved Second Edition

To the Instructor

The title of this textbook is not a joke. It is meant to signify our intention to offer an alternative approach to the traditional course called "Writing about Literature" or "Introduction to Literature." By substituting the concept of *text* for the traditional concept of *literature,* we accomplish a number of things. We allow for the presentation of a wider range of material and a broader spectrum of approaches to literary study. And we close or reduce the gaps that have separated reading from writing, creative from critical work, and literature from ordinary language.

In this book the traditional literary genres have their places. We attend to narrative, dramatic, and poetic texts—but not in isolation from explanatory, meditative, and persuasive texts. We discuss reading and interpretation, but we do not restrict ourselves to those modes of study. Our aim is to help students to feel at home in the universe of textuality: to understand the workings of power and pleasure in all kinds of texts.

We begin with the simplest and most accessible materials and concepts, working from story and scene through metaphor, intertextuality, and experiment. We introduce concepts from linguistics and literary theory at appropriate points. But this is not a book *about* literature; it is a text for working *with* literature. Textual interaction is the guiding principle throughout. At any point, including, of course, the end, the teacher may profitably bring in supplementary material. This is an inclusive, not an exclusive, approach. It is, however, presented in a highly developmental manner. Later sections assume the mastery of concepts and techniques stressed in the earlier sections. We guarantee that students using this book will have interesting discussions and will produce interesting texts themselves. And that is what it is all about.

New to This Edition

Among the many comments we have received on *Text Book,* a general consensus has prevailed that the material brought together in the first edition worked well but the text might be fruitfully expanded in new directions. Consequently, this second edition encompasses new and, we believe, exciting material while keeping changes in the retained selections to a minimum.

The most significant expansion, of course, is the addition of an entirely new Chapter 5, "Experiments with Texts: Text and Research." This chapter summarizes and synthesizes the principal lessons of the first four chapters while breaking new ground of its own by developing a textualist approach to the researched essay, to be (provisionally) realized here in a new genre of research writing we have called the "mystory." Textualist research and writing is distinguished from conventional scholarship by its exploration of a personal (ideological) relationship to the object of study. Textualism puts the traditional practice of literary study into the frame provided by Nietzsche, who challenged authors not to be satisfied with either biography or bibliography, but to find that secret point at which the anecdote of life and the aphorism of thought amount to the same thing. Using the experimental method of "mystory" suggested by the readings, students discover how to experience the methods of scholarship as a kind of personal memory.

Another significant addition appears in Chapter 3 with a new section called "Identifying with Texts," which asks students to consider the relation of identity formation to texts from popular culture. This section, along with Chapter 5, redresses the one blind spot most often noted by users and reviewers of the first edition by bringing a new, explicitly cultural and ideological dimension to *Text Book*'s treatment of textuality.

Finally, we have chosen some new readings throughout the text wherever our discussion seemed in need of stronger illumination.

Acknowledgments

We would like once again to thank Tom Broadbent and Nancy Perry, the first for originally envisioning this project and the second for seeing it through its first edition. Thanks also to the staff at St. Martin's Press, especially Edward Hutchinson and Nicholas Webb, and to Robyn Feller for their work on this new and improved second edition.

We would like to thank the instructors at the University of Tennessee at Knoxville and our colleagues at Queens College, CUNY, the University of Florida at Gainesville, and Brown University who have used *Text Book* and given us useful feedback. The following instructors took time to give detailed written comments on *Text Book,* and we are very grateful to them: David Adams, Queens College, CUNY; Marianne Ahokus, University of Minnesota; Doree Allen, Stanford University; Robin Avner, Johns Hopkins University; Michael Bechler, Montana State University; Gwen Bindas, Northeastern University; Richard Boyd, University of California at Riverside; Anne Boyle, Wake Forest University; Louis Burkhardt, University of Colorado; Terry Caesar, Clarion University; Thomas Couser, Hofstra University; Patricia Craddock, University of Florida at Gainesville; Sandra Donaldson, University of North Dakota; Mary Dunlop, Iowa State University; Irene Fairley, Northeastern

University; Clayton Hudnall, University of Hartford; Michael Jarrett, Pennsylvania State University, York Campus; Kenneth R. Johnston, Indiana University; James Kissane, Grinnell College; Pamela Koehlinger, Indiana University; Melissa Kort, Santa Rosa Junior College; Kathleen Krager, Walsh College; Marilyn Krysl, University of Colorado; Zoran Kuzmanovich, Davidson College; Paulino Lim, California State University at Long Beach; J. Livingstone-Webber, Western Illinois University; Nancy McLelland, Mendocino College; Eric Mendelsohn, Queens College, CUNY; Jonathan Middlebrook, San Francisco State University; A. L. Mitch, Bethany College; Anthony O'Brien, Queens College, CUNY; Stanley Oropesa, East Los Angeles College; Patrick Pacheco, Santa Rosa Junior College; Steven Reese, Youngstown State University; Robin Roberts, Louisiana State University; Epifanio San Juan, University of Connecticut; Jo C. Searles, Pennsylvania State University, Altoona Campus; Michael Sexson, Montana State University; Robert Smart, Bradford College; Ann Spector, Fairfield University; Linda Strahan, University of California at Riverside; Michele Thomas, Indiana University; Sheryl Thompson, California State University at Northridge; Samuel Umland, Kearney State College; Paula M. Uruburu, Hofstra University; Sara Varhus, SUNY College at Oswego; Ulrich Wicks, University of Maine.

Robert Scholes
Nancy R. Comley
Gregory L. Ulmer

Contents

A Letter to the Student

You may, of course, have read our preface to this edition, or reviewed the table of contents, or even skimmed through a reading selection. Nevertheless, in these few paragraphs we will assume that you have just opened this book for the first time and want to know why you are using this book of all books, and what you may get out of using it. We consider these fair questions and will try to answer them fairly, but first we must warn you that verbal education is a lot like physical education. You build your mind in the same way you build your body: through your own efforts. We can provide the most interesting and useful material for you to work on, based on the most recent information about language and literature, but the benefits to you will depend on your own efforts, "No pain, no gain," as the iron pumpers say.

Our goal is to help you to a better mastery of your verbal environment. We all live in a world that constantly bombards us with texts. To survive—and above all to do more than just survive: to flourish—we need to deal with all kinds of texts confidently. This book is called *Text Book* because it offers an entrance into the world of textuality: to the higher and more developed forms of reading and writing.

As you enter this book you will find all kinds of texts: some are usually called "literary" and some are not. This mixture is essential to our method. We do *not* want to offer you a collection of "master" works that ask for your passive submission, but a set of texts that you can work and play with, increasing your own understanding of fundamental textual processes and your own ability to use the written word. We hope to help you feel more at home in the house of language, and we are confident that a better command of written language will contribute to a better life. That is saying a lot, we realize, but we want you to know that, though this book is often playful, we are serious about its purpose. It is different from other books, and that has made it harder to write—and more fun. We have worked on it for years, trying to make it as effective and attractive as we could.

Come on in and see for yourself.

Sincerely,

Robert Scholes
Nancy R. Comley
Gregory L. Ulmer

TEXT BOOK

An Introduction to
Literary Language

SECOND EDITION

Chapter 1
Texts and People

In this chapter we will explore the ways in which people and their actions get into texts. Human events can be recounted (narrative) or enacted (drama), but either way they become *textualized,* taking on a certain formal structure that is found in much the same form in every culture: the structure of stories, which extends from personal anecdotes to literary novels and plays. That this should be the case is interesting in itself, but even more interesting is the way this formal structure returns into our lives, shaping our thoughts and actions. If you have ever found yourself wondering how something that was happening to you would sound in the telling, you know what we mean. If you have ever wondered how some experience in your life would "come out," you were applying a concept from storytelling to the interpretation of your own experience, even as it was happening: because experience does not "come out"—it just goes on and on.

The point of all this is that texts and life exist in a very complex relationship. Our thinking and even our feeling are shaped by texts in ways that we are dimly aware of in our normal day-to-day existence. We all use narrative structures and dramatic devices every day in our thoughts and in our actions—living out stories, playing roles, recounting events, enacting gestures and deeds. To learn more about how narrative and dramatic texts work, then, is to be a little more conscious of our own situations, a little more in control of our own lives.

The reading, discussion, and writing opportunities presented in this chapter are designed to help you strengthen your command of narrative and dramatic processes, building on the awareness you already have—having come this far in life—of narrative and dramatic forms. We will present you with some texts designed to reveal connections between these "literary" forms and ordinary life, and with some opportunities to move back and forth between the forms, developing your awareness and mastery of textual processes.

Story and Storyteller

Natural Narrative

Mary Louise Pratt

We think of literature as something special, as something above or beyond the way we use language in our daily lives—and so, in certain respects, it is. Literature is language used with special care and precision, or special energy and imagination. But the forms taken by literary works, and even the language used by poets and playwrights, are based on forms and ways of speaking that we all use, all the time. Literature is different from other uses of language, but it is also the same; it overlaps ordinary speech. Most approaches to the study of literature emphasize the differences, concentrating on the unique powers of literature. Without denying that these powers exist, we are taking the opposite tack in this book. We are going to emphasize the continuities, showing how literary forms and uses of language are connected to the ways that we use language on ordinary occasions. The point of doing it this way is to show that the passage from ordinary language to literature can be negotiated by any of us. It is not some impassable abyss that only a genius can leap across. It is a craft, a skill, that will benefit from study, effort, and practice. Our presentation begins with the anecdote, a basic form of storytelling that links the personal narratives we tell one another with the literary narratives produced by professional writers.

A few years ago Mary Louise Pratt, a literary critic, discovered that the great novels of world literature were similar in their structure to the personal narratives exchanged among people with very little formal education. She based her discovery on studies of inner-city speech by the sociolinguist William Labov. In the following selection we have reprinted a section of the second chapter of her book, A Speech-Act Theory of Literary Discourse, *in which she presents Labov's work and discusses its significance.*

For our purposes, the most important thing to learn from Pratt is the six-part structure of the ordinary personal narrative. You will find versions of this structure—or interesting deviations from it—in every kind of text that presents a story.

Much of Labov's research over the past ten years has been devoted to documenting dialect variations in American English and above all to exploring the ways in which those divisions reflect and reinforce a speaker's place in the class hierarchy of the larger speech community. He has concentrated especially on those dialects of American English considered by most Americans 1 to be not only nonstandard but also substandard. In his first book, *The Social Stratification of English in New York City* (1966), Labov showed that phonological variation in the speech of New Yorkers could not be systematically specified independently of the social pressures acting on the speakers in the given speech situation. This was an important realization for linguistics since it provided support for building information about social context into the grammar.

Labov's interest in oral narrative stems mainly from a study of Black 2
English Vernacular (BEV), "that relatively uniform dialect spoken by the majority of black youth in most parts of the United States today, especially in the inner city areas" (Labov, 1972:xiii). The project, which resulted in the volume of essays titled *Language in the Inner City* (1972), was originally undertaken to find out whether dialect differences had anything to do with the consistent reading problems of inner city black children. It was conducted in Harlem. As he analyzed the phonological and grammatical differences between BEV and Standard English, Labov made an important observation:

> The major reading problems did not stem from structural interference in any simple sense. . . . The major causes of reading failure are political and cultural conflicts in the classroom, and dialect differences are important because they are symbols of this conflict. We must then understand the way in which the vernacular culture uses language and how verbal skills develop in this culture. (Labov, 1972:xiv)

BEV speakers had trouble reading not because they lacked verbal skills (the contrary proved to be the case) but because the verbal skills they had were of no use in school. All this seems a far cry from aesthetics, and it is true that Labov's interest in "verbal art" rose from his research quite indirectly. I quote here Labov's own description of this development. The passage is long but worthwhile as an introduction to my own discussion to follow:

> In the course of our studies of vernacular language, we have developed a number of devices to overcome the constraints of the face-to-face interview and obtain large bodies of tape-recorded casual speech. The most effective of these techniques produce *narratives of personal experience,* in which the speaker becomes deeply involved in rehearsing or even reliving events of his past. The "Danger of Death" question is the prototype and still the most generally used: at a certain point in the conversation, the interviewer asks, "Were you ever in a situation where you were in serious danger of being killed, where you said to yourself—'*This is it'?*" In the section of our interview schedule that deals with fights, we ask "Were you ever in a fight with a guy bigger than you?" When the subject says "Yes" we pause and then ask simply, "What happened?" The

> narratives that we have obtained by such methods form a large body of data on comparative verbal skills, ranging across age levels, classes and ethnic groups. Because they occur in response to a specific stimulus in the interview situation, they are not free of the interactive effect of the outside observer. The form they take is in fact typical of discourse directed to someone outside of the immediate peer group of the speaker. But because the experience and emotions involved here form an important part of the speaker's biography, he seems to undergo a partial reliving of that experience, and he is no longer free to monitor his own speech as he normally does in face-to-face interviews. (1972: 354–55)

Labov was fascinated by the high degree of verbal virtuosity displayed by 3
many of his informants in these narratives and by the high value placed on that virtuosity by the vernacular speech communities. This interest and the fact that, despite cultural differences, the narratives had great structural similarities led him to attempt a structural description of the oral narrative of personal experience as a speech act. The results of his study are found in two papers, "Narrative Analysis: Oral Versions of Personal Experience" (1967), written in collaboration with Joshua Waletzky, and "The Transformation of Experience in Narrative Syntax," in *Language in the Inner City*. (Unless otherwise specified, all subsequent references are to the latter article.) Before presenting Labov's analysis of these narratives, let me offer two contrasting examples, both taken from Labov's data. The first is a story told by a middle-aged white male speaker from Martha's Vineyard:

(1)

> I never believed a whole lot in licking. I was never— with my children, and I never—when it was with my animals, dogs; I never licked a dog, I never had to. A dog knew what I meant; when I hollered at a dog, he knew the—what I meant. I could—I had dogs that could do everything but talk. And by gorry, sir, I never licked 'em.
>
> I never come nearer bootin' a dog in my life. I had a dog—he was a wonderful retriever, but as I say he could do everything but talk. I could waif him that way, I could waif him on, I could waif him anywhere. If I shot a crippled duck he went after it; he didn't see it in the water, he'd always turn around look at me, and I'd waif him over there, if the duck was there, or if it was on the other side of where we're on, I could waif him straight ahead, and he'd turn and he'd go. If he didn't see me, he'd turn around, he'd look at me, and I'd keep

a-waifin' him on. And he'd finally catch sight of him, and the minute he did, you know, he would beeline and get that duck.

I was gunnin' one night with that dog—we had to use live decoys in those days—a fellow named Jack Bumpus was with me; I was over at a place called Deep Bottom, darker than pitch. And—uh—heard a quackin' off shore. And I said to Jack, "keep quiet. There's one comin' in." And uh—finally Jack said to me, "I think I see 'im." I said, "Give 'im a gun. Give 'im a gun. Try it."

So he shot, and this duck went for the shore with his wings a-goin' like that for the shore. Went up on the shore. Well this dog never lost a crippled duck on shore, he'd take a track just the same as a hound would take a rabbit track. And I sent him over. I said, "Go ahead."

So he went over there. And—gone a while and come back and he didn't have the duck. And that was unusual—I said, "You git back there and get that duck!" And he went back there; and he stayed a little while longer, longer than he did the first time, and he come back and he didn't have the duck.

And I never come nearer shootin' a dog. By gorry, I come pretty near. "*You git back there and get that duck!*" And that dog went back there, and he didn't come back. And he didn't come back. By gorry, we went over there—I walked over there, and here he was; one of my tame ducks that I had tethered out there had got the strap off her leg, and had gone out there, and when this fellah shot he hadn't hit the duck. The duck came to the shore, he hadn't hit the duck; but the duck was scared and come for the shore. My dog was over there, and he had his paw right on top of that duck, holdin' him down just as tight as could be, and—by gorry, boy, I patted that dog, I'll tell you if I had ever walloped that dog I'd have felt some bad. He knew more'n I did; the dog knew more than I did. He knew that was that tame duck; he wasn't gonna pick him up in his mouth and bring him, you know. He was just holdin' him right down on the ground.

(Labov, 1967:14–15)

The second is a fight story told by a black adolescent male from Harlem referred to as Larry:

(2)

An' then, three weeks ago I had a fight with this other dude outside. He got mad 'cause I wouldn't give him a cigarette Ain't that a bitch? (Oh yeah?)

Yeah, you know, I was sittin' on the corner an' shit, smokin' my cigarette, you know. I was high, an' shit. He walked over to me:

"Can I have a cigarette?"

He was a little taller than me, but not that much. I said:

"I ain't got no more, man."

'Cause, you know, all I had was one left. An' I ain't gon' give up my last cigarette unless I got some more. So I said:

"I don't have no more, man."

So he, you know, dug on the pack, 'cause the pack was in my pocket. So he said:

"Eh, man, I can't get a cigarette, man? I mean—I mean we supposed to be brothers, an' shit."

So I say:

"Yeah, well, you know, man, all I got is one, you dig it?"

An' I won't give up my las' one to nobody. So you know, the dude, he looks at me, an' he—I 'on' know—he jus' thought he gon' rough that motherfucker up. He said:

"I can't get a cigarette."

I said:

"Tha's what I said, my man."

You know, so he said:

"What you supposed to be *bad* an' shit?"

So I said:

"Look here, my man, I don't think I'm bad, you understand? But I mean, you know, if I had it, you could git it. I like to see you with it, you dig it? But the sad part about it, you get to do without it. That's all, my man."

So the dude, he 'on' to pushin' me, man.

(Oh, he pushed you?)

An' why he do that? *Everytime somebody fuck with me,* why they do it? I put that cigarette down, an' boy let me tell you. I beat the shit outa that motherfucker. I tried to *kill* 'im—over one cigarette! I tried to *kill* 'im. Square business! After I got through stompin' him in the face, man, you know, all of a sudden I went crazy! I jus' went crazy. An' I jus' wouldn't stop hittin' the motherfucker. Dig, it, I couldn't stop hittin' 'im, man, till the teacher pulled me off o' him. An' guess what? After all that I gave the dude the cigarette, after all that. Ain't that a bitch?

(How come you gave 'im the cigarette?)
I 'on' know. I jus' gave it to him. An' he smoked it, too!
(Labov, 1972:356–58)

Labov's (1972) analysis of these "natural narratives," as they are commonly called, will seem self-evident to literary critics, and it is for precisely this reason that I want to outline it here. Labov defines narrative as: 4

> one method of recapitulating past experience by matching a verbal sequence of clauses to the sequence of events which (it is inferred) actually occurred. . . . Within this conception of narrative, we can define a *minimal narrative,* as a sequence of two clauses which are *temporally ordered:* that is, a change in their order will result in a change in the temporal sequence of the original semantic interpretation. (p. 360)

Narrative clauses are clauses with a simple preterite verb or, in some styles, a verb in the simple present. Here is an adult "danger of death" narrative which consists of four such ordered clauses: (This and all further examples in this chapter are taken from Labov's data.) 5

(3) Well, this person had a little too much to drink and he attacked me and the friend came in and she stopped it.

Narratives like (3), which consist only of narrative clauses, are not very interesting, nor are they very common. A fully developed natural narrative, according to Labov, is made up of the following sections:

1. abstract
2. orientation
3. complicating action
4. evaluation
5. result or resolution
6. coda

"A complete narrative," he concludes, "begins with an orientation, proceeds to the complicating action, is suspended at the focus of evaluation before the resolution, concludes with the resolution, and returns the listener to the present time with the coda." I shall summarize briefly Labov's description of the six sections:

Complicating action and *resolution* are, of course, the core of the narrative. The former begins with the first narrative clause in the speech act; the latter usually ends with the last such clause. 6

The *abstract* is a short (usually one or two sentence) summary of the story 7
that narrators generally provide before recounting the story proper. The abstract "encapsulates the point of the story." In narrative (1) above, the single sentence "I never come nearer bootin' a dog in my life" has this function; in narrative (2), lines 1–2 are the abstract.

The *orientation* serves to "identify in some way the time, place, persons, 8
and their activity or situation" and occurs immediately before the first narrative clause, as a rule. The orientation often includes "an elaborate portrait of the main character" as in (1), whose narrator describes at length the prowess of his retriever before going on to the situation orientation (ll. 20–22). In (2), some information is already available in the abstract, and the orientation section (ll. 4–5) gives a more detailed picture of the situation. Syntactically, orientations often contain many past progressive verbs "sketching the kind of thing that was going on before the first event of the narrative occurred or during the entire episode."

The *coda*'s general function is to "close off the sequence of complicating 9
actions and indicate that none of the events that followed were important to the narrative." In addition to this mechanical function, "a good coda . . . leaves the listener with a feeling of satisfaction and completeness that matters have been rounded off and accounted for." Labov notes a number of forms codas can take. Sometimes they consist of a single sentence like "And that was that"; sometimes they "bring the narrator and the listener back to the point at which they entered the narrative," as does this coda, which closes out a story in which the teller was saved from drowning:

(4) And you know, that man who picked me out of the water? He's a detective in Union City, and I see him every now and again.

and this coda to a fight story:

(5) Ever since then I haven't seen the guy 'cause I quit. I quit, you know. No more problems.

In narrative (1) above, the narrative proper ends at "just as tight as could be" (1.49) and the coda, starting with a pause and the phrase "by gorry," echoes the abstract ("If I had ever walloped. . . . ") and provides an additional explication and recapitulation of the story's climax. In narrative (2), the fight story ends with the teacher's intervention, and the coda, beginning with "Guess what?" (1.41), contains additional information about the ultimate effects of the events, as in (5) above. The narrator of (2), like that of (1), echoes the abstract in the coda, here by repeating the line "Ain't that a bitch?"

Evaluation is considered by Labov to be "perhaps the most important 10
element in addition to the basic narrative clause." By evaluation, Labov means

"the means used by the narrator to indicate the point of the narrative, its raison d'être: why it was told and what the narrator was getting at." He elaborates:

> There are many ways to tell the same story, to make very different points, or to make no point at all. Pointless stories are met (in English) with the withering rejoinder, "So what?" Every good narrator is continually warding off this question; when his narrative is over, it should be unthinkable for a bystander to say, "So what?" Instead, the appropriate remark would be "He did?" or similar means of registering the reportable character of the events of the narrative. (p. 366)
>
> To identify the evaluative portion of a narrative, it is necessary to know why this narrative—or any narrative—is felt to be tellable; in other words, why the events of the narrative are reportable. Most of the narratives cited here concern matters that are always reportable: danger of death or of physical injury. These matters occupy a high place on an unspoken permanent agenda. . . . The narrators of most of these stories were under social pressure to show that the events involved were truly dangerous and unusual, or that someone else really broke the normal rules in an outrageous and reportable way. Evaluative devices say to us: this was terrifying, dangerous, weird, wild, crazy; or amusing, hilarious and wonderful; more generally, that it was strange, uncommon, or unusual—that is, worth reporting. (p. 371)

The evaluation of a natural narrative is usually concentrated in one section 11
immediately preceding the resolution. However, as Labov notes, evaluative devices are generally strung throughout the entire narrative, forming what he calls "a secondary structure." Labov's discussion of evaluation is long, and I shall only partially summarize here his preliminary typology of the evaluative devices used by his informants. Again, the examples are Labov's.

A. *Evaluative commentary*

The narrator interrupts the progress of the narrative with a statement reaffirming the tellability of the story or assessing the situation. Such commentary may be

1. *External:* The narrator himself asserts the point of the story as in statements like "it was quite an experience" or "it was the strangest feeling" and so on.
2. *Internal:* The evaluative statements are embedded in the story. The narrator may
   a. present the statement as having occurred to him at the time in the story, e.g., "I just closed my eyes, I said, 'O my God, Here it is!' "

b. present the evaluation as statements addressed by himself to another character. Larry's evaluation, addressed (in rhymed couplets, no less) to his adversary (ll.28–31) is an example of this type.

c. attribute evaluative remarks to a witness or neutral observer in the story as in this example, referring to a knife wound: "And the doctor says, 'Just about this much more' he says, 'And you'd a been dead!' "

(a) to (c), you will notice, involve progressively deeper embedding of the evaluation in the story. As Labov notes, the more deeply embedded the evaluation, the more effective it is.

B. *Sentence-internal evaluation devices*

1. *Intensifiers:* These are devices superimposed or added onto the basic narrative syntax without affecting the unmarked (simple past) form of the narrative verb phrase. Examples:
   a. gestures.
   b. expressive phonology such as lengthened vowels ("a loooong time").
   c. repetition; there are many examples in (1) and (2).
   d. ritual interjections like "Well, sir," "By gorry," and so on.
2. *Comparators:* These are devices which involve the use of some verb phrase construction other than the simple past of the narrative clause. They include negatives, futures, modals, questions, commands, comparatives, and others.

The category called comparators merits some explanation. Labov 12
observed that complex auxiliary constructions tended to be concentrated in the evaluation sections of natural narratives, and he concluded upon analysis that most, if not all, verb constructions that depart from the simple past tense in natural narrative can be shown to be performing an evaluative role. The comparators do so by referring to hypothetical events that are then compared to the observed events. Comparators, in other words, "draw upon a cognitive background considerably richer than the set of events which were observed." Negatives, for example, talk about what didn't happen but could have; futures allude to what could happen but hasn't yet; modals refer to hypothetical events; questions and commands are attempts to produce future events and function often as disguised threats in narratives, implying future consequences (see, for example, narrative (2) above). Generally speaking "a comparator moves away from the line of narrative events to consider unrealized possibilities and compare them with events that did occur." Labov uses the following evaluation taken from a schoolboy's narrative of a fight with "the baddest girl in the neighborhood" to exemplify the evaluative role played by complex auxiliary structures:

(6) So I says to myself, "There's *gonna* be times my mother won't give me money, because we're a poor family and I *can't* take this every time she *don't* give me any money." So I say, "Well, I just *gotta* fight this girl. She *gonna hafta* whup me. I hope she *don't* whup me" (emphasis mine).

The passage contains four negatives, four futures, and three modals, all involving speculation about hypothetical events or situations which are compared to the present state of affairs. In the resolution of the story which follows, the simple narrative syntax is restored:

(7) I hit the girl, powww! I put something on it. I win the fight.

Larry's fight narrative above (ll.7–12 and elsewhere) is similarly organized. The grammatical comparative of course always performs an evaluative function, as do similes and metaphors. Interestingly, such overt comparisons are found mainly in the syntax of older, more highly skilled narrators like that of (1) (see for example, ll. 7, 30, 52).

One of the most striking aspects of Labov's model, as I suggested earlier, is 13
its self-evidence. I think it is self-evident for two reasons. First, the oral narrative of personal experience is a speech act exceedingly familiar to us all, regardless of what dialect we speak. We all spend enormous amounts of conversational time exchanging anecdotes, though these may only occasionally involve fights or danger of death. Most speakers of English have a distinctive speech style for this type of narration with special intonation and in many cases special grammatical constructions not used in other contexts.* We are all perfectly aware of the "unspoken agenda" by which we assess an experience's tellability. We know that anecdotes, like novels, are expected to have endings. We know that for an anecdote to be successful, we must introduce it into the conversation in an appropriate way, provide our audience with the necessary background information, keep the point of the story in view at all times, and so on. And as with any speech situation, literary or otherwise, we form firm judgments all the time about how "good" an anecdote was and how well it was brought off by its teller; in fact, we are expected to express this judgment as soon as an anecdote ends. We recognize narrative expertise when we hear it, and when narrative

*For example, adverbial constructions like "down we fell" or "over it went" are apparently exclusively narrative. In many languages, including North American English, speakers often switch to the present tense for narration or alternate between present and simple past as in "so yesterday he comes into my office and I told him he was fired." Many North American English dialects use irregular first person forms like "I says," "I comes," "I runs" exclusively for narration. Needless to say, these phenomena are much in need of study, but their very existence strongly supports the hypothesis that, independent of any literary considerations, narration must be identified as a speech act in its own right.

speech acts fail, we can almost always say why: the experience was trivial, the teller long-winded, or we "missed the point." Should anyone be in doubt about any of these points, I would urge him to spend an hour some day listening to real "everyday language," watching for narratives and for people's responses to them.

14 The second reason Labov's analysis seems so obvious is that his subdivision of the narrative into six main components corresponds very closely indeed to the kind of organization we are traditionally taught to observe in narrative literature. Every high school student knows that novels and plays have an introduction, a gradual rising action, a climax followed by a swift dénouement and resolution with the option of an epilogue at the end. That novels and natural narratives both have a structurally similar "narrative core" is not so surprising, since both are attempts to render experience. . . .

For Discussion and Writing

1. *Complicating action* and *resolution* are two elements of narrative that Pratt does not discuss at length, because she assumes that "every high school student knows that novels and plays have an introduction, a gradual rising action, a climax followed by a swift dénouement and resolution with the option of an epilogue at the end." Is she right? Do you know these things? In any case, it might be a good idea to review your understanding by discussing the complicating action and resolution of the two complete examples Pratt quotes from Labov. Try to summarize the *action* of each narrative, ignoring the other elements of the speech act. Can you locate a "rising" action, climax, and dénouement or resolution in both cases?
2. What makes a good anecdote good? Discuss the two examples given by Pratt. How much depends upon the events narrated and how much upon the way the narrator handles such matters as abstract, orientation, evaluation, and coda?
3. Take Pratt's example (3), which presents a whole story in a single sentence, and make something of it. That is, retell it as a full-fledged anecdote, using all six elements and adding descriptive details that will make it interesting. (This can be done as a group project.)
4. In preparation for writing your own anecdote (exercise 5 below), your instructor may ask you to tell your anecdote to the class, or to a group of students. As you listen to one another's anecdotes, take note of the evaluative commentary used by each speaker. You might want to discuss the writing strategies necessary to substitute for gestures used by the speaker to emphasize a point. Remember, it is not easy to convey a tone of voice in writing.
5. Write an anecdote based on personal experience. Your narrative may concern something that happened to you, or it may concern something that you witnessed but that happened to someone else. You may, like most

of Labov's speakers, tell about a situation when you felt yourself to be in danger, but, as Labov points out, memorable events can be "weird, wild, crazy; or amusing, hilarious and wonderful" as well. After you have written out your anecdote, refer to Pratt's list of six parts of the anecdote to make sure that yours is formally complete.

Four "Literary" Anecdotes

Mary Louise Pratt has helped us to understand that all narratives—from a story told in the street to a great literary novel—share the same formal building blocks. Every story is "literary" to some degree. Still, there are differences of degree possible. Having looked at some anecdotes, thought about the anecdote as a form of narrative, and produced an anecdote of your own, you should be ready to consider the ways in which even the anecdote—that simplest of narrative forms—can be made more literary in the hands of a skilled writer. Many a musician can carry a tune, but the great improvisers—in classical variations on a theme, or in jazz, or any other musical form—will do things that make a simple melody endlessly fascinating.

Here are four examples of writers playing with the anecdote form, using the six features identified by Labov, but rearranging them or omitting some, or playing games with time and space. We ask you, in reading and discussing them, to use the six basic elements as a way of looking at these texts, to help you see what is and is not going on in them. Remember, the point is not to check for all six and take points away for any that are missing. The point is to see what these professional writers do with the basic form. To see that, of course, you have to start by looking for it.

Anecdote (1)

Ordnance

Walter Benjamin

"Ordnance" refers to gunnery. A metaphor of gunpowder (a "magazine" is a supply of explosive powder) runs through this anecdote. Riga is a city in Latvia. This story takes place in the 1920s. Walter Benjamin, a literary critic and cultural philosopher, died trying to escape the Nazis during the Second World War.

I had arrived in Riga to visit a woman friend. Her house, the town, the language were unfamiliar to me. Nobody was expecting me, no one knew me.

For two hours I walked the streets in solitude. Never again have I seen them so. From every gate a flame darted, each cornerstone sprayed sparks, and every streetcar came toward me like a fire engine. For she might have stepped out of the gateway, around the corner, been sitting in the streetcar. But of the two of us I had to be, at any price, the first to see the other. For had she touched me with the match of her eyes, I should have gone up like a magazine.

Anecdote (2)

Polar Bears

Patricia J. Williams

This is a fragment of a larger essay in which the polar bears return more than once, but it is also readable in itself as an anecdote about the refusal to tell anecdotes, among other things. Patricia J. Williams, an African American, is a professor of law and writer on women's issues and racial questions. Professor Williams prefaces this anecdote with a quotation from Walter Benjamin's essay, "The Storyteller."

"Familiar though his name may be to us, the storyteller in his living immediacy is by no means a present force. He has already become something remote from us and something that is getting even more distant. . . . Less and less frequently do we encounter people with the ability to tell a tale properly. . . . It is as if something that seemed inalienable to us, the securest among our possessions, were taken from us: the ability to exchange experiences" (from *Illuminations,* New York: Schocken, 1969, p. 83). 1

My mother's cousin Marjorie was a storyteller. From time to time I would press her to tell me the details of her youth, and she would tell me instead stories about a child who wandered into a world of polar bears, who was prayed over by the polar bears, and in the end eaten. The child's life was not in vain because the polar bears had been made holy by its suffering. The child had been a test, a message from god for polar bears. In the polar bear universe, she would tell me, the primary object of creation was polar bears, and the rest of the living world was fashioned to serve polar bears. The clouds took their shape from polar bears, trees were designed to give shelter and shade to polar bears, and humans were ideally designed to provide polar bears with meat. 2

The truth, the truth, I would laughingly insist as we sat in her apartment eating canned fruit and heavy roasts, mashed potatoes, pickles and vanilla pudding, cocoa, Sprite, or tea. What about roots and all that, I coaxed. But the voracity of her amnesia would disclaim and disclaim and disclaim, and she 3 would go on telling me about the polar bears until our places were full of emptiness and I became large in the space which described her emptiness and I gave in to the emptiness of words.

Anecdote (3)

Departures

Storm Jameson

This selection is the conclusion of a chapter from Margaret Storm Jameson's autobiography, Journey from the North. ***In it she begins to tell of a train journey from Yorkshire (in the north of England) to London made with her husband during the First World War. But, in the telling, her mind moves back through memories of other departures to an anecdote of an earlier departure from Yorkshire, this one with her mother (the wife of a sea captain). Jameson was the author of many novels and other books.***

The September day we left for London was cold and cloudily sunny. In the few minutes as the train drew out past the harbour, I felt myself isolated by a barrier of ice from every living human being, including the husband facing me. Like a knot of adders uncoiling themselves one departure slid from another behind my eyes—journeys made feverish by unmanageable longings and ambitions, night journeys in wartime, the darkened corridors crammed with young men in clumsy khaki, smoking, falling asleep, journeys with a heavy baby in one arm. At last I come to the child sitting in a corner of a third-class carriage, waiting, silent, tense with anxiety, for the captain's wife to return from the ticket office. A bearded gentleman in a frock coat—the stationmaster—saunters up to the open door and says, smiling, something she makes no attempt to hear. Her mother walks lightly across the platform. "Ah, there you are, Mrs. Jameson. Your little girl was afraid you weren't coming," he said amiably. Nothing less amiable than Mrs. Jameson's coldly blue eyes turned on him, and cold voice. 1

"Nonsense. My child is never afraid." 2

Not true... 3

Anecdote (4)

L.

Richard Huelsenbeck

Richard Huelsenbeck was one of the founders of the Dada movement, a group of anti-art artists, writers, and musicians who started out—in a café in Zürich, Switzerland, inspired by the madness of the First World War—on a protest against practically everything. They were inspired jokers whose jokes were a way of fighting senselessness with nonsense. The following two anecdotes, taken from his book **Memoirs of a Dada Drummer,** ***concern Huelsenbeck's "wedding night" with a young woman that he had courted for some time and with the way he finally lost her at the movies.***

Needless to say my "nuptial night" with L. was extremely disappointing. 1
Her friend who had married an engineer was sympathetic and let us use a room that she had given up after her wedding. . . .

The outcome was total chaos. I behaved as well as I might, but I couldn't 2
reconcile my dadaist "wildness" with L.'s reserve. Although, as I have said, I greatly sympathized with the conventional, I was still a very poor comforter and savior. There is nothing more sensitive on earth than a man's potency. Every kind of love-making involves freedom, real or imaginary. Here, however, we found ourselves in a hopeless bramble of violently contradictory feelings. So we had no choice but to leave the apartment that had been so generously offered to us. We walked wordlessly through nighttime Zurich, which in those days did not as yet illuminate its venerable buildings with neon lights.

It was really dark, very dark. I wanted to take hold of L.'s arm but she 3
pushed me away, and in the Drahtzugstrasse—I'll never forget the name of the street—L. became icy cold and bitter. I felt that our relationship had come to an end.

Nevertheless, I went out with L. from time to time; the real end was so 4
peculiar that I have to mention it. I lost L. in a movie house in which a panic had broken out. It's hard to believe, but in a small room—cinemas weren't very large in those days—a man in the back row uttered such a grotesque moan that several people in the audience screamed. Next, others stood up, and eventually the entire audience began rioting. They shoved their way to the exits, stamped about, called for help; but no one could find out what had happened. Fire? Murder? Revolution? Nobody knew, and nobody cared. All they wanted to do was get out, get away, run off. It was what the Australian farmers and cattlemen called a stampede, an effective English word because it expresses the stamping of the cattle onomatopoetically. The herd starts moving suddenly and for no reason. It flees, it stamps, a sinister sight, and woe to anyone landing under its

hoofs. Thus, I lost L. in a stampede in a Zurich movie theater many years ago and never saw her again. I hope that since then she found what she deserved. Despite her great limitations, she was a fine woman.

For Discussion and Writing

1. Counting the two separate anecdotes in selection (4), there are five "literary" anecdotes collected here. If we think of Labov's six elements as a basic plan for all anecdotes, consider the ways in which each of these five deviates from the basic plan, either by rearrangement of the basic six or by omission of one or more. For instance, checking the first anecdote against Labov's list, we might get something like this:

    1. abstract? missing
    2. orientation? yes, explanation of reason for visit
    3. complicating action? yes, wandering the streets
    4. evaluation? yes, in the last sentence
    5. result or resolution? no—we are never told what happened
    6. coda? yes, combined with evaluation, and no, since the resolution is missing. Because the last sentence is not in the simple past tense of narration but in the conditional (*if* she *had* even looked at him, he *would* have exploded), the story cannot be resolved as a story is resolved. Narration requires the past tense.

    This simple analysis would then enable us to probe further into the "literary" quality of this anecdote. It establishes suspense but then, instead of providing a result or resolution it shifts the point of the tale to the evaluation, suggesting that what actually happened is not as important as the state of the author's emotions at the time—feeling like a powder keg ready to explode under the gaze of his friend. By shifting the emphasis from the events to the metaphor of explosive longing, the author has moved the anecdote in the direction of the "literary."

    The question to begin with, then, has two parts:

    a. check each anecdote against Labov's six elements of narrative;
    b. consider the effect of any omissions or modifications in the use of these elements.

2. Later on, you may study metaphor more formally. For the moment, however, it will be enough to consider metaphor as a sort of comparison, a way of talking about one thing in terms of another. For instance, as we have noted, Benjamin's anecdote depends upon the metaphor or comparison of his emotional state to an explosive charge needing only a match to set it off. Examine the other anecdotes for their use of compari-

son or metaphor: the polar bears in (2), for instance, the snakes (adders) in (3), the bramble and stampede in (4). What do the comparisons contribute toward the "literary" quality of those anecdotes?

3. Anecdote (2) begins with a quotation from the author of (1) about the loss of the ability to "tell a tale properly." Consider all of the anecdotes in relation to what it means to "tell a tale properly"—and do not worry if you cannot reach absolutely firm conclusions about this. Does Benjamin himself tell his tale "properly"?

   Benjamin is talking partly about the loss of a tradition of oral storytelling and its replacement by written narratives, which were more "literary" but perhaps less satisfactory as stories. Considering the five anecdotes collected here, do you find any particularly good or bad, strong or weak? Try to explain your judgment—to yourself and others. That is, try not only to justify your opinion but to explore the reasons why you came to it in the first place. This could be done in the form of an essay about the anecdote(s), which could also include discussion of the anecdotes considered in Pratt's essay (pp. 2–12).

4. In writing these questions, we have been putting the word "literary" in quotation marks to indicate that the category of "literature" is not something fixed and given but is itself a matter of discussion and debate. We have suggested that *literary* may mean nothing more than "what is written" as opposed to what is told orally, or it can mean something that is inventive, surprising. "Literature" can also refer to texts that seem to refer more widely to common experiences than others. An anecdote is always a singular story, a tale of some one thing that happened to some one person (or possibly to a group of people). A literary anecdote might be seen as a story about one person who becomes the representative of others, as the scared girl and tough mother in (3) might represent the childish fears and maternal toughness of other children and mothers. Consider each of these anecdotes from this point of view. That is, to what extent can the anecdotes they tell be seen as representative of more common or general experiences?

5. If the notion of "dada"—art against Art, nonsense against senselessness—interests you, find out more about the Dada movement and prepare a report on it for the class. This could be a group activity or a panel discussion. You could even put on a Dada performance for your classmates. (If you do, be prepared for resistance.)

The Use of Force

William Carlos Williams

The following selection is a personal experience recounted by the American poet William Carlos Williams. Williams was a physician, a general practitioner, and this is a story drawn from his practice.

They were new patients to me, all I had was the name, Olson. Please come down as soon as you can, my daughter is very sick. 1

When I arrived I was met by the mother, a big startled looking woman, very clean and apologetic who merely said, Is this the doctor? and let me in. In the back, she added. You must excuse us, doctor, we have her in the kitchen where it is warm. It is very damp here sometimes. 2

The child was fully dressed and sitting on her father's lap near the kitchen table. He tried to get up, but I motioned for him not to bother, took off my overcoat and started to look things over. I could see that they were all very nervous, eyeing me up and down distrustfully. As often, in such cases, they weren't telling me more than they had to, it was up to me to tell them; that's why they were spending three dollars on me. 3

The child was fairly eating me up with her cold, steady eyes, and no expression to her face whatever. She did not move and seemed, inwardly, quiet; an unusually attractive little thing, and as strong as a heifer in appearance. But her face was flushed, she was breathing rapidly, and I realized that she had a high fever. She had magnificent blonde hair, in profusion. One of those picture children often reproduced in advertising leaflets and the photogravure sections of the Sunday papers. 4

She's had a fever for three days, began the father and we don't know what it comes from. My wife has given her things, you know, like people do, but it don't do no good. And there's been a lot of sickness around. So we tho't you'd better look her over and tell us what is the matter. 5

As doctors often do I took a trial shot at it as a point of departure. Has she had a sore throat? 6

Both parents answered me together, No . . . No, she says her throat don't hurt her. 7

Does your throat hurt you? added the mother to the child. But the little girl's expression didn't change nor did she move her eyes from my face. 8

Have you looked? 9

I tried to, said the mother, but I couldn't see. 10

As it happens we had been having a number of cases of diphtheria in the school to which this child went during that month and we were all, quite apparently, thinking of that, though no one had as yet spoken of the thing. 11

Well, I said, suppose we take a look at the throat first. I smiled in my best 12
professional manner and asking for the child's first name I said, come on, Mathilda, open your mouth and let's take a look at your throat.

Nothing doing. 13

Aw, come on, I coaxed, just open your mouth wide and let me take a look. 14
Look, I said opening both hands wide, I haven't anything in my hands. Just open up and let me see.

Such a nice man, put in the mother. Look how kind he is to you. Come on, 15
do what he tells you to. He won't hurt you.

At that I ground my teeth in disgust. If only they wouldn't use the word 16
"hurt" I might be able to get somewhere. But I did not allow myself to be hurried or disturbed but speaking quietly and slowly I approached the child again.

As I moved my chair a little nearer suddenly with one catlike movement 17
both her hands clawed instinctively for my eyes and she almost reached them too. In fact she knocked my glasses flying and they fell, though unbroken, several feet away from me on the kitchen floor.

Both the mother and father almost turned themselves inside out in 18
embarrassment and apology. You bad girl, said the mother, taking her and shaking her by one arm. Look what you've done. The nice man . . .

For heaven's sake, I broke in. Don't call me a nice man to her. I'm here to 19
look at her throat on the chance that she might have diphtheria and possibly die of it. But that's nothing to her. Look here, I said to the child, we're going to look at your throat. You're old enough to understand what I'm saying. Will you open it now by yourself or shall we have to open it for you?

Not a move. Even her expression hadn't changed. Her breaths however 20
were coming faster and faster. Then the battle began. I had to do it. I had to have a throat culture for her own protection. But first I told the parents that it was entirely up to them. I explained the danger but said that I would not insist on a throat examination so long as they would take the responsibility.

If you don't do what the doctor says you'll have to go to the hospital, the 21
mother admonished her severely.

Oh yeah? I had to smile to myself. After all, I had already fallen in love with 22
the savage brat, the parents were contemptible to me. In the ensuing struggle they grew more and more abject, crushed, exhausted while she surely rose to magnificent heights of insane fury of effort bred of her terror of me.

The father tried his best, and he was a big man but the fact that she was his 23
daughter, his shame at her behavior and his dread of hurting her made him release her just at the critical times when I had almost achieved success, till I wanted to kill him. But his dread also that she might have diphtheria made him tell me to go on, go on though he himself was almost fainting, while the mother moved back and forth behind us raising and lowering her hands in an agony of apprehension.

Put her in front of you on your lap, I ordered, and hold both her wrists. 24

But as soon as he did the child let out a scream. Don't, you're hurting me. 25
Let go of my hands. Let them go I tell you. Then she shrieked terrifyingly, hysterically. Stop it! Stop it! You're killing me!

Do you think she can stand it, doctor! said the mother. 26

You get out, said the husband to his wife. Do you want her to die of 27
diphtheria?

Come on now, hold her, I said. 28

Then I grasped the child's head with my left hand and tried to get the 29
wooden tongue depressor between her teeth. She fought, with clenched teeth, desperately! But now I also had grown furious—at a child. I tried to hold myself down but I couldn't. I know how to expose a throat for inspection. And I did my best. When finally I got the wooden spatula behind the last teeth and just the point of it into the mouth cavity, she opened up for an instant but before I could see anything she came down again and gripping the wooden blade between her molars she reduced it to splinters before I could get it out again.

Aren't you ashamed, the mother yelled at her. Aren't you ashamed to act 30
like that in front of the doctor?

Get me a smooth-handled spoon of some sort, I told the mother. We're 31
going through with this. The child's mouth was already bleeding. Her tongue was cut and she was screaming in wild hysterical shrieks. Perhaps I should have desisted and come back in an hour or more. No doubt it would have been better. But I have seen at least two children lying dead in bed of neglect in such cases, and feeling that I must get a diagnosis now or never I went at it again. But the worst of it was that I too had got beyond reason. I could have torn the child apart in my own fury and enjoyed it. It was a pleasure to attack her. My face was burning with it.

The damned little brat must be protected against her own idiocy, one says 32
to one's self at such times. Others must be protected against her. It is a social necessity. And all these things are true. But a blind fury, a feeling of adult shame, bred of a longing for muscular release are the operatives. One goes on to the end.

In a final unreasoning assault I overpowered the child's neck and jaws. I 33
forced the heavy silver spoon back of her teeth and down her throat till she gagged. And there it was—both tonsils covered with membrane. She had fought valiantly to keep me from knowing her secret. She had been hiding that sore throat for three days at least and lying to her parents in order to escape just such an outcome as this.

Now truly she was furious. She had been on the defensive before but now 34
she attacked. Tried to get off her father's lap and fly at me while tears of defeat blinded her eyes.

For Discussion and Writing

1. Later in this book, we will discuss more formally the question of how to produce "interpretations" of literary texts. For the moment we can think of interpretation simply as an extension of what Labov calls evaluation. It is a matter of explaining the significance or meaning of the events narrated. In Williams's story there is actually very little evaluation. You might confirm this by checking the text of the story against the six Labovian features of narrative. The absence of overt evaluation in many literary texts is a way of drawing the reader into the creative process. The reader must supply an appropriate evaluation for the events in order to complete the narrative structure.

   With this in mind, how do you evaluate or interpret the events in this story. What is the story about? What does it mean? You might begin by locating anything in the text that does seem to you to belong to orientation or evaluation. What about the title, for instance? Would you consider that a step toward an interpretation of the story? Try to develop, either in writing or in discussion, a full evaluation or interpretation of the story.
2. At this point, you might begin discussing the similarities and differences between the natural narratives of Labov and Pratt and the literary anecdote or story as exemplified by "The Use of Force." What seem to you to be the important features common to both types of narrative, and what differences do you find notable? Which seem to you the most important—the similarities or the differences?

The Kiss

Kate Chopin

This selection is a short story by the American writer Kate Chopin, who lived in Louisiana a century ago. She was unique for her time, in that she wrote frequently about a powerful female sexuality trapped within an elaborate code of manners.

It was still quite light out of doors, but inside with the curtains drawn and the smouldering fire sending out a dim, uncertain glow, the room was full of deep shadows. 1

Brantain sat in one of these shadows; it had overtaken him and he did not mind. The obscurity lent him courage to keep his eyes fastened as ardently as he liked upon the girl who sat in the firelight. 2

She was very handsome, with a certain fine, rich coloring that belongs to the healthy brune type. She was quite composed, as she idly stroked the satiny coat of the cat that lay curled in her lap, and she occasionally sent a slow glance 3 into the shadow where her companion sat. They were talking low, of indifferent things which plainly were not the things that occupied their thoughts. She knew that he loved her—a frank, blustering fellow without guile enough to conceal his feelings, and no desire to do so. For two weeks past he had sought her society eagerly and persistently. She was confidently waiting for him to declare himself and she meant to accept him. The rather insignificant and unattractive Brantain was enormously rich; and she liked and required the entourage which wealth could give her.

During one of the pauses between their talk of the last tea and the next 4
reception the door opened and a young man entered whom Brantain knew quite well. The girl turned her face toward him. A stride or two brought him to her side, and bending over her chair—before she could suspect his intention, for she did not realize that he had not seen her visitor—he pressed an ardent, lingering kiss upon her lips.

Brantain slowly arose; so did the girl arise, but quickly, and the newcomer 5
stood between them, a little amusement and some defiance struggling with the confusion in his face.

"I believe," stammered Brantain, "I see that I have stayed too long. I—I 6
had no idea—that is, I must wish you good-by." He was clutching his hat with both hands, and probably did not perceive that she was extending her hand to him, her presence of mind had not completely deserted her; but she could not have trusted herself to speak.

"Hang me if I saw him sitting there, Nattie! I know it's deuced awkward for 7
you. But I hope you'll forgive me this once—this very first break. Why, what's the matter?"

"Don't touch me; don't come near me," she returned angrily. "What do you 8
mean by entering the house without ringing?"

"I came in with your brother, as I often do," he answered coldly, in 9
self-justification. "We came in the side way. He went upstairs and I came in here hoping to find you. The explanation is simple enough and ought to satisfy you that the misadventure was unavoidable. But do say that you forgive me, Nathalie," he entreated, softening.

"Forgive you! You don't know what you are talking about. Let me pass. It 10
depends upon—a good deal whether I ever forgive you."

At that next reception which she and Brantain had been talking about she 11
approached the young man with a delicious frankness of manner when she saw him there.

"Will you let me speak to you a moment or two, Mr. Brantain?" she asked 12
with an engaging but perturbed smile. He seemed extremely unhappy; but when she took his arm and walked away with him, seeking a retired corner, a ray of hope mingled with the almost comical misery of his expression. She was apparently very outspoken.

"Perhaps I should not have sought this interview, Mr. Brantain; but—but, 13
oh, I have been very uncomfortable, almost miserable since that little encoun-

ter the other afternoon. When I thought how you might have misinterpreted it, and believed things"—hope was plainly gaining the ascendancy over misery in Brantain's round, guileless face—"of course, I know it is nothing to you, but for my own sake I do want you to understand that Mr. Harvy is an intimate friend of long standing. Why, we have always been like cousins—like brother and sister, I may say. He is my brother's most intimate associate and often fancies that he is entitled to the same privileges as the family. Oh, I know it is absurd, uncalled for, to tell you this; undignified even," she was almost weeping, "but it makes so much difference to me what you think of—of me." Her voice had grown very low and agitated. The misery had all disappeared from Brantain's face.

"Then you do really care what I think, Miss Nathalie? May I call you Miss 14
Nathalie?" They turned into a long, dim corridor that was lined on either side with tall, graceful plants. They walked slowly to the very end of it. When they turned to retrace their steps Brantain's face was radiant and hers was triumphant.

Harvy was among the guests at the wedding; and he sought her out in a 15
rare moment when she stood alone.

"Your husband," he said, smiling, "has sent me over to kiss you." 16

A quick blush suffused her face and round polished throat. "I suppose it's 17
natural for a man to feel and act generously on an occasion of this kind. He tells me he doesn't want his marriage to interrupt wholly that pleasant intimacy which has existed between you and me. I don't know what you've been telling him," with an insolent smile, "but he has sent me here to kiss you."

She felt like a chess player who, by the clever handling of his pieces, sees 18
the game taking the course intended. Her eyes were bright and tender with a smile as they glanced up into his; and her lips looked hungry for the kiss which they invited.

"But, you know," he went on quietly, "I didn't tell him so, it would have 19
seemed ungrateful, but I can tell you. I've stopped kissing women; it's dangerous."

Well, she had Brantain and his million left. A person can't have everything 20
in this world; and it was a little unreasonable of her to expect it.

For Discussion and Writing

1. **This is a sophisticated story of a sophisticated world. Begin your study of it by comparing its structure to that of "natural" narratives. Does it have all six of Labov's analytic elements? Discuss what is omitted, compressed, or rearranged in this story.**
2. **Retell the story as a personal narrative recounted by Mr. Harvy. Imagine him in his club, telling this tale to a small circle of intimate friends. You will have to develop his character and motivation a bit to do this, but try to keep your additions in harmony with the material in Chopin's version of this story. Aim for a "complete" narrative, with all six Labovian elements.**

3. In a written essay take up the question of the relationship between "natural" narratives and "literary" narratives, exploring both their similarities and differences. Use Pratt and Chopin as your primary sources, but feel free to add material from the anecdotes of Benjamin, Williams, Jameson, Huelsenbeck, or from William Carlos Williams if you have studied this material. Try to reach some conclusion about which is more important: the differences or the similarities between popular and literary storytelling.

Character and Confrontation

Spring Awakening *(a scene from the play)*

Frank Wedekind

In the previous section the object of study was the basic structure of narrative texts. Beginning with personal or "natural" narrative, we considered the ways in which Labov's six elements of narrative can be applied to texts of every size and shape. In the present section we will approach the study of dramatic texts through the ways in which they resemble and differ from narrative, using Labov's six elements as the basis of our comparison.

To begin with, let us consider a sample of dramatic literature that is drawn closely from ordinary life. The following selection is a scene from a play by Frank Wedekind, written in Germany over half a century ago. In this scene Wedekind presents the drama that occurs when a girl insists that her mother tell her the "facts of life." Later, you may wish to consider how such domestic scenes have changed in the past seventy years, but to begin you should simply read the scene over a couple of times and be prepared to act it out or stage a reading of it in class. You should know that until quite recently it was common for children in Germany and in the United States to be told that babies were delivered by the Stork, who was often pictured in cartoons flying along holding a baby's diapers or swaddling clothes in his beak, with the infant dangling down beneath him.

SCENE II.

Wendla's room, empty. Mrs. Bergmann, her hat on, her shawl round her shoulders, a basket on her arm, enters with beaming face.

Mrs. Bergmann Wendla! Wendla!

Wendla [Appearing, half dressed, at the other door.] What is it, Mother?

Mrs. Bergmann Up already, dear? Well! That's nice of you.

Wendla Have you been out already?

Mrs. Bergmann Hurry up now and get dressed! You must go straight down to Ina's and take this basket to her.

Wendla [Finishing dressing during the following.] Have you been at Ina's? How is Ina feeling? Isn't she ever going to get better?

Mrs. Bergmann Just think, Wendla: the stork came to her last night and brought her a new little boy!

Wendla A boy?—A boy?—Oh, that's grand!—So it was for that she's been sick so long with influenza!

Mrs. Bergmann A splendid boy!

Wendla I've got to see him, Mother!—So now I'm an aunt for the third time—one niece and two nephews!

Mrs. Bergmann And what fine nephews they are!—That's just the way of it when one lives so close to the church roof.—It'll be just two [and a half?] years to-morrow since she went up those steps in her wedding-dress!

Wendla Were you with her when he brought him, mother?

Mrs. Bergmann He had just that minute flown away again!—Don't you want to pin a rose on here? *[At the front of her dress.]*

Wendla Why didn't you get there a little bit sooner, Mother?

Mrs. Bergmann Why, I do believe, almost, that he brought you something too—a brooch or something like that.

Wendla *[Losing patience.]* Oh, it's really too bad!

Mrs. Bergmann But I tell you that he did bring you a brooch too!

Wendla I've got brooches enough. . . .

Mrs. Bergmann Why, then be happy, darling. What are you troubled about?

Wendla I'd like to have known, so much, whether he flew in by the window or down the chimney.

Mrs. Bergmann You must ask Ina about that. *[Laughing.]* You must ask Ina about that, dear heart! Ina will tell you all about it exactly. Didn't Ina spend a whole half-hour talking to him?

Wendla I'll ask Ina as soon as I get down there.

Mrs. Bergmann Be sure you don't forget, you angel child! Really, I'm interested myself in knowing if he came in by the window or the chimney!

Wendla Or how about asking the chimney-sweep, rather?—The chimney-sweep must know better than anybody whether he flies down the chimney or not.

Mrs. Bergmann No, not the chimney-sweep, dear; not the chimney-sweep! What does the chimney-sweep know about the stork? He'll fill you chuck-full of nonsense he doesn't believe himself. . . . Wha-what are you staring down the street so at?

Wendla A man, mother, three times as big as an ox!—with feet like steam-boats—!

Mrs. Bergmann *[Plunging to the window.]* Impossible! Impossible!

Wendla *[Right after her.]* He's holding a bedstead under his chin and fiddling "The Watch on the Rhine" on it—now he's just turned the corner. . . .

Mrs. Bergmann Well! You are and always were a little rogue! To put your simple old mother into such a fright!—Go get your hat. I wonder when you'll ever get any sense! I've given up hope!

Wendla So have I, Mother; so've I. It's pretty sad about my sense! Here I have a sister who's been married two and a half years; here I am an aunt three times over; and I haven't the least idea how it all happens! . . . Don't be cross, motherkin! don't be cross! Who in the world should I ask about it but you? Please, Mother dear, tell it to me! Tell me, darling motherkin! I feel ashamed at myself! Please, please, mother, speak! Don't scold me for asking such a thing. Tell me about it—how does it happen—how does it all come about?—Oh, you can't seriously expect me still to believe in the stork when I'm fourteen!

Mrs. Bergmann But, good Lord, child, how queer you are! What things do occur to you! Really, I just can't do that!

Wendla But why not, mother? Why not? It can't be anything ugly, surely, when everyone feels so glad about it!

Mrs. Bergmann Oh, oh, God defend me!—Have I deserved to——Go and put your things on, girl,—put your things on.

Wendla I'm going . . . and supposing your child goes out now and asks the chimney-sweep?

Mrs. Bergmann Oh, but that's enough to drive me crazy!—Come, child, come here: I'll tell you. . . . Oh, Almighty Goodness!—only not to-day, Wendla! To-morrow, day after, next week, whenever you want, dear heart!

Wendla Tell it to me to-day, mother. Tell it to me now; now, at once. Now that I've seen you so upset, it's all the more impossible for me to quiet down again until you do!

Mrs. Bergmann I just can't, Wendla.

Wendla Oh, but why can't you, motherkin?—Here I'll kneel at your feet and put my head in your lap. Cover my head with your apron and talk and talk as if you were sitting all soul alone in the room. I won't move a muscle, I won't make a sound; I'll keep perfectly still and listen, no matter what may come!

Mrs. Bergmann Heaven knows, Wendla, it isn't my fault! The good God knows me.—Come, in His name!—I will tell you, little girl, how you came into this world—so listen, Wendla. . . .

Wendla [Under her apron.] I'm listening.

Mrs. Bergmann [Incoherent.] But it's no use, child! That's all! I can't justify it.—I know I deserve to be put in prison,—to have you taken from me . . .

Wendla [Under her apron.] Pluck up heart, Mother!

Mrs. Bergmann Well, then, listen. . . .

Wendla [Trembling.] O God, O God!

Mrs. Bergmann To have a child—you understand me, Wendla?——

Wendla Quick, mother! I can't bear it much longer!

Mrs. Bergmann To have a child—one must love the man—to whom one is married—love him, I say,—as one can only love a man! You must love him so utterly—with all your heart—that—that—it can't be told! You must love him, Wendla, as you at your age can't possibly love anyone yet. . . . Now you know.

Wendla [Getting up.] Great—God—in Heaven!

Mrs. Bergmann Now you know what tests lie before you!

Wendla And that is all?

Mrs. Bergmann God help me, yes, all!—Now pick up the basket there and go down to Ina. You'll get some chocolate there, and cakes with it.—Come here—let me just look you over—laced boots, silk gloves, sailor-blouse, a rose in your hair. . . . But your little dress is really getting too short now, Wendla!

Wendla Have you got meat for dinner already, motherkin?

Mrs. Bergmann God bless you and keep you!—I must find time to sew another breadth of ruffles round your skirt.

CURTAIN

For Discussion and Writing

1. Stage a reading of the scene.
2. Plays are meant to be acted. We often forget this little fact when we encounter the texts of plays in books. A printed play is more like a printed story than an acted play is. For one thing, a printed play usually has stage directions. At this point we would like you to consider the full range of differences between narration and enactment as ways of representing events. What seem to you the special strengths and limitations of each form? What do plays have that stories don't—and vice versa? Base your answers on the texts you have already considered in this course. You might also consider the difference between your private reading of Wedekind's text and the public staging or reading of it that you have just witnessed. The point of this inquiry is to refine your understanding of the ways that events are made into texts in these different forms. If you have a preference for one form over the other, try to explain the reasons for your preference.
3. Write your own version of a contemporary scene in which a child (of either sex) asks a parent (of either sex) about the facts of life. Remember to specify the age of the child. (How old is Wendla?)
4. Using Wedekind's scene as a source, write a personal narrative in which Wendla (or her mother) tells a friend about this moment in her life. You will have to decide how long after the scene this telling takes place, since narration is always some distance after the events narrated, and the length of this distance can affect the telling.

The Kiss *(dialogue from the story)*

Kate Chopin

This selection should look familiar to you. It consists of all of the spoken dialogue from Kate Chopin's little story, "The Kiss." Look this material over before considering the assignment.

Brantain: I believe, I see that I have stayed too long. I—I had no idea—that is, I must wish you good-by.

Harvy: Hang me if I saw him sitting there, Nattie! I know it's deuced awkward for you. But I hope you'll forgive me this once—this very first break. Why, what's the matter?

Nathalie: Don't touch me; don't come near me. What do you mean by entering the house without ringing?

Harvy: I came in with your brother, as I often do. We came in the side way. He went upstairs and I came in here hoping to find you. The explanation is simple enough and ought to satisfy you that the misadventure was unavoidable. But do say you forgive me, Nathalie.

Nathalie: Forgive you! You don't know what you're talking about. Let me pass. It depends upon—a good deal whether I ever forgive you.

Nathalie: Will you let me speak to you a moment or two, Mr. Brantain?

Nathalie: Perhaps I should not have sought this interview, Mr. Brantain; but—but, oh, I have been very uncomfortable, almost miserable since that little encounter the other afternoon. When I thought how you might have misinterpreted it, and believed things—of course, I know it is nothing to you, but for my sake I do want you to understand that Mr. Harvy is an intimate friend of long standing. Why, we have always been like cousins—like brother and sister, I may say. He is my brother's most intimate associate and often fancies that he is entitled to the same privileges as the family. Oh, I know it is absurd, uncalled for, to tell you this; undignified even, but it makes so much difference to me what you think of—of me.

Brantain: Then you really do care what I think, Miss Nathalie? May I call you Miss Nathalie?

Harvy: Your husband has sent me over to kiss you.

Harvy: I suppose it's natural for a man to feel and act generously on an occasion of this kind. He tells me he doesn't want his marriage to interrupt wholly that pleasant intimacy which has existed between you and me. I don't know what you've been telling him, but he has sent me over here to kiss you.

Harvy: But you know, I didn't tell him so, it would have seemed ungrateful, but I can tell you. I've stopped kissing women; it's dangerous.

For Discussion and Writing

Your task is to add everything that is needed to make this into a play that is as complete as the story from which it has been taken. You might begin by considering what is missing from this version that is in the story, using Labov's formula to aid your investigation. Then consider how to compensate for what is lacking. Some of the things you should consider adding are these:

a. scene divisions and settings
b. stage directions
c. additional dialogue (monologue? soliloquy?)
d. additional characters (a confidante? a commentator?)

You should undertake your revision of the dialogue with a staged production in mind: something that could be performed in class.

Character Contests

Erving Goffman

A personal narrative or a dramatic scene can be thought of as a form imposed upon the chaos of life—and we are often encouraged to think of literature in this way. But in fact, as sociologists have been demonstrating for some time, such forms are already present in life itself. Because life is social, it often has many of the features of a scene played before an audience. No one has developed this view more eloquently than Erving Goffman, a sociologist who has studied the dramatic or literary aspects of ordinary human interaction.

Ordinary interaction is not always ordinary, of course, and Goffman has argued persuasively that the smooth running of society requires a rhythm of crisis and relaxation, a rhythm caused by attempts of individuals to live out the roles or characters that they have adopted in order to function within a social structure. Our characters, says Goffman, are illusions encouraged by society. Our behavior in moments of crisis or confrontation depends upon our feeling that what we do will reveal what we are. Goffman puts it this way:

> And now we can begin to see character for what it is. On the one hand, it refers to what is essential and unchanging about the individual—what is *characteristic* of him. On the other, it refers to attributes that can be generated and destroyed in a few fateful moments.
>
> (*Interaction Ritual,* p. 238)

Because we want to have a good character—to be known as brave or honest or faithful—we try to behave in moments of stress so as to enact our ideas of bravery, honesty, fidelity. *For Goffman one of the most interesting social moments arrives when the characters of two individuals are at stake in a contest. He describes the "character contest"—a form of life that is also a form of art—in* Interaction Ritual, *as "a special form of moral game":*

These engagements occur, of course, in games and sports where opponents are balanced and marginal effort is required to win. But character contests are also found under conditions less obviously designed for contesting, subjecting us all to a stream of little losses and gains. Every day in many ways we can try to score points, and every day in many ways we can be shot down. (Perhaps a slight residue remains from each of these trials, so that the moment one individual approaches another, his manner and face may betray the consequences that have been usual for him, and subtly set the interaction off on a course that develops and terminates as it always seems to do for him.) Bargaining, threatening, promising—whether in commerce, diplomacy, warfare, card games, or personal relations—allow a contestant to pit his capacity for dissembling intentions and resources against the other's capacity to rile or cajole the secretive into readability. Whenever individuals ask for or give excuses, proffer or receive compliments, slight another or are slighted, a contest of self-control can result. Similarly, the tacit little flirtations occurring between friends and between strangers produce a contest of unavailability—if usually nothing more than this. And when banter occurs or "remarks" are exchanged, someone will have out-poised another. The territories of the self have boundaries that cannot be literally patrolled. Instead, border disputes are sought out and indulged in (often with glee) as a means of establishing where one's boundaries are. And these disputes are character contests. 1

The character contest is of interest to a social scientist like Goffman because it is a place where individual actions reveal the social codes by which people judge others and themselves. As he says, "When a contest occurs over whose treatment of self and other is to prevail, each individual is engaged in providing evidence to establish a definition of himself at the expense of what can remain for the other." Human behavior has a certain literary quality built in, as individuals play roles (dramatically) in order to define (verbally) themselves. Goffman is especially interested in what happens when human interaction is carried to the point of serious conflict. When one person offends or challenges another and neither will apologize or give in, we have what Goffman calls a "run-in," which is an especially intense form of character contest. Such encounters, it should be emphasized, are not just about who gets to have their way but about character itself: who is seen to have acted with what the social group—and the individuals themselves—consider to be good character. This is the way he elaborates on the possibilities of the run-in:

When the run-in has occurred and the contest begun, the characterological implications of the play can unfold in different ways, and not necessarily with "zero-sum" restrictions. 2

One party can suffer a clear-cut defeat on the basis of properties of character: he proves to have been bluffing all along and is not really prepared 3 to carry out his threatened deed; or he loses his nerve, turns tail and runs, leaving his opponent in the comfortable position of not having to demonstrate how seriously he was prepared to carry through with the contest; or he collapses as an opponent, abases himself and pleads for mercy, destroying his own status as a person of character on the tacit assumption that he will then be unworthy as an opponent and no longer qualify as a target of attack.

Both parties can emerge with honor and good character affirmed—an 4
outcome carefully achieved, apparently, in most formal duels of honor, a considerable achievement since injury was also usually avoided.

And presumably both parties can lose, just as one party may lose while the 5
other gains little. Thus, that ideal character contest, the "chicken run," may end with both vehicles swerving, neither vehicle swerving, or one swerving so early as to bring great dishonor to its driver but no particular credit to the opponent.

Obviously, the characterological outcome of the contest is quite in- 6
dependent of what might be seen as the "manifest" result of the fray. An overmatched player can gamely give everything he has to his hopeless situation and then go down bravely, or proudly, or insolently, or gracefully, or with an ironic smile on his lips.[1] A criminal suspect can keep his cool in the face of elaborate techniques employed by teams of police interrogators, and later receive a guilty sentence from the judge without flinching. Further, a well-matched player can grimly suffer while his opponent stoops to dishonorable but decisive techniques, in which case a duel is lost but character is won. Similarly, an individual who pits himself against a weak opponent may acquire the character of a bully through the very act of winning the match. And a bully who ties is lost indeed, as this news story from Fresno, California illustrates:

> A barmaid and a bandit played a game of "chicken" with loaded pistols early yesterday and although no shots were fired, the barmaid won.
>
> The action took place at The Bit, a proletarian beer and wine oasis on the southern fringe of town, where lovely Joan O'Higgins was on duty behind the bar.
>
> Suddenly a towering bandit walked into the establishment, ordered a beer, flashed a small pistol and commanded Miss O'Higgins to clean out the cash register.
>
> The barmaid placed $11 on the bar, an amount that failed to satisfy the bandit, whose height was estimated at six feet five.

[1] One of the reasons unexpected rescues are employed in action stories is that only in this way can the hero be given a chance to demonstrate that even in the face of quite hopeless odds he will not cry uncle. Second leads are allowed to prove this the hard way, being expendable in the plot.

"Give me the rest," he demanded.

Barmaid O'Higgins reached into a drawer for the main money bag and the .22 caliber pistol beneath it.

She pointed the gun at the man and asked:

"Now, what do you want to do?"

The bandit, realizing that he had met his match in The Bit, blinked at the sight of the gun and left, leaving his beer and the $11 behind.[2]

For Discussion and Writing

1. Goffman suggests that we make up and enact fictions about ourselves—that our real lives are penetrated by fictional concepts. Do you agree or disagree? If there are any aspects of Goffman's essay that you find difficult to understand or to accept, present them for discussion.
2. According to Goffman, when two people have a "run-in" in real life, this takes a form quite similar to a scene from a play. Does your own experience support this view? Can you recall a run-in that you have either seen or participated in yourself? Could it be reenacted as a dramatic scene? Can you describe how this might be done?
3. Character contests involve what Goffman calls the "boundaries" or "borders" of the self. They also involve matters of "honor" or "principle." Discuss the scene from Frank Wedekind's *Spring Awakening* (above, pp. 26–30) in Goffman's terms. In what sense does that scene record a "character contest"? Are matters of honor, principle, or boundaries of the self at stake in that scene? Is there a winner or a loser?
4. Consider Kate Chopin's story "The Kiss" as a character contest. What is at stake? Who wins or loses?
5. Consider William Carlos Williams's story "The Use of Force" as a character contest. What is at stake? Who wins or loses?
6. The "run-in" is an especially dramatic form of character contest. Which of the anecdotes you studied earlier can be described as a run-in? Rewrite a personal anecdote of your own in the form of a dramatic run-in, so that a reader will have no trouble assigning gains and losses to the characters involved. Use the dramatic rather than the narrative form of presentation.
7. In the run-in between the "bandit" and the "barmaid" the bandit is described as "towering" and the barmaid as "lovely." How important to the success of the story as a story are these details?
8. Suppose the barmaid had shot and killed the bandit. Would the result make as good a story? What would be lost with respect to this event's quality as a "character contest"?

[2] *San Francisco Chronicle,* July 14, 1966.

9. How important are the barmaid's exact words to the function of this episode as a little drama or character contest?
10. The following is a brief but complete newspaper item about an event similar to the run-in between bandit and barmaid:

French Robbers Flee Barrage of Pastries
United Press International

St. Etienne, France—Two would-be robbers were driven away from a pastry shop by a hail of creme pies, cakes and pastries thrown by the 65-year-old owner, her daughter and two grandchildren, police said. 1

The two men armed with a tear-gas bomb and a pistol entered Armand Davier's pastry shop Sunday in the industrial city on the Loire River in southeastern France and demanded the contents of the cash box, officers said. 2

They ran from a fusillade of pies and cakes hurled at them by the owner, her daughter and two grandchildren, police said. 3

Your task is to make a complete little drama out of this, with three scenes:

1. The bandits before the raid.
2. The shop before, during, and after the raid.
3. The bandits after they have fled.

Try to make any gains or losses of character apparent, but try also to make your presentation as affective and amusing as possible. In particular, you should consider how this event may have changed the characters of the two bandits and the relationship between them.

The Stronger

August Strindberg

The following one-act play was written almost a hundred years ago by the Swedish playwright, August Strindberg, who is known for his dramatizations of psychological and sexual problems within and around family life. This particular play is unusual in several respects. Only one character speaks, while the others (and one other in particular) listen and react. The speaking character tells and interprets a narrative of events involving her, her husband, and the woman she is addressing. The title of the play suggests that the events that are narrated—and their narration on this occasion—

constitute a character contest over which woman is "the stronger." As you read you will need to put some effort into reconstructing a narrative of the events that have preceded the play.

CHARACTERS
Mrs. X, actress, married
Miss Y, actress, unmarried
A Waitress

Scene: A corner of a ladies' café (in Stockholm in the eighteen eighties). Two small wrought-iron tables, a red plush settee and a few chairs. Miss Y is sitting with a half-empty bottle of beer on the table before her, reading an illustrated weekly which from time to time she exchanges for another. Mrs. X enters, wearing a winter hat and coat and carrying a decorative Japanese basket.

Mrs. X Why, Millie, my dear, how are you? Sitting here all alone on Christmas Eve like some poor bachelor.

Miss Y looks up from her magazine, nods, and continues to read.

Mrs. X You know it makes me feel really sad to see you. Alone. Alone in a café and on Christmas Eve of all times. It makes me feel as sad as when once in Paris I saw a wedding party at a restaurant. The bride was reading a comic paper and the bridegroom playing billiards with the witnesses. Ah me, I said to myself, with such a beginning how will it go, and how will it end? He was playing billiards on his wedding day! And she, you were going to say, was reading a comic paper on hers. But that's not quite the same.

A waitress brings a cup of chocolate to Mrs. X and goes out.

Mrs. X Do you know, Amelia, I really believe now you would have done better to stick to him. Don't forget I was the first who told you to forgive him. Do you remember? Then you would be married now and have a home. Think how happy you were that Christmas when you stayed with your fiancé's people in the country. How warmly you spoke of domestic happiness! You really quite longed to be out of the theatre. Yes, Amelia dear, home is best—next best to the stage, and as for children—but you couldn't know anything about that.

Miss Y's expression is disdainful. Mrs. X sips a few spoonfuls of chocolate, then opens her basket and displays some Christmas presents.

Mrs. X Now you must see what I have bought for my little chicks. *[Takes out a doll.]* Look at this. That's for Lisa. Do you see how she can roll her eyes and turn her head. Isn't she lovely? And here's a toy pistol for Maja. *[She loads the pistol and shoots it at Miss Y, who appears frightened.]*

Mrs. X Were you scared? Did you think I was going to shoot you? Really, I didn't think you'd believe that of me. Now if *you* were to shoot *me* it wouldn't be so surprising, for after all I did get in your way, and I know you never forget it—although I was entirely innocent. You still think I intrigued to get you out of the Grand Theatre, but I didn't. I didn't, however much you think I did. Well, it's no good talking, you will believe it was me . . . [*Takes out a pair of embroidered slippers.*] And these are for my old man, with tulips on them that I embroidered myself. As a matter of fact I hate tulips, but he has to have tulips on everything.

Miss Y looks up, irony and curiosity in her face.

Mrs. X [putting one hand in each slipper] Look what small feet Bob has, hasn't he? And you ought to see the charming way he walks—you've never seen him in slippers, have you?

Miss Y laughs.

Mrs. X Look, I'll show you. *[She makes the slippers walk across the table, and Miss Y laughs again.]*

Mrs. X But when he gets angry, look, he stamps his foot like this. "Those damn girls who can never learn how to make coffee! Blast! That silly idiot hasn't trimmed the lamp properly!" Then there's a draught under the door and his feet get cold. "Hell, it's freezing, and the damn fools can't even keep the stove going!" *[She rubs the sole of one slipper against the instep of the other Miss Y roars with laughter.]*

Mrs. X And then he comes home and has to hunt for his slippers, which Mary has pushed under the bureau . . . Well, perhaps it's not right to make fun of one's husband like this. He's sweet anyhow, and a good, dear husband. You ought to have had a husband like him, Amelia. What are you laughing at? What is it? Eh? And, you see, I know he is faithful to me. Yes, I know it. He told me himself—what *are* you giggling at?—that while I was on tour in Norway that horrible Frederica came and tried to seduce him. Can you imagine anything more abominable? *[Pause.]* I'd have scratched her eyes out if she had come around while I was at home. *[Pause.]* I'm glad Bob told me about it himself, so I didn't just hear it from gossip. *[Pause.]* And, as a matter of fact, Frederica wasn't the only one. I can't think why, but all the women in the Company seem to be crazy about my husband. They must think his position gives him some say in who is engaged at the Theatre. Perhaps you have run after him yourself? I don't trust you very far, but I know he has never been attracted by you, and you always seemed to have some sort of grudge against him, or so I felt.

Pause. They look at one another guardedly.

Mrs. X Do come and spend Christmas Eve with us tonight, Amelia—just to show that you're not offended with us, or anyhow not with me. I don't know why, but it seems specially unpleasant not to be friends with you. Perhaps it's because I did get in your way that time . . . [*slowly*] or—I don't know—really, I don't know at all why it is.

Pause. Miss Y gazes curiously at Mrs. X.

Mrs. X [thoughtfully] It was so strange when we were getting to know one another. Do you know, when we first met, I was frightened of you, so frightened I didn't dare let you out of my sight. I arranged all my goings and comings to be near you. I dared not be your enemy, so I became your friend. But when you came to our home, I always had an uneasy feeling, because I saw my husband didn't like you, and that irritated me—like when a dress doesn't fit. I did all I could to make him be nice to you, but it was no good—until you went and got engaged. Then you became such tremendous friends that at first it looked as if you only dared show your real feelings then—when you were safe. And then, let me see, how was it after that? I wasn't jealous—that's queer. And I remember at the christening, when you were the godmother, I told him to kiss you. He did, and you were so upset . . . As a matter of fact I didn't notice that then . . . I didn't think about it afterwards either . . . I've never thought about it—I didn't think about it afterwards either . . . I've never thought about it—until *now! [Rises abruptly.]* Why don't you say something? You haven't said a word all this time. You've just let me go on talking. You have sat there with your eyes drawing all these thoughts out of me—they were there in me like silk in a cocoon—thoughts . . . Mistaken thoughts? Let me think. Why did you break off your engagement? Why did you never come to our house after that? Why don't you want to come to us tonight?

Miss Y makes a motion, as if about to speak.

Mrs. X No. You don't need to say anything, for now I see it all. That was why—and why—and why. Yes. Yes, that's why it was. Yes, yes, all the pieces fit together now. That's it. I won't sit at the same table as you. *[Moves her things to the other table.]* That's why I have to embroider tulips, which I loathe, on his slippers—because you liked tulips. *[Throws the slippers on the floor.]* That's why we have to spend the summer on the lake—because you couldn't bear the seaside. That's why my son had to be called Eskil—because it was your father's name. That's why I had to wear your colours, read your books, eat the dishes you liked, drink your drinks—your chocolate, for instance. That's why—oh my God, it's terrible to think of, terrible! Everything, everything came to me from you—even your passions. Your soul bored into mine like a worm into an apple, and ate and ate and burrowed and burrowed, till nothing was left but the skin and a little black mould. I wanted to fly from you, but I couldn't. You were there like a snake, your black eyes fascinating me. When I spread my wings, they only dragged me down. I lay in the water with my feet tied together, and the harder I worked my arms, the deeper I sank—down, down, till I reached the bottom, where you lay in waiting like a giant crab to catch me in your claws—and now here I am. Oh how I hate you! I hate you, I hate you! And you just go on sitting there, silent, calm, indifferent, not caring whether the moon is new or full, if it's Christmas or New Year, if other people are happy or unhappy. You don't know how to hate or to love. You just sit there without moving—like a cat at a mouse-hole. You can't drag your prey out, you can't chase it, but you can out-stay it. Here you sit in your corner—you know they call it the rat-trap after you—reading the papers to see if anyone's ruined or wretched or been thrown out of the Company. Here you sit sizing up your victims and weighing your chances—like a pilot his shipwrecks for the salvage. *[Pause.]* Poor Amelia! Do you know, I couldn't be more sorry for you. I know you are miserable, miserable like some wounded creature, and vicious because you are wounded. I can't be angry with you. I should like to be, but after all you are the small one—and as for your affair with Bob, that doesn't worry me in the least. Why should it matter to me? And if you, or somebody else, taught me to drink chocolate, what's the difference? *[Drinks a spoonful. Smugly.]* Chocolate is very wholesome anyhow. And if I learnt from you how to dress, *tant mieux!*—that only gave me a stronger hold over my husband, and you have lost what I gained. Yes, to judge from various signs, I think you have now lost him. Of course, you meant me to walk out, as you once did, and which you're now regretting. But I won't do that, you may be sure. One shouldn't be narrow-minded, you know. And why should nobody else want what I have? *[Pause.]* Perhaps, my dear, taking everything into consideration, at this moment it is I who am the stronger. You never got anything from me, you just gave away from yourself. And now, like the thief in the night, when you woke up I had what you had lost. Why was it then that everything you touched became worthless and sterile? You couldn't keep a man's love—for all your tulips and your passions—but I could. You couldn't learn the art of living from your books—but I learnt it. You bore no little Eskil, although that was your father's name. *[Pause.]* And why is it you are silent—everywhere, always silent? Yes, I used to think this was strength, but perhaps it was because you hadn't anything to say, because you couldn't think of anything. *[Rises and picks up the slippers.]* Now I am going home, taking the tulips with me—*your* tulips. You couldn't learn from others, you couldn't bend, and so you broke like a dry stick. I did not. Thank you, Amelia, for all your good lessons. Thank you for teaching my husband how to love. Now I am going home—to love him.

Exit.

For Discussion and Writing

1. **Discuss the history of the relationships that have led to this little scene. That is, from the evidence given in the play, construct the story of the relevant portions of the characters' lives.**
2. **Discuss Goffman's theory of character contests as a way of interpreting the play. To do this, you must examine what is enacted and said in the play in the light of Goffman's concepts of why and how people behave the way they do. How much of what happens in the play can be explained by Goffman's theory? Are there aspects of the play that seem to elude Goffman's theory—perhaps things that belong to art rather than life?**

3. Write a revised version of the play in which Miss Y does all the talking and Mrs. X is silent. To do this you should make the following assumptions: first, that Mrs. X's monologue is simply a version of events interpreted in a way that is satisfying for Mrs. X; second that Miss Y would not only interpret the "same" events differently, she might also remember the events differently and might even remember somewhat different events; that is, you should assume that something happened between Mr. X and Miss Y that roughly corresponds to the description provided by Mrs. X, but may not correspond to that description in every respect. Your job is to keep the same large structure—an affair between Mr. X and Miss Y that ended with Mr. X still married to Mrs. X—but allow Miss Y to tell a version of the events that shows her to be "the stronger." We say there are two sides to every story. This is your chance to show what that expression means.
4. Assume that the waitress overhears this whole scene and that she knows more about the history of the Xs and Miss Y than emerges from Mrs. X's speeches. Has the waitress known Mr. X intimately? You decide. At any rate, your assignment here is to narrate the waitress's version of this scene. Assume she is telling a friend about it—or writing a letter to a friend about it—and go on from there.

Aristotle and the Advertisers: The Television Commercial as Drama *(passages from the essay)*

Martin Esslin

Dramatic form not only shapes our social behavior but confronts us regularly as a form of persuasive manipulation. A major literary critic, Martin Esslin, has even argued that much of television advertising is dramatic in structure. Centuries ago Aristotle pointed out that dramatic plots can be reduced to two simple forms and two complex developments of those forms. In one basic form the fortunes of the central character or protagonist (hero) are improved during the course of the action. This is the basic comic plot. In the other simple form—the tragic—the protagonist experiences a fall in fortune.

The more complex plots involve a reversal in the course of the hero's fortunes: first a rise, followed by a fall; or first a fall, then a rise. Aristotle's word for such a reversal of fortune was peripeteia. *In classic drama, reversals were often brought about by the intervention of a god, whose descent from the heavens was simulated by lowering the god or goddess onto the stage with a machine like a derrick or backhoe. The Latin term for such a "god from a machine" is* deus ex machina, *a term we still use for divine intervention or other mechanical methods of reversing a character's fortunes in a play.*

Aristotle also believed that plots are more interesting if they lead to a change from ignorance to knowledge. He called such a change recognition or anagnorisis, *and the new way of thinking brought about by recognition he called* dianoia. *He was surely right about the importance of these features, for they are the basis of every detective story as well as of Aristotle's favorite play, the* Oedipus *of Sophocles. In a murder mystery the* anagnorisis *and* dianoia *lead to the* peripeteia *of the murderer. The structures Aristotle identified are still very much with us, so it should come as no surprise that Martin Esslin finds them active in TV commercials. Here are selections from his essay "Aristotle and the Advertisers":*

We have all seen it a hundred times, and in dozens of variations: that short 1
sequence of images in which a husband expresses disappointment and distress at his wife's inability to provide him with a decent cup of coffee and seems inclined to seek a better tasting potion outside the home, perhaps even at the bosom of another lady; the anxious consultation, which ensues between the wife and her mother or an experienced and trusted friend, who counsels the use of another brand of coffee; and finally, the idyllic tableau of the husband astonished and surprised by the excellence of his wife's new coffee, demanding a second—or even a third!—cup of the miraculously effective product.

A television commercial. And, doubtless, it includes elements of drama, 2
yet is it not too short, too trivial, too contemptible altogether to deserve serious consideration? That seems the generally accepted opinion. But in an age when, through the newly discovered technologies of mechanical reproduction and dissemination, drama has become one of the chief instruments of human expression, communication, and indeed, thought, all uses of the dramatic form surely deserve study. If the television commercial could be shown to be drama, it would be among the most ubiquitous and the most influential of its forms and hence deserve the attention of the serious critics and theoreticians of that art, most of whom paradoxically still seem to be spellbound by types of drama (such as tragedy) that are hallowed by age and tradition, though practically extinct today. And surely, in a civilization in which drama, through the mass media, has become an omnipresent, all-pervasive, continuously available, and unending stream of entertainment for the vast majority of individuals in the so-called developed world, a comprehensive theory, morphology, and typology of drama is urgently needed. Such a theory would have to take cognizance of the fact that the bulk of drama today is to be found not on the stage but in the mechanized mass media, the cinema, television, and in most civilized countries, radio; that, both on the stage and in the mass media, drama exists in a

multitude of new forms, which might even deserve to be considered genres unknown to Aristotle—from mime to musicals, from police serials to science fiction, from westerns to soap opera, from improvisational theatre to happenings—and that, among all these, the television commercial might well be both unprecedented and highly significant.

The coffee commercial cited above, albeit a mere thirty to fifty seconds in 3
length, certainly exhibits attributes of drama. Yet to what extent is it typical of the television commercial in general? Not all TV commercials use plot, character, and spoken dialogue to the same extent. Nevertheless, I think it can be shown that most, if not all, TV commercials are essentially dramatic, because basically they use mimetic action to produce a semblance of real life, and the basic ingredients of drama—character and a story line—are present in the great majority of them, either manifestly or by implication.

Take another frequently occurring type: a beautiful girl who tells us that 4
her hair used to be lifeless and stringy, while now, as she proudly displays, it is radiantly vital and fluffy. Is this not just a bare announcement, flat and undramatic? I should argue that, in fact, there is drama in it, implied in the clearly fictitious character who is telling us her story. What captures our interest and imagination is the radiant girl, and what she tells us is an event which marked a turning point in her life. Before she discovered the miraculous new shampoo she was destined to live in obscurity and neglect, but now she has become beautiful and radiant with bliss. Are we not, therefore, here in the presence of that traditional form of drama in which a seemingly static display of character and atmosphere evokes highly charged, decisive events of the past that are now implicit in the present—the type of drama, in fact, of which Ibsen's *Ghosts* is a frequently cited specimen?

What, though, if the lady in question is a well-known show business or 5
sporting personality and hence a *real* rather than a fictitious character? Do we not then enter the realm of reality rather than fictional drama? I feel that there are very strong grounds for arguing the opposite: for film stars, pop singers, and even famous sporting personalities project not their real selves but a carefully tailored fictional image. There has always, throughout the history of drama, been the great actor who essentially displayed no more than a single, continuous personality rather than a series of differing characters (witness the harlequins and other permanent character types of the *commedia dell'arte;* great melodrama performers like Frédéric Lemaître; great comics like Chaplin, Buster Keaton, Laurel and Hardy, or the Marx Brothers; or indeed, great film stars like Marilyn Monroe or John Wayne—to name but a very few). Such actors do not enact parts so much as lend their highly wrought and artistically crafted fictitious personality to a succession of roles that exist merely to display that splendid artifact. Hence if Bob Hope or John Wayne appear as spokesmen for banking institutions, or Karl Malden as the advocate of a credit card, no one is seriously asked to believe that they are informing us of their real experience with these institutions; we all know that they are speaking a preestablished,

carefully polished text, which, however brief it may be, has been composed by a team of highly skilled professional writers, and that they are merely lending them the charisma of their long-established—and fictional—urbanity, sturdiness, or sincerity.

There remains, admittedly, a residue of nondramatic TV commercials: those which are no more than newspaper advertisements displaying a text and a symbol, with a voice merely reading it out to the less literate members of the audience, and those in which the local car or carpet salesman more or less successfully tries to reel off a folksy appeal to his customers. But these commercials tend to be the local stations' fill-up material. The bulk of the major, nationally shown commercials are profoundly dramatic and exhibit, in their own peculiar way, in minimal length and maximum compression, the basic characteristics of the dramatic mode of expression in a state of particular purity—precisely because here it approaches the point of zero extension, as though the TV commercial were a kind of differential calculus of the aesthetics of drama. 6

Let us return to our initial example: the coffee playlet. Its three-beat basic structure can be found again and again. In the first beat the exposition is made and the problem posed. Always disaster threatens: persistent headaches endanger the love relationship or success at work of the heroine or hero (or for headaches read constipation, body odor, uncomfortable sanitary pads, ill-fitting dentures, hemorrhoids, lost credit cards, inefficient detergents that bring disgrace on the housewife). In the second beat a wise friend or confidant suggests a solution. And this invariably culminates in a moment of insight, of conversion, in fact the classical anagnorisis that leads to dianoia and thus to the peripeteia, the turning point of the action. The third beat shows the happy conclusion to what was a potentially tragic situation. For it is always and invariably the hero's or heroine's ultimate happiness that is at stake: his health or job or domestic peace. In most cases there is even the equivalent of the chorus of ancient tragedy in the form of an unseen voice, or indeed, a choral song, summing up the moral lesson of the action and generalizing it into a universally applicable principle. And this is, almost invariably, accompanied by a visual epiphany of the product's symbol, container, trademark, or logo—in other words the allegorical or symbolic representation of the beneficent power that has brought about the fortunate outcome and adverted the ultimate disaster; the close analogy to the *deus ex machina* of classical tragedy is inescapable. 7

All this is compressed into a span of from thirty to fifty seconds. Moreover such a mini-drama contains distinctly drawn characters, who, while representing easily recognizable human types (as so many characters of traditional drama), are yet individualized in subtle ways, through the personalities of the actors portraying them, the way they are dressed, the way they speak. The setting of the action, however briefly it may be glimpsed, also greatly contributes to the solidity of characterization: the tasteful furnishings of the home, 8 not too opulent, but neat, tidy, and pretty enough to evoke admiring sympathy and empathy; the suburban scene visible through the living room or kitchen window, the breakfast table that bears witness to the housewifely skills of the heroine—and all subtly underlined by mood music rising to a dramatic climax at the moment of anagnorisis and swelling to a triumphant coda at the fortunate conclusion of the action. Of all the art forms only drama can communicate such an immense amount of information on so many levels simultaneously within the span of a few seconds. That all this has to be taken in instantaneously, moreover, ensures that most of the impact will be subliminal—tremendously suggestive while hardly ever rising to the level of full consciousness. It is this which explains the great effectiveness of the TV commercial and the inevitability of its increasing employment of dramatic techniques. Drama does not simply translate the abstract idea into concrete terms. It literally incarnates the abstract message by bringing it to life in a human personality and a human situation. Thus it activates powerful subconscious drives and the deep animal magnetisms that dominate the lives of men and women who are always interested in and attracted by other human beings, their looks, their charm, their mystery.

For Discussion and Writing

1. **Look back at the various narratives and dramas you have already considered, from the personal narratives of Pratt to the character contests of Goffman. Which of them have clear reversals, recognitions, or both? Is Aristotle right? Are the texts with reversals and recognitions the most interesting? Discuss any exceptions you find. It would be especially useful to consider your own dramatizations and personal narratives in the light of Aristotle's views.**
2. **Watch commercials on TV until you find one that follows the Aristotelian principles described by Esslin. If you have access to a VCR, record the commercial you are going to use so that you can study it carefully. If you don't have a VCR, do the best you can. You may have to see a commercial several times before you can complete your project.**

   This project has two parts. First, develop a written version of your chosen commercial, in the form of a play, with stage directions and everything else you would need for someone to act out the commercial. (An alternative to this would be to have someone with access to a VCR provide a written version that the whole class could use.) Second, write an alternative version of the same commercial, in which some event happens or something is said that subverts or destroys the commercial function of the play. Try to make the smallest changes possible that will achieve the result that is being aimed at here. With some help from your classmates, act out your altered version.

Chapter 2

Texts, Thoughts, and Things

In this chapter we ask you to shift your attention from the large or "macro" structures of narrative and drama to the small or "micro" structure of language itself. In particular we will focus on a single crucial element of language: the creative principle of metaphor.

A friend of ours who became a writer and teacher himself told us that his whole attitude toward language was changed when a teacher said to him — somewhat brutally — "Words are razor blades. You use them as if they were bricks." The point, of course, was that careless, clumsy use of language could be dangerous: that a certain awareness, a certain delicacy, is demanded by language. A razor blade can be a tool, a weapon, or a hazard, but you ignore its sharp edges at your peril. The point was forcefully made by the teacher's own use of the blade of metaphor, drawing the student's attention to a potential danger in language that he had overlooked.

We do not intend to draw any blood here, nor do we recommend wounding people to get their attention, but we hope this fragment of an anecdote will help explain why we have singled out metaphor as a dimension of language that should receive special attention. The reading and writing work in this chapter is designed to help you develop your awareness of the presence and function of metaphor in all sorts of texts. This awareness should help you attain greater precision and power as a writer. It should also enhance your pleasure and ability as a reader. Metaphor is at the heart of the creative process embodied in human language.

The Linguistic Basis of Metaphor

It is widely understood that metaphor is a basic element of poetry. It is also true, however, that metaphor is a fundamental building block of ordinary language and of such forms of written prose as the essay. We begin our investigation of metaphor with two passages from a book called *Words and Things* by the psycholinguist Roger Brown.

In the first passage Brown uses the case of the Wild Boy of Aveyron as a way of directing our attention to the linguistic problem of names for things—or nouns, as we call them. By clarifying for us the way in which nouns refer not to individual things but to "universals," or categories of things, Brown lays the basis for an understanding of metaphor.

In a metaphor the name of one thing is applied to another, so that, as in certain chemical reactions, there is an exchange of particles between the two. That is, when we say, "Words are razor blades," certain defining attributes of the category *razor blades* are transferred to the category *words:* namely, delicacy and dangerousness. This is the way metaphor works. In the second passage included here, Brown helps us understand why the transfer takes place. He also suggests that all nouns are to some extent metaphorical. Language grows by a kind of metaphorical extension. Metaphor is thus not an ornament added on top of language, but a principle built in at the most fundamental level of linguistic behavior.

The following selections by Roger Brown are clear but dense—packed with meaning. Please read them slowly and carefully. Your understanding of metaphor will depend on your understanding of how words refer to things. That is, Brown's discussion of metaphor in the second selection depends upon his discussion of reference and categories in the first. To understand metaphor, we must be aware of how delicate and complicated is the connection between language and all the things we use language to discuss.

What Words Are: Reference and Categories

Roger Brown

"A child of eleven or twelve, who some years before had been seen 1
completely naked in the Caune Woods seeking acorns and roots to eat, was met in the same place toward the end of September 1797 by three sportsmen who

seized him as he was climbing into a tree to escape from their pursuit." In these words Dr. Jean-Marc-Gaspard Itard began his first report on the education of the wild boy found in the Department of Aveyron. The discovery of a human creature who had lived most of his life outside of all human society excited the greatest interest in Paris. Frivolous spirits looked forward with delight to the boy's astonishment at the sights of the capital. Readers of Rousseau expected to see an example of man as he was "when wild in woods the noble savage ran." There were even some who counted on hearing from the boy mankind's original unlearned language—they conjectured that it was most likely to be Hebrew. The savage of Aveyron disappointed all of these expectations. He was a dirty, scarred, inarticulate creature who trotted and grunted like a beast, ate the most filthy refuse, and bit and scratched those who opposed him. In Paris he was exhibited to the populace in a cage, where he ceaselessly rocked to and fro like an animal in the zoo, indifferent alike to those who cared for him and those who stared. The great psychiatrist Pinel, who taught France to treat the insane as patients rather than as prisoners, was brought to examine the boy. After a series of tests Pinel pronounced him a congenital idiot unlikely to be helped by any sort of training.

Many came to believe that the so-called savage was merely a poor subnormal child whose parents had recently abandoned him at the entrance to some woods. However, a young physician from the provinces, Dr. Itard, believed that the boy's wildness was genuine, that he had lived alone in the woods from about the age of seven until his present age of approximately twelve, and there was much to support this view. The boy had a strong aversion to society, to clothing, furniture, houses, and cooked food. He trotted like an animal, sniffed at everything that was given him to eat, and masticated with his incisors in the same way as certain wild beasts. His body showed numerous scars, some of them apparently caused by the bites of animals and some which he had had for a considerable time. Above all, a boy of his general description had been seen running wild in the same forest some five years earlier. 2

Dr. Itard had read enough of Locke and Condillac to be convinced that most of the ideas a man possesses are not innate but, rather, are acquired by experience. He believed that the apparent feeble-mindedness of the boy of Aveyron was caused by his prolonged isolation from human society and his ignorance of any language and that the boy could be cured by a teacher with patience and a knowledge of epistemology. Itard asked for the job. He had been appointed physician to the new institute for deaf mutes in Paris and so asked to take Victor there to be civilized and, most interesting for us, to learn the French language. Permission was granted and Itard worked with the boy, whom he called Victor, for five years. Itard had little success in teaching Victor to speak. However, he had considerable success in teaching Victor to understand language and, especially, to read simple words and phrases. . . . 3

In teaching Victor to understand speech, Itard found that he must, in the beginning, set aside the question of meaning and simply train the boy to 4 identify speech sounds. In the first period after his capture Victor paid no attention to the human voice but only to sounds of approach or movement in his vicinity—noises that would be important to a creature living in the forest. Itard devised an instructive game for teaching Victor to distinguish one vowel from another. Each of the boy's five fingers was to stand for one of five French vowels. When Itard pronounced a vowel, Victor was to raise the appropriate finger. Victor was blindfolded and the vowels were pronounced in an unpredictable order so that if the boy made correct responses it must be because he could distinguish the vowels. In time Victor learned to play the game, but he was never very good at it. Thus Itard decided that the boy's vision was more acute than his hearing and thought he might be taught to read more easily than he could be taught to understand speech.

5 Again Itard came up with an ingenious game designed to teach Victor to identify the forms of the written and printed language, even though he could not yet understand their meanings. The same collection of words was written on two blackboards, making the order of words on one board unrelated to the order on the other. Itard would point to a word on his board and it was Victor's task to point to its counterpart on the other board. When the boy made a mistake, teacher and pupil "spelled" the word together; Itard pointed to the first letter of his word and Victor did the same with his supposed match, and they proceeded in this fashion until they came to two letters where Victor saw a difference. After a time Victor could read quite a large number of words, some of them very much alike. As yet, however, this was not reading with understanding but simply the identification of empty forms.

6 The time had come to teach Victor something about the meanings of words. Itard arranged several objects on a shelf in the library, including a pen, a key, a box, and a book. Each thing rested on a card on which its name was written, and Victor had already learned to identify the names. Itard next disarranged the objects and cards and indicated to Victor that he was to match them up again. After a little practice the boy did this very well. Itard then removed all the objects to a corner of the room. He showed Victor one name and gave him to understand that he was to fetch the object named. Victor also learned this very quickly, and Itard grew increasingly optimistic.

7 The next test went badly at first. Itard locked away in a cupboard all of the particular objects with which Victor had practiced, but made sure that there were in his study other objects of the same kinds—other pens, keys, boxes, and books. He then showed Victor a word, e.g., *livre,* and indicated that the boy was to bring the referent. Victor went to the cupboard for the familiar book and finding the cupboard locked had to give up the task. He showed no interest in any other book. The same failure occurred with the other words. Victor had understood each word to name some particular thing rather than a category of things.

8 Itard then spread out a variety of books, turning their pages to show what they had in common. He indicated that the word *livre* could go with any of

them. After this lesson, when shown the word *livre,* Victor was able to fetch a book other than the specific book of his training. However, he did not correctly constitute the book category at once, for he brought a handful of paper at one time and a pamphlet and magazine at another. As his errors were corrected, however, he learned to distinguish books from other sorts of publications and also to recognize such categories as are named *key, pen,* and *box.* The crucial test for understanding of the referent category was always Victor's ability to identify new instances.

Itard next approached the difficult problem of conveying an understand- 9
ing of words that name qualities and relations rather than objects that have size, shape, and weight. He took out two books, one large and one small, and Victor promptly labelled each with the word *livre.* Itard then took Victor's hand and spread it flat on the front of the large volume showing how it failed to cover the full surface. The same hand spread out on the smaller book did cover that surface. Victor then seemed puzzled as if wondering that one word should name these two different objects. Itard gave him new cards labelled *grand livre* and *petit livre* and matched them with the appropriate books. Now came the test to see whether Victor had learned specific habits or had abstracted a general relationship. Itard produced two nails, one large and one small, and asked that the cards *grand* and *petit* be correctly assigned. Victor learned this relationship and others besides.

Itard had another good idea for verbs that name actions. He took a familiar 10
thing, e.g., a book, and made it the object of some action—pounding it or dropping it or opening it or kissing it. In each case he gave the boy the appropriate verb in the infinitive form. The test was for the boy to label such actions when their object was changed, e.g., to a key or a pen. This too Victor learned.

The end of all this imaginative teaching was that Victor learned to read 11
with understanding quite a large number of words and phrases. He would obey simple written commands and also use the word cards to signal his own desires. In addition to all this he assumed the manners and appearance of a civilized young man. However, Itard's final word was discouraging. Although Victor had been greatly improved by education, diminishing returns on his efforts convinced Itard that the boy was performing to the limits permitted by his intellectual endowment and these limits, unfortunately, were subnormal.

Reference and Categories

When Dr. Itard wanted to give Victor some idea of the meanings of words, 12
he hit upon a way of showing that each word stood for something, that each word had a referent. This is the sort of thing each of us would do to convey to a small child the meanings of his first words; it is also the usual recourse in trying to communicate with a foreigner who understands no English. The use of language to make reference is the central language function which is prerequi-

site to all else. It is the beginning of the psychology of language and is, accordingly, the focus of this book.

What Victor learned about reference was at first too specific. Words do not 13
name particular things as Victor thought; they name classes or categories. Someone who properly understands the word *book* is prepared to apply it to any and all particular books. I see in the room where I sit a novel in a highly colored dust jacket and quite near it one numbered volume of a sober encyclopedia; on the floor is a Penguin paperback, and asleep in the hall the telephone directory. Although they differ in many respects, all of these are, nevertheless, books. They have the printed pages and stiff covers that define the category.

Actually we do not badly stretch the notion of the category if we treat even 14
a single particular book as a category. The single book, the single anything, is a category of sense impressions. Victor must have seen the book that was used in his early training on many occasions, in various positions, and from different angles. At one time a book is a rectangular shape lying on a table; at another time the same book is only the back of a binding on the library shelf. While it is possible to say that these various experiences constitute a category, that category must be distinguished from the sort named by *book* in general. The various appearances of one book have a continuity in space-time that makes us think of them as one thing preserving its identity through change. The various individual books around my room do not have this kind of continuity. So let us agree to call all referents categories but to distinguish the particular referent from the general by calling it an "identity" category.

Itard's later training procedures show that not all referents are objects 15
with size, shape, and weight. Actions like dropping and kissing are referents and so are such qualities as large and small or red and green. Clearly too, these referents are categories. The act of dropping changes many of its characteristics from one occasion to the next but preserves something invariant that defines the action. Any sort of recurrence in the non-linguistic world can become the referent of a name and all such recurrences will be categories because recurrences are never identical in every detail. Recurrence always means the duplication of certain essential features in a shifting context of non-essentials.

It is quite easy to see that the referents of words are categories but 16
somewhat less easy to see that language forms, the names of referents, are also categories. Variations in the production of a language form are probably more obvious in the written or printed version than in the spoken. Differences in handwriting and of type are so great that it is actually difficult to specify what all the renderings of one word have in common. Even the individual letter is a category of forms changing considerably in their numerous productions. Variations in pronunciation are also certainly ubiquitous but our early extensive training in disregarding the dimensions of speech that are not significant for distinguishing English words causes us to overlook them. So long as phonetic essentials are preserved we identify utterances as the same, although

they change greatly in loudness, pitch, quaver, breathiness, and the like. From acoustic studies we know that even one speaker "repeating" the same vowel does not produce identical sounds. Itard's productions of the French vowels cannot have been identical from one time to another and neither, we may be sure, were the "matched" words he wrote on the two blackboards. In these first games Victor was learning to categorize the empty forms of language, to pick out the essential recurrent features and to overlook the non-essential variations.

For Discussion and Writing

1. **It is easy to understand Brown when he says that the word *book* refers to a "category" that includes all the books that one could possibly encounter. But things get more complicated when he says that any particular book is also a category—what he calls an "identity category." Reconsider Brown's fourteenth paragraph and discuss the notion of "identity category." Define this term in your own words, and illustrate your definition with examples.**
2. **Every word, even every letter, says Brown, is also a "category of forms." Looking over paragraph 16, define "category of forms" in your own words, and illustrate the way in which a word may be described as a "category of forms."**

What Words Are: Metaphor

Roger Brown

When someone invents a new machine, or forms a concept, or buys a dog, 1
or manufactures a soap powder his first thought is to name it. These names are almost never arbitrary creations produced by juggling the sounds of the language into a novel sequence. We think hard and ask our friends to help us find a "good" name, a name that is appropriate in that its present meaning suggests the new meaning it is to have.

Sometimes new words are introduced by borrowing words or mor- 2
phemes[1] from classical languages. The biological sciences have been especially partial to this practice as *photosynthesis, streptoneura,* and *margaritifera* testify. In order to savor the appropriateness of these names a classical education is required and so, for most of us, they are functionally arbitrary.

The usual method of creating a new name is to use words or morphemes 3
already in the language, either by expanding the semantic range of some word or by recombining morphemes. Every word has a history of former meanings and, traced back far enough, an ancestor that belongs to another language. The

[1] morpheme: the smallest unit of meaning in any given language. In English the word *dog* is a morpheme. The word *dogged* adds a second morpheme—Editor.

modern French *lune* derives from the Latin *lux.* The extension of the Latin word for *light* to the moon is appropriate and may once have been experienced as appropriate. Today, however, because of phonetic change and loss of the earlier meaning, the metaphor in *lune* must be overlooked by most French speakers even as we overlook the metaphor in our *moon* which is a remote cognate of Latin *mensis* for month. Both languages arrived at their word for the moon by metaphorical means, though the metaphors are constructed on different attributes of the referent—its luminosity for the French, its periodic cycle for the English. In both cases the whole process dates so far back that the appropriateness of these names like that of *margaritifera* or *photosynthesis* is evident only to scholars.

Many new names are still very familiar in an older reference and so their 4
appropriateness to the new referent is easy to see. There are dogs called *Spot* or *Rover;* detergents and soaps are called *Surf, Rinso,* and *Duz;* one kind of personality is said, by clinical psychologists, to be *rigid.* Compounds like *overcoat, railroad train,* and *fireplace* have familiar constituents. While the origins of these names are obvious enough they probably are not ordinarily noticed. It seems to be necessary to take a special attitude toward language, quite different from our everyday attitude, to discern the metaphors around us.

The metaphor in a word lives when the word brings to mind more than a 5
single reference and the several references are seen to have something in common. Sometime in the past someone or other noticed that the foot of a man bears the same relation to his body as does the base of a mountain to the whole mountain. He thought of extending the word *foot* to the mountain's base. This word *foot* then referred to two categories. These categories share a relational attribute which makes them one category. Within this superordinate category, which we might name *the foundations* or *lower parts of things,* are two subordinate categories—the man's foot and the mountain's base. These two remain distinct within the larger category because the members of each subordinate category share attributes that are not shared with the members of the other subordinate category. The *man's foot* is made of flesh and has toes, which is not true of the base of any mountain. Thus far the relationship is like that of any set of superordinate and subordinate categories, e.g., *polygons* as superordinate to triangles and squares. The subordinates have something in common which makes them species of one genus but they are distinct because members of one subordinate have still more in common. Metaphor differs from other superordinate-subordinate relations in that the superordinate is not given a name of its own. Instead, the name of one subordinate is extended to the other and this, as we shall see, has the effect of calling both references to mind with their differences as well as their similarities. The usual superordinate name, e.g., polygons, calls to mind only the shared attributes of the various varieties of polygon.

The use of *foot* to name a part of the mountain results in the appearance of 6
foot in certain improbable phrase contexts. One hears, for the first time, the

foot of the mountain or *mountain's foot.* Until someone saw the similarity that generated the metaphor these sayings were not heard. They cause the metaphor to live for others who have not noticed the similarity in question. The anatomical reference is called to mind by the word *foot* which has been its unequivocal name. The context *of the mountain* is one in which this word has never appeared. The phrase suggests such forms as *peak* or *top* or *slope* or *height* or *base;* it is a functional attribute of all these. Only one of these forms has a referent that is like the anatomical foot and that one is *base.* There is a click of comprehension as the similarity is recognized and some pleasure at the amusing conceit of a mountain with toes, a mountain anthropomorphized. If the metaphor was created for a poem about the mountain climber's struggle with his almost human antagonist—the mountain itself—then the metaphor might figure importantly in communicating the sense of the poem.

This metaphor blazed briefly for the person who created it and it lights up 7
again when anyone hears it for the first time, but for most of us it is dead. This is because with repetition of the phrase *foot of the mountain* the word *foot* loses its exclusive connection with anatomy. The word may be used of mountain as often as of man. When that is true there is nothing in the phrase *foot of the mountain* to suggest a man's foot and so the phrase is experienced as a conventional name for the lower part of a mountain. Part of the phrase is accidentally homophonic with part of the phrase *foot of a man* but there is no more reason for one to call the other to mind than there is for *board of wood* to remind us of *board of directors, bored with psycholinguistics,* or *bored from within.* In the interest of univocal reference we attend to the context in which each form occurs and do not consider the meanings it might have in other contexts.

The word *foot,* in isolation, is ambiguous. It has many referents including 8
the mountainous and the anatomical. That special attitude toward language which brings out the potential metaphors now seems to me to involve attending to forms in isolation, deliberately ignoring context. In this last sentence, for instance, consider the word *attending* and disregard its surroundings. *Attending* names at least two kinds of behavior; there is "attending a lecture" and "attending to a lecture." The latter behavior is notoriously not the same as the former. In the sentence above only the intellectual attention sense of *attending* comes to mind; the other is ruled out by context.

A metaphor lives in language so long as it causes a word to appear in 9
improbable contexts, the word suggesting one reference, the context another. When the word becomes as familiar in its new contexts as it was in the old the metaphor dies. This has happened with *foot of the mountain.* Sometimes there is a further stage in which the older set of contexts dies altogether and also the older reference. In these circumstances one speaks of a historical semantic change in the word. The term *strait-laced* is applied nowadays to people who follow an exceptionally severe, restrictive moral code. An older sense can be revived by placing the term in one of its older contexts: "Mrs. Mather was

miserable in her strait-laced bodice." In the days when people laced their clothing *strait* meant *tight* and to be *strait-laced* was literally to be rather tightly trussed up. It is not difficult to see the attributes of this condition that resulted first in a metaphor and then in a semantic change. Whether one is tightly laced into his clothing or into his conscience he will feel confined, he may strain against his bonds and burst them, or, when no one else is about, he may secretly relax them a little. The metaphor is so rich that we should not be surprised to find it in poetry as well as in the history of linguistic change.

In fact there exists a poem founded on the very similarities that caused 10
strait-laced to change in meaning.

Delight in Disorder

A sweet disorder in the dress
Kindles in clothes a wantonness.
A lawn about the shoulders thrown
Into a fine distraction;
An erring lace, which here and there
Enthrals the crimson stomacher;
A cuff neglectful, and thereby
Ribbands to flow confusedly;
A winning wave, deserving note,
In the tempestuous petticoat;
A careless shoestring, in whose tie
I see a wild civility;—
Do more bewitch me, than when art
Is too precise in every part.

Robert Herrick

Herrick lived in seventeenth century England, through the period of 11
Puritan rule into the restoration of Charles II. F. W. Bateson . . . points out that the poem reproduced above is concerned with more than disorder of costume. It is not only the clothes but also the wearers that Herrick would have *sweet, wanton, distracted, erring, neglectful, winning, tempestuous, wild,* and *bewitching.* The poem is a plea for disorder of manners and morals as well as of dress. It is a statement of anti-Puritanism.

How does Herrick communicate these depth meanings? The poem by its 12
title professes to be concerned with dress. The word *disorder* can be applied to dress, to manners, to politics, to morals, or even to a man's wits. The fact that we are reading a poem makes us receptive to multiple meanings but the title alone does not indicate what secondary meanings, if any, are relevant. In the first line

sweet sounds a trifle odd since it is not often said of disorder in dress. *Sweet* starts several auxiliary lines of thought having to do, perhaps, with girl friends, small children, and sugar cane. Only one of these is reinforced by what follows. *Kindles* and *wantonness* in the second line rule out children and sugar cane. Thoughts about girls and loose behavior are supported by words like *distraction, enthrals,* and *tempestuous.* All of these words can be used in talking about clothes. However, their choice is improbable enough to call for some explanation. Since the improbable words are all drawn from a set of terms having to do with girls and their behavior a second group of consistent references is created.

A scientist might call Herrick's message ambiguous since he uses words 13 that have several different referents and does not clearly sort these out with critical contexts. Behind that judgment is the assumption that the poet intends, as a scientist might, to call attention to just one kind of reference. In fact, however, Herrick wanted to talk simultaneously about clothing, ladies, and morality and to do so in a very compact way. Rather than string out three unequivocal vocabularies he uses one vocabulary which is able to make three kinds of reference.

When a poet uses simile he explicitly invites us to note the similarities and 14 differences in two referents as in "My love is like a red, red rose." When he uses metaphor a word is used in a context that calls for a different word as in "The *lion* of England" or "My *rose* smiled at me." The context evokes one reference, the word another and the meaning is enriched by their similarities and differences. *Lion* and *king, rose* and *love* concentrate on similarities. There is an extraordinary sentence of e. e. cummings' . . . in which the difference in the two references is the main thing: "And although her health eventually failed her she kept her sense of humor to the *beginning.*" The most probable word for final position in that sentence is *end.* This is not only different from *beginning,* it is the antonym. The probability of *end* is so great that the reader is bound to anticipate it. Finding instead its antonym almost makes us feel reprimanded. Our worldly outlook has made us too prone to think of death as the end.

For Discussion and Writing

1. **At the end of paragraph 4, Brown says that "it seems to be necessary to take a special attitude toward language, quite different from our everyday attitude, to discern the metaphors around us." Try to define or describe the attitude Brown is discussing.**
2. **Adopting the attitude of a student of metaphor, examine the metaphors that Brown himself employs—as in the first sentence of paragraph 7, for instance. Does his use of metaphor differ from that of a poet like Robert Herrick?**
3. **Examine more closely the poem by Herrick. Brown has discussed the major system of metaphor in the poem, but the poetic text is enlivened by**

other instances of metaphoric language. Discuss the range of meaning evoked by some of the following words in the poem:

kindles (line 2)
enthrals (line 6)
flow, wave, tempestuous (lines 8, 9, 10)

How do you understand a phrase like "wild civility"?

4. Produce, in your own words, a working definition of metaphor, with some appropriate illustrative examples. You will need some clear notion of metaphor to begin your study of the workings of this feature of language in poems, dreams, essays, and advertisements.

Metaphor in Three Poems

Metaphor is a vital principle of all language, but it is especially important in poetry. If metaphors grow like weeds—in ordinary language—poets cultivate them, extend them, and combine them to make new hybrids that might never occur in nature but are exotic and exciting in those formal gardens we call poems.

Our study of the workings of metaphor will take us ultimately to essays, arguments, and advertising—back toward ordinary life. But we begin with three short poems, as laboratory specimens designed to illustrate some of the principles of metaphoric language. Please read them carefully and consider the questions for discussion and writing after each poem.

Separation

Your absence has gone through me
Like thread through a needle
Everything I do is stitched with its color.

W. S. Merwin

For Discussion and Writing

1. It has been said that a good simile or metaphor is both unexpected and appropriate. Consider Merwin's poem in the light of this view. How would you expect someone to complete the phrase "Your absence has gone through me like . . . "?
2. If someone said "Your absence has gone through me like a dagger," that would signify that separation is painful. What does Merwin's metaphor signify?

"Let us honor . . . "

Let us honor if we can
The vertical man
Though we value none
But the horizontal one.

W. H. Auden

For Discussion and Writing

This very small poem was sent by Wystan Hugh Auden to his friend Christopher Isherwood, and later appeared at the beginning of a volume of Auden's poetry. The poem depends upon the use of two words that are nearly synonyms (*honor* and *value*) and two words that form an abstract, geometrical opposition (*vertical* and *horizontal*). The reader is invited to make his or her own interpretive distinction between the meanings of *honor* and *value* and also to supply some concrete interpretations for *vertical* and *horizontal.* One way to do this is simply to rewrite the poem by filling in the blanks:

Let us ________ if we can
The ________ man
Though we ________ none
But the ________ one.

The assumption you must make in filling in these blanks is that *horizontal* and *vertical* are metaphors for something: for instance, death and life, slackness and probity. By supplying your interpretation, you collaborate in the completion of the poem.

Compare your version with others. Are some more satisfying than others? Is any one so satisfying that you feel like adopting it as "correct" and labeling the others wrong? Are any so unsatisfying that you want to rule them out entirely? Does the idea of interpretation as a collaborative or creative activity please or displease you? Discuss these matters.

Metaphors

I'm a riddle in nine syllables,
An elephant, a ponderous house,
A melon strolling on two tendrils.
O red fruit, ivory, fine timbers!
This loaf's big with its yeasty rising.
Money's new-minted in this fat purse.
I'm a means, a stage, a cow in calf.
I've eaten a bag of green apples,
Boarded the train there's no getting off.

Sylvia Plath

For Discussion and Writing

1. This poem is a riddle, with each line providing a metaphoric clue to its solution. Solve the riddle, and consider how the relationships between the metaphors contribute to its solution.
2. Compose your own riddle poem to present to the class for solution. Your subject should be something with which the class is familiar, such as a physical or emotional state (sleepiness, hunger, happiness, envy), or a place (classroom, fast-food restaurant), or a thing (car, TV, pizza). To get started, make a list of the qualities of your subject that first come to mind. Consider which quality or qualities best describe your subject, and concentrate on developing metaphors that will make your audience experience your subject from your point of view.

Metaphor and Dream

For centuries people have believed that dreams are messages from somewhere, perhaps in a code that disguises their meaning. In our century a new theory of dreams has dominated discussion, the theory developed by Sigmund Freud. According to Freud, dreams are messages from the human unconscious, in a code designed to pass the censorship of our conscious mind. These messages, which have to do with our most primal needs and desires—especially those relating to sexuality—must be censored because we do not wish to admit that we could even "think" such things, since they conflict with our status as civilized, reasonable beings.

Freud has a name for the psychic process or mechanism that transforms our desires into acceptable shape. He calls it the *dream-work.* For our purposes Freud's dream-work is interesting on two counts. First, it operates much as do those linguistic devices called figures of speech, of which metaphor is especially important. Second, Freud calls the process of making sense of dreams *interpretation,* and what he means by interpretation is very close to what literary critics mean by the interpretation of poems.

Dreams and poems are texts that work in similar ways—to a certain extent. We are concerned here with both the similarities and the differences. But before discussing them, we should examine Freud's own definitions of his key terms. We have numbered and arranged these definitions here, but the language is Freud's (from the English translation of his *Introductory Lectures on Psychoanalysis*). We have added explanatory comments after each quotation from Freud.

From *Introductory Lectures on Psychoanalysis*

Sigmund Freud

1. *Latent* and *manifest*

We will describe what the dream actually tells us as the *manifest dream-content* and the concealed material, which we hope to reach by pursuing the ideas that occur to the dreamer, as the *latent dream-thoughts.*

Comment: Freud's theory depends upon a metaphor of surface and depth. What is manifest *is what is visible on the surface. What is* latent *is hidden in the depths. For instance, a dream about the loss of a wedding ring (manifest) might signify a (latent) wish for separation from a spouse. What is manifest can be read directly. What is latent must be interpreted.*

2. *Dream-work* and *work of interpretation*

The work which transforms the latent dream into its manifest one is called the *dream-work.* The work which proceeds in the contrary direction, which endeavors to arrive at the latent dream from the manifest one, is our work of *interpretation.* This work of interpretation seeks to undo the dream-work.

Comment: Freud here gives a name to the unconscious process that enables our real feelings to be expressed in a disguised manner. Thus disguised, thoughts and feelings we would censor or "repress" if we were awake can find expression in the form of dreams. He calls this process of transformation the dream-work. *For our purposes what is most important is that Freud's dream-work operates by means of metaphors and other forms of verbal displacement. The dream-work functions poetically.*

3. *Condensation*

The first achievement of the dream work is *condensation.* . . . Condensation is brought about (1) by the total omission of certain latent dream elements, (2) by only a fragment of some complexes in the latent dream passing over into the manifest one and (3) by latent elements which have something in common being combined and fused into a single unity in the manifest dream. . . . The dream-work tries to condense two different thoughts by seeking out (like a joke) an ambiguous word in which the two thoughts come together.

Comment: The first two forms of condensation mentioned by Freud are both ways of leaving out part of the whole complex of feelings behind the dream. The third, however, is a way of getting such thoughts or feelings into the dream by disguising them in some way. Freud points out that this process also occurs in slips of the tongue, sometimes now called "Freudian slips." A woman we know once found herself saying, "I don't believe in Freudian strips." *She became a believer on the spot. The expression, "Freudian strips," of course combines or condenses the notion of the slip of the tongue with the notion of undressing or laying bare the latent content—what is under the clothing or behind the words. It is a perfect illustration of what Freud meant by condensation.*

4. *Displacement*

The second achievement of the dream-work is displacement. . . . It manifests itself in two ways: in the first, a latent element is replaced not by a component part of itself but by something more remote—that is by an allusion; and in the second, the psychical accent is shifted so that the dream appears differently centered and strange.

Comment: Freud is speaking here about the way in which meaning is displaced. For example, in the dream we mentioned earlier, about the loss of a wedding ring, the manifest and latent content are very close together, since the ring is a component part of the marriage. But suppose one dreamed of the loss of a donut. To interpret this dream as a dream of the end of marriage one would have to see the donut as an allusion to the ring based on their shared form. And this could happen in a dream that seemed to be about a tea party like the one in Alice in Wonderland, *in which everything is differently centered and strange.*

5. *Imagery*

The third achievement of the dream-work is psychologically the most interesting. It consists in transforming thoughts into visual images. [Freud suggests that we can imagine how this works by trying to translate a political editorial into pictures.] In so far as the article mentioned people and concrete objects you will replace them easily and perhaps even advantageously by pictures; but your difficulties will begin when you come to the representation of abstract words and of all those parts of speech which indicate relations between thoughts—such as particles, conjunctions, and so on. In the case of abstract words . . . you will recall that most abstract words are "watered down" concrete ones, and you will for that reason hark back as often as possible to the original concrete meaning of such words. Thus you will be pleased to find out that you can represent the "possession" of an object by a real, physical sitting down on it.

Comment: Once again, Freud's description of the dream-work sounds much like the work of a poetical imagination, finding concrete images in which to embody abstract ideas. The interpretation of dreams and the interpretation of poetical language have very much in common because what Freud called the dream-work and found to be active in the construction of dreams is actually modeled on the work of poets. Or, to put it another way, dreaming and poetry are both rooted in the human unconscious, though poetry is a way of trying to harness the unconscious to the demands of consciousness.

As we can see from Freud's definitions, the dream-work functions in order to conceal meaning. But it conceals meaning in order to express it. Its motto might be, "Better disguised expression than no expression at all." The language of poetry uses metaphor and other ways of displacing and condensing meaning for similar ends. In most poetry, however, meanings are displaced and condensed consciously, so as to give the reader an active role in constructing meanings for a poetic text, through the process that we call interpretation.

Poetic meaning, however, is not simply a matter of a poet's having a clear meaning and then disguising it. A poem is often a search for meaning on the part of the poet, who seeks—like the dream-work—to find signs and symbols for feelings that lie too deep within his or her psyche to have a definite mental shape. Poetic metaphor, then, is a way of pointing to meanings that can only be made clear by an act of interpretation.

You will have a chance to do some interpreting of poetic texts later on, but now we would like you to consider briefly some instances of poets using metaphor in a way especially close to the manner in which Freud says the dream-work functions. These poets, who called themselves "surrealists," tried to push metaphor to the point of nonsense, as a way of allowing the unconscious to speak in images. In the next section you will have a chance to examine for yourself the relationship between poems and dreams.

Surrealist Metaphor

How far can metaphor be extended? If all naming is metaphorical, moving toward the unknown by analogies with what is already known and safely named, perhaps a poet can suggest new realities by metaphorically linking unusual or incompatible things. The surrealist movement in art and literature is based on disrupting our habitual sense of reality so as to allow us glimpses of a deeper reality. Consider, for instance, what the surrealist poet André Breton (1896–1966) said about the images that combine to make metaphors:

> For me, the strongest is one that presents
> the highest degree of arbitrariness . . . ; one
> that requires the longest time to translate
> into practical language, either because it
> contains an enormous dose of apparent
> contradiction, or because one of the terms
> is strangely hidden, or because it appears
> to unravel feebly after heralding itself as
> sensational . . . , or because it very naturally
> lays the masque of the concrete upon abstract
> things, or vice versa, or because it implies
> the negation of some elementary physical
> property, or because it unleashes laughter.
>
> (Cauvin and Caws, xix)

If a balanced view of poetic metaphor insists on images that are combined in a way that is both surprising *and* appropriate, the surrealists take an extreme position in favor of the surprising combination, as in the following lines from one of Breton's poems:

> . . . there go the fuses blown again
> Here's the squid with his elbows on the window sill
> And here wondering where to unfold his sparkling sewer grill
> Is the clown of the eclipse in his white outfit
> Eyes in his pocket. . . .

The impossibility of a squid leaning elbows (of all things) on a window sill is perhaps the most striking thing about this language. Its parts just won't go together to form a "normal" image. But the possibility that this bizarre image is a metaphor for something else is both tantalizing and a little threatening. Is there some particular meaning that we are intended to decode? And are we stupid if we can't discover it?

Above all, the surrealists want to disabuse their readers of the notion that they have hidden a correct meaning behind every metaphor. They have allowed their unconscious minds to interrupt the logic of consciousness. If meanings have been generated, the surrealist poet and his or her readers will have to look for them together. Breton hopes that his images will have a high degree of arbitrariness, that they will require time and effort to be translated into "practical language." Notice that he does not say that they should be impossible to translate, only that they should offer resistance. Breton would like the reader's unconscious to enter into the process of translation. He wants us to play with his images until we begin to see how to connect and interpret them. Try, for instance, playing with the "clown of the eclipse" until you generate some reason for him to have "eyes in his pocket."

For Discussion

At this point it will be helpful for you to compare what Breton said in the quotation above (p. 64) to Freud's description of the dream-work quoted in the previous section (pp. 60–62). If we reduce Breton's statement to its purely descriptive notions, we get something like this:

1. apparent contradiction
2. hidden term
3. concrete for abstract
4. abstract for concrete
5. negation of physical property

This is not the same as Freud's list, by any means, but there is some overlap. Discuss these five processes until you understand what is meant by each one, and then compare this list to Freud's description of the dream-work. Note both the common features and the differences. This development of your analytical terminology will help you in doing the assignments to come.

Two Poems

Some of our finest poets have been influenced by the surrealists. Both W. S. Merwin and Wallace Stevens like to develop metaphoric images that set our ordinary perceptions back on their heels. In one of his poems Stevens tells us, in words very similar to Breton's, that "The poem must resist the intelligence/Almost successfully." The "almost" is important, but most of the major modern poets have believed that the intelligence must be "resisted" in order to free the imagination to discover things that mere intelligence would not notice. This is one reason why some poems are

difficult—not to embarrass their readers but to challenge us and stimulate our own creativity.

Read the following two poems by Breton and Stevens with this in mind, and consider the points raised for discussion.

Broken Line

for Raymond Roussel

We plain bread and water in the prisons of the sky
We the paving stones of love all the interrupted signals
Who personify the charms of this poem
Nothing expresses us beyond death
At this hour when night puts on its polished ankle-boots to go out
We take our times as it comes
Like a party wall adjoining that of our prisons
Spiders bring the ship into the harbor
One has only to touch there is nothing to see
Later you shall learn who we are
Our labors are still well protected
But it's dawn on the last shore the weather is worsening
Soon we'll carry our cumbersome luxury elsewhere
We'll carry the luxury of the plague elsewhere
We a little hoarfrost on human firewood
And that's all
Brandy dresses wounds in a cellar through the vent from which one glimpses a road lined with great empty patience-docks
Don't ask where you are
We plain bread and water in the prisons of the sky
Card game under the stars
We scarcely lift the veil by its edge
The mender of crockery is working on a ladder
He looks young despite the concession
We wear yellow mourning for him
The pact is not yet signed
The sisters of charity provoke
Escapes on the horizon
Perhaps we palliate at the same time evil and good
Thus it is that the will of dreams is done
People you who could
Our rigors become lost in the regret of all that crumbles
We are the popular idols of the more terrible seduction
Ragman Morning's hook on flowery tatters
Casts us to the fury of long-toothed treasures

Don't add anything to the shame of your own pardon
'Tis enough to arm toward a bottomless end
Your eyes with these ridiculous tears that relieve us
The belly of words is golden this evening and nothing is in vain any more

André Breton

For Discussion and Writing

1. Breton's poem is called "Broken Line," and it celebrates, among other things, "the interrupted signals/Who personify the charms of this poem." Speculate, for a moment, on the connections among broken lines, interrupted signals, and poetic charms.
2. Certain individual lines of Breton's poem can provoke interesting thoughts if we simply meditate on what they mean to *us,* without worrying about whether these meanings are "intended" or "correct." Using one of the following lines from the poem (or any other single line of your choice) write a few sentences on what the line means to you or what it leads you to think about:

    line 13 Soon we'll carry our cumbersome luxury elsewhere
    line 28 Perhaps we palliate at the same time evil and good
    line 29 Thus it is that the will of dreams is done
    line 32 We are the popular idols of the more terrible seduction
    line 35 Don't add anything to the shame of your own pardon

3. Many of Breton's lines would not be shocking or difficult at all if one or two words were changed to give the line a consistent topic. Consider the following revisions, for instance:

    line 8 Spiders bring the ship into the harbor
    Tugboats bring the ship into the harbor
    line 22 The mender of crockery is working on a ladder
    The mender of crockery is working on a pot
    line 32 We are the popular idols of the more terrible seduction
    We are the popular idols of the more fashionable seduction
    line 35 Don't add anything to the shame of your own pardon
    Don't add anything to the shame of your own crime.

    By giving these—and other—lines a simple prose sense we can begin to see how the surrealistic effect is managed—and we can also see why some of these lines are simply startling while others are both startling and interesting. Discuss the lines presented here, and then write a paper in which you extend your research in this direction: Take a line from

Breton's poem and translate it—with minimal change—into simple prose. Then discuss the differences between the meanings of the two versions of the line. Perform the same operation with one or two additional lines. Use your analyses as the basis for some speculation about the method and uses of surrealist poetry.

4. Go back to the poem by Robert Herrick quoted by Roger Brown on p. 54. Starting with the title, make a few changes in every line so as to turn "Delight in Disorder" into a surrealist poem. Try to produce something in the spirit of Breton. Don't worry if the lines lose their rhythm or rhyme. In class, exchange poems and discuss the most interesting poems or lines with their authors. The point of this exercise is to confront the problems of interpretation and the problems of composition together.
5. Reconsider Breton's "Broken Line" in the light of his discussion of the metaphoric image. Try to locate the specific devices he mentions in his own poetic lines. For instance, is line 8 a case of "negation of some elementary physical property" or a line that "appears to unravel feebly after heralding itself as sensational"—or both?

Domination of Black

At night, by the fire,
The colors of the bushes
And of the fallen leaves,
Repeating themselves,
Turned in the room,
Like the leaves themselves
Turning in the wind.
Yes: but the color of the heavy hemlocks
Came striding.
And I remembered the cry of the peacocks.

The colors of their tails
Were like the leaves themselves
Turning in the wind,
In the twilight wind.
They swept over the room,
Just as they flew from the boughs of the hemlocks
Down to the ground.
I heard them cry—the peacocks.
Was it a cry against the twilight
Or against the leaves themselves
Turning in the wind,
Turning as the flames

Turned in the fire,
Turning as the tails of the peacocks
Turned in the loud fire,
Loud as the hemlocks
Full of the cry of the peacocks?
Or was it a cry against the hemlocks?

Out of the window,
I saw how the planets gathered
Like the leaves themselves
Turning in the wind.
I saw how the night came,
Came striding like the color of the heavy hemlocks.
I felt afraid.
And I remembered the cry of the peacocks.

Wallace Stevens

For Discussion and Writing

In some respects this resembles a surrealist poem. Its images are striking, unexpected. The poem resists interpretation, but it is not meant to resist successfully. For one thing, we can locate a single situation in the poem: a person in a room, with a fire going in a fireplace, in autumn, at night, thinking about darkness. We can also find certain images repeated in the poem, giving it a higher degree of coherence than a surrealist poem.

To interpret the poem, we need to understand how the images are connected. How, for instance, are autumn leaves and peacocks' tails connected? There are only a few clusters of images in the poem: the autumn leaves, the hemlock bushes, the peacocks, the firelight, and the darkness. Write a short paper in which you express in your own words the meaning of the poem. Among other things, you should explore the connections among images, the meaning of the title, and the significance of the cry of the peacocks.

Poetic Uses of Metaphor

What follows is a minianthology of poems selected because each of them is short and makes some interesting use of metaphor. Some of them are about the poetic process and about metaphor in particular. Others are about other things but employ similes or other kinds of metaphoric process as a way of presenting their ideas.

If you have attended to the previous work on metaphor in this book, you should be in a position now to write an essay on the way metaphors work in poetry. We ask you, then, to write such an essay, using the following minianthology as your source for examples. You are not being asked to write an interpretation of each poem, but to draw from the poems certain metaphors to illustrate your discussion.

In writing your essay you should consider some of the following matters:

1. Why do poets use metaphors so frequently?
2. What does the use of metaphor have to do with the "difficulty" of poetry?
3. What does the use of metaphor have to do with the pleasures of poetry?
4. What makes an interesting metaphor interesting?
5. How do metaphors contribute to the power of poetry to move us emotionally or to amuse us?

In the course of your discussion, you should consider some specific metaphors drawn from these poems, exploring and explaining the meanings generated by each metaphor. In the case of an extended comparison, you should examine the way that the details of description apply to both of the things being compared. For instance, Robert Francis's poem "Pitcher" describes what a baseball pitcher does in such a way that it becomes a metaphor for what a poet does. The result changes our way of thinking about both activities: pitching and writing poetry. But the effectiveness of the poem depends upon the way that the details of the description support both ends of the comparison, and that is the sort of analysis that you should make in your essay. To make it, of course, you have to understand that the comparison is being made—that the description is not just description but metaphoric. You need to be an alert reader and to read each poem over until you have a real grip on its meanings. If the poet is the pitcher, you are the batter—but in this case you can make him keep on throwing the same pitch until you really get a hold of it.

Remember, you are not being asked to go through each poem and write about what it means. You are being asked to draw from the poems the material that will enable you to produce your own essay on why and how poets use metaphor.

"Doesn't he realize . . ."

Doesn't he realize
that I am not
like the swaying kelp
in the surf,
where the seaweed gatherer
can come as often as he wants.

Ono no Komachi
Translated from Japanese by
K. Rexroth and I. Atsumi

Word

The word bites like a fish.
Shall I throw it back free
Arrowing to that sea
Where thoughts lash tail and fin?
Or shall I pull it in
To rhyme upon a dish?

Stephen Spender

Pitcher

His art is eccentricity, his aim
How not to hit the mark he seems to aim at,

His passion how to avoid the obvious,
His technique how to vary the avoidance.

The others throw to be comprehended. He
Throws to be a moment misunderstood.

Yet not too much. Not errant, arrant, wild,
But every seeming aberration willed.

Not to, yet still, still to communicate
Making the batter understand too late.

Robert Francis

Ars Poetica

The goose that laid the golden egg
Died looking up its crotch
To find out how its sphincter worked.

Would you lay well? Don't watch.

X. J. Kennedy

Cottonmouth Country

Fish bones walked the waves off Hatteras.
And there were other signs
That Death wooed us, by water, wooed us
By land: among the pines
An uncurled cottonmouth that rolled on moss
Reared in the polluted air.
Birth, not death, is the hard loss.
I know. I also left a skin there.

Louise Glück

Sonnet to My Mother

Most near, most dear, most loved and most far,
Under the window where I often found her
Sitting as huge as Asia, seismic with laughter,
Gin and chicken helpless in her Irish hand,
Irresistible as Rabelais but most tender for
The lame dogs and hurt birds that surround her,—
She is a procession no one can follow after
But be like a little dog following a brass band.
She will not glance up at the bomber or condescend
To drop her gin and scuttle to a cellar,
But lean on the mahogany table like a mountain
Whom only faith can move, and so I send
O all my faith and all my love to tell her
That she will move from mourning into morning.

George Barker

"You fit into me"

you fit into me
like a hook into an eye

a fish hook
an open eye

Margaret Atwood

"A narrow Fellow in the Grass"

A narrow Fellow in the Grass
Occasionally rides—
You may have met Him—did you not
His notice sudden is—

The Grass divides as with a Comb—
A spotted shaft is seen—
And then it closes at your feet
And opens further on—

He likes a Boggy Acre
A Floor too cool for Corn—
Yet when a Boy, and Barefoot—
I more than once at Noon
Have passed, I thought, a Whip lash
Unbraiding in the Sun
When stooping to secure it
It wrinkled, and was gone—

Several of Nature's People
I know, and they know me—
I feel for them a transport
Of cordiality—

But never met this Fellow
Attended, or alone
Without a tighter breathing
And Zero at the Bone—

Emily Dickinson

You don't understand me,

you gulp, a frog suddenly on my dinner
plate hopping through the buttered noodles
blinking cold eyes of reproach.

I can interpret the language of your hands
warm under calluses. Your body speaks into mine.
We are native users of the same jangling American.

A casual remark lets ants loose in your ears.
The wrong tone drips ice water on your nape.
Waiting I finger the bruise-colored why.

Look, I can't study you like the engine
of an old car coughing into silence on wet mornings.
Can't read the convolutions of your brain through the skull.

You want hieroglyphs at the corners of your squint decoded
in perfect silence that folds into your ribbed side,
a woman of soft accordion-pleated wool with healer's hands.

I don't understand you: you are not a book,
an argument, a theory. Speak to me.
I listen, and I speak back.

Marge Piercy

Moving in Winter

Their life, collapsed like unplayed cards,
is carried piecemeal through the snow:
Headboard and footboard now, the bed
where she has lain desiring him
where overhead his sleep will build
its canopy to smother her once more;
their table, by four elbows worn
evening after evening while the wax runs down;
mirrors grey with reflecting them,
bureaus coffining from the cold
things that can shuffle in a drawer,
carpets rolled up around those echoes
which, shaken out, take wing and breed
new altercations, the old silences.

Adrienne Rich

Inscription Facing Western Sea

Lord of each wave comes in
campaign finished ten thousand miles
years clashes winds dead moons
riderless horses no messages
he lays down flag bowing quickly and retires
his flag
sun waits to take him home
flag fades
sand
stars gather again to watch the war

W. S. Merwin

The Motive for Metaphor

You like it under the trees in autumn,
Because everything is half dead.
The wind moves like a cripple among the leaves
And repeats words without meaning.

In the same way, you were happy in spring,
With the half colors of quarter-things,
The slightly brighter sky, the melting clouds,
The single bird, the obscure moon—

The obscure moon lighting an obscure world
Of things that would never be quite expressed,
Where you yourself were never quite yourself
And did not want nor have to be,

Desiring the exhilarations of changes:
The motive for metaphor, shrinking from
The weight of primary noon,
The A B C of being,

The ruddy temper, the hammer
Of red and blue, the hard sound—
Steel against intimation—the sharp flash,
The vital, arrogant, fatal, dominant X.

Wallace Stevens

Metaphor as a Basis for Thought

In the last section we considered metaphor as a way of structuring poetry. Here we will be looking not only at metaphor as a way of structuring prose but also at the ways in which metaphor structures our thinking. How this structuring is revealed in our everyday language has been of primary interest to linguists George Lakoff and Mark Johnson. The material presented here is from their book *Metaphors We Live By*.

From *Metaphors We Live By*

George Lakoff and Mark Johnson

Concepts We Live By

Metaphor is for most people a device of the poetic imagination and the rhetorical flourish—a matter of extraordinary rather than ordinary language. Moreover, metaphor is typically viewed as characteristic of language alone, a matter of words rather than thought or action. For this reason, most people think they can get along perfectly well without metaphor. We have found, on the contrary, that metaphor is pervasive in everyday life, not just in language but in thought and action. Our ordinary conceptual system, in terms of which we both think and act, is fundamentally metaphorical in nature. 1

The concepts that govern our thought are not just matters of the intellect. They also govern our everyday functioning, down to the most mundane details. Our concepts structure what we perceive, how we get around in the world, and how we relate to other people. Our conceptual system thus plays a central role in defining our everyday realities. If we are right in suggesting that our conceptual system is largely metaphorical, then the way we think, what we experience, and what we do every day is very much a matter of metaphor. 2

But our conceptual system is not something we are normally aware of. In most of the little things we do every day, we simply think and act more or less automatically along certain lines. Just what these lines are is by no means obvious. One way to find out is by looking at language. Since communication is based on the same conceptual system that we use in thinking and acting, language is an important source of evidence for what that system is like. 3

Primarily on the basis of linguistic evidence, we have found that most of our ordinary conceptual system is metaphorical in nature. And we have found a way to begin to identify in detail just what the metaphors are that structure how we perceive, how we think, and what we do. 4

To give some idea of what it could mean for a concept to be metaphoric- 5
al and for such a concept to structure an everyday activity, let us start with the concept ARGUMENT and the conceptual metaphor ARGUMENT IS WAR. This metaphor is reflected in our everyday language by a wide variety of expressions:

Argument Is War

Your claims are *indefensible.*
He *attacked every weak point* in my argument.
His criticisms were *right on target.*
I *demolished* his argument.
I've never *won* an argument with him.
You disagree? Okay, *shoot!*
If you use that *strategy,* he'll *wipe you out.*
He *shot down* all of my arguments.

It is important to see that we don't just *talk* about arguments in terms of 6
war. We can actually win or lose arguments. We see the person we are arguing with as an opponent. We attack his positions and we defend our own. We gain and lose ground. We plan and use strategies. If we find a position indefensible, we can abandon it and take a new line of attack. Many of the things we *do* in arguing are partially structured by the concept of war. Though there is no physical battle, there is a verbal battle, and the structure of an argument—attack, defense, counterattack, etc.—reflects this. It is in this sense that the ARGUMENT IS WAR metaphor is one that we live by in this culture; it structures the actions we perform in arguing.

Try to imagine a culture where arguments are not viewed in terms of 7
war, where no one wins or loses, where there is no sense of attacking or defending, gaining or losing ground. Imagine a culture where an argument is viewed as a dance, the participants are seen as performers, and the goal is to perform in a balanced and aesthetically pleasing way. In such a culture, people would view arguments differently, experience them differently, carry them out differently, and talk about them differently. But *we* would probably not view them as arguing at all: they would simply be doing something different. It would seem strange even to call what they were doing "arguing." Perhaps the most neutral way of describing this difference between their culture and ours would be to say that we have a discourse form structured in terms of battle and they have one structured in terms of dance.

This is an example of what it means for a metaphorical concept, namely, 8
ARGUMENT IS WAR, to structure (at least in part) what we do and how we understand what we are doing when we argue. *The essence of metaphor is*

understanding and experiencing one kind of thing in terms of another. It is not that arguments are a subspecies of war. Arguments and wars are different kinds of things—verbal discourse and armed conflict—and the actions performed are different kinds of actions. But ARGUMENT is partially structured, understood, performed, and talked about in terms of WAR. The concept is metaphorically structured, the activity is metaphorically structured, and, consequently, the language is metaphorically structured.

Moreover, this is the *ordinary* way of having an argument and talking about one. The normal way for us to talk about attacking a position is to use the words "attack a position." Our conventional ways of talking about arguments presuppose a metaphor we are hardly ever conscious of. The metaphor is not merely in the words we use—it is in our very concept of an argument. The language of argument is not poetic, fanciful, or rhetorical; it is literal. We talk about arguments that way because we conceive of them that way—and we act according to the way we conceive of things.

Some Further Examples

We have been claiming that metaphors partially structure our everyday concepts and that this structure is reflected in our literal language. Before we can get an overall picture of the philosophical implications of these claims, we need a few more examples. In each of the ones that follow we give a metaphor and a list of ordinary expressions that are special cases of the metaphor. The English expressions are of two sorts: simple literal expressions and idioms that fit the metaphor and are part of the normal everyday way of talking about the subject.

Theories (and Arguments) Are Buildings

Is that the *foundation* for your theory? The theory needs more *support.* The argument is *shaky.* We need some more facts or the argument will *fall apart.* We need to *construct* a *strong* argument for that. I haven't figured out yet what the *form* of the argument will be. Here are some more facts to *shore up* the theory. We need to *buttress* the theory with *solid* arguments. The theory will *stand* or *fall* on the *strength* of that argument. The argument *collapsed.* They *exploded* his latest theory. We will show that theory to be without *foundation.* So far we have put together only the *framework* of the theory.

Ideas Are Food

What he said *left a bad taste in my mouth.* All this paper has in it are *raw facts, half-baked ideas, and warmed-over theories.* There are too many facts here for me to *digest* them all. I just can't *swallow* that claim. That argument *smells fishy.* Let me *stew* over that for a while. Now there's a theory you can really *sink your teeth into.* We need to let that idea *percolate* for a while. That's *food for thought.* He's a *voracious* reader. We don't need to *spoon-feed* our students. He *devoured* the book. Let's let that idea *simmer on the back burner* for a while. This is the *meaty* part of the paper. Let that idea *jell* for a while. That idea has been *fermenting* for years.

With respect to life and death IDEAS ARE ORGANISMS, either PEOPLE or PLANTS. 11

Ideas Are People

The theory of relativity *gave birth to* an enormous number of ideas in physics. He is the *father* of modern biology. Whose *brain-child* was that? Look at what his ideas have *spawned.* Those ideas *died off* in the Middle Ages. His ideas will *live on* forever. Cognitive psychology is still in its *infancy.* That's an idea that ought to be *resurrected.* Where'd you *dig up* that idea? He *breathed new life into* that idea.

Ideas Are Plants

His ideas have finally come to *fruition.* That idea *died on the vine.* That's a *budding* theory. It will take years for that idea to *come to full flower.* He views chemistry as a mere *offshoot* of physics. Mathematics has many *branches.* The *seeds* of his great ideas were *planted* in his youth. She has a *fertile* imagination. Here's an idea that I'd like to *plant* in your mind. He has a *barren* mind.

Ideas Are Products

We're really *turning (churning, cranking, grinding) out* new ideas. We've *generated* a lot of ideas this week. He *produces* new ideas at an astounding rate. His *intellectual productivity* has decreased in recent years. We need to *take the rough edges off* that idea, *hone it down, smooth it out.* It's a rough idea; it needs to be *refined.*

Ideas Are Commodities

It's important how you *package* your ideas. He won't *buy* that. That idea just won't *sell.* There is always a *market* for good ideas. That's a *worthless* idea. He's been a source of *valuable* ideas. I wouldn't *give a plugged nickel for* that idea. Your ideas don't have a chance in the *intellectual marketplace.*

Ideas Are Resources

He *ran out of* ideas. Don't *waste* your thoughts on small projects. Let's *pool* our ideas. He's a *resourceful* man. We've *used up* all our ideas. That's a *useless* idea. That idea will *go a long way.*

Ideas Are Money

Let me put in my *two cents' worth.* He's *rich* in ideas. That book is a *treasure trove* of ideas. He has a *wealth* of ideas.

Ideas Are Cutting Instruments

That's an *incisive* idea. That *cuts right to the heart of* the matter. That was a *cutting* remark. He's *sharp.* He has a *razor* wit. He has a *keen* mind. She *cut* his argument *to ribbons.*

Ideas Are Fashions

That idea went *out of style* years ago. I hear sociobiology *is in* these days. Marxism is currently *fashionable* in western Europe. That idea is *old hat!* That's an *outdated* idea. What are the new *trends* in English criticism? *Old-fashioned* notions have no place in today's society. He keeps *up-to-date* by reading the New York Review of Books. Berkeley is a center of *avant-garde* thought. Semiotics has become quite *chic.* The idea of revolution is no longer *in vogue* in the United States. The transformational grammar *craze* hit the United States in the mid-sixties and has just made it to Europe.

Understanding Is Seeing; Ideas Are Light-Sources; Discourse Is a Light-Medium

I *see* what you're saying. It *looks* different from my *point of view.* What is your *outlook* on that? I *view* it differently. Now I've got the *whole picture.* Let me *point something out* to you. That's an *insightful* idea. That was a *brilliant* remark. The argument is *clear.* It was a *murky* discussion. Could you *elucidate* your remarks? It's a *transparent* argument. The discussion was *opaque.*

Love Is a Physical Force (Electromagnetic, Gravitational, etc.)

I could feel the *electricity* between us. There were *sparks.* I was *magnetically drawn* to her. They are uncontrollably *attracted* to each other. They *gravitated* to each other immediately. His whole life *revolves* around her. The *atmosphere* around them is always *charged.* There is incredible *energy* in their relationship. They lost their *momentum.*

Love Is a Patient

This is a *sick* relationship. They have a *strong, healthy* marriage. The marriage is *dead*—it can't be *revived.* Their marriage is *on the mend.* We're getting *back on our feet.* Their relationship is *in really good shape.* They've got a *listless* marriage. Their marriage is *on its last legs.* It's a *tired* affair.

Love Is Madness

I'm *crazy* about her. She *drives me out of my mind.* He constantly *raves* about her. He's gone *mad* over her. I'm just *wild* about Harry. I'm *insane* about her.

Love Is Magic

She *cast her spell* over me. The *magic* is gone. I was *spellbound.* She had me *hypnotized.* He has me *in a trance.* I was *entranced* by him. I'm *charmed* by her. She is *bewitching.*

Love Is War

He is known for his many rapid *conquests.* She *fought for* him, but his mistress *won out.* He *fled from* her *advances.* She *pursued* him *relentlessly.* He is slowly *gaining ground* with her. He *won* her hand in marriage. He *overpowered* her. She is *besieged* by suitors. He has to *fend* them *off.* He *enlisted the aid* of her friends. He *made an ally* of her mother. Theirs is a *misalliance* if I've ever seen one.

Wealth Is a Hidden Object

He's *seeking* his fortune. He's flaunting his *new-found* wealth. He's a *fortune-hunter.* She's a *gold-digger.* He *lost* his fortune. He's *searching for* wealth.

Significant Is Big

He's a *big* man in the garment industry. He's a *giant* among writers. That's the *biggest* idea to hit advertising in years. He's *head and shoulders above* everyone in the industry. It was only a *small* crime. That was only a *little* white lie. I was astounded at the *enormity* of the crime. That was one of the *greatest* moments in World Series history. His accomplishments *tower over* those of *lesser* men.

Seeing Is Touching; Eyes Are Limbs

I can't *take* my eyes *off* her. He sits with his eyes *glued* to the TV. Her eyes *picked out* every detail of the pattern. Their eyes *met.* She never *moves* her eyes *from* his face. She *ran* her eyes *over* everything in the room. He wants everything *within reach* of his eyes.

The Eyes Are Containers for the Emotions

I could see the fear *in* his eyes. His eyes were *filled* with anger. There was passion *in* her eyes. His eyes *displayed* his compassion. She couldn't *get* the fear *out* of her eyes. Love *showed in* his eyes. Her eyes *welled* with emotion.

Emotional Effect Is Physical Contact

His mother's death *hit* him *hard.* That idea *bowled me over.* She's a *knockout.* I was *struck* by his sincerity. That really *made an impression* on me. He *made his mark on* the world. I was *touched* by his remark. That *blew me away.*

Physical and Emotional States Are Entities Within a Person

He has a pain *in* his shoulder. Don't *give* me the flu. My cold has *gone from my head to my chest.* His pains *went away.* His depression *returned.* Hot tea and honey will *get rid of* your cough. He could barely *contain* his joy. The smile *left* his face. *Wipe* that sneer *off* your face, private! His fears *keep coming back.* I've got to *shake off* this depression—it keeps *hanging on.* If you've got a cold, drinking lots of tea will *flush it out* of your system. There isn't a *trace* of cowardice *in* him. He hasn't got *an honest bone in his body.*

Vitality Is a Substance

She's *brimming* with vim and vigor. She's *overflowing* with vitality. He's *devoid* of energy. I don't *have* any energy *left* at the end of the day. I'm *drained.* That *took a lot out of* me.

Life Is a Container

I've had a *full* life. Life is *empty* for him. There's *not much left* for him *in* life. Her life is *crammed* with activities. *Get the most out of life.* His life *contained* a great deal of sorrow. Live your life *to the fullest.*

Life Is a Gambling Game

I'll *take my chances.* The *odds are against me.* I've got an *ace up my sleeve.* He's *holding all the aces.* It's a *toss-up.* If you *play your cards right,* you can do it. He *won* big. He's a real *loser.* Where is he when the *chips are down?* That's my *ace in the hole.* He's *bluffing.* The president is *playing it close to his vest.* Let's *up the ante.* Maybe we need to *sweeten the pot.* I think we should *stand pat.* That's *the luck of the draw.* Those are *high stakes.*

In this last group of examples we have a collection of what are called "speech formulas," or "fixed-form expressions," or "phrasal lexical items." 12
These function in many ways like single words, and the language has thousands of them. In the examples given, a set of such phrasal lexical items is coherently structured by a single metaphorical concept. Although each of them is an instance of the LIFE IS A GAMBLING GAME metaphor, they are typically used to speak of life, not of gambling situations. They are normal

ways of talking about life situations, just as using the word "construct" is a normal way of talking about theories. It is in this sense that we include them in what we have called literal expressions structured by metaphorical concepts. If you say "The odds are against us" or "We'll have to take our chances," you would not be viewed as speaking metaphorically but as using the normal everyday language appropriate to the situation. Nevertheless, your way of talking about, conceiving, and even experiencing your situation would be metaphorically structured.

The Partial Nature of Metaphorical Structuring

Up to this point we have described the systematic character of metaphorically 13
defined concepts. Such concepts are understood in terms of a number of different metaphors (e.g., TIME IS MONEY, TIME IS A MOVING OBJECT, etc.). The metaphorical structuring of concepts is necessarily partial and is reflected in the lexicon of the language, including the phrasal lexicon, which contains fixed-form expressions such as "to be without foundation." Because concepts are metaphorically structured in a systematic way, e.g., THEORIES ARE BUILDINGS, it is possible for us to use expressions *(construct, foundation)* from one domain (BUILDINGS) to talk about corresponding concepts in the metaphorically defined domain (THEORIES). What *foundation,* for example, means in the metaphorically defined domain (THEORY) will depend on the details of how the metaphorical concept THEORIES ARE BUILDINGS is used to structure the concept THEORY.

The parts of the concept BUILDING that are used to structure the 14
concept THEORY are the foundation and the outer shell. The roof, internal rooms, staircases, and hallways are parts of a building not used as part of the concept THEORY. Thus the metaphor THEORIES ARE BUILDINGS has a "used" part (foundation and outer shell) and an "unused" part (rooms, staircases, etc.). Expressions such as *construct* and *foundation* are instances of the used part of such a metaphorical concept and are part of our ordinary literal language about theories.

But what of the linguistic expressions that reflect the "unused" part of a 15
metaphor like THEORIES ARE BUILDINGS? Here are four examples:

> His theory has thousands of little rooms and long, winding corridors.
> His theories are Bauhaus in their pseudofunctional simplicity.
> He prefers massive Gothic theories covered with gargoyles.
> Complex theories usually have problems with the plumbing.

These sentences fall outside the domain of normal literal language and are part of what is usually called "figurative" or "imaginative" language. Thus, literal expressions ("he has constructed a theory") and imaginative expressions ("His theory is covered with gargoyles") can be instances of the same general metaphor (THEORIES ARE BUILDINGS).

Here we can distinguish three different subspecies of imaginative (or nonliteral) metaphor: 16

> Extensions of the used part of a metaphor, e.g., "These facts are the bricks and mortar of my theory." Here the outer shell of the building is referred to, whereas the THEORIES ARE BUILDINGS metaphor stops short of mentioning the materials used.
>
> Instances of the unused part of the literal metaphor, e.g., "His theory has thousands of little rooms and long, winding corridors."
>
> Instances of novel metaphor, that is, a metaphor not used to structure part of our normal conceptual system but as a new way of thinking about something, e.g., "Classical theories are patriarchs who father many children, most of whom fight incessantly." Each of these subspecies lies outside the *used* part of a metaphorical concept that structures our normal conceptual system.

We note in passing that all of the linguistic expressions we have given to characterize general metaphorical concepts are figurative. Examples are TIME IS MONEY, TIME IS A MOVING OBJECT, CONTROL IS UP, IDEAS ARE FOOD, THEORIES ARE BUILDINGS, etc. None of these is literal. This is a consequence of the fact that only *part* of them is used to structure our normal concepts. Since they necessarily contain parts that are not used in our normal concepts, they go beyond the realm of the literal. 17

Each of the metaphorical expressions we have talked about so far (e.g., the time *will come;* we *construct* a theory, *attack* an idea) is used within a whole system of metaphorical concepts—concepts that we constantly use in living and thinking. These expressions, like all other words and phrasal lexical items in the language, are fixed by convention. In addition to these cases, which are parts of whole metaphorical systems, there are idiosyncratic metaphorical expressions that stand alone and are not used systematically in our language or thought. These are well-known expressions like the *foot* of the mountain, a *head* of cabbage, the *leg* of a table, etc. These expressions are isolated instances of metaphorical concepts, where there is only one instance of a used part (or maybe two or three). Thus the *foot* of the mountain is the only used part of the metaphor A MOUNTAIN IS A PERSON. In normal discourse we do not speak of the *head, shoulders,* or *trunk* of a mountain, though in special contexts it is possible to construct novel metaphorical expressions based on these unused parts. In fact, there is an aspect of the metaphor A MOUNTAIN IS A PERSON in which mountain climbers will speak of the *shoulder* of a mountain (namely, a ridge near the top) and of *conquer-* 18 *ing, fighting,* and even *being killed by* a mountain. And there are cartoon conventions where mountains become animate and their peaks become heads. The point here is that there are metaphors, like A MOUNTAIN IS A PERSON, that are marginal in our culture and our language; their used part may consist of only one conventionally fixed expression of the language, and they do not systematically interact with other metaphorical concepts because so little of them is used. This makes them relatively uninteresting for our purposes but not completely so, since they can be extended to their unused part in coining novel metaphorical expressions, making jokes, etc. And our ability to extend them to unused parts indicates that, however marginal they are, they do exist.

Examples like the *foot* of the mountain are idiosyncratic, unsystematic, 19
and isolated. They do not interact with other metaphors, play no particularly interesting role in our conceptual system, and hence are not metaphors that we live by. The only signs of life they have is that they can be extended in subcultures and that their unused portions serve as the basis for (relatively uninteresting) novel metaphors. If any metaphorical expressions deserve to be called "dead," it is these, though they do have a bare spark of life, in that they are understood partly in terms of marginal metaphorical concepts like A MOUNTAIN IS A PERSON.

It is important to distinguish these isolated and unsystematic cases from 20
the systematic metaphorical expressions we have been discussing. Expressions like *wasting time, attacking positions, going our separate ways,* etc., are reflections of systematic metaphorical concepts that structure our actions and thoughts. They are "alive" in the most fundamental sense: they are metaphors we live by. The fact that they are conventionally fixed within the lexicon of English makes them no less alive.

For Discussion and Writing

1. **Lakoff and Johnson begin by defining what they call *metaphorical concepts.* Exactly what do they mean by this expression? What is the difference between a metaphor and a metaphorical concept? Base your explanation on a discussion of the "further examples" presented in the text.**
2. **In paragraph 18 Lakoff and Johnson discuss the metaphor *foot of the mountain.* Compare their discussion with Roger Brown's treatment of this same metaphor. Sum up in your own words the points each essay makes using this same example. Do these two views complement each other, or are they in conflict at any point?**
3. **In Sylvia Plath's poem "Metaphors" we can find references to common expressions such as "big as a house" and "big as an elephant." Find other references to common metaphors in any of the other poems in this text. What happens when a poet works with a common metaphorical concept?**

What role do the normally unused parts of such concepts play in the construction of poetic metaphors?

4. In your local newspaper or in a national news or sports magazine, find an editorial in which metaphor plays an important part, either because many metaphorical expressions are used in it or because the whole piece is based on one or more metaphorical concepts, or both. Write an essay in which you discuss the way metaphor functions in your chosen editorial. That is, show how metaphors are presented to influence the reader's response or how metaphorical concepts have operated to structure the writer's thinking.
5. Take one of Lakoff and Johnson's examples of a metaphorical concept, such as "ideas are fashions" or "love is madness," and use it to structure a short essay in which you explore, through the examples given, the cultural attitude that is reflected there. Feel free to provide additional examples of your own.

Metaphorical Concepts

Metaphorical concepts function in every aspect of life, from business to health. The following two selections will serve to illustrate some of the ways in which metaphorical thinking shapes our thought and our actions in areas that seem a long way from poetry, such as business and medicine. The first selection is an article that appeared in the financial section of the *New York Times.* It was written by a management consultant from a major business school and addressed to an audience of corporate executives and would-be executives. It illustrates the way a particular set of metaphorical concepts—drawn from sports—operates in the thinking of corporate America.

The second selection is by the cultural critic and writer Susan Sontag. It consists of two chapters from her book *AIDS and Its Metaphors,* in which she explores the ways in which certain metaphors of disease have operated to shape thinking about quite different matters—political affairs, for instance.

A New Game for Managers to Play

Robert W. Keidel

As the football season gradually gives way to basketball, corporate managers would do well to consider the differences between these games. For just as football mirrors industrial structures of the past, basketball points the way to the corporate structure of the future. 1

It's the difference between the former chief executive officer of I.T.T., Harold Geneen, the master football coach who dictates his players' roles and actions, and Donald Burr, the People Express Airlines chief executive officer, who puts his players on the floor and lets them manage themselves. 2

Football is, metaphorically, a way of life in work today—the corporate sport. This is reflected in the language many managers use: 3

"It's taken my staff and me a sizable chunk of time, but we now have a solid game plan for the XYZ job. Jack, I want you to quarterback this thing all the way into the end zone. Of course, a lot of it will be making the proper assignments—getting the right people to run interference and the right ones to run with the ball. But my main concern is that we avoid mistakes. No fumbles, no interceptions, no sacks, no penalties. I don't want us to have to play catch-up; no two-minute drills at the end. I want the game plan executed exactly the way it's drawn. When we're done we want to look back with pride at a win—and not have to Monday-morning-quarterback a loss." 4

Does this football language represent more than just a convenient shorthand? Almost certainly it does, because the metaphors we use routinely are the means by which we structure experience. Thus, football metaphors may well 5 reflect—and reinforce—underlying organizational dynamics. But football, despite its pervasiveness, is the wrong model for most corporations.

Consider the scenario above. Planning has been neatly separated from implementation; those expected to carry out the game plan have had no part in creating it. Also, the communication flow is one-way: from the head coach (speaker) to the quarterback (Jack)—and, presumably, from the quarterback to the other players. And the thrust of the message is risk-averse; the real name of the game is control—minimizing mistakes. But perhaps most significant is the assumption of stability—that nothing will change to invalidate the corporate game plan. "No surprises!" as Mr. Geneen likes to say. 6

Stability is a realistic assumption in football, even given the sport's enormous complexity, because of the time available to coaches—between games and between plays. A pro football game can very nearly be programmed. Carl Peterson, formerly with the Philadelphia Eagles and now president of the United States Football League's champions, the Baltimore Stars, has estimated that managing a game is 75 percent preparation and only 25 percent adjustment. 7

Thus, football truly is the realm of the coach—the head coach, he who calls the shots. (Most pro quarterbacks do not call their own plays.) As Bum Phillips has said in tribute to the head coach of the Miami Dolphins, Don Shula, "He can take his'n and beat your'n, or he can take your'n and beat his'n." 8

But football is not an appropriate model for most businesses precisely because instability is an overwhelming fact of life. Market competition grows ever more spastic, product life-cycles shrink unimaginably and technology courses on paths of its own. 9

In this milieu, corporate "players" simply cannot perform effectively if they must wait for each play to be called for them, and remain in fixed positions—or in narrowly defined roles—like football players; increasingly, they need to deploy themselves flexibly, in novel combinations. 10

Thirty years ago it may have been possible to regard core business functions—R&D, manufacturing and marketing—as separate worlds, with little need for interaction. R&D would design the product and then lob it over the wall to manufacturing; manufacturing would make the product and lob it over another wall to the customer. 11

No need to worry about problems that do not fit neatly into the standard departments; these are inconsequential and infrequent. And when they do arise, they are simply bumped up the hierarchy to senior management—the head coach and his staff. 12

In effect, performance is roughly the sum of the functions—just as a football team's performance is the sum of the performances of its platoons—offense, defense and special teams. Clearly, this view of the corporation is anachronistic. Yet it remains all too common. 13

Business's "season" is changing, and a new metaphor is needed. While football will continue to be a useful model for pursuing machinelike efficiency 14 and consistency—that is, for minimizing redundancies, bottlenecks and errors—this design favors stability at the expense of change. Since now more than ever businesses must continuously innovate and adapt, a more promising model is basketball.

To begin with, basketball is too dynamic a sport to permit the rigid separation of planning and execution that characterizes football. Unlike football teams, basketball teams do not pause and regroup after each play. As the former star player and coach Bill Russell has noted, "Your game plan may be wiped out by what happens in the first minute of play." Success in basketball depends on the ability of the coach and players to plan and adjust while in motion. Such behavior requires all-around communication—just as basketball demands all-around passing, as opposed to football's linear sequence of "forward," one-way passing. 15

Basketball also puts a premium on generalist skills. Although different players will assume somewhat different roles on the court, all must be able to dribble, pass, shoot, rebound and play defense. Everyone handles the ball—a far cry from what happens on the gridiron. Indeed, basketball is much more player-oriented than football—a sport in which players tend to be viewed as interchangeable parts. 16

If football is a risk-averse game, basketball is risk-accepting. In basketball, change is seen as normal, not exceptional; hence, change is regarded more as the source of opportunities than of threats. Mr. Geneen has claimed that "Ninety-nine percent of all surprises in business are negative." 17

Mr. Geneen's perspective is classic football and is tenable in stable, "controllable" environments. But such environments are becoming rare. The future increasingly belongs to managers like Mr. Burr or James Treybig, the founder of Tandem Computers, who thrive on change rather than flee from it. 18

We need fewer head coaches and more player-coaches, less scripted teamwork and more spontaneous teamwork. We need to integrate planning and doing—managing and working—far more than we have to date. Are you playing yesterday's game—or tomorrow's? 19

For Discussion and Writing

1. **In paragraph 5 Keidel makes an important point about metaphor. Try to restate it in your own terms. What does he mean by *structure* in the expression "the means by which we structure experience"?**
2. **Keidel is arguing that corporate managers should replace one set of metaphors with another. Why do you suppose he doesn't suggest getting rid of metaphor altogether and thinking of business *as* business?**
3. **If you have ever played an organized sport, you know that coaches use metaphors. That is, they talk about sports in terms of something else. Discuss some of the metaphors you have encountered within the world of sports. If you have ever had a coach whose speech was memorable, try to**

describe what you remember about the way he or she spoke. A coach (who shall remain nameless here) of a college soccer team used to crack up his team by telling them to "pair up in three"—not a metaphor exactly, but a piece of almost surrealist speech. You must have encountered similar poetic phrases. Share them with your classmates—especially any notable uses of metaphor. Where do most sports metaphors come from?

4. Write an essay in which you describe any common aspect of life in terms of one or two sports. That is, begin with an idea of this order: "Marriage is more like tennis than like boxing." Then explore all the parallels and contrasts between your subject matter and the sport (or sports) you have chosen as the basis for your metaphors. Some functions of life that you might wish to consider are school, family, friendship, love, and work, but choose something that interests you and discuss it in terms of appropriate sporting metaphors.

From *AIDS and Its Metaphors*

Susan Sontag

Just as one might predict for a disease that is not yet fully understood as well as extremely recalcitrant to treatment, the advent of this terrifying new disease, new at least in its epidemic form, has provided a large-scale occasion for the metaphorizing of illness. 1

Strictly speaking, AIDS—acquired immune deficiency syndrome—is not the name of an illness at all. It is the name of a medical condition, whose consequences are a spectrum of illnesses. In contrast to syphilis and cancer, which provide prototypes for most of the images and metaphors attached to AIDS, the very definition of AIDS requires the presence of other illnesses, so-called opportunistic infections and malignancies. But though not in *that* sense a single disease, AIDS lends itself to being regarded as one—in part because, unlike cancer and like syphilis, it is thought to have a single cause. 2

AIDS has a dual metaphoric genealogy. As a micro-process, it is described as cancer is: an invasion. When the focus is transmission of the disease, an older metaphor, reminiscent of syphilis, is invoked: pollution. (One gets it from the blood or sexual fluids of infected people or from contaminated blood products.) But the military metaphors used to describe AIDS have a somewhat different focus from those used in describing cancer. With cancer, the metaphor scants the issue of causality (still a murky topic in cancer research) and picks up at the point at which rogue cells inside the body mutate, eventually moving out from an original site or organ to overrun other organs or systems—a domestic subversion. In the description of AIDS the enemy is what causes the disease, an infectious agent that comes from the outside: 3

> The invader is tiny, about one sixteen-thousandth the size of the head of a pin. . . . Scouts of the body's immune system, large cells called macrophages, sense the presence of the diminutive foreigner and promptly alert the immune system. It begins to mobilize an array of cells that, among other things, produce antibodies to deal with the threat. Single-mindedly, the AIDS virus ignores many of the blood cells in its path, evades the rapidly advancing defenders and homes in on the master coordinator of the immune system, a helper T cell. . . .

This is the language of political paranoia, with its characteristic distrust of a pluralistic world. A defense system consisting of cells "that, among other things, produce antibodies to deal with the threat" is, predictably, no match for an invader who advances "single-mindedly." And the science-fiction flavor, already present in cancer talk, is even more pungent in accounts of AIDS—this one comes from *Time* magazine in late 1986—with infection described like the high-tech warfare for which we are being prepared (and inured) by the fantasies of our leaders and by video entertainments. In the era of Star Wars and Space Invaders, AIDS has proved an ideally comprehensible illness:

> On the surface of that cell, it finds a receptor into which one of its envelope proteins fits perfectly, like a key into a lock. Docking with the cell, the virus penetrates the cell membrane and is stripped of its protective shell in the process. . . .

Next the invader takes up permanent residence, by a form of alien takeover familiar in science-fiction narratives. The body's own cells *become* the invader. With the help of an enzyme the virus carries with it,

> the naked AIDS virus converts its RNA into . . . DNA, the master molecule of life. The molecule then penetrates the cell nucleus, inserts itself into a chromosome and takes over part of the cellular machinery, directing it to produce more AIDS viruses. Eventually, overcome by its alien product, the cell swells and dies, releasing a flood of new viruses to attack other cells. . . .

As viruses attack other cells, runs the metaphor, so "a host of opportunistic diseases, normally warded off by a healthy immune system, attacks the body," whose integrity and vigor have been sapped by the sheer replication of "alien product" that follows the collapse of its immunological defenses. "Gradually weakened by the onslaught, the AIDS victim dies, sometimes in months, but almost always within a few years of the first symptoms." Those who have not already succumbed are described as "under assault, showing the telltale symptoms of the disease," while millions of others "harbor the virus, vulnerable at any time to a final, all-out attack."

4 Cancer makes cells proliferate; in AIDS, cells die. Even as this original model of AIDS (the mirror image of leukemia) has been altered, descriptions of how the virus does its work continue to echo the way the illness is perceived as infiltrating the society. "AIDS Virus Found to Hide in Cells, Eluding Detection by Normal Tests" was the headline of a recent front-page story in *The New York Times* announcing the discovery that the virus can "lurk" for years in the macrophages—disrupting their disease-fighting function without killing them, "even when the macrophages are filled almost to bursting with virus," and without producing antibodies, the chemicals the body makes in response to "invading agents" and whose presence has been regarded as an infallible marker of the syndrome.* That the virus isn't lethal for *all* the cells where it takes up residence, as is now thought, only increases the illness-foe's reputation for wiliness and invincibility.

5 What makes the viral assault so terrifying is that contamination, and therefore vulnerability, is understood as permanent. Even if someone infected were never to develop any symptoms—that is, the infection remained, or could by medical intervention be rendered, inactive—the viral enemy would be forever within. In fact, so it is believed, it is just a matter of time before something awakens ("triggers") it, before the appearance of "the telltale symptoms." Like syphilis, known to generations of doctors as "the great masquerader," AIDS is a clinical construction, an inference. It takes its identity from the presence of *some* among a long, and lengthening, roster of symptoms (no one has everything that AIDS could be), symptoms which "mean" that what the patient has is this illness. The construction of the illness rests on the invention not only of AIDS as a clinical entity but of a kind of junior AIDS, called AIDS-related complex (ARC), to which people are assigned if they show "early" and often intermittent symptoms of immunological deficit such as fevers, weight loss, fungal infections, and swollen lymph glands. AIDS is progressive, a disease of time. Once a certain density of symptoms is attained, the course of the illness can be swift, and brings atrocious suffering. Besides the commonest

*The larger role assigned to the macrophages—"to serve as a reservoir for the AIDS virus because the virus multiplies in them but does not kill them, as it kills T-4 cells"—is said to explain the not uncommon difficulty of finding infected T-4 lymphocytes in patients who have antibodies to the virus and symptoms of AIDS. (It is still assumed that antibodies will develop once the virus spreads to these "key target" cells.) Evidence of presently infected populations of cells has been as puzzlingly limited or uneven as the evidence of infection in the populations of human societies—puzzling, because of the conviction that the disease is everywhere, and must spread. "Doctors have estimated that as few as one in a million T-4 cells are infected, which led some to ask where the virus hides. . . . " Another resonant speculation, reported in the same article (*The New York Times*, June 7, 1988): "Infected macrophages can transmit the virus to other cells, possibly by touching the cells."

"presenting" illnesses (some hitherto unusual, at least in a fatal form, such as a rare skin cancer and a rare form of pneumonia), a plethora of disabling, disfiguring, and humiliating symptoms make the AIDS patient steadily more infirm, helpless, and unable to control or take care of basic functions and needs.

The sense in which AIDS is a slow disease makes it more like syphilis, 6
which is characterized in terms of "stages," than like cancer. Thinking in terms of "stages" is essential to discourse about AIDS. Syphilis in its most dreaded form is "tertiary syphilis," syphilis in its third stage. What is called AIDS is generally understood as the last of three stages—the first of which is infection with a human immunodeficiency virus (HIV) and early evidence of inroads on the immune system—with a long latency period between infection and the onset of the "telltale" symptoms. (Apparently not as long as syphilis, in which the latency period between secondary and tertiary illness might be decades. But it is worth noting that when syphilis first appeared in epidemic form in Europe at the end of the fifteenth century, it was a rapid disease, of an unexplained virulence that is unknown today, in which death often occurred in the second stage, sometimes within months or a few years.) Cancer *grows* slowly: it is not thought to be, for a long time, latent. (A convincing account of a process in terms of "stages" seems invariably to include the notion of a normative delay or halt in the process, such as is supplied by the notion of latency.) True, a cancer is "staged." This is a principal tool of diagnosis, which means classifying it according to its gravity, determining how "advanced" it is. But it is mostly a spatial notion: that the cancer advances through the body, traveling or migrating along predictable routes. Cancer is first of all a disease of the body's geography, in contrast to syphilis and AIDS, whose definition depends on constructing a temporal sequence of stages.

Syphilis is an affliction that didn't have to run its ghastly full course, to 7
paresis (as it did for Baudelaire and Maupassant and Jules de Goncourt), and could and often did remain at the stage of nuisance, indignity (as it did for Flaubert). The scourge was also a cliché, as Flaubert himself observed. "SYPHILIS. Everybody has it, more or less" reads one entry in the *Dictionary of Accepted Opinions,* his treasury of mid-nineteenth-century platitudes. And syphilis did manage to acquire a darkly positive association in late-nineteenth- and early-twentieth-century Europe, when a link was made between syphilis and heightened ("feverish") mental activity that parallels the connection made since the era of the Romantic writers between pulmonary tuberculosis and heightened emotional activity. As if in honor of all the notable writers and artists who ended their lives in syphilitic witlessness, it came to be believed that the brain lesions of neurosyphilis might actually inspire original thought or art. Thomas Mann, whose fiction is a storehouse of early-twentieth-century disease myths, makes this notion of syphilis as muse central to his *Doctor Faustus,* with its protagonist a great composer whose voluntarily contracted syphilis—the

Devil guarantees that the infection will be limited to the central nervous system—confers on him twenty-four years of incandescent creativity. E. M. Cioran recalls how, in Romania in the late 1920s, syphilis-envy figured in his adolescent expectations of literary glory: he would discover that he had contracted syphilis, be rewarded with several hyperproductive years of genius, then collapse into madness. This romanticizing of the dementia characteristic of neurosyphilis was the forerunner of the much more persistent fantasy in this century about mental illness as a source of artistic creativity or spiritual originality. But with AIDS—though dementia is also a common, late symptom—no compensatory mythology has arisen, or seems likely to arise. AIDS, like cancer, does not allow romanticizing or sentimentalizing, perhaps because its association with death is too powerful. In Krzysztof Zanussi's film *Spiral* (1978), the most truthful account I know of anger at dying, the protagonist's illness is never specified; therefore, it *has* to be cancer. For several generations now, the generic idea of death has been a death from cancer, and a cancer death is experienced as a generic defeat. Now the generic rebuke to life and to hope is AIDS. . . .

"Plague" is the principal metaphor by which the AIDS epidemic is un- 8
derstood. And because of AIDS, the popular misidentification of cancer as an epidemic, even a plague, seems to be receding: AIDS has banalized cancer.

Plague, from the Latin *plaga* (stroke, wound), has long been used 9
metaphorically as the highest standard of collective calamity, evil, scourge—Procopius, in his masterpiece of calumny, *The Secret History,* called the Emperor Justinian worse than the plague ("fewer escaped")—as well as being a general name for many frightening diseases. Although the disease to which the word is permanently affixed produced the most lethal of recorded epidemics, being experienced as a pitiless slayer is not necessary for a disease to be regarded as plague-like. Leprosy, very rarely fatal now, was not much more so when at its greatest epidemic strength, between about 1050 and 1350. And syphilis has been regarded as a plague—Blake speaks of "the youthful Harlot's curse" that "blights with plagues the Marriage hearse"—not because it killed often, but because it was disgracing, disempowering, disgusting.

It is usually epidemics that are thought of as plagues. And these mass 10
incidences of illness are understood as inflicted, not just endured. Considering illness as a punishment is the oldest idea of what causes illness, and an idea opposed by all attention to the ill that deserves the noble name of medicine. Hippocrates, who wrote several treatises on epidemics, specifically ruled out "the wrath of God" as a cause of bubonic plague. But the illnesses interpreted in antiquity as punishments, like the plague in *Oedipus,* were not thought to be shameful, as leprosy and subsequently syphilis were to be. Diseases, insofar as

they acquired meaning, were collective calamities, and judgments on a community. Only injuries and disabilities, not diseases, were thought of as individually merited. For an analogy in the literature of antiquity to the modern sense of a shaming, isolating disease, one would have to turn to Philoctetes and his stinking wound.

11 The most feared diseases, those that are not simply fatal but transform the body into something alienating, like leprosy and syphilis and cholera and (in the imagination of many) cancer, are the ones that seem particularly susceptible to promotion to "plague." Leprosy and syphilis were the first illnesses to be consistently described as repulsive. It was syphilis that, in the earliest descriptions by doctors at the end of the fifteenth century, generated a version of the metaphors that flourish around AIDS: of a disease that was not only repulsive and retributive but collectively invasive. Although Erasmus, the most influential European pedagogue of the early sixteenth century, described syphilis as "nothing but a kind of leprosy" (by 1529 he called it "something worse than leprosy"), it had already been understood as something different, because sexually transmitted. Paracelsus speaks (in Donne's paraphrase) of "that foule contagious disease which then had invaded mankind in a few places, and since overflowes in all, that for punishment of generall licentiousnes God first inflicted that disease." Thinking of syphilis as a punishment for an individual's transgression was for a long time, virtually until the disease became easily curable, not really distinct from regarding it as retribution for the licentiousness of a community—as with AIDS now, in the rich industrial countries. In contrast to cancer, understood in a modern way as a disease incurred by (and revealing of) individuals, AIDS is understood in a premodern way, as a disease incurred by people both as individuals and as members of a "risk group"—that neutral-sounding, bureaucratic category which also revives the archaic idea of a tainted community that illness has judged.

12 Not every account of plague or plague-like diseases, of course, is a vehicle for lurid stereotypes about illness and the ill. The effort to think critically, historically, about illness (about disaster generally) was attempted throughout the eighteenth century: say, from Defoe's *A Journal of the Plague Year* (1722) to Alessandro Manzoni's *The Betrothed* (1827). Defoe's historical fiction, purporting to be an eyewitness account of bubonic plague in London in 1665, does not further any understanding of the plague as punishment or, a later part of the script, as a transforming experience. And Manzoni, in his lengthy account of the passage of plague through the duchy of Milan in 1630, is avowedly committed to presenting a more accurate, less reductive view than his historical sources. But even these two complex narratives reinforce some of the perennial, simplifying ideas about plague.

13 One feature of the usual script for plague: the disease invariably comes from somewhere else. The names for syphilis, when it began its epidemic sweep through Europe in the last decade of the fifteenth century, are an

exemplary illustration of the need to make a dreaded disease foreign.* It was the "French pox" to the English, *morbus Germanicus* to the Parisians, the Naples sickness to the Florentines, the Chinese disease to the Japanese. But what may seem like a joke about the inevitability of chauvinism reveals a more important truth: that there is a link between imagining disease and imagining foreignness. It lies perhaps in the very concept of wrong, which is archaically identical with the non-us, the alien. A polluting person is always wrong, as Mary Douglas has observed. The inverse is also true: a person judged to be wrong is regarded as, at least potentially, a source of pollution.

The foreign place of origin of important illnesses, as of drastic changes in 14
the weather, may be no more remote than a neighboring country. Illness is a species of invasion, and indeed is often carried by soldiers. Manzoni's account of the plague of 1630 (chapters 31 to 37) begins:

> The plague which the Tribunal of Health had feared might enter the Milanese provinces with the German troops had in fact entered, as is well known; and it is also well known that it did not stop there, but went on to invade and depopulate a large part of Italy.

Defoe's chronicle of the plague of 1665 begins similarly, with a flurry of ostentatiously scrupulous speculation about its foreign origin:

> It was about the beginning of September, 1664, that I, among the rest of my neighbours, heard in ordinary discourse that the plague was returned again in Holland; for it had been very violent there, and particularly at Amsterdam and Rotterdam, in the year 1663, whither, they say, it was brought, some said from Italy, others from the Levant, among some

*As noted in the first accounts of the disease: "This malady received from different peoples whom it affected different names," writes Giovanni di Vigo in 1514. Like earlier treatises on syphilis, written in Latin—by Nicolo Leoniceno (1497) and by Juan Almenar (1502)—the one by di Vigo calls it *morbus Gallicus,* the French disease. (Excerpts from this and other accounts of the period, including *Syphilis; Or a Poetical History of the French Disease* [1530] by Girolamo Fracastoro, who coined the name that prevailed, are in *Classic Descriptions of Disease,* edited by Ralph H. Major [1932].) Moralistic explanations abounded from the beginning. In 1495, a year after the epidemic started, the Emperor Maximilian issued an edict declaring syphilis to be an affliction from God for the sins of men.

The theory that syphilis came from even farther than a neighboring country, that it was an entirely new disease in Europe, a disease of the New World brought back to the Old by sailors of Columbus who had contracted it in America, became the accepted explanation of the origin of syphilis in the sixteenth century and is still widely credited. It is worth noting that the earliest medical writers on syphilis did not accept the dubious theory. Leoniceno's *Libellus de Epidemia, quam vulgo morbum Gallicum vocant* starts by taking up the question of whether "the French disease under another name was common to the ancients," and says he believes firmly that it was.

> goods which were brought home by their Turkey fleet; others said it was brought from Candia; others from Cyprus. It mattered not from whence it came; but all agreed it was come into Holland again.

The bubonic plague that reappeared in London in the 1720s had arrived from Marseilles, which was where plague in the eighteenth century was usually thought to enter Western Europe: brought by seamen, then transported by soldiers and merchants. By the nineteenth century the foreign origin was usually more exotic, the means of transport less specifically imagined, and the illness itself had become phantasmagorical, symbolic.

At the end of *Crime and Punishment* Raskolnikov dreams of plague: "He 15
dreamt that the whole world was condemned to a terrible new strange plague that had come to Europe from the depths of Asia." At the beginning of the sentence it is "the whole world," which turns out by the end of the sentence to be "Europe," afflicted by a lethal visitation from Asia. Dostoevsky's model is undoubtedly cholera, called Asiatic cholera, long endemic in Bengal, which had rapidly become and remained through most of the nineteenth century a worldwide epidemic disease. Part of the centuries-old conception of Europe as a privileged cultural entity is that it is a place which is colonized by lethal diseases coming from elsewhere. Europe is assumed to be by rights free of disease. (And Europeans have been astoundingly callous about the far more devastating extent to which they—as invaders, as colonists—have introduced *their* lethal diseases to the exotic, "primitive" world: think of the ravages of smallpox, influenza, and cholera on the aboriginal populations of the Americas and Australia.) The tenacity of the connection of exotic origin with dreaded disease is one reason why cholera, of which there were four great outbreaks in Europe in the nineteenth century, each with a lower death toll than the preceding one, has continued to be more memorable than smallpox, whose ravages increased as the century went on (half a million died in the European smallpox pandemic of the early 1870s) but which could not be construed as, plague-like, a disease with a non-European origin.

Plagues are no longer "sent," as in Biblical and Greek antiquity, for the 16
question of agency has blurred. Instead, peoples are "visited" by plagues. And the visitations recur, as is taken for granted in the subtitle of Defoe's narrative, which explains that it is about that "which happened in London during the Last Great Visitation in 1665." Even for non-Europeans, lethal disease may be called a visitation. But a visitation on "them" is invariably described as different from one on "us." "I believe that about one half of the whole people was carried off by this visitation," wrote the English traveler Alexander Kinglake, reaching Cairo at a time of the bubonic plague (sometimes called "oriental plague"). "The Orientals, however, have more quiet fortitude than Europeans under afflictions of this sort." Kinglake's influential book *Eothen* (1844)—suggestively subtitled "Traces of Travel Brought Home from the East"—illustrates many of the enduring Eurocentric presumptions about others,

starting from the fantasy that peoples with little reason to expect exemption from misfortune have a lessened capacity to *feel* misfortune. Thus it is believed that Asians (or the poor, or blacks, or Africans, or Muslims) don't suffer or don't grieve as Europeans (or whites) do. The fact that illness is associated with the poor—who are, from the perspective of the privileged, aliens in one's midst—reinforces the association of illness with the foreign: with an exotic, often primitive place.

Thus, illustrating the classic script for plague, AIDS is thought to have started in the "dark continent," then spread to Haiti, then to the United States and to Europe, then . . . It is understood as a tropical disease: another infestation from the so-called Third World, which is after all where most people in the world live, as well as a scourge of the *tristes tropiques.* Africans who detect racist stereotypes in much of the speculation about the geographical origin of AIDS are not wrong. (Nor are they wrong in thinking that depictions of Africa as the cradle of AIDS must feed anti-African prejudices in Europe and Asia.) The subliminal connection made to notions about a primitive past and the many hypotheses that have been fielded about possible transmission from animals (a disease of green monkeys? African swine fever?) cannot help but activate a familiar set of stereotypes about animality, sexual license, and blacks. In Zaire and other countries in Central Africa where AIDS is killing tens of thousands, the counterreaction has begun. Many doctors, academics, journalists, government officials, and other educated people believe that the virus was sent to Africa from the United States, an act of bacteriological warfare (whose aim was to decrease the African birth rate) which got out of hand and has returned to afflict its perpetrators. A common African version of this belief about the disease's provenance has the virus fabricated in a CIA-Army laboratory in Maryland, sent from there to Africa, and brought back to its country of origin by American homosexual missionaries returning from Africa to Maryland.* 17

*The rumor may not have originated as a KGB-sponsored "disinformation" campaign, but it received a crucial push from Soviet propaganda specialists. In October 1985 the Soviet weekly *Literaturnaya Gazeta* published an article alleging that the AIDS virus had been engineered by the U.S. government during biological-warfare research at Fort Detrick, Maryland, and was being spread abroad by U.S. servicemen who had been used as guinea pigs. The source cited was an article in the Indian newspaper *Patriot.* Repeated on Moscow's "Radio Peace and Progress" in English, the story was taken up by newspapers and magazines throughout the world. A year later it was featured on the front page of London's conservative, mass-circulation *Sunday Express.* ("The killer AIDS virus was artificially created by American scientists during laboratory experiments which went disastrously wrong—and a massive cover-up has kept the secret from the world until today.") Though ignored by most American newspapers, the *Sunday Express* story was recycled in virtually every other country. As recently as the summer of 1987, it appeared in newspapers in Kenya, Peru, Sudan, Nigeria, Senegal, and Mexico. Gorbachev-era policies have since produced an official denial of the allegations by two eminent members of the Soviet Academy of Sciences, which was published in *Izvestia* in October 1987. But the story is still being repeated—from Mexico to Zaire, from Australia to Greece.

At first it was assumed that AIDS must become widespread elsewhere in the same catastrophic form in which it has emerged in Africa, and those who still think this will eventually happen invariably invoke the Black Death. The plague metaphor is an essential vehicle of the most pessimistic reading of the epidemiological prospects. From classic fiction to the latest journalism, the standard plague story is of inexorability, inescapability. The unprepared are taken by surprise; those observing the recommended precautions are struck down as well. *All* succumb when the story is told by an omniscient narrator, as in Poe's parable "The Masque of the Red Death" (1842), inspired by an account of a ball held in Paris during the cholera epidemic of 1832. Almost all—if the story is told from the point of view of a traumatized witness, who will be a benumbed survivor, as in Jean Giono's Stendhalian novel *Horseman on the Roof* (1951), in which a young Italian nobleman in exile wanders through cholera-stricken southern France in the 1830s.

Plagues are invariably regarded as judgments on society, and the metaphoric inflation of AIDS into such a judgment also accustoms people to the inevitability of global spread. This is a traditional use of sexually transmitted diseases: to be described as punishments not just of individuals but of a group ("generall licentiousnes"). Not only venereal diseases have been used in this way, to identify transgressing or vicious populations. Interpreting any catastrophic epidemic as a sign of moral laxity or political decline was as common until the later part of the last century as associating dreaded diseases with foreignness. (Or with despised and feared minorities.) And the assignment of fault is not contradicted by cases that do not fit. The Methodist preachers in England who connected the cholera epidemic of 1832 with drunkenness (the temperance movement was just starting) were not understood to be claiming that *everybody* who got cholera was a drunkard: there is always room for "innocent victims" (children, young women). Tuberculosis, in its identity as a disease of the poor (rather than of the "sensitive"), was also linked by late-nineteenth-century reformers to alcoholism. Responses to illnesses associated with sinners and the poor invariably recommended the adoption of middle-class values: the regular habits, productivity, and emotional self-control to which drunkenness was thought the chief impediment.* Health itself was eventually identified with these values, which were religious as well as mercantile, health being evidence of virtue as disease was of depravity. The dictum that

*According to the more comprehensive diagnosis favored by secular reformers, cholera was the result of poor diet and "indulgence in irregular habits." Officials of the Central Board of Health in London warned that there were no specific treatments for the disease, and advised paying attention to fresh air and cleanliness, though "the true preventatives are a healthy body and a cheerful, unruffled mind." Quoted in R. J. Morris, *Cholera 1832* (1976).

cleanliness is next to godliness is to be taken quite literally. The succession of cholera epidemics in the nineteenth century shows a steady waning of religious interpretations of the disease; more precisely, these increasingly coexisted with other explanations. Although, by the time of the epidemic of 1866, cholera was commonly understood not simply as a divine punishment but as the consequence of remediable defects of sanitation, it was still regarded as the scourge of the sinful. A writer in *The New York Times* declared (April 22, 1866): "Cholera is especially the punishment of neglect of sanitary laws; it is the curse of the dirty, the intemperate, and the degraded."*

20 That it now seems unimaginable for cholera or a similar disease to be regarded in this way signifies not a lessened capacity to moralize about diseases but only a change in the kind of illnesses that are used didactically. Cholera was perhaps the last major epidemic disease fully qualifying for plague status for almost a century. (I mean cholera as a European and American, therefore a nineteenth-century, disease; until 1817 there had never been a cholera epidemic outside the Far East.) Influenza, which would seem more plague-like than any other epidemic in this century if loss of life were the main criterion, and which struck as suddenly as cholera and killed as quickly, usually in a few days, was never viewed metaphorically as a plague. Nor was a more recent epidemic, polio. One reason why plague notions were not invoked is that these epidemics did not have enough of the attributes perennially ascribed to plagues. (For instance, polio was construed as typically a disease of children—of the innocent.) The more important reason is that there has been a shift in the focus of the moralistic exploitation of illness. This shift, to diseases that can be interpreted as judgments on the individual, makes it harder to use epidemic disease as such. For a long time cancer was the illness that best fitted this secular culture's need to blame and punish and censor through the imagery of disease. Cancer was a disease of an individual, and understood as the result not of an action but rather of a failure to act (to be prudent, to exert proper self-control, or to be properly expressive). In the twentieth century it has become almost impossible to moralize about epidemics—except those which are transmitted sexually. . . .

21 The persistence of the belief that illness reveals, and is a punishment for, moral laxity or turpitude can be seen in another way, by noting the persistence of descriptions of disorder or corruption as a disease. So indispensable has been the plague metaphor in bringing summary judgments about social crisis that its use hardly abated during the era when collective diseases were no longer treated so moralistically—the time between the influenza and encephalitis pandemics of the early and mid-1920s and the acknowledgment of a new, mysterious epidemic illness in the early 1980s—and when great infectious epidemics were so often and confidently proclaimed a thing of the

*Quoted in Charles E. Rosenberg, *The Cholera Years: The United States in 1832, 1849, and 1866* (1962).

past.* The plague metaphor was common in the 1930s as a synonym for social and psychic catastrophe. Evocations of plague of this type usually go with rant, with antiliberal attitudes: think of Artaud on theatre and plague, of Wilhelm Reich on "emotional plague." And such a generic "diagnosis" necessarily promotes antihistorical thinking. A theodicy as well as a demonology, it not only stipulates something emblematic of evil but makes this the bearer of a rough, terrible justice. In Karel Čapek's *The White Plague* (1937), the loathsome pestilence that has appeared in a state where fascism has come to power afflicts only those over the age of forty, those who could be held morally responsible.

Written on the eve of the Nazi takeover of Czechoslovakia, Čapek's allegor- 2
ical play is something of an anomaly—the use of the plague metaphor to convey the menace of what is defined as barbaric by a mainstream European liberal. The play's mysterious, grisly malady is something like leprosy, a rapid, invariably fatal leprosy that is supposed to have come, of course, from Asia. But Čapek is not interested in identifying political evil with the incursion of the foreign. He scores his didactic points by focusing not on the disease itself but on the management of information about it by scientists, journalists, and politicians. The most famous specialist in the disease harangues a reporter ("The disease of the hour, you might say. A good five million have died of it to date, twenty million have it and at least three times as many are going about their business, blithely unaware of the marble-like, marble-sized spots on their bodies"); chides a fellow doctor for using the popular terms, "the white plague" and "Peking leprosy," instead of the scientific name, "the Cheng Syndrome"; fantasizes about how his clinic's work on identifying the new virus and finding a cure ("every clinic in the world has an intensive research program") will add to the prestige of science and win a Nobel Prize for its discoverer; revels in hyperbole when it is thought a cure has been found ("it was the most dangerous disease in all history, worse than the bubonic plague"); and outlines plans for sending those with symptoms to well-guarded detention camps ("Given that every carrier of the disease is a potential spreader of the disease, we *must* protect the uncontaminated from the contaminated. All sentimentality in this regard is fatal and therefore criminal"). However cartoonish Čapek's ironies may seem, they are a not improbable sketch of catastrophe (medical, ecological) as a managed public event in modern mass society. And however conventionally he deploys the plague metaphor, as an agency of retribution (in the end the plague strikes down the dictator himself), Čapek's feel for public relations leads him to make explicit in the play the understanding of disease *as*

*As recently as 1983, the historian William H. McNeill, author of *Plagues and Peoples,* started his review of a new history of the Black Death by asserting: "One of the things that separate us from our ancestors and make contemporary experience profoundly different from that of other ages is the disappearance of epidemic disease as a serious factor in human life" (*The New York Review of Books,* July 21, 1983). The Eurocentric presumption of this and many similar statements hardly needs pointing out.

a metaphor. The eminent doctor declares the accomplishments of science to be as nothing compared with the merits of the dictator, about to launch a war, "who has averted a far worse scourge: the scourge of anarchy, the leprosy of corruption, the epidemic of barbaric liberty, the plague of social disintegration fatally sapping the organism of our nation."

Camus's *The Plague,* which appeared a decade later, is a far less literal use of plague by another great European liberal, as subtle as Čapek's *The White Plague* is schematic. Camus's novel is not, as is sometimes said, a political allegory in which the outbreak of bubonic plague in a Mediterranean port city represents the Nazi occupation. This plague is not retributive. Camus is not protesting anything, not corruption or tyranny, not even mortality. The plague is no more or less than an exemplary event, the irruption of death that gives life its seriousness. His use of plague, more epitome than metaphor, is detached, stoic, aware—it is not about bringing judgment. But, as in Čapek's play, characters in Camus's novel declare how unthinkable it is to have a plague in the twentieth century . . . as if the belief that such a calamity could not happen, could not happen *anymore,* means that it must. 23

For Discussion and Writing

1. Summarize in your own words the major points of Sontag's text.
2. According to Sontag, what are the major metaphors used to speak about AIDS?
3. As Sontag demonstrates, we not only speak of disease in metaphors drawn from other aspects of life, we also use metaphors *from* disease to speak of other things. What aspects of her discussion do you find most surprising, interesting, or controversial? What connections do you find between her essay and Lakoff and Johnson's view of metaphor?
4. Sontag's book *AIDS and Its Metaphors* was published in 1988. What changes, if any, have you noticed in metaphors used to discuss AIDS since the publication of her book? Consider metaphors used by those with AIDS as well as by those without it. You may want to look beyond such obvious sources as *Time* and *Newsweek* to discuss drama, fiction, poetry, essays, medical journalism, and AIDS-prevention literature. Write a short essay in which you discuss the metaphors used in one or more of your sources.

Arguing with Metaphor: Analogy and Parable

As we have seen, metaphor is a crucial element of language and thought. In particular, it functions powerfully in texts designed to argue a position or persuade a reader to adopt a particular attitude. The form of metaphor most common in argument is *analogy.*

Basic strategy in the use of analogy is to claim that situation X, which is under disputation, is like or analogous to situation Y, about which there is no dispute. In extreme forms, such arguments go beyond the assertion of likeness and assert sameness. One says not "Abortion is *like* murder," but "Abortion *is* murder." In arguing for such analogies, the writer tends to suppress what Lakoff and Johnson call the "unused" parts of metaphorical concepts. Therefore, counterargument will often consist of using these unused elements, thus calling into question the whole analogy.

A creative element in argument is the generation of fresh analogies that force a reappraisal of the situation. Such arguments may take the form "X is not much like Y; it is more like Z." Often an argument that has a logical structure will be animated by creatively designed analogies, as in the following text by Judith Jarvis Thomson. In her discussion of ethical questions related to abortion, Thomson uses both *analogy* and *parable* to make abstract issues concrete and to support her own views. A parable is simply an extended analogy in the form of an anecdote: the metaphorical principle developed in narrative form. As you read Thomson, pay particular attention to her use of both analogy and parable.

Abortion and Ethics

Judith Jarvis Thomson

Most opposition to abortion relies on the premise that the fetus is a human being, a person from the moment of conception. The premise is argued for, but, as I think, not well. But I shall not discuss any of this. For it seems to me to be of great interest to ask what happens if, for the sake of argument, we allow the premise. How, precisely, are we supposed to get from there to the conclusion that abortion is morally impermissible? Opponents of abortion commonly spend most of their time establishing that the fetus is a person, and hardly any time explaining the step from there to the impermissibility of abortion. Perhaps they think the step too simple and obvious to require much comment. Or perhaps instead they are simply being economical in argument. Many of those 1 who defend abortion rely on the premise that the fetus is not a person, but only a bit of tissue that will become a person at birth; and why pay out more arguments than you have to? Whatever the explanation, I suggest that the step they take is neither easy nor obvious, that it calls for closer examination than it is commonly given, and that when we do give it this closer examination we shall feel inclined to reject it.

I propose, then, that we grant that the fetus is a person from the moment of 2
conception. How does the argument go from here? Something like this, I take it. Every person has a right to life. So the fetus has a right to life. No doubt the mother has a right to decide what shall happen in and to her body; everyone would grant that. But surely a person's right to life is stronger and more stringent than the mother's right to decide what happens in and to her body, and so outweighs it. So the fetus may not be killed; an abortion may not be performed.

It sounds plausible. But now let me ask you to imagine this. You wake up in 3
the morning and find yourself back to back in bed with an unconscious violinist. A famous unconscious violinist. He has been found to have a fatal kidney ailment, and the Society of Music Lovers has canvassed all the available medical records and found that you alone have the right blood type to help. They have therefore kidnapped you, and last night the violinist's circulatory system was plugged into yours, so that your kidneys can be used to extract poisons from his blood as well as your own. The director of the hospital now tells you, "Look, we're sorry the Society of Music Lovers did this to you—we would never have permitted it if we had known. But still, they did it, and the violinist now is plugged into you. To unplug you would be to kill him. But never mind, it's only for nine months. By then he will have recovered from his ailment, and can safely be unplugged from you." Is it morally incumbent on you to accede to this situation? No doubt it would be very nice of you if you did, a great kindness. But do you *have* to accede to it? What if it were not nine months, but nine years? Or longer still? What if the director of the hospital says, "Tough luck, I agree, but you've now got to stay in bed, with the violinist plugged into you, for the rest of your life. Because remember this. All persons have a right to life, and violinists are persons. Granted you have a right to decide what happens in and to your body, but a person's right to life outweighs your right to decide what happens in and to your body. So you cannot ever be unplugged from him." I imagine you would regard this as outrageous, which suggests that something really is wrong with that plausible-sounding argument I mentioned a moment ago.

In this case, of course, you were kidnapped; you didn't volunteer for the 4
operation that plugged the violinist into your kidneys. Can those who oppose abortion on the ground I mentioned make an exception for a pregnancy due to rape? Certainly. They can say that persons have a right to life only if they didn't come into existence because of rape; or they can say that all persons have a right to life, but that some have less of a right to life than others, in particular,

that those who came into existence because of rape have less. But these statements have a rather unpleasant sound. Surely the question of whether you have a right to life at all, or how much of it you have, shouldn't turn on the question of whether or not you are the product of a rape. And in fact the people who oppose abortion on the ground I mentioned do not make this distinction, and hence do not make an exception in case of rape.

Nor do they make an exception for a case in which the mother has to 5
spend the nine months of her pregnancy in bed. They would agree that would be a great pity, and hard on the mother; but all the same, all persons have a right to life, the fetus is a person, and so on. I suspect, in fact, that they would not make an exception for a case in which, miraculously enough, the pregnancy went on for nine years, or even the rest of the mother's life.

Some won't even make an exception for a case in which continuation of 6
the pregnancy is likely to shorten the mother's life; they regard abortion as impermissible even to save the mother's life. Such cases are nowadays very rare, and many opponents of abortion do not accept this extreme view. All the same, it is a good place to begin: a number of points of interest come out in respect to it.

Let us call the view that abortion is impermissible even to save the 7
mother's life "the extreme view." I want to suggest first that it does not issue from the argument I mentioned earlier without the addition of some fairly powerful premises. Suppose a woman has become pregnant, and now learns that she has a cardiac condition such that she will die if she carries the baby to term. What may be done for her? The fetus, being a person, has a right to life, but as the mother is a person too, so has she a right to life. Presumably they have an equal right to life. How is it supposed to come out that an abortion may not be performed? If mother and child have an equal right to life, shouldn't we perhaps flip a coin? Or should we add to the mother's right to life her right to decide what happens in and to her body, which everybody seems to be ready to grant—the sum of her rights now outweighing the fetus' right to life?

The most familiar argument here is the following. We are told that 8
performing the abortion would be directly killing[1] the child, whereas doing nothing would not be killing the mother, but only letting her die. Moreover, in killing the child, one would be killing an innocent person, for the child has committed no crime, and is not aiming at his mother's death. And then there are a variety of ways in which this might be continued: (1) but as directly killing an innocent person is always and absolutely impermissible, an abortion may not be performed. (2) As directly killing an innocent person is murder, and murder is always and absolutely impermissible, an abortion may

[1] The term "direct" in the arguments I refer to is a technical one. Roughly, what is meant by "direct killing" is either killing as an end in itself, or killing as a means of some end, for example, the end of saving someone else's life.

not be performed.[2] (3) As one's duty to refrain from directly killing an innocent person is more stringent than one's duty to keep a person from dying, an abortion may not be performed. (4) If one's only options are directly killing an innocent person or letting a person die, one must prefer letting the person die, and thus an abortion may not be performed.[3]

Some people seem to have thought that these are not further premises 9
which must be added if the conclusion is to be reached, but that they follow from the very fact that an innocent person has a right to life.[4] But this seems to me to be a mistake, and perhaps the simplest way to show this is to bring out that while we must certainly grant that innocent persons have a right to life, the theses in (1) through (4) are all false. Take (2), for example. If directly killing an innocent person is murder, and thus is impermissible, then the mother's directly killing the innocent person inside her is murder, and thus is impermissible. But it cannot seriously be thought to be murder if the mother performs an abortion on herself to save her life. It cannot seriously be said that she *must* refrain, that she *must* sit passively by and wait for her death. Let us look again at the case of you and the violinist. There you are, in bed with the violinist, and the director of the hospital says to you, "It's all most distressing, and I deeply sympathize, but you see this is putting an additional strain on your kidneys, and you'll be dead within the month. But you *have* to stay where you are all the same. Because unplugging you would be directly killing an innocent violinist, and that is murder, and that's impermissible." If anything in the world is true, it is that you do not commit murder, you do not do what is impermissible, if you reach around to your back and unplug yourself from that violinist to save your life.

[2] Cf. *Encyclical Letter of Pope Pius XI on Christian Marriage,* St. Paul Editions, Boston, p. 32: "However much we may pity the mother whose health and even life is gravely imperiled in the performance of the duty allotted to her by nature, nevertheless what could ever be a sufficient reason for excusing in any way the direct murder of the innocent? This is precisely what we are dealing with here." Noonan, in *The Morality of Abortion,* reads this as follows: "What cause can ever avail to excuse in any way the direct killing of the innocent? For it is a question of that."

[3] The thesis in (4) is in an interesting way weaker than those in (1), (2), and (3): they rule out abortion even in cases in which both mother *and* child will die if the abortion is not performed. By contrast, one who held the view expressed in (4) could consistently say that one needn't prefer letting two persons die to killing one.

[4] Cf. the following passage from Pius XII, *Address to the Italian Catholic Society of Midwives:* "The baby in the maternal breast has the right to life immediately from God. Hence there is no man, no human authority, no science, no medical, eugenic, social, economic or moral 'indication' which can establish or grant a valid juridical ground for a direct deliberate disposition of an innocent human life, that is a disposition which looks to its destruction either as an end or as a means to another end perhaps in itself not illicit. The baby, still not born, is a man in the same degree and for the same reason as the mother" (quoted in Noonan, *The Morality of Abortion,* p. 45).

The main focus of attention in writings on abortion has been on what a third party may or may not do in answer to a request from a woman for an abortion. This is in a way understandable. Things being as they are, there isn't much a woman can safely do to abort herself. So the question asked is what a third party may do, and what the mother may do, if it is mentioned at all, is deduced, almost as an afterthought, from what it is concluded that third parties may do. But it seems to me that to treat the matter in this way is to refuse to grant to the mother that very status of person which is so firmly insisted on for the fetus. For we cannot simply read off what a person may do from what a third party may do. Suppose you find yourself trapped in a tiny house with a growing child. I mean a very tiny house, and a rapidly growing child—you are already up against the wall of the house and in a few minutes you'll be crushed to death. The child on the other hand won't be crushed to death; if nothing is done to stop him from growing he'll be hurt, but in the end he'll simply burst open the house and walk out a free man. Now I could well understand it if a bystander were to say, "There's nothing we can do for you. We cannot choose between your life and his, we cannot be the ones to decide who is to live, we cannot intervene." But it cannot be concluded that you too can do nothing, that you cannot attack it to save your life. However innocent the child may be, you do not have to wait passively while it crushes you to death. Perhaps a pregnant woman is vaguely felt to have the status of house, to which we don't allow the right of self-defense. But if the woman houses the child, it should be remembered that she is a person who houses it.

I should perhaps stop to say explicitly that I am not claiming that people have a right to do anything whatever to save their lives. I think, rather, that there are drastic limits to the right of self-defense. If someone threatens you with death unless you torture someone else to death, I think you have not the right, even to save your life, to do so. But the case under consideration here is very different. In our case there are only two people involved, one whose life is threatened, and one who threatens it. Both are innocent: the one who is threatened is not threatened because of any fault; the one who threatens does not threaten because of any fault. For this reason we may feel that we bystanders cannot intervene. But the person threatened can.

In sum, a woman surely can defend her life against the threat to it posed by the unborn child, even if doing so involves its death. And this shows not merely that the theses in (1) through (4) are false; it shows also that the extreme view of abortion is false, and so we need not canvass any other possible ways of arriving at it from the argument I mentioned at the outset.

The extreme view could of course be weakened to say that while abortion is permissible to save the mother's life, it may not be performed by a third party, but only by the mother herself. But this cannot be right either. For what we have to keep in mind is that mother and the unborn child are not like two tenants in a small house which has, by an unfortunate mistake, been rented to both: the mother *owns* the house. The fact that she does adds to the offensiveness of deducing that the mother can do nothing from the supposition that third parties can do nothing. But it does more than this: it casts a bright light on the supposition that third parties can do nothing. Certainly it lets us see that a third party who says "I cannot choose between you" is fooling himself if he thinks this is impartiality. If Jones has found and fastened on a certain coat, which he needs to keep him from freezing, but which Smith also needs to keep him from freezing, then it is not impartiality that says, "I cannot choose between you" when Smith owns the coat. Women have said again and again, "This body is *my* body!" and they have reason to feel angry, reason to feel that it has been like shouting into the wind. Smith, after all, is hardly likely to bless us if we say to him, "Of course it's your coat, anybody would grant that it is. But no one may choose between you and Jones who is to have it."

We should really ask what it is that says "no one may choose" in the face of 14
the fact that the body that houses the child is the mother's body. It may be simply a failure to appreciate this fact. But it may be something more interesting, namely, the sense that one has a right to refuse to lay hands on people, even where it would be just and fair to do so, even where justice seems to require that somebody do so. Thus justice might call for somebody to get Smith's coat back from Jones, and yet you have a right to refuse to be the one to lay hands on Jones, a right to refuse to do physical violence to him. This, I think, must be granted. But then what should be said is not "no one may choose, but only "*I* cannot choose," and indeed not even this, but "*I* will not *act*," leaving it open that somebody else can or should, and in particular that anyone in a position of authority, with the job of securing people's rights, both can and should. So this is no difficulty. I have not been arguing that any given third party must accede to the mother's request that he perform an abortion to save her life, but only that he may.

I suppose that in some views of human life the mother's body is only on 15
loan to her, the loan not being one which gives her any prior claim to it. One who held this view might well think it impartiality to say "I cannot choose." But I shall simply ignore this possibility. My own view is that if a human being has any just, prior claim to anything at all, he has a just, prior claim to his own body. And perhaps this needn't be argued for here anyway, since, as I mentioned, the arguments against abortion we are looking at do grant that the woman has a right to decide what happens in and to her body.

But although they do grant it, I have tried to show that they do not take 16
seriously what is done in granting it. I suggest the same thing will reappear even more clearly when we turn away from cases in which the mother's life is at stake, and attend, as I propose we now do, to the vastly more common cases in which a woman wants an abortion for some less weighty reason than preserving her own life.

Where the mother's life is not at stake, the argument I mentioned at the 17
outset seems to have a much stronger pull. "Everyone has a right to life, so the unborn person has a right to life." And isn't the child's right to life weightier

than anything other than the mother's own right to life, which she might put forward as ground for an abortion?

This argument treats the right to life as if it were unproblematic. It is not, 1
and this seems to me to be precisely the source of the mistake.

For we should now, at long last, ask what it comes to, to have a right to life. 1
In some views having a right to life includes having a right to be given at least the bare minimum one needs for continued life. But suppose that what in fact *is* the bare minimum a man needs for continued life is something he has no right at all to be given? If I am sick unto death, and the only thing that will save my life is the touch of Henry Fonda's cool hand on my fevered brow, then all the same, I have no right to be given the touch of Henry Fonda's cool hand on my fevered brow. It would be frightfully nice of him to fly in from the West Coast to provide it. It would be less nice, though no doubt well meant, if my friends flew out to the West Coast and carried Henry Fonda back with them. But I have no right at all against anybody that he should do this for me. Or again, to return to the story I told earlier, the fact that for continued life that violinist needs the continued use of your kidneys does not establish that he has a right to be given the continued use of your kidneys. He certainly has no right against you that you should give him continued use of your kidneys. For nobody has any right to use your kidneys unless you give him such a right; and nobody has the right against you that you shall give him this right—if you do allow him to go on using your kidneys, this is a kindness on your part, and not something he can claim from you as his due. Nor has he any right against anybody else that *they* should give him continued use of your kidneys. Certainly he had no right against the Society of Music Lovers that they should plug him into you in the first place. And if you now start to unplug yourself, having learned that you will otherwise have to spend nine years in bed with him, there is nobody in the world who must try to prevent you, in order to see to it that he is given something he has a right to be given.

Some people are rather stricter about the right to life. In their view, it does not include the right to be given anything, but amounts to, and only to, the right not to be killed by anybody. But here a related difficulty arises. If everybody is to refrain from killing that violinist, then everybody must refrain from doing a great many different sorts of things. Everybody must refrain from slitting his throat, everybody must refrain from shooting him—and everybody must refrain from unplugging you from him. But does he have a right against everybody that they shall refrain from unplugging you from him? To refrain from doing this is to allow him to continue to use your kidneys. It could be argued that he has a right against us that *we* should allow him to continue to use your kidneys. That is, while he had no right against us that we should give him the use of your kidneys, it might be argued that he anyway has a right against us that we shall not now intervene and deprive him of the use of your kidneys. I shall come back to third-party interventions later. But certainly the violinist has no right against you that *you* shall allow him to continue to use your kidneys. As I said, if you do allow him to use them, it is a kindness on your part, and not something you owe him.

The difficulty I point to here is not peculiar to the right to life. It reappears 21
in connection with all the other natural rights; and it is something which an adequate account of rights must deal with. For present purposes it is enough just to draw attention to it. But I would stress that I am not arguing that people do not have a right to life—quite to the contrary, it seems to me that the primary control we must place on the acceptability of an account of rights is that it should turn out in that account to be a truth that all persons have a right to life. I am arguing only that having a right to life does not guarantee having either a right to be given the use of or a right to be allowed continued use of another person's body—even if one needs it for life itself. So the right to life will not serve the opponents of abortion in the very simple and clear way in which they seem to have thought it would.

There is another way to bring out the difficulty. In the most ordinary sort of 22
case, to deprive someone of what he has a right to is to treat him unjustly. Suppose a boy and his small brother are jointly given a box of chocolates for Christmas. If the older boy takes the box and refuses to give his brother any of the chocolates, he is unjust to him, for the brother has been given a right to half of them. But suppose that, having learned that otherwise it means nine years in bed with that violinist, you unplug yourself from him. You surely are not being unjust to him, for you gave him no right to use your kidneys, and no one else can have given him any such right. But we have to notice that in unplugging yourself, you are killing him; and violinists, like everybody else, have a right to life, and thus in the view we were considering just now, the right not to be killed. So here you do what he supposedly has a right you shall not do, but you do not act unjustly to him in doing it.

The emendation which may be made at this point is this: the right to life 23
consists not in the right not to be killed, but rather in the right not to be killed unjustly. This runs a risk of circularity, but never mind: it would enable us to square the fact that the violinist has a right to life with the fact that you do not act unjustly toward him in unplugging yourself, thereby killing him. For if you do not kill him unjustly, you do not violate his right to life, and so it is no wonder you do him no injustice.

But if this emendation is accepted, the gap in the argument against 24
abortion stares us plainly in the face: it is by no means enough to show that the fetus is a person, and to remind us that all persons have a right to life—we need to be shown also that killing the fetus violates its right to life, i.e., that abortion is unjust killing. And is it?

I suppose we may take it as a datum that in a case of pregnancy due to rape 25
the mother has not given the unborn person a right to the use of her body for food and shelter. Indeed, in what pregnancy could it be supposed that the

mother has given the unborn person such a right? It is not as if there were unborn persons drifting about the world, to whom a woman who wants a child says "I invite you in."

But it might be argued that there are other ways one can have acquired a 26
right to the use of another person's body than by having been invited to use it by that person. Suppose a woman voluntarily indulges in intercourse, knowing of the chance it will issue in pregnancy, and then she does become pregnant; is she not in part responsible for the presence, in fact, the very existence, of the unborn person inside her? No doubt she did not invite it in. But doesn't her partial responsibility for its being there itself give it a right to the use of her body? If so, then her aborting it would be more like the boy's taking away the chocolates, and less like your unplugging yourself from the violinist—doing so would be depriving it of what it does have a right to, and thus would be doing it an injustice.

And then, too, it might be asked whether or not she can kill it even to save 27
her own life: If she voluntarily called it into existence, how can she now kill it, even in self-defense?

The first thing to be said about this is that it is something new. Opponents 28
of abortion have been so concerned to make out the independence of the fetus, in order to establish that it has a right to life, just as its mother does, that they have tended to overlook the possible support they might gain from making out that the fetus is *dependent* on the mother, in order to establish that she has a special kind of responsibility for it, a responsibility that gives it rights against her which are not possessed by any independent person—such as an ailing violinist who is a stranger to her.

On the other hand, this argument would give the unborn person a right to 29
its mother's body only if her pregnancy resulted from a voluntary act, undertaken in full knowledge of the chance a pregnancy might result from it. It would leave out entirely the unborn person whose existence is due to rape. Pending the availability of some further argument, then, we would be left with the conclusion that unborn persons whose existence is due to rape have no right to the use of their mothers' bodies, and thus that aborting them is not depriving them of anything they have a right to and hence is not unjust killing.

And we should also notice that it is not at all plain that this argument really 30
does go even as far as it purports to. For there are cases and cases, and the details make a difference. If the room is stuffy, and I therefore open a window to air it, and a burglar climbs in, it would be absurd to say, "Ah, now he can stay, she's given him a right to the use of her house—for she is partially responsible for his presence there, having voluntarily done what enabled him to get in, in full knowledge that there are such things as burglars, and that burglars burgle." It would be still more absurd to say this if I had had bars installed outside my windows, precisely to prevent burglars from getting in, and a burglar got in only because of a defect in the bars. It remains equally absurd if we imagine it is not a burglar who climbs in, but an innocent person who blunders or falls in.

Again, suppose it were like this: people-seeds drift about in the air like pollen, and if you open your windows, one may drift in and take root in your carpets or upholstery. You don't want children, so you fix up your windows with fine mesh screens, the very best you can buy. As can happen, however, and on very, very rare occasions does happen, one of the screens is defective; and a seed drifts in and takes root. Does the person-plant who now develops have a right to the use of your house? Surely not—despite the fact that you voluntarily opened your windows, you knowingly kept carpets and upholstered furniture, and you knew that screens were sometimes defective. Someone may argue that you are responsible for its rooting, and it does have a right to your house, because after all you *could* have lived out your life with bare floors and furniture, or with sealed windows and doors. But this won't do—for by the same token anyone can avoid a pregnancy due to rape by having a hysterectomy, or anyway by never leaving home without a (reliable!) army.

It seems to me that the argument we are looking at can establish at most that there are *some* cases in which the unborn person has a right to the use of its mother's body, and therefore *some* cases in which abortion is unjust killing. There is room for much discussion and argument as to precisely which, if any. But I think we should sidestep this issue and leave it open, for at any rate the argument certainly does not establish that all abortion is unjust killing. 31

There is room for yet another argument here, however. We surely must all grant that there may be cases in which it would be morally indecent to detach a person from your body at the cost of his life. Suppose you learn that what the violinist needs is not nine years of your life, but only one hour: all you need to do to save his life is to spend one hour in bed with him. Suppose also that letting him use your kidneys for that one hour would not affect your health in the slightest. Admittedly you were kidnapped. Admittedly you did not give anyone permission to plug him into you. Nevertheless it seems to me plain you *ought* to allow him to use your kidneys for that hour—it would be indecent to refuse. 32

Again, suppose pregnancy lasted only an hour, and constituted no threat to life or health. And suppose that a woman becomes pregnant as a result of rape. Admittedly she did not voluntarily do anything to bring about the existence of a child. Admittedly she did nothing at all which would give the unborn person a right to the use of her body. All the same it might well be said, as in the newly emended violinist story, that she *ought* to allow it to remain for that hour—that it would be indecent in her to refuse. 33

Now some people are inclined to use the term "right" in such a way that it follows from the fact that you ought to allow a person to use your body for the hour he needs, that he has a right to use your body for the hour he needs, even though he has not been given that right by any person or act. They may say that it follows also that if you refuse, you act unjustly toward him. This use 34 of the term is perhaps so common that it cannot be called wrong; nevertheless it seems to me to be an unfortunate loosening of what we would do better to keep a tight rein on. Suppose that box of chocolates I mentioned earlier had not been given to both boys jointly, but was given only to the older boy. There he sits, stolidly eating his way through the box, his small brother watching enviously. Here we are likely to say, "You ought not to be so mean. You ought to give your brother some of those chocolates." My own view is that it just does not follow from the truth of this that the brother has any right to any of the chocolates. If the boy refuses to give his brother any, he is greedy, stingy, callous—but not unjust. I suppose that the people I have in mind will say it does follow that the brother has a right to some of the chocolates, and thus that the boy does act unjustly if he refuses to give his brother any. But the effect of saying this is to obscure what we should keep distinct, namely, the difference between the boy's refusal in this case and the boy's refusal in the earlier case, in which the box was given to both boys jointly, and in which the small brother thus had what was from any point of view clear title to half.

A further objection to so using the term "right" that from the fact that A 35
ought to do a thing for B, it follows that B has a right against A that A do it for him, is that it is going to make the question of whether or not a man has a right to a thing turn on how easy it is to provide him with it; and this seems not merely unfortunate, but morally unacceptable. Take the case of Henry Fonda again. I said earlier that I had no right to the touch of his cool hand on my fevered brow, even though I needed it to save my life. I said it would be frightfully nice of him to fly in from the West Coast to provide me with it, but that I had no right against him that he should do so. But suppose he isn't on the West Coast. Suppose he has only to walk across the room, place a hand briefly on my brow—and lo, my life is saved. Then surely he ought to do it, it would be indecent to refuse. Is it to be said, "Ah, well, it follows that in this case she has a right to the touch of his hand on her brow, and so it would be an injustice in him to refuse"? So that I have a right to it when it is easy for him to provide it, though no right when it's hard? It's rather a shocking idea that anyone's rights should fade away and disappear as it gets harder and harder to accord them to him.

So my own view is that even though you ought to let the violinist use 36
your kidneys for the one hour he needs, we should not conclude that he has a right to do so—we should say that if you refuse, you are, like the boy who owns all the chocolates and will give none away, self-centered and callous, indecent in fact, but not unjust. And similarly, that even supposing a case in which a woman pregnant due to rape ought to allow the unborn person to use her body for the hour he needs, we should not conclude that he has a right to do so; we should conclude that she is self-centered, callous, indecent, but not unjust, if she refuses. The complaints are no less grave; they are just different. However, there is no need to insist on this point. If anyone does not

wish to deduce "he has a right" from "you ought," then all the same he must surely grant that there are cases in which it is not morally required of you that you allow that violinist to use your kidneys, and in which he does not have a right to use them, and in which you do not do him an injustice if you refuse. And so also for mother and unborn child. Except in such cases as the unborn person has a right to demand it—and we were leaving open the possibility that there may be such cases—nobody is morally *required* to make large sacrifices, of health, of all other interests and concerns, of all other duties and commitments, for nine years, or even for nine months, in order to keep another person alive.

We have in fact to distinguish between two kinds of Samaritan: the 37
Good Samaritan and what we might call the Minimally Decent Samaritan. The story of the Good Samaritan, you will remember, goes like this:

> A certain man went down from Jerusalem to Jericho, and fell among thieves, which stripped him of his raiment, and wounded him, and departed, leaving him half dead.
>
> And by chance there came down a certain priest that way; and when he saw him, he passed by on the other side.
>
> And likewise a Levite, when he was at the place, came and looked on him, and passed by on the other side.
>
> But a certain Samaritan, as he journeyed, came where he was; and when he saw him he had compassion on him.
>
> And went to him, and bound up his wounds pouring in oil and wine, and set him on his own beast, and brought him to an inn, and took care of him.
>
> And on the morrow, when he departed, he took out two pence, and gave them to the host, and said unto him, "Take care of him; and whatsoever thou spendest more, when I come again, I will repay thee."
>
> (Luke 10:30–35)

The Good Samaritan went out of his way, at some cost to himself, to help one in need of it. We are not told what the options were, that is, whether or not the priest and the Levite could have helped by doing less than the Good Samaritan did, but assuming they could have, then the fact they did nothing at all shows they were not even Minimally Decent Samaritans, not because they were not Samaritans, but because they were not even minimally decent.

These things are a matter of degree, of course, but there is a difference, 38
and it comes out perhaps most clearly in the story of Kitty Genovese, who, as you will remember, was murdered while thirty-eight people watched or listened, and did nothing at all to help her. A Good Samaritan would have rushed out to give direct assistance against the murderer. Or perhaps we had better allow that it would have been a Splendid Samaritan who did this, on the ground that it would have involved a risk of death for himself. But the

thirty-eight not only did not do this, they did not even trouble to pick up a phone to call the police. Minimally Decent Samaritanism would call for doing at least that, and their not having done it was monstrous.

After telling the story of the Good Samaritan, Jesus said, "Go, and do thou 39
likewise." Perhaps he meant that we are morally required to act as the Good Samaritan did. Perhaps he was urging people to do more than is morally required of them. At all events it seems plain that it was not morally required of any of the thirty-eight that he rush out to give direct assistance at the risk of his own life, and that it is not morally required of anyone that he give long stretches of his life—nine years or nine months—to sustaining the life of a person who has no special right (we were leaving open the possibility of this) to demand it.

Indeed, with one rather striking class of exceptions, no one in any 40
country in the world *is legally* required to do anywhere near as much as this for anyone else. The class of exceptions is obvious. My main concern here is not the state of the law in respect to abortion, but it is worth drawing attention to the fact that in no state in this country is any man compelled by law to be even a Minimally Decent Samaritan to any person; there is no law under which charges could be brought against the thirty-eight who stood by while Kitty Genovese died. By contrast, in most states in this country women are compelled by law to be not merely Minimally Decent Samaritans, but Good Samaritans to unborn persons inside them. This doesn't by itself settle anything one way or the other, because it may well be argued that there should be laws in this country—as there are in many European countries—compelling at least Minimally Decent Samaritanism.[5] But it does show that there is a gross injustice in the existing state of the law. And it shows also that the groups currently working against liberalization of abortion laws, in fact working toward having it declared unconstitutional for a state to permit abortion, had better start working for the adoption of Good Samaritan laws generally, or earn the charge that they are acting in bad faith.

I should think, myself, that Minimally Decent Samaritan laws would be 41
one thing, Good Samaritan laws quite another, and in fact highly improper. But we are not here concerned with the law. What we should ask is not whether anybody should be compelled by law to be a Good Samaritan, but whether we must accede to a situation in which somebody is being compelled—by nature, perhaps—to be a Good Samaritan. We have, in other words, to look now at third-party interventions. I have been arguing that no person is morally required to make large sacrifices to sustain the life of

[5] For a discussion of the difficulties involved, and a survey of the European experience with such laws, see *The Good Samaritan and the Law,* ed. James M. Ratcliffe, New York, 1966.

another who has no right to demand them, and this even where the sacrifices do not include life itself; we are not morally required to be Good Samaritans or anyway Very Good Samaritans to one another. But what if a man cannot extricate himself from such a situation? What if he appeals to us to extricate him? It seems to me plain that there are cases in which we can, cases in which a Good Samaritan would extricate him. There you are, you were kidnapped, and nine years in bed with that violinist lie ahead of you. You have your own life to lead. You are sorry, but you simply cannot see giving up so much of your life to the sustaining of his. You cannot extricate yourself, and ask us to do so. I should have thought that—in light of his having no right to the use of your body—it was obvious that we do not have to accede to your being forced to give up so much. We can do what you ask. There is no injustice to the violinist in our doing so.

Following the lead of the opponents of abortion, I have throughout been 42
speaking of the fetus merely as a person, and what I have been asking is whether or not the argument we began with, which proceeds only from the fetus's being a person, really does establish its conclusion. I have argued that it does not.

But of course there are arguments and arguments, and it may be said that 43
I have simply fastened on the wrong one. It may be said that what is important is not merely the fact that the fetus is a person, but that it is a person for whom the woman has a special kind of responsibility issuing from the fact that she is its mother. And it might be argued that all my analogies are therefore irrelevant—for you do not have that special kind of responsibility for that violinist, Henry Fonda does not have that special kind of responsibility for me. And our attention might be drawn to the fact that men and women both *are* compelled by law to provide support for their children.

I have in effect dealt (briefly) with this argument above; but a (still 44
briefer) recapitulation now may be in order. Surely we do not have any such "special responsibility" for a person unless we have assumed it, explicitly or implicitly. If a set of parents do not try to prevent pregnancy, do not obtain an abortion, and then at the time of birth of the child do not put it out for adoption, but rather take it home with them, then they have assumed responsibility for it, they have given it rights, and they cannot *now* withdraw support from it at the cost of its life because they now find it difficult to go on providing for it. But if they have taken all reasonable precautions against having a child, they do not simply by virtue of their biological relationship to the child who comes into existence have a special responsibility for it. They may wish to assume responsibility for it, or they may not wish to. And I am suggesting that if assuming responsibility for it would require large sacrifices, then they may refuse. A Good Samaritan would not refuse—or anyway, a Splendid Samaritan, if the sacrifices that had to be made were enormous. But then so would a Good Samaritan assume responsibility for that violinist; so

would Henry Fonda, if he is a Good Samaritan, fly in from the West Coast and assume responsibility for me.

My argument will be found unsatisfactory on two counts by many of 45
those who want to regard abortion as morally permissible. First, while I do argue that abortion is not impermissible, I do not argue that it is always permissible. There may well be cases in which carrying the child to term requires only Minimally Decent Samaritanism of the mother, and this is a standard we must not fall below. I am inclined to think it a merit of my account precisely that it does *not* give a general yes or a general no. It allows for and supports our sense that, for example, a sick and desperately frightened fourteen-year-old schoolgirl, pregnant due to rape, may *of course* choose abortion, and that any law which rules this out is an insane law. And it also allows for and supports our sense that in other cases resort to abortion is even positively indecent. It would be indecent in the woman to request an abortion, and indecent in a doctor to perform it, if she is in her seventh month, and wants the abortion just to avoid the nuisance of postponing a trip abroad. The very fact that the arguments I have been drawing attention to treat all cases of abortion, or even all cases of abortion in which the mother's life is not at stake, as morally on a par ought to have made them suspect at the outset.

Second, while I am arguing for the permissibility of abortion in some 46
cases, I am not arguing for the right to secure the death of the unborn child. It is easy to confuse these two things in that up to a certain point in the life of the fetus it is not able to survive outside the mother's body; hence removing it from her body guarantees its death. But they are importantly different. I have argued that you are not morally required to spend nine months in bed, sustaining the life of that violinist; but to say this is by no means to say that if, when you unplug yourself, there is a miracle and he survives, you then have a right to turn round and slit his throat. You may detach yourself even if this costs him his life; you have no right to be guaranteed his death, by some other means, if unplugging yourself does not kill him. There are some people who will be dissatisfied by this feature of my argument. A woman may be utterly devastated by the thought of a child, a bit of herself, put out for adoption and never seen or heard of again. She may therefore want not merely that the child be detached from her, but more, that it die. Some opponents of abortion are inclined to regard this as beneath contempt—thereby showing insensitivity to what is surely a powerful source of despair. All the same, I agree that the desire for the child's death is not one which anybody may gratify, should it turn out to be possible to detach the child alive.

For Discussion and Writing

1. **As a certain point in her argument, Thomson introduces and quotes the biblical parable of the Good Samaritan. What is a parable, and how does it**

work? Have you any idea why Jesus speaks in parables? What is the relationship between parable, analogy, and metaphor? Is the plugged-in violinist a parable?

2. Discuss Thomson's use of analogies and metaphors. Which of her analogies do you find most effective? Which least effective?
3. There are several ways to counter the use of analogy in argument. One is by offering a better analogy that supports a counterargument. Another is by examining the analogy critically, pointing out the "unused" or suppressed features of the analogy so as to weaken or negate its argumentative thrust. One may also attack the logic of the argument—but we are not really concerned with the logic of argumentation at the present time. We suggest, therefore, that you produce a response to Thomson's views in terms of your own values. You should examine critically the "unused" portions of the analogies she uses, and you should also try to develop an alternative to the analogy of the plugged-in violinist that supports your own position.
4. Consider some controversial subject of the moment—either local or national—and present a position on that subject, basing your presentation on an analogy that you develop for the occasion, such as Thomson's image of being plugged in to a violinist. Use your analogy as the basis for explaining your own position on the issue you have chosen to discuss.

Metaphor and Metonymy: Advertising

Metaphor plays a major role in one kind of text that we encounter every day: advertising. To analyze the role of metaphor in advertising we will need one more technical term: *metonymy.* We have been using the term *metaphor* to cover all the ways of talking about one thing in terms of another, but actually we can make an important distinction between metaphor proper and another metaphoric device. This device is called *metonymy.* Metaphor proper is based upon some resemblance between the two things that are brought together in the metaphor. Robert Francis can speak of poetry and baseball in the same language because a poet and a baseball pitcher share certain attributes (p. 71). There is an analogy between the two elements of the metaphor.

We use metonymy, on the other hand, whenever we speak of one thing in terms of another that is usually associated with it. When we say "The White House says . . . " we don't mean that the building actually spoke but that the person who lives there, the president, has taken the position attributed to the building. Cartoonists use this same metonymy whenever they draw a picture of the White House with words coming out of it. A frequently used type of metonymy called *synecdoche* is the substitution of part of something for the whole of it. If we asked a rancher "How many cattle do you own?" he might reply, "Seven hundred head." Obviously, he owns the rest of the beasts also, not just the heads. You can keep clear the difference between metaphor and metonymy by remembering these examples: (1) *head of beer* is a metaphor, based on resemblance, and (2) *head of cattle* is metonymy, based on association—in this case synecdoche, a part for the whole.

In advertising, metonymy or association is very important. When a celebrity endorses a product, an association is formed between them. When a basketball player endorses a basketball shoe, we have a natural metonymy. Such shoes are already associated with the player. What the advertiser wants, however, and will sometimes make very explicit, is to have this metonymy interpreted as a metaphor. That is, the maker of basketball shoes wants us (subconsciously or consciously) to attribute the quality of the player to the shoe. But it would be a courageous maker of baseball gloves who hired Bob Uecker, who has a well-established image as having been a *not* very good player, to endorse his product. Uecker instead advertises beer. Most beer commercials establish a metonymic connection between good times and beer, hoping that the viewer will accept a further metaphoric connection and finally a cause-and-effect connection: the beer *is* good and a *cause* of good times.

Some ads make a very skillful use of metaphor and metonymy to push

their products. You owe it to yourself to understand exactly how they are trying to manipulate you. We provide analyses of three ads here and then invite you to do some analytical work of your own.

"Light My Lucky"

At this point we would like to describe an advertisement for Lucky Strike cigarettes, because cigarette ads are among the cleverest and most technically perfect that one can find, and because their use raises interesting moral problems about the functioning of advertising in general. We assume that you have seen Lucky Strike ads so that you will be able to follow our description without too much trouble. (Originally we intended to reprint the ad, but the company denied us permission to do so.) The ad is very simple. It presents a photo of a young woman (perhaps twenty-three or twenty-four years old) in a sweater, in a field or meadow, wearing a scarf, with one hand in her pocket and the other resting lightly on her windblown hair, holding an unlighted cigarette. She gazes straight out of the frame. The words "Light My Lucky" appear in quotation marks, very prominently displayed, starting just below her chin and extending across to the right margin of the page. In the lower right corner of the frame, also superimposed over the photographic image of the woman, is a large image of an opened package of Lucky Strike Lights. At the bottom of the frame, on the left, is the well-known warning from the Surgeon General, which says: "Smoking By Pregnant Women May Result in Fetal Injury, Premature Birth, and Low Weight." You can visualize the ad, we are sure, or find a comparable ad in a current magazine.

The young woman in the ad is very beautiful. She is outdoors and dressed in outdoorsy clothing, a thick scarf and a heavy sweater. The background is blurred, but it looks like a field or wooded area. What has all this got to do with cigarettes? She is holding an unlighted cigarette in a hand that rests on top of her windblown blonde hair. She looks serious, or perhaps sultry. We read the written phrase in quotation marks as what she says, though she does not appear to be speaking—what she might say, perhaps, but certainly what she wants: "Light My Lucky."

The woman is lightly but carefully made up: an unobtrusive lipstick, delicate but effectively applied eye makeup. The ad makes her the central figure in a cluster of metonymic associations: woman/cigarette/outdoors. This is a healthy, vigorous woman. The makers of the ad expect some of these positive healthy values to attach themselves (in the reader's subconscious mind) to the cigarette.

The woman is also extremely good-looking. Asking someone for a light is a classic sexual approach, presented in countless films, and turned into a metaphor for sex itself in rock songs like "Light My Fire." The phrase in the ad—"Light My Lucky"—quite deliberately suggests these other texts that are now part of our cultural memory. We call this sort of allusion *intertextuality*. (The concept will be presented more fully in the next chapter, but we should note at this point that intertextuality is, like metaphor and metonymy, a way of presenting two or more things at the same time in the same text.) The ad thus associates the cigarette with beauty, health, and erotic pleasures. These metonymies are deliberate: the cigarette is meant to acquire the associations as permanent attributes.

It is worth noting that the word *light* is used in a punning way in the ad, and that a pun, like metaphor and metonymy, is a way of bringing two meanings together in a single place—in a single word, in fact. *Light* is used as a verb to mean set on fire: light my cigarette, light a fire. By a common metaphorical extension it means "inflame" or "arouse," as in "light my fire." But *light* (as opposed to heavy) is used in our weight-conscious and health-conscious society to mean "free from bad ingredients." Light beer has fewer calories; light cigarettes have less tar and nicotine. These uses are slightly metaphorical in themselves. The "light" in "Light My Lucky" thus refers to both the classic sexual approach and the relative healthiness of the "light" cigarette, just as the image of an attractive woman in outdoor clothing refers to the same two things. Always, in such ads, the hope is held out that the desirable qualities metonymically connected to the product will come to the reader if he or she uses the product. Do you want to be healthy and attractive, and experience erotic pleasure? Smoke Lucky Strike Lights.

The "Surgeon General's Warning" that appears in the corner of the ad refers to pregnant women. But the woman in the ad is anything but pregnant. She is as emphatically unattached as she is positively healthy. The Surgeon General associates smoking, pregnancy, and ill-health. The ad associates smoking, sex, and good health. The idea that smoking is unhealthy is obliterated by these contradictory messages, leaving only pregnancy connected to ill health. This is an extremely clever and well-made ad.

"Finally, Life Insurance as Individual as You Are"

The Prudential Life Insurance Company logo, visible at the bottom of the ad, is a stylized image of the Rock of Gibraltar. By selecting the physical object as their company symbol, the Prudential Company obviously hoped for a metaphorical transfer of qualities from the Rock to the company in the mind of the consumer. Rocks are an ancient symbol of strength and solidity. In the Gospel of Matthew (16:18) Jesus says to Peter, "Thou art Peter, and upon this rock I will build my church." In saying these words, Jesus is playing upon a pun in the name Peter, which means rock (*pet*rified, for instance, means turned into stone). The qualities of a rock—strength, solidity, firmness—are to be ex-

With Prudential offering more types of life insurance than any other insurance company, we're confident we have a policy that's designed to meet your individual needs.

For instance, we have one policy for people who want high interest on their contract fund while taking life easy with a fixed premium schedule.

*There's another policy that earns high interest while giving you high premium flexibility.**

There are also two kinds of policies that let you invest in one or more of five accounts—stock, bond, money market, an aggressively managed account and a conservatively managed account.** All these products offer you guaranteed lifetime protection.*

In addition, Prudential offers competitively priced Term insurance. And a new Permanent Life insurance portfolio with current dividend schedules based on today's higher interest rates.

Of course, whichever life insurance matches your lifestyle, you know it is from The Prudential, one of the world's largest, most trusted financial institutions.

Let a Prudential/Pruco Securities representative review your needs to help you put your finger on the one policy that is unmistakably yours.

* *These products are offered through Prudential subsidiaries: Pruco Life Insurance Company and Pruco Life Insurance Company of New Jersey*
** *For more complete information, including fees and expenses, send for a prospectus. Read it carefully before you invest or send money.*
Sold through Pruco Securities Corporation, Newark, New Jersey
Interest rates may vary from year to year.

© 1985 The Prudential Insurance Company of America, Newark, N J

tended metaphorically to the institution of a church by means of a man whose character can be described metaphorically in terms of those rocky qualities.

The Rock of Gibraltar is in fact a rocky mountain that looms over the harbor of Gibraltar, on the southern tip of Spain at the gateway to the Mediterranean Sea. A harbor of enormous strategic importance, it is almost impregnable because the Rock makes attacking it from the land side difficult. It has been a major outpost of the British empire for over a century, and thus can stand metaphorically for power and stability beyond any ordinary rock. The viewer doesn't have to know any of these details, of course. He or she has only to perceive the company in terms of the qualities signified by this enormous rock. So Prudential chose the Rock for its symbol, its logo, and has used it in dozens of ads and TV commercials.

The company, like many other insurance companies, faces another advertising problem. If potential customers feel that it is big, strong, safe, and stable, they may also feel that it is enormous, cold, and indifferent. In making the ad we are examining, Prudential needed to find something that would indicate its concern for the individual. The company might be a rock, but it is a delicate, precise, *caring* sort of rock, who treats everybody as a person rather than a number.

What is unique about each one of us? Physically speaking, the handiest method of establishing each person's uniqueness is through the use of fingerprints. Our fingerprints are in fact indexical signs of each one of us, powerful metonyms that can, for instance, indicate that we were present at the scene of a crime. Because each one of us has his or her own set of prints, the fingerprint can function as a metaphor for uniqueness and individuality. Thus, the Prudential Company can use fingerprints to symbolize individuality. By shaping its rocky symbol *out of* a fingerprint in this ad, it hopes to add individuality to the other qualities that are metaphorically signified by the rock.

However, metaphors are not mathematical, and it is not easy to add them together and reach a predictable result. At this point we ask you to stop and make your own interpretation of the metaphors in the Prudential ad. What do the images of rock and fingerprint, taken together, mean to you? What associations or connotations do they arouse in your mind? Compare your reactions to those of your classmates in trying to assess the effectiveness of the use of metaphors in this ad. Whatever you decide, these two ads taken together, help to illustrate some of the ways in which advertising and poetry draw upon the same aspects of language for their power. One further example should show how important figurative language can be in advertising.

Vista

Though it may not appear so in our black and white reproduction of it, the Vista ad is visually striking. The tanned diver is dressed in red trunks and T-shirt. The water in the foreground is very shallow and transparent, showing the brown sand under it. The sea is green with bright whitecaps. The upper half of the picture is all bright blue sky, without a cloud. The diver is plunging into no more than two or three inches of water. It is a dramatic, arresting picture, and it arrests the viewer's eye as well. What is going on here, we wonder, and what will come of it? Why would anyone dive into two inches of water, anyway?

For answers, we must go to the small white sentences printed over the blue sky in the upper left of the frame. What they tell us is that we shouldn't read the picture literally. It is not about diving but about things for which such a dive may be a metaphor. The printed text picks up these metaphors from the visual image and interprets them in such a way as to connect them to the product being advertised. It says,

> When you dive into a client
> presentation.
> When you hit the dirt in a
> business skirmish.
> When you make a splash with
> the higher-ups.
> And the higher higher-ups.
> When you finally crest the
> wave.
> Come test our waters.

After this it introduces the product, a chain of hotels seeking businessmen as customers. The ad takes a collection of dead or inert metaphors that have come to function as clichés about business, and revitalizes them by connecting them to a single, startling visual image. What the image does is take them literally—dive, hit the dirt, make a splash, crest the wave, test our waters. It shows someone doing all these things—or almost doing all these things. After all, it is not easy to hit the dirt and make a splash at the same time. This sounds, in fact, like a clumsily mixed metaphor, but the picture shows how one can indeed hit the dirt and make a splash at the same time. You just dive into two inches of water. This whole process does many of the same things that poems do. It revives inert metaphors that have become clichés; it gives you metaphor where you expect literal meaning and literal meaning where you expect figures of speech. It is also a little bit like a riddle or puzzle on the order of Sylvia Plath's poem "Metaphors." Is it a good ad? Will it sell the product? It is hard to say but it certainly is an attention-getter, and the visual image does indeed lead us to look at the text to find out what is going on here. For our purposes, of course, it also demonstrates once again how poetry and advertising often employ the same dimensions of language for their different purposes.

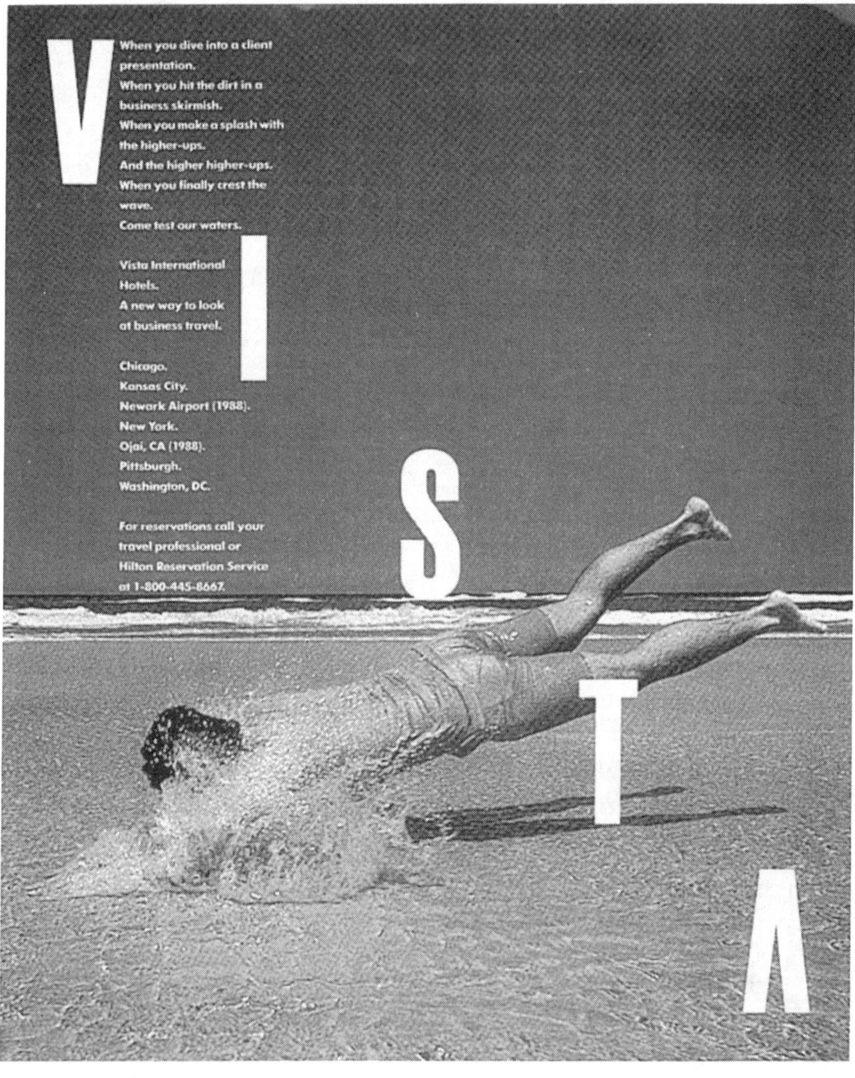

For Discussion and Writing

1. Even without the example of these discussions before you, you know a lot about advertising because you see many ads every day. Find two different full-page ads for a particular type of product such as designer perfume, cigarettes, bran cereal, or luxury automobiles. (We suggest a slick magazine designed for a general audience, such as *Sports Illustrated, The New Yorker, Esquire,* or *Vogue* as your best source of skillfully done ads.) Write an essay in which you compare and discuss the metaphoric and metonymic qualities of the two ads. Try to reach some conclusions about how and why certain things work in advertising.
2. Knowing what you know about the workings of advertisements, you should be able to design an ad that works the wrong way. Imagine, for instance, replacing the sultry, outdoorsy blonde in the "Lucky" ad with an obviously pregnant woman. Given the "Surgeon General's Warning" that appears in the ad, this would be a disaster—even if the woman were as lovely and healthy in appearance as the woman now in the ad. Your task is to take an existing ad and make a substitution or two that will ruin the ad for its intended purpose. You should not be too blatant or obvious in your changes nor make too many of them. Just do something that spoils the intended result as you understand it.

Chapter 3
Texts and Other Texts

In the previous two chapters we have examined aspects of language and textuality that have been considered important since Aristotle's time. At this point, however, we begin to shift our attention to things that have been the special concerns of modern literature and recent literary theory. As you might expect, from here on, things get more complicated. Our principles, however, remain the same. We will continue to share with you the theory that we have used to shape our presentation of ideas and materials. We will also continue to offer you opportunities to grasp this theory by actual application of it to textual situations.

Our emphasis in this chapter, as you will soon see, is on the way that texts are always related to and dependent upon other texts. In our culture we have tended to stress "originality" as a supreme value in writing. The pressure to be "original" has often worked to inhibit writers—especially student writers—and thus to prevent them from actually developing their ideas. One of our purposes in this chapter is to reduce the anxiety about originality.

Once you realize that all texts are reworkings of other texts, that writing comes out of reading, that writing is always rewriting, you can see that the desirable quality we call "originality" does not mean creating something out of nothing but simply making an interesting change in what has been done before you. One develops as a writer by playing with material already in existence. The "new" emerges as a function of this play. With this in mind we invite you to enter the world of intertextuality—where you have actually lived all along.

Intertextuality

One of the surest tests is the way a poet borrows. Immature poets imitate; mature poets steal.

—*T. S. Eliot*

In their traffic with art, artists employ preformed images as they employ whatever else feeds into their work. Between their experience of nature and their experience of other art they allow no functional difference.

—*Leo Steinberg*

Artists and writers do not simply look at nature—or into their own hearts—and transcribe what they find there. This is so because for them the very act of looking is already shaped by the art and writing of the past, as well as by other cultural conventions. The eye of an adult human being is never innocent. The eye of a baby may be "innocent" in some sense, but it is also untrained, and the untrained eye does not see much. As observers of life, we go from ignorance to prejudice without ever passing through the mythical land of objectivity. What a scientist learns is how to see with the prejudices of his or her own science. An artist sees through the prejudices of art.

This is simply the way things are for human beings in this world. Learning to see nature or the human heart is learning how to notice certain things and disregard others. But that is only one side of the problem facing the artist or writer. The writer must not only notice and disregard things. The writer must transcribe the things that he or she notices. That is, the writer must find ways to put experience into verbal form. Experience need not come in the form of an anecdote or a play, but it must be expressed in these or other forms that already exist. A writer, we may say, has one eye on experience and the other on writing that has already been done. No text is produced without awareness of other texts. This is why Labov (see Chapter 1) finds a repeated structural pattern in anecdotes told by ordinary speakers. These speakers have already listened to many anecdotes themselves. They know the anecdotal forms.

When a group of people are exchanging anecdotes, stories, or jokes, a further development will be noticed: relationships may be generated between what one person and another person recount. Sometimes the connection is just similarity or association. You will hear a speaker say "That reminds me of . . . " But other times one story will be told in opposition to another, to prove an opposite point or illustrate an alternative view of someone or something. In an extended session, the relationship of one story to another can become very complicated. With written texts—and especially the durable written texts we call literature—such relationships are often of the most elaborate and complex kinds. The technical term for such relationships is *intertextuality*.

Wherever there are texts, there is intertextuality. Even in what we may call minimal texts, like bumper stickers, we can find intertextuality. For instance, in a certain tiny New England state, environmentalists display a red bumper sticker that says SAVE THE BAY. The bay in question suffers from pollution that is a threat to health, to commercial shellfishing, and to the quality of life in general. Many of those concerned with these matters have joined an organization working to preserve or restore the quality of this bay's water. Hence the bumper sticker: SAVE THE BAY.

There are those, however, who do not love environmentalists and do not care about the quality of the bay. They have originated and proudly display a black sticker with their own slogan: PAVE THE BAY. Whatever one's view of the rights and wrongs of the matter, if you are a student of literary language, you have to admit that PAVE THE BAY is the more interesting of the two signs. It is interesting because it is more concrete (so to speak), because it suggests something that is hardly possible (since the bay in question is thirty miles long and five miles wide), and because it is more clearly intertextual.

Paving the bay is sufficiently unlikely to violate our sense of the possible. We readers of this bumper text are forced by this impossibility to find a second way to read the text. If it cannot be meant *literally,* it must, if it means anything, have what we call a *figurative* meaning. That is, it must function like a metaphor. We cannot simply read it; we must interpret it. What does PAVE THE BAY mean? Its meaning depends upon its intertextuality. Without SAVE THE BAY, PAVE THE BAY would be close to nonsense, a mere impossibility. But alongside SAVE THE BAY, from which it is distinguishable by only a single letter, PAVE THE BAY signifies, among other things, the rejection or negation of the environmentalist position that is textualized in SAVE THE BAY. PAVE THE BAY means "Don't let these wimpy environmentalists push you around."

A similar relationship exists between another bumper sticker, WARNING: I BRAKE FOR ANIMALS, and its anti-text, WARNING: I SPEED UP TO HIT LITTLE ANIMALS (both actually exist). Even here the second text signifies mainly a rejection of the first. That is, WARNING: I BRAKE FOR ANIMALS is meant to refer literally to the behavior of the driver; whereas WARNING: I SPEED UP TO HIT LITTLE ANIMALS does not necessarily tell you about the driver's intentions. It does tell you about his attitude toward the sentiment displayed on the first sign. It refers, then, not literally to the world of action but intertextually to the other sign, which it negates.

PAVE THE BAY is a more interesting negation for two reasons. First, it is so economical: a major change in meaning is achieved through the alteration of just one letter. Second, it presents a more startling concept than speeding up to hit animals: It suggests a slightly different world, where strange feats of engineering are possible, whereas going out of one's way to inflict pain on defenseless creatures is distressingly familiar to us. The attitudes motivating the two signs may not be terribly different. They are rooted in dislike of environmentalists who interfere with the rights of others. But one of the two stickers is more interesting than the other—and both are more interesting than their pre-texts, precisely because they are intertextual.

In another case, the "wimps" have the last word. The sticker PRESERVE YOUR RIGHT TO BEAR ARMS has been answered by PRESERVE YOUR RIGHT TO ARM BEARS. Again, the second sign is more interesting because it is both intertextual and figurative. Giving guns to bears is not a possible project in this world. The text that advocates this impossibility thus forces us to look for a nonliteral meaning. To read it we must see it as a transformation of its literal predecessor: ARM BEARS is another minimal change, using exactly the same letters as BEAR ARMS, but inverting the words and relocating the *s* to make ARM a verb and BEARS a noun. Maximum change of meaning with minimal verbal change seems to be a rule of quality here. The second text, which would be nonsense without the first, becomes supersense when connected with its pre-text. For the reader to interpret the second text, he or she must see it as a *transformation* of the first. That is a crucial principle. Intertextuality is active when the reader is aware of the way one text is connected to others.

There are many forms of intertextuality. One text may contain a mention of another, for instance, or a quotation or citation of an earlier text. One text may devote itself extensively to a discussion of another, offering commentary, interpretation, counterstatement, or criticism. One text may be a translation of another, an imitation, an adaptation, a pastiche, or parody. In this chapter, we shall be exploring many—though not all—of these possible relationships. As an introduction to the practice of intertextuality, we ask you to consider and discuss the following three texts. Text (1) is a passage from the Bible's Old Testament, in the translation produced in England in the early seventeenth century. Text (2) is a speech delivered by a messenger in a play written in England in the later seventeenth century. Text (3) is an advertisement that appeared in a popular magazine in the later twentieth century.

Text (1)

Judges 16: Samson

21 But the Philistines took him, and put out his eyes, and brought him down to Gaza, and bound him with fetters of brass; and he did grind in the prison house.

22 Howbeit the hair of his head began to grow again after he was shaven.

23 Then the lords of the Philistines gathered them together for to offer a great sacrifice unto Dagon their god, and to rejoice: for they said, Our god hath delivered Samson our enemy into our hand.

24 And when the people saw him, they praised their god: for they said,
Our god hath delivered into our hands our enemy, and the destroyer of our
country, which slew many of us.
25 And it came to pass, when their hearts were merry, that they said, Call
for Samson, that he may make us sport. And they called for Samson out of the
prison house; and he made them sport: and they set him between the pillars.
26 And Samson said unto the lad that held him by the hand, Suffer me that
I may feel the pillars whereupon the house standeth, that I may lean upon them.
27 Now the house was full of men and women; and all the lords of the
Philistines were there; and *there were* upon the roof about three thousand men
and women, that beheld while Samson made sport.
28 And Samson called unto the Lord, and said, O Lord God, remember
me, I pray thee, and strengthen me, I pray thee, only this once, O God, that I
may be at once avenged of the Philistines for my two eyes.
29 And Samson took hold of the two middle pillars upon which the house
stood, and on which it was borne up, of the one with his right hand, and of the
other with his left.
30 And Samson said, Let me die with the Philistines. And he bowed
himself with *all his* might; and the house fell upon the lords, and upon all the
people that *were* therein. So the dead which he slew at his death were more
than *they* which he slew in his life.
31 Then his brethren and all the house of his father came down, and took
him, and brought *him* up, and buried him between Zorah and Eshtaol in the
buryingplace of Manoah his father. . . .

Text (2)

From Samson Agonistes

John Milton

Messenger. Occasions drew me early to this city,
And as the gates I entered with sun-rise,
The morning trumpets festival proclaimed
Through each high street. Little I had despatched
When all abroad was rumored that this day
Samson should be brought forth to shew the people
Proof of his mighty strength in feats and games;
I sorrowed at his captive state, but minded
Not to be absent at that spectacle.
The building was a spacious theater
Half round on two main pillars vaulted high,

With seats where all the lords and each degree
Of sort, might sit in order to behold,
The other side was open, where the throng
On banks and scaffolds under sky might stand;
I among these aloof obscurely stood.
The feast and noon grew high, and sacrifice
Had filled their hearts with mirth, high cheer, and wine,
When to their sports they turned. Immediately
Was Samson as a public servant brought,
In their state livery clad; before him pipes
And timbrels, on each side went armed guards,
Both horse and foot before him and behind
Archers, and slingers, cataphracts and spears
At sight of him the people with a shout
Rifted the air clamoring their god with praise,
Who had made their dreadful enemy their thrall.
He patient but undaunted where they led him,
Came to the place, and what was set before him
Which without help of eye, might be assayed,
To heave, pull, draw, or break, he still performed
All with the incredible, stupendious force,
None daring to appear antagonist.
At length for intermission sake they led him
Between the pillars; he his guide requested
(For so from such as nearer stood we heard)
As over-tired to let him lean a while
With both his arms on those two massy pillars
That to the arched roof gave main support.
He unsuspicious led him; which when Samson
Felt in his arms, with head a while inclined,
And eyes fast fixed he stood, as one who prayed,
Or some great matter in his mind revolved.
At last with head erect thus cried aloud,
"Hitherto, Lords, what your commands imposed
I have performed, as reason was, obeying,
Not without wonder or delight beheld.
Now of my own accord such other trial
I mean to show you of my strength, yet greater;
As with amaze shall strike all who behold."
This uttered, straining all his nerves he bowed;
As with the force of winds and waters pent
When mountains tremble, those two massy pillars
With horrible convulsion to and fro
He tugged, he shook, till down they came and drew

The whole roof after them, with burst of thunder
Upon the heads of all who sat beneath,
Lords, ladies, captain, counsellors, or priests,
Their choice nobility and flower, not only
Of this but each Philistian city round
Met from all parts to solemnize this feast.
Samson with these immixed, inevitably
Pulled down the same destruction on himself;
The vulgar only scaped, who stood without.

Text (3)

For Discussion and Writing

1. The biblical text is itself, no doubt, a written version of material that was transmitted orally before being set down in the Hebrew Bible. The English version is a translation made in the early 1600s. It is the immediate pre-text for Milton's verse drama, *Samson Agonistes,* though Milton knew his Bible in Hebrew as well. In the passage we have quoted, a messenger recounts the same crucial events covered by the biblical passage. Discuss the changes Milton has made and the possible reasons for them. How, in other words, has he used his pre-text?
2. Looking at the third text, how can we tell it is part of the same textual network as the others? What specific features indicate this connection? How does this text use the Samson textual network? Try to consider every detail of text (3), such as things like the meaning of "ultimate," for instance.

Transforming Texts (1)

In this section we will be considering some of the more obvious ways in which new texts are created out of old ones. We can begin with a textual finger exercise devised by the French writer Raymond Queneau. In his book *Transformations,* Queneau presents a very short account of two trivial incidents that do not even make a simple story. He then proceeds to re-present these incidents a hundred times, using a different stylistic principle every time. We have reprinted here, in English translation, Queneau's original "Notation" and six of his revisions. We would like you to examine each of his transformations and discuss exactly what he has done and how he has done it, before proceeding to some transformations of your own.

From Transformations

Raymond Queneau

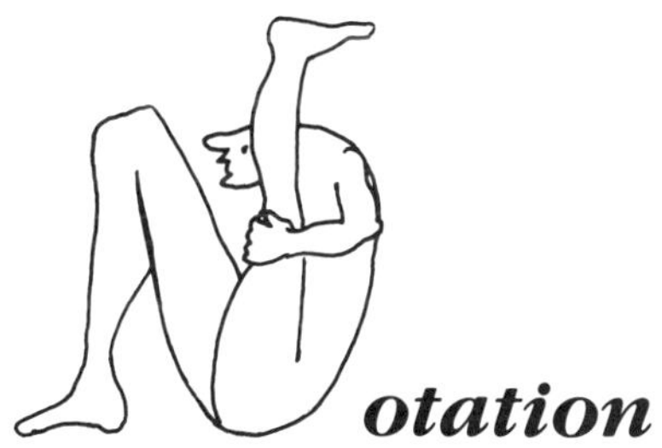

otation

In the S bus, in the rush hour. A chap of about 26, felt hat with a cord instead of a ribbon, neck too long, as if someone's been having a tug-of-war with it. People getting off. The chap in question gets annoyed with one of the men standing next to him. He accuses him of jostling him every time anyone goes past. A snivelling tone which is meant to be aggressive. When he sees a vacant seat he throws himself on to it.

Two hours later, I meet him in the Cour de Rome, in front of the gare Saint-Lazare. He's with a friend who's saying: "You ought to get an extra button put on your overcoat." He shows him where (at the lapels) and why.

ouble ntry

Towards the middle of the day and at midday I happened to be on and got on to the platform and the balcony at the back of an S-line and of a Contrescarpe-Champerret bus and passenger transport vehicle which was packed and to all intents and purposes full. I saw and noticed a young man and an old adolescent who was rather ridiculous and pretty grotesque; thin neck and skinny windpipe, string and cord round his hat and tile. After a scrimmage and scuffle he says and states in a lachrymose and snivelling voice and tone that his neighbour and fellow-traveller is deliberately trying and doing his utmost to push him and obtrude himself on him every time anyone gets off and makes an exit. This having been declared and having spoken he rushes headlong and wends his way towards a vacant and a free place and seat.

Two hours after and a-hundred-and-twenty minutes later, I meet him and see him again in the Cour de Rome and in front of the gare Saint-Lazare. He is with and in the company of a friend and pal who is advising and urging him to have a button and vegetable ivory disc added and sewn on to his overcoat and mantle.

recision

In a bus of the S-line, 10 metres long, 3 wide, 6 high, at 3 km. 600 m. from its starting point, loaded with 48 people, at 12.17 P.M., a person of the masculine sex aged 27 years 3 months and 8 days, 1 m. 72 cm. tall and weighing 65 kg. and wearing a hat 35 cm. in height round the crown of which was a ribbon 60 cm. long, interpollated a man aged 48 years 4 months and 3 days, 1 m. 68 cm. tall and weighing 77 kg., by means of 14 words whose enunciation lasted 5 seconds and which alluded to some involuntary displacements of from 15 to 20 mm. Then he went and sat down about 1 m. 10 cm. away.

57 minutes later he was 10 metres away from the suburban entrance to the gare Saint-Lazare and was walking up and down over a distance of 30 m. with a friend aged 28, 1 m. 70 cm. tall and weighing 71 kg. who advised him in 15 words to move by 5 cm. in the direction of the zenith a button which was 3 cm. in diameter.

Narrative

One day at about midday in the Parc Monceau district, on the back platform of a more or less full S bus (now No. 84), I observed a person with a very long neck who was wearing a felt hat which had a plaited cord round it instead of a ribbon. This individual suddenly addressed the man standing next to him, accusing him of purposely treading on his toes every time any passengers got on or off. However he quickly abandoned the dispute and threw himself on to a seat which had become vacant.

Two hours later I saw him in front of the gare Saint-Lazare engaged in earnest conversation with a friend who was advising him to reduce the space between the lapels of his overcoat by getting a competent tailor to raise the top button.

Passive

It was midday. The bus was being got into by passengers. They were being squashed together. A hat was being worn on the head of a young gentleman, which hat was encircled by a plait and not by a ribbon. A long neck was one of the characteristics of the young gentleman. The man standing next to him was being grumbled at by the latter because of the jostling which was being inflicted on him by him. As soon as a vacant seat was espied by the young gentleman it was made the object of his precipitate movements and it became sat down upon.

The young gentleman was later seen by me in front of the gare Saint-Lazare. He was clothed in an overcoat and was having a remark made to him by a friend who happened to be there to the effect that it was necessary to have an extra button put on it.

aiku[1]

Summer S long neck
plait hat toes abuse retreat
station button friend

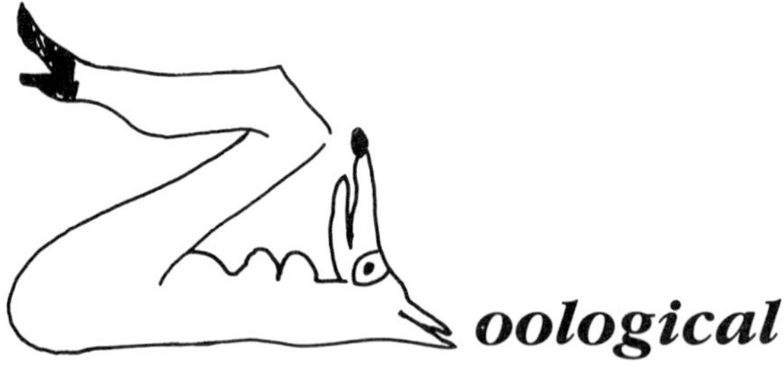

oological

In the dog days while I was in a bird cage at feeding time I noticed a young puppy with a neck like a giraffe who, like the toad, ugly and venomous, wore yet

[1] Haiku: a Japanese poem composed of three lines, of 5, 7, and 5 syllables respectively, and presenting one theme.

a precious beaver upon his head. This queer fish obviously had a bee in his bonnet and was quite bats, he started yakking at a wolf in sheep's clothing claiming that he was treading on his dogs with his beetle-crushers. But the sucker got a flea in his ear; that foxed him, and quiet as a mouse he ran like a hare for a perch.

I saw him again later in front of the Zoo with a young buck who was telling him to bear in mind a certain drill about his fevvers.

For Discussion and Writing

1. Compare "Notation" with each of its transformations. What, specifically, has been done in each adaptation to make it different from the others? How would you describe the "voice" in each one?
2. Using Queneau's six transformations as models, write a set of your own. Use as your "Notation" a short anecdote of your own, or a newspaper report, such as a police report, or the article reprinted here on pp. 137–41
3. Which transformation was easiest for you to write? Why? Which was most difficult. Why?
4. Try to imagine that "Precision" was written by someone whose composition teacher was always telling him or her to "be more precise" in his writing. What other rules of good writing are being parodied in Queneau's transformations?

Transforming Texts (2)

Writers are always borrowing, or—as T. S. Eliot said in the quotation at the beginning of this chapter—stealing from one another. This is a basic element of textuality. Texts are produced through a combination of the writer's experiences as a human being and the writer's knowledge of earlier texts. Sometimes, however, the intertextual relationship is very much in the foreground: this is true in translation, interpretation, adaptation, and parody. Translation from one language to another is not our concern in this book. Interpretation will be taken up in the next section of this chapter. At the moment, we are concerned with *adaptation* and that special form of adaptation called *parody.*

Adaptation occurs whenever a writer rewrites an earlier work, making significant changes in the original. Raymond Queneau's *Transformations* (pp. 137–41) is one kind of adaptation. The versions of Samson's story produced by John Milton and by the Nike company's copywriters (pp. 133–35) are also adaptations. Milton's adaptation is a reverent development and extension of the biblical original. The Nike ad is more an allusion to the original than a full adaptation of it, but it represents a tendency toward that kind of irreverent adaptation we call *parody.*

A parody is an adaptation that makes fun of its original by exaggerating its most striking and unusual features or by relocating it to a context that renders the original absurd, as in the Nike ad. Exaggeration parodies the form of the original. Relocation parodies its content or meaning. Because it has a critical function, parody points the way to more formal kinds of interpretation and criticism. Parody and other forms of adaptation assume that the original still has some life in it if certain aspects of it are modified, others eliminated, and some new things added. In the following pages, we are going to present for your consideration some adaptations of a well-known text, the fairy tale "Hansel and Gretel," originally published in German by Jacob and Wilhelm Grimm in the year 1812. To begin with, here is a good modern translation of "Hansel and Gretel." We ask you to read it and then move on to the first adaptation.

Hansel and Gretel

Jacob and Wilhelm Grimm

At the edge of a large forest there lived a poor woodcutter with his wife and two children. The little boy's name was Hansel, and the little girl's was Gretel. There was never much to eat in the house, and once, in time of famine, there wasn't even enough bread to go around. One night the woodcutter lay in bed thinking, tossing and turning with worry. All at once he sighed and said to his wife: "What's to become of us? How can we feed our poor children when we haven't even got enough for ourselves?" His wife answered: "Husband, listen to me. Tomorrow at daybreak we'll take the children out to the thickest part of the forest and make a fire for them and give them each a piece of bread. Then we'll leave them and go about our work. They'll never find the way home again and that way we'll be rid of them." "No, Wife," said the man. "I won't do it. How can I bring myself to leave my children alone in the woods? The wild beasts will come and tear them to pieces." "You fool!" she said. "Then all four of us will starve. You may as well start planing the boards for our coffins." And she gave him no peace until he consented. "But I still feel badly about the poor children," he said.

The children were too hungry to sleep, and they heard what their step- 2
mother said to their father. Gretel wept bitter tears and said: "Oh, Hansel, we're lost." "Hush, Gretel," said Hansel. "Don't worry. I'll find a way." When the old people had fallen asleep, he got up, put on his little jacket, opened the bottom half of the Dutch door, and crept outside. The moon was shining bright, and the pebbles around the house glittered like silver coins. Hansel crouched down and stuffed his pocket full of them. Then he went back and said to Gretel: "Don't worry, little sister. Just go to sleep, God won't forsake us," and went back to bed.

At daybreak, before the sun had risen, the woman came and woke the two 3
children. "Get up, you lazybones. We're going to the forest for wood." Then she gave each a piece of bread and said: "This is for your noonday meal. Don't eat it too soon, because there won't be any more." Gretel put the bread under her apron, because Hansel had the pebbles in his pocket. Then they all started out for the forest together. When they had gone a little way, Hansel stopped still and looked back in the direction of their house, and every so often he did it again. His father said: "Hansel, why do you keep looking back and lagging behind? Wake up and don't forget what your legs are for." "Oh, father," said Hansel, "I'm looking at my white kitten; he's sitting on the roof, trying to bid me good-bye." The woman said: "You fool, that's not your white kitten. It's the morning sun shining on the chimney." But Hansel hadn't been looking at his kitten. Each time, he had taken a shiny pebble from his pocket and dropped it on the ground.

When they came to the middle of the forest, the father said: "Start gather- 4
ing wood, children, and I'll make a fire to keep you warm." Hansel and Gretel gathered brushwood till they had a little pile of it. The brushwood was kindled and when the flames were high enough the woman said: "Now, children, lie down by the fire and rest. We're going into the forest to cut wood. When we're done, we'll come back and get you."

Hansel and Gretel sat by the fire, and at midday they both ate their pieces 5
of bread. They heard the strokes of an ax and thought their father was nearby. But it wasn't an ax, it was a branch he had tied to a withered tree, and the wind was shaking it to and fro. After sitting there for some time, they became so tired

that their eyes closed and they fell into a deep sleep. When at last they awoke, it was dark night. Gretel began to cry and said: "How will we ever get out of this forest?" But Hansel comforted her: "Just wait a little while. As soon as the moon rises, we'll find the way." And when the full moon had risen, Hansel took his little sister by the hand and followed the pebbles, which glistened like newly minted silver pieces and showed them the way. They walked all night and reached their father's house just as day was breaking. They knocked at the door, and when the woman opened it and saw Hansel and Gretel, she said: "Wicked children! Why did you sleep so long in the forest? We thought you'd never get home." But their father was glad, for he had been very unhappy about deserting them.

A while later the whole country was again stricken with famine, and the 6
children heard their mother talking to their father in bed at night: "Everything has been eaten up. We still have half a loaf of bread, and when that's gone there will be no more. The children must go. We'll take them still deeper into the forest, and this time they won't find their way home; it's our only hope." The husband was heavy-hearted, and he thought: "It would be better if I shared the last bite with my children." But the woman wouldn't listen to anything he said, she only scolded and found fault. Once you've said yes, it's hard to say no, and so it was that the woodcutter gave in again.

But the children were awake; they had heard the conversation. When the 7
old people had fallen asleep, Hansel got up again. He wanted to pick up some more pebbles, but the woman had locked the door and he couldn't get out. But he comforted his little sister and said: "Don't cry, Gretel. Just go to sleep, God will help us."

Early in the morning the woman came and got the children out of bed. She 8
gave them their pieces of bread, but they were smaller than the last time. On the way to the forest, Hansel crumbled his bread in his pocket. From time to time he stopped and dropped a few crumbs on the ground. "Hansel," said his father, "why are you always stopping and looking back? Keep moving." "I'm looking at my little pigeon," said Hansel. "He's sitting on the roof, trying to bid me good-bye." "Fool," said the woman. "That's not your little pigeon, it's the morning sun shining on the chimney." But little by little Hansel strewed all his bread on the ground.

The woman led the children still deeper into the forest, to a place where 9
they had never been in all their lives. Again a big fire was made, and the mother said: "Just sit here, children. If you get tired, you can sleep awhile. We're going into the forest to cut wood, and this evening when we've finished we'll come and get you." At midday Gretel shared her bread with Hansel, who had strewn his on the ground. Then they fell asleep and the afternoon passed, but no one came for the poor children. It was dark night when they woke up, and Hansel comforted his little sister. "Gretel," he said, "just wait till the moon rises; then we'll see the breadcrumbs I strewed and they'll show us the way home." When the moon rose, they started out, but they didn't find any breadcrumbs, because

the thousands of birds that fly around in the forests and fields had eaten them all up. Hansel said to Gretel: "Don't worry, we'll find the way," but they didn't find it. They walked all night and then all day from morning to night, but they were still in the forest, and they were very hungry, for they had nothing to eat but the few berries they could pick from the bushes. And when they were so tired their legs could carry them no farther, they lay down under a tree and fell asleep.

It was already the third morning since they had left their father's house. 10
They started out again, but they were getting deeper and deeper into the forest, and unless help came soon, they were sure to die of hunger and weariness. At midday, they saw a lovely snow-white bird sitting on a branch. It sang so beautifully that they stood still and listened. When it had done singing, it flapped its wings and flew on ahead, and they followed until the bird came to a little house and perched on the roof. When they came closer, they saw that the house was made of bread, and the roof was made of cake and the windows of sparkling sugar. "Let's eat," said Hansel, "and the Lord bless our food. I'll take a piece of the roof. You, Gretel, had better take some of the window; it's sweet." Hansel reached up and broke off a bit of the roof to see how it tasted, and Gretel pressed against the windowpanes and nibbled at them. And then a soft voice called from inside:

"Nibble nibble, little mouse,
Who's that nibbling at my house?"

The children answered:

"The wind so wild,
The heavenly child,"

and went right on eating. Hansel liked the taste of the roof, so he tore off a big chunk, and Gretel broke out a whole round windowpane and sat down on the ground to enjoy it. All at once the door opened, and an old, old woman with a crutch came hobbling out. Hansel and Gretel were so frightened they dropped what they were eating. But the old woman wagged her head and said: "Oh, what dear children! However did you get here? Don't be afraid, come in and stay with me. You will come to no harm." She took them by the hand and led them into her house. A fine meal of milk and pancakes, sugar, apples, and nuts was set before them. And then two little beds were made up clean and white, and Hansel and Gretel got into them and thought they were in heaven.

But the old woman had only pretended to be so kind. Actually she was a 11
wicked witch, who waylaid children and had built her house out of bread to entice them. She killed, cooked, and ate any child who fell into her hands, and that to her was a feast day. Witches have red eyes and can't see very far, but they

have a keen sense of smell like animals, so they know when humans are coming. As Hansel and Gretel approached, she laughed her wicked laugh and said with a jeer: "Here come two who will never get away from me." Early in the morning, when the children were still asleep, she got up, and when she saw them resting so sweetly with their plump red cheeks, she muttered to herself: "What tasty morsels they will be!" She grabbed Hansel with her scrawny hand, carried him to a little shed, and closed the iron-barred door behind him. He screamed for all he was worth, but much good it did him. Then she went back to Gretel, shook her awake, and cried: "Get up, lazybones. You must draw water and cook something nice for your brother. He's out in the shed and we've got to fatten him up. When he's nice and fat, I'm going to eat him." Gretel wept bitterly, but in vain; she had to do what the wicked witch told her.

The best of food was cooked for poor Hansel, but Gretel got nothing but 1
crayfish shells. Every morning the old witch crept to the shed and said: "Hansel, hold out your finger. I want to see if you're getting fat." But Hansel held out a bone. The old woman had weak eyes and couldn't see it; she thought it was Hansel's finger and wondered why he wasn't getting fat. When four weeks had gone by and Hansel was still as skinny as ever, her impatience got the better of her and she decided not to wait any longer. "Ho there, Gretel," she cried out. "Go and draw water and don't dawdle. Skinny or fat, I'm going to butcher Hansel tomorrow and cook him." Oh, how the little girl wailed at having to carry the water, and how the tears flowed down her cheeks! "Dear God," she cried, "oh, won't you help us? If only the wild beasts had eaten us in the forest, at least we'd have died together." "Stop that blubbering," said the witch. "It won't do you a bit of good."

Early in the moring Gretel had to fill the kettle with water and light the fire. 1
"First we'll bake," said the old witch. "I've heated the oven and kneaded the dough." And she drove poor Gretel out to the oven, which by now was spitting flames. "Crawl in," said the witch, "and see if it's hot enough for the bread." Once Gretel was inside, she meant to close the door and roast her, so as to eat her too. But Gretel saw what she had in mind and said: "I don't know how. How do I get in?" "Silly goose," said the old woman. "The opening is big enough. Look. Even I can get in." She crept to the opening and stuck her head in, whereupon Gretel gave her a push that sent her sprawling, closed the iron door and fastened the bolt. Eek! How horribly she screeched! But Gretel ran away and the wicked witch burned miserably to death.

Gretel ran straight to Hansel, opened the door of the shed, and cried: 1
"Hansel, we're saved! The old witch is dead." Hansel hopped out like a bird when someone opens the door of its cage. How happy they were! They hugged and kissed each other and danced around. And now that there was nothing to be afraid of, they went into the witch's house and in every corner there were boxes full of pearls and precious stones. Hansel stuffed his pockets full of them and said: "These will be much better than pebbles," and Gretel said: "I'll

take some home too," and filled her apron with them. "We'd better leave now," said Hansel, and "get out of this bewitched forest." When they had walked a few hours, they came to a big body of water. "How will we ever get across?" said Hansel. "I don't see any bridge." "And there's no boat, either," said Gretel, "but over there I see a white duck. She'll help us across if I ask her." And she cried out:

> "Duckling, duckling, here is Gretel,
> Duckling, duckling, here is Hansel.
> No bridge or ferry far and wide—
> Duckling, come and give us a ride."

Sure enough, the duck came over to them and Hansel sat down on her 15
back and told his sister to sit beside him. "No," said Gretel, "that would be too much for the poor thing; let her carry us one at a time." And that's just what the good little duck did. And when they were safely across and had walked a little while, the forest began to look more and more familiar, and finally they saw their father's house in the distance. They began to run, and they flew into the house and threw themselves into their father's arms. The poor man hadn't had a happy hour since he had left the children in the forest, and in the meantime his wife had died. Gretel opened out her little apron, the pearls and precious stones went bouncing around the room, and Hansel reached into his pockets and tossed out handful after handful. All their worries were over, and they lived together in pure happiness. My story is done, see the mouse run; if you catch it, you may make yourself a great big fur cap out of it.

Transformation (1)

The Gingerbread House

Robert Coover

This is a story called "The Gingerbread House" by the contemporary writer Robert Coover. It consists of forty-two numbered paragraphs that present parts of a story that is clearly an adaptation of "Hansel and Gretel." Read it slowly, pausing after each paragraph to consider its relationship to the Grimm brothers' version of "Hansel and Gretel." Be especially careful to note what Coover has taken from the original, what he has ignored, what he has added, and what he has taken but changed in some significant way. Then consider the points we have raised for discussion and writing.

1

A pine forest in the midafternoon. Two children follow an old man, dropping breadcrumbs, singing nursery tunes. Dense earthy greens seep into the darkening distance, flecked and streaked with filtered sunlight. Spots of red, violet, pale blue, gold, burnt orange. The girl carries a basket for gathering flowers. The boy is occupied with the crumbs. Their song tells of God's care for little ones.

2

Poverty and resignation weigh on the old man. His cloth jacket is patched and threadbare, sunbleached white over the shoulders, worn through on the elbows. His feet do not lift, but shuffle through the dust. White hair. Parched skin. Secret forces of despair and guilt seem to pull him earthward.

3

The girl plucks a flower. The boy watches curiously. The old man stares impatiently into the forest's depths, where night seems already to crouch. The girl's apron is a bright orange, the gay color of freshly picked tangerines, and is stitched happily with blues and reds and greens; but her dress is simple and brown, tattered at the hem, and her feet are bare. Birds accompany the children in their singing and butterflies decorate the forest spaces.

4

The boy's gesture is furtive. His right hand trails behind him, letting a crumb fall. His face is half-turned toward his hand, but his eyes remain watchfully fixed on the old man's feet ahead. The old man wears heavy mud-spattered shoes, high-topped and leather-thonged. Like the old man's own skin, the shoes are dry and cracked and furrowed with wrinkles. The boy's pants are a bluish-brown, ragged at the cuffs, his jacket a faded red. He, like the girl, is barefoot.

5

The children sing nursery songs about May baskets and gingerbread houses and a saint who ate his own fleas. Perhaps they sing to lighten their young hearts, for puce wisps of dusk now coil through the trunks and branches of the thickening forest. Or perhaps they sing to conceal the boy's subterfuge. More likely, they sing for no reason at all, a thoughtless childish habit. To hear themselves. Or to admire their memories. Or to entertain the old man. To fill the silence. Conceal their thoughts. Their expectations.

6

The boy's hand and wrist, thrusting from the outgrown jacket (the faded red cuff is not a cuff at all, but the torn limits merely, the ragged edge of the soft worn sleeve), are tanned, a little soiled, childish. The fingers are short and plump, the palm soft, the wrist small. Three fingers curl under, holding back crumbs, kneading them, coaxing them into position, while the index finger and thumb flick them sparingly, one by one, to the ground, playing with them a moment, balling them, pinching them as if for luck or pleasure, before letting them go.

7

The old man's pale blue eyes float damply in deep dark pouches, half-shrouded by heavy upper lids and beetled over by shaggy white brows. Deep creases fan out from the moist corners, angle down past the nose, score the tanned cheeks and pinch the mouth. The old man's gaze is straight ahead, but at what? Perhaps at nothing. Some invisible destination. Some irrecoverable point of departure. One thing can be said about the eyes: they are tired. Whether they have seen too much or too little, they betray no will to see yet more.

8

The witch is wrapped in a tortured whirl of black rags. Her long face is drawn and livid, and her eyes glow like burning coals. Her angular body twists this way and that, flapping the black rags—flecks of blue and amethyst wink and flash in the black tangle. Her gnarled blue hands snatch greedily at space, shred her clothes, claw cruelly at her face and throat. She cackles silently, then suddenly screeches madly, seizes a passing dove, and tears its heart out.

9

The girl, younger than the boy, skips blithely down the forest path, her blonde curls flowing freely. Her brown dress is coarse and plain, but her apron is gay and white petticoats wink from beneath the tattered hem. Her skin is fresh and pink and soft, her knees and elbows dimpled, her cheeks rosy. Her young gaze flicks airily from flower to flower, bird to bird, tree to tree, from the boy to the old man, from the green grass to the encroaching darkness, and all of it seems to delight her equally. Her basket is full to overflowing. Does she even know the boy is dropping crumbs? or where the old man is leading them? Of course, but it's nothing! a game!

10

There is, in the forest, even now, a sunny place, with mintdrop trees and cotton candy bushes, an air as fresh and heady as lemonade. Rivulets of honey flow over gumdrop pebbles, and lollypops grow wild as daisies. This is the place of the gingerbread house. Children come here, but, they say, none leave.

11

The dove is a soft lustrous white, head high, breast filled, tip of the tail less than a feather's thickness off the ground. From above, it would be seen against the pale path—a mixture of umbers and grays and the sharp brown strokes of pine needles—but from its own level, in profile, its pure whiteness is set off glowingly against the obscure mallows and distant moss greens of the forest. Only its small beak moves. Around a bread crumb.

12

The song is about a great king who won many battles, but the girl sings alone. The old man has turned back, gazes curiously but dispassionately now at the boy. The boy, too, has turned, no longer furtive, hand poised but no crumb dropping from his fingertips. He stares back down the path by which they three have come, his mouth agape, his eyes startled. His left hand is raised, as if arrested a moment before striking out in protest. Doves are eating his bread-crumbs. His ruse has failed. Perhaps the old man, not so ignorant in such matters after all, has known all along it would. The girl sings of pretty things sold in the market.

13

So huddled over her prey is the witch that she seems nothing more than a pile of black rags heaped on a post. Her pale long-nailed hands are curled inward toward her breast, massaging the object, her head lower than her hunched shoulders, wan beaked nose poked in among the restless fingers. She pauses, cackling softly, peers left, then right, then lifts the heart before her eyes. The burnished heart of the dove glitters like a ruby, a polished cherry, a brilliant, heart-shaped bloodstone. It beats still. A soft radiant pulsing. The black bony shoulders of the witch quake with glee, with greed, with lust.

14

A wild blur of fluttering white: the dove's wings flapping! Hands clutch its body, its head, its throat, small hands with short plump fingers. Its wings flail against the dusky forest green, but it is forced down against the umber earth. The boy falls upon it, his hands bloodied by beak and claws.

15

The gingerbread house is approached by flagstones of variegated wafers, through a garden of candied fruits and all-day suckers in neat little rows.

16

No song now from the lips of the girl, but a cry of anguish. The basket of flowers is dropped, the kings and saints forgotten. She struggles with the boy for the bird. She kicks him, falls upon him, pulls his hair, tears at his red jacket. He huddles around the bird, trying to elbow free of the girl. Both children are weeping, the boy of anger and frustration, the girl of pain and pity and a bruised heart. Their legs entangle, their fists beat at each other, feathers fly.

17

The pale blue eyes of the old man stare not ahead, but down. The squint, the sorrow, the tedium are vanished; the eyes focus clearly. The deep creases fanning out from the damp corners pinch inward, a brief wince, as though at some inner hurt, some certain anguish, some old wisdom. He sighs.

18

The girl has captured the bird. The boy, small chest heaving, kneels in the path watching her, the anger largely drained out of him. His faded red jacket is torn; his pants are full of dust and pine needles. She has thrust the dove protectively beneath her skirt, and sits, knees apart, leaning over it, weeping softly. The old man stoops down, lifts her bright orange apron, her skirt, her petticoats. The boy turns away. The dove is nested in her small round thighs. It is dead.

19

Shadows have lengthened. Umbers and lavenders and greens have grayed. But the body of the dove glows yet in the gathering dusk. The whiteness of the ruffled breast seems to be fighting back against the threat of night. It is strewn with flowers, now beginning to wilt. The old man, the boy, and the girl have gone.

20

The beams of the gingerbread house are licorice sticks, cemented with taffy, weatherboarded with gingerbread, and coated with caramel. Peppermint-stick chimneys sprout randomly from its chocolate roof and its windows are laced with meringue. Oh, what a house! and the best thing of all is the door.

21

The forest is dense and deep. Branches reach forth like arms. Brown animals scurry. The boy makes no furtive gestures. The girl, carrying her flowerbasket, does not skip or sing. They walk, arms linked, eyes wide open and staring ahead into the forest. The old man plods on, leading the way, his heavy old leather-thonged shoes shuffling in the damp dust and undergrowth.

22

The old man's eyes, pale in the sunlight, now seem to glitter in the late twilight. Perhaps it is their wetness picking up the last flickering light of day. The squint has returned, but it is not the squint of weariness: resistance, rather. His mouth opens as though to speak, to rebuke, but his teeth are clenched. The witch twists and quivers, her black rags whirling, whipping, flapping. From her lean bosom, she withdraws the pulsing red heart of a dove. How it glows, how it rages, how it dances in the dusk! The old man now does not resist. Lust flattens his face and mists his old eyes, where glitter now reflections of the ruby heart. Grimacing, he plummets forward, covering the cackling witch, crashing through brambles that tear at his clothes.

23

A wild screech cleaves the silence of the dusky forest. Birds start up from branches and the undergrowth is alive with frightened animals. The old man stops short, one hand raised protectively in front of him, the other, as though part of the same instinct, reaching back to shield his children. Dropping her basket of flowers, the girl cries out in terror and springs forward into the old man's arms. The boy blanches, shivers as though a cold wind might be wetly wrapping his young body, but manfully holds his ground. Shapes seem to twist and coil, and vapors seep up from the forest floor. The girl whimpers and the old man holds her close.

24

The beds are simple but solid. The old man himself has made them. The sun is setting, the room is in shadows, the children tucked safely in. The old man tells them a story about a good fairy who granted a poor man three wishes. The wishes, he knows, were wasted, but so then is the story. He lengthens the tale with details about the good fairy, how sweet and kind and pretty she is, then lets the children complete the story with their own wishes, their own dreams. Below, a brutal demand is being forced upon him. Why must the goodness of all wishes come to nothing?

25

The flowerbasket lies, overturned, by the forest path, its wilting flowers strewn. Shadows darker than dried blood spread beneath its gaping mouth. The shadows are long, for night is falling.

26

The old man has fallen into the brambles. The children, weeping, help pull him free. He sits on the forest path staring at the boy and girl. It is as though he is unable to recognize them. Their weeping dies away. They huddle more closely together, stare back at the old man. His face is scratched, his clothes torn. He is breathing irregularly.

27

The sun, the songs, the breadcrumbs, the dove, the overturned basket, the long passage toward night: where, the old man wonders, have all the good fairies gone? He leads the way, pushing back the branches. The children follow, silent and frightened.

28

The boy pales and his heart pounds, but manfully he holds his ground. The witch writhes, her black rags fluttering, licking at the twisted branches. With a soft seductive cackle, she holds before him the burnished cherry-red heart of a dove. The boy licks his lips. She steps back. The glowing heart pulses gently, evenly, excitingly.

29

The good fairy has sparkling blue eyes and golden hair, a soft sweet mouth and gentle hands that caress and soothe. Gossamer wings sprout from her smooth back; from her flawless chest two firm breasts with tips bright as rubies.

30

The witch, holding the flaming pulsing heart out to the boy, steps back into the dark forest. The boy, in hesitation, follows. Back. Back. Swollen eyes aglitter, the witch draws the ruby heart close to her dark lean breast, then past her shoulder and away from the boy. Transfixed, he follows it, brushing by her. The witch's gnarled and bluish fingers claw at his poor garments, his pale red jacket and bluish-brown pants, surprising his soft young flesh.

31

The old man's shoulders are bowed earthward, his face is lined with sorrow, his neck bent forward with resignation, but his eyes glow like burning coals. He clutches his shredded shirt to his throat, stares intensely at the boy. The boy stands alone and trembling on the path, staring into the forest's terrible darkness. Shapes whisper and coil. The boy licks his lips, steps forward. A terrible shriek shreds the forest hush. The old man grimaces, pushes the whimpering girl away, strikes the boy.

32

No more breadcrumbs, no more pebbles, no more songs or flowers. The slap echoes through the terrible forest, doubles back on its own echoes, folding finally into a sound not unlike a whispering cackle.

33

The girl, weeping, kisses the struck boy and presses him close, shielding him from the tormented old man. The old man, taken aback, reaches out uncertainly, gently touches the girl's frail shoulder. She shakes his hand off—nearly a shudder—and shrinks toward the boy. The boy squares his shoulders, color returning to his face. The familiar creases of age and despair crinkle again the old man's face. His pale blue eyes mist over. He looks away. He leaves the children by the last light of day.

34

But the door! The door is shaped like a heart and is as red as a cherry, always half-open, whether lit by sun or moon, is sweeter than a sugarplum, more enchanting than a peppermint stick. It is red as a poppy, red as an apple, red as a strawberry, red as a bloodstone, red as a rose. Oh, what a thing is the door of that house!

35

The children, alone in the strange black forest, huddle wretchedly under a great gnarled tree. Owls hoot and bats flick menacingly through the twisting branches. Strange shapes writhe and rustle before their weary eyes. They hold each other tight and, trembling, sing lullabyes, but they are not reassured.

36

The old man trudges heavily out of the black forest. His way is marked, not by breadcrumbs, but by dead doves, ghostly white in the empty night.

37

The girl prepares a mattress of leaves and flowers and pine needles. The boy gathers branches to cover them, to hide them, to protect them. They make pillows of their poor garments. Bats screech as they work and owls blink down on their bodies, ghostly white, young, trembling. They creep under the branches, disappearing into the darkness.

38

Gloomily, the old man sits in the dark room and stares at the empty beds. The good fairy, though a mystery of the night, effuses her surroundings with a lustrous radiance. Is it the natural glow of her small nimble body or perhaps the star at the tip of her wand? Who can tell? Her gossamer wings flutter rapidly, and she floats, ruby-tipped breasts downward, legs dangling and dimpled knees bent slightly, glowing buttocks arched up in defiance of the night. How good she is! In the black empty room, the old man sighs and uses up a wish: he wishes his poor children well.

39

The children are nearing the gingerbread house. Passing under mintdrop trees, sticking their fingers in the cotton candy bushes, sampling the air as heady as lemonade, they skip along singing nursery songs. Nonsense songs about dappled horses and the slaying of dragons. Counting songs and idle riddles. They cross over rivulets of honey on gumdrop pebbles, picking the lollypops that grow as wild as daffodils.

40

The witch flicks and flutters through the blackened forest, her livid face twisted with hatred, her inscrutable condition. Her eyes burn like glowing coals and her black rags flap loosely. Her gnarled hands claw greedily at the branches, tangle in the night's webs, dig into tree trunks until the sap flows beneath her nails. Below, the boy and girl sleep an exhausted sleep. One ghostly white leg, with dimpled knee and soft round thigh, thrust out from under the blanket of branches.

41

But wish again! Flowers and butterflies. Dense earthly greens seeping into the distance, flecked and streaked with midafternoon sunlight. Two children following an old man. They drop breadcrumbs, sing nursery songs. The old man walks leadenly. The boy's gesture is furtive. The girl—but it's no use, the doves will come again, there are no reasonable wishes.

42

The children approach the gingerbread house through a garden of candied fruits and all-day suckers, hopping along on flagstones of variegated wafers. They sample the gingerbread weatherboarding with its caramel coating, lick at the meringue on the windowsills, kiss each other's sweetened lips. The boy climbs up on the chocolate roof to break off a peppermint-stick chimney, comes sliding down into a rainbarrel full of vanilla pudding. The girl, reaching out to catch him in his fall, slips on a sugarplum and tumbles into a sticky rock garden of candied chestnuts. Laughing gaily, they lick each other clean. And how grand is the red-and-white striped chimney the boy holds up for her! how bright! how sweet! But the door: here they pause and catch their breath. It is heart-shaped and bloodstone-red, its burnished surface gleaming in the sunlight. Oh, what a thing is that door! Shining like a ruby, like hard cherry candy, and pulsing softly, radiantly. Yes, marvelous! delicious! insuperable! but beyond: what is that sound of black rags flapping?

For Discussion and Writing

1. **What are the most striking differences between Coover's version and the Grimms'? Discuss the significance of some of these differences.**
2. **Select a passage where Coover seems to be following the Grimms' version closely. How does his style of presentation differ from theirs?**
3. **Consider the sequence of paragraphs 13–18. A critic has observed that paragraph 15 "presents a Disneyfied version of the scene." What do you suppose this means? How does paragraph 15 fit into this sequence of four paragraphs? Are the others Disneyfied also?**

How do you interpret these paragraphs? What does the behavior of each character mean? What parallels do you find between the behavior of one character and another? What significant contrasts do you find?

4. Consider Coover's story as an interpretation of the Grimms'. What is Coover telling us about the meaning of this story? Examine in particular any images he returns to frequently. Write an essay in which you discuss "The Gingerbread House" as a creative reading or interpretation of "Hansel and Gretel."

Transformation (2)

The Little Brother and the Little Sister

Jacob and Wilhelm Grimm

We have been speaking of "Hansel and Gretel" as the "original" text, of which Coover made a transformation. But actually the Grimm brothers were the first transformers. They wrote down stories told to them by various informants. These written manuscripts were then transformed into the first published versions of the tales. As new editions of the book appeared, tales continued to be transformed. For many of them, we have four significantly different versions. The original manuscripts were destroyed, but copies of some of them have survived. What follows here is an English translation of a copy of the Grimms' original manuscript of a story entitled "The Little Brother and the Little Sister."

There was once a poor woodcutter, who lived in front of a great forest. He fared so miserably, that he could scarcely feed his wife and his two children. Once he had no bread any longer, and suffered great anxiety, then his wife said to him in the evening in bed: take the two children tomorrow morning and take them into the great forest, give them the bread we have left, and make a large fire for them and after that go away and leave them alone. The husband did not want to for a long time, but the wife left him no peace, until he finally agreed. 1

But the children had heard everything that the mother had said. The little sister began to weep a lot, the little brother said to her she should be quiet and comforted her. Then he quietly got up and went outside in front of the door, the moon shone there and the white pebbles shone in front of the house. The boy picked them up carefully and filled his little coat pocket with them, as many as he could put there. Then he went back to his little sister into bed, and went to sleep. 2

Early next morning, before the sun had risen, the father and mother came and woke the children up, who were to go with them into the great forest. They 3 gave each a little piece of bread, little sister took it under her little apron, for the little brother had his pocket full of pebbles. Then they set off on their way to the great forest. As they were walking like this, the little brother often stood still, and looked back at their little house. The father said: why are you always standing and looking back; oh, answered the little brother, I am looking at my little white cat, it is sitting on the roof and wants to say goodbye to me but secretly he kept letting one of the little white pebbles drop. The mother spoke: just keep going, it's not your little cat, it is the morning glow which is shining on the chimney. But the boy kept looking back and kept letting another little stone drop.

They walked like this for a long time and at last came to the middle of the 4
great forest. Then the father made a great fire, and the mother says: sleep a while children, we will go into the forest and look for wood, wait until we come back. The children sat down by the fire, and they both ate their little piece of bread. They wait a long time until it was night, but the parents did not come back. Then the little sister began to weep, but the little brother comforted her and took her by the hand. Then the moon shone, and the little white pebbles shone, and showed them the way. And the little brother led the little sister through the whole night. And in the morning they came again in front of the house. The father was glad, for he had not done it willingly; but the mother was angry.

Soon after they had no bread again, and the little brother heard again in 5
the evening in bed, how the mother said to the father, he should take the children out into the great forest again. Then the little sister began again to sob her heart out, and the little brother got up again, and wanted to look for little stones. When he got to the door, however, it was bolted by the mother, then the little brother began to feel sad, and could not comfort the little sister.

They got up again before daybreak, each received a little piece of bread 6
again. When they were on their way, the little brother looks back often. The father said: my child why are you always standing still and looking back towards the little house? Oh! answered the little brother, I am looking at my little dove, it is sitting on the roof, and wants to say goodbye to me, but secretly he crumbled his little piece of bread, and kept letting a crumb fall. The mother spoke: just keep going, it's not your little dove, it's the morning glow shining on the chimney. But the little brother still kept looking back, and kept letting another little crumb drop.

When they had come to the middle of the great forest, the father again 7
made a great fire, the mother again said the same words and both went away. The little sister gave the little brother a half of her little piece of bread, for the little brother had thrown his onto the path. And they waited until evening, then the little brother wanted to lead the little sister back by the moonshine. But the little birds had eaten up the little crumbs of bread and they could not find the way. They walked further and further and got lost in the great forest. On the third day they came to a little house that was made of bread, the roof was

covered with cake and the windows of sugar. The children were glad when they saw it and the little brother ate some of the roof and the little sister some of the window. As they stook like this and enjoyed it, a delicate voice cried out:

> nibble, nibble, gnaw!
> who is nibbling at my little house?

The children were badly startled; soon after a small old woman came out, she took the children by the hand in a kindly way, took them into the house, and give them something good to eat, and put them in a nice bed. But the next morning she put the little brother in a little stable, he was to be a little pig, and the little sister had to bring him water and good food. Every day she went to it then the little brother had to stick out his finger, and she felt if it was already fat. He always stuck out in place of it a little bone, then she thought that he was still not fat, and this went on for a long time. She gave to the little sister nothing to eat but crab-shells, because she was not to be fattened. After four weeks she said in the evening to the little sister, go and fetch water, and heat it tomorrow morning, we will slaughter and boil your little brother, meanwhile I'll make the dough, so that we can also bake as well. The next morning, when the water was hot, she called the little sister to the oven, and said to her: sit on the board, I will push you into the oven, see if the bread is already done; but she wanted to leave the little sister in there and roast her. The little sister notices this and said to her: I don't understand that, sit there first yourself, I will push you in. The old woman sat on it, and the little sister pushed her in, shut the door, and the witch burned to death. Then she went to the little brother and opens his little stable for him. They found the whole little house full of jewels, filled all their pockets with them, and took them to their father, who became a rich man; but the mother was dead.

For Discussion and Writing

1. **We can see now that what we thought was the "original" text was itself a transformation of another "original," a transformation that rewrites significant features of the manuscript version. Please note and discuss the major changes you find, taking "The Little Brother and the Little Sister" as the original and "Hansel and Gretel" as the transformation.**
2. **Write an essay in which you use the transformation made by the Grimms as your starting point for a discussion of transformation as a form of writing. Consider the possible reasons why the Grimms made the changes they did, moving on to why Coover seems to have undertaken his transformation. What is there in the fairy tale that leads people to maintain such a strong interest in it that they wish to rewrite it in a different way? Finally, you might consider how your knowledge of the Grimms' first text changes your view of the other two. Scholars have only recently, and with**

great reluctance, come to realize how actively the Grimms transformed their source material. To what extent are the Grimms and Coover doing something different? To what extent are they doing the same thing?

3. You, too, can be a transformer. Take some well-known fairy tale and produce your own purposeful transformation of it. This will work best if you look up some familiar story and work with the printed text in front of you. You may follow the leads of the Grimms and Coover or find your own principle of transformation, but don't just imitate. Steal! That is, *change* the text you are transforming sufficiently to make it your own.

Completing Texts: The Reader's Work

Texts are lazy machineries that ask someone to do part of their job.
—Umberto Eco

What do we do when we read? What does it mean to "complete" a text? Here we shall be considering the act of reading as an act of writing in both a figurative and literal sense. In his book *The Role of the Reader,* Italian semiotician Umberto Eco discusses reading as a collaborative act in which "a well-organized text on the one hand presupposes a model of competence coming, so to speak, from outside the text, but on the other hand works to build up, by merely textual means, such a competence." As readers, we provide "models of competence," bringing to a text our own intellectual equipment to help us understand what we are reading. At the same time, the text directs that reading. When we look at a text that starts out "Once upon a time" or "Once there was" we know we are in the presence of a fairy tale and we therefore accept the conventions of that genre—talking frogs, wicked stepmothers, handsome princes—when we encounter them in the text. In recognizing a text as a particular kind of text, such as fairy tale, mystery, or historical romance, we are drawing on our intertextual knowledge—our reading of other texts like the one in front of us. As Eco reminds us, "no text is read independently of other texts."

When we read the first sentence of William Carlos Williams's story "The Use of Force"—"They were new patients to me, all I had was the name, Olson"—the text assumes that we will know that the speaker is a doctor. When the speaker describes his patient as "One of those picture children often reproduced in advertising leaflets and the photogravure sections of the Sunday papers," the text assumes the reader shares a common cultural frame of reference; specifically, that the reader has seen those American advertisements that feature children, and knows what part the "Sunday papers" play in American culture, and is familiar with the magazine section in them, as well as the type of child (blond and blue-eyed) likely to be featured there as a "beautiful child." These are small examples of the reader's work, and much of this work occurs subconsciously as we read.

The reader's work increases when there is a gap in the narrative and the reader is called upon to infer what took place during that missing time. In Eco's terms, this is called writing (in one's head) a "ghost chapter":

> Frequently, given a series of causally and linearly connected events *a . . . e,* a text tells the reader about the event *a* and, after a while, about the event *e,* taking for granted that the reader has already

> anticipated the dependent events *b, c, d* (of which *e* is the consequence, according to many intertextual frames). Thus the text implicitly validates a "ghost chapter," tentatively written by the reader.

Writing this ghost chapter in your head can be a very straightforward operation when the information in the gap does not affect the events in the story. If the story tells us, for example, the "John got on the bus in New York," and in the next sentence, "John arrived in Providence," the reader quickly infers that the trip between New York and Providence was both safe and uneventful. The ghost chapter we write between event *a,* "John got on the bus in New York" and event *e,* "John arrived in Providence," might logically contain event *b,* John gave his ticket to the bus driver; event *c,* John found a seat; and event *d,* John watched the scenery go by. We know from our own experience that these are the events most likely to occur on any bus ride between one city and another, and because this is common knowledge, the text does not have to provide this information.

In Kate Chopin's story "The Kiss," there are two gaps in time, the first between the kiss and the reception, and the second between the reception and the wedding. Those jumps in time are appropriate to a story with a heroine who acts to get what she wants rather than sitting and brooding about it. Again, the reader may, in writing a ghost chapter, infer that whatever happens in those time periods is not important to the story. Yet Nathalie's final statement before the first gap in time (kiss—reception), "It depends upon—a good deal whether I ever forgive you," leaves the reader as well as Harvy speculating about what the gap in Nathalie's statement signifies: "depends upon—" what? The reader may also be busy speculating as to the nature of the relationship between Nathalie and Harvy. During a second reading of the text, the reader might wonder what plans ran through Nathalie's head; namely, how she plotted the moves that are described to us in the next sequence: the entrapment of Brantain at the reception. (And what information in the text allows us to use the term "entrapment"?) In the second gap, between the reception and the wedding, the reader can logically infer from common knowledge that Brantain and Nathalie become engaged, that she is given an engagement ring, that wedding plans are made. But it is also possible to speculate here about Harvy's reaction to this forthcoming event and to try to forecast what will take place in the final sequence of events.

In other texts, there are gaps that are not so easily filled by the reader because the text wishes to create suspense and so information is deliberately withheld from the reader. At these moments, the reader constructs a *possible world.* Say heroine X enters a room and finds her lover Y in the arms of another woman Z, and the text closes the door in our faces and changes the scene to the battlefield at Waterloo. The thwarted reader, desiring to know what happened in that room, may draw on his or her own frame of reference—"I know what I would do if I were X"—and create a possible world in which the scene is completed, though the imagined completion may be at variance with what actually is to take place in the text. This act is the creation by the reader of a possible world, a new text.

In Eco's terms, possible worlds are "sketches for another story, the story the actual one could have been had things gone differently. . . . They are worlds imagined, believed, wished." A fictional text is itself a possible world because it is composed of a possible set of events chosen by its author. As readers, we most frequently construct possible worlds from texts in which we have become deeply involved, and because we want their stories to continue, we construct our own, adding new endings, proposing new situations. Fans of that problematical heroine Scarlett O'Hara, of *Gone With the Wind,* may construct a possible world in which Scarlett marries Ashley Wilkes, her one true love. But this possible world would have little to do with the possible world that is actualized in Margaret Mitchell's novel, since that world is structured on the proposition that Ashley marries Melanie.

So when we talk about completing a text, we're not being entirely accurate. A text can never be completed. Each reader brings a unique model of competence to a text, and so each reader will fill gaps in the text differently. Because the fictional text is directed at the imagination of the reader, there will always be variables in the interpretation possible in the imaginative spaces of the text. However, a well-organized fictional text will not allow just any interpretation; rather, it directs the reader toward a certain number of possible readings. It is because of the extension of these possible readings by an infinite number of readers, each with a different model of competence, that an infinite number of readings of a text is possible. Which is to say, when John gets on the bus in New York, reader A will put him on a green and white bus; reader B will put him on a blue and white bus; reader C will give him a bumpy ride to Providence; reader D, who has taken that bus ride, will make John bored during the seemingly endless barren stretch from the Connecticut line to East Greenwich, Rhode Island; and so on and on. John's bus ride has endless variations.

In this section, you will be asked to put your work as a reader into the actual writing of ghost chapters and possible worlds. When you compare your reading with those of your classmates, you will have a very clear idea of what we mean by variables in interpretation.

The Boarding House

James Joyce

This story, which James Joyce termed "a story of adolescence," is one of a group called* Dubliners. *The stories draw on Joyce's experience of growing up in Dublin, Ireland, at the turn of the century.

Mrs. Mooney was a butcher's daughter. She was a woman who was quite able to keep things to herself: a determined woman. She had married her father's foreman and opened a butcher's shop near Spring Gardens. But as soon as his father-in-law was dead Mr. Mooney began to go to the devil. He drank, plundered the till, ran headlong into debt. It was no use making him take the pledge: he was sure to break out again a few days after. By fighting his wife in the presence of customers and by buying bad meat he ruined his business. One night he went for his wife with the cleaver and she had to sleep in a neighbor's house. 1

After that they lived apart. She went to the priest and got a separation from him with care of the children. She would give him neither money nor food nor house-room; and so he was obliged to enlist himself as a sheriff's man. He was a shabby stooped little drunkard with a white face and a white moustache and white eyebrows, pencilled above his little eyes, which were pink-veined and raw; and all day long he sat in the bailiff's room, waiting to be put on a job. Mrs. Mooney, who had taken what remained of her money out of the butcher business and set up a boarding house in Hardwicke Street, was a big imposing woman. Her house had a floating population made up of tourists from Liverpool and the Isle of Man and, occasionally, *artistes* from the music halls. Its resident population was made up of clerks from the city. She governed her house cunningly and firmly, knew when to give credit, when to be stern and when to let things pass. All the resident young men spoke of her as *The Madam.* 2

Mrs. Mooney's young men paid fifteen shillings a week for board and lodgings (beer or stout at dinner excluded). They shared in common tastes and occupations and for this reason they were very chummy with one another. They discussed with one another the chances of favorites and outsiders. Jack Mooney, the Madam's son, who was clerk to a commission agent in Fleet Street, had the reputation of being a hard case. He was fond of using soldiers' obscenities: usually he came home in the small hours. When he met his friends he had always a good one to tell them and he was always sure to be on to a good thing—that is to say, a likely horse or a likely *artiste.* He was also handy with the mits and sang comic songs. On Sunday nights there would often be a reunion in Mrs. Mooney's front drawing-room The music-hall *artistes* would oblige; and Sheridan played waltzes and polkas and vamped accompaniments. Polly Mooney, the Madam's daughter, would also sing. She sang: 3

I'm a . . . naughty girl.
You needn't sham:
You know I am.

Polly was a slim girl of nineteen; she had light soft hair and a small full mouth. Her eyes, which were grey with a shade of green through them, had a habit of glancing upwards when she spoke with anyone, which made her look like a little perverse madonna. Mrs. Mooney had first sent her daughter to be a typist in a corn-factor's office but, as a disreputable sheriff's man used to come every other day to the office, asking to be allowed to say a word to his daughter, she had taken her daughter home again and set her to do housework. As Polly was very lively the intention was to give her the run of the young men. Besides, young men like to feel that there is a young woman not very far away. Polly, of course, flirted with the young men but Mrs. Mooney, who was a shrewd judge, knew that the young men were only passing the time away: none of them meant business. Things went on so for a long time and Mrs. Mooney began to think of sending Polly back to typewriting when she noticed that something was going on between Polly and one of the young men. She watched the pair and kept her own counsel.

Polly knew that she was being watched, but still her mother's persistent silence could not be misunderstood. There had been no open complicity between mother and daughter, no open understanding but, though people in the house began to talk of the affair, still Mrs. Mooney did not intervene. Polly began to grow a little strange in her manner and the young man was evidently perturbed. At last, when she judged it to be the right moment, Mrs. Mooney intervened. She dealt with moral problems as a cleaver deals with meat: and in this case she had made up her mind.

It was a bright Sunday morning of early summer, promising heat, but with a fresh breeze blowing. All the windows of the boarding house were open and the lace curtains ballooned gently towards the street beneath the raised sashes. The belfry of George's Church sent out constant peals and worshippers, singly or in groups, traversed the little circus before the church, revealing their purpose by their self-contained demeanor no less than by the little volumes in their gloved hands. Breakfast was over in the boarding house and the table of the breakfast-room was covered with plates on which lay yellow streaks of eggs with morsels of bacon-fat and bacon-rind. Mrs. Mooney sat in the straw arm-chair and watched the servant Mary remove the breakfast things. She made Mary collect the crusts and pieces of broken bread to help to make Tuesday's bread-pudding. When the table was cleared, the broken bread collected, the sugar and butter safe under lock and key, she began to reconstruct the interview which she had had the night before with Polly. Things were as she had suspected; she had been frank in her questions and Polly had been frank in her answers. Both had been somewhat awkward, of course. She had been made awkward by her not wishing to receive the news in too cavalier a fashion or to seem to have connived and Polly had been made awkward not merely because allusions of that kind always made her awkward but also because she did not wish it to be thought that in her wise innocence she had divined the intention behind her mother's tolerance.

Mrs. Mooney glanced instinctively at the little gilt clock on the mantelpiece 7
as soon as she had become aware through her revery that the bells of George's Church had stopped ringing. It was seventeen minutes past eleven: she would have lots of time to have the matter out with Mr. Doran and then catch short twelve at Marlborough Street. She was sure she would win. To begin with she had all the weight of social opinion on her side: she was an outraged mother. She had allowed him to live beneath her roof, assuming that he was a man of honor, and he had simply abused her hospitality. He was thirty-four or thirty-five years of age, so that youth could not be pleaded as his excuse; nor could ignorance be his excuse since he was a man who had seen something of the world. He had simply taken advantage of Polly's youth and inexperience: that was evident. The question was: What reparation would he make?

There must be reparation made in such cases. It is all very well for the man: 8
he can go his ways as if nothing had happened, having had his moment of pleasure, but the girl has to bear the brunt. Some mothers would be content to patch up such an affair for a sum of money; she had known cases of it. But she would not do so. For her only one reparation could make up for the loss of her daughter's honor: marriage.

She counted all her cards again before sending Mary up to Mr. Doran's 9
room to say that she wished to speak with him. She felt sure she would win. He was a serious young man, not rakish or loud-voiced like the others. If it had been Mr. Sheridan or Mr. Meade or Bantam Lyons her task would have been much harder. She did not think he would face publicity. All the lodgers in the house knew something of the affair; details had been invented by some. Besides, he had been employed for thirteen years in a great Catholic wine-merchant's office and publicity would mean for him, perhaps, the loss of his sit. Whereas if he agreed all might be well. She knew he had a good screw for one thing and she suspected he had a bit of stuff put by.

Nearly the half-hour! She stood up and surveyed herself in the pier-glass. 10
The decisive expression of her great florid face satisfied her and she thought of some mothers she knew who could not get their daughters off their hands.

Mr. Doran was very anxious indeed this Sunday morning. He had made 11
two attempts to shave but his hand had been so unsteady that he had been obliged to desist. Three days' reddish beard fringed his jaws and every two or three minutes a mist gathered on his glasses so that he had to take them off and polish them with his pocket-handkerchief. The recollection of his confession of the night before was a cause of acute pain to him; the priest had drawn out every ridiculous detail of the affair and in the end had so magnified his sin

that he was almost thankful at being afforded a loophole of reparation. The harm was done. What could he do now but marry her or run away? He could not brazen it out. The affair would be sure to be talked of and his employer would be certain to hear of it. Dublin is such a small city: everyone knows everyone else's business. He felt his heart leap warmly in his throat as he heard in his excited imagination old Mr. Leonard calling out in his rasping voice: *Send Mr. Doran here, please.*

All his long years of service gone for nothing! All his industry and 1
diligence thrown away! As a young man he had sown his wild oats, of course; he had boasted of his free-thinking and denied the existence of God to his companions in public-houses. But that was all passed and done with . . . nearly. He still bought a copy of *Reynolds's Newspaper* every week but he attended to his religious duties and for nine-tenths of the year lived a regular life. He had money enough to settle down on; it was not that. But the family would look down on her. First of all there was her disreputable father and then her mother's boarding house was beginning to get a certain fame. He had a notion that he was being had. He could imagine his friends talking of the affair and laughing. She *was* a little vulgar; sometimes she said *I seen* and *If I had've known.* But what would grammar matter if he really loved her? He could not make up his mind whether to like her or despise her for what she had done. Of course, he had done it too. His instinct urged him to remain free, not to marry. Once you are married you are done for, it said.

While he was sitting helplessly on the side of the bed in shirt and 1
trousers she tapped lightly at his door and entered. She told him all, that she had made a clean breast of it to her mother and that her mother would speak with him that morning. She cried and threw her arms round his neck, saying:

—O, Bob! Bob! What am I to do? What am I to do at all? 1

She would put an end to herself, she said. 1

He comforted her feebly, telling her not to cry, that it would be all right, 1
never fear. He felt against his shirt the agitation of her bosom.

It was not altogether his fault that it had happened. He remembered 1
well, with the curious patient memory of the celibate, the first casual caresses her dress, her breath, her fingers had given him. Then late one night as he was undressing for bed she had tapped at his door, timidly. She wanted to relight her candle at his for hers had been blown out by a gust. It was her bath night. She wore a loose open combing-jacket of printed flannel. Her white instep shone in the opening of her furry slippers and the blood glowed warmly behind her perfumed skin. From her hands and wrists too as she lit and steadied her candle a faint perfume arose.

On nights when he came in very late it was she who warmed up his 1
dinner. He scarcely knew what he was eating, feeling her beside him alone, at night, in the sleeping house. And her thoughtfulness! If the night was anyway cold or wet or windy there was sure to be a little tumbler of punch ready for him. Perhaps they could be happy together. . . .

19 They used to go upstairs together on tiptoe, each with a candle, and on the third landing exchange reluctant good-nights. They used to kiss. He remembered well her eyes, the touch of her hand and his delirium. . . .

20 But delirium passes. He echoed her phrase, applying it to himself: *What am I to do?* The instinct of the celibate warned him to hold back. But the sin was there; even his sense of honor told him that reparation must be made for such a sin.

21 While he was sitting with her on the side of the bed Mary came to the door and said that the missus wanted to see him in the parlor. He stood up to put on his coat and waistcoat, more helpless than ever. When he was dressed he went over to her to comfort her. It would be all right, never fear. He left her crying on the bed and moaning softly: *O my God!*

22 Going down the stairs his glasses became so dimmed with moisture that he had to take them off and polish them. He longed to ascend through the roof and fly away to another country where he would never hear again of his trouble, and yet a force pushed him downstairs step by step. The implacable faces of his employer and of the Madam stared upon his discomfiture. On the last flight of stairs he passed Jack Mooney who was coming up from the pantry nursing two bottles of *Bass.* They saluted coldly; and the lover's eyes rested for a second or two on a thick bulldog face and a pair of thick short arms. When he reached the foot of the staircase he glanced up and saw Jack regarding him from the door of the return-room.

23 Suddenly he remembered the night when one of the music-hall *artistes,* a little blond Londoner, had made a rather free allusion to Polly. The reunion had been almost broken up on account of Jack's violence. Everyone tried to quiet him. The music-hall *artiste,* a little paler than usual, kept smiling and saying that there was no harm meant: but Jack kept shouting at him that if any fellow tried that sort of a game on with *his* sister he'd bloody well put his teeth down his throat, so he would.

24 Polly sat for a little time on the side of the bed, crying. Then she dried her eyes and went over to the looking-glass. She dipped the end of the towel in the water-jug and refreshed her eyes with the cool water. She looked at herself in profile and readjusted a hairpin above her ear. Then she went back to the bed again and sat at the foot. She regarded the pillows for a long time and the sight of them awakened in her mind secret amiable memories. She rested the nape of her neck against the cool iron bed-rail and fell into a revery. There was no longer any perturbation visible on her face.

25 She waited on patiently, almost cheerfully, without alarm, her memories gradually giving place to hopes and visions of the future. Her hopes and visions were so intricate that she no longer saw the white pillows on which her gaze was fixed or remembered that she was waiting for anything.

26 At last she heard her mother calling. She started to her feet and ran to the banisters.

—Polly! Polly! 2

—Yes, mamma? 2

—Come down, dear. Mr. Doran wants to speak to you. 2

Then she remembered what she had been waiting for. 3

For Discussion and Writing

1. In paragraph 5, the reader must draw on a set of inferences if such phrases as the following are to be interpreted:

   "no open complicity"

   "her mother's persistent silence could not be misunderstood"

   "the affair"

   "a little strange"

   "the young man was evidently perturbed"

   "the right moment"

   "moral problems as a cleaver deals with meat"

   What information in the first four paragraphs can be drawn on by the reader in order to interpret these phrases? How much does the text depend on the reader's model of competence here? What phrases lack interpretive information and act to pique the reader's interest in forthcoming events?
2. Write a ghost chapter of the confrontation of Mr. Doran and Mrs. Mooney. Decide what persuasive strategies Mrs. Mooney will employ to win her case, and how much, if any, resistance Mr. Doran will exhibit. Your chapter may be written as a narrative describing what was said by both parties or as a combination of narrative and dialogue.

You Were Perfectly Fine

Dorothy Parker

A New York writer of verse, fiction, plays, and filmscripts, Dorothy Parker was most celebrated for her wit in the 1920s and 1930s. In the story that follows, she presents the aftermath of a fashionable New York dinner party.

The pale young man eased himself carefully into the low chair, and rolled his head to the side, so that the cool chintz comforted his cheek and temple. 1

"Oh, dear," he said, "Oh, dear, oh, dear, oh, dear. Oh." 2

The clear-eyed girl, sitting light and erect on the couch, smiled brightly at him 3

"Not feeling so well today?" she said. 4

"Oh, I'm great," he said. "Corking, I am. Know what time I got up? Four 5
o'clock this afternoon, sharp. I kept trying to make it, and every time I took my
head off the pillow, it would roll under the bed. This isn't my head I've got on
now. I think this is something that used to belong to Walt Whitman. Oh, dear,
oh, dear, oh, dear."

"Do you think maybe a drink would make you feel better?" she said. 6

"The hair of the mastiff that bit me?" he said, "Oh, no, thank you. Please 7
never speak of anything like that again. I'm through. I'm all, all through. Look at
that hand; steady as a humming-bird. Tell me, was I very terrible last night?"

"Oh, goodness," she said, "everybody was feeling pretty high. You were all 8
right."

"Yeah," he said. "I must have been dandy. Is everybody sore at me?" 9

"Good heavens, no," she said. "Everyone thought you were terribly funny. 10
Of course, Jim Pierson was a little stuffy, there for a minute at dinner. But
people sort of held him back in his chair, and got him calmed down. I don't
think anybody at the other tables noticed it at all. Hardly anybody."

"He was going to sock me?" he said. "Oh, Lord. What did I do to him?" 11

"Why, you didn't do a thing," she said. "You were perfectly fine. But you 12
know how silly Jim gets, when he thinks anybody is making too much fuss over
Elinor."

"Was I making a pass at Elinor?" he said. "Did I do that?" 13

"Of course you didn't," she said. "You were only fooling, that's all. She 14
thought you were awfully amusing. She was having a marvelous time. She only
got a little tiny bit annoyed just once, when you poured the clam-juice down her
back."

"My God," he said. "Clam-juice down that back. And every vertebra a little 15
Cabot. Dear God. What'll I ever do?"

"Oh, she'll be all right," she said. "Just send her some flowers, or some- 16
thing. Don't worry about it. It isn't anything."

"No, I won't worry," he said. "I haven't got a care in the world. I'm sitting 17
pretty. Oh, dear, oh, dear. Did I do any other fascinating tricks at dinner?"

"You were fine," she said. "Don't be so foolish about it. Everybody was 18
crazy about you. The maître d'hôtel was a little worried because you wouldn't
stop singing, but he really didn't mind. All he said was, he was afraid they'd
close the place again, if there was so much noise. But he didn't care a bit,
himself. I think he loved seeing you have such a good time. Oh, you were just
singing away, there, for about an hour. It wasn't so terribly loud, at all."

"So I sang," he said. "That must have been a treat. I sang." 19

"Don't you remember?" she said. "You just sang one song after another. 20
Everybody in the place was listening. They loved it. Only you kept insisting that
you wanted to sing some song about some kind of fusiliers or other, and
everybody kept shushing you, and you'd keep trying to start it again. You were
wonderful. We were all trying to make you stop singing for a minute, and eat
something, but you wouldn't hear of it. My, you were funny."

"Didn't I eat any dinner?" he said.

"Oh, not a thing," she said. "Every time the waiter would offer you something, you'd give it right back to him, because you said that he was your long-lost brother, changed in the cradle by a gypsy band, and that anything you had was his. You had him simply roaring at you."

"I bet I did," he said. "I bet I was comical. Society's Pet, I must have been. And what happened then, after my overwhelming success with the waiter?"

"Why, nothing much," she said. "You took a sort of dislike to some old man with white hair, sitting across the room, because you didn't like his necktie and you wanted to tell him about it. But we got you out, before he got really mad."

"Oh, we got out," he said. "Did I walk?"

"Walk? Of course you did," she said. "You were absolutely all right. There was that nasty stretch of ice on the sidewalk, and you did sit down awfully hard, you poor dear. But good heavens, that might have happened to anybody."

"Oh, surely," he said. "Mrs. Hoover or anybody. So I fell down on the sidewalk. That would explain what's the matter with my—Yes. I see. And then what, if you don't mind?"

"Ah, now, Peter!" she said. "You can't sit there and say you don't remember what happened after that! I did think that maybe you were just a little tight at dinner—oh, you were perfectly all right, and all that, but I did know you were feeling pretty gay. But you were so serious, from the time you fell down—I never knew you to be that way. Don't you know, how you told me I had never seen your real self before? Oh, Peter, I just couldn't bear it, if you didn't remember that lovely long ride we took together in the taxi! Please, you do remember that, don't you? I think it would simply kill me, if you didn't."

"Oh, yes," he said. "Riding in the taxi. Oh, yes, sure. Pretty long ride, hmm?"

"Round and round and round the park," she said. "Oh, and the trees were shining so in the moonlight. And you said you never knew before that you really had a soul."

"Yes," he said. "I said that. That was me."

"You said such lovely, lovely things," she said. "And I'd never known, all this time, how you had been feeling about me, and I'd never dared to let you see how I felt about you. And then last night—oh, Peter dear, I think that taxi ride was the most important thing that ever happened to us in our lives."

"Yes," he said. "I guess it must have been."

"And we're going to be so happy," she said. "Oh, I just want to tell everybody! But I don't know—I think maybe it would be sweeter to keep it all to ourselves."

"I think it would be," he said.

"Isn't it lovely?" she said.

"Yes," he said. "Great."

"Lovely!" she said.

"Look here," he said, "do you mind if I have a drink? I mean, just medicinal- 39
ly, you know. I'm off the stuff for life, so help me. But I think I feel a collapse coming on."

"Oh, I think it would do you good," she said. "You poor boy, it's a shame 40
you feel so awful. I'll go make you a highball."

"Honestly," he said, "I don't see how you could ever want to speak to me 41
again, after I made such a fool of myself, last night. I think I'd better go join a monastery in Tibet."

"You crazy idiot!" she said. "As if I could ever let you go away now! Stop 42
talking like that. You were perfectly fine."

She jumped up from the couch, kissed him quickly on the forehead, and 43
ran out of the room.

The pale young man looked after her and shook his head long and slowly, 44
then dropped it in his damp and trembling hands.

"Oh, dear," he said. "Oh, dear, oh, dear, oh dear." 45

For Discussion and Writing

1. **In this story, the reader and the young man learn together the events of the previous evening. Both reader and young man must re-create out of the girl's report of those events a narrative of the dinner party and its aftermath. The young man will write a ghost chapter, because the events of the previous evening constitute a gap in his life; the reader is asked to construct a possible world of the previous evening, to imagine from the information given what may have actually occurred. In order to do this, the reader must pay attention to the girl's presentation of information and to the young man's interpretation of it. What differences do you find between the two?**
2. **It is later the same day. The young man's head is beginning to clear and he is beginning to remember more details of the night before. Write a narrative of the evening's events from the young man's point of view. You might want him to answer some questions raised in the text, such as why he made a pass at Elinor, why he disliked the old man's tie, and how he really feels about the girl he was with.**
3. **Retell the events of the night before as a series of short narratives told by three or more of the following:**
   a. **Jim Pierson**
   b. **Elinor**
   c. **the maître d'hôtel**
   d. **the waiter**
   e. **the old man with white hair**
   f. **the taxi driver**

Interpreting Texts

Schoolchildren are expected to be able to infer something called the character of Macbeth from indices scattered about Shakespeare's text.
—Frank Kermode

Directed to art, interpretation means plucking a set of elements (the X, the Y, the Z, and so forth) from the whole work. The task of interpretation is virtually one of translation. The interpreter says, Look, don't you see that X is really—or, really means—A? That Y is really B? That Z is really C?
—Susan Sontag

As the word *interpretation* is normally used in literary study, it means transforming a story, play, or poem into an essay. We have already considered transformation as a form of intertextuality, but the transformations we considered were mainly transformations *within* the same genre: fiction into fiction. We have also considered the way readers must construct ghost chapters and possible worlds in order to complete the texts they read. Both of these activities, transformation and completion, are interpretive. So is the translation of figurative language into literal prose. In short, we have already considered many of the dimensions of interpretation, though not all, but we have not yet faced squarely the problem of writing the interpretive essay.

The purpose of the interpretive essay is not simply to repeat in the form of an essay what has already been said in a story, poem, or play. It *is* that to some extent, but, if that were all, interpretation would be a trivial enterprise. The major function of interpretation is to say what a previous text has left unsaid: to unravel its complications, to make explicit its implications, and to raise its concrete and specific details to a more abstract and general level. That is, as we shall illustrate a few paragraphs later on, the interpreter must find a way of writing about the general principles of human behavior that are embodied in the specific situations and events of any story. The interpreter must say what the story is *about.*

We should also note that interpretation is not something that is entirely avoided in plays, poems, and stories themselves. Authors will often attempt to control the way their texts are read by offering self-interpretations within those texts. Samuel Beckett parodied this desire of the author to control meaning by adding what he called "Addenda" to the end of his novel *Watt,* noting that "The following precious and illuminating material should be carefully studied. Only fatigue and disgust prevented its incorporation." The last addendum reads simply, "no symbols where none intended."

By forbidding the reader to find symbolic or figurative meanings except where the author intended them to be found, Beckett symbolized the desire of most authors to control the interpretation of their own texts. By saying it so bluntly, he also made this desire faintly ridiculous. But did he *intend* this statement to symbolize what we say it symbolizes? That is a matter of interpretation. We say that when Beckett wrote "no symbols where none intended" he was joking, because he knew that no one can control meanings or even realize their intentions perfectly. And we would support our interpretation by pointing to other places where Beckett seems to be saying something similar—an easy task since *Watt* is devoted to the distressing gap between words and things, the constant slippage of meaning. Furthermore, we would add, the expression itself doesn't even specify whose intention is required to make an object into a symbol. If the rule is to be "no symbols where none intended," then perhaps the reader's intention would satisfy the rule in this instance. Then, of course, it would be *our* symbol, and not Beckett's. But doesn't interpretation mean that it must be *his* symbol that we understand? What is the writer's share in meaning and what is the reader's? These are vexed and difficult questions, much debated in literary theory. We cannot and should not try to settle them here. What we hope to accomplish instead is to clarify the possibilities of interpretive writing a bit and to offer a few practical suggestions for entering the world of interpretive discourse.

You may remember the story by William Carlos Williams included in Chapter 1 of this book, about a doctor who must struggle physically to diagnose the fever of a lovely and ferocious little girl (pp. 19–21). The story itself is very sparing with interpretive commentary, but it nevertheless makes a strong effort to direct our interpretation of it. The effort is most apparent in the title provided by the author: "The Use of Force." This title takes the concrete events narrated in the text and gathers them under the interpretive umbrella of "force." That is one of the major features of interpretive discourse. Interpretation is constituted by our moving from saying "The story is about a doctor and a child" to saying "The story is about the use of force." This move, from the concrete details of doctor and child to the abstraction "use of force" is what interpretation is all about. In this case, the author tries hard to guide the interpretive move by providing his own interpretive abstraction in the title of his text.

Kate Chopin, in her story "The Kiss," does not provide us with such guidance. Her title simply names the initial action of the story. To produce an interpretation, we must find our own way of discussing the significance of the events narrated in the text. We might decide the story is about "deception," for instance, and base our interpretation upon this decision. The important point to remember is that interpretation always involves a move from the specific details named in the text to a more general level: from the doctor prying open the child's mouth with a spoon to the abstract concept *force.*

In the epigraph by Frank Kermode at the beginning of this discussion, we can locate one type of interpretation. The reader takes a set of details from a play and constructs from them an abstraction called the "character" of

Macbeth. One could do the same for characters in many of the plays and stories we have read. This sort of interpretation appears to be "natural," since we do it all the time, but it is based upon certain assumptions about the psychic unity of human beings and the importance of the individual person that are not, in fact, universal assumptions. Many forms of storytelling exist in which the individuals named in the text are not important in themselves but as representations of something else. This is the case in fables, parables, allegories, and other forms of symbolic fiction. In reading such narratives, the interpreter does what Susan Sontag describes in the epigraph from her essay, "Against Interpretation," quoted at the head of this discussion. That is, the interpreter says, "X is really A, Y is really B."

Being able to say "X is really A" involves knowing the system of values and beliefs that gives the concept "A" its meaning. For instance, Christianity is a system of values and beliefs. The story of Samson, from the Old Testament—a Jewish scripture—is read by Christian interpreters in accordance with their own system of beliefs. Reading and interpreting in this way, they say that Samson is really Christ, or, more technically, that Samson is a "type" of Christ, a symbol of Christ. By his sacrifice of his own life, Samson contributes to the salvation of his people. His death in the temple of the Philistines is equivalent to the death of Jesus at the hands of the Romans; and, just as the Philistines were defeated by Samson's sacrificial death, Rome was Christianized, ultimately conquered, by the One the Romans captured and tortured. This is how interpretation according to a system of values and beliefs works.

Christianity is one of a number of such systems used in literary interpretation. Psychoanalytical systems, such as the Freudian, are also widely used, and so are socioeconomic systems, such as Marxism. It is extremely difficult to generate such interpretations without serious study of the systems involved, which is one of the reasons why we will not ask you to undertake this kind of work. It is possible, however, for someone who is not an expert but is willing to pay close attention to comment on such interpretations, to extend them, and to revise, question, and even reject them. If you have worked on the transformations of "Hansel and Gretel" in the previous section of this book, you are now something of an expert on that story. Therefore, you are in a good position to respond to the following two interpretive essays. The first, from a book by Jack Zipes called *Breaking the Magic Spell,* is a Marxist reading of two tales, including "Hansel and Gretel." The second, from *The Uses of Enchantment* by the noted child psychologist Bruno Bettelheim, is a Freudian interpretation of "Hansel and Gretel."

The Politics of Fairy Tales

Jack Zipes

Perhaps the best-known and most widely circulated collection of folk tales is that of the Brothers Grimm. These *Märchen* were recorded during the first decade of the nineteenth century in the Rhineland. They were told in dialect, largely by servants, housewives, a watchman and inhabitants from towns and small cities and were stylized and transcribed into High German by the Grimms. Consequently, a thorough analysis of the tales must take into account the background of the narrators and their communities, the social upheavals of the times caused by the Napoleonic Wars, the advent of mercantilism and the perspective of the Grimms, including their reasons for choosing certain folk tales for their collection. In dealing with the politics of the tales I want to limit my discussion to an analysis of the socio-historical conditions as reflected in two tales, *How Six Travelled through the World* and *Hansel and Gretel,* to demonstrate how links might be established with the actual struggles of that period. In the first, *How Six Travelled through the World,* the elements of class struggle are most apparent, and the entire feudal system is placed in question. In the second, *Hansel and Gretel,* which is more widely known and has been watered down in modern versions, the social references are at first not as clear. For audiences of the eighteenth and early nineteenth centuries, particularly for the peasantry, the social and political signs were unmistakable. 1

How Six Travelled through the World concerns a man, who "was well-versed in all kinds of skills," served a king valiantly during a war, but was miserably paid and dismissed by the king when the war ended. The soldier swears that he will avenge himself if he can find the right people to help him. Indeed, he encounters five peasants who possess extraordinary powers and agree to assist him. The soldier seeks out the king, who has declared in the meantime that anyone who can defeat his daughter in a foot race can marry her. If she happens to win, death is the reward. With the help of his friends and their supernatural gifts, the soldier wins the race. However, the king is annoyed, and his daughter even more so, that such a common soldier formerly in his employ should win the wager. The king plots to kill the soldier and his friends, but they outsmart him. The king promises the soldier all the gold he can carry if he renounces his claim to the princess. The soldier agrees and has one of his friends, who has enormous strength, to carry away the entire wealth of the kingdom. The king sends the royal army after the soldier and his friends to retrieve the gold. Of course, they easily defeat the army, divide the gold amongst themselves, and live happily ever after. 2

It is obvious that this tale treats a social problem of utmost concern to the lower classes. In the eighteenth century it was customary for the state to recruit soldiers for standing armies, treat them shabbily and abandon them when there was no more use for them. Here the perspective of the story is clearly that 3 of the people, and though its origins are pre-capitalist, the narrator and the Grimms were probably attracted to its theme because of its relation to the Napoleonic Wars and perhaps even the Napoleonic Code (instituted in the Rhineland). Common soldiers were indeed treated miserably during these wars; yet, the Code gave rise to hopes for greater democratization. In this tale a common man shows himself to be the equal of a king if not better. The miraculous talents—the magic—are symbolic of the real hidden qualities which he himself possesses, or they might represent the collective energies of small people, the power they actually possess. When these talents are used properly, that is, when they are used to attain due justice and recompense, the people are invincible, a theme common to many other folk tales such as *The Bremen Town Musicians.* Thus, the imaginative elements have a real reference to history and society, for the peasant uprisings and the French Revolution in the eighteenth century were demonstrations of how the oppressed people could achieve limited victories against the nobility. To be sure, these victories were often of short duration, and the peasants and lower estates could be divided or pacified with money as is the case in this tale, where the social relations are not changed. Still, it is important that the tale does *illustrate how common people can work together, assert themselves actively* and achieve clear-cut goals, using their skills and imagination.

The story of "Hansel and Gretel" is also a story of hope and victory. Again 4
the perspective is plebeian. A woodcutter does not have enough food to feed his family. His wife, the stepmother of his children, convinces him that they must abandon *his* children in the woods in order to survive. The children are almost devoured by a witch, but they use their ingenuity to trick and kill her. No fooling around here. Then Hansel and Gretel return home with jewels and embrace their father.

The struggle depicted in this tale is against poverty and against witches 5
who have houses of food and hidden treasures. Here again the imaginative and magic elements of the tale had specific meanings for a peasant and lower-class audience at the end of the eighteenth century. The wars of this period often brought with them widespread famine and poverty which were also leading to the breakdown of the feudal patronage system. Consequently, peasants were often left to shift on their own and forced to go to extremes to survive. These extremes involved banditry, migration or abandonment of children. The witch (as parasite) could be interpreted here to symbolize the entire feudal system or the greed and brutality of the aristocracy, responsible for the difficult conditions. The killing of the witch is symbolically the realization of the hatred which the peasantry felt for the aristocracy as hoarders and oppressors. It is important to note that the children do not turn against their father or stepmother as one might think they would. On the contrary, they reluctantly comprehend the situation which forces their parents to act as they do. That is, they understand the social forces as being responsible for their plight and do

not personalize them by viewing their parents as their enemies. The objectification of the tale is significant, for it helps explain the tolerant attitude toward the stepmother (which is not always the case). It must be remembered that women died young due to frequent child-bearing and insanitary conditions. Thus, stepmothers were common in households, and this often led to difficulties with the children by former wives. In this respect, the tale reflects the strained relations but sees them more as a result of social forces. The stepmother is not condemned, either by the narrator or the children. They return home, unaware that she is dead. They return home with hope and jewels to put an end to *all* their problems.

In both these tales class conflict is portrayed in the light of pre-capitalist 6
social conditions which were common in the late eighteenth and early nineteenth centuries in Germany. In neither tale is there a political revolution. What is important is that the contradictions are depicted, whereby the prejudices and injustices of feudal ideology are exposed. The magic and fantastic elements are closely tied to the real possibilities for the peasantry to change conditions, albeit in a limited way. The emphasis is on hope and action. The soldier and his friends *act* and *defeat* the king whenever they are tested. Hansel and Gretel *act* and *kill* the witch. The form of the tale, its closed, compact nature, is shaped by the individual carriers who distribute the stories and allow the common people to learn how they might survive in an unjust society and struggle with hope. Whatever symbols and magic are used can clearly be understood when placed in the historical context of the transition from feudalism to early capitalism.

Naturally it could be argued that the folk tale has nothing to do with the 7
socio-political conditions of feudalism. That is, the folk tale originated thousands of years ago, and we cannot be entirely certain about the conditions which gave rise to them. But we do know that it was cultivated in an oral tradition by the people and passed on from generation to generation in essentially 35 different basic patterns which have been kept intact over thousands of years. As Vladimir Propp has shown, there have been transformations of elements within the patterns, and these changes depend on the social realities of the period in which the tales are told. Linda Dégh clarifies this point in her thorough examination of the social function of the storyteller in a Hungarian peasant community: "Our knowledge of European folktale material stems from two sources: literary works and oral tradition. The most striking characteristic of the traditional tale lies in the fact that the social institutions and concepts which we discover in it reflect the age of feudalism. Thus the question of the origin of the folktale coincides with that of the origin of literature in general." Clearly the folk tales collected in the seventeenth, eighteenth and nineteenth centuries, though they preserved aesthetic patterns derived from pre-capitalist societies, did so because these patterns plus the transformed elements and motifs continued to reflect and speak to the conditions of the

people and the dominant ideology of the times to a great degree. Though primitive in origin, the folk tale in Germany, as told in the late eighteenth century and collected by the Grimms in the early nineteenth, related to and was shaped by feudal conditions.

Hansel and Gretel

Bruno Bettelheim

"Hansel and Gretel" begins realistically. The parents are poor, and they worry about how they will be able to take care of their children. Together at night they discuss their predicament, and how they can deal with it. Even taken on this surface level, the folk fairy tale conveys an important, although unpleasant, truth: poverty and deprivation do not improve man's character, but rather make him more selfish, less sensitive to the sufferings of others, and thus prone to embark on evil deeds. 1

The fairy tale expresses in words and actions the things which go on in children's minds. In terms of the child's dominant anxiety, Hansel and Gretel believe that their parents are talking about a plot to desert them. A small child, awakening hungry in the darkness of the night, feels threatened by complete rejection and desertion, which he experiences in the form of fear of starvation. By projecting their inner anxiety onto those they fear might cut them off, Hansel and Gretel are convinced that their parents plan to starve them to death! In line with the child's anxious fantasies, the story tells that until then the parents had been able to feed their children, but had now fallen upon lean times. 2

The mother represents the source of all food to the children, so it is she who now is experienced as abandoning them, as if in a wilderness. It is the child's anxiety and deep disappointment when Mother is no longer willing to meet all his oral demands which leads him to believe that suddenly Mother has become unloving, selfish, rejecting. Since the children know they need their parents desperately, they attempt to return home after being deserted. In fact, Hansel succeeds in finding their way back from the forest the first time they are abandoned. Before a child has the courage to embark on the voyage of finding himself, of becoming an independent person through meeting the world, he can develop initiative only in trying to return to passivity, to secure for himself eternally dependent gratification. "Hansel and Gretel" tells that this will not work in the long run. 3

The children's successful return home does not solve anything. Their effort to continue life as before, as if nothing had happened, is to no avail. The frustrations continue, and the mother becomes more shrewd in her plans for getting rid of the children. 4

By implication, the story tells about the debilitating consequences of 5
trying to deal with life's problems by means of regression and denial, which reduce one's ability to solve problems. The first time in the forest Hansel used his intelligence appropriately by putting down white pebbles to mark the path home. The second time he did not use his intelligence as well—he, who lived close to a big forest, should have known that birds would eat the bread crumbs. Hansel might instead have studied landmarks on the way in, to find his way back out. But having engaged in denial and regression—the return home—Hansel has lost much of his initiative and ability to think clearly. Starvation anxiety has driven him back, so now he can think only of food as offering a solution to the problem of finding his way out of a serious predicament. Bread stands here for food in general, man's "life line"—an image which Hansel takes literally, out of his anxiety. This shows the limiting effects of fixations to primitive levels of development, engaged in out of fear.

The story of "Hansel and Gretel" gives body to the anxieties and learning 6
tasks of the young child who must overcome and sublimate his primitive incorporative and hence destructive desires. The child must learn that if he does not free himself of these, his parents or society will force him to do so against his will, as earlier his mother had stopped nursing the child when she felt the time had come to do so. This tale gives symbolic expression to these inner experiences directly linked to the mother. Therefore, the father remains a shadowy and ineffectual figure throughout the story, as he appears to the child during his early life when Mother is all-important, in both her benign and her threatening aspects.

Frustrated in their ability to find a solution to their problem in reality 7
because reliance on food for safety (bread crumbs to mark the path) fails them, Hansel and Gretel now give full rein to their oral regression. The gingerbread house represents an existence based on the most primitive satisfactions. Carried away by their uncontrolled craving, the children think nothing of destroying what should give shelter and safety, even though the birds' having eaten the crumbs should have warned them about eating up things.

By devouring the gingerbread house's roof and window, the children 8
show how ready they are to eat somebody out of house and home, a fear which they had projected onto their parents as the reason for their desertion. Despite the warning voice which asks, "Who is nibbling at my little house?" the children lie to themselves and blame it on the wind and "[go] on eating without disturbing themselves."

The gingerbread house is an image nobody forgets: how incredibly 9
appealing and tempting a picture this is, and how terrible the risk one runs if one gives in to the temptation. The child recognizes that, like Hansel and Gretel, he would wish to eat up the gingerbread house, no matter what the dangers. The house stands for oral greediness and how attractive it is to give in to it. The fairy tale is the primer from which the child learns to read his mind in

the language of images, the only language which permits understanding before intellectual maturity has been achieved. The child needs to be exposed to this language, and must learn to be responsive to it, if he is to become master of his soul.

The preconscious content of fairy-tale images is much richer than even the 10
following simple illustrations convey. For example, in dreams as well as in fantasies and the child's imagination, a house, as the place in which we dwell, can symbolize the body, usually the mother's. A gingerbread house, which one can "eat up," is a symbol of the mother, who in fact nurses the infant from her body. Thus, the house at which Hansel and Gretel are eating away blissfully and without a care stands in the unconscious for the good mother, who offers her body as a source of nourishment. It is the original all-giving mother, whom every child hopes to find again later somewhere out in the world, when his own mother begins to make demands and to impose restrictions. This is why, carried away by their hopes, Hansel and Gretel do not heed the soft voice that calls out to them, asking what they are up to—a voice that is their externalized conscience. Carried away by their greediness, and fooled by the pleasures of oral satisfaction which seem to deny all previous oral anxiety, the children "thought they were in heaven."

But, as the story tells, such unrestrained giving in to gluttony threatens 11
destruction. Regression to the earliest "heavenly" state of being—when on the mother's breast one lived symbiotically off her—does away with all individuation and independence. It even endangers one's very existence, as cannibalistic inclinations are given body in the figure of the witch.

The witch, who is a personification of the destructive aspects of orality, is 12
as bent on eating up the children as they are on demolishing her gingerbread house. When the children give in to untamed id impulses, as symbolized by their uncontrolled voraciousness, they risk being destroyed. The children eat only the symbolic representation of the mother, the gingerbread house; the witch wants to eat the children themselves. This teaches the hearer a valuable lesson: dealing in symbols is safe when compared with acting on the real thing. Turning the tables on the witch is justified also on another level: children who have little experience and are still learning self-control are not to be measured by the same yardstick as older people, who are supposed to be able to restrain their instinctual desires better. Thus, the punishment of the witch is as justified as the children's rescue.

The witch's evil designs finally force the children to recognize the dangers 13
of unrestrained oral greed and dependence. To survive, they must develop initiative and realize that their only recourse lies in intelligent planning and acting. They must exchange subservience to the pressures of the id for acting in accordance with the ego. Goal-directed behavior based on intelligent assessment of the situation in which they find themselves must take the place of wish-fulfilling fantasies: the substitution of the bone for the finger, tricking the witch to climb into the oven.

Only when the dangers inherent in remaining fixed to primitive orality 14
with its destructive propensities are recognized does the way to a higher stage of development open up. Then it turns out that the good, giving mother was hidden deep down in the bad, destructive one, because there are treasures to be gained: the children inherit the witch's jewels, which become valuable to them after their return home—that is, after they can again find the good parent. This suggests that as the children transcend their oral anxiety, and free themselves of relying on oral satisfaction for security, they can also free themselves of the image of the threatening mother—the witch—and rediscover the good parents, whose greater wisdom—the shared jewels—then benefit all.

On repeated hearing of "Hansel and Gretel," no child remains unaware of 15
the fact that birds eat the bread crumbs and thus prevent the children from returning home without first meeting their great adventure. It is also a bird which guides Hansel and Gretel to the gingerbread house, and thanks only to another bird do they manage to get back home. This gives the child—who thinks differently about animals than older persons do—pause to think: these birds must have a purpose, otherwise they would not first prevent Hansel and Gretel from finding their way back, then take them to the witch, and finally provide passage home.

Obviously, since all turns out for the best, the birds must have known that 16
it is preferable for Hansel and Gretel not to find their way directly back home out of the forest, but rather to risk facing the dangers of the world. In consequence of their threatening encounter with the witch, not only the children but also their parents live much more happily ever afterward. The different birds offer a clue to the path the children must follow to gain their reward.

After they have become familiar with "Hansel and Gretel," most children 17
comprehend, at least unconsciously, that what happens in the parental home and at the witch's house are but separate aspects of what in reality is one total experience. Initially, the witch is a perfectly gratifying mother figure, as we are told how "she took them both by the hand, and led them into her little house. Then good food was set before them, milk and pancakes with sugar, apples, and nuts. Afterwards two pretty little beds were covered with clean white linen, and Hansel and Gretel lay down in them, and thought they were in heaven." Only on the following morning comes a rude awakening from such dreams of infantile bliss. "The old woman had only pretended to be so kind; she was in reality a wicked witch . . . "

This is how the child feels when devastated by the ambivalent feelings, 18
frustrations, and anxieties of the oedipal stage of development, as well as his previous disappointment and rage at failures on his mother's part to gratify his needs and desires as fully as he expected. Severely upset that Mother no longer serves him unquestioningly but makes demands on him and devotes herself ever more to her own interest—something which the child had not permitted to come to his awareness before—he imagines that Mother, as she nursed him

and created a world of oral bliss, did so only to fool him—like the witch of the story.

Thus, the parental home "hard by a great forest" and the fateful house in 19
the depths of the same woods are on an unconscious level but the two aspects of the parental home: the gratifying one and the frustrating one.

The child who ponders on his own the details of "Hansel and Gretel" finds 20
meaning in how it begins. That the parental home is located at the very edge of the forest where everything happens suggests that what is to follow was imminent from the start. This is again the fairy tale's way to express thoughts through impressive images which lead the child to use his own imagination to derive deeper understanding.

Mentioned before was how the behavior of the birds symbolizes that the 21
entire adventure was arranged for the children's benefit. Since early Christian times the white dove has symbolized superior benevolent powers. Hansel claims to be looking back at a white dove that is sitting on the roof of the parental home, wanting to say goodbye to him. It is a snow-white bird, singing delightfully, which leads the children to the gingerbread house and then settles on its roof, suggesting that this is the right place for them to arrive at. Another white bird is needed to guide the children back to safety: their way home is blocked by a "big water" which they can cross only with the help of a white duck.

The children do not encounter any expanse of water on their way in. 22
Having to cross one on their return symbolizes a transition, and a new beginning on a higher level of existence (as in baptism). Up to the time they have to cross this water, the children have never separated. The school-age child should develop consciousness of his personal uniqueness, of his individuality, which means that he can no longer share everything with others, has to live to some degree by himself and stride out on his own. This is symbolically expressed by the children not being able to remain together in crossing the water. As they arrive there, Hansel sees no way to get across, but Gretel spies a white duck and asks it to help them cross the water. Hansel seats himself on its back and asks his sister to join him. But she knows better: this will not do. They have to cross over separately, and they do.

The children's experience at the witch's house has purged them of their 23
oral fixations; after having crossed the water, they arrive at the other shore as more mature children, ready to rely on their own intelligence and initiative to solve life's problems. As dependent children they had been a burden to their parents; on their return they have become the family's support, as they bring home the treasures they have gained. These treasures are the children's new-won independence in thought and action, a new self-reliance which is the opposite of the passive dependence which characterized them when they were deserted in the woods.

It is females—the stepmother and the witch—who are the inimical 24
forces in this story. Gretel's importance in the children's deliverance reassures

the child that a female can be a rescuer as well as a destroyer. Probably even more important is the fact that Hansel saves them once and then later Gretel saves them again, which suggests to children that as they grow up they must come to rely more and more on their age mates for mutual help and understanding. This idea reinforces the story's main thrust, which is a warning against regression, and an encouragement of growth toward a higher plane of psychological and intellectual existence.

"Hansel and Gretel" ends with the heroes returning to the home from 25
which they started, and now finding happiness there. This is psychologically correct, because a young child, driven into his adventures by oral or oedipal problems, cannot hope to find happiness outside the home. If all is to go well in his development, he must work these problems out while still dependent on his parents. Only through good relations with his parents can a child successfully mature into adolescence.

Having overcome his oedipal difficulties, mastered his oral anxieties, 26
sublimated those of his cravings which cannot be satisfied realistically, and learned that wishful thinking has to be replaced by intelligent action, the child is ready to live happily again with his parents. This is symbolized by the treasures Hansel and Gretel bring home to share with their father. Rather than expecting everything good to come from the parents, the older child needs to be able to make some contribution to the emotional well-being of himself and his family.

As "Hansel and Gretel" begins matter-of-factly with the worries of a poor 27
woodcutter's family unable to make ends meet, it ends on an equally down-to-earth level. Although the story tells that the children brought home a pile of pearls and precious stones, nothing further suggests that their economic way of life was changed. This emphasizes the symbolic nature of these jewels. The tale concludes: "Then all worries ended, and they lived together in perfect joy. My tale is ended; there runs a mouse, who catches it may make himself a big fur cap out of it." Nothing has changed by the end of "Hansel and Gretel" but inner attitudes; or, more correctly, all has changed because inner attitudes have changed. No more will the children feel pushed out, deserted, and lost in the darkness of the forest; nor will they seek for the miraculous gingerbread house. But neither will they encounter or fear the witch, since they have proved to themselves that through their combined efforts they can outsmart her and be victorious. Industry, making something good even out of unpromising material (such as by using the fur of a mouse intelligently for making a cap), is the virtue and real achievement of the school-age child who has fought through and mastered the oedipal difficulties.

"Hansel and Gretel" is one of many fairy tales where two siblings cooper- 28
ate in rescuing each other and succeed because of their combined efforts. These stories direct the child toward transcending his immature dependence on his parents and reaching the next higher stage of development: cherishing also the support of age mates. Cooperating with them in meeting life's tasks will

eventually have to replace the child's single-minded reliance on his parents only. The child of school age often cannot yet believe that he ever will be able to meet the world without his parents; that is why he wishes to hold on to them beyond the necessary point. He needs to learn to trust that someday he will master the dangers of the world, even in the exaggerated form in which his fears depict them, and be enriched by it.

29 The child views existential dangers not objectively but fantastically exaggerated in line with his immature dread—for example, personified as a child-devouring witch. "Hansel and Gretel" encourages the child to explore on his own even the figments of his anxious imagination, because such fairy tales give him confidence that he can master not only the real dangers which his parents told him about, but even those vastly exaggerated ones which he fears exist.

30 A witch as created by the child's anxious fantasies will haunt him; but a witch he can push into her own oven and burn to death is a witch the child can believe himself rid of. As long as children continue to believe in witches—they always have and always will, up to the age when they no longer are compelled to give their formless apprehensions humanlike appearance—they need to be told stories in which children, by being ingenious, rid themselves of these persecuting figures of their imagination. By succeeding in doing so, they gain immensely from the experience, as did Hansel and Gretel.

For Discussion and Writing

1. **Both Zipes and Bettelheim say things that take the form mentioned by Sontag: "X is really A, Y is really B." Locate some instances of this in each essay. Are you persuaded in all, some, or none of these instances that X really is A, and so on? What are your reasons? What qualities make such assertions acceptable or unacceptable?**
2. **Because of your previous research, you know some things about "Hansel and Gretel" that Zipes and Bettelheim do not. In particular, you have access to the early version of the tale. Using this knowledge and your own good sense and critical awareness, write a critique of the interpretations of "Hansel and Gretel" by Zipes and Bettelheim. Discuss the strengths and weaknesses of each interpretation as you see them. You may also indicate which interpretation you prefer. Try to be fair, judicious, and critical. Incorporate your own interpretation of the tale in your discussion.**

   You are not being asked here to criticize Zipes and Bettelheim from the inside, knowing as much as they do about the interpretive methods they use. This is really a chance for you to express your own opinion. What do they say that makes sense to you? What do they say that seems absurd or simply wrong to you? Knowing whatever you know about life and ways of putting life into story form, discuss these two interpretations, considering what they showed you that you hadn't seen before and whether you are

persuaded by what they have shown you. Try to make your criticisms as clearly and persuasively as you can, with reasons for every judgment.

3. Looking back at "The Use of Force" or "The Kiss," write an interpretation of one of these stories. Make it as complete and satisfying as you can. To get started it may help you to reread the introduction to this section on interpretation.
4. Select another tale or children's story (don't rely on your memory; find and reread a version of your choice). Write a script or treatment for a video documentary version of the story. Use Coover's "Gingerbread House" version of "Hansel and Gretel" as a model, since its style is quite similar to that of a script for a filmed translation of the story. But add to the Coover model the part of a narrator or commentator—a Zipes or Bettelheim, or both—who interrupts the action to offer explanations or interpretations of the events.

Identifying with Texts

Let's extend our thinking about intertextuality from folk culture into popular culture. How do works of entertainment—stories represented in the popular media such as cinema, television, or journalism—function as "texts"? The interpretive acts by Zipes and Bettelheim reflect the critical attitude toward popular culture the promotion of which is one of the primary functions of schooling. The daily-life attitude to narrative is equally interpretive, but not necessarily critical, in that consumers of stories outside of school tend to *identify* with the entertainment narratives they enjoy.

Many critics contend that, precisely by virtue of this identification, entertainment texts serve an *ideological* purpose. *Ideology* is often thought of as a pejorative term alluding to "false consciousness"—thought that is merely deluded belief, unaware of the real conditions of one's life. A more neutral sense of *ideology* is equally applied, however, referring to "the set of ideas that arise from a given set of material circumstances," ideas by means of which the general public (without access to critical science) becomes conscious of its condition. This more neutral sense of the term acknowledges the fact that ideology is inescapable and irreducible, even if it is subject to analysis by critical science. The categories of ideology, that is, name the fundamental elements of individual identity: race, ethnicity, sexuality, gender, religion, class, age, nationality. Until recently the preferred ideological identity of our society was white, European, heterosexual, masculine, Protestant, bourgeois, young, and American.

What ideas do we have about these aspects of our identity? What conduct is "proper" according to one's status in each of these categories? We all have learned and internalized these codes of conduct and preferred behaviors from our experiences with our family and with our entertainment culture, long before we ever encounter the critical methods of interpretive analysis in school. Another often-misunderstood term may be used to clarify the effects of popular storytelling as a vehicle for the construction of identity: *propaganda.* The kind of propaganda we are most familiar with as such is what critics refer to as "agitational," understood as oppositional and subversive with the purpose of overthrowing the established order. Such propaganda is also used by the establishment in times of crisis to rally its citizens and distress its enemies. Another type of propaganda is equally prevalent however: the propaganda of integration (to use the terms provided by Jacques Ellul), which promotes acceptance of the status quo, conformity, passivity. Modern revolutionary societies have had to negotiate the complex shift from the agitational propaganda used to help get into power to the integrative propaganda used to stay in power. Each new administration in the American democratic system has to practice its own version of this shift from running against the bureaucracy to defending it.

In textual terms, the insight of ideological and propagandistic readings of popular entertainment is that stories play a crucial role in the symbolic life of a culture; the capacity for making meaning through the experience of reading is one way that individuals are gathered into a community. Values and beliefs in popular culture are not imposed by some external power, however, but negotiated in a kind of collective dialogue whose operations are still not fully understood. Critics have begun to recognize the positive side of entertainment by noting the way fans transform their favorite works into texts—the way *Star Trek* fans, for example, rewrite the story to suit their own interests and fantasies. It turns out that even while readers identify with their favorite stories they do not simply accept the dominant values and beliefs expressed within them. Rather, a familiarity with popular culture in general and various subcultures in particular constitutes a "language" for the individual. Citizens of a given national culture "speak" it the way they speak their native language: they may use the stories, characters, scenes, images, and songs to think more or less creatively about their own lives. In our terms we could say that the native readers fashion an intertextual consciousness out of the stories they consume.

Typical of this intertextual function of popular stories is the classic cult film *Casablanca*. *Casablanca*, based on *Everybody Comes to Rick's* (which the critic James Agee called "one of the world's worst plays"), is ranked third behind *Gone With the Wind* and *Citizen Kane* on the American Film Institute poll of the best American films of all time. Directed by Michael Curtiz and starring Humphrey Bogart and Ingrid Bergman, *Casablanca* premiered on Thanksgiving day, 1942, and went on to win Oscars for best director, best screenplay, and best picture. The following set of readings about how films in general—and *Casablanca* in particular—present scenes of instruction about values and belief, are offered as a point of departure for thinking and writing about intertextuality and ideology.

Bambi: A Boy's Story

Russell Banks

This selection introduces you to the cinema as a place in which we receive integrative propaganda about how we ought to behave or, at least, about the kind of behavior that our dominant culture deems most valuable. Russell Banks writes about Bambi *rather than about* Casablanca, *but his account of the effect on him of this simple children's story helps clarify what is at stake in more complex stories (whatever their medium). It also helps explain the pleasure derived from watching the brief cartoon* Bambi Meets Godzilla. *Russell Banks, the author of numerous books of fiction, teaches at Princeton University.*

Who can say that one and only one movie changed his life? Who can name with confidence *the* movie that accomplished so much? No, there have been many movies—or "films," as I called them in my late teens and twenties—which altered my thinking about the world and thus about myself and which, therefore, could be said, to a greater or lesser degree, to have changed my life. (Although I must say that there have not been as many movies as books that have had this effect—but that's in the nature of a more or less bookish adult life, isn't it?) 1

Even so, I am an American child of the twentieth century, so that, before books began to change my life—books, and then travel, sex, death, and divorce—which is to say, before I reached adolescence, there were surely movies to do the serious work, and in my childhood, in the absence of books, in the absence of even a merely provincial cinematic context against which I could place and measure the movie, and, going back still further, in the absence of *any* world larger than the one provided by my immediate family, in the absence, then, of church, school, community, in the absence of a conscious culture of any kind, yes, a single movie did have the capacity to alter and then shape my inner life with a power, clarity, and speed that would never be available to me again. Not in movies, anyhow, and certainly not in books. 2

I was little more than a baby at the time, but a person nonetheless; no tabula rasa, no amorphous unformed amoeba of a consciousness, but a true *person;* and I recently discovered that there was a single winter afternoon at the movies that did indeed change my life, and in such a thoroughgoing way that I am utterly unable to remember today the person I was before the moment I sat down in the Scenic Theater, the only movie house in the small mill town of Pittsfield, New Hampshire, with my younger brother Steve on one side, my cousin Neil, also younger, and Uncle Bud Eastman on the other, and the lights went out. One person—a child very much like the newborn fawn Bambi, of no particular gender, a creature whose destiny was shaped merely by his species—seems to have died that afternoon; and another—a child defined by his gender—got born. 3

The power and clarity and speed of ritual is what I'm referring to here. My secularized New England Protestant bar mitzvah. Though I had long remembered the event, the name of the movie, the circumstances surrounding my viewing, and a few vivid details, until I happened in recent months to see it again, I recalled little else of it. And exactly who I was before I first saw the movie is lost to me now, except as I'm able to observe him in another child that age or younger; and who I was afterward remains to a disturbing degree the person I am today. That's how powerful it is, or was—*Bambi,* the Disney movie version of the Felix Salten story, which I saw at the age of four. 4

How do I know this took place, this transformation? The truth is, I was taught it by a child and, in part, by another Disney movie. I have a three-year-old granddaughter, Sarah, and last summer Sarah spent a week, without her 5 parents, visiting my wife and me in our home in the Adirondack Mountains in upstate New York.

I am a relatively young grandfather, and my wife (not Sarah's grandmother) is even younger, but nevertheless we soon tired of carting this energetic, curious, but easily bored child to Santa's Workshop, Frontiertown, and the Great Escape Amusement Park. We began to look for diversions for her that were located closer to home and that we ourselves would find amusing, too. 6

There is very little television programming for children her age, especially way up in the north country, where the only channel we receive, and receive badly at that, is the NBC affiliate from Plattsburgh. We tuned in, but most of the children's shows seemed alternately hysterical and simple-minded. Sarah was neither, and we liked her that way, as did she. 7

But she seemed too young for movies—she was barely three, and too sidereal and digressive in her perceptions of time to care for plot, too curious about background to bother distinguishing it from foreground, and too far outside the economy to have her fantasy life targeted for colonization by sexual imagery. She was, we thought, media innocent. Possibly media immune. 8

We concluded all this when we rented the more popular children's movies and played them for her one after the other on the VCR. She watched them, *Mary Poppins, Cinderella, Peter Pan,* even *The Wizard of Oz;* but she watched them obediently, passively, sleepily, as if narcotized by a little too much cough medicine; and reluctantly (*we* were interested, after all), we rewound the movies halfway through, with no protest from her, and returned them to the video outlet in nearby Elizabethtown. 9

Then, one evening, for the first time we ran a movie that instantly seized her attention, drew her forward in her seat and engaged her emotionally in a way that none of the others had so far. She had locked onto it like a heat-seeking missile. It was Disney's *The Little Mermaid.* Relieved, my wife and I brought in a bowl of popcorn and sat down to watch it with her, but after a few moments, to our dismay and slight embarrassment, we realized that *The Little Mermaid* was essentially a dramatized tract designed to promote the virtues and rewards of female submissiveness and silence. Not the sort of thing we wanted our granddaughter to watch while in our care. She was *not* too young, it now seemed, to have her fantasy life structured and rearranged by sexual imagery, not too young to be colonized by the masters of the medium. 10

She wept when we rewound the film and removed it from the VCR. We replaced it with *Bambi,* the last of the children's films in Elizabethtown that was not science fiction or horror. My wife, born in 1950, had not seen *Bambi* since her own early childhood and remembered it no more clearly than I, although she at least knew that Bambi was a boy, which I did not. All I'd remembered of it, as I said, was that I had seen it at the Scenic in Pittsfield when I was four, with my brother and cousin and uncle. In my memory, it was a *girl's* story about a 11 fawn—Bambi is a girl's name, right?—and there was a forest fire, and Bambi's mother had died somehow. Which was sad, to be sure, but it was only one episode and not the dramatic point of the movie, and the Disney people had handled the tragedy with gentleness and tact, as I recalled. The ending I remembered vaguely as uplifting. There were several memorable secondary characters, a mischievous rabbit with a foot spasm named Thumper and a winsome skunk named Flower. Nothing very promising; certainly nothing dangerous.

I did remember it as having been a visually thrilling movie, however, filled with gorgeously painted scenery—endless northern forests, fields of wildflowers, falling leaves, snow and ice, lofty mountains, and turbulent skies—lyrical pictures of a world not unlike the one that I had grown up in and that actually surrounded us now in the Adirondacks. A world I hoped to honor and celebrate with my granddaughter. 12

It opened with a trailer for *The Little Mermaid,* a preview. We winced and waited. This stuff is inescapable. Perhaps Sarah thought the trailer was the opening scene of the new movie; or the final scene of the movie we had just removed, a lingering afterimage. 13

No matter. From the first frame, *Bambi* was of an entirely different aesthetic and moral order than *The Little Mermaid.* We approved of this. We may have been forced to deprive our granddaughter of the pleasure of watching the story of Ariel, the free-swimming mermaid who surrenders her beautiful voice, becomes a bimbo in a bikini—Barbie with fins—and lands her prince, but we had given her instead the story of *Bambi,* which, from the scene unfolding behind the credits, we realized would be a story about love between mother and child, with possibly an early Green theme tossed in—the enemy, the outsider, would be Man, we could see. The central image appeared to be that of the Edenic garden before the arrival of the wars between the species. Nice. We approved. And where *The Little Mermaid* had opened like Andre Agassi's wardrobe, a frantic disco-dance of primary colors, of garish neon red and orange and fluorescent green and purple, the colors and rhythms of *Bambi* were soft and muted, opening slowly like the wings of a butterfly in shades of pale green and blue-gray, shifting to rose to speckled sunlight. This was a visual lyricism we could understand and value, one we wanted to share with Sarah. 14

It's the slow dawning of a spring day in the deep forest. Behind the images, the voices of a male tenor and chorus, hymnlike, rise up singing. . . . 15

My obligations to oversee the moral education of my granddaughter met, I was free now to sit back, relax, and watch the movie for myself, and suddenly I was gone, lost inside the world of the movie, and found again inside my four-year-old self. It was a startling transformation, instantaneous and complete. I was at once and once again a country child on the cusp of boyhood, a creature just emerging from the polymorphous envelope of infancy and facing for the first time the beginnings of a terrifying, bewildering male life with others. An owl returns to his huge oak from his nighttime haunts, and flocks of 16 birds waken the rest of the world with song. The dappled forest floor fills with parents and their newborn babes—quail, mice, squirrels, rabbits—all performing their morning ablutions, breaking their fasts, when a bluebird, fluttering from tree to tree, excitedly brings the news, "It's happened! It's happened!" What's happened? we all wonder. "The prince is born!" the bird exclaims. "The prince is born!"

Everyone hurries to what can only be called an adoration scene, a crèche, practically, in the thicket, where a lovely large-eyed doe nudges her newborn fawn into view. It's straight from the New Testament. Like a benign Dr. Johnson, Friend Owl, urging reverence, explains to the excited onlookers, especially the agitated, somewhat bewildered young: "This is quite an occasion. It isn't every day a new Prince is born." 17

Indeed. And that is why this dawn is different from all other dawns. The story of stories, your own story, if you happen to have just figured out this week that you yourself are a new prince, has begun. 18

The irrepressible Thumper asks what we all want to ask but don't dare. "Whacha gonna call Him?" 19

"I think I'll call Him," says his mother, in a voice that can only come from the mouth of a madonna, " . . . Bambi." (Not Jesus, but, to these ears, almost; or, more likely, what I heard was, "I think I'll call Him . . . Russell.") 20

After we have paused and admired the mother and child, the adoration is appropriately terminated by Friend Owl, and we cut away and move through the tangled woods to a slowly rising shot of a powerful stag on a mountaintop in the distance. It's the magnificent Hartford Insurance stag in profile, silent on a peak in Darien, nobly examining the horizon. The Father. Our gaze has gone from the son to the father, from adoration of the young prince to contemplation of the old. Time and destiny have entered the story. 21

Strong stuff. At least, for me it was. In seconds, the movie had shattered my personal time, had broken it into bits and swept away all the intervening years in which I had struggled, and mostly failed, to live out the story of Bambi, returning me to the moment when the story first took me over. I suddenly remembered (oddly, remembered with my right hand, which began to move, as if holding a pencil or crayon between thumb and forefinger) how for years I had obsessively drawn that hugely antlered male deer, the old prince of the forest. Seated now on my living room sofa next to my granddaughter and wife, I reproduced the drawing invisibly in air, just as I had done over and over again when I was a boy—a single swift line that traced the outline of the noble stag, covering brown paper grocery bags with it, filling schoolbook margins and endpapers, drawing it all over my notebooks, even in wet sand at Wells Beach and in new snow in the backyard. 22

The story of Bambi, subtitled in Felix Salten's book "A Life in the Woods," is both simple and amazingly complete. From birth to death, it describes and proscribes the territory of a male life in a sequence that follows exactly the Victorian and modern middle-class view of that life properly lived. It's a 23 rigorous, wholly believable, moral story. Believable because, although it has no irony, no sly winking inside jokes between knowing adults, it has an abundance of humor. And while, as everyone knows, it has heartbreak aplenty, the movie, as few of us remember, is nonetheless not sentimental. It's downright Darwinian. *Bambi* has danger to be faced, great peril, obstacles to be overcome; and, at crucial moments, the movie shows us death. Both kinds—death that is sudden, violent, and inexplicable and death that comes late and is unavoidable, natural, necessary. It has sex, to be sure, but no Hollywood sleaze, no puritanical prurience—males and females are simply drawn to one another, where they go mad with procreative desire ("twitter-pated," Friend Owl explains) and rush off to couple with one another and quickly produce offspring, all done with pleasure, great good gusto, and not a single salacious nudge or apology. No one, after all, wears clothes in this movie. In fact, the pleasures of the body—eating, sleeping, bathing, sport, and sex—are presented as straightforwardly satisfying and natural as in *Tom Jones.*

Bambi makes all the stops on the life-circuit, and does so in a rigorously 24
structured, comprehensive, and rhythmically patterned way, as precise and inclusive as a Catholic mass or a cycle of myths. Which, of course, makes it feel universal. And from that feeling proceeds its moral imperative. *Bambi* may be agitprop, but it's agitprop of a very high order.

Not for everyone, however. Recently, a friend of mine took his son to see 25
the movie in a Manhattan theater. My friend is a large and gentle feminist of a man; his son is a bright six-year-old boy, older perhaps by several lifetimes than I was when I first saw the movie. In the scene that follows the death of Bambi's mother, when Bambi's father arrives at the thicket and, basso profundo, says to him, "Your mother can't be with you any more . . . ," my friend's son asked, "Didn't the father help the mother?" My friend had to say no. After all, the movie said no. "Then we'd better get out of here," the boy said, and they did, father and son, barely a third of the way through the movie.

On Manhattan's Upper West Side in 1990, *Bambi,* the boy's story, was not 26
their story, that's for sure. Not the way it had been mine in the middle 1940s in small-town New Hampshire. My father had a rack of antlers and was absent on a hill, too—a plumber working all week on the construction of the weather station at the top of Mount Washington, coming home only on weekends, taking up my mother's time with his needs and watching over me from a vast, powerfully masculine, fixed distance. "Were you a good boy this week? Did you do all your chores? Did you obey your mother, take care of your younger brother, learn the ways of the forest?"

There are the usual differences between the movie and the book that 27
generated it, *Bambi: A Life in the Woods,* by Felix Salten, translated in 1928 by Whittaker Chambers, of all people, with a wry foreword by John Galsworthy ("I particularly recommend it to sportsmen . . . "). The story has been simplified, streamlined, slightly sanitized. But there is, to me, an amazing and shrewd faithfulness to the overall structure of the book (everything is cyclic and occurs

in triplets—three acts, three seasonal sequences, three distinct stages of life) and to Salten's realistic description of "a life in the woods." His is not a kind and gentle woods; it's nature with fang and frost, with hunger and hardship, with violence that is natural and necessary (there are carnivores in the forest, after all) and the perverse, gratuitous violence of Man the Hunter. And although there is much in Salten's novel concerning the relations between the genders that is explicit and didactic, in Disney's movie that same material is implicit, is dramatized, and is no less thematically central or seductive for that. Quite the opposite.

At bottom, they are both, novel and movie, moral tales about the proper relations between the genders, told for boys from the Victorian male point of view. In the book, after having seen a passing pair of grown male deer for the first time, Bambi asks his mother, " 'Didn't they see us?' 28

"His mother understood what he meant and replied, 'Of course, they saw all of us.' 29

"Bambi was troubled. He felt shy about asking questions, but it was too much for him. 'Then why . . . ,' he began, and stopped. 30

"His mother helped him along. 'What is it you want to know, son?' she asked. 31

" 'Why didn't they stay with us?' 32

" 'They don't ever stay with us,' his mother answered, 'only at times.' 33

"Bambi continued, 'But why didn't they speak to us?' 34

"His mother said, 'They don't speak to us now; only at times. We have to wait till they come to us. And we have to wait for them to speak to us. They do it whenever they like.' " 35

And a little further on, his mother says, " 'If you live, my son, if you are cunning and don't run into danger, you'll be as strong and handsome as your father is sometime, and you'll have antlers like his, too.' 36

"Bambi breathed deeply. His heart swelled with joy and expectancy." 37

As did mine. Hunkered down in my seat in the darkness in the Scenic Theater, and now here, forty-six years later, in front of a TV screen in my living room, I was on both occasions located at precisely the age when a child can be most easily colonized by the gender-specific notions of his or her culture, the age when the first significant moves toward individuation are occurring at a recklessly fast rate and in the explicit terms of one's inescapable biology. 38

At that moment, at the telling of one's story, one's heart cannot help swelling with joy and expectancy. Just as, earlier, Sarah's heart, perhaps, had swelled at the telling of Ariel's story in *The Little Mermaid*. And was apparently not moved in the slightest by the telling of Bambi's and mine. For this was, as she surely knew, a boy's story, and thus was not for her, was irrelevant, if pleasantly distracting. For, after all, the birds were pretty, the thump-footed rabbit funny, the shy skunk sweet, and there was the excitement of the forest fire, the scary presence of the hunters. All that seemed more than mildly interesting to her, but in no way capable of changing her life. 39

40 She needed *The Little Mermaid* for that, I'm afraid. I have no regrets that my wife and I kept it from her, however. And though it probably would have done me in the long run no good at all, I wish that someone—my uncle Bud Eastman, maybe, or a kindly grandfather conscious of the pain, confusion, and cruelty that come as soon as a boy marches into such territory—someone, had taken a quick look at the opening scenes of *Bambi* that Saturday afternoon and had said to himself, This movie is only going to drive the kid deeper into sexual stereotyping. It's going to validate the worst attitudes of the adult world that surrounds him. It's going to speed the end of his innocence.

41 "Let's get out of here, boys," he might then have said to me and my brother Steve and cousin Neil. He'd have needed to know back then only what my friend's six-year-old son knows now. "Let's go down the street to Varney's for an ice cream soda," he might have said, "and come back next week for a Zorro double feature, or maybe for Gene Autry, the Singing Cowboy. Let's come back when they're showing a movie that *won't* change your life."

From *Play It Again, Sam*

Woody Allen

"Play It Again, Sam"—a play by Woody Allen, made into a 1972 film starring Allen and directed by Herb Ross—is a prototype for intertextual effects at all levels. It may be read as a dramatized essay on the ideological function of intertextuality both in the story of the nebbish Allan who is a fan of Bogart and in the form of the film itself, which is a kind of remake of Casablanca. *The character Allan demonstrates (no doubt in an exaggerated way for comic effect) how a fan obsessed with a particular celebrity or star icon might manipulate experience to reproduce the scenes of certain stories. For example, at the end of* Play It Again, Sam, *Allan is able to break off his affair with his best friend's wife by quoting one of the most famous speeches in* Casablanca*—the "hill of beans" speech: "I'm no good at being noble, but it doesn't take much to see that the problems of three little people don't amount to a hill of beans in this crazy world. Someday you'll understand that. Not now. Here's looking at you, kid."*

In the scene from the play excerpted here, Allan has invited Linda over for dinner while his best friend, Dick, is out of town on a business trip. During the seduction scene on the couch, Allan, who has no idea how to relate with women, gets some advice from the spirit of Bogart—or rather, from the persona of some of the characters Bogart played. (In both the play and the film, "Bogart" is visible to the audience and to Allan, but to none of the other characters—one of many devices that ensure our identification with Allan.) The interest of this scene is that it dramatizes one of the central ideas of ideological criticism—that all *popular narratives instruct the*

audience in how to behave according to their position in society (all popular works are guides to etiquette). Part of the value of looking at works from an earlier period, for our critical purposes, is that the beliefs that were taken for granted then become dated and hence more easily recognized* as *beliefs (rather than as truths) by later audiences. The racist attitudes that seemed normal to viewers of D. W. Griffith's film,* The Birth of a Nation, *are painfully obvious to viewers today. Similarly, the sexism that informs the comedy in* Play It Again, Sam, *written in 1968, (as will be perhaps even shockingly evident in this selection) is no longer considered funny. The value of such examples, however, is that they remind us that the entertainment narratives we enjoy today are as filled with the stereotypes and prejudices of our current ideology as are the works from an earlier period. Indeed,* ideology *has been defined as "that which goes without saying."

Allan. (*Pacing* R. *and* L.) Look, Let's not get carried away. I'm not an appealing guy. The thought that a girl like Linda could go for me . . . I'm kidding myself. Where the hell is she? By now she could have had her steak and been home. *(Door BUZZES.* Allan *opens it.* Linda *enters for real with bag of groceries.)*

Linda. I feel so light. That Librium is beginning to work.

Allan. *(Takes bag.)* Maybe you better not have any champagne.

Linda. *(Takes candles from bag.)* Oh, no, what the hell—if I get too out of hand you can always call the police.

Allan. *(Into kitchen with bag.)* How long did you say Dick was out of town for?

Linda. He'll be back tomorrow.

Allan. *(Enters from kitchen.)* There's a new Godard film at the Sutton . . . I thought maybe we could go—

Linda. *(Gets candlesticks from shelf above bar.)* Come on—you're kidding . . . we're all set for here. . . . Besides, it's starting to rain. Besides, I remembered that great Ida Lupino movie is on Channel Four . . . you know, where she's married and she suddenly becomes involved with her husband's best friend.

Allan. How does it end?

Linda. *(Sits on sofa, puts candles in sticks.)* She kills them and herself.

Allan. (*Crosses down to sofa* R.) Let's go out.

Linda. *(Puts candles on mantel, turns on sconce switch, then picks up pillows near fireplace.)* I want to see that Ida Lupino movie. It's a fascinating theme. You think it's possible to love two people at once?

Allan. (*To* C. *sofa.)* What do you mean?

Linda. *(Crosses in to* Allan *at sofa, puts one pillow on sofa.)* A wife, happily married, suddenly finds she loves another man . . . not that she doesn't love her husband . . . just that . . . she loves someone else . . . you think it's very possible?

Allan. Do you?

Linda. Very. Very possible and probably very common. Love is such a strange phenomenon . . . strange and exquisite. . . .

Bogart. (Appears L. C. *slot.)* Go ahead. Make your move.

Allan. Uh—

Bogart. (Crosses in to Allan *on sofa* R.) Go ahead. Take her and kiss her.

Allan. Uh—*(Paralyzed to act on this advice.)* Uh—

Linda. Is something wrong?

Bogart. Go ahead. She wants it.

Allan. Wrong? No—I—

Linda. I better begin our food.

Bogart. Go ahead. Kiss her.

Linda. Yes?

Bogart. Hurry! Before she moves out of position.

Allan. I—can't do it.

Bogart. Kiss her, kid!

Allan. I—I—can't!

Linda. I'll be right back. *(Turns and goes off to kitchen, puts other pillow on sofa.)*

Bogart. (Sits swivel.) Well, kid! You blew it.

Allan. I can't do it. She'll misunderstand it. I invite her over and I come on like a sex degenerate! How does it look? What am I, a rapist?

Bogart. You're getting carried away. You think too much. Just do it.

Allan. We're Platonic friends. I can't spoil that by suddenly coming on. She'll slap my face.

Bogart. I've had my face slapped plenty of times.

Allan. Yeah, but your glasses don't go flying across the room.

Bogart. (Rises, crosses up above R. *corner of sofa.)* You're going to disappoint her.

Linda. (Enters with two glasses of champagne.) Here we are. Start on this. *(Hands him glass, crosses below coffee table to* L. *corner of sofa.)* Hey, did you read in the papers, another Queens woman was raped?

Allan. (Practically spits up his first swallow.) Oh, really? I was nowhere near Queens! Do they know who did it?

Linda. (Sits on sofa, L. *end.)* No. They haven't a clue. He must be very clever.

Allan. (Sits R. *end of sofa.)* You've got to have something on the ball to rape so many women and get away with it. Ah-ha . . . *(He's trying to be light. He looks at* Bogart *who doesn't smile.)*

Linda. I think if anyone ever tried to rape me I'd pretend to go along with it and then right in the middle pick up the nearest heavy object and let him have it. (Bogart *and* Allan *look troubled.*) Unless, of course, I was enjoying it. (Both Men *brighten.*)

Allan. They say it's the secret desire of every woman.

Linda. Well, I guess it depends on who does the raping.

Allan. Well look, why dwell on morbid things? Odds are you'll never get raped.

Linda. Not with my luck. *(Closes her eyes happily.)* Um—I feel so light. The drink went right to my head. I'm floating.

Allan. Um. *(Agreeing.)*

Bogart. Go ahead, kiss her.

Allan. I can't.

Bogart. She's ready.

Allan. How do you know?

Bogart. Believe me. I know.

Allan. She'll pull back. I feel it.

Bogart. She's sitting and waiting. Don't screw up.

Allan. O.K.—I'm going to try. . . . But I'm gonna go slow . . . *(Begins inching into position. Very scared.)* If she jumps I'll pretend it was a joke.

Bogart. Hurry.

Allan. She better laugh. *(Just as he's about to strike, the PHONE RINGS with shattering clarity and he jumps with a near heart attack.)* Ohmigod! Didn't expect that! *(He goes to pick up phone.)* What a start. . . . *(Into phone.)* Hello? Dick? Hi . . . What? Yes . . . she is. She dropped over—very unexpectedly. I had a Polish date.—Two good friends—we're going to have one fast dinner, then right out.—Huh? Yes, I'm all right. I'm fine. Say, aren't you in Cleveland? Oh, then this call is costing you money. . . . I'll put her on. . . . *(Offers her phone.)* He wants to speak to you. From Cleveland. (Bogart *crosses above sofa.*)

Linda. *(To* Allan, *en route to phone.)* Are you upset over anything?

Allan. Oh no . . . I was just startled. . . . (Linda *sits on bench, speaks into phone.* Allan *crosses* L. *to* L. *end of sofa.*) This is ridiculous. I'm going to cause an international incident. I want her out. I can't handle this.

Linda. Hello, darling.

Allan. Hello, darling. She loves him. Why am I kidding myself?

Bogart. *(Crosses down to* L. *corner of sofa.)* Will you relax. You're as nervous as Lizabeth Scott was before I blew her brains out. All you gotta do is make your move and you're home free.

Allan. This is crazy. We'll all wind up on the front page of the *National Enquirer.*

Linda. Okay. Goodbye. I will. *(Hangs up.)* Dick sounded a little down. I think he's having some trouble in Cleveland.

Allan. How come he never takes you with him when he goes on those out-of-town trips?

Linda. (*Crosses to sofa, sits* R.) I'm afraid to fly. My analyst thinks that's an excuse. He never asks me along, though. Who knows? Maybe he's got something going on the side. *(This last said jokingly.)*

Allan. *(Sits on sofa* L. *of Linda.)* Would that bother you?

Linda. Sure. I mean not if I didn't know.

Allan. I know he'd be very hurt if you ever had a casual affair with somebody else.

Linda. I don't think I could have a casual affair.

Allan. No?

Linda. I don't take those things lightly. If I fell for another man there'd have to be something more there than a little fling. I'd have to feel something more serious, in which case my marriage would be in question. Are you shaking?

Allan. I'm chilly.

Linda. It's not very cold. I'm not the type, though. I don't think I could take the excitement involved. Anyway, I'm not glamorous enough.

Allan. Oh, you are. You're uncommonly beautiful.

Linda. When I go to a discotheque and see all those beautiful young girls I feel like life has passed me by. I should be selling chocolates at Fanny Farmer.

Allan. You're crazy! Those girls are not in your league.

Linda. Keep talking. You're saving my life. I have such an inferiority complex.

Bogart. Say, you're handling yourself very well. Now kiss her.

Allan. Please—

Bogart. You built up to it beautifully.

Allan. I just don't have the nerve.

Bogart. Tell her how beautiful she is again.

Allan. I just told her!

Bogart. Again.

Allan. Y'know, you are really one of the most beautiful girls I've ever known.

Linda. I don't know what to say to that.

Allan. I mean really beautiful—unbelievably beautiful—fantastically beautiful—

Bogart. All right already.

Linda. It's been so long since anybody said that to me.

Bogart. Now move closer to her.

Allan. How close?

Bogart. The length of your lips.

Allan. That's very close.

Bogart. Come on. Move. (Allan *does.*)

Allan. Now what?

Bogart. Tell her that she moves something in you that you can't control.

Allan. You're kidding.

Bogart. Go ahead.

Allan. From me it's corny.

Bogart. She'll love it.

Allan. It's like Fred Astaire looks great in tails, I look silly.

Bogart. Leave Fred Astaire out of this. Say something.

Allan. I love the time we've spent together.

Linda. So have I.

Allan. Was that all right?—I don't want to use your other line about moving something in me.
Bogart. You're doing fine, kid. Tell her she has the most irresistible eyes you've ever seen.
Allan. Eyes you,—you eyes—you—you have the *most* eyes of anybody . . .
Linda. Your hand is trembling.
Allan. It is?
Bogart. That's because you're near.
Allan. Pardon me?
Bogart. Tell her that!
Allan. That's because you're near.
Linda. You always know what to say, don't you?
Bogart. Tell her you've met a lot of dames but she's really something special.
Allan. That she won't believe.
Bogart. No?
Allan. I've met a lot of dames but you are really something special.
Linda. Really?
Allan. She bought it.
Bogart. Now put your right hand around her shoulder and draw her near.
Allan. I don't want to—I'm afraid.
Bogart. Go ahead. (Allan *does it.*) Now get ready for the big move and do exactly as I tell you. . . .
Linda. Well, I guess I'll start the steaks.
Allan. Linda, your eyes are like two thick steaks. *(Has summoned his courage and tries to kiss her. She bangs backwards, knocking over the standing lamp on the sofa table.)*
Linda. Allan, don't! I'll pay for the lamp.
Allan. It's all right! I think I love you!
Linda. I insist on paying for the lamp!
Allan. *(Still in a wrestle.)* Forget the lamp!
Linda. I'm so clumsy—will you take ten dollars!
Allan. *(Still going for her bobbing head.)* Forget the damn lamp! Give me five bucks, we'll call it square!
Linda. *(Disengaged, she rises and gets purse from bench.)* Allan—don't—
Allan. Don't get the wrong idea—it was a joke—I was testing you—you don't think—I meant a Platonic kiss—not a whole kiss—here—
Linda. I better go.
Allan. *(Following.)* Linda . . .
Linda. I really better go.
Allan. Linda.
Linda. Please. I'll be fine. *(Awkwardly, she goes.)*
Allan. *(Alone, frantic.)* I attacked her! What did I do? I'm a vicious jungle beast! She's going to tell Dick! She's panicky now! By the time she gets home she'll be hysterical! She'll probably go right to Police Headquarters! What

kind of idiot am I to try a fool thing like that! I'm not Bogart. I never will be Bogart. What'll I tell Dick? I'm a disgrace to my sex. I should work in an Arabian palace as a eunuch. *(BUZZ.)* There's the Vice Squad. *(Turns. Opens door.* Linda *enters.)*

Linda. Did you say you loved me? *(They kiss.)*

Allan. Play it again, Sam! *(MUSIC up.)*

CURTAIN

The Culmination of Classic Hollywood: *Casablanca*

Robert B. Ray

In this authoritative history of American cinema, Robert Ray explains how popular films, typified by* Casablanca, *respond to specific historical situations by conveying implicit instructions about the beliefs and values relevant to the given moment. Robert Ray is director of film studies at the University of Florida in Gainesville. He is also the leader of a rock band called the Vulgar Boatmen.

Casablanca's plot confronted Rick with a series of choices: Should he help Laszlo to escape and thereby forfeit his own safe neutrality? Should he keep Ilsa with him? Should he avoid the situation altogether and do nothing? In turn, the film appeared to demand that its audience decide between two sets of values, Rick's outlaw hero code and Laszlo's official morality. This dichotomy resulted from the film's sustained contrasting of the two men. 1

Appearance: As played by Paul Henreid, standing erect in a white dress suit, Victor Laszlo perfectly embodied the official hero. Indeed, Henreid's clear eyes, chiseled Roman nose, high forehead, and strong jaw (with the hint of an underbite) made Laszlo resemble George Washington, the arch-official hero of American culture. 2

If Henreid gave Laszlo a kind of classical good looks, Bogart lent Rick an irregular handsomeness, with weary, cynical eyes, a rather plain nose, and an idiosyncratic mouth. The important thing about this attractiveness was its individuality; its refusal to conform to any preconceived notions of handsomeness duplicated the character's stubborn independence. 3

Attitude toward Women: While Laszlo was married (and even more tellingly, comfortable with being so), Rick was another example of what Fiedler has called "a long line of heroes in flight from woman and home." An early scene confirmed Rick's attitude. Confronted by an ex-girlfriend trying to pin 4 him down to some commitment, he brushed her off with the casual disdain of a man interested in women only for sexual entertainment:

Yvonne: Where were you last night?
Rick: That's so long ago I don't remember.
Yvonne: Will I see you tonight?
Rick: I never make plans that far ahead.

Finally getting the message, Yvonne uttered the classic complaint of all women abandoned by an outlaw hero: "What a fool I was to fall for a man like you."

Significantly, too, Rick operated and lived above a saloon, a place which, as 5
Fiedler points out, "was for a long time felt as the anti-type of the home, a refuge for escaping males nearly as archetypal as the wilderness and the sea." Rick's bar was no different, a man's world where women were nightly bought and sold in exchange for exit visas.

Origins: With their different origins, the American Rick and the European 6
Laszlo embodied the contradictory sources of the American ideology. For while the official heroes (e.g., Jefferson, Franklin) provided continuity with the manners, learning, and sophistication of the Old World, the outlaw hero represented the instinctive repudiation of Europe and its culture.

Significantly, Rick's outlaw status depended on more than simply the 7
imagery of self-containment that surrounded him. Like Shane and the typical gunfighter, he had an ambiguous past: "Richard Blaine, American, Age 37. Cannot return to his country," Strasser read to Rick. "The reason is a little vague." Renault also showed interest:

Renault: I've often speculated on why you don't return to America. Did you abscond with the church funds? Did you run off with the Senator's wife? I'd like to think that you killed a man. It's the romantic in me.
Rick: It was a combination of all three.

The truth about Rick's past remained the undisclosed secret of *Casablan-* 8
ca; the film never revealed why Rick could not go home, as *Shane* refused to specify the exact nature of what its hero refused to discuss.

Casablanca, however, did indicate that while Laszlo was in Morocco for a specific purpose (to escape the Nazis), Rick had come for apparently no reason at all:

Renault: And what in heaven's name brought you to Casablanca?
Rick: My health. I came to Casablanca for the waters.
Renault: What waters? We're in the desert.
Rick: I was misinformed.

This denial of rational motivation represented a characteristic American ideological tendency to deny past events their capacity to control present circumstances. As an assertion, it derived from the frontier mythology of perpetual renewal which encouraged escapism. Not surprisingly, however, Rick's apparent fresh start concealed a previous disappointment. Like Jay Gatsby (another hero with mysterious origins), he was obsessed with a past that he sought simultaneously to obliterate. In maintaining this ambiguous relationship with his own history, Rick represented not only the typical frontiersman, but also America itself.

Attitudes toward Politics and Ideology: Laszlo was first and foremost a 9
public figure, driven by abstract principles at once rational and supra-individualistic. Trying to explain his character to Rick, Ilsa spoke of "knowledge and thoughts and ideals," the chief symbols of the official values. Significantly, too, Laszlo led a collective movement, the Pan-European underground. Thanking Rick at the end, he spoke of "*our* side."

Rick's pragmatic skepticism contrasted strongly with Laszlo's idealism. 1
"You are a very cynical person," Ugarte told him, and nothing Rick said disproved that characterization. "The problems of the world are not in my department," he insisted, and having heard Ilsa's moralizing about Laszlo's cause, he refused to help: "I'm not fighting for anything anymore except myself. I'm the only cause I'm interested in." With his distrust of abstract principles, Rick confirmed Tocqueville's observation that in America, "each man is narrowly shut up in himself, and from that basis makes the pretension to judge the world."

While Laszlo's absorption in political activities confirmed his official hero 1
status, Rick's evident leisure connected him further to the western hero described by Robert Warshow:

> The Westerner is *par excellence* a man of leisure. Even when he wears the badge of a marshal or, more rarely, owns a ranch, he appears to be unemployed. We see him standing at a bar, or playing poker—a game which expresses perfectly his talent for remaining relaxed in the midst of tension—or perhaps camping out on the plains on some extraordinary errand. If he does own a ranch, it is in the background; we are not actually aware that he owns anything except his horse, his guns, and the one worn suit of clothing which is likely to remain unchanged all through the movie. It comes as a surprise to see him take money from his saddlebags. As a rule we do not even know where he sleeps at night and don't think of asking. Yet it never occurs to us that he is a poor man. . . . [1]

This passage described Rick almost exactly. He owned the casino, but his work seemed limited to signing checks and vouchers, breaking up occasional fights, and refusing to drink with customers. In this context, the information that his cash reserves could withstand the café's closing for "two weeks, maybe three" *was* surprising. He seemed never to think of money.

[1] Robert Warshow, *The Immediate Experience* (New York: Atheneum, 1972).

Attitudes toward the Law: Casablanca repeatedly emphasized Rick's and Laszlo's contrasting views of the law, an issue traditionally dividing the official hero and the renegade. Rick was clearly another version of Robin Hood, operating outside a corrupt legal system in the name of some higher, private notion of justice. Like the original Robin, he made all the decisions for a loyal band of followers (Carl the waiter, Sacha the bartender, the croupier, and most important, Sam the piano player). Like Robin (or the American gunfighter variants: Jesse James, Bonnie and Clyde, John Wesley Hardin), Rick robbed from the rich to give to the poor, manipulating his own roulette wheel to provide refugees with money for exit visas. When after one instance of remarkable "luck" by one of Rick's favored, another customer asked, "Say, are you sure this place is honest?" Carl's ironic reply reaffirmed the outlaw hero's private standard: "Honest? As honest as the day is long." 12

While Rick represented an extralegal morality, Laszlo relied on a legal principle for his safety. The movie's basic premise was the neutrality of the "frontier" town Casablanca, an abstract principle that Laszlo repeatedly asserted. "You won't dare to interfere with me here," he warned Strasser. "This is still unoccupied France. Any violation would reflect on Captain Renault." 13

Having established Laszlo's dependence on the law, however, *Casablanca* used the stock western depiction of the legal system's ultimate inadequacy as a guarantor of the official hero's safety. As in most westerns, the villains in *Casablanca* could control the legal mechanism to their own advantage. "The Germans have *outlawed* miracles," Ferrari warned Laszlo, and Renault used the flimsiest legal pretext to close Rick's café: "I'm shocked! Shocked to find that gambling is going on here!" he proclaimed, pocketing his own roulette winnings. Unlike Laszlo, Rick recognized the Germans' eagerness to manipulate the law. His proposed scheme to deliver Laszlo into the Gestapo's hands offered an apparent certitude of legal proof: Laszlo would be apprehended in the act of purchasing the stolen letters of transit, thereby making himself an accessory to the German couriers' murder. 14

While Laszlo relied on the law, Rick, like all western heroes, took it into his own hands, replacing an insufficient, corrupt system with his individual standards of right and wrong. His willingness to operate outside the law preserved Laszlo, who, left to his own devices, might never have escaped Casablanca. 15

Although Rick and Laszlo clearly represented the two strains of American culture, *Casablanca* demonstrated their imbalance. For Bogart was the film's star, and no matter how badly he behaved early on, the interest center remained with him. Renault made this focus overt, describing Rick to Ilsa as "the kind of man that, well, if I were a woman, and I weren't around, I should be in love with Rick," an ironic version of Mark Twain's encomium to Tom Blankenship, the model for Huck: "He was the only really independent person—boy or man—in the community," Twain remembered in his *Autobiography,* adding in *Tom Sawyer* that all the other children "wished they dared be like him." 16

As *Casablanca*'s moral center, Laszlo was more ambiguous. While his principles were rationally acceptable, he represented too many of the things traditionally disparaged by the frontier mythology: marriage, political commitment, collective action, the denial of individualism. At moments, the movie allowed the implicit sense of Laszlo's coldness to surface in thin disguise: "We read five times that you were killed in five different places," a fellow underground fighter whispered. "As you see," Laszlo replied, seeming to acknowledge the cost of idealism to the human elements of his character, "it was true every single time." 1

In a cinematic tradition so dependent on audience identification, Laszlo's glacial perfection diminished his appeal. In contrast to Rick's emotional drunk scene, his control suggested a less passionate attachment to Ilsa. As Rick observed, she seemed mostly another "part of his work, the thing that keeps him going"—the conventional western's low estimate of married love. Rick's love, the movie assured, was the genuine article. 1

Having established Rick and Laszlo as representatives of the two divergent strains of American mythology, *Casablanca* assumed the national ideology's basic project: their reconciliation. . . . 1

Throughout this discussion of *Casablanca,* I have made deliberate references to *Huckleberry Finn.* For part of the movie's authority derived from its reworking of many of the motifs of Twain's novel, which Hemingway referred to as the source for all American literature. Indeed, *Casablanca*'s particularly close connection to *Huck Finn* was merely one instance of Classic Hollywood's characteristic, and probably unconscious, repetitions of that literature's fundamental themes. 2

Casablanca not only made Rick a reincarnation of the renegade Huck; it also imitated basic elements of Twain's plot. The opening map sequence of *Casablanca,* with its dark, moving line representing "a tortuous, roundabout refugee trail," simulated a river, in the midst of which the city of Casablanca, and Rick's café, lay like a raft. Like Huck, Rick lived on this "raft" with a black companion (Sam), and this "river" (like the Mississippi) provided an escape route from oppression. *Casablanca* divided the character of Jim, the runaway slave, into two figures: the black friend, Sam, and the white man, Laszlo, who assumed Jim's problem, the need to escape. 2

Furthermore, Rick repeated Huck's pattern of being apolitical, of trying to avoid the entire issue of helping Laszlo with its complicated issues of right and wrong. Sam, who was more like Tom Sawyer than Jim, pleaded with his boss to get away from the dilemma. Sounding like Jake Barnes in *The Sun Also Rises* proposing the trip to Spain to Bill Gorton, Sam begged, "We'll take the car and drive all night. We'll get drunk. We'll go fishin' and stay away until she's gone." 2

But Rick, like Huck, ended up helping Laszlo, almost in spite of himself. His plan, which involved deceiving Ilsa and Laszlo until the last moment, repeated the kind of elaborate trickery that Tom and Huck had inflicted on Jim. Above all, *Casablanca* reaffirmed *Huck Finn*'s assurance that the outsider's 2 freedom could survive the entanglements required by helping someone else. The movie depicted any such commitment as only temporary, an emergency measure without lasting implications. As Huck ended by "light[ing] out for the Territory," staying one step ahead of civilization, Rick told Louis, "I could use a trip," and set out for the mysterious "Free French garrison over at Brazzaville," a phrase whose exotic, Foreign Legion remoteness effectively converted French North Africa into another frontier.

Casablanca's ending was crucial to the success of the film's ideological project: the avoidance of choice between autonomy and commitment. Rick's intervention assumed the typical western form, the gunfight, as he outdrew the German officer trying to prevent Laszlo's escape. But as in all westerns, the crucial issue in *Casablanca* turned on the woman. Ingrid Bergman's well-known account of the scriptwriters' uncertainty about whether Ilsa would stay with Rick or leave with Laszlo misleadingly suggests the relative appropriateness of either conclusion. In fact, however, as a disguised western intent on demonstrating the impermanence of all interventions in society's affairs, *Casablanca* could not have conceivably allowed its outlaw hero to keep the girl. For the frontier mythology persistently portrayed the real danger to that hero's independence not as intervention for the good of others, but as marriage. *Casablanca* reassured its male audience (the source of the national anxiety regarding World War II intervention) that one could accept responsibilities without forfeiting autonomy, if one could evade the symbolic entanglements offered by the Good Good Girl. 24

The power of *Casablanca*'s ending, like *The Maltese Falcon*'s, derived from the coincidence of ideological need (to send the woman away) with official morality: in *The Maltese Falcon,* the woman had to be turned over to the police because she was the murderer; in *Casablanca,* because she had to remain with her legal husband. The striking visual resemblances between the two conclusions merely suggested the frequency with which Classic Hollywood resorted to this basic western trope. 25

In both films, the woman played the sacrificial lamb which allowed the audience to avoid choosing between the outlaw code and the official morality. Freed of Ilsa, Rick could light out for the Territory with Renault, their banter encouraging the film's audience to consider such temporary commitments as fun. . . . 26

For Discussion and Writing

1. **Watch the films *Play It Again, Sam* and *Casablanca* and analyze them using the terms provided by Gerard Genette. Genette supplied some terms, that is, to describe the palimpsest-like or intertextual relationship that exists between the Curtiz and Allen films. The source film in Genette's terms is called the "hypotext," and the receiving film is called the "hypertext" (although the latter term is less specific now that it is associated with**

multilinked interactive works for the computer). As Genette has shown at length in his scholarly study *Palimpsestes,* the use of an earlier work as the basis for generating one's own new work is an ancient tradition, with its most famous modern example being James Joyce's rewriting of Homer's *Odyssey* in a novel called *Ulysses.* In your analysis, decide exactly how Woody Allen made use of the source material.

2. Umberto Eco used *Casablanca* as the prototype for defining the formal characteristics of a classic cult film. His argument is worth quoting at some length, since it shows the intertextual nature of the experience of fandom.

> In order to transform a work into a cult object, one must be able to break, dislocate, unhinge it so that one can remember only parts of it, irrespective of their original relationship with the whole. In the case of a book one can unhinge it, so to speak, physically, reducing it to a series of excerpts. A movie, on the contrary, must be already ramshackle, rickety, unhinged in itself. A perfect movie, since it cannot be reread every time we want, from the point we choose, as happens with a book, remains in our memory as a whole, in the form of a central idea or emotion; only an unhinged movie survives as a disconnected series of images, of peaks, of visual icebergs. It should display not one central idea but many. It should not reveal a coherent philosophy of composition. It must live on, and because of, its glorious ricketiness.[1]

This ramshackle quality of the cult film facilitates viewer identification, who recognize in certain disjointed sequences certain archetypes that have been internalized as the frames of their experience. "The term *archetype,*" Eco adds, "serves only to indicate a preestablished and frequently reappearing narrative situation, cited or in some way recycled by innumerable other texts and provoking in the addressee a sort of intense emotion accompanied by the vague feeling of a déjà vu that everybody yearns to see again." Eco notes that when he has reviewed *Casablanca* with groups assembled for the purpose of counting all such archetypes, the process takes many hours. Similarly, Ray's interpretation of the film frequently cites parallel archetypes from other classic American texts. Try this inventory process yourself, to see how many standard types and scenarios you recognize. In your inventory keep in mind Eco's distinction between "common frames" ("data-structures for representing stereotyped situations such as dining at a restaurant coded by our normal experience") and "intertextual frames" ("stereotyped situations derived from preceding textual tradition and recorded by our encyclopedia, such as the standard duel between the sheriff and the bad guy").

[1]Umberto Eco, *Travels in Hyperreality,* trans. William Weaver (San Diego: Harcourt Brace Jovanovich, 1986).

3. Use Russell Banks's essay about *Bambi* as a model for your own discussion of a favorite or significant film. Select the film in the same way that Banks does—by reflecting a bit, to discover a film that has most stayed in your memory. If the film is available on tape, watch it again and analyze the story as an "allegory" about the preferred values of our culture. Banks argues that *Bambi* represents an allegory about gender expectations in a certain period of our culture. *Allegory* here means that the characters are viewed as "personifications" of ideological concepts. The relations among the characters in *Play It Again, Sam* likewise represent an allegory about gender expectations. Compare the two allegories, and relate them to your own beliefs about the conduct that is proper for men and women in our society.
4. Select a celebrity figure or star whom you find interesting. Use the scene from *Play It Again, Sam* as a model for composing your own version of a scene of ideological instruction. Think of a situation that involves one of the ideological categories of identity (for example, race, class, or gender). Imagine that you are in that situation, and write a script in which the spirit of this star shows up to give you advice. In deciding what sort of advice the celebrity might give, notice that the Bogart figure in Woody Allen's film is really a composite of several of Bogart's roles, and not just an incarnation of the character of Rick from *Casablanca.*
5. Make a list of some of the best-known classic popular icons that you can think of (such as James Dean, Marilyn Monroe, and so forth). Discuss the kinds of values, beliefs, and behaviors that have come to be associated with these figures. Select one of the figures and do some background research on the ideological interpretations that might have been applied to him or her. Make a second list of contemporary or current celebrities and compare the two lists. Collectively, is the second list just an update of the first one? That is, are the values associated with the two lists similar, but with the "archetype" passing to a new carrier? Or do you notice a shift in the values, a revision that requires some new types or a modification of the classic icons? For example, compare Marilyn Monroe and Madonna in ideological terms.
6. Robert Ray argues that *Casablanca* displays a pattern that may be found in many other American films. Test his claim by applying his analysis of *Casablanca* to a current film or television show to see if the same sorts of archetypes (in Eco's terms) are present. What are the similarities? What has changed?

Chapter 4

Experiments with Texts: Fragments and Signatures

Textuality

A major theme of *Text Book* has been the interplay between the use of language in ordinary life and the practices of literacy. In the first chapter, we learned from Pratt and Labov the extent to which literature derives its structure and content from the forms and experiences of everyday life. But literacy can repay in full the debt it owes to ordinary language, as we shall see in this chapter.

The experiments to which you will be introduced in this chapter combine creative and critical writing to investigate your own experience as citizen of a specific culture and language. In some of the earlier chapters, you attempted to capture in literary forms certain life experiences, to express in language something you had already done, thought, felt, or believed. The experimental use of a text in a sense reverses the relationship between writing and knowing, in that you start out with a form and a procedure and use them to invent an idea, to produce or generate a text whose features you may not be able to predict in advance. Instead of trying to make language conform to what you already know, now you may let the form lead you, let the form tell you something or show you something about your cultural existence. In Chapter 3 you learned that literary writing can function as a kind of critical or analytical method. The transformations, adaptations, and ghost chapters introduced there took extant works of literature as their raw material. The rewriting of available works, producing new texts from old ones, is already a kind of experimentation with literature, revealing as well as does any analytical procedure how a work produces effects of meaning, emotion, or style.

Our next experiments carry this critical function of literary invention one step farther, and at the same time bring us fully into the practice of textuality in its specialized sense, summarized by the philosopher Martin Heidegger as the feeling that we do not speak language, language speaks us.

This notion of text as *productivity* rather than as representation or communication, giving full play to the generative power of language while reducing its descriptive function, was developed most extensively in France during the 1960s and 1970s. The strategy of "giving the lead to language" is as old as poetry, of course. The new element in the experiments created by two of the leaders of the French school of textuality—Roland Barthes and Jacques Derrida—is the attempt to apply this technique of creative writing to the ends of critical thinking.

The Fragment

One of Roland Barthes's principal contributions to the practice of textuality was the idea that critical and creative writing are essentially the same—that the old distinction separating fact and fiction, truth and imagination, is less important than the more general condition in which all experience (science as well as art) is equally mediated by language. To explore the consequences of this insight, Barthes developed a hybrid essay combining aspects of critical analysis and artistic expression. One of the texts resulting from this procedure is *A Lover's Discourse: Fragments.*

The poetic or artistic dimension of *Fragments* includes the telling of a love story. The story or anecdote at the heart of this text focuses on the *crisis* or *critical* moment of the love affair. While waiting for the beloved to keep their date at a café (in vain, as it turns out: the beloved stands him up), the lover reads a famous Romantic novel, *The Sorrows of Young Werther,* by Goethe. He begins to compare his own unhappy situation with the story of unrequited love recounted in the novel, which ends with the suicide of the protagonist, Werther. Attempting to free himself from the pain of rejection and jealousy, the lover-reader here decides to end the affair.

This story is never told directly in *A Lover's Discourse,* only in fragments distributed throughout the text, cast in the frame of the lover's meditations. The critical or analytical dimension of *Fragments* thus consists of Barthes casting this highly emotional experience into a collection of stereotypes and clichés that appear in all such love stories. He distances himself from the strong emotions by ordering or classifying the elements of the experience in a scientific manner. Part of his purpose is to identify those aspects of our personal, private attitudes and actions that are in fact directed by public, social, and cultural conventions and beliefs (ideology). He hopes in this way to combine in one text the effects of truth and beauty.

Barthes himself provided a set of instructions at the beginning of *Fragments* itemizing the rhetorical components of his experiment, which could be summarized as follows—as in Pratt's inventory (page 2) of the parts of a natural narrative.

A. Selecting the figures:

1. Each separate fragment ("Waiting," "The Heart," etc.) is one *figure, pose,* or *topic.* The lover's situation includes a set of poses that anyone who enters into a dating relationship is likely to employ—like the "character contests" described by Goffman (page 31), courting is a "ritual" process. With the term *pose,* Barthes alludes not only to "role playing" but also to dance figures, a standardized set of movements with which a choreographer might design a ballet.
2. A figure in the lover's discourse is recognizable to the extent that it is something clearly outlined as *memorable.* "You know you have a

figure when you can say 'That is so true: I recognize that scene of language.' "

B. Writing the figures:

1. Each figure or topic has a *title* (e.g., "Show me whom to desire," a *heading* (e.g., "induction"), and an *argument* (e.g., "The loved being is desired because another . . . "). The point of departure for a figure is always something the lover might *say,* even if only to himself or herself, perhaps only unconsciously, in that situation (hence the *discourse*). The argument is a paraphrase *describing* that saying. The figures are arranged in alphabetical order, according to the spelling of the headings (hence the translator had to retain the French—*cacher* comes before *coeur*).
2. Of the body (numbered paragraphs) the following may be observed:
   a. Only the topic headings and arguments are general. The meditations or reflections recorded within each topic will be specific to each user of the discourse, who must fill in the figure with his or her own experience (thoughts, feelings, actions) of the pose.
   b. The figures do not tell the love story, but instead record the "asides" that might accompany the story, as if one had kept a running commentary on one's experience (not in the manner of a diary, but an analysis, like the color commentary that embellishes the action of a sports broadcast).
   c. The content of the commentary in the body is drawn from a combination of three areas of reference, each acknowledged briefly in the margins:
      (1) a primary work of art (Goethe's *Sorrows of Young Werther* in this case) relevant to the concerns of the discourse.
      (2) the speaker's specialized culture (schooling, training).
      (3) the speaker's everyday-life culture—popular arts, mass-media experience, conversations with friends, and the like.

From A Lover's Discourse

Roland Barthes

Here are four complete "figures" from Barthes's text. As you read them, notice the regular structure (title, heading, argument, and body) and the irregular or flexible size and shape of the body itself. The regular structure directs and stimulates writing; the flexible body allows the writer to stop when he has nothing more to say. As you read, be thinking of how your own meditation on these figures would be different, governed by different cultural and personal experiences.

So it is a Lover who Speaks and who Says:

Waiting

attente / waiting

Tumult of anxiety provoked by waiting for the loved being, subject to trivial delays (rendezvous, letters, telephone calls, returns).

1. I am waiting for an arrival, a return, a promised sign. This can be futile, or immensely pathetic: in *Erwartung (Waiting),* a woman waits for her lover, ***Schönberg*** at night, in the forest; I am waiting for no more than a telephone call, but the anxiety is the same. Everything is solemn: I have no sense of *proportions.*

2. There is a scenography of waiting: I organize it, manipulate it, cut out a portion of time in which I shall mime the loss of the loved object and provoke all the effects of a minor mourning. This is then acted out as a play.

The setting represents the interior of a café; we have a rendezvous, I am waiting. In the Prologue, the sole actor of the play (and with reason), I discern and indicate the other's delay; this delay is as yet only a mathematical, computable entity (I look at my watch several times); the Prologue ends with a brainstorm: I decide to "take it badly," I release the anxiety of waiting. Act I now begins; it is occupied by suppositions: was there a misunderstanding as to the time, the place? I try to recall the moment when the rendezvous was made, the details which were supplied. What is to be done (anxiety of behavior)? Try another café? Telephone? But if the other comes during these absences? Not seeing me, the other might leave, etc. Act II is the act of anger; I address violent reproaches to the absent one: "All the same, he (she) could have . . . "

"He (she) knows perfectly well . . . " Oh, if she (he) could be here, so that I could reproach her (him) for not being here! In Act III, I attain to (I obtain?) anxiety in the pure state: the anxiety of abandonment; I have just shifted in a ***Winnicott*** second from absence to death; the other is as if dead: explosion of grief: I am internally *livid.* That is the play; it can be shortened by the other's arrival; if the other arrives in Act I, the greeting is calm; if the other arrives in Act II, there is a "scene"; if in Act III, there is recognition, the action of grace: I breathe deeply, like Pelléas emerging from the underground chambers and ***Pelléas*** rediscovering life, the odor of roses.

(The anxiety of waiting is not continuously violent; it has its matte moments; I am waiting, and everything around my waiting is stricken with unreality: in this café, I look at the others who come in, chat, joke, read calmly: they are not waiting.)

3. Waiting is an enchantment: I have received *orders not to move.* Waiting for a telephone call is thereby woven out of tiny unavowable interdictions *to infinity:* I forbid myself to leave the room, to go to the toilet, even to telephone (to keep the line from being busy); I suffer torments if someone else telephones me (for the same reason); I madden myself by the thought that at a certain (imminent) hour I shall have to leave, thereby running the risk of missing the healing call, the return of the Mother. All these diversions which solicit me are so many wasted moments for waiting, so many impurities of anxiety. For the anxiety of waiting, in its pure state, requires that I be sitting in a chair within reach of the telephone, without doing anything.

4. The being I am waiting for is not real. Like the mother's breast for the

Winnicott infant, "I create and re-create it over and over, starting from my capacity to love, starting from my need for it": the other comes here where I am waiting, here where I have already created him/her. And if the other does not come, I hallucinate the other: waiting is a delirium.

The telephone again: each time it rings, I snatch up the receiver, I think it will be the loved being who is calling me (since that being should call me); a little more effort and I "recognize" the other's voice, I engage in the dialogue, to the point where I lash out furiously against the importunate outsider who wakens me from my delirium. In the café, anyone who comes in, bearing the faintest resemblance, is thereupon, in a first impulse, *recognized.*

And, long after the amorous relation is allayed, I keep the habit of hallucinating the being I have loved: sometimes I am still in anxiety over a telephone call that is late, and no matter who is on the line, I imagine I recognize the voice I once loved: I am an amputee who still feels pain in his missing leg.

5. "Am I in love?—Yes, since I'm waiting." The other never waits. Sometimes I want to play the part of the one who doesn't wait; I try to busy myself elsewhere, to arrive late; but I always lose at this game: whatever I do, I find myself there, with nothing to do, punctual, even ahead of time. The lover's fatal identity is precisely: *I am the one who waits.*

(In transference, one always waits—at the doctor's, the professor's, the analyst's. Further, if I am waiting at a bank window, an airport ticket counter, I immediately establish an aggressive link with the teller, the stewardess,

---

Winnicott: *Playing and Reality.*

whose indifference unmasks and irritates my subjection; so that one might say that wherever there is waiting there is transference: I depend on a presence which is shared and requires time to be bestowed—as if it were a question of lowering my desire, lessening my need. *To make someone wait:* the constant *E.B.* prerogative of all power, "age-old pastime of humanity.")

6. A mandarin fell in love with a courtesan. "I shall be yours," she told him, "when you have spent a hundred nights waiting for me, sitting on a stool, in my garden, beneath my window." But on the ninety-ninth night, the mandarin stood up, put his stool under his arm, and went away.

The Heart

coeur / heart

This word refers to all kinds of movements and desires, but what is constant is that the heart is constituted into a gift-object—whether ignored or rejected.

1. The heart is the organ of desire (the heart swells, weakens, etc., like the sexual organs), as it is held, enchanted, within the domain of the Image-repertoire. What will the world, what will the other do with my desire? That is the anxiety in which are gathered all the heart's movements, all the heart's "problems."

2. Werther complains of Prince von X: "He esteems my mind and my talents more than this heart of mine, which yet is my one pride . . . Ah, whatever I *Werther* know, anyone may know—I alone have my heart."

You wait for me where I do not want to go: you love me where I do not exist. Or again: the world and I are not interested in the same thing; and to my misfortune, this divided thing is myself; I am not interested (Werther says) in my mind; you are not interested in my heart.

3. The heart is what I imagine I give. Each time this gift is returned to me, then it is little enough to say, with Werther, that the heart is what remains of me, once all the wit attributed to me and undesired by me is taken away: the heart is what remains *to me,* and this heart that lies heavy on my heart is heavy with the ebb which has filled it with itself (only the lover and the child have a heavy heart).

E.B.: Letter.

(X is about to leave for some weeks, and perhaps longer; at the last moment, he wants to buy a watch for his trip; the clerk simpers at him: "Would you like mine? You would have been a little boy when they cost what this one did," etc.; she doesn't know that *my heart is heavy within me.*)

Images

image / image

In the amorous realm, the most painful wounds are inflicted more often by what one sees than by what one knows.

1. ("Suddenly, coming back from the coatroom, he sees them in intimate conversation, leaning close to one another.")

The image is presented, pure and distinct as a letter: it is the letter of what pains me. Precise, complete, definitive, it leaves no room for me, down to the last finicky detail: I am excluded from it as from the primal scene, which may exist only insofar as it is framed within the contour of the keyhole. Here then, at last, is the definition of the image, of any image: that from which I am excluded. Contrary to those puzzle drawings in which the hunter is secretly figured in the confusion of the foliage, I am not in the scene: the image is without a riddle.

2. The image is peremptory, it always has the last word; no knowledge can contradict it, "arrange" it, refine it. Werther knows perfectly well that Charlotte is betrothed to Albert, and in fact only suffers vaguely from the fact; but "his whole body shudders when Albert embraces her slender waist." *I know perfectly well* that Charlotte does not belong to me, says Werther's reason, *but all the same,* Albert is stealing her from me, says the image which is before his eyes.

Werther

3. The images from which I am excluded are cruel, yet sometimes I am caught up in the image (reversal). Leaving the outdoor café where I must *leave behind* the other with friends, I *see myself* walking away alone, shoulders bowed, down the empty street. I convert my exclusion into an image. This image, in which my absence is reflected as in a mirror, is a *sad* image.

A romantic painting shows a heap of icy debris in a polar light; no man, no object inhabits this desolate space; but for this very reason, provided I am suffering an amorous sadness, this void requires that I fling myself into it; I project myself there as a tiny figure, seated on a block of ice, abandoned forever. "I'm cold," the lover says, "let's go back"; but there is no road, no way, the boat is wrecked. There is a *coldness* particular to the lover, the chilliness of the child (or of any young animal) that needs maternal warmth. ***Caspar David Friedrich***

4. What wounds me are the *forms* of the relation, its images; or rather, what others call *form* I experience as force. The image—as the example for the obsessive—is *the thing itself.* The lover is thus an artist; and his world is in fact a world reversed, since in it each image is its own end (nothing beyond the image). . . .

"How blue the sky was"

rencontre / encounter

The figure refers to the happy interval immediately following the first ravishment, before the difficulties of the amorous relationship begin.

1. Though the lover's discourse is no more than a dust of figures stirring according to an unpredictable order, like a fly buzzing in a room, I can assign to love, at least retrospectively, according to my Image-repertoire, a settled course: it is by means of this *historical* hallucination that I sometimes make love into a romance, an adventure. This would appear to assume three stages (or three acts): first comes the instantaneous capture (I am ravished by an image); then a series of encounters (dates, telephone calls, letters, brief trips), during which I ecstatically "explore" the perfection of the loved being, i.e., the unhoped-for correspondence between an object and my desire: this is the sweetness of the beginning, the interval proper to the idyll. This happy period acquires its identity (its limits) from its opposition (at least in memory) to the "sequel": the "sequel" is the long train of sufferings, wounds, anxieties, distresses, resentments, despairs, embarrassments, and deceptions to which I fall prey, ceaselessly living under the threat of a downfall which would envelop at once the other, myself, and the glamorous encounter that first revealed us to each other. ***Ronsard***

2. Some lovers do not commit suicide: it is possible for me to emerge from that "tunnel" which follows the amorous encounter. I see daylight again, either because I manage to grant unhappy love a dialectical outcome (retain-

---

Friedrich: *The Wreck of the "Hope."*

Ronsard: *"Quand je fus pris au doux commencement*
D'une douceur si doucettement douce . . ."
When I was caught up in the sweet beginning
Of a sweetness so deliciously sweet . . . *("Doux fut le trait")*

ing the love but getting rid of the hypnosis) or because I abandon that love altogether and set out again, trying to reiterate, with others, the encounter whose dazzlement remains with me: for it is of the order of the "first pleasure" and I cannot rest until it recurs: I affirm the affirmation, I begin again, without repeating.

(The encounter is radiant; later on, in memory, the subject will telescope into one the three moments of the amorous trajectory; he will speak of "love's dazzling tunnel.")

3. In the encounter, I marvel that I have found someone who, by successive touches, each one successful, unfailing, completes the painting of my hallucination; I am like a gambler whose luck cannot fail, so that his hand unfailingly lands on the little piece which immediately completes the puzzle of his desire. This is a gradual discovery (and a kind of verification) of affinities, ***Chateaubriand*** complicities, and intimacies which I shall (I imagine) eternally sustain with the other, who is thereby becoming "my other": I am totally given over to this discovery (I tremble within it), to the point where any intense curiosity for someone encountered is more or less equivalent to love (it is certainly love which the young Moraïte feels for the traveler Chateaubriand, greedily watching his slightest gesture and following him until his departure). At every moment of the encounter, I discover in the other another myself: *You like* ***Bouvard and Pécuchet*** *this? So do I! You don't like that? Neither do I!* When Bouvard and Pécuchet meet for the first time, they marvel over the catalogue of their shared tastes: the scene, beyond all doubt, is a love scene. The Encounter casts upon the (already ravished) amorous subject the dazzlement of a supernatural stroke of luck: love belongs to the (Dionysiac) order of the Cast of the dice.

(Neither knows the other yet. Hence they must tell each other: "This is what I am." This is narrative bliss, the kind which both fulfills and delays knowledge, ***R.H.*** in a word, *restarts* it. In the amorous encounter, I keep rebounding—I am *light.*)

For Discussion and Writing

1. For each of Barthes's four figures, identify the areas of reference drawn upon by the writer. Adapting Barthes's system to our own purposes, it will be useful to classify these references into three broad categories: (1) literature, classical music, fine art; (2) popular culture, including music, proverbs or clichés, films, advertising; and (3) personal experience, including both things that have happened and things that have been said to the lover. When you understand Barthes's method you will be in a position to adapt it to your own writing. As a first step toward that

---

Chateaubriand: *Travels in Egypt, Palestine, Greece and Barbary.*
R. H.: Conversation.

understanding, select one of Barthes's figures and replace its body with your own numbered paragraphs. Begin by jotting down notes from your own cultural repertory: books, films, TV, things you have heard or said that have to do with the figure you have selected. Then, using your notes for inspiration, compose your own meditation on your chosen figure.

2. We have reprinted only four figures from the eighty in Barthes's book. Assuming that the lover's discourse Barthes describes is shared by many people in Western cultures, try to add some of the missing pieces of this scenario. Make a list of some of the other objects, events, and expressions that constitute the lover's "scenes of language." In class discussion, try to construct the argument that should go with each figure. As a group, begin to list some of the cultural items that would help you compose the bodies of these figures. You can only go so far with this as a group project, because at some point the general cultural discourse (all lovers) must be supplemented by your personal repertory of texts (your own experiences as stored in memory).

3. One way to test the validity and value of an experiment is to see if it is replicable, or if it is applicable to other problems or issues. Write a set of figures, entitled *Fragments of a Student's Discourse,* modeled after Barthes's *Fragments,* applying Barthes's form and procedure to the discourse of the student. You are to write about the conventions and stereotypes of the student experience, identifying the conventions and clichés, figures and poses, myths and expectations of the student life. Do for the student's life*style* what Barthes did for the lover's style of conduct. Use the following questions to guide your extrapolation from the lover's to the student's discourse:

   Are any of the figures used in the lover's discourse also relevant to the student's discourse? Of the ones that might be directly translatable across discourses, do they mean the same thing, or function the same way, in both contexts? Some of the figures may not be directly transferable but might have equivalents in the new setting. For example, if the heart is the organ of love sentiment, would the brain be equivalent for the student's situation? What does it mean to *be* "a brain"? Is this the same as *having* one? Can a student be too brainy? What are the sources of a student's anxiety, hope, joy, pain? What are the crucial moments or events in a student's life? Where does this scene of life and language begin? Where does it end? What objects are important to a student? What words, phrases, sayings, clichés preside over our lives as students? To help stimulate your thinking along these lines, we have presented a few cultural references for you to read before composing your fragments. You need neither "cover" them nor be limited by them.

References for Fragments of a Student's Discourse

The two pieces included here may be used in the same way Barthes used Goethe's novel about Werther—as the literary texts to help you identify the conventions of student life as they are represented in writing in our culture. Compare your own experience of the student life with the themes, attitudes, and events of these pieces. Identify any common figures or poses (those items about which you can say, "That's so true!"). Note also those items with which you cannot identify. In writing the *Fragments of a Student's Discourse,* your purpose is to "make a text" for yourself that articulates the central clichés our culture holds regarding "the best years of your life"—college. Part of the interest of Barthes's *Fragments* is the tension that sometimes exists between the general topic and heading and the individual experience of the pose. As you compose your student *Fragments,* you might reflect on the stereotyped notion people tend to have about the student lifestyle. By putting his figures in alphabetical order, Barthes avoids telling the story of love, but he makes this comment about that commonplace anecdote of the unhappy lover:

> every amorous episode can be, of course, endowed with a meaning: it is generated, develops, and dies; it follows a path which it is always possible to interpret according to a causality or a finality—even, if need be, which can be moralized ("I was out of my mind, I'm over it now" "Love is a trap which must be avoided from now on" etc.): this is the *love story,* subjugated to the great narrative Other, to that general opinion which disparages any excessive force and wants the subject himself to reduce the great imaginary current, the orderless, endless stream which is passing through him, to a painful, morbid crisis of which he must be cured, which he must "get over": the love story (the "episode," the "adventure") is the tribute the lover must pay to the world in order to be reconciled with it.

What is the equivalent for the student? What story must the student tell to the great moralizing Other (relatives, friends, parents, employers) in response to the question, "How are things going at school?"

Graduation

Maya Angelou

In her four volumes of autobiography, Maya Angelou (b. 1928) has written vividly of her struggles to achieve success as an actress, a dancer, a songwriter, a teacher, and a writer. An active worker in the civil rights movement in the 1960s, Angelou continues to focus much of her writing on racial issues. The following selection is from* I Know Why the Caged Bird Sings *(1969), in which she writes, "I speak to the Black experience, but I am always talking about the human condition."

The children in Stamps trembled visibly with anticipation.[1] Some adults 1
were excited too, but to be certain the whole young population had come down with graduation epidemic. Large classes were graduating from both the grammar school and the high school. Even those who were years removed from their own day of glorious release were anxious to help with preparations as a kind of dry run. The junior students who were moving into the vacating classes' chairs were tradition-bound to show their talents for leadership and management. They strutted through the school and around the campus exerting pressure on the lower grades. Their authority was so new that occasionally if they pressed a little too hard it had to be overlooked. After all, next term was coming, and it never hurt a sixth grader to have a play sister in the eighth grade, or a tenth-year student to be able to call a twelfth grader Bubba. So all was endured in a spirit of shared understanding. But the graduating classes themselves were the nobility. Like travelers with exotic destinations on their minds, the graduates were remarkably forgetful. They came to school without their books, or tablets or even pencils. Volunteers fell over themselves to secure replacements for the missing equipment. When accepted, the willing workers might or might not be thanked, and it was of no importance to the pregraduation rites. Even teachers were respectful of the now quiet and aging seniors, and tended to speak to them, if not as equals, as beings only slightly lower than themselves. After tests were returned and grades given, the student body, which acted like an extended family, knew who did well, who excelled, and what piteous ones had failed.

Unlike the white high school, Lafayette County Training School dis- 2
tinguished itself by having neither lawn, nor hedges, nor tennis court, nor climbing ivy. Its two buildings (main classrooms, the grade school and home economics) were set on a dirt hill with no fence to limit either its boundaries or those of bordering farms. There was a large expanse to the left of the school which was used alternately as a baseball diamond or basketball court. Rusty hoops on swaying poles represented the permanent recreational equip-

[1] Stamps: a town in Arkansas. [Eds.]

ment, although bats and balls could be borrowed from the P.E. teacher if the borrower was qualified and if the diamond wasn't occupied.

Over this rocky area relieved by a few shady tall persimmon trees the graduating class walked. The girls often held hands and no longer bothered to speak to the lower students. There was a sadness about them, as if this old world was not their home and they were bound for higher ground. The boys, on the other hand, had become more friendly, more outgoing. A decided change from the closed attitude they projected while studying for finals. Now they seemed not ready to give up the old school, the familiar paths and classrooms. Only a small percentage would be continuing on to college—one of the South's A & M (agricultural and mechanical) schools, which trained Negro youths to be carpenters, farmers, handymen, masons, maids, cooks and baby nurses. Their future rode heavily on their shoulders, and blinded them to the collective joy that had pervaded the lives of the boys and girls in the grammar school graduating class. 3

Parents who could afford it had ordered new shoes and ready-made clothes for themselves from Sears and Roebuck or Montgomery Ward. They also engaged the best seamstresses to make the floating graduating dresses and to cut down secondhand pants which would be pressed to a military slickness for the important event. 4

Oh, it was important, all right. Whitefolks would attend the ceremony, and two or three would speak of God and home, and the Southern way of life, and Mrs. Parsons, the principal's wife, would play the graduation march while the lower-grade graduates paraded down the aisles and took their seats below the platform. The high school seniors would wait in empty classrooms to make their dramatic entrance. 5

In the Store I was the person of the moment. The birthday girl. The center. Bailey had graduated the year before,[2] although to do so he had had to forfeit all pleasures to make up for his time lost in Baton Rouge. 6

My class was wearing butter-yellow piqué dresses, and Momma launched out on mine. She smocked the yoke into tiny crisscrossing puckers, then shirred the rest of the bodice. Her dark fingers ducked in and out of the lemony cloth as she embroidered raised daisies around the hem. Before she considered herself finished she had added a crocheted cuff on the puff sleeves, and a pointy crocheted collar. 7

I was going to be lovely. A walking model of all the various styles of fine hand sewing and it didn't worry me that I was only twelve years old and merely graduating from the eighth grade. Besides, many teachers in Arkansas Negro schools had only that diploma and were licensed to impart wisdom. 8

The days had become longer and more noticeable. The faded beige of former times had been replaced with strong and sure colors. I began to see my classmates' clothes, their skin tones, and the dust that waved off pussy 9

[2]Bailey: the brother of the author. [Eds.]

willows. Clouds that lazed across the sky were objects of great concern to me. Their shiftier shapes might have held a message that in my new happiness and with a little bit of time I'd soon decipher. During that period I looked at the arch of heaven so religiously my neck kept a steady ache. I had taken to smiling more often, and my jaws hurt from the unaccustomed activity. Between the two physical sore spots, I suppose I could have been uncomfortable, but that was not the case. As a member of the winning team (the graduating class of 1940) I had outdistanced unpleasant sensations by miles. I was headed for the freedom of open fields.

10 Youth and social approval allied themselves with me and we trammeled memories of slights and insults. The wind of our swift passage remodeled my features. Lost tears were pounded to mud and then to dust. Years of withdrawal were brushed aside and left behind, as hanging ropes of parasitic moss.

11 My work alone had awarded me a top place and I was going to be one of the first called in the graduating ceremonies. On the classroom blackboard, as well as on the bulletin board in the auditorium, there were blue stars and white stars and red stars. No absences, no tardinesses, and my academic work was among the best of the year. I could say the preamble to the Constitution even faster than Bailey. We timed ourselves often: "WethepeopleoftheUnitedStatesinordertoformamoreperfectunion . . . " I had memorized the Presidents of the United States from Washington to Roosevelt in chronological as well as alphabetical order.

12 My hair pleased me too. Gradually the black mass had lengthened and thickened, so that it kept at last to its braided pattern, and I didn't have to yank my scalp off when I tried to comb it.

13 Louise and I had rehearsed the exercises until we tired out ourselves. Henry Reed was class valedictorian. He was a small, very black boy with hooded eyes, a long, broad nose and an oddly shaped head. I had admired him for years because each term he and I vied for the best grades in our class. Most often he bested me, but instead of being disappointed I was pleased that we shared top places between us. Like many Southern Black children, he lived with his grandmother, who was as strict as Momma and as kind as she knew how to be. He was courteous, respectful and soft-spoken to elders, but on the playground he chose to play the roughest games. I admired him. Anyone, I reckoned, sufficiently afraid or sufficiently dull could be polite. But to be able to operate at a top level with both adults and children was admirable.

14 His valedictory speech was entitled "To Be or Not to Be." The rigid tenth-grade teacher had helped him write it. He'd been working on the dramatic stresses for months.

15 The weeks until graduation were filled with heady activities. A group of small children were to be presented in a play about buttercups and daisies and bunny rabbits. They could be heard throughout the building practicing

their hops and their little songs that sounded like silver bells. The older girls (nongraduates, of course) were assigned the task of making refreshments for the night's festivities. A tangy scent of ginger, cinnamon, nutmeg and chocolate wafted around the home economics building as the budding cooks made samples for themselves and their teachers.

In every corner of the workshop, axes and saws split fresh timber as the 16
woodshop boys made sets and stage scenery. Only the graduates were left out of the general bustle. We were free to sit in the library at the back of the building or look in quite detachedly, naturally, on the measures being taken for our event.

Even the minister preached on graduation the Sunday before. His sub- 17
ject was, "Let your light so shine that men will see your good works and praise your Father, Who is in Heaven." Although the sermon was purported to be addressed to us, he used the occasion to speak to backsliders, gamblers and general ne'er-do-wells. But since he had called our names at the beginning of the service we were mollified.

Among Negroes the tradition was to give presents to children going only 18
from one grade to another. How much more important this was when the person was graduating at the top of the class. Uncle Willie and Momma had sent away for a Mickey Mouse watch like Bailey's. Louise gave me four embroidered handkerchiefs. (I gave her crocheted doilies.) Mrs. Sneed, the minister's wife, made me an undershirt to wear for graduation, and nearly every customer gave me a nickel or maybe even a dime with the instruction "Keep on moving to higher ground," or some such encouragement.

Amazingly the great day finally dawned and I was out of bed before I 19
knew it. I threw open the back door to see it more clearly, but Momma said, "Sister, come away from that door and put your robe on."

I hoped the memory of that morning would never leave me. Sunlight 20
was itself young, and the day had none of the insistence maturity would bring it in a few hours. In my robe and barefoot in the backyard, under cover of going to see about my new beans, I gave myself up to the gentle warmth and thanked God that no matter what evil I had done in my life He had allowed me to live to see this day. Somewhere in my fatalism I had expected to die, accidentally, and never have the chance to walk up the stairs in the auditorium and gracefully receive my hard-earned diploma. Out of God's merciful bosom I had won reprieve.

Bailey came out in his robe and gave me a box wrapped in Christmas 21
paper. He said he had saved his money for months to pay for it. It felt like a box of chocolates, but I knew Bailey wouldn't save money to buy candy when we had all we could want under our noses.

He was as proud of the gift as I. It was a soft-leather-bound copy of a 22
collection of poems by Edgar Allan Poe, or, as Bailey and I called him, "Eap." I turned to "Annabel Lee" and we walked up and down the garden rows, the cool dirt between our toes, reciting the beautifully sad lines.

Momma made a Sunday breakfast although it was only Friday. After we finished the blessing, I opened my eyes to find the watch on my plate. It was a dream of a day. Everything went smoothly and to my credit. I didn't have to be reminded or scolded for anything. Near evening I was too jittery to attend to chores, so Bailey volunteered to do all before his bath. 23

Days before, we had made a sign for the Store, and as we turned out the lights Momma hung the cardboard over the doorknob. It read clearly: CLOSED. GRADUATION. 24

My dress fitted perfectly and everyone said that I looked like a sunbeam in it. On the hill, going toward the school, Bailey walked behind with Uncle Willie, who muttered, "Go on, Ju." He wanted him to walk ahead with us because it embarrassed him to have to walk so slowly. Bailey said he'd let the ladies walk together, and the men would bring up the rear. We all laughed, nicely. 25

Little children dashed by out of the dark like fireflies. Their crepe paper dresses and butterfly wings were not made for running and we heard more than one rip, dryly, and the regretful "uh uh" that followed. 26

The school blazed without gaiety. The windows seemed cold and unfriendly from the lower hill. A sense of ill-fated timing crept over me, and if Momma hadn't reached for my hand I would have drifted back to Bailey and Uncle Willie, and possibly beyond. She made a few slow jokes about my feet getting cold, and tugged me along to the now-strange building. 27

Around the front steps, assurance came back. There were my fellow "greats," the graduating class. Hair brushed back, legs oiled, new dresses and pressed pleats, fresh pocket handkerchiefs and little handbags, all homesewn. Oh, we were up to snuff, all right. I joined my comrades and didn't even see my family go in to find seats in the crowded auditorium. 28

The school band struck up a march and all classes filed in as had been rehearsed. We stood in front of our seats, as assigned, and on a signal from the choir director, we sat. No sooner had this been accomplished than the band started to play the national anthem. We rose again and sang the song, after which we recited the pledge of allegiance. We remained standing for a brief minute before the choir director and the principal signaled to us, rather desperately I thought, to take our seats. The command was so unusual that our carefully rehearsed and smooth-running machine was thrown off. For a full minute we fumbled for our chairs and bumped into each other awkwardly. Habits change or solidify under pressure, so in our state of nervous tension we had been ready to follow our usual assembly pattern: the American national anthem, then the pledge of allegiance, then the song every Black person I knew called the Negro National Anthem. All done in the same key, with the same passion and most often standing on the same foot. 29

Finding my seat at last, I was overcome with a presentiment of worse things to come. Something unrehearsed, unplanned, was going to happen, and we were going to be made to look bad. I distinctly remember being 30 explicit in the choice of pronoun. It was "we," the graduating class, the unit, that concerned me then.

The principal welcomed "parents and friends" and asked the Baptist minister to lead us in prayer. His invocation was brief and punchy, and for a second I thought we were getting on the high road to right action. When the principal came back to the dais, however, his voice had changed. Sounds always affected me profoundly and the principal's voice was one of my favorites. During assembly it melted and lowed weakly into the audience. It had not been in my plan to listen to him, but my curiosity was piqued and I straightened up to give him my attention. 31

He was talking about Booker T. Washington, our "late great leader," who said we can be as close as the fingers on the hand, etc. . . . Then he said a few vague things about friendship and the friendship of kindly people to those less fortunate than themselves. With that his voice nearly faded, thin, away. Like a river diminishing to a stream and then to a trickle. But he cleared his throat and said, "Our speaker tonight, who is also our friend, came from Texarkana to deliver the commencement address, but due to the irregularity of the train schedule, he's going to, as they say, 'speak and run.' " He said that we understood and wanted the man to know that we were most grateful for the time he was able to give us and then something about how we were willing always to adjust to another's program, and without more ado—"I give you Mr. Edward Donleavy." 32

Not one but two white men came through the door off-stage. The shorter one walked to the speaker's platform, and the tall one moved to the center seat and sat down. But that was our principal's seat, and already occupied. The dislodged gentleman bounced around for a long breath or two before the Baptist minister gave him his chair, then with more dignity than the situation deserved, the minister walked off the stage. 33

Donleavy looked at the audience once (on reflection, I'm sure that he wanted only to reassure himself that we were really there), adjusted his glasses and began to read from a sheaf of papers. 34

He was glad "to be here and to see the work going on just as it was in the other schools." 35

At the first "Amen" from the audience, I willed the offender to immediate death by choking on the word. But Amens and Yes, sir's began to fall around the room like rain through a ragged umbrella. 36

He told us of the wonderful changes we children in Stamps had in store. The Central School (naturally, the white school was Central) had already been granted improvements that would be in use in the fall. A well-known artist was coming from Little Rock to teach art to them. They were going to have the newest microscopes and chemistry equipment for their laboratory. Mr. Donleavy didn't leave us long in the dark over who made these improvements available to Central High. Nor were we to be ignored in the general betterment scheme he had in mind. 37

38 He said that he had pointed out to people at a very high level that one of the first-line football tacklers at Arkansas Agricultural and Mechanical College had graduated from good old Lafayette County Training School. Here fewer Amens were heard. Those few that did break through lay dully in the air with the heaviness of habit.

39 He went on to praise us. He went on to say how he had bragged that "one of the best basketball players at Fisk sank his first ball right here at Lafayette County Training School."

40 The white kids were going to have a chance to become Galileos and Madame Curies and Edisons and Gauguins, and our boys (the girls weren't even in on it) would try to be Jesse Owenses and Joe Louises.

41 Owens and the Brown Bomber were great heroes in our world, but what school official in the white-goddom of Little Rock had the right to decide that those two men must be our only heroes? Who decided that for Henry Reed to become a scientist he had to work like George Washington Carver, as a boot-black, to buy a lousy microscope? Bailey was obviously always going to be too small to be an athlete, so which concrete angel glued to what country seat had decided that if my brother wanted to become a lawyer he had to first pay penance for his skin by picking cotton and hoeing corn and studying correspondence books at night for twenty years?

42 The man's dead words fell like bricks around the auditorium and too many settled in my belly. Constrained by hard-learned manners I couldn't look behind me, but to my left and right the proud graduating class of 1940 had dropped their heads. Every girl in my row had found something new to do with her handkerchief. Some folded the tiny squares into love knots, some into triangles, but most were wadding them, then pressing them flat on their yellow laps.

43 On the dais, the ancient tragedy was being replayed. Professor Parsons sat, a sculptor's reject, rigid. His large, heavy body seemed devoid of will or willingness, and his eyes said he was no longer with us. The other teachers examined the flag (which was draped stage right) or their notes, or the windows which opened on our now-famous playing diamond.

44 Graduation, the hush-hush magic time of frills and gifts and congratulations and diplomas, was finished for me before my name was called. The accomplishment was nothing. The meticulous maps, drawn in three colors of ink, learning and spelling decasyllabic words, memorizing the whole of *The Rape of Lucrece*[3]—it was for nothing. Donleavy had exposed us.

45 We were maids and farmers, handymen and washerwomen, and anything higher that we aspired to was farcical and presumptuous.

46 Then I wished that Gabriel Prosser and Nat Turner had killed all whitefolks in their beds and that Abraham Lincoln had been assassinated

[3] *The Rape of Lucrece:* a 1,855-line narrative poem by William Shakespeare. [Eds.]

before the signing of the Emancipation Proclamation,[4] and that Harriet Tubman had been killed by that blow on her head and Christopher Columbus had drowned in the *Santa Maria.*[5]

It was awful to be a Negro and have no control over my life. It was brutal 4
to be young and already trained to sit quietly and listen to charges brought against my color with no chance of defense. We should all be dead. I thought I should like to see us all dead, one on top of the other. A pyramid of flesh with the whitefolks on the bottom, as the broad base, then the Indians with their silly tomahawks and teepees and wigwams and treaties, the Negroes with their mops and recipes and cotton sacks and spirituals sticking out of their mouths. The Dutch children should all stumble in their wooden shoes and break their necks. The French should choke to death on the Louisiana Purchase (1803) while silkworms ate all the Chinese with their stupid pigtails. As a species, we were an abomination. All of us.

Donleavy was running for election, and assured our parents that if he 4
won we could count on having the only colored paved playing field in that part of Arkansas. Also—he never looked up to acknowledge the grunts of acceptance—also, we were bound to get some new equipment for the home economics building and the workshop.

He finished, and since there was no need to give any more than the most 4
perfunctory thank-you's, he nodded to the men on the stage, and the tall white man who was never introduced joined him at the door. They left with the attitude that now they were off to something really important. (The graduation ceremonies at Lafayette County Training School had been a mere preliminary.)

The ugliness they left was palpable. An uninvited guest who wouldn't 5
leave. The choir was summoned and sang a modern arrangement of "Onward, Christian Soldiers," with new words pertaining to graduates seeking their place in the world. But it didn't work. Elouise, the daughter of the Baptist minister, recited "Invictus,"[6] and I could have cried at the impertinence of "I am the master of my fate, I am the captain of my soul."

My name had lost its ring of familiarity and I had to be nudged to go and 5
receive my diploma. All my preparations had fled. I neither marched up to the stage like a conquering Amazon, nor did I look in the audience for Bailey's nod of approval. Marguerite Johnson, I heard the name again, my honors were read, there were noises in the audience of appreciation, and I took my place on the stage as rehearsed.

I thought about colors I hated: ecru, puce, lavender, beige and black. 5

[4] Gabriel Prosser and Nat Turner: leaders of slave rebellions during the early 1800s in Virginia. [Eds.]

[5] Harriet Tubman: an escaped slave who conducted others to freedom on the Underground Railroad and worked as an abolitionist. [Eds.]

[6] "Invictus": a poem by the nineteenth-century English poet, William Ernest Henley. Its inspirational conclusion is quoted here. [Eds.]

There was shuffling and rustling around me, then Henry Reed was giving his valedictory address, "To Be or Not to Be." Hadn't he heard the whitefolks? We couldn't *be,* so the question was a waste of time. Henry's voice came out clear and strong. I feared to look at him. Hadn't he got the message? There was no "nobler in the mind" for Negroes because the world didn't think we had minds, and they let us know it. "Outrageous fortune"? Now, that was a joke. When the ceremony was over I had to tell Henry Reed some things. That is, if I still cared. Not "rub," Henry, "erase." "Ah, there's the erase." Us. 53

Henry had been a good student in elocution. His voice rose on tides of promise and fell on waves of warnings. The English teacher had helped him to create a sermon winging through Hamlet's soliloquy. To be a man, a doer, a builder, a leader, or to be a tool, an unfunny joke, a crusher of funky toadstools. I marveled that Henry could go through with the speech as if we had a choice. 54

I had been listening and silently rebutting each sentence with my eyes closed; then there was a hush, which in an audience warns that something unplanned is happening. I looked up and saw Henry Reed, the conservative, the proper, the A student, turn his back to the audience and turn to us (the proud graduating class of 1940) and sing, nearly speaking, 55

"Lift ev'ry voice and sing
Till earth and heaven ring
Ring with the harmonies of Liberty . . . "

It was the poem written by James Weldon Johnson. It was the music composed by J. Rosamond Johnson. It was the Negro National Anthem. Out of habit we were singing it.

Our mothers and fathers stood in the dark hall and joined the hymn of encouragement. A kindergarten teacher led the small children onto the stage and the buttercups and daisies and bunny rabbits marked time and tried to follow: 56

"Stony the road we trod
Bitter the chastening rod
Felt in the days when hope, unborn, had died.
Yet with a steady beat
Have not our weary feet
Come to the place for which our fathers sighed?"

Each child I knew had learned that song with his ABC's and along with "Jesus Loves Me This I Know." But I personally had never heard it before. Never heard the words, despite the thousands of times I had sung them. Never thought they had anything to do with me. 57

On the other hand, the words of Patrick Henry had made such an impression on me that I had been able to stretch myself tall and trembling 58 and say, "I know not what course others may take, but as for me, give me liberty or give me death."

And now I heard, really for the first time: 59

"We have come over a way that with tears
has been watered,
We have come, treading our path through
the blood of the slaughtered."

While echoes of the song shivered in the air, Henry Reed bowed his 60
head, said "Thank you," and returned to his place in the line. The tears that slipped down many faces were not wiped away in shame.

We were on top again. As always, again. We survived. The depths had 61
been icy and dark, but now a bright sun spoke to our souls. I was no longer simply a member of the proud graduating class of 1940; I was a proud member of the wonderful, beautiful Negro race.

Oh, Black known and unknown poets, how often have your auctioned 62
pains sustained us? Who will compute the lonely nights made less lonely by your songs, or the empty pots made less tragic by your tales?

If we were a people much given to revealing secrets, we might raise 63
monuments and sacrifice to the memories of our poets, but slavery cured us of that weakness. It may be enough, however, to have it said that we survive in exact relationship to the dedication of our poets (include preachers, musicians and blues singers).

From Of This Time, of That Place

Lionel Trilling

The second "primary reference" consists of a series of excerpts from a story published in 1943 by Lionel Trilling, a prominent professor of literature at Columbia University for many years. The excerpts dramatize the figures of the classroom and the office visit.

I

. . . He reached the campus as the hour was striking. The students were 1
hurrying to their classes. He himself was in no hurry. He stopped at his dim cubicle of an office and lit a cigarette. The prospect of facing his class had suddenly presented itself to him and his hands were cold, the lawful seizure of power he was about to make seemed momentous. Waiting did not help. He put out his cigarette, picked up a pad of theme paper and went to his classroom.

As he entered, the rattle of voices ceased and the twenty-odd freshmen settled themselves and looked at him appraisingly. Their faces seemed gross, his heart sank at their massed impassivity, but he spoke briskly. 2

"My name is Howe," he said and turned and wrote it on the blackboard. The carelessness of the scrawl confirmed his authority. He went on, "My office is 412 Slemp Hall and my office hours are Monday, Wednesday, and Friday from eleven-thirty to twelve-thirty." 3

He wrote, "M., W., F., 11:30–12:30." He said, I'll be very glad to see any of you at that time. Or if you can't come then, you can arrange with me for some other time." 4

He turned again to the blackboard and spoke over his shoulder. "The text for the course is Jarman's *Modern Plays,* revised edition. The Co-op has it in stock." He wrote the name, underlined "revised edition" and waited for it to be taken down in the new notebooks. 5

When the bent heads were raised again he began his speech of prospectus. "It is hard to explain—," he said, and paused as they composed themselves. "It is hard to explain what a course like this is intended to do. We are going to try to learn something about modern literature and something about prose composition." 6

As he spoke, his hands warmed and he was able to look directly at the class. Last year on the first day the faces had seemed just as cloddish, but as the term wore on they became gradually alive and quite likable. It did not seem possible that the same thing could happen again. 7

"I shall not lecture in this course," he continued. "Our work will be carried on by discussion and we will try to learn by an exchange of opinion. But you will soon recognize that my opinion is worth more than anyone else's here." 8

He remained grave as he said it, but two boys understood and laughed. The rest took permission from them and laughed too. All Howe's private ironies protested the vulgarity of the joke but the laughter made him feel benign and powerful. 9

When the little speech was finished, Howe picked up the pad of paper he had brought. He announced that they would write an extemporaneous theme. Its subject was traditional, "Who I am and why I came to Dwight College." By now the class was more at ease and it gave a ritualistic groan of protest. Then there was a stir as fountain-pens were brought out and the writing arms of the chairs were cleared and the paper was passed about. At last all the heads bent to work and the room became still. 10

Howe sat idly at his desk. The sun shone through the tall clumsy windows. The cool of the morning was already passing. There was a scent of autumn and of varnish, and the stillness of the room was deep and oddly touching. Now and then a student's head was raised and scratched in the old elaborate students' pantomime that calls the teacher to witness honest intellectual effort. 11

Suddenly a tall boy stood within the frame of the open door. "Is this," he said, and thrust a large nose into a college catalogue, "is this the meeting place of English 1A? The section instructed by Dr. Joseph Howe?" 12

He stood on the very sill of the door, as if refusing to enter until he was perfectly sure of all his rights. The class looked up from work, found him absurd and gave a low mocking cheer. 13

The teacher and the new student, with equal pointedness, ignored the disturbance. Howe nodded to the boy, who pushed his head forward and then jerked it back in a wide elaborate arc to clear his brow of a heavy lock of hair. He advanced into the room and halted before Howe, almost at attention. In a loud clear voice he announced, "I am Tertan, Ferdinand R., reporting at the direction of Head of Department Vincent." 14

The heraldic formality of this statement brought forth another cheer. Howe looked at the class with a sternness he could not really feel, for there was indeed something ridiculous about this boy. Under his displeased regard the rows of heads dropped to work again. Then he touched Tertan's elbow, led him up to the desk, and stood so as to shield their conversation from the class. 15

"We are writing an extemporaneous theme," he said. "The subject is, 'Who I am and why I came to Dwight College.' " 16

He stripped a few sheets from the pad and offered them to the boy. Tertan hesitated and then took the paper but he held it only tentatively. As if with the effort of making something clear, he gulped, and a slow smile fixed itself on his face. It was at once knowing and shy. 17

"Professor," he said, "to be perfectly fair to my classmates"—he made a large gesture over the room—"and to you"—he inclined his head to Howe—"this would not be for me an extemporaneous subject." 18

Howe tried to understand. "You mean you've already thought about it—you've heard we always give the same subject? That doesn't matter." 19

Again the boy ducked his head and gulped. It was the gesture of one who wishes to make a difficult explanation with perfect candor. "Sir," he said, and made the distinction with great care, "the topic I did not expect but I have given much ratiocination to the subject." 20

Howe smiled and said, "I don't think that's an unfair advantage. Just go ahead and write." 21

Tertan narrowed his eyes and glanced sidewise at Howe. His strange mouth smiled. Then in quizzical acceptance, he ducked his head, threw back the heavy dank lock, dropped into a seat with a great loose noise and began to write rapidly. 22

The room fell silent again and Howe resumed his idleness. When the bell rang, the students who had groaned when the task had been set now groaned again because they had not finished. Howe took up the papers and held the class while he made the first assignment. When he dismissed it, Tertan bore down on him, his slack mouth held ready for speech. 23

"Some professors," he said, "are pedants. They are Dryasdusts. However, 24 some professors are free souls and creative spirits. Kant, Hegel, and Nietzsche were all professors." With this pronouncement he paused. "It is my opinion," he continued, "that you occupy the second category."

Howe looked at the boy in surprise and said with good-natured irony, 25
"With Kant, Hegel, and Nietzsche?"

Not only Tertan's hand and head but his whole awkward body waved 26
away the stupidity. "It is the kind and not the quantity of the kind," he said sternly.

Rebuked, Howe said as simply and seriously as he could, "It would be 27
nice to think so." He added, "Of course I am not a professor."

This was clearly a disappointment but Tertan met it. "In the French 28
sense," he said with composure. "Generically, a teacher."

Suddenly he bowed. It was such a bow, Howe fancied, as a stage-director 29
might teach an actor playing a medieval student who takes leave of Abelard—stiff, solemn, with elbows close to the body and feet together. Then, quite as suddenly, he turned and left.

A queer fish, and as soon as Howe reached his office he sifted through 30
the batch of themes and drew out Tertan's. The boy had filled many sheets with his unformed headlong scrawl. "Who am I?" he had begun. "Here, in a mundane, not to say commercialized academe, is asked the question which from time long immemorably out of mind has accreted doubts and thoughts in the psyche of man to pester him as a nuisance. Whether in St. Augustine (or Austin as sometimes called) or Miss Bashkirtsieff or Frederic Amiel or Empedocles, or in less lights of the intellect than these, this posed question has been ineluctable."

Howe took out his pencil. He circled "academe" and wrote "vocab," in 31
the margin. He underlined "time long immemorably out of mind" and wrote "Diction!" But this seemed inadequate for what was wrong. He put down his pencil and read ahead to discover the principle of error in the theme. "Today as ever, in spite of gloomy prophets of the dismal science (economics) the question is uninvalidated. Out of the starry depths of heaven hurtles this spear of query demanding to be caught on the shield of the mind ere it pierces the skull and the limbs be unstrung."

Baffled but quite caught, Howe read on. "Materialism, by which is meant 32
the philosophic concept and not the moral idea, provides no aegis against the question which lies beyond the tangible (metaphysics). Existence without alloy is the question presented. Environment and heredity relegated aside, the rags and old clothes of practical life discarded, the name and the instrumentality of livelihood do not, as the prophets of the dismal science insist on in this connection, give solution to the interrogation which not from the professor merely but veritably from the cosmos is given. I think, therefore I am (cogito etc.) but who am I? Tertan I am, but what is Tertan? Of this time, of that place, of some parentage, what does it matter?"

Existence without alloy: the phrase established itself. Howe put aside 33
Tertan's paper and at random picked up another. "I am Arthur J. Casebeer Jr."

he read. "My father is Arthur J. Casebeer and my grandfather was Arthur J. Casebeer before him. My mother is Nina Wimble Casebeer. Both of them are college graduates and my father is in insurance. I was born in St. Louis eighteen years ago and we still make our residence there."

Arthur J. Casebeer, who knew who he was, was less interesting than 3
Tertan, but more coherent. Howe picked up Tertan's paper again. It was clear that none of the routine marginal comments, no "sent. str." or "punct." or "vocab." could cope with this torrential rhetoric. He read ahead, contenting himself with underscoring the errors against the time when he should have the necessary "conference" with Tertan. . . .

II

The question was, At whose door must the tragedy be laid? 3

All night the snow had fallen heavily and only now was abating in sparse 3
little flurries. The windows were valanced high with white. It was very quiet, something of the quiet of the world had reached the class and Howe found that everyone was glad to talk or listen. In the room there was a comfortable sense of pleasure in being human.

Casebeer believed that the blame for the tragedy rested with heredity. 3
Picking up the book he read, "The sins of the fathers are visited on their children." This opinion was received with general favor. Nevertheless Johnson ventured to say that the fault was all Pastor Manders' because the Pastor had made Mrs. Alving go back to her husband and was always hiding the truth. To this Hibbard objected with logic enough, "Well then, it was really all her husband's fault. He *did* all the bad things." De Witt, his face bright with an impatient idea, said that the fault was all society's. "By society I don't mean upper-crust society," he said. He looked around a little defiantly, taking in any members of the class who might be members of upper-crust society. "Not in that sense. I mean the social unit."

Howe nodded and said, "Yes, of course." 3

"If the society of the time had progressed far enough in science," De Witt 3
went on, "then there would be no problem for Mr. Ibsen to write about. Captain Alving plays around a little, gives way to perfectly natural biological urges, and he gets a social disease, a venereal disease. If the disease is cured, no problem. Invent salvarsan and the disease is cured. The problem of heredity disappears and li'l Oswald just doesn't get paresis. No paresis, no problem—no problem, no play."

This was carrying the ark into battle and the class looked at De Witt with 4
respectful curiosity. It was his usual way and on the whole they were sympathetic with his struggle to prove to Howe that science was better than literature. Still, there was something in his reckless manner that alienated them a little.

"Or take birth control, for instance," De Witt went on. "If Mrs. Alving had had some knowledge of contraception, she wouldn't have had to have li'l Oswald at all. No li'l Oswald, no play." 41

The class was suddenly quieter. In the back row Stettenhover swung his great football shoulders in a righteous sulking gesture, first to the right, then to the left. He puckered his mouth ostentatiously. Intellect was always ending up by talking dirty. 42

Tertan's hand went up and Howe said, "Mr. Tertan." The boy shambled to his feet and began his long characteristic gulp. Howe made a motion with his fingers, as small as possible, and Tertan ducked his head and smiled in apology. He sat down. The class laughed. With more than half the term gone, Tertan had not been able to remember that one did not rise to speak. He seemed unable to carry on the life of the intellect without this mark of respect for it. To Howe the boy's habit of rising seemed to accord with the formal shabbiness of his dress. He never wore the casual sweaters and jackets of his classmates. Into the free and comfortable air of the college classroom he brought the stuffy sordid strictness of some crowded metropolitan high school. 43

"Speaking from one sense," Tertan began slowly, "there is no blame ascribable. From the sense of determinism, who can say where the blame lies? The preordained is the preordained and it cannot be said without rebellion against the universe, a palpable absurdity." 44

In the back row Stettenhover slumped suddenly in his seat, his heels held out before him, making a loud dry disgusted sound. His body sank until his neck rested on the back of his chair. He folded his hands across his belly and looked significantly out of the window, exasperated not only with Tertan but with Howe, with the class, with the whole system designed to encourage this kind of thing. There was a certain insolence in the movement and Howe flushed. As Tertan continued to speak, Howe walked casually toward the window and placed himself in the line of Stettenhover's vision. He stared at the great fellow, who pretended not to see him. There was so much power in the big body, so much contempt in the Greek-athlete face under the crisp Greek-athlete curls, that Howe felt almost physical fear. But at last Stettenhover admitted him to focus and under his disapproving gaze sat up with slow indifference. His eyebrows raised high in resignation, he began to examine his hands. Howe relaxed and turned his attention back to Tertan. 45

"Flux of existence," Tertan was saying, "produces all things, so that judgment wavers. Beyond the phenomena, what? But phenomena are adumbrated and to them we are limited." 46

Howe saw it for a moment as perhaps it existed in the boy's mind—the world of shadows which are cast by a great light upon a hidden reality as in the old myth of the Cave. But the little brush with Stettenhover had tired him and he said irritably, "But come to the point, Mr. Tertan." 47

He said it so sharply that some of the class looked at him curiously. For three months he had gently carried Tertan through his verbosities, to the vaguely respectful surprise of the other students, who seemed to conceive that there existed between this strange classmate and their teacher some special understanding from which they were content to be excluded. Tertan looked at him mildly and at once came brilliantly to the point. "This is the summation of the play," he said and took up his book and read," 'Your poor father never found any outlet for the overmastering joy of life that was in him. And I brought no holiday into his home, either. Everything seemed to turn upon duty and I am afraid I made your poor father's home unbearable to him, Oswald.' Spoken by Mrs. Alving."

Yes, that was surely the "summation" of the play and Tertan had hit it, as he hit, deviously and eventually, the literary point of almost everything. But now, as always, he was wrapping it away from sight. "For most mortals," he said, "there are only joys of biological urgings, gross and crass, such as the sensuous Captain Alving. For certain few there are the transmutations beyond these to a contemplation of the utter whole."

Oh, the boy was mad. And suddenly the word, used in hyperbole, intended almost for the expression of exasperated admiration, became literal. Now that the word was used, it became simply apparent to Howe that Tertan was mad.

It was a monstrous word and stood like a bestial thing in the room. Yet it so completely comprehended everything that had puzzled Howe, it so arranged and explained what for three months had been perplexing him that almost at once its horror became domesticated. With this word Howe was able to understand why he had never been able to communicate to Tertan the value of a single criticism or correction of his wild, verbose themes. Their conferences had been frequent and long but had done nothing to reduce to order the splendid confusion of the boy's ideas. Yet, impossible though its expression was, Tertan's incandescent mind could always strike for a moment into some dark corner of thought.

And now it was suddenly apparent that it was not a faulty rhetoric that Howe had to contend with. With his new knowledge he looked at Tertan's face and wondered how he could have so long deceived himself. Tertan was still talking and the class had lapsed into a kind of patient unconsciousness, a coma of respect for words which, for all that most of them knew, might be profound. Almost with a suffusion of shame, Howe believed that in some dim way the class had long ago had some intimation of Tertan's madness. He reached out as decisively as he could to seize the thread of Tertan's discourse before it should be entangled further.

"Mr. Tertan says that the blame must be put upon whoever kills the joy of living in another. We have been assuming that Captain Alving was a wholly bad man, but what if we assume that he became bad only because Mrs. Alving, when they were first married, acted toward him in the prudish way she says she did?"

It was a ticklish idea to advance to freshmen and perhaps not profitable. 54
Not all of them were following.

"That would put the blame on Mrs. Alving herself, whom most of you 55
admire. And she herself seems to think so." He glanced at his watch. The hour was nearly over. "What do you think, Mr. De Witt?"

De Witt rose to the idea, wanted to know if society couldn't be blamed 56
for educating Mrs. Alving's temperament in the wrong way. Casebeer was puzzled, Stettenhover continued to look at his hands until the bell rang.

Tertan, his brows louring in thought, was making as always for a private 57
word. Howe gathered his books and papers to leave quickly. At this moment of his discovery and with the knowledge still raw, he could not engage himself with Tertan. Tertan sucked in his breath to prepare for speech and Howe made ready for the pain and confusion. But at that moment Casebeer detached himself from the group with which he had been conferring and which he seemed to represent. His constituency remained at a tactful distance. The mission involved the time of an assigned essay. Casebeer's presentation of the plea—it was based on the freshmen's heavy duties at the fraternities during Carnival Week—cut across Tertan's preparations for speech. "And so some of us fellows thought," Casebeer concluded with heavy solemnity, "that we could do a better job, give our minds to it more, if we had more time."

Tertan regarded Casebeer with mingled curiosity and revulsion. Howe 58
not only said that he would postpone the assignment but went on to talk about the Carnival and even drew the waiting constituency into the conversation. He was conscious of Tertan's stern and astonished stare, then of his sudden departure. . . .

Howe, as he lectured on the romantic poets, became conscious of 59
Blackburn emanating wrath. Blackburn did it well, did it with enormous dignity. He did not stir in his seat, he kept his eyes fixed on Howe in perfect attention, but he abstained from using his notebook, there was no mistaking what he proposed to himself as an attitude. His elbow on the writing-wing of the chair, his chin on the curled fingers of his hand, he was the embodiment of intellectual indignation. He was thinking his own thoughts, would give no public offense, yet would claim his due, was not to be intimidated. Howe knew that he would present himself at the end of the hour.

Blackburn entered the office without invitation. He did not smile, there 60
was no cajolery about him. Without invitation he sat down beside Howe's desk. He did not speak until he had taken the blue-book from his pocket. He said, "What does this mean, sir?"

It was a sound and conservative student tactic. Said in the usual way it 61
meant, "How could you have so misunderstood me?" or "What does this

mean for my future in the course?" But there were none of the humbler tones in Blackburn's way of saying it.

Howe made the established reply, "I think that's for you to tell me."

Blackburn continued icy. "I'm sure I can't, sir."

There was a silence between them. Both dropped their eyes to the blue-book on the desk. On its cover Howe had penciled: "F. This is very poor work."

Howe picked up the blue-book. There was always the possibility of injustice. The teacher may be bored by the mass of papers and not wholly attentive. A phrase, even the student's handwriting, may irritate him unreasonably. "Well," said Howe, "let's go through it."

He opened the first page. "Now here: you write, 'In *The Ancient Mariner,* Coleridge lives in and transports us to a honey-sweet world where all is rich and strange, a world of charm to which we can escape from the humdrum existence of our daily lives, the world of romance. Here, in this warm and honey-sweet land of charming dreams we can relax and enjoy ourselves.' "

Howe lowered the paper and waited with a neutral look for Blackburn to speak. Blackburn returned the look boldly, did not speak, sat stolid and lofty. At last Howe said, speaking gently, "Did you mean that, or were you just at a loss for something to say?"

"You imply that I was just 'bluffing'?" The quotation marks hung palpable in the air about the word.

"I'd like to know. I'd prefer believing that you were bluffing to believing that you really thought this."

Blackburn's eyebrows went up. From the height of a great and firm-based idea he looked at his teacher. He clasped the crags for a moment and then pounced, craftily, suavely. "Do you mean, Dr. Howe, that there aren't two opinions possible?"

It was superbly done in its air of putting all of Howe's intellectual life into the balance. Howe remained patient and simple. "Yes, many opinions are possible, but not this one. Whatever anyone believes of *The Ancient Mariner,* no one can in reason believe that it represents a—a honey-sweet world in which we can relax."

"But that is what I *feel,* sir."

This was well done too. Howe said, "Look, Mr. Blackburn. Do you really relax with hunger and thirst, the heat and the sea-serpents, the dead men with staring eyes, Life in Death and the skeletons? Come now, Mr. Blackburn."

Blackburn made no answer and Howe pressed forward. "Now you say of Wordsworth, 'Of peasant stock himself, he turned from the effete life of the salons and found in the peasant the hope of a flaming revolution which would sweep away all the old ideas. This is the subject of his best poems.' "

Beaming at his teacher with youthful eagerness, Blackburn said, "Yes, sir, a rebel, a bringer of light to suffering mankind. I see him as a kind of Prothemeus."

"A kind of what?" 76

"Prothemeus, sir." 77

"Think, Mr. Blackburn. We were talking about him only today and I 78
mentioned his name a dozen times. You don't mean Prothemeus. You mean—" Howe waited but there was no response.

"You mean Prometheus." 79

Blackburn gave no assent and Howe took the reins. "You've done a bad 80
job here, Mr. Blackburn, about as bad as could be done." He saw Blackburn stiffen and his genial face harden again. "It shows either a lack of preparation or a complete lack of understanding." He saw Blackburn's face begin to go to pieces and he stopped.

"Oh, sir," Blackburn burst out, "I've never had a mark like this before, 81
never anything below a B, never. A thing like this has never happened to me before."

It must be true, it was a statement too easily verified. Could it be that 82
other instructors accepted such flaunting nonsense? Howe wanted to end the interview. "I'll set it down to lack of preparation," he said. "I know you're busy. That's not an excuse but it's an explanation. Now suppose you really prepare and then take another quiz in two weeks. We'll forget this one and count the other."

Blackburn squirmed with pleasure and gratitude. "Thank you, sir. You're 83
really very kind, very kind."

Howe rose to conclude the visit. "All right then—in two weeks." 84

For Discussion and Writing

1. Compare these pieces with your own experience. Has schooling changed very much in the 1990s from what it was in the 1940s? What figures do you recognize? What aspects of the student's discourse do these authors ignore?

   Think about the way stereotypes function in life and the way they are used as organizing devices in literature, film, television. What *image* of teachers and students predominates in the popular media today? Can you think of any examples of times you have been treated as a "typical student" rather than as an individual?

   Has your experience of college lived up to your expectations?
2. As a group project, assemble all the figures identified in the individual papers on *Fragments of a Student's Discourse.* Distribute this composite thesaurus and use it, reversing the direction of Barthes's project, to tell the story of the "typical student." In other words, you should transform the alphabetized figures into a narrative or dramatic representation of the story you might tell in response to the question "How's school going?" or to the observation "College—the best years of your life."

The Signature

Another leader in the development of textualism is the French philosopher Jacques Derrida. Like Roland Barthes, Derrida experiments with a kind of writing that combines creativity and criticism. He no longer wants to write *about* literature but *with* literature. The reason for this approach is the textualist belief that literature cannot be fully understood by the traditional methods of interpretation, description, and analysis. For the textualist, a work of literature becomes intelligible through imitation of the work's own principle of composition—that is, the critic explains the work by using the artist's compositional technique to produce a new text. The textualist no longer tries to tell artists or students what a work of literature means, but seeks to learn from literature how to write criticism. To write as a textualist one must transfer the artist's invention strategy from fiction or poetry to criticism or theory.

To test his theory that literature functions not only as an object of study but as a source of knowledge, Derrida designed an experiment involving one of the oldest and most honored topics in the humanistic tradition—"know thyself." In previous epochs, this project had been understood as an attempt to comprehend one's identity in terms of life experience by means of introspection. In our own time, in which language has become the model for explaining everything else, Derrida proposes to investigate not so much our identity in "life" but our identity in language—the identity not of our person but of our name.

By calling his experiment the "signature," Derrida reminds us of an ancient belief in the similarity or correspondence between the world outside and the interior life of a person, between the macro and micro worlds. The link mediating nature and society, joining one's biological existence to one's cultural experience, is language, with one's proper name bridging these dimensions of reality. The experiment includes the musical sense of "signature"—the set of signs at the beginning of a staff indicating the key (and/or time) of the piece. The letters of the proper name constitute the "key" in which one's life is played out. We shall be returning to Derrida's technique of the "signature" after an excursion through the world of names. We can begin with the question asked by Shakespeare's teenage hero, Juliet.

What's in a Name

From Romeo and Juliet *(II.ii.33–61)*

William Shakespeare

The scene is set in the Italian city of Verona, four centuries ago. In a dark corner of the orchard behind the house of the Capulet family stands Romeo, young son of the Capulets' bitter enemies, the Montagues. He has just met and fallen in love with the Capulet daughter Juliet. At that moment Juliet comes to a window of the house (or out on a balcony, as it is often staged) brooding to herself about this young Montague, who has obviously caught her fancy.

This is, of course, one of the most famous love scenes in all of literature—but we ask you to read it in another way, as a scene about language: specifically, as an interrogation of the relationship between words and things. We pick up the action just as Juliet's frustration bursts out in speech. She is not aware, of course, that the person on her mind is actually lurking in her father's orchard, where he will hear every word she says.

Juliet O Romeo Romeo! wherefore art thou Romeo?
Deny thy father and refuse thy name;
Or, if thou wilt not, be but sworn my love,
And I'll no longer be a Capulet.
Romeo [aside] Shall I hear more, or shall I speak at this?
Juliet 'Tis but thy name that is my enemy.
Thou art thyself, though not a Montague.
What's Montague? It is nor hand, nor foot,
Nor arm, nor face, nor any other part
Belonging to a man. O, be some other name!
What's in a name? That which we call a rose
By any other name would smell as sweet.
So Romeo would, were he not Romeo called,
Retain that dear perfection which he owes
Without that title. Romeo, doff thy name;
And for thy name, which is no part of thee,
Take all myself
Romeo I take thee at thy word.
Call me but love, and I'll be new baptized;
Henceforth I never will be Romeo.
Juliet What man art thou that, thus bescreened in night,
So stumblest on my counsel?

Romeo By a name
I know not how to tell thee who I am.
My name, dear saint, is hateful to myself,
Because it is an enemy to thee.
Had I it written, I would tear the word.
Juliet My ears have yet not drunk a hundred words
Of thy tongue's uttering, yet I know the sound.
Art thou not Romeo, and a Montague?
Romeo Neither, fair maid, if either thee dislike.

For Discussion and Writing

1. Make a list of all the statements about names in the text. Separate them into statements about proper names (Romeo, Montague) and statements about common nouns (rose, love). First, try to put each statement into your own words. Then discuss the larger implications of each statement. What assumptions about the way names work are being made by the speaker?
2. What aspects of names and naming are causing the problems here? What can and cannot be changed with respect to names? Could we call a rose something else? Try to imagine how you might go about changing the common name for something. What about proper names? What does it mean to be "Romeo, and a Montague"?

The History of Names

The essay we excerpt here is designed to provide you with background on the subject of proper names, before you undertake some research into your own.

Names and Professions (*from* Destiny in Names)

A. A. Roback

It is well known that most of our surnames are derived from the occupation of an individual's progenitors. Thus we have Smith and Baker and Taylor and Butcher, Fisher, and Clark and all the rest. Since the decline of the guilds, and the free choice of a person's calling, it would become quite uncommon to find a man actually in the vocation designated by his surname. 1

Occasionally, especially among Jews, we might find a dynasty of cantors, musicians, who preserve the rationale of their surname (Eddie Cantor, Zimbalist, and Fiedler are several illustrations of such namings), and the Cohens, Kahns, Kohns, Kagans, Kaplans, Katzes (abbreviation of *Kohen Tzedek,* "righteous priest"), are still to be regarded, for religious purposes, priests, descended from Aaron, the first of the caste, but most of them are not aware of their function and keep assimilating their name to something in keeping with the name-patterns of the ruling culture. (Coan, Conway, Cowan, Kuhn, Coburn, Kane, etc.)

If, then, after many removes from the original bearer, we still find, as if 2
through an atavistic throwback, an individual whose name corresponds with his profession, we think of it as a curiosity. That General Marshall should have risen to the first place in the American army, which, in European countries, would earn for him the title of Chief Marshal, is certainly a notable coincidence, if destiny plays no part here. Or let us, for a moment, scan the name of the man who led all the forces against the Nazis and succeeded in squelching their power through the invasion of France. Is it not worth reflecting that this man's surname is "a hewer of iron" (*Eisenhower* is, in the original German, *Eisenhauer*)? If an honorific sobriquet were to be pondered for the purpose, in recognition of his feat, it could not be more appropriate than the name which he actually inherited. Surely it is just as fitting as the nickname Martel, i.e., "the hammer," which was given to Charles, grandfather of Charlemagne, in celebration of his victory over the Saracens. Another of our first-line generals, Van Fleet, does not seem to be quite at home, onomastically, but after all the fleet and the army are only complementary to one another.

This interlinking, or rather cross linking, is not rare with the army, air 3
force, and navy. We can cite, e.g., Bryant L. M. Boatner, commanding general of the air proving grounds, as one illustration, while his brother, H. J. Boatner, who has become a major general, is not out of place as a high land officer. In W. M. Fechteler (in German *fechten* means to fight), commander-in-chief of the Atlantic Fleet, we have another patronymic worthy of its bearer and vice versa.

All these are names with which any newspaper reader must be familiar. A 4
full list of the high ranking officers in the armed forces would, no doubt, disclose many more such coincidences.

In a sphere far removed from warfare and destruction we have a more 5
agreeable circumstance in the name of Pissarev ("writer") the famous Russian critic and that of Sir Russell Brain, probably the most eminent authority on the nervous system, and particularly the brain. Inasmuch as Brain is such an uncommon name, there must be something more than coincidence in this correspondence. In an adjacent sphere, we have the name of Freud, who tells us that because of his sex theories, his name, a contraction of *Freude,* meaning joy, was used as a taunt by his bitter opponents, associating it with

the *filles de joie,* in other words implying that his scientific profession coincided with the world's oldest profession.

For Discussion and Writing

1. Whether or not a name determines one's destiny, there is evidence that people do form an impression of someone based on that person's name. It was recently reported in the newspapers that half the businessmen on Little Tokyo Street in Los Angeles did not want it renamed after *Challenger* astronaut Ellison Onizuka (killed in the shuttle explosion). One reason for this opposition had to do with Onizuka's name. Although it is a fairly common Japanese surname, the archaic meaning of Onizuka is "place where the devil lives." More troubling are the studies that show that a student's name influences the grade a paper receives (papers signed with common, strong names receive higher marks than those signed with odd, unusual names). Anyone who has ever been teased about his or her name (and who has not at some time during childhood?) knows that we are vulnerable through our names, that our name is an important feature of our identity. Write or tell an anecdote about such teasing, either that you experienced yourself or that you witnessed.
2. You know something about names in general. What do you know about your own names—or what can you find out? Using your library's resources (where you should find information on specific proper names and family names) and calling upon older members of your family, find out what you can about the meaning and history of the names you use regularly. If your names mean something in some other language, find out about that, too. (Don't neglect nicknames and pet names.) Assemble your material so that you can present information about your names in the form of an oral or written report. And *save this material.* You will be using it more creatively later on.

The Power of Names

Here are two discussions of the power of names. The first is a brief selection from an autobiographical essay by the well-known black writer Ralph Ellison in which he reveals his full name and discusses its significance and its influence on his own life. The second is from a book on women and language by the social critic Dale Spender, who shows how the absence of names affects the place of women in history, and how titles like "Mr." and "Mrs." reveal structures of cultural power.

From Hidden Name and Complex Fate

Ralph Ellison

Let Tar Baby, that enigmatic figure from Negro folklore, stand for the world. He leans, black and gleaming, against the wall of life utterly noncommittal under our scrutiny, our questioning, starkly unmoving before our naïve attempts at intimidation. Then we touch him playfully and before we can say *Sonny Liston!* we find ourselves stuck. Our playful investigations become a labor, a fearful struggle, an *agon.* Slowly we perceive that our task is to learn the proper way of freeing ourselves to develop, in other words, technique. 1

Sensing this, we give him our sharpest attention, we question him carefully, we struggle with more subtlety; while he, in his silent way, holds on, demanding that we perceive the necessity of calling him by his true name as the price of our freedom. It is unfortunate that he has so many, many "true names"—all spelling chaos; and in order to discover even one of these we must first come into the possession of our own names. For it is through our names that we first place ourselves in the world. Our names, being the gift of others, must be made our own. 2

Once while listening to the play of a two-year-old girl who did not know she was under observation, I heard her saying over and over again, at first with questioning and then with sounds of growing satisfaction, "I am Mimi Livisay? . . . *I* am Mimi Livisay. I *am* Mimi Livisay . . . I am *Mimi* Li-vi-say! I am Mimi . . . " 3

And in deed and in fact she was—or became so soon thereafter, by working playfully to establish the unit between herself and her name. 4

For many of us this is far from easy. We must learn to wear our names within all the noise and confusion of the environment in which we find ourselves; make them the center of all of our associations with the world, with man and with nature. We must charge them with all our emotions, our hopes, hates, loves, aspirations. They must become our masks and our shields and the containers of all those values and traditions which we learn and/or imagine as being the meaning of our familial past. 5

And when we are reminded so constantly that we bear, as Negroes, names originally possessed by those who owned our enslaved grandparents, we are apt, especially if we are potential writers, to be more than ordinarily concerned with the veiled and mysterious events, the fusions of blood, the furtive couplings, the business transactions, the violations of faith and loyalty, the assaults; yes, and the unrecognized and unrecognizable loves through which our names were handed down unto us. 6

So charged with emotion does this concern become for some of us, that 7
we have, earlier, the example of the followers of Father Divine and, now, the Black Muslims, discarding their original names in rejection of the blood-stained, the brutal, the sinful images of the past. Thus they would declare new identities, would clarify a new program of intention and destroy the verbal evidence of a willed and ritualized discontinuity of blood and human intercourse.

Not all of us, actually only a few, seek to deal with our names in this 8
manner. We take what we have and make of them what we can. And there are even those who know where the old broken connections lie, who recognize their relatives across the chasm of historical denial and the artificial barriers of society, and who see themselves as bearers of many of the qualities which were admirable in the original sources of their common line (Faulkner has made much of this); and I speak here not of mere forgiveness, nor of obsequious insensitivity to the outrages symbolized by the denial and the division, but of the conscious acceptance of the harsh realities of the human condition, of the ambiguities and hypocrisies of human history as they have played themselves out in the United States.

Perhaps, taken in aggregate, these European names which (sometimes 9
with irony, sometimes with pride, but always with personal investment) represent a certain triumph of the spirit, speaking to us of those who rallied, reassembled and transformed themselves and who under dismembering pressures refused to die. "Brothers and sisters," I once heard a Negro preacher exhort, "let us make up our faces before the world, and our names shall sound throughout the land with honor! For we ourselves are our *true* names, not their epithets! So let us, I say, Make Up Our Faces and Our Minds!"

Perhaps my preacher had read T. S. Elliot, although I doubt it. And in 10
actuality, it was unnecessary that he do so, for a concern with names and naming was very much part of that special area of American culture from which I come, and it is precisely for this reason that this example should come to mind in a discussion of my own experience as a writer.

Undoubtedly, writers begin their *conditioning* as manipulators of words 11
long before they become aware of literature—certain Freudians would say at the breast. Perhaps. But if so, that is far too early to be of use at this moment. Of this, though, I am certain: that despite the misconceptions of those educators who trace the reading difficulties experienced by large numbers of Negro children in Northern schools to their Southern background, these children are, in *their* familiar South, facile manipulators of words. I know, too, that the Negro community is deadly in its ability to create nicknames and to spot all that is ludicrous in an unlikely name or that which is incongruous in conduct. Names are not qualities; nor are words, in this particular sense, actions. To assume that they are could cost one his life many times a day. Language skills depend to a large extent upon a knowledge of the details, the

manners, the objects, the folkways, the psychological patterns, of a given environment. Humor and wit depend upon much the same awareness, and so does the suggestive power of names.

"A small brown bowlegged Negro with the name 'Franklin D. Roosevelt Jones' might sound like a clown to someone who looks at him from the outside," said my friend Albert Murray, "but on the other hand he just might turn out to be a hell of a fireside operator. He might just lie back in all of that comic juxtaposition of names and manipulate you deaf, dumb and blind—and you not even suspecting it, because you're thrown out of stance by his name! There you are, so dazzled by the F.D.R. image—which you *know* you can't see—and so delighted with your own superior position that you don't realize that it's *Jones* who must be confronted." 12

Well, as you must suspect, all of this speculation on the matter of names has a purpose, and now, because it is tied up so ironically with my own experience as a writer, I must turn to my own name. 13

For in the dim beginnings, before I ever thought consciously of writing, there was my own name, and there was, doubtless, a certain magic in it. From the start I was uncomfortable with it, and in my earliest years it caused me much puzzlement. Neither could I understand what a poet was, nor why, exactly, my father had chosen to name me after one. Perhaps I could have understood it perfectly well had he named me after his own father, but that name had been given to an older brother who died and thus was out of the question. But why hadn't he named me after a hero, such as Jack Johnson, or a soldier like Colonel Charles Young, or a great seaman like Admiral Dewey, or an educator like Booker T. Washington, or a great orator and abolitionist like Frederick Douglass? Or again, why hadn't he named me (as so many Negro parents had done) after President Teddy Roosevelt? 14

Instead, he named me after someone called Ralph Waldo Emerson, and then, when I was three, he died. It was too early for me to have understood his choice, although I'm sure he must have explained it many times, and it was also too soon for me to have made the connection between my name and my father's love for reading. Much later, after I began to write and work with words, I came to suspect that he was aware of the suggestive powers of names and of the magic involved in naming. 15

I recall an odd conversation with my mother during my early teens in which she mentioned their interest in, of all things, prenatal culture! But for a long time I actually knew only that my father read a lot, and that he admired this remote Mr. Emerson, who was something called a "poet and philosopher"—so much so that he named his second son after him. 16

I knew, also, that whatever his motives, the combination of names he'd given me caused me no end of trouble from the moment when I could talk well enough to respond to the ritualized question which grownups put to very young children. Emerson's name was quite familiar to Negroes in Oklahoma during those days when World War I was brewing, and adults, 17 eager to show off their knowledge of literary figures, and obviously amused by the joke implicit in such a small brown nubbin of a boy carrying around such a heavy moniker, would invariably repeat my first two names and then to my great annoyance, they'd add "Emerson."

And I, in my confusion, would reply, "No, *no, I'm* not Emerson, he's the little boy who lives next door." Which only made them laugh all the louder. "Oh, no," they'd say, "*you're* Ralph Waldo Emerson," while I had fantasies of blue murder. 18

For a while the presence next door of my little friend, Emerson, made it unnecessary for me to puzzle too often over this peculiar adult confusion. And since there were other Negro boys named Ralph in the city, I came to suspect that there was something about the combination of names which produced their laughter. Even today I know of only one other Ralph who had as much comedy made out of his name, a campus politician and deep-voiced orator whom I knew at Tuskegee, who was called in friendly ribbing, *Ralph Waldo Emerson Edgar Allan Poe,* spelled Powe. This must have been quite a trial for him, but I had been initiated much earlier. 19

During my early school years the name continued to puzzle me, for it constantly evoked in the faces of others some secret. It was as though I possessed some treasure or some defect, which was invisible to my own eyes and ears; something which I had but did not *possess,* like a piece of property in South Carolina, which was mine but which I could not have until some future time. I recall finding, about this time, while seeking adventure in back alleys—which possess for boys a superiority over playgrounds like that which kitchen utensils possess over toys designed for infants—a large photographic lens. I remember nothing of its optical qualities, of its speed or color correction, but it gleamed with crystal mystery and it was beautiful. 20

Mounted handsomely in a tube of shiny brass, it spoke to me of distant worlds of possibility. I played with it, looking through it with squinted eyes, holding it in shafts of sunlight, and tried to use it for a magic lantern. But most of this was as unrewarding as my attempts to make the music come from a phonograph record by holding the needle in my fingers. 21

I could burn holes through newspapers with it, or I could pretend that it was a telescope, the barrel of a cannon, or the third eye of a monster—*I* being the monster—but I could do nothing at all about its proper function of making images, nothing to make it yield its secret. But I could not discard it. 22

Older boys sought to get it away from me by offering knives or tops, agate marbles or whole zoos of grass snakes and horned toads in trade, but I held on to it. No one, not even the white boys I knew, had such a lens, and it was my own good luck to have found it. Thus I would hold on to it until such time as I could acquire the parts needed to make it function. Finally I put it aside and it remained buried in my box of treasures, dusty and dull, to be lost and forgotten as I grew older and became interested in music. 23

I had reached by now the grades where it was necessary to learn 24 something about Mr. Emerson and what he had written, such as the "Concord Hymn" and the essay "Self-Reliance," and in following his advice, I reduced the "Waldo" to a simple and, I hoped, mysterious "W.," and in my own reading I avoided his works like the plague. I could no more deal with my name—I shall never really master it—than I could find a creative use for my lens. Fortunately there were other problems to occupy my mind. . . .

The Male Line (*from* Man Made Language)

Dale Spender

Studies of language have revealed that semantics is only one of the forms through which sexism operates. . . . One of the other features of English language practices which is inherently sexist is the use of names. In our society "only men have real names" in that their names are permanent and they have "accepted the permanency of their names as one of the rights of being male." . . . This has both practical and psychological ramifications for the construction—and maintenance—of male supremacy. 1

Practically it means that women's family names do not count and that there is one more device for making women invisible. Fathers pass their names on to their sons and the existence of daughters can be denied when in the absence of a male heir it is said that a family "dies out." One other direct result of this practice of only taking cognizance of the male name has been to facilitate the development of history as the story of the male line, because it becomes almost impossible to trace the ancestry of women—particularly if they do not come into the male-defined categories of importance. 2

Very little is known about women, says Virginia Woolf . . . for "the history of England is the history of the male line" . . . this point was brought home to Jill Liddington and Jill Norris . . . when they undertook to document the story of women's suffrage in Lancashire for "this vital contribution had been largely neglected by historians." . . . They had difficulty with sources and one difficulty was not one which would be encountered in tracing men . . . : 3

> Sometimes we seemed to be forever chasing down blind alleys. For instance, one of the most active women, Helen Silcock, a weavers' union leader from Wigan, seemed to disappear after 1902. We couldn't think why, until we came across a notice of 'congratulations to Miss Silcock on her marriage to Mr Fairhurst' in a little known labour journal, the *Women's Trade Union Review* . . . it was an object lesson for us in the difficulties of tracing women activists.

It is also an extremely useful device for eliminating women from history and for making it exceedingly difficult to perceive a continuum and develop a tradition.

When females have no right to "surnames," to family names of their own, the concept of women as the property of men is subtly reinforced (and this is of course assisted by the title *Mrs.*). Currently many women are changing their names and instead of taking the name of either their father or their husband they are coining new, autonomous names for themselves: for example, Cheris Kramer has become Cheris Kramarae, Julia Stanley has become Julia Penelope—there are almost countless examples of this change. A common practice has become that of taking the first name of a close female friend or relative—such as mother—as the new family name (for example, Janet Robyn, Elizabeth Sarah). When asked why she had legally dropped her surname and retained her first two given names, Margaret Sandra stated that a "surname" was intended as an indication of the "sire" and was so closely linked socially with the ownership of women that there was no "surname" that she found acceptable. 4

Although attempts have been made to trivialize these new naming activities among women, such activities are serious and they do undermine patriarchal practices. At the very least they raise consciousness about the role men's names have played in the subordination of women, and at best they confound traditional patriarchal classification schemes which have not operated in women's interest. I have been told that it makes it very difficult to "pigeon-hole" women, to "place" them, if they persist with this neurotic practice of giving themselves new names. One male stated quite sincerely that it was becoming "jolly difficult to work out whether women were married these days because of the ridiculous practice of not taking their husband's names." In order to operate in the world, however, it has *never* been necessary to know from a name whether someone is married or single, as women can testify. Men have not thought that *not* changing their name upon marriage should present difficulties to women and once more the bias of language practices is revealed. 5

But many males are confused, and not without cause. The language has helped to create the representation of females as sex objects; it has also helped to signal when a sex object is not available and is the property of another male. The patriarchal order has been maintained by such devices and when women consciously and intentionally abolish them men have reason to feel insecure; they do not however have reason to protest.... 6

For Discussion and Writing

1. **Consider any points in these two excerpts that seem to you especially interesting, surprising, or controversial. See if your classmates agree with your judgment. Try to resolve any differences.**
2. **What can you find out about the female names in your own heritage? How far back can you go beyond your mother, her mother, and so on? Do you**

have equal information about the male and female parts of your heritage? Note any interesting names from the female side of your family. Compare your findings with those of others.

3. Consider some of the aspects of naming raised by Ellison. Do you know anyone whose last name was acquired at some recent point in history (for example, through Americanization or religious conversion)? Do you know anyone descended from slaves whose name comes from the family that owned the person's ancestors? Do you know of any well-known people who have changed their names? Have you ever heard of a *nom de plume,* or pen name? How many actors and musicians use their "own" names? What is one's "own" name? Have we "problematized" for you the notion of having a name of one's own?

   If you could have any names you wanted, with no fuss, what names would you take? Why? If you decided to change your names in actuality, would there be a fuss? Who would make it? Why?

   Do you know anyone named after a famous person? If so, how has this affected his or her life? Would you like to bear a famous name? Do you believe that names are important? What's in a name?

Writing from Signatures

Let us begin with a brief discussion of the ancient practice of *blazoning.* In 1484 King Richard III of England chartered the Herald's College, whose purpose was to assign coats of arms and trace lineages. Within a century a set of rules for *blazoning* (giving a concise verbal description of a shield bearing a coat of arms) had been standardized. Aristocratic families all had a coat of arms, and the practice continues today, with coats of arms being displayed by colleges and universities, fraternal organizations and business. There are even people who will provide an "authentic" coat of arms for any of us willing to pay for such a thing.

Derrida's signature experiment is in part an adaptation to the generation (note the pun on lineage) of texts out of one's names of the techniques originally developed for representing symbolically on a shield the lineage of a family name. Some of the terms you will encounter when reading Derrida are derived from the art of heraldry. Besides the term *blazon,* Derrida also refers to the *abyss,* which means in this context the central point or heart of the shield. A coat of arms often contains at the abyss point a miniature shield representing the paternal (most important) coat of arms (or sometimes the arms of a line to which the "armiger" held a claim). The shield within a shield creates an effect of infinite regression, like that of the label on Morton salt, with the girl pictured holding a package of the salt with a label also picturing the girl holding the package, and so on. The implication of this "putting into the abyss" for the experiment is that the microcosm (in this case the name of the author) constitutes a representation of the macrocosm (the work written by the one who signs that name).

The designers of coats of arms used poetic techniques such as the pun and the rebus. The mottoes inscribed on banners draped above or below the shield, for example, frequently were based on a pun on the family name (replacing the war cries of days of old). The Seton family motto is "Set On." The Bernard family, whose shield bore the image of a bear, covered by a crest with a smaller bear, had the motto "Bear and Forbear." The Winlaw's motto is "What I Win I Keep." The best known of such mottoes is that of the Vernons—*Ver non semper viret*—which may be translated either as "The spring is not always green," or, as intended, "Vernon always flourishes."

A member of the Grafton family devised a rebus of the name, composed of a graft issuing from a *tun* (heraldic name for a beer or wine keg). Arms and crests, in other words, frequently deduce their origin from the family name in the same manner as mottoes, in which case they are called *Armes Parlantes* or Canting Heraldry. The families of Salmon, Sturgeon, Lucy, Herring, Shelley, Talbot, Wolf, Rabbitt, Falconer, and the like, bear the image of their namesake (lucies are pike, shelley is whelk-stalk, talbot is a hound). The Cardingtons bear three wool-cards, and the Harrows three harrows.

As you read the following selections from James Joyce and Jacques Derrida keep in mind that both writers alluded to the herald's system of blazoning a name as one of the models for their use of language.

Shem the Penman (*from* Finnegans Wake)

James Joyce

Everyone knows that James Joyce is a major modern writer, with a reputation for being difficult. And some people know that Finnegans Wake *is his last and most complicated text, one which he kept revising for years and years, always making it more complicated. Only those who have actually looked at it, however, also know that it is a funny book, chock full of jokes and puns. Among other things, it is also a book about names and naming, and the way we are all full of ready-made language that we apply to things and people left and write (to use a Joycean sort of pun).*

In the pages that follow we present you with three versions of a tiny excerpt from Joyce's dream-book: some scraps from the first draft, the same section from a later draft, and the same section as it appears in the published book. In this section of the book Joyce is writing about a character named Shem the Penman, who is a writer very much like himself, Shem being a version of his own first name. In short, Joyce is

playing with his signature here, and especially with the similarity of Shem and Sham. Read his work for some clues on how you might do this sort of thing yourself. And please don't be too solemn about it. Joyce is just playing with his names, playing with language, playing with himself, following a process that sociolinguists now recognize as the standard operation of nicknaming in our culture.

From the First Draft of Finnegans Wake

Shem is as short for Shemus as Jim is for Jacob. Originally of respectable connections his back life simply won't stand being written about.

* * * * * *

Cain—Ham (Shem)—Esau—Jim the Penman

---

wellknown for violent abuse of self and others.

lives in inkbottlehouse

boycotted, local publican refuse to supply books, papers, ink,
foolscap, makes his own from dried dung sweetened with spittle (ink)
writes universal history on his own body (parchment)

hospitality, all drunk & rightly indignant

1 eye halfopen, 1 arm, 42 hairs on his head, 17 on upper lip, 5 on
chin, 3 teeth, no feet, 10 thumbs, ½ a buttock, ½ & ½ a
testicle,—when is a man not a man?

a forger, can imitate all styles, some of his own.

1st copies of most original masterpieces slipped from his pen

From a Later Draft of Finnegans Wake

Shem is as short for Shemus as Jim is joky for Jacob. A few are still found who say that originally he was of respectable connections (——was among his cousins) but every honest to goodness man in the land knows that his back life will not stand being written about. Putting truth and lies together some shot may be made at how this hybrid actually looked. His bodily makeup, it seems, included 1 halfopen eye, 1 arm, 42 hairs on his crown, 18 on his upper lip, 5 on his chin, all ears, no feet, 5 thumbs, 2 fifths of a buttocks, a testicle & a half,—so that even Shem himself, when playing with words in the nursery asked his brothers & sisters the first riddle of the universe: When is a man not a man?: offering a prize of a crabapple to the winner. One said when the heavens are rocking, another said when other lips, a third said when the fair land of Poland, the next one said when those angel faces smile, still another said when the wine is in, one of the youngest said when father papered the parlour, still one said when you are old & grey & full of tears, and still another when we were boys, & another when you come down the vale, another *et enim imposuit manus episcopas fecit illum altissimis sacerdotum* & one when pigs begin to fly. All were wrong, he said. So Shem took the cake, the correct solution being, when he is a sham.

From Section I, Part vii, of **Finnegans Wake**

Shem is as short for Shemus as Jem is joky for Jacob. A few toughnecks 1
are still getatable who pretend that aboriginally he was of respectable stemming (he was an outlex between the lines of Ragonar Blaubarb and Horrild Hairwire and an inlaw to Capt. the Hon. and Rev. Mr. Bbyrdwood de Trop Blogg was among his most distant connections) but every honest to goodness man in the land of the space of today knows that his back life will not stand being written about in black and white. Putting truth and untruth together a shot may be made at what this hybrid actually was like to look at.

Shem's bodily getup, it seems, included an adze of a skull, an eight of a 2
larkseye, the whoel of a nose, one numb arm up a sleeve, fortytwo hairs off his uncrown, eighteen to his mock lip, a trio of barbels from his megageg chin (sowman's son), the wrong shoulder higher than the right, all ears, an artificial tongue with a natural curl, not a foot to stand on, a handful of thumbs, a blind stomach, a deaf heart, a loose liver, two fifths of two buttocks, one gleetsteen avoirdupoider for him, a manroot of all evil, a salmonkelt's thinskin, eelsblood in his cold toes, a bladder tristended, so much so that young Master Shemmy on his very first debouch at the very dawn of protohistory seeing himself such and such, when playing with thistlewords in their garden nursery, Griefotrofio, at Phig Streat III, Shuvlin, Old Hoeland, (would we go back there now for sounds, pillings and sense? would we now for annas and annas? Would we for fullscore eight and a liretta? for twelve blocks one bob? for four testers one groat? not for a dinar! not for jo!) dictited to of all his little brothron and sweestureens the first riddle of the universe: asking, when is a man not a man?: telling them take their time, yungfries, and wait till the tide stops (for from the first his day was a fortnight) and offering the prize of a bittersweet crab, a little present from the past, for their copper age was yet unminted, to the winner. One said when the heavens are quakers, a second said when Bohemeand lips, a third said when he, no, when hold hard a jiffy, when he is a gnawstick and detarmined to, the next one said when the angel of death kicks the bucket of life, still another said when the wine's at witsends, and still another when lovely wooman stoops to conk him, one of the littliest said me, me, Sem, when pappa papared the harbour, one of the wittiest said, when he yeat ye abblokooken and he zmear hezelf zo

zhooken, still one said when you are old I'm grey fall full wi sleep, and still another when wee deader walkner, and another when he is just only after having being semisized, another when yea, he hath no mananas, and one when dose pigs they begin now that they will flies up intil the looft. All were wrong, so Shem himself, the doctator, took the cake, the correct solution being—all give it up?—; when he is a—yours till the rending of the rocks,—Sham.

For Discussion and Writing

1. Does your family have a crest or coat of arms? How much do you know about it? How do these family coats of arms relate to the crests adopted by fraternities and sororities? corporations? Are the logos devised by businesses to represent their companies, or the emblems devised by advertisers to represent products, similar to family crests?

   Imagine that you have been knighted in recognition of your good works, and that you have permission to suggest the design of your own coat of arms. What would it look like?
2. With the three drafts of *Finnegans Wake* before us we can see the progression of the passage both at the level of style and of theme. What is the organizing idea of the piece? What is the stylistic principle? Evaluate the final draft according to the standards of writing normally applied to student essays.
3. Discuss the *Wake* in terms of the theory of nicknames found in it. Write a short self-portrait in the style of Joyce based on your experience with nicknames.

Signing (The Proper Name)

According to the French philosopher, Jacques Derrida, there are at least three ways in which an author signs a work. The first dimension or register of signing is the signature "proper"—the proper name placed on the title page identifying the source of the writing. The second register refers to what is commonly called "style"—"the inimitable idiom of an artist's work"—such that even without the availability of the proper name an experienced reader might recognize the author of a work. (This second register has been the basis for many an exam question.) There remains, however, one more way in which a piece of writing carries the mark of its owner. This third register of the signature is the most complex, involving the heraldic placement of the name in the depths of the text. At this level the writer's name is seen as the seed out of which the text has grown, by a process of metaphorical and intertextual development. Retracing this process, an interpreter can find the author's name, hidden in the depths—or, to use Derrida's word, the "abyss"—of the text.

As we learned from the reading by Roger Brown in Chapter 2, a common noun is the name of a general category—"book" for example. A proper noun, in contrast, is said to have no "meaning" in the ordinary sense of the term. It refers exclusively, picking out in the world not a category of things but a specific individual thing. All the people named "James" or "Robert" do not constitute a set or category in the way that everything named "book" does, because the shared name does not promise any other relationship among the people (other than the fact that people have names), unlike the term "book," which promises that everything by that name will possess certain qualities or attributes.

Or at least such has been the thinking about the operation of proper nouns or names until Derrida came along. Derrida asks us to reconsider the question of how names refer, that is, of the relationship between language and lived reality. We know from some of the readings in this section and from our familiarity with naming practices in non-Western societies, that in some cultures there is a looser, freer passage between common and proper nouns, between a general category and a particular individual who shares some of the qualities of that category; as in nicknames, which continue this tradition of naming a person according to personal attributes, such that the name not only identifies the person, but connotes some aspects of the person's "style."

Derrida's point of departure for reopening the study of reference is the naming process as practiced in literature. Unlike ordinary life in our society in which a person's name is arbitrarily assigned and denotes without connotation the bearer of the name, in literature a name often tells a great deal about a person. One of the first tricks a reader learns about the great symbol hunt for meaning in reading literature is to notice the names of the characters. If a character bears the name "Christian," the reader may expect to find certain religious themes of some use in understanding the work. But what about in life? If you meet people named "Christian" do you expect them to be Christians? And if they are, that is hardly surprising in our culture.

But there is more to it than that, for Derrida finds that not only do authors often give "motivated" names to their characters, but these names also may bear a significant relationship to the author's identity. Jean Genet, the French novelist and dramatist, a reformed criminal, named many of his characters after flowers. His own name, "Genet," means "broomflower" in French, as well as "horse" (among other things). This relationship between the real and fictional proper names is only the beginning of the textual phenomenon identified by Derrida, whose research revealed that the rhetorical figure of antonomasia—taking a common noun for a proper name or a proper name for a common noun—is the key to the process by which the third level of the signature takes place.

At the third level of signing, the relationship between an author's name and his or her literary style becomes the basis for a "poetics"—a theory of the production or making of texts. Derrida calls this process the "double bind" or "double band" of the signature, in which the proper name moves from designating a particular individual to become the key to a general theory of how texts are constructed. Genet provides one model for this process, folding all three levels into one scene in which the botanical properties of the flowers in his books refer both to the proper name "Genet" and to a theory of rhetorical invention. Therefore writing may be produced that follows the linguistic equivalent of the reproductive processes of the specific plants concerned (hence the careful description of "dissemination," or the spreading of seeds as manifested in certain species—cryptogams, angiosperms, and the like).

Derrida's area of application of this idea is unusual, but the metaphor itself is ancient. Fertilization and reproduction in the plant and animal kingdoms have long served as metaphors for creativity in the arts. Indeed, the procedure Derrida uses in the following excerpt—juxtaposing the categories (and vocabulary) of botany and textiles, and these in turn with the terms of literature—is familiar to us from the readings on metaphor in Chapter 2. His suggestion that we can find in our own names the conceptual category modeling a personal style of creativity is unusual and provocative, not to mention controversial. Derrida has used the signature theory to read a number of major figures in the fields of literature and philosophy ("Ponge" as "sponge," "Blanchot" as "white water," "Kant" as "edge," and so forth), converting their proper names into common nouns using the literal meanings of the name, or puns on the name, to identify the conceptual category which is the clue to that author's principle of invention. In the exercise assigned in this section, you will have an opportunity to extend this experiment to the investigation of your own signature at all three levels, in order to discover, perhaps, your own principle of thinking and writing. Derrida has researched "signing" only with writers, but he intends it to be a theory of language adaptable to thinking in any discipline or field of knowledge. Thus, the style you discover in your experiment based on the readings in this section should be applicable to your work regardless of your intended or eventual major.

In the following excerpt from *Glas* (the book in which he discusses Genet), Derrida offers some elements of his signature theory along with citations from Genet's writings, including statements from autobiographical as well as from fictional works (genres that are not clearly differentiated in Genet's work nor in the signature theory in general) which are meant to support or illustrate the argument.

The blurbs on Genet's books describe him as "the foremost prince in the lineage of French *poètes maudites*—cursed magicians whose lives are as colorful as their work is dangerous, and who distinguish themselves as outlaws as well as masters of language." His peers in American literature would be the likes of Henry Miller and William Burroughs. Genet's masterpiece, *Our Lady of the Flowers,* was written in a prison cell, on brown paper from which the prisoners were supposed to make bags. In 1948 he was condemned to life imprisonment (he was a habitual thief and pervert), but was pardoned by the president of France at the request of France's most eminent writers. Our excerpts from *Glas* do not include the discussions of the more "perverse" themes of Genet's works, but the basic elements of the signature theory come through clearly enough.

From Glas*

Jacques Derrida

Apparently, yielding to the Passion of Writing, Genet has made himself into a flower. . . . What is rhetoric, if the flower (or rhetoric) is the figure of figures and the place of places? Why does the flower dominate all the fields to which it nonetheless belongs? Why does it stop belonging to the series of bodies or objects of which it forms a part? . . . 1

The name of the person who seems to affix, append here his seal (Genet) is the name, as we know, of his mother. . . . *Genêt* names a plant with flowers—yellow flowers (*sarothamnus scoparius, genista;* broom, *genette, genêt-à-balais,* poisonous and medicinal, as distinct from the dyer's broom, 2

*Translated by John P. Leavey, Jr., and Richard Rand (Lincoln: U. of Nebraska Press).

dyer's greenweed, woodwaxen, an herb for dying yellow); *genet* a kind of horse. Of Spain, a country of great importance in the text.

If all his literature sings and weaves a funerary hymen to nomination, 3
Genet never sets any value, *noblesse oblige,* on anything but naming himself.

He rides horse(back) on his proper name. He holds it by the bit 4
(mors). . . .

Departed are those who thought the flower signified, symbolized, 5
metaphorized, metonymized, that one was devising repertories of signifiers and anthic figures, classifying flowers of rhetoric, combining them, ordering them, binding them up in a sheaf or a bouquet around the phallic arch. . . .

Departed then are, save certain exceptions, duly so considered, the 6
archaeologists, philosophers, hermeneuts, semioticians, semanticians, psychoanalysts, rhetoricians, poeticians, even perhaps all those readers who still believe, in literature or anything else.

Those still in a hurry to recognize are patient for a moment: provided 7
that it be anagrams, anamorphoses, somewhat more complicated, deferred and diverted semantic insinuations capitalized in the depths of a crypt, cleverly dissimulated in the play of letters and forms. Genet would then rejoin this powerful, occulted tradition that was long preparing its coup, its haywire start from sleep, while hiding its work from itself, anagrammatizing proper names, anamorphosing signatures and all that follows. Genet, by one of those movements in (n)*ana,* would have, knowing it or not, silently, laboriously, minutely, obsessionally, compulsively, and with the moves of a thief in the night, set his signatures in (the) place of all the missing objects. In the morning, expecting to recognize familiar things, you find his name all over the place, in big letters, small letters, as a whole or in morsels deformed or recomposed. He is no longer there, but you live in his mausoleum or his latrines. You thought you were deciphering, tracking down, pursuing, you are included. He has affected everything with his signature. He has affected it with everything. . . .

(. . .) 8

The rhetorical flower organizing this antitrope, this metonymy simulat- 9
ing autonymy, I baptize it anthonymy. One could also say anthonomasia. Antonomasia is a "kind of synecdoche that consists in taking a common noun for a proper name, or a proper name for a common noun" (Littré).

"I was born in Paris on December 19, 1910. As a ward of the *Assistance* 10
Publique, it was impossible for me to know anything but my civil state. When I was twenty-one, I obtained a birth certificate. My mother's name was Gabrielle Genet. My father remains unknown. I came into the world at 22 Rue d'Assas.

" 'I'll find out something about my origin,' I said to myself, and went to 11
the Rue d'Assas. Number 22 was occupied by the Maternity Hospital. They refused to give me any information. I was raised in Le Morvan by peasants. Whenever I come across genêt (broom) flowers on the heaths—especially at

twilight on my way back from a visit to the ruins of Tiffauges where Gilles de Rais lived—I feel a deep sense of kinship with them. I regard them solemnly, with tenderness. My emotion seems ordained by all nature. I am alone in the world, and I am not sure that I am not their king—perhaps the fairy of these flowers. They render homage as I pass, bow without bowing, but recognize me. They know that I am their living, moving, agile representative, conqueror of the wind. They are my natural emblem, but through them I have roots in that French soil which is fed by the powdered bones of the children and youths screwed, massacred and burned by Gilles de Rais."

"Through that spiny plant of the Cevennes [Spain], I take part in the 12
criminal adventures of Vacher. Thus, through her whose name I bear, the vegetable kingdom is my familiar. I can regard all flowers without pity; they are members of my family. If, through them, I rejoin the nether realms—though it is to the bracken and their marshes, to the algae, that I should like to descend—I withdraw further from men." . . .

So this flower name would be a cryptogram or a cryptonym. It is not 13
proper because it is common. On the other hand, . . . it is not proper because it also leads back to the nether realms, to the marshes, verily to the depths of the sea. Above the sea, with heavy sides but carried by it, the galley. In the depths of the sea, algae.

Alga is a cryptogam, one of those plants that hide their sexual organs. 14
Like ferns, which in general multiply themselves through the dispersion of spores. Whether one remarks them or not on the surface, the text is full of them. The "ferns" of the "Man Condemned to Death" are "rigid." Certain brackens unfold their fronds several meters below the ground. Cryptogams are evidently not flowers. . . .

The stamin, *l'étamine,* names not only the light material in which nuns 15
are sometimes veiled, or through which precious liquids are filtered. But *étamine,* stamen, is also the male sex organ of plants: according to the *navette* [shuttle, rape]—that's the word—running between the textile code and the botanical code. Situated around the style and its stigma, stamens generally form a thin thread, or filaments *(stamina).* Above the thin thread, a connective with four pollen sacs (microsporangia) that "elaborate and disperse the pollen seeds." . . .

No more than for the flower, is there any univocal semantic or morpho- 16
logical definition of *étamine. Etamine* deviates itself from itself, bursts its sheath, at the risk of disseminating the pollen. This always open risk affects not only the androecium, but also the gynoecium. One must argue from the fact that the seed can always burst or remain dormant.

It is concerning the seed, a fertilized ovule, that one thinks one is literally 17
[*proprement*] speaking of dissemination (with angiosperms or gymnosperms). The seeds are sometimes thrown in every direction [*sens*] by the bursting of the fruit. More often, they escape from it through slits or holes

open in its wall; wind or animals disperse them. Germination is therefore immediate only if light and moisture permit. . . .

"Botanists know a variety of *genêt which they call winged-genêt.* It 18
describes its flight and theft in the *Journal:*

"As the theft was indestructible, I decided to make it the origin of a state 19
of moral perfection. . . . 'I want to cover the world with its loathsome progeny.' . . . A kind of dissatisfaction inflated each of my acts, including the most simple. I would have liked a visible, dazzling glory to be manifest at my fingertips, would have liked my potency to lift me from the earth, to explode within me and dissolve me, to shower me to the four winds. I would have rained over the world. My powder, my pollen . . . would have touched the stars."

For Discussion and Writing

1. Derrida introduces a neologism in his commentary—"anthonymy"—to name the figure of antonomasia specific to Genet's practice. What is the justification for his invention of this hybrid critical term (notice its similarity with "anthology")? What other terms appearing in the selection did you not recognize? In *Glas* Derrida cites many passages from encyclopedic dictionaries, juxtaposing scientific information about botany with Genet's discussion of writing and his descriptions of the sexual life of the characters in his novels. He points out that certain words appear in the vocabularies of both botany and literature. What is the botanical meaning of "style"? Derrida suggests that the punning relationship between the two meanings of "style" justifies a conceptual gathering of the two sets into one category (the signature). Does this possibility make any sense? Look through a glossary of another specialized discipline that interests you, and compare its terminology with a glossary of literary terms.
2. Select an author whose works are at least somewhat familiar to you and test the signature theory. Write a short account in the manner of Derrida's *Glas* discussing whether or not, or in what way, the author's names are "in the abyss" of the work(s).
3. Drawing on all the readings and exercises provided in this chapter relevant to the proper name, write a text exploring the words and information that may be generated out of your given and surnames. First identify a "key list" of such terms and topics, then construct a composition (organized as much for aesthetic effect as for the exposition of your discoveries) by writing out a variety of presentations expanding your vocabulary into an account of the third level of the signature. To make the original list you should use every available means to find the common nouns or names that translate your proper names into ordinary

discourse. Check the dictionary definitions in the original language of your heritage, as well as encyclopedic dictionaries relevant to the names. You may also use poetic techniques to produce words out of your names—puns, anagrams might be especially useful. You might also want to include photocopied images depicting the things you find in your names. Several of the readings suggest analogies which might guide your experiment: think of the project as a written version of your coat of arms (a kind of improvised blazoning); or as a nicknaming process. Comment along the way on any signs of fate or destiny you notice in the results of your research. Are you "well-named"? Remember finally that the goal of the project is to take whatever material your names provide and turn it into a model for a theory (general description) of how to write.

The following text, composed as an experiment in the signature signing by James Michael Jarrett, provides a model for your own composition. Jarrett writes for a jazz magazine and teaches literature for a living, which accounts for at least part of the content of his signature. Your content will be different, but the kind of thing you do with the content produced out of your name should resemble Jarrett's procedure.

A Jarrett in Your Text

James Michael Jarrett

For me, Francis Ponge is someone first of all who has known that, in order to know what goes on in the name and the thing, one has to get busy with one's own, let oneself be occupied by it. . . .

—(Signsponge, 26)

The text—this text almost mad in its need to obey the law of my (im)possible signature—always begins at a stopping (stoppering or corking) place. It represents the end of false starts for the one who inscribes it. Like the mason jars that lined my Grandmother Jarrett's pantry—full of pole beans, okra, corn, tomatoes, bread 'n' butter pickles, and all kinds of preserves (peach, pear, watermelon rind, blackberry, and muscadine, to name only five)—it silently marks the work (it is the trace) of canning. (In the South, "puttin' up stuff in cans" is to put up stuff in jars.) And like mason jars, signed and dated, covered and sealed with paraffin (like tomes or tombs "sealed unto the day of redemption"), which wait standing with their strong, well-formed legs locked at attention, the text as jar—a cornucopia—exists to become part of a feast. 1

But you will notice (for you have opened my jar, are feasting now), the text-jar is not used up. It fills itself as fast as it is emptied. To emphasize this 2

James M. Jarrett

Jarrett
Jarrette
Jarrete
J'arrete
J'arrête

point, consider the following biblical passage which describes Elijah the prophet's visit to the drought stricken town of Zarephath and to a widow whom God promised would provide sustenance:

> [Elijah] arose and went to Zarephath. And when he came to the gate of the city, indeed a widow was there gathering sticks. And he called to her and said, "Please bring me a little water in a cup, that I may drink." And as she was going to get it, he called to her and said, "Please bring me a morsel of bread in your hand." Then she said, "As the LORD your God lives, I do not have bread, only a handful of flour in a bin, and a little oil in a jar; and see, I am gathering a couple of sticks that I may go in and prepare it for myself and my son, that we may eat it, and die." And Elijah said to her, "Do not fear; go and do as you have said, but make me a small cake from it first, and bring it to me; and afterward make some for yourself and your son. For thus says the LORD God of Israel: 'The bin of flour shall not be used up, nor shall the jar of oil run dry, until the day the LORD sends rain on the earth.' " So she went away and did according to the the word of Elijah; and she and he and her household ate for many days. The bin of flour was not used up, nor did the jar of oil run dry, according to the word of the LORD which He spoke by Elijah. (I Kings 17:10-16)

Clearly the jar of Zarephath forms this passage's cynosure. It is a hedge against the wasteland. Because of its fecundity (always enjoyed "out of season" and removed from the place of generation), death becomes pregnant. The oil that flows out of its mouth or orifice (associated with the anointing or sanctifying work of God and his prophet) produces new life.

"Can it!"

But I am way ahead of myself, so I stop.

I stop to start. I "close (a finger hole of a wind instrument) or press down (a violin string, etc.) to produce a desired tone" (*Webster's New World Dictionary,* "stop"). But my stopping will not be noted, or rather notated, in

Michael Jarrett

this particular manner again. Instead, it is sufficient to see that every punctuation mark, every white space, the breaking off of every letter to make another heralds (like a band of angels) a stopping, marks my signature.

My model for this experiment in composition is Derrida's *Signsponge*. 6
Hence, I use my "own signation to investigate [to invaginate] a field of study," a field of studs. To make my intentions transparent (so they will be perfectly clear) and straightforward, merely observe that I ret ("to impute, ascribe, or attribute"—OED) to composition an essentially jar-like function. This essay, therefore, tests sound principles of canning. It is itself a recipe for making the most heavenly (literally Godlike) jams and jars, and it follows this recipe:

JAMES MICHAEL JARRETT JAM
(straightforward version)

1 signature (James Michael Jarrett)

1 literary object (genre of satire or Menippea)

1 pinch of content

Write an introduction using the generative principle of signature and add a pinch of content; cook until moderately thick; write the recipe. Remark the proper name's generative principle by exposing the grid of common nouns produced by exploring etymological and associative (homonyms, anagrams, and such) possibilities of the signature. Copiously elaborate the terms of the grid into a text by straining the Menippea (the literary object) through the grid. Season and serve as a specific example of an inexhaustible, general compositional principle.

The above recipe (which both goes before and follows the essay) also 7
follows the following recipe for "Muscadine Jam," which Mrs. S. R. Dull (who signs her Foreword as Henrietta Stanley Dull) recorded in her book *Southern Cooking*—a text "gleaned from over forty years of . . . experience" and written in response to "the need for an authoritative source of information on the preparation of foodstuffs the 'Southern Way' ":

Muscadine Jam

5 lbs. fruit

3 lbs. sugar

Pulp grapes and put pulp to cook in small quantity of water; cook until broken. Put through coarse strainer to remove seed. To the hulls put sufficient water to boil until tender. Mix the two together, add sugar and cook slowly, stirring often to prevent scorching. Season with any spices liked. (p. 333)

Inexplicably, Mrs. Dull omits any reference to the jars that traditionally hold jam. Many reasons could be suggested, but several possibilities seem especially promising:

(1) The jars are present, but because they constitute the received container of jam making, they are invisible.

(2) The jars are absent. Dull—"the first lady of cooking in Georgia"—can only conceive of jars in Tennessee (or they are absent to spite Wallace Stevens).

(3) The jars are both absent and present, and the absent/present opposition is jammed by the jars (as texts or marks). Mrs. Dull's omission typifies logocentrism's habit of establishing dualisms, that is, of privileging content over form, inside over outside, and presence over absence.

My signature, though, explicitly demonstrates the interpenetration, or at least the interdependence, of jams and jars.

My papa Jarrett was named James—James Lloyd. But when I think of my 8
first name, the memory usually recalled is not an image of Papa, but of the hand-tinted photograph that hung over the bed I slept in when visiting my grandparents. This photograph, which both comforted and frightened me as a child, portrayed my uncle James—who died of leukemia when he was three

CARROT
JARRETT

years old. My father—Richard Eugene, the only surviving son and oldest of three children—never saw his brother, so, of course, neither did I.

On December 10, 1953, my parents named me James Michael Jarrett. 9
They decided that I would be called Michael (a law broken by telephone solicitors and teachers on the first day of school). However, when I sign my signature, I sign it as James M. Jarrett, because my father said that was best. Thus, in the signing of my name, Michael all but erases itself, and James—the mark of the ghost-like, absent child—appears. I mark his absence, his never appearing, as his mark in turn marks mine.

James, the Hellenistic version of Jacob (Iakobŏs), means supplanter 10
(supplement) or literally "heel-catcher." A man always in a tight spot, Jacob usually improvised a way to get out of sticky situations. For instance, at his birth, foreshadowing the Olympic games (now held in gyms), Jacob ham-strung his older twin Esau. Nevertheless, God loved Jacob and hated Esau (Romans 9:13). God thought Jacob had the potential to become a real gem.

When I was in Junior High School, people called me Micajarrett, one 11
word, said real fast. And I loved it, for its rhythm and for its association with mica.

No mineral matched mica. Its thin, somewhat flexible, crystalline layers 12
(called isinglass), which could be separated into transparent planes with one's fingernail, fascinated me. I looked at the freckles it made in granite. I searched for it in the red, Georgia clay. And I marveled at the tops of electric fuses—little windows of mica resistant to heat and electricity. If Jacob was God's gem, mica was mine.

Mica, actually Michael, asks the question, "Who is like God?" I know the 13
answer well. Its emphatic "nobody"—an answer that certainly demonstrates its asker's unwillingness to elicit the banter of light conversation—booms like Pavarotti singing through an expensive microphone. But herein lies a problem: who asks the question of Michael, and to whom is the question addressed? What questions are raised in my signature, and what shall I make of this apocalyptic scene?

Gently but firmly tap on Jarrett, and it will easily open up, making its 14
contents available. Cut it in half with a jarrit ("a wooden javelin, about five feet long, used in games by Persian, Turkish, and Arabian horsemen"—OED), and it will reveal two parts as distinct as a *jaret* (a "*variété de prune*"—Littré). It will neatly divide into a common noun—"jar"—and an uncommon verb—"ret." But before I investigate this (reveal its contents to you), notice my Mother's maiden name—"Jordan." Its origin is uncertain, but

> the suggestion has been made that *Jordan* is short for *Jordan-bottle,* and meant originally a bottle of water brought from the Jordan by crusaders or pilgrims; that it was thence transferred to 'a pot or vessel used by physicians and alchemists', and thence to the chamber utensil.

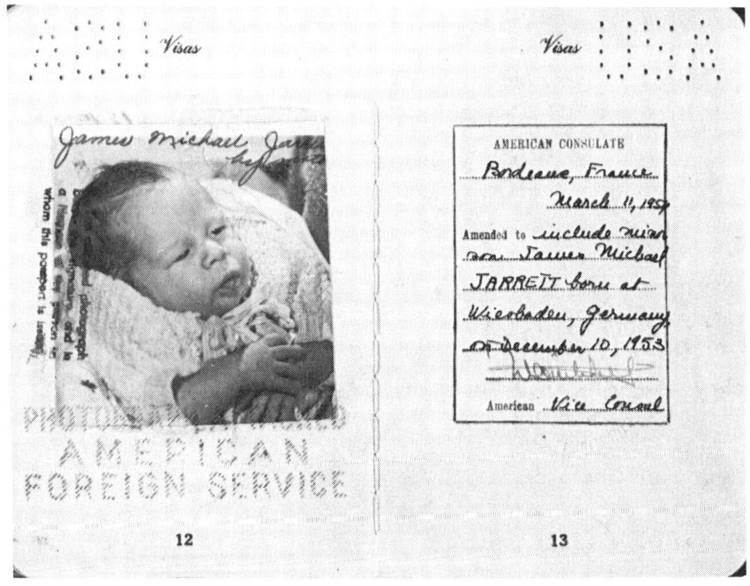

Visas

Visas

AMERICAN CONSULATE
Bordeaux, France
March 11, 195
Amended to include minor son James Michael JARRETT born at Wiesbaden, Germany on December 10, 1953
American Vice Consul

AMERICAN
FOREIGN SERVICE

12

13

WIESBADEN Hauptbahnhof Aufnahme K. H. Mitschke

> But the earlier steps of this conjecture apparently rest upon nothing but the later form of the word (which may actually be a corruption of something else), and the external probabilities of such an origin. (OED)

Thus, "jordan" involves a complex series of displacements, until finally patriarchal law (the law of Dick Jarrett and the OED) puts a lid on the whole subject, screws meaning down, and declares that, henceforth jordan shall be:

(1) a kind of pot or vessel formerly used by physicians and alchemists,
(2) a chamber-pot,
(3) applied derisively to a person (OED),
(4) or, in a word, a jarrett.

Jarrett supplements jordan. The alchemist's vessel of healing/poison becomes a piss-pot. The little jar relegates the jordan to "The Lady's Dressing Room," declares it unclean—a *pharmakos*—or at very best a "frail *China* Jar [ready to] receive a Flaw" (*Rape of the Lock,* Canto II). But undeniably a trace or whiff of jordan remains, for, after all, a jarrett is a jordan as we have seen, and as I shall point out again.

I married Pamela Gail Dill. She now signs her name Pamela Gail Jarrett. 15
Did I take her name? Was it freely given? Did I erase her name? Does it palimpsestically remain? What is the nature of the idiomatic law by which dill (a plant of the carrot family) disappears into the abyss of a pickle jar only to emblazon itself upon the label or signature of the jar? In what way do the three boys she bore resemble (remark) a pickle jar, which at once carries the signature of both mother and father? These are questions I shall only pose, preserve (for later) by placing them into this text-jar, this *jahr's* text.

As I noted earlier, Jarrett—to measure out, sound out, or partly open its 16
principle of generation—yields a "jar" and a "ret." *Jar,* whose noun form rates three separate entries in the OED (a kind of jar in its own rite), suggests: (1) a harsh, inharmonious, grating sound or combination of sounds, which by extension signifies dissension, discord, dispute, and want of harmony, (2) a vessel without spout or handle (or having two handles) usually more or less cylindrical in form, and hence, a measure of volume, and (3) something (like a door) "on the turn, partly open." *Ret,* a verb, signifies the actions of: (1) accusing, charging, reckoning, imputing, and ascribing, (2) soaking (especially flax or hemp) in water and exposing to moisture, in order to soften or season, and (3) rotting (e.g., hay spoiled by water). Ret is also an obsolete form ("3 sing. pres. indic.") of "read." Jarrett, I ret, equals (among other things) a rotten, slightly opened jar. A jarrett is a jordan—a truly jarring fact.

In French, the definition of *jarret* is expressed as: (1) "bend of the knee, 17
popliteal space, ham (in man); hough, hock (of horse, etc.)," (2) "knuckle (of veal); shin (of beef)," and (3) "unevenness, bulge, break of outline (in curve of arch, etc.)" or "an elbow, knee-joint (of pipe)" *(Heath's Standard French and English Dictionary).* Phrases employing my signature are as follows:

Plier le jarret, to bend the knee.
Avoir du jarret, to be strong in the leg.
Couper les jarrets à quelqu' un, to take the wind out of someone's sails.
S' avancer le jarret tendu, (i) (of courtier, etc.) to advance making a leg, (ii) (of fencer, etc.) to advance on his toes.
Couper les jarrets à un cheval, to hamstring a horse.

Also, note that *jarrettes* are socks or half-hose. The verb *jarreter* refers to the act of putting on one's garters or stockings or to stripping a tree of its side branches.

Obviously, then, I find myself attracted to Menippean satire because my 18
signature makes the genre possible. I say this, rather write this, because as I study the menippea, it seems purely fanciful (i.e., scientific) to think that my signature—myself as subject—can remain outside the text (establishing an inside and outside of the text). Therefore I insert my signature into the genre (or jar) called menippea, but in so doing, I lose my identity, my title of ownership over the text. I let james michael jarrett—a chain of common nouns—"become a moment or a part of the [menippean] text" (*Signsponge,* 56).

On the simplest level this means that I like satire for its jars. For example, 19
Petronius' character, Seleucus, asked:

> What are men anyway but balloons on legs, a lot of blown-up bladders? Flies, that's what we are. No, not even flies. Flies have something inside. But a man's a bubble, all air, nothing else. (*Satyricon,* trans. Arrowsmith, 50)

People, to Seleucus, were empty jars, and whatever Petronius' position on this issue was, one thing is clear. The *Satyricon* concerned itself with what was later called the Cartesian jar/jelly split. Swift worked the same image when he wrote:

> in most corporeal beings, which have fallen under my cognizance, the outside hath been infinitely preferable to the in; whereof I have been farther convinced from some late experiments. Last week I saw a woman flayed, and you will hardly believe how much it altered her person for the worse.
>
> Yesterday I ordered the carcass of a beau to be stripped in my presence, when we were all amazed to find so many unsuspected faults

> under one suit of clothes. Then I laid open his brain, his heart, and his spleen; but I plainly perceived at every operation, that the farther we proceeded, we found the defects increase upon us in number and bulk. (*A Tale of a Tub,* Section IX)

This often cited passage presents a jarrish or jordanean episteme. It 20
forcefully argues that people are jelly jars—tubs. It implies that *A Tale of a Tub* should be renamed *A Tale of a Jarrett.*

The menippea features tons of other famous jars. Here are a few ex- 21
amples. Rabelais organized the whole of *Gargantua and Pantagruel* around "the Holy Bottle of Bacbuc." Sir Thomas Browne wrote a piece entitled *Urne Buriall.* Voltaire wrote *CANdide.* Sterne has Mr. Shandy call his servant-girl, Susannah's mind "a leaky vessel" (Vol. IV, ch. 14). And Carlyle, following Swift's lead, wrote *Sartor Resartus* or the *Canner Recanned* or the *Jarrer Rejarred. . . .*

Or look at it another way. The menippea is a kind of jazz; (jazz is a kind 22
of menippea, forming a body of work that aurally satirizes mainstream, Caucasian music, art and culture). When it really cooks—lets out all the stops and hams it up—the result is a high quality jam. This jam, what Duke Ellington called "such sweet thunder," jars ("cuts") established (generic) ways of playing tunes, because it foregrounds the solo or group improvisation. Stated succinctly, jazz and the menippea follow the law of the signature (a hymen making the fold of ensembles and solos); classical music and literature (e.g., romance and tragedy) follow

Jazziz: You've been viewed as something of a musical satirist, something along the lines of Brecht and Weill. I've even seen references to Swift and Aristophanes. Are you a satirist?

Bley[1]: No, I used to be, and I'm not anymore. I'm terribly serious.

Jazziz: So you're not satirizing anyone?

Bley: No!

Jazziz: No more barbs?

Bley: Well they all think I still am. And that's o.k., if they want to think that—if that makes it more acceptable.

Jazziz: What kind of music does your new sextet demonstrate a love for?

Bley: It's music that helps you get through the day—or the night. And not music that's educational, or interesting, or modern or any of that. Deep down it's trying to make people feel better, trying to be music that puts people into a very back of the brain mood—like way back without your thought processes. I don't know what that's called.

the law of the preestablished score.

[1] Carla Bley, a jazz musician interviewed by Jarrett for *Jazziz* magazine.

What, then, of this essay? Does it follow the law of the subject (the idiom) 23
or the law of the object (the recipe)? Hopefully, by miming the motions of signation, it folds the two laws together. If this is the case, perhaps a new recipe for essaying is called for, one that can be written only after all cooking, canning, and jamming is done.

TURN BACK!

JAMES MICHAEL JARRETT JAM

(Revised Unstandard Version)

1 signature

1 literary object (genre of satire or menippea)

Chapter 5

Experiments with Texts: Text and Research

In this concluding section you have an opportunity to bring together in one final experiment all the devices of textual writing that you have learned in the preceding chapters. Traditionally, composition textbooks often include a unit on "writing the research paper." *Text Book* also conforms to this rule, except that textualist research is conducted somewhat differently than research directed by the rules of argumentative writing. Our name for this new mode of research is *mystory.*

The point of departure for our research experiment is Roland Barthes's definition of "text" as being constituted by the work (object of study) plus the reader. Textual meaning concerns the relationship of the reader to the work. To do textual research is to write from this position or experience of the affected reader. A research paper as text, then, is a kind of autobiography, in that the purpose of the research is to explore and discover one's own (the reader's) relationship to the traditions, institutions, and discourses that have provided the contexts and tools the reader uses to understand not just a given work, but the self, the world, and everything in the world.

Rather than imitating the attempt of conventional research in the natural and social sciences to attain impersonal objectivity, with the aim of establishing consensus that is collective and universal, text research is a methodology for the humanities designed to take responsibility for knowledge that is individual, particular, singular, idiomatic. This methodology of "difference," however, has been applied successfully in the natural sciences in at least one case—the research of the Nobel laureate Barbara McClintock, who discovered genetic transposition while working with corn plants. McClintock's capacity "to see one kernel of maize that is different, and make that understandable" resonates with the "mystorical" methodology of empathy and identification with the object of study. "No two plants are exactly alike," McClintock says. "I start with the seedling, and I don't want to leave it. I don't feel I really know the story if I don't watch the plant all the way along. So I know every plant in the field. I know them intimately and I find it a great pleasure to know them." As Evelyn Fox Keller reported, McClintock "has the ability to write the 'autobiography' of every plant she works with."

The two experiments conducted in Chapter 4, which together constitute a "student's signature," provide an introduction to text as research. Such research carries the experience of signing a text—the experience of how "language speaks us"—into the scholarly methods of arts and letters. The more specific version of the experience now is to learn how the existing works of high culture speak us as well. Evelyn Fox Keller characterizes a similar attitude on McClintock's part toward nature as "humility": "Precisely because the complexity of nature exceeds our own imaginative possibilities, it becomes essential to 'let the experiment tell you what to do.' " The signature strategy is conducted in a similar spirit of humility, as a way to attend to the exceptional and the anomalous (as a way to open oneself up to culture, not as a way to reduce what is different to one's own experience). In the same way that the institution of the family assigns individuals their places in society by means of the proper name, so do other institutions (school, business, government) contribute to the formation of identity by supplying names or titles for practices and positions internalized by participants. The same sort of identification with parents, and then with celebrities that occurs in popular culture (noted at the end of Chapter 3), also operates in the learned setting of high culture. Scholars not only know about their objects of study—they *identify* with them (thus collapsing the distinction between subjective and objective writing).

Text research, then, complements traditional argumentative research in that while the latter concentrates on the knowledge about the object of study, the former foregrounds the "subject" of knowledge (the person who wants to know). The act of research presumes a desire—the desire to know something. It turns out that the object of study often serves as a metaphor for the subject of the researcher, as a vehicle that, read in the right way, offers a reflection or figure of the desire motivating the research. As a research method, text is a way to investigate one's own style of thought. This autobiographical approach to research has much to learn from the analytical approach of critique that uses the abstract categories of ideology to locate the way a given work carries the values, beliefs, and mythologies of the culture that produced it. As discussed in Chapter 3, these ideological categories of identity include race, ethnicity, sexuality, gender, religion, class, age, nationality. Having seen how works of popular culture, such as *Casablanca*, support ideological identity, we now want to explore how these same processes are at work in the materials of the learned disciplines.

Mystory

The following series of readings and exercises are designed to lead to the formation of a new genre for academic research called the *mystory.* Mystory is a neologism formed by analogy with the generation of the term "herstory" out of "history," to name the collective story of women within the patriarchal story of Western civilization. Mystory extends this revision of history to represent the development of any individual's education: mystory is to the individual learning experience what history is to the changes reflected in a collective story such as the story of the American nation. Indeed, "nation" is one of the few categories of ideology all the citizens of a state supposedly have in common. As Benedict Anderson noted in *Imagined Communities,* a nation is an "idea" that exists only so long as people believe in it and act upon that belief. He also demonstrates that print literacy in both its popular and high culture forms is essential to the establishment and maintenance of nationality. The creators of great literature in a national language contribute in an essential and necessary way to our experience of belonging to a specific nation. To find out exactly *what* we are part of—to gain access to this collectively maintained idea—requires that we exercise one of the basic skills associated with literacy: research.

The purpose of this final project is twofold: first, to design the rules or conventions for this new kind of research. The rules for the textualist research project do not exist prior to the project itself. Indeed, one goal of the project is to invent these rules. Second, the rules thus discovered must be tested by writing a mystorical text. The readings included here should not be considered *models* of a mystory, but *relays* that may be used to guide you to your own design or recipe. In short, this project is an experiment. What are the goals of the experiment exactly? The first is to compose an intellectual self-portrait as a way to discover the resources available for personal use within the archives of literacy. The second is to test the value of the learning experience that comes from including within research writing the making of images, metaphors, and narratives (to add to the arguments and interpretations we have come to expect).

The following selections should be read and discussed as *relays,* then, as figurative, indirect, partial, yet exemplary instructions for making a new kind of research called *mystory,* in which what guides the acts of research and composition is the pattern provided by the signature or personal style of the writer. Each of the following readings adds some feature or procedure to the mix; the exercises accompanying the selections are guides to some of these important features of the relay and clues for the construction of the poetics or rules for your new research paper. The challenge is to adapt the lessons of the samples to your own case, to find the pattern repeated in the individual pieces that might be abstracted into a useful formula. In reading the samples that follow the questions below, keep in mind your goal: to find in the excerpts the instructions for writing a new kind of research paper.

For Discussion and Writing

1. Many of the composition books available in the library—the various introductions to argumentative and expository writing—provide a section or chapter on writing the research paper. Write a short analysis in which you compare the rules and guidelines for the conventional academic research paper with the principles of textual research that you have already explored in Chapter 4 in the experiments with fragments and signatures. To get started with the process of designing your new poetics, make a list of all the features recommended in the standard textbook accounts of the research paper, then generate an alternative set of features by listing something that is the *opposite* of each item in the first list. Typical of the rules or recommendations you will encounter are statements such as these: "Somewhere in the introduction you must ask your thesis question"; "Since you are presenting yourself as a disinterested researcher . . . the best choice is to present the opposing view first." In contrast, then, a mystory will have no thesis statement and will not adopt a tone of disinterested objectivity. Or, to restate these negative rules of thumb more positively, a mystory discovers its thesis as it goes along, and its tone is personal. In generating your antonymic list of counter-rules, keep in mind that most authorities on creativity agree that the first ingredient in making something new is simply the determination to do things "differently," no matter what.
2. What is the relationship between the strategies suggested for gathering information (known in rhetorical terms as *inventio*) in the standard textbook and the standard form recommended for arranging the results of that research into a composition *(dispositio)*? Compare, that is, the method of gathering the information and the form for writing it up. To what extent does the form of the research paper limit and determine the kind of information you gather and what you are able to say about it? If instead of putting the information you gathered for a standard research paper into argumentative form you simply told the story of how you went about your research, would your narrative still be classifiable as a "research paper"? Contrast these two methods (the expository and the narrative) with the method recommended by the radical composer John Cage, who selected the books for his assignments by using the random combinations of the *I Ching* to generate library call numbers.

Archive for a Mystorical Method

From The Autobiographer as *Torero*

Michel Leiris

Perhaps the best way to clarify, textually, the strategy of using figures, analogies, images, and metaphors to guide the practice of research might be to consider Michel Leiris's use of a metaphor to define the genre of autobiography—keeping in mind the differences between institutions, between school and art, and hence between the mystory (adapting the autobiography to the practices of scholarly research) and the confession developed by Michel Leiris as an investigation into his erotic existence. The "erotic" theme that Leiris addresses serves as a figure for the "desire to know" that mystory is meant to make intelligible. In fact, one purpose of the mystory that distinguishes it from history is its reminder that writing is used to communicate not only with others but also with oneself.

Michel Leiris grew up in France between the two World Wars, and developed and extended in one hybrid method the tendencies of surrealism and of anthropology—the worlds of dreams and of science. Claude Lévi-Strauss, the great structuralist anthropologist, wrote that Leiris's autobiography demonstrated "that every attempt to know others must start in an even more passionate attempt to understand oneself." Conducting a kind of self-anthropology, a study of the sources of his own imagination in the experience of growing up, Leiris found himself to be obsessed with two images of "woman" given expression in two paintings by Cranach, representing the female figures Lucrece and Judith—figures of the woman as martyr and as murderess. By "arbitrarily" attaching an allegorical significance to these two figures, Leiris was able to tell his life story as "a confession based on Cranach's paintings." While this allegorical strategy of using a work of art to explore one's own emotional reality is important to mystory, the following selection is taken from the afterword to Manhood, *in which Leiris offers a metaphor for the method itself of writing a confessional work.*

If it seemed to me, originally, that to set down an account of my life from an 1
erotic point of view (a preferential one, since sexuality then seemed to me the cornerstone in the structure of the personality), if it seemed to me that a confession bearing on what Christianity calls "the works of the flesh" was

enough to make me, by the act this represents, a kind of *torero,*[1] I must still consider whether the rule I had imposed upon myself—a rule whose rigor, I was satisfied to note, endangered me—is actually comparable, relation to danger aside, to that which dictates the *torero*'s movements.

In a general way, one might say that the bullfighting code pursues one essential goal: aside from the fact that it obliges a man to incur serious danger (while arming him with an indispensable technique), and not to dispatch his adversary just anyhow, it prevents the combat from being a mere slaughter; as punctilious as a ritual, it presents a tactical aspect (put the bull in a state to receive the final thrust though without having exhausted the animal more than was necessary), but also an aesthetic aspect: to the degree that the man is "exposed in profile," as he must be when giving his sword thrust, there is an arrogance in his posture; to the degree that his feet remain motionless throughout a series of close and fluid passes, the cape moving slowly, he forms with the beast that glamorous amalgamation in which man, material, and the huge horned mass seem united by a play of reciprocal influences; everything combines, in a word, to imprint upon the confrontation of bull and *torero* a *sculptural* character. 2

Looking on my enterprise as a sort of photomontage and choosing for my expression a tone as objective as possible, trying to gather my life into a single solid block (an object I can touch, as though to insure myself against death, even when, paradoxically, I am claiming to risk everything), even if I opened my door to dreams (a psychologically justified element but tinged with romanticism, just as the *torero*'s cape work, technically useful, is also a series of lyrical flights), I was imposing on myself a rule quite as severe as if I intended to compose a classical work. And it is ultimately this very severity, this "classicism"—not excluding such excess as one finds in even our most formalized tragedies and relying not only on considerations of form but on the notion of thereby achieving a maximum of veracity—which seems to me to have afforded my undertaking (if I have managed to succeed at all) something analogous to what constitutes for me the exemplary value of the *corrida* and which the imaginary bull's horn could not have contributed by itself. 3

To use materials of which I was not the master and which I had to take as I found them (since my life was what it was and I could not alter, by so much as a comma, my past, a primary *datum* representing for me a fate as unchallengeable as for the *torero* the beast that runs into the ring), to say everything and say it without "doctoring," without leaving anything to the imagination and as though obeying a necessity—such was the risk I accepted and the law I had fixed for myself, such the ceremony with which I could make no compromise. Though the desire to *expose myself* (in every sense of 4

[1] Bullfighter

the term) has constituted the first impulse, the fact remained that this *necessary* condition was not a *sufficient* condition, and that, further, it was from this original goal that the form to be adopted had to be deduced, with the almost automatic force of an obligation. These images I gathered together, this tone I employed—at the same time that they deepened and sharpened my self-awareness—had to be (unless I failed) what would accord my emotion a better chance of being shared. Similarly, the order of the *corrida* (a rigid framework imposed on an action in which, theatrically, chance must appear to be dominated) is a technique of combat and at the same time a ritual. It was therefore necessary that this method I had imposed upon myself—dictated by the desire to see into myself as clearly as possible—function simultaneously and effectively as a rule of composition. Identity, so to speak, of form and content, but, more precisely, a unique procedure revealing the content to me as I gave it form, a form that could be of interest to others and (at its extreme) allow them to discover in themselves something homophonous to this content I had discovered in myself.

Obviously I am formulating this quite *a posteriori,* in order to define as 5
well as I can the procedure I used, and without being qualified, of course, to decide if this "tauromachic" code, a guide for action and a guarantee against complacency, has turned out to be capable of such effectiveness as a means of style, or even (as to certain details) if what I claimed to see as a necessity of method did not actually correspond to an ulterior motive concerning composition.

I distinguish in literature a genre of major significance to me, which 6
would include those works where the horn is present in one form or another, where the author assumes the direct risk either of a confession or of a subversive work, a work in which the human condition is confronted directly or "taken by the horns" and which presents a conception of life "engaging" its partisan—or its victim; works showing an attitude of something like humor or madness toward things, and the intent to make oneself the mouthpiece of the great themes of human tragedy. I can suggest in any case—but no doubt this is battering down an open door?—that it is precisely to the degree that one cannot see in a work any other rule of composition than the Ariadne's thread the author followed throughout the explanation he was making (by successive approaches or at point-blank range) to himself that works of this genre can be regarded, in literary terms, as "authentic." This by definition, from the moment one admits that literary activity, in its specific aspect as a mental discipline, cannot have any other justification than to *illuminate certain matters for oneself at the same time as one makes them communicable to others,* and that one of the highest goals that can be assigned to literature's pure form, by which I mean poetry, is to restore by means of words certain intense states, concretely experienced and become significant, to be thus put into words.

For Discussion and Writing

1. Leiris's example suggests that an important ingredient for the invention of the mystory, both the recipe for how to make one and the actual practice itself, is the identification of an analogy with some other practice that might guide the design process. Leiris used the practices of the bullfight to generate ideas for a method of writing a confession. Perform a commutation test on Leiris's choice of "vehicle" by replacing his use of the bullfight with another practice. Try out not only dangerous occupations but also practices of other kinds (for example, compare the confession to "moving from one house to another"). Use this exercise to think about an analogy for the methodology of the mystory.
2. Notice that Leiris's choice of the bullfight scene allows him to elaborate upon two proverbs or "sayings" that are also available in English: "to take the bull by the horns," and to be "stuck on the horns of a dilemma." In a way his analogy could be read as a way of revitalizing the dead metaphors in these sayings. Review some of the proverbs and contemporary sayings with which you are familiar to see if they allude to or contain material that could be reattached to a larger scene in the same way that Leiris resituated the proverbs back into the fully imagined scene of the bullfight.
3. In the first set of questions for discussion in this section, you generated some ideas for the poetics of mystory by contrast with or opposition to the features of the standard research paper recommended in most composition textbooks. Now consider how the analogy you came up with in the question above could be used to produce a positive set of features of your new research method. In the library find a reference book of rhetorical or literary devices, such as *A Dictionary of Literary Devices* by Bernard Dupriez (translated by Albert W. Halsall). Try to find specific "moves" that may be made with language that are comparable to the moves of the *torero.* Apply the comparison to your own alternative analogy.

History of an Encounter

Eunice Lipton

In what could be considered an example of "herstory," the art historian Eunice Lipton demonstrates the possibility of the researcher openly identifying with the object of study, but in a way that puts in question, rather than simply reproducing, the dominant values of the discipline. Researchers probably have always identified with their objects of study, but the conventions of objectivity prevented them from admitting this, or even recognizing it. Herstory has produced some of the most innovative work of our time and is a major force in the transformation of the humanities not only in its politics but also in its methodologies. The feminist slogan—"the personal is political"—has been extended also to disciplinary research, with artists leading the way into a new mode of study.

An example of the artistic practices that anticipate Lipton's personal approach to research is the "artist's book" Extraordinary/Ordinary *by May Stevens, which the artist described as "a collage of words and images of Rosa Luxemburg, Polish/German revolutionary leader, theoretician, and murder victim (1871–1919) juxtaposed with images and words of Alice Stevens (born 1895–), housewife, mother, washer and ironer, inmate of hospitals and nursing homes." To compose this "juxtaportrait" Stevens researched the life and works of Luxemburg, gathering such materials as "thoughts from intimate notes sent from prison to her comrade and lover, Leo Jogiches, and to her friends; from agit-prop published in* Die Rote Fahne; *and from her serious scientific writings. Images from her girlhood, her middle life, and the final photograph of her murdered head." The point to emphasize is that before Stevens could use the historical figure of Rosa Luxemburg as a metaphor for her feelings about her mother, she had to do some conventional research in the library. What is new here is the application of the research to emotional and poetic rather than strictly informational ends.*

Eunice Lipton's feminist politics led her to shift her attention away from the "author" (Manet) of a famous painting ("Olympia") and away from the abstract form of the painting (the approved method of her discipline) to focus instead on the life of the artist's model. Lipton's research into the life and career of the model, Victorine Meurent, is conducted explicitly as an analogy for understanding the researcher's own condition as a woman and as a professional. The form of the research is a narrative recounting Lipton's travels and interviews as she tracked down information about the elusive Meurent.

I don't remember when I first saw Victorine Meurent, but I wouldn't have recognized her or known her name at the time. No one would have. She was just another naked woman in a painting. Maybe I remarked that the man who made the picture was called Manet or that the work itself was named *Olympia,* but that would have been it. When I was at college in the late 1950s, works of art were considered things of beauty. Period. One would never pay attention to a painting's literal content. One wouldn't even risk noticing that De Kooning's *Woman II* had a woman in it. 1

Even as I became a professional art historian in the 1960s, the look of *Olympia* did not change. The naked white woman on the bed seemed like 2 any odalisque, Venus, or Danaë—idealized flesh made into art. I was taught to appreciate Manet's particularly modern vocabulary, his tonal contrasts, flattened spaces, outlined forms, that is, his fundamentally abstract intentions. It was Manet who was placed first in the pantheon of modernist painting; we were told that before anyone else, he had seen people and events for what they really were: abstract pictorial forms.

But one day in 1970, try as I may, I could not shake the feeling that there 3
was an event unfolding in *Olympia* and that the naked woman was staring quite alarmingly out of the picture. I could not make her recede behind the abstract forms I knew—I had been taught so fervently to believe—were the true content of the work. Her face kept swimming forward, her eyes demanded attention. I saw that unlike other naked women in paintings, Olympia did not drape herself suggestively upon her bed, or supplicate prospective lovers, or droop resignedly. Nor did she smile flirtatiously. Rather she reigned imperiously, reclining upon silken pillows, her steady gaze a dare, her tight little body and proprietary hand an omen. Now I could see that even the stilted pose of the black maid and overarching cat gave the lie to scenarios of seduction. Olympia, alert and dignified, resembled a noble consort on an Etruscan funerary monument far more than an inviting Greek or Oriental courtesan. This was a woman who could say "yes," *or* she could say "no."

Her contemporaries knew this in the nineteenth century though they 4
didn't say it in so many words. In fact, Manet was greatly distressed over how his painting was received; he even considered destroying it. What happened was this. In May of 1865 *Olympia* was exhibited in the Salon, the official exhibition forum of the time. The press took an instant and bellicose dislike to the work, using words like: "The vicious strangeness of [this] . . . woman of the night"; "a sort of female gorilla, a grotesque. . . . " "Such indecency! . . . " Before anyone knew what was happening, respectable Parisians were sweeping through the Salon's drafty halls brandishing walking sticks and umbrellas; they were heading toward *Olympia* with murder on their minds. The authorities were taken aback, and took the unprecedented step of cordoning off the painting. But the damage was done. Manet fled to Spain thinking: Titian had done it, so had Giorgione and Velazquez—he meant painted naked women—why is everyone so angry at me? This may have been the first time in modern history that a painting incited people to such public agitation. . . .

I can't say when it was exactly that my wonder about Olympia and the 5
treatment she received turned to impatience, but I began to hear the rampaging walking sticks and umbrellas, and to feel the heat and rage the painting produced in commentators, the barely contained anger squeezed into stylish commentary about artist-geniuses and their pathetic models. I know it was about the same time that I met Linda, and also read an article in the *Village Voice* entitled "The Next Great Moment in History Is Theirs." In it, Vivian Gornick wrote that "women in this country are gathering themselves into a

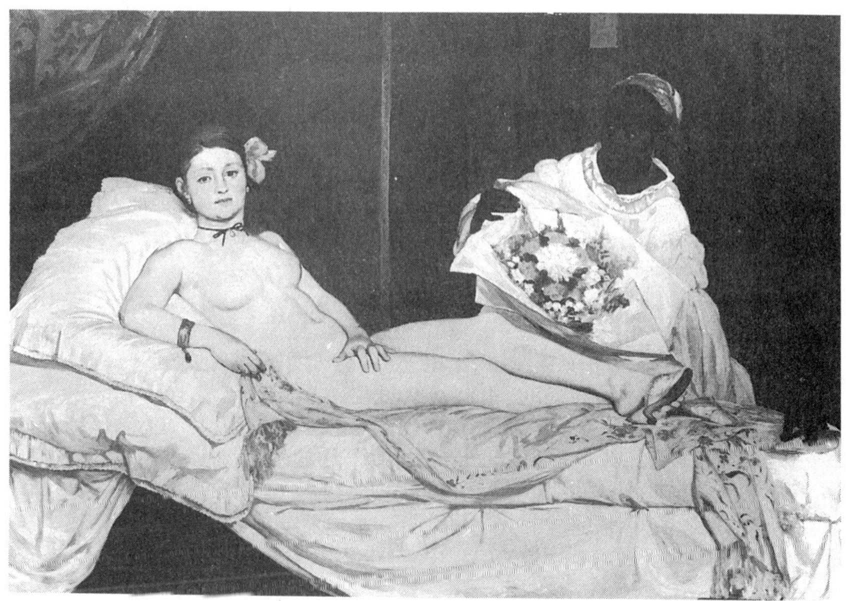

Edouard Manet. *Olympia,* 1863. Giraudan/Art Resources, NY

sweat of civil revolt.... [Their] energy ... lies trapped and dormant like a growing tumor, and at its center there is despair, hot, deep, wordless. ... [They have been] deprived ... of the right to say 'I' and have it mean something. This understanding ... underlies the current wave of feminism. It is felt by thousands of women today, it will be felt by millions tomorrow."

The next thing I knew I was throwing Kate Millett's *Sexual Politics* across the room, demanding, "How can this be true, this silencing of women, this enforced invisibility? And what the hell did that professor mean when he said I had too many ideas?" 6

Then it was August 26, 1970, and a march was called to commemorate the Nineteenth Amendment to the Constitution, the establishing of women's right to vote. I went with my friend Marcia. We made our way to Fifth Avenue and Fifty-ninth Street. As we approached, what we saw took our breath away. Women were everywhere—thousands and thousands and thousands of women. Marcia grabbed my arm and said the oddest thing: "What *would* my mother have made of this?" I wouldn't have thought of my mother at such a moment. I never thought of my mother as a woman. 7

But what a sight the avenue was, women filling all the spaces, banishing the cars, the honking, the men. How we gazed upon each other. With what amazement and pleasure we talked and laughed and wept as we flooded that capacious boulevard. And with what confidence we lured the hesitant from the sidelines. How they fell into the arms of the river that we became that day, we women of all shapes, sizes, and ages marveling at each other. 8

We also handed each other leaflets and flyers that said: "Join the National Organization of Women!" "Come to meetings of Redstockings" " . . . The New York Radical Feminists" " . . . The Feminists!" And we did. We met in churches, in school rooms, in libraries. Then in each other's homes. We organized by neighborhood, ten to twelve in a cadre. We met weekly, and we talked our hearts out. We divulged secrets we didn't know we had. Nothing was off limits. We talked about sex and orgasm, ambition, marriage, homosexuality, our fathers, our siblings, our mothers. The rage at our families, our lovers, our teachers was staggering. And maybe for the first time in our lives, we turned that fury on to the world, away from ourselves. 9

The listening, the uninterrupted speaking, made us realize how smart we were, and how inhibited. For most of us, this talking—this consciousness-raising—was the first time we heard each other speaking discursively and analytically about our lives. Bit by little bit, our talking, our weeping, and our anger added up to an emotional and political history. And a strategy. 1

What better emblem for the time—those opening salvos of the Women's Movement—than *Olympia,* a woman whose naked body said: "See this? It's mine. I will not be the object of your gaze, invisible to my own. This is my body, my life." 1

Yes, I marveled at the intricate psychological drama surrounding *Olympia,* which on the one hand elicited men's attraction—so many had written *some*thing about her at a time when models were usually nameless and invisible—but on the other provoked ridicule and contempt. *All that writing about her.* In our own time, in 1977, an entire book on *Olympia* written by Theodore Reff, and again in 1985, T. J. Clark, the most dazzling bad boy in the Art History community, published a notably long, obfuscating, and tortured essay on *Olympia* in his book on Manet. Every prominent scholar of nineteenth-century art planted himself in front of her, writing paraphernalia at hand. All thought their engagement disinterested, but it wasn't. They circled her from above, close up, on top. What did they mean to do with all those words? Describe her? Analyze her? Situate her? *Or:* Possess her? Control her? Silence her? No one admitted his emotions, neither the irritation nor the fascination. None could acknowledge what amounted to a professional obsession that spanned a century and a half. And continues. 1

More and more I brought Meurent up in my classes as if I could somehow redress the balance by at least speaking her name, acknowledging her corporeality as Victorine Meurent, a real woman of the nineteenth century. Musingly, I'd say, "Some day I'm going to find this woman," and the more I said it, the more I meant it. It became a promise. I took her to myself, unconsciously, unwittingly. That face, those eyes. I wanted what she had: her confidence, her dignity, her "no." 1

Many things came between us though. My career for one, books and articles about geniuses—Picasso, Degas, Manet. And my own ambivalent self 1 stuck in a conservative profession. And a culture that enjoined girls to behave themselves. Plus—I rationalized—all I know is Meurent's name, that she worked for Manet, traveled to the United States, exhibited a few times at the Paris Salon. She was only a model. What is there really to say?

15 I had no idea what the ramifications of the search would be. I didn't even realize that our names were the same: "Eunice" is a translation from the Greek of "Evnike;" it means "Happy Victory." And I certainly didn't *intend* to end up a redhead. All I knew was that I envied Meurent her autonomy even as I acknowledged the paradox that I was a well-paid American professor in the late twentieth century, and she was a working-class model in nineteenth-century Paris. I was convinced that she had had more choices than I, and that she had acted on them. The dare of her gaze was the proof.

16 As I set out in earnest to find Meurent, I kept losing my way. A two-step of desire and longing crossed by withdrawal and passivity. I had learned this dance as a child, but coming of age in the era of McCarthyism, Eisenhower, and Doris Day refined it immeasurably. Across this faraway history I started looking for Meurent.

17 This is the record of my search.

For Discussion and Writing

1. **Lipton's example clarifies how to undertake a study of the abstractions of ideological identity in a specific embodied case. She helps us see how to recognize in Leiris's "erotic" inquiry the ideological categories of "sexuality" and "gender." There is no agreement about the politics of art, as may be seen in the case of "Olympia." On several college campuses, charges of sexual harassment have been brought by women relating to a similar painting (Goya's "Naked Maja"). The argument is that displaying representations of nudes (even of ones characterized as "masterpieces") in public places is demeaning to women and creates an environment that is not conducive to equal status of all participants. What are the issues involved in such a controversy? Would Lipton support or oppose efforts to remove a copy of "Olympia" from your classroom? As a compromise some administrators have proposed pairing the female nude with a similarly classical male nude (such as a reproduction of Michelangelo's "David"). What do you think of this suggestion?**
2. **Lipton's project illustrates how the ideological category of gender may motivate research. Suppose that someone identified with the black woman in "Olympia" rather than with the white one. How would adding the category of race change the research? A good example of how to use race to organize research was Glenn Ligon's exhibition (held at the Hirshhorn Museum) entitled "To Disembark." Ligon explored his ideological autobiography by gathering together four elements:**

> Wooden boxes, using international symbols that define fragility, emit barely audible sounds (a heartbeat, Billie Holiday singing "Strange Fruit," and "Traveling Light," disco music by Royal House). The boxes take their proportions from the one in which a slave, Henry "Box" Brown, was shipped from Richmond, Virginia, to freedom in Philadelphia in 1849. In the same gallery are lithographs imitating nineteenth-century advertisements for the return of escaped slaves. All name and describe the artist himself (he asked friends to describe him without giving a reason and used their descriptions to create the prints). In another part of the exhibition, three quotes from an essay by Zora Neale Hurston are stenciled directly on the walls. Accompanying them are etchings that mimic frontispieces of the nineteenth-century narratives published by white abolitionists in which former slaves recounted their lives under slavery and the stories of their escapes. Ligon replaces the Bible verses and antislavery poems that often appeared on the title pages of the nineteenth-century narratives with quotes from contemporary authors such as Hilton Als, bell hooks, and others. Like the runaway posters that describe him, these narratives tell the story of the artist. ("Glenn Ligon: To Disembark." Exhibition brochure. Washington, D.C.: Hirshhorn Museum, 1993.)

How could you translate an exhibition such as Ligon's into a project done on paper? What parallels with Ligon's identification as an African-American with the escape of Henry "Box" Brown might you find to describe your own position in one of the ideological categories? Find a historical example that manifests the heroism of your collective group.

Incloser

Susan Howe

Susan Howe's text suggests how a photomontage or collage method may be applied to written materials. Her writing is associated with a school of poetics known as the "Language" group, which includes such figures as Charles Bernstein, Clark Coolidge, and Bob Perelman, to name only a few participants in the movement. "Incloser" takes up all the issues mentioned by Michel Leiris—collage form, autobiography, confession, and desire—but in the context that views composition from a position based on the "death of the author." This is the position from which Charles Bernstein argues, for example, that "it is a mistake to posit the self as the primary organizing feature of writing. As many others have pointed out, a poem exists in a matrix of social and historical relations [among them

its relation to its reader, who also exists in a matrix of social and historical relations] that are more significant to the formation of an individual text than any personal qualities of the life or voice of an author."

Howe's **Defenestration of Prague** ***has been described as an attempt to collapse the medieval into the contemporary, with the connections established not by means of argument or historical research, but by means of poetic association. In "Incloser" a similar operation is applied to the colonial period of New England.***

***EN-CLŌSE. See* INCLOSE.**

IN - CLŌSE,′ *v.t.* [Fr. *enclos;* Sp. It. *incluso;* L. *inclusus, includo; in* and *claudo,* 1
or *cludo.*]

1. To surround; to shut in, to confine on all sides; as, to *inclose* a field with a fence; to *inclose* a fort or an army with troops; to *inclose* a town with walls.
2. To separate from common grounds by a fence; as, to *inclose* lands.
3. To include; to shut or confine; as, to *inclose* trinkets in a box.
4. To environ; to encompass.
5. To cover with a wrapper or envelope; to cover under seal; as, to *inclose* a letter or a bank note.

IN - CLŌS′ER, *n.* He or that which incloses; one who separates land from common grounds by a fence.

—Noah Webster, *An American Dictionary of the English Language*

THOMAS SHEPARD
Anagram: O, a map's thresh'd
(W 3:513)

The first and least of those books [by Shepard] is called, **"The Sincere** 2
Convert:" ***which the Author would commonly call,*** **his ragged child;** ***and once, even after its fourth edition, wrote unto Mr. Giles Firmin thus concerning it: "That which is called,*** **'The Sincere Convert:'** ***I have not the book: I once saw it: it was a collection of such notes in a dark town in*** **England,** ***which one procuring of me, published them without my will or my privity. I scarce know what it contains, nor do I like to see it; considering the many*** **Σφαλματα Typographica,** ***most absurd; and the confession of him that published it, that it comes out much altered from what was first written. (M I:389)***

—Cotton Mather, ***Magnalia Christi Americana***

* * *

My writing has been haunted and inspired by a series of texts, woven in shrouds and cordage of classic American nineteenth-century works; they are the buried ones, they body them forth. 3

The selection of particular examples from a large group is always a social act. By choosing to install certain narratives somewhere between history, mystic speech, and poetry, I have enclosed them in an organization, although I know there are places no classificatory procedure can reach, where connections between words and things we thought existed break off. For me, paradoxes and ironies of fragmentation are particularly compelling. 4

Every statement is a product of collective desires and divisibilities. Knowledge, no matter how I get it, involves exclusion and repression. National histories hold ruptures and hierarchies. On the scales of global power, what gets crossed over? Foreign accents mark dialogues that delete them. Ambulant vagrant bastardy comes looming through assurance and sanctification. 5

THOMAS SHEPARD: A long story of conversion, and a hundred to one if some lie or other slip not out with it. Why, the secret meaning is, I pray admire me. (W 2:284) 6

When we move through the positivism of literary canons and master narratives, we consign ourselves to the legitimation of power, chains of inertia, an apparatus of capture. 7

BROTHER CRACKBONE HIS WIFE: So I gave up and I was afraid to sing because to sing a lie, Lord teach me and I'll follow thee and heard Lord will break the will of His last work. (C 140) 8

* * *

A printed book enters social and economic networks of distribution. Does the printing modify an author's intention, or does a text develop itself? Why do certain works go on saying something else? Pierre Macherey says, in *A Theory of Literary Production,* "The work has its beginnings in a break from the usual ways of speaking and writing—a break which sets it apart from all other forms of ideological expression" (TP 52). Roman Jakobson says, in "Dialogue on Time in Language and Literature": "One of the essential differences between spoken and written language can be seen clearly. The former has a purely temporal character, while the latter connects time and space. While the sounds that we hear disappear, when we read we usually have immobile letters before us and the time of the written flow of words is reversible" (V 20). Gertrude Stein says, in "Patriarchal Poetry": "They said they said. / They said they said when they said men. / Men many men many how many many many many men men men said many here" (YS 132). Emily Dickinson writes to her sister-in-law, Susan Gilbert Dickinson: "Moving 9 on in the Dark like Loaded Boats at Night, though there is no Course, there is Boundlessness—" (L 871).

Strange translucencies: letters, phonemes, syllables, rhymes, shorthand 10
segments, alliteration, assonance, meter, form a ladder to an outside state outside of States. Rungs between escape and enclosure are confusing and compelling.

BROTHER CRACKBONE HIS WIFE: And seeing house burned down, I thought it was 11
just and mercy to save life of the child and that I saw not after again my children there. And as my spirit was fiery so to burn all I had, and hence prayed Lord would send fire of word, baptize me with fire. And since the Lord hath set my heart at liberty. (C 140)

* * *

There was the last refuge from search and death; so here. (W 2.196) 12

I am a poet writing near the close of the twentieth century. 13

Little by little sound grew to be meaning. I cross an invisible line spoken 14
in the first word "Then." Every prescriptive grasp assertion was once a hero reading Samson. There and here I encounter one vagabond formula another pure Idea. To such a land. Yet has haunts. The heart of its falls must be crossed and re-crossed. October strips off cover and quiet conscience.

New England is the place I am. Listening to the clock and the sun whirl 15
dry leaves along. Distinguishing first age from set hour. The eternal and spirit in them.

A poem can prevent onrushing light going out. Narrow path in the teeth 16
of proof. Fire of words will try us. Grace given to few. Coming home though bent and bias for the sake of why so. Awkward as I am. Here and there invincible things as they are.

I write quietly to her. She is a figure of other as thin as paper. 17

Sorrow for uproar and wrongs of this world. You covenant to love. 18

* * *

EMILY DICKINSON:

Master.
If you saw a bullet
hit a Bird—and he told you
he was'nt shot—you might weep
at his courtesy, but you would
certainly doubt his word—
(ML 32)

If history is a record of survivors, Poetry shelters other voices. 19

Dickinson, Melville, Thoreau, and Hawthorne guided me back to what I 20
once thought was the distant seventeenth century. Now I know that the arena in which Scripture battles raged among New Englanders with originary fury is part of our current American system and events, history and structure.

GOODWIFE WILLOWS: Then I had a mind for New England and I thought I should 21
know more of my own heart. So I came and thought I saw more than ever I could have believed that I wondered earth swallowed me not up. And 25 Matthew 5—foolish virgins saw themselves void of all grace. I thought I was so and was gone no farther. And questioned all that ever the Lord had wrought, I'll never leave thee. I could now apprehend that yet desired the Lord not to leave me nor forsake me and afterward I thought I was now discovered. Yet hearing He would not hide His face forever, was encouraged to seek. But I felt my heart rebellious and loathe to submit unto Him. (C 151)

An English relation of conversion spoken at a territorial edge of America 22
is deterritorialized and deterred by anxiety crucial to iconoclastic Puritan piety. Inexplicable acoustic apprehension looms over assurance and sanctification, over soil subsoil sea sky.

Each singular call. As the sound is the sense is. Severed on this side. Who 23
would know there is a covenant. In a new world morphologies are triggered off. . . .

* * *

Finding is the First Act (MBED 1043)

After the beaver population in New England had been decimated by 24
human greed, when roads were cut through unopened countryside, the roadbuilders often crossed streams on abandoned beaver dams, instead of taking time to construct wooden bridges. When other beaver dams collapsed from neglect, they left in their wake many years' accumulation of dead bark, leaves, twigs, and silt. Ponds they formed disappeared with the dams, leaving rich soil newly opened to the sun. These old pond bottoms, often many acres wide, provided fertile agricultural land. Here grass grew as high as a person's shoulder. Without these natural meadows many settlements could not have been established as soon as they were.

Early narratives of conversion and first captivity narratives in New Eng- 25
land are often narrated by women. A woman, afraid of not speaking well, tells her story to a man who writes it down. The participant reporters follow and

fly out of Scripture and each other. All testimonies are bereft, brief, hungry, pious, *authorized.*

Shock of God's voice speaking English. 26

Sound moves over the chaos of place in people. In this hungry world 27
anyone may be eaten. What a nest and litter. A wolf lies coiled in the lamb.

Silence becomes a Self. Open your mouth. 28

In such silence women were talking. Undifferentiated powerlessness 29
swallowed them. When did the break at this degree of distance happen?

Silence calls me himself. Open your mouth. 30

Whosoever. Not found written in the book of life. 31

During a later Age of Reason eighteenth-century Protestant gentlemen 32
signed the Constitution in the city of Philadelphia. These first narratives from wide-open places re-place later genial totalities.

During the 1850s, when the Republic was breaking apart, newly exposed 33
soil from abandoned narratives was as rich and fresh as a natural meadow.

Emily Dickinson and Herman Melville are bridge builders. Their writing 34
vaults the streams. They lead me in nomad spaces. They sieve cipherings, hesitations, watchings, survival of sound-meaning associations: the hound and cry, track and call. So much strangeness from God. What is saved to be said.

Once dams, narratives are bridges. 35

In 1850, when Melville wrote about American literary expression, he 36
called the essay "Hawthorne and His Mosses" and chose a fragment from Hawthorne's story of Puritan doubt.

" 'Faith!' shouted Goodman Brown, in a voice of agony and desperation; 37
and the echoes of the forest mocked him, crying—'Faith! Faith!' as if bewildered wretches were seeking her all through the wilderness" (PT 251).

* * *

THOMAS SHEPARD:

Object. But Christ is in heaven; how can I receive him and his love? 38

Ans. A mighty prince is absent from a traitor; he sends his herald with a letter 39
of love, he gives it him to read; how can he receive the love of the prince when absent? *Ans.* He sees his love in his letter, he knows it came from him, and so at a distance closeth with him by this means; so here, he that was dead, but now is alive, writes, sends to thee; O, receive his love here in his word; this is receiving "him by faith." (W 2:599–600)

In Europe, Protestant tradition since Luther had maintained that no one 40
could fully express her sins. In New England, for some reason hard to determine, Protestant strictures were reversed. Bare promises were insufficient. Leaders and followers had to voice the essential mutability they

suddenly faced. Now the minister's scribal hand copied down an applicant for church membership's narrative of mortification and illumination.

In *The Puritan Conversion Narrative: The Beginnings of American Expression,* Patricia Caldwell points out that during the 1630s, in the Bay Colony, a disclaimer about worthlessness and verbal inadequacy had to be followed by a verbal performance strong enough to convince the audience-congregation of the speaker's sincerity. 41

New England's first isolated and independent clerics must have wrestled with many conflicting impulses and influences. Rage against authority and rage for order, desire for union with the Father and the guilty knowledge they had abandoned their own mothers and fathers. In the 1630s a new society was being shaped or shaping itself. Oppositional wreckers and builders considered themselves divine instruments committed to the creation of a holy commonwealth. In 1636 the antinomian controversy erupted among this "Singular Prospect of Churches erected in an *American* Corner of the World, on purpose to express and pursue the Protestant *Reformation*" (MC 172). 42

The antinomian controversy circled around a woman, Anne Hutchinson, and what was seen to be "the Flewentess of her Tonge and her Willingness to open herselfe and to divulge her Opinions and to sowe her seed in us that are but highway side and Strayngers to her" (AC 353). Thomas Shepard made this accusation. Paradoxically, he was one of the few ministers who required women to recite their confessions of faith publicly, before the gathered congregation. Hugh Peter lectured Anne Hutchinson in court: "You have stept out of your place, *you have rather bine a Husband than a Wife and a preacher than a Hearer; and a Magistrate than a Subject.* And soe you have thought to carry all Thinges in Church and Commonwealth, as you would and have not bine humbled for this" (AC 382–83). 43

Peter, Cotton, Winthrop, Eliot, Wilson, Dudley, Shepard, and other men had stepped out of their places when they left England. She was humbled by them for their Transgression. Anne Hutchinson was the community scapegoat. "The Mother Opinion of all the rest. . . . From the womb of this *fruitful opinion,* and from the countenance here by given to immediate and unwarranted revelations, 'tis not easie to relate how many monsters, worse than African, arose in these regions of *America:* But a *synod* assembled at *Cambridge,* whereof Mr. Shepard was no small part, most happily crushed them all" (M I:386). 44

NOAH WEBSTER:

SCĀPE´-GŌAT, *n.* [*escape* and *goat*] In *the Jewish ritual,* a goat which was brought to the door of the tabernacle, where the high priest laid his hands upon him, confessing the sins of the people, and putting them on the head of the goat; after which the goat was sent into the wilderness, bearing the iniquities of the people. *Lev.* xvi. (WD 986) 45

Kenneth Burke says, in *A Grammar of Motives,* "Dialectic of the 46
Scapegoat": "When the attacker chooses for himself the object of attack, it is usually his blood brother; the debunker is much closer to the debunked than others are; Ahab was pursued by the white whale he was pursuing" (GM 406–7).

René Girard says, in *The Scapegoat,* "What is a Myth?": "Terrified as they 47
[the persecutors] are by their own victim, they see themselves as completely passive, purely reactive, totally controlled by this scapegoat at the very moment when they rush to his attack. They think that all initiative comes from him. There is only room for a single cause in their field of vision, and its triumph is absolute, it absorbs all other causality: it is the scapegoat" (S 43).

I say that the Scapegoat Dialectic and mechanism is peculiarly open to 48
violence if the attacker is male; his bloodbrother, female. Kenneth Burke and René Girard dissect grammars and mythologies in a realm of discourse structured, articulated, and repeated by men.

THOMAS SHEPARD: We are all in Adam, as a whole country in a parliament man; 49
the whole country doth what he doth. And although we made no particular choice of Adam to stand for us, yet the Lord made it for us; who, being goodness itself, bears more good will to man than he can or could bear to himself; and being wisdom itself, made the wisest choice, and took the wisest course for the good of man. (W I:24)

* * *

A Short Story

GOVERNOR WINTHROP: She thinkes that the Soule is annihilated by the Judge- 50
ment that was sentenced upon Adam. Her Error springs from her Mistaking of the Curse of God upon Adam, for that Curse doth not implye Annihilation of the soule and body, but only a dissolution of the Soule and Body.

MR. ELIOT: She thinks the Soule to be Nothinge but a Breath, and so vanisheth. 51
I pray put that to her.

MRS. HUTCHINSON: *I thinke the soule to be nothing but Light.* (AC 356) 52

* * *

The Erroneous Gentlewoman

GOVERNOR WINTHROP: We have thought good to send for you to understand 53
how things are, that if you be in an erroneous way we may reduce you that so you may become a profitable member here among us. (AC 312)

THOMAS SHEPARD: I confes I am wholy unsatisfied in her Expressions to some of the Errors. Any Hereticke may bringe a slye Interpritation, upon any of thease Errors and yet hould them to thear Death: therfor I am unsatisfied. (AC 377) 54

ANNE HUTCHINSON: My Judgment is not altered though my Expression alters. 55

BROTHER WILLSON: Your Expressions, whan your Expressions are soe contrary to the Truth. (AC 378) 56

NOAH WEBSTER: EX-PRES´SION, (eks-presh´un,) *n.* The act of expressing; the act of forcing out by pressure, as juices and oils from plants. 57

2. The act of uttering, declaring, or representing; utterance; declaration; 58
representation; as, an *expression* of the public will. (WD 426)

MRS. HUTCHINSON: I doe not acknowledge it to be an Error but a Mistake. *I doe acknowledge my Expression to be Ironious but my Judgment was not Ironious,* for I held befor as you did but could not express it soe. (AC 361) 59

NOAH WEBSTER: ER-RO´NE-OUS, *a.* [L.-*erroneus,* from *erro,* to err.] 60

1. Wandering; roving; unsettled.

They roam
Erroneous and disconsolate. *Philips.*

2. Deviating; devious; irregular; wandering from the right course.

Erroneous circulation of blood *Arbuthnot.* (WD 408)

ANNE HUTCHINSON: *So thear was my Mistake. I tooke Soule for Life.* (AC 360) 61

NOAH WEBSTER: Noah is here called *Man.* (WD xxiii) 62

* * *

KEY

AC Hall, David D. *The Antinomian Controversy, 1636–1638: A Documentary History.* Edited by David D. Hall. Middletown, Conn.: Wesleyan University Press, 1968.

C Shepard, Thomas. *Thomas Shepard's "Confessions."* Edited by George Selement and Bruce C. Woolley. In *Collections of the Colonial Society of Massachusetts,* vol. 58. Boston: The Society, 1981.

GM Burke, Kenneth. *A Grammar of Motives.* New York: Georges Braziller, 1955.

L Dickinson, Emily. *The Letters of Emily Dickinson.* 3 vols. Edited by Thomas H. Johnson and Theodora Ward. Cambridge, Mass.: The Belknap Press, Harvard University Press, 1958.

M Mather, Cotton. *Magnalia Christi Americana: or, The Ecclesiastical History of New-England.* 2 vols. Hartford, Conn.: Silus Andrus & Son, 1855.

MBED Dickinson, Emily. *The Manuscript Books of Emily Dickinson.* 2 vols. Edited by R. W. Franklin. Cambridge, Mass.: The Belknap Press, Harvard University Press, 1981.

ML Dickinson, Emily. *The Master Letters of Emily Dickinson.* Edited by R. W. Franklin. Amherst, Mass.: Amherst College Press, 1986.

PT Melville, Herman. *The Piazza Tales, and Other Prose Pieces.* Edited by Harrison Hayford, Alma A. MacDougall, and G. Thomas Tanselle. Evanston and Chicago: Northwestern University Press and the Newberry Library, 1987.

S Girard, Rene. *The Scapegoat.* Translated by Yvonne Freccero. Baltimore: Johns Hopkins University Press, 1986.

TP Macherey, Pierre. *A Theory of Literary Production.* Translated by Geoffrey Wall. London: Routledge & Kegan Paul, 1978.

V Jakobson, Roman. *Verbal Art, Verbal Sign, Verbal Time.* Edited by Krystyna Pomorska and Stephen Rudy. Minneapolis: University of Minnesota Press, 1985.

W Shepard, Thomas. *The Works of Thomas Shepard.* 3 vols. Edited by John A. Albro. 1853. Reprint, New York: AMS, 1967.

WD Webster, Noah. *An American Dictionary of the English Language.* Revised and enlarged by Chauncey A. Goodrich. Springfield, Mass.: George and Charles Merriam, 1852.

YS Stein, Gertrude. *The Yale Gertrude Stein.* Edited by Richard Kostelanetz. New Haven, Conn.: Yale University Press, 1980.

For Discussion and Writing

1. What effect does Howe achieve by shifting the orientation of her composition, by rearranging the elements of subjectivity and objectivity. The objective element is present in that she has researched the historical archive of the colonial period. At the same time, she conveys the idea that her references to the autobiography of the Puritan Thomas Shepard and the life of Anne Hutchinson and their context is a way to think about her own autobiography. How does she use external scholarly materials (citations from Shepard, accounts of certain historical events or conditions) to evoke inner experience or personal emotion? What is the ideological or political effect of "Incloser"? With whom does the author identify? with Shepard? with Anne Hutchinson?
2. Do some background research on the figures included in "Incloser." Assuming that Howe is using the historical information allegorically or metaphorically, what sort of commentary effect is created by juxtaposing the Puritan setting with our contemporary circumstances? Use a literary history to locate some typical writers of another period of American letters (or of another culture). Compose a collage of citations, historical events, and personal reflections in the manner of Howe's composition. Use her technique of investigating certain specific terms found in the writings (such as "inclose") as an organizing device.
3. Howe's selection of materials to include in her composition is guided not only by her ideological concerns as a woman and as an American, but also by her interests as a poet. In her reflexive statements about writing

"Incloser" she refers frequently to the "sound" of the words she is using: "Little by little sound grew to be meaning." Locate passages that seem to be included for their "acoustic" interest as much as for their historical value. What is the effect of mixing the styles of citation, commentary, and poetry in this piece?

From How to Become Paranoia-Critical

Salvador Dali

As Gregory Bateson wrote in Steps to an Ecology of Mind, *"We might regard patterning or predictability as the very essence of communication; communication is the creation of redundancy or patterning." Working within the movement of surrealism, Salvador Dali developed a method of research he called "paranoia-critical activity." That is to say, Dali imitated the systematic associations peculiar to paranoid behavior, which he turned into an experimental method of research, his paranoia-critical activity, a "spontaneous method of irrational understanding based upon the interpretative critical association of delirious phenomena; an organizational and productive force of objective chance." Dali's strategy may be imitated in the mystory by applying it to the information produced through the research into figures of identification (as in the cases of Lipton and Howe). The chance or coincidental convergence of details linking one set of information with another provides an organizing structure with which to pull together the disparate materials of one's mystory. Mystory, in other words, achieves coherence not at the level of generality—of concepts or abstractions that embrace and unify diverse particulars under one category—but at the level of the particular itself, through the repetition of concrete details within the words (sounds and images) of the text.*

As Susan Howe said, "The selection of particular examples from a large group is always a social act." Dali also foregrounds his act of selection as meaningful—as itself an act of writing—although he characterizes his motive as "obsessional." Dali and Howe equally draw upon the aesthetics of "correspondences," in which the materials of arts and history are used to explore or project inner experience. Salvador Dali, a Spaniard who settled in Paris in 1929, is best known for paintings that combine fantasy with meticulously realistic representation, such as his picture of soft or melting watches. Because of his genius for self-promotion, he became the best-known representative of surrealism in the public mind. ("Gala" is Dali's wife.) Dali's discussion of a train station as a representation of his personal "standard of measure" shows how the mystory poses particular, idiosyncratic categories of organization against

"universal," consensual ones and, in so doing, reveals the equally arbitrary character of the latter.

Every year, when we leave Cadaqués for Paris, our old Cadillac takes us 1
to the station at Perpignan, where I wait in the waiting room while Gala checks the baggage. There are people all around me. I feel as if isolated and that is when I have an instant of absolute pleasure. I have just left my Cadaqués studio and its stimulating climate of creative work in which I live in a state of perpetual alert, and am on my way to Paris with its gastronomical feasts, its erotic celebrations. I sit on my bench as at a border crossing, I feel myself available, and intense jubilation invades me, a monumental joyfulness.

At this precise moment I visualize the painting I ought to have painted 2
during the summer. I buy a scientific journal at the newsstand and read that, in operating for glaucoma, the eye anesthetic used is a "diffusion factor" made from wasp venom. I immediately recall that one day a wasp fell into my paint-pan and the fusion of the color pigments took place with miraculous flexibility and ductility. I wonder whether wasp venom could not be used as a color solvent. Since then, based on my intuition, I have had such a medium made and it is one of the secrets of my art of painting.

So, for years, the station at Perpignan has been a source of enlighten- 3
ment, a cathedral of intuition to me. I long thought it was because genius needed a trivial place in which to assert itself. The Parthenon and Niagara Falls are too overwhelming! The absurd and the anodyne are better handmaidens to enlightenment. The memories of the unconscious let their passages get through only when the mind is vacant, and toilet seats are a high place for the state of grace, quite as good as the Perpignan station.

Then in 1966, I found out that it was at Perpignan that the measure of 4
earth, the standard meter, had been established. On a straight line twelve kilometers long, from Vernet to the outskirts of Salses, north of Perpignan, Pierre Méchain, in 1796, set the bases for the triangulation that led to determining the standard meter. I understood the fundamental metaphysical significance of this research. The standard meter is not only one ten-millionth of a quarter of the earth's meridian, it is also the formula for the density of God, and this place appears to me privileged among all places. The Perpignan station becomes a truly high place.

I then took a taxi and went slowly around the station, inspecting it as if it 5
were some esoteric monument of which I had to find the meanings. The setting sun was ablaze and the flood of its light created flames on the facades and especially the central skylight of the station that seemed to become the center of an atomic explosion. About the station I could see a radiating aura in a perfect circle: the metal trolley cables of the streetcars that ringed the edifice and gave it a crown of glinting light. My penis sprang to attention with joy and ecstasy: I had seized truth, I was living it. Everything became overpoweringly evident. The center of the universe was there before me.

Physical, mathematical, and astronomical sciences are split over whether the world is finite or infinite. No one has yet answered that key question. At that moment, I knew that the world is limited on *only one side,* which is its *axis.* I cannot put into words the vision and certainty I had, but from that moment on there was no longer any doubt in me: cosmic space began in front of the facade of the Perpignan station in the area marked off by the circle of cables, and the universe ended at the same point. 6

This very limit was the proof of the existence of the universe; it showed that the hypothesis of permanent expansion was erroneous. Non-Euclidian space stopped at the point where it met the dimension of the mind. This limit could not be defined but could appear only as a vision, a snapshot of absolute time-space that illuminated me viscerally. I decided to have the Perpignan station cast in gold as a transcendent image of truth. To me it is the laboratory in which the absolute values of the universe can be followed, and I inspect it with passion. Under the impulse of my paranoiac delirium, I have had attentive analyses of the monument made. All its measurements have been noted. Not only the general dimensions, but those of windows, doors, ticket windows, benches. I have had the posters photographed, and the timetables which in enlargement show me all the shapes of objective chance, and starting from my delirious impressions I will be able to set up a kind of seismographic system of the relationships of the universe with itself. The point is to bring total truth out of this microcosm of the universe. I am persuaded that the bible of the world is symbolically represented in the Perpignan station; I know this in my innermost self: all that is needed is to find the decoding key. 7

Each year supplies me with new proofs. Do you know that the only drawing Sigmund Freud ever made is a sketch of his student bedroom, which is exactly the same shape as the waiting room of the Perpignan station? 8

I am like the alchemist trying to apprehend the non-measurable through the measurable, and the power of my paranoia-critical delirium will see me through. A meter is now defined as equal to 1,650,753.73 times the wavelength in a vacuum of the difference between the levels of 2 P 10 and 5 D 5 of a krypton atom, or the orange-red radiation of krypton 86, but this precision to the thousandth of a micron is insignificant compared to my ability to conceive that the x of the radiations of krypton is an equivalence of God, whose temple is the quite derisory, anodyne Perpignan station, so made in order that none may suspect its importance, but which I have now designated as the focal point of all universality of thought. 9

For Discussion and Writing

1. **Discuss the role of research in Dali's obsessive relationship with the Perpignan railway station. The strategy of using "paranoia" in a critical way is to decide to take personally the phenomena of culture. Once an**

item, object, place, or product is selected for this attention (either intuitively or arbitrarily), one researches the selection to find the surprising link between the objective and subjective materials. Language (including discourse and all the productions of culture) is the meeting ground of the individual with the collective context. André Breton (the official founder of surrealism), for example, observed the date 1713 in his initials. A number one set very closely to a number seven with a crossed vertical leg (a European custom) resembles an A with a flat rather than a pointed top (17). A number one set very closely to a number three resembles a B (13). In his version of the signature experiment Breton then researched the events of 1713 to find an allegorical commentary on his own existence. In the library find a reference book that explains the features of paranoid behavior. Make a list of the qualities of paranoia and use it to generate a list of instructions for analyzing a work of art.

2. Discuss Dali's strategy as an analogy in comparison with Leiris's analogy with the bullfight. In a reference book find another symptomology for a different mental or physical disorder and use it to generate a list of practices for a research or composition methodology. Test your new method by applying it as instructions for writing about a work of art or letters.
3. One of the useful features of Dali's relay is the way it turns a specific place familiar to the artist into a pattern for ordering other information. Select a place with which you are familiar and research its background or history. Use the paranoia-critical method to relate this place to your experience and to books you have read (including *Text Book*). Keep in mind the architect Rem Koolhaas's definition. "Paranoia is a delirium of interpretation. Each fact, event, force, observation is caught in one system of speculation and 'understood' by the afflicted individual in such a way that it absolutely confirms and reinforces his thesis—that is, the initial delusion which is his point of departure. Just as in a magnetic field metal molecules align themselves to exert a collective, cumulative pull, so, through unstoppable, systematic and in themselves strictly rational associations, the paranoiac turns the whole world into a magnetic field of facts, all pointing in the same direction."

From The Way to Rainy Mountain

N. Scott Momaday

N. Scott Momaday shows how to put together the elements articulated in the preceding relays into an overall arrangement in a way that is very useful for the mystory. Using a tripartite form, clearly marking the separate levels of discourse, Momaday juxtaposes three levels of his cultural experience: the Kiowa myths that he learned from his grandmother; the actual history of the Kiowa symbolized in these myths; his personal recollections of his childhood on the reservation. While these three levels are similar to those Susan Howe mentions in her reflections on her own method ("history, mystic speech, and poetry"), Momaday makes his personal experience a more explicit part of the composition. In this example we observe the use of identification (with his grandmother Aho and grandfather Mammedaty); the use of pattern (the unity of each section is created by the repetition of a detail within the information across the three levels); the use of setting to express feeling (the memories of scenes from the reservation). Most important is the location of Momaday's memories of childhood in the context of the traditional stories and actual history of his group (the Kiowa), thus bringing the three levels of his symbolic experience into contact—personal, historical, mythical. Note the resemblance of Momaday's use of fragments and anecdotes with Barthes's tripartite structure in A Lover's Discourse.

N. Scott Momaday, professor of English and comparative literature at the University of Arizona, won the Pulitzer Prize in 1969 for his novel House Made of Dawn. *He has become perhaps the best-known American-Indian writer. His mother was one-eighth Cherokee and his father was Kiowa.* The Way to Rainy Mountain *is a collection of thirty-four three-paragraph units (plus an introduction and epilogue) and is illustrated with drawings by Momaday's father.*

I

You know, everything had to begin, and this is how it was: the Kiowas came one by one into the world through a hollow log. They were many more than now, but not all of them got out. There was a woman whose body was swollen up with child, and she got stuck in the log. After that, no one could get through, and that is why the Kiowas are a small tribe in number. They looked all around and saw the world. It made them glad to see so many things. They called themselves *Kwuda,* "coming out." 1

They called themselves Kwuda *and later* Tepda, *both of which mean "coming out." And later still they took the name* Gaigwu, *a name which can be taken to indicate something of which the two halves differ from each other in appearance. It was once a custom among Kiowa warriors that they cut their hair on the right side of the head only and on a line level with the lobe of the ear, while on the left they let the hair grow long and wore it in a thick braid wrapped in otter skin. "Kiowa" is indicated in sign language by holding the hand palm up and slightly cupped to the right side of the head and rotating it back and forth from the wrist. "Kiowa" is thought to derive from the softened Comanche form of* Gaigwu. 2

I remember coming out upon the northern Great Plains in the late spring. There were meadows of blue and yellow wildflowers on the slopes, and I could see the still, sunlit plain below, reaching away out of sight. At first there is no discrimination in the eye, nothing but the land itself, whole and impenetrable. But then smallest things begin to stand out of the depths—herds and rivers and groves—and each of these has perfect being in terms of distance and of silence and of age. Yes, I thought, now I see the earth as it really is; never again will I see things as I saw them yesterday or the day before. 3

III

Before there were horses the Kiowas had need of dogs. That was a long time ago, when dogs could talk. There was a man who lived alone; he had been thrown away, and he made his camp here and there on the high ground. Now it was dangerous to be alone, for there were enemies all around. The man spent his arrows hunting food. He had one arrow left, and he shot a bear; but the bear was only wounded and it ran away. The man wondered what to do. Then a dog came up to him and said that many enemies were coming; they were close by and all around. The man could think of no way to save himself. But the dog said: "You know, I have puppies. They are young and weak and they have nothing to eat. If you will take care of my puppies, I will show you how to get away." The dog led the man here and there, around and around, and they came to safety. 4

A hundred years ago the Comanche Ten Bears remarked upon the great number of horses which the Kiowas owned. "When we first knew you," he said, "you had nothing but dogs and sleds." It was so; the dog is primordial. Perhaps it was dreamed into being. 5

The principal warrior society of the Kiowas was the Ka-itsenko, *"Real Dogs," and it was made up of ten men only, the ten most brave. Each of these men wore a long ceremonial sash and carried a sacred arrow. In*

time of battle he must by means of this arrow impale the end of his sash to the earth and stand his ground to the death. Tradition has it that the founder of the **Ka-itsenko** ***had a dream in which he saw a band of warriors, outfitted after the fashion of the society, being led by a dog. The dog sang the song of the*** **Ka-itsenko,** ***then said to the dreamer: "You are a dog; make a noise like a dog and sing a dog song."***

There were always dogs about my grandmother's house. Some of them were nameless and lived a life of their own. They belonged there in a sense that the word "ownership" does not include. The old people paid them scarcely any attention, but they should have been sad, I think, to see them go. 6

XXI

Mammedaty was the grandson of Guipahgo, and he was well-known on that account. Now and then Mammedaty drove a team and wagon out over the plain. Once, in the early morning, he was on the way to Rainy Mountain. It was summer and the grass was high and meadowlarks were calling all around. You know, the top of the plain is smooth and you can see a long way. There was nothing but the early morning and the land around. Then Mammedaty heard something. Someone whistled to him. He looked up and saw the head of a little boy nearby above the grass. He stopped the horses and got down from the wagon and went to see who was there. There was no one; there was nothing there. He looked for a long time, but there was nothing there.

There is a single photograph of Mammedaty. He is looking past the camera and a little to one side. In his face there is calm and good will, strength and intelligence. His hair is drawn close to the scalp, and his braids are long and wrapped with fur. He wears a kilt, fringed leggings, and beaded moccasins. In his right hand there is a peyote fan. A family characteristic: the veins stand out in his hands, and his hands are small and rather long. 8

Mammedaty saw four things that were truly remarkable. This head of the child was one, and the tracks of the water beast another. Once, when he walked near the pecan grove, he saw three small alligators on a log. No one had ever seen them before and no one ever saw them again. Finally, there was this: something had always bothered Mammedaty, a small aggravation that was never quite out of mind, like a name on the tip of the tongue. He had always wondered how it is that the mound of earth which a mole makes around the opening of its burrow is so fine. It is nearly as fine as powder, and it seems almost to 9 have been sifted. One day Mammedaty was sitting quietly when a mole came out of the earth. Its cheeks were puffed out as if it had been a squirrel packing nuts. It looked all around for a moment, then blew the fine dark earth out of its mouth. And this it did again and again, until there was a ring of black, powdery earth on the ground. That was a strange and meaningful thing to see. It meant that Mammedaty had got possession of a powerful medicine.

XXIV

10 East of my grandmother's house, south of the pecan grove, there is buried a woman in a beautiful dress. Mammedaty used to know where she is buried, but now no one knows. If you stand on the front porch of the house and look eastward towards Carnegie, you know that the woman is buried somewhere within the range of your vision. But her grave is unmarked. She was buried in a cabinet, and she wore a beautiful dress. How beautiful it was! It was one of those fine buckskin dresses, and it was decorated with elk's teeth and beadwork. That dress is still there, under the ground.

11 ***Aho's high moccasins are made of softest, cream-colored skins. On each instep there is a bright disc of beadwork—an eight-pointed star, red and pale blue on a white field—and there are bands of beadwork at the soles and ankles. The flaps of the leggings are wide and richly ornamented with blue and red and green and white and lavender beads.***

12 East of my grandmother's house the sun rises out of the plain. Once in his life a man ought to concentrate his mind upon the remembered earth, I believe. He ought to give himself up to a particular landscape in his experience, to look at it from as many angles as he can, to wonder about it, to dwell upon it. He ought to imagine that he touches it with his hands at every season and listens to the sounds that are made upon it. He ought to imagine the creatures there and all the faintest motions of the wind. He ought to recollect the glare of noon and all the colors of the dawn and dusk.

For Discussion and Writing

1. Momaday is a good relay for what mystory is trying to achieve in that in his Native American culture the individual readily acknowledges his or her part in a collective order. Reflecting the point of view of an oral culture, the Native American author treats the public traditions of the tribe as a personal memory. As a research collage, *Rainy Mountain* tells the Kiowa story from four perspectives, as Kenneth Lincoln explains:

> The tribal or folkloric memory speaks through Aho, the grandmother muse; the pictorial or visual mode projects through the senior Momaday's drawings to illustrate his mother's stories to her grandson; the historical or public medium documents events through James Mooney's *Calendar History of the Kiowa Indians* (1898), borrowings from Elsie Clews Parson's *Kiowa Tales* (1929), and parallels with Mildred P. Mayhall's *The Kiowas* (1962); the personal or impressionist voice elegizes a journey through Momaday's own re-created pilgrimage from Montana to Oklahoma, occasioned by Aho's death.

Place Momaday on the list of ideological categories. Use Momaday's example to compose a list of your own equivalents of the groups and individuals with whom Momaday identifies. Do some research to locate the collective and personal resources available for citation in your own version of *Rainy Mountain.*

2. What are the formal lessons of *Rainy Mountain?* Notice how the three parts of each unit in Momaday's composition are linked. In the opening paragraph of *Mind Tools: The Five Levels of Mathematical Reality,* Rudy Rucker observes that "mathematics is the study of pure pattern, and everything in the cosmos is a kind of pattern." Look for the pattern that appears in the information you gathered in exercise 1 above. Compare your pattern with the patterns constructed by each of the authors represented in this chapter.
3. One goal of mystory as an experiment is to learn how to replace argumentation with mood as a way to guide research. Mystory thus shares some of the same attitudes expressed by a new generation of graphic designers who are inventing a hybrid approach to visualization that draws equally on the arts and industrial design. "It may address a problem," Rich Poyner has argued in the design magazine *I.D.,* "but it is absolved from the need to find a solution in the closed, objective, rational sense that still informs so much rhetoric about graphic design." The opposition between style and idea, he says, "is misleading because it never seems to acknowledge that the solution to a communication problem might be a mood, emotion, or atmosphere." One motive for this shift is to leave a place for the reader in the construction of the text (interactive texts are written from the position of receiver rather than author—a receiver of the traditions of existing high and popular culture). If there are to be any arguments made, the reader of the mystory, not the composer, supplies them.

   The emotion generated during the process of composition is "objective" in that it does not necessarily exist prior to the activity of research; the writer does not express this emotion. Rather, the experiment shows a potential scene of emotion to the writer, who then decides to grasp it, research it, and repeat it through a series of elaborations and enlargements to learn what it has to say about the relation of the writer to the cultural contexts brought together in the mystory. The text creates the experience; it does not "represent" a prior experience within the standards of a realism. The writer is free to reject the comment of the miniaturized pattern or to interpret it. At the same time, the metaphor that emerges during the stage of *inventio* (of research, of finding and collecting the items of information from each context) may be manipulated by the writer, since an extensive number of details may be found that repeat across these discourses. The emotion functions to hold the diverse materials together in memory, more than to express an authentic reality.

The final assignment is not simply to write a mystory (whatever that might be) but to write a "discourse on method" for the mystory. Analyze and compare the readings collectively to find their pattern, to see what features they manifest that, when added together, constitute a set of instructions for making a mystory. Notice in the form and style of the relays how each one both tells about how the author wants to write and how the author performs this kind of writing at the same time. Your discourse on method (like most examples of this genre) should combine these two levels of information about the mystory in one composition: explanations of how and why one could compose a mystory; and a demonstration showing what research composed mystorically might look like. The mystory is experimental, and it could be organized in the form often used to write up the results of a scientific experiment, which would require separating the statement of what the experiment is to be, the conduct of the experiment itself, and the evaluation of the results. A discourse on method, however, combines these elements into one document that says what it does; it tells and shows the method.

Acknowledgments

Woody Allen, from *Play It Again, Sam.* Copyright © 1969 by Woody Allen. *Caution:* Professionals and amateurs are hereby warned that *Play It Again, Sam,* being fully protected under the copyright laws of the United States of America, the British Commonwealth countries, including Canada, and the other countries of the Copyright Union, is subject to a royalty. All rights, including professional, amateur, motion picture, recitation, public reading, radio, television and cable broadcasting, and the rights of translation into foreign languages, are strictly reserved. Any inquiry regarding the availability of performance rights, or the purchase of individual copies of the authorized acting edition, must be directed to Samuel French, Inc., with locations in New York, Hollywood, and Toronto, Canada.

Maya Angelou, "Graduation," from *I Know Why the Caged Bird Sings* by Maya Angelou. Copyright © 1969 by Maya Angelou. Reprinted by permission of Random House, Inc.

Margaret Atwood, "You fit into me." From *Power Politics* by Margaret Atwood. Copyright © 1971 House of Anansi Press Ltd. Reprinted with the permission of Stoddart Publishing Co. Ltd, Don Mills, Ontario.

W. H. Auden, "Let us honor . . .," Copyright 1934 and renewed 1962 by W. H. Auden. Reprinted from *W. H. Auden: Collected Poems* edited by Edward Mendelson, by permission of Random House, Inc., and Faber and Faber Ltd.

Russell Banks. "*Bambi:* A Boy's Story" by Russell Banks. From *The Movie That Changed my Life* by David Rosenberg. Copyright © by David Rosenberg. Used by permission of Viking Penguin, a division of Penguin Books USA, Inc.

George Barker. "Sonnet to my Mother." From *Collected Poems* by George Barker. Reprinted by permission of Faber and Faber Ltd.

Roland Barthes, "Waiting," "The Heart," "Images," and "Encounter," from *A Lover's Discourse* by Roland Barthes, English translation by Richard Howard. Translation copyright © 1978 by Farrar, Straus and Giroux, Inc. Reprinted by permission of Hill & Wang, a division of Farrar, Straus and Giroux, Inc.

Bruno Bettelheim, "Hansel and Gretel," from *The Uses of Enchantment: The Meaning and Importance of Fairy Tales* by Bruno Bettelheim. Copyright © 1975, 1976 by Bruno Bettelheim. Reprinted by permission of Alfred A. Knopf, Inc.

André Breton, "Broken Line." Reprinted from *Poems of André Breton: A Bilingual Anthology,* translated and edited by Jean-Pierre Cauvin and Mary Ann Caws, copyright © 1982. By permission of the University of Texas Press.

Roger Brown. Reprinted with the permission of The Free Press, a Division of Macmillan, Inc., from *Words and Things* by Roger Brown. Copyright © 1958, 1968 by The Free Press.

Robert Coover, "The Gingerbread House," from *Pricksongs and Descants* by Robert Coover. Copyright © 1969 by Robert Coover. Used by permission of Dutton Signet, a division of Penguin Books USA, Inc.

Salvador Dali, from *The Unspeakable Confessions of Salvador Dali* by Salvador Dali, pp. 156–159, as told to André Parinaud, trans. Harold J. Salemson. Translation copyright © 1976 by Harold J. Salemson. By permission of William Morrow & Co., Inc.

Jacques Derrida, reprinted from *Glas* by Jacques Derrida, English translation by John P. Leavey, Jr. and Richard Rand, by permission of University of Nebraska Press. Copyright 1986 by the University of Nebraska Press.

Jacques Derrida. From *Signesponge.* Copyright by Columbia University Press, New York. Reprinted with permission of the publisher.

Emily Dickinson, reprinted by permission of the publishers and the Trustees of Amherst College from *The Poems of Emily Dickinson,* edited by Thomas H. Johnson, Cambridge, Mass.: The Belknap Press of Harvard University Press.

Copyright 1951, © 1955, 1979, 1983 by the President and Fellows of Harvard College.

Ralph Ellison, "Hidden Name and Complex Fate." Copyright © 1964 by Ralph Ellison. Reprinted from *Shadow and Act* by Ralph Ellison, by permission of Random House, Inc.

Martin Esslin, "Aristotle and the Advertisers," reprinted by permission of Louisiana State University Press from *Meditations: Essays on Brecht, Beckett, and the Media* by Martin Esslin. Copyright © 1962, 1965, 1966, 1967, 1970, 1971, 1974, 1975, 1976, 1977, 1980 by Martin Esslin.

Robert Francis, "Pitcher." Copyright © 1953 by Robert Francis. Reprinted from *The Orb Weaver* by permission of Wesleyan University Press.

Sigmund Freud, excerpts reprinted from *Introductory Lectures on Psychoanalysis* by Sigmund Freud translated and edited by James Strachey. By permission of Liveright Publishing Corporation. Copyright © 1966 by W. W. Norton & Company, Inc. Copyright © 1965, 1964, 1963 by James Strachey. Copyright 1920, 1934 by Edward L. Bernays. Reprinted by permission of Sigmund Freud Copyrights Ltd., The Institute of Psycho-Analysis, and The Hogarth Press from *The Standard Edition of the Complete Psychological Works of Sigmund Freud* translated and edited by James Strachey.

Louise Glück, "Cottonmouth Country." Copyright © 1968 by Louise Glück. From *Firstborn* by Louise Glück, published by The Ecco Press in 1983. Reprinted by permission.

Erving Goffman, "Character Contests," from *Interaction Ritual* by Erving Goffman. Reprinted by permission of Gillian Sankoff, Executrix for Erving Goffman, Dechert, Price & Rhods, Philadelphia, PA 19102.

Brothers Grimm, "Hansel and Gretel," from *Grimm's Tales for Young and Old* by the Brothers Grimm, translated by Ralph Manheim. Translation copyright © 1977 by Ralph Manheim. Reprinted by permission of Doubleday & Company, Inc.

Brothers Grimm, "The Little Brother and the Little Sister," from *One Fairy Story Too Many* by John Ellis. Reprinted by permission of The University of Chicago Press and John Ellis.

David Hayman, reprinted from *A First-Draft of* Finnegans Wake edited and annotated by David Hayman. Copyright © 1963, by permission of David Hayman.

Susan Howe, "Incloser." Reprinted from *The Birthmark*. © 1993 by Susan Howe, Wesleyan University Press. By permission of University Press of New England.

Richard Huelsenbeck, from *Memoirs of a Dada Drummer* by Richard Huelsenbeck, edited by Hans Kleinschmidt. Copyright © 1969 by Richard Huelsenbeck; English translation. Copyright © 1974 by The Viking Press, Inc.; Intro & notes. Copyright © 1974 by Hans Kleinschmidt. Used by permission of Viking Penguin, a division of Penguin Books USA, Inc.

James Jarrett, "A Jarret in Your Text," reprinted by permission of the author.

James Joyce, "The Boarding House," from *Dubliners* by James Joyce. Copyright 1916 by B. W. Huebsch. Definitive text copyright © 1967 by the Estate of James Joyce. Reprinted by permission of Viking Penguin, Inc.

James Joyce, "Shem the Penman," from *Finnegans Wake* by James Joyce. Copyright 1939 by James Joyce. Copyright renewed © 1967 by George Joyce and Lucia Joyce. Reprinted by permission of Viking Penguin, Inc.

X. J. Kennedy, "Ars Poetica," from *Nude Descending a Staircase*. Reprinted by permission of Curtis Brown Ltd. Copyright © 1961 by X. J. Kennedy.

Robert W. Keidel, "A New Game for Managers to Play." Copyright © 1985 by The New York Times Company. Reprinted by permission.

Ono no Komachi, "Doesn't he realize . . .," from Kenneth Rexroth. *Women Poets of*

Japan. Copyright © 1977 by Kenneth Rexroth and Ikuko Atsumi. Reprinted by permission of New Directions Publishing Corporation.

George Lakoff and Mark Johnson, excerpts from *Metaphors we live by.* Copyright © 1980 by University of Chicago Press. Reprinted by permission.

Michel Leiris, from *Manhood: A Journey from Childhood into the Fierce Order of Virility,* trans. Richard Howard. Originally published by Grossman Publishers, New York, 1963. Published 1992 by the University of Chicago Press. Copyright © 1992 by University of Chicago Press. All rights reserved.

Eunice Lipton. Reprinted with the permission of Charles Scribner's Sons, an imprint of Macmillan Publishing Company from *Alias Olympia* by Eunice Lipton. Copyright © 1992 by Eunice Lipton.

W. S. Merwin, "Inscription Facing Western Sea," from *The Carrier of Ladders.* Copyright © 1970 by W. S. Merwin. Reprinted with the permission of Georges Borchardt, Inc.

W. S. Merwin, "Separation," from *The Moving Target.* Copyright © 1963 W. S. Merwin. Reprinted with the permission of Georges Borchardt, Inc.

N. Scott Momaday. Reprinted from *The Way to Rainy Mountain* by N. Scott Momaday. © 1969, The University of New Mexico Press. Reprinted with permission of the publishers.

Dorothy Parker, "You Were Perfectly Fine," from *The Portable Dorothy Parker,* edited by Brendan Gill. Copyright 1929, renewed 1957 by Dorothy Parker. Originally published in *The New Yorker.* Reprinted by permission of Viking Penguin, Inc.

Marge Piercy, "You don't understand me," from *Stone, Paper, Knife* © 1983 by Marge Piercy. Reprinted by permission of Alfred A. Knopf, Inc., a division of Random House, Inc.

Sylvia Plath, "Metaphors," from *Crossing the Water* by Sylvia Plath. Copyright © 1960 by Ted Hughes. Copyright renewed. Reprinted by permission of HarperCollins Publishers, Inc. and Faber and Faber, Ltd.

Mary Louise Pratt, "Natural Narratives," from *Toward a Speech Act Theory of Literary Discourse.* Reprinted by permission of Indiana University Press.

Raymond Queneau, "Transformations," from *Exercises in Style.* Copyright 1947 by Editions Gallimard. Translated by Barbara Wright. Reprinted by permission of New Directions Publishing Corporation.

Robert Ray, from *A Certain Tendency of the American Cinema, 1930–1980.* © 1985 by Princeton University Press. Reprinted by permission of Princeton University Press.

Adrienne Rich, "Moving in Winter," from *The Fact of a Doorframe: Poems Selected and New, 1950–1984,* by Adrienne Rich, reprinted by permission of W. W. Norton & Company, Inc. Copyright © 1984 by Adrienne Rich.

Susan Sontag, excerpts from *AIDS and Its Metaphors* by Susan Sontag. Copyright © 1988, 1989 by Susan Sontag. Reprinted by permission of Farrar, Straus and Giroux, Inc.

Dale Spender, "The Male Line," from *Man Made Language.* Reprinted by permission of Routledge & Kegan Paul.

Stephen Spender, "Word." Copyright 1948 by Stephen Spender. Reprinted from *Selected Poems* by Stephen Spender, by permission of Random House, Inc. and Faber and Faber, Ltd.

Wallace Stevens, "Domination of Black." Copyright © 1923 and renewed 1951 by Wallace Stevens. Reprinted from *The Collected Poems* by Wallace Stevens. Reprinted by permission of Alfred A. Knopf, Inc.

Wallace Stevens, "The Motive for Metaphor." Copyright © 1947 by Wallace Stevens. Reprinted from *The Collected Poems* by Wallace Stevens. Reprinted by permission of Alfred A. Knopf, Inc.

August Strindberg, "The Stronger," translated by Elizabeth Sprigge. Copyright © 1955 by Elizabeth Sprigge. Reprinted by permission of A. P. Watt, Ltd. on behalf of Ruth Lumley-Smith.

Judith Jarvis Thomson, from "A Defense of Abortion," *Philosophy and Public Affairs* 1, no. 1 (Fall 1971). Copyright © 1971 by Princeton University Press. Reprinted with permission of Princeton University Press.

Lionel Trilling, "Of This Time, of That Place," from *Of This Time, of That Place* by Lionel Trilling, copyright © 1979 by Diana Trilling and James Trilling. Reprinted by permission of Harcourt Brace & Company.

Patricia J. Williams, from "On Being the Object of Property," from *Signs: Journal of Women in Culture and Society.* Vol. 14:1, 1988. Reprinted by permission of the University of Chicago Press, Journals Division, and Patricia J. Williams.

William Carlos Williams, "The Use of Force," from *The Doctor Stories.* Copyright 1938 by William Carlos Williams. Reprinted by permission of New Directions Publishing Corporation.

Jack Zipes, "The Politics of Fairy Tales," reprinted from Jack Zipes, *Breaking the Magic Spell: Radical Theories of Folk and Fairy Tales.* Copyright © 1979. By permission of the University of Texas Press.

Art Permissions

Nike advertisement courtesy of Chiat-Day Adv./Gary McGuire Photo. Reprinted with permission.

Prudential "Life Insurance as Individual as You Are" reprinted with permission.

W. B. Roddenbery's Whole Dill Pickles label reprinted with permission.

Vista advertisement reprinted courtesy of Hilton International/Vista International Hotels, Cydney Roach-Lawrence copy writer. Agency: Doyle Graf Mabley.

Index

Instructor's Manual to Accompany

Instructor's Manual

to accompany

<u>TEXT BOOK</u>

An Introduction to Literary Language

Second Edition

Instructor's Manual

to accompany

TEXT BOOK

An Introduction to Literary Language

Second Edition

Robert Scholes
Nancy R. Comley
Gregory L. Ulmer

St. Martin's Press New York

Manufactured in the United States of America.

9 8 7 6 5
f e d c b a

For information, write:
St. Martin's Press, Inc.
175 Fifth Avenue
New York, NY 10010

ISBN: 0-312-10123-6

Preface

In <u>Text Book</u> we have proposed a new method of introducing students to literature at the college level, a method in which literature is seen not as a body of texts to be covered but as a way of thinking to be mastered. Our aim is to help students learn to think in the modes and to recognize the modes that are best exemplified in literary texts. Each of the first three chapters of the book emphasizes a different mode: First, the representative mode of narration and drama, in which human deeds and situations are recounted or enacted; second, the analogical mode of metaphor, in which one thing is presented in terms of another; and third, the mode of intertextuality, in which one text is seen as a development or transformation of earlier texts. In each of these cases our aim is to show how literary texts use processes that are also found in other kinds of speech and writing.

This whole conception of literary study is heavily influenced by recent developments in literary theory--but this is not a course in theory. Our book is <u>not</u> crammed with difficult theoretical readings. Nor do you need to be a theoretician to use it. All you need is a love for literature and an open mind. This is because the theory that informs this book has led us to present literature in a democratic way--not as a set of untouchable great works, each on its pedestal, but as a way of thinking and writing to which we all have access, indeed to which we all need access if we are to realize our full potential as citizens of a democracy. This is why we present literary texts as objects of interaction and emulation rather than worship.

The first two chapters of the book follow a traditional course, treating fiction, drama, and poetry primarily, though not in the traditional way. The third chapter is more unusual, because in it we introduce the concept of "intertextuality" as a key to literary thought and especially to those modes of writing we call interpretation and criticism. In this way, we situate academic ways of writing about literature in relation to literary processes in general, as simply one sort of intertextuality among others. This is a little unusual, but we feel that our gradual approach to this concept makes it possible for all students to comprehend and practice interpretive and critical writing--surely goals of a course like those this book is intended to serve.

The fourth and fifth chapters are more radical departures from the norm. It may well be that on first using this book, you will not feel ready to tackle these chapters. That is fine. There is plenty of material in the other chapters for a semester's work, and it should be easy to supplement the material in the earlier chapters with additional texts of your own choosing, if you want to spend more time on a particular form of literature, or if you simply have some favorite works that your want to include because you think your students should read them.

On the other hand, if you and your students are ready for a challenge, then you should consider doing one or both of the last two chapters. Whichever you choose will demand some time for preparation and discussion in class of some rather difficult material. The reward will come when your students write on the major assignments provided in these two chapters. If they have covered the reading and discussed it thoroughly enough to understand what they are undertaking, their writing will astonish both you and themselves. We tend, all too often, to underestimate the creative energy of our students. The trick is to find ways of unleashing the capabilities that are actually there. Accomplishing just that is a major purpose of Text Book, as it should be of all courses that introduce students to literary ways of thought. The addition, in this edition, of Chapter 5, "Experiments with Texts: Text and Research," should prove especially welcome for those whose courses require research assignments. In any case, the writing produced will prove rewarding for the student and for the teacher.

In this manual, we provide some practical advice on how to use the readings and writing assignments in Text Book, we report on our own experiences in field-testing this material, and we include some samples of student writing that demonstrate the kind of creative energy released by these assignments. We have attempted, in fact, to do everything in our power to encourage you to give the book a serious try, and to assist you in the actual use of it, should you decide to put it to the test. We are convinced that the results of such a test will be the strongest argument that could be made on behalf of this book. A course in literary study must find its justification in the way students who have taken such a course can then use language in reading, thinking, and writing. Their own writing will be the best measure of all this. That is why we have oriented our book to the production of interesting writing by students.

CONTENTS

Setting Up the Course
The Syllabus

You will of course want to design your own syllabus, but sometimes it is useful to have something to react against. Therefore we are providing two possible versions of a syllabus for a course that uses Text Book as the sole text for a semester's work. Obviously, you can follow a plan like either of these and feed into it works from an anthology or materials from any other source. What we are providing here is meant to be a skeleton that can be the basis for your own planning.

Version 1: Our basic assumption in this version is that you will use all five sections of the book for about equal periods of time. Recognizing that quarters and semesters vary considerably in length from school to school, we have designed this typical syllabus for fourteen units, that we call "weeks," which can be adjusted to fit other actual quarters or semesters.

Week 1: Concentrate on the first part of Chapter 1: Story and Storyteller. Assign and discuss Pratt, "Natural Narrative." Students write a personal anecdote. Assign and discuss some of the "literary" anecdotes and/or Williams. Raise question of relationship between "natural" and "literary" narratives. Assign Chopin. Second writing assignment on Chopin.

Week 2: Concentrate on the second part of Chapter 1: Character and Confrontation. Assign either Wedekind or Chopin, followed by a writing assignment on drama. Use some class time for performances.

Week 3: Conclude Chapter 1. Assign Goffman. Discuss in class. Then move to either the Strindberg for more drama or the Esslin for an approach to television. A writing assignment can come from either the Goffman or the later reading in this section.

Week 4: Begin Chapter 2 with Roger Brown's material on language. This is crucial for the rest of the chapter; make sure in discussion that everyone understands this. During the rest of the week, work with the three short poems and the related writing and discussion exercises, to make sure all students begin to get a feel for metaphor. Bring in other poems if you like.

Week 5: Attend to Freud and the surrealists. This is fairly difficult material, so you may wish to go slowly. Students should write on surrealism this week. If you have time, you can begin looking at the poems in the next section.

Week 6: Writing a paper on metaphor should be the main business of this week, based on the minianthology included in the text. Close with a discussion of Lakoff and Johnson.

Week 7: We recommend an extra week on metaphor at this point, concentrating on either argument or advertising. Begin with the Keidel and Sontag readings (assuming you have already discussed Lakoff and Johnson, which is crucial).

Week 8: Begin the study of Chapter 3, with the introduction on intertextuality and the three examples provided. You may want to use the Queneau material for in-class writing, or to move on to the Coover and Grimm material to prepare your students for the writing of a fairy tale transformation.

Weeks 9 and 10: Complete Chapter 3, choosing among "Completing Texts," "Interpreting Texts," or "Identifying with Texts."

Weeks 11 and 12: Choose one of the two sections in Chapter 4. Both lead to substantial writing assignments. Some of the reading may prove challenging, so allow time for adequate class discussion. For this assignment, as for others, you will also want to allow time for the reading and discussion of the students' writing.

Weeks 13 and 14: The material in Chapter 5 will prove especially useful for courses requiring a researched paper. Whether your course does or not, students' time will be well spent, not only in working through the material provided, but in using it as a model for their own "Mystory."

A Possible Addendum to the Syllabus

You may wish to give your students a version of the handout we include here, or simply to use it as a guide for a discussion about the course and its purpose. If you wish to duplicate and distribute it, you have our permission.

The Interrogation of Texts

One of the goals of this course is to teach you to use models. These models include not only various forms of writing, but also certain styles of speaking. Success in school depends not only on the ability to write, but also on the ability to ask questions and to develop strategies for accessing the information stored in whatever materials you are asked to treat. The university requires this class of all students because of the belief that what you learn about reading, writing, speaking, and thinking in this class will be transferable to other parts of the curriculum. If this goal is to be realized, you must become an independent learner, able to use the learning strategies demonstrated in this course without continual prompting by an instructor. Rather, you must learn to prompt yourself, and to interrogate actively the readings and instructions that you encounter. The following list of questions indicates the kinds of things you should know about all the readings in this class.

While it is not exhaustive, the list should also be useful in other classes. While some if not all of the questions are quite obvious, it is our experience that many students are content to leave them unformulated, or unanswered.

1. What is the assignment? Exactly what kind of writing am I expected to produce?
2. What is the model I am to follow? What are its specific features? How is it put together? What techniques or devices does the author use?
3. What is the purpose of the supporting readings? How do they contribute to an understanding of the model?
4. Is it possible to reduce the model to a formula? to a precise generalized description of a few steps that must be followed or a few fundamental techniques that must be performed? If so, what are these steps? Can I think of the model as a blueprint or pattern for making more items of its kind?
5. What is the interest of the readings in their own right? What issues do they raise that might be worth discussing, questioning, challenging? Is the form of the model in any way necessary to the topic it talks about? If it were written in some other manner, would that affect my response to the themes?
6. How do earlier sections of the course readings help me understand the present assignment and model?
7. Assuming that the readings supply most if not all of the information needed to define and carry out the project, which selections are the most helpful? which parts are most confusing or difficult?

Instructor's Manual

to accompany

TEXT BOOK

An Introduction to Literary Language

Second Edition

Chapter 1: TEXTS AND PEOPLE

Story and Storyteller

Mary Louise Pratt, "Natural Narrative" (p. 2) The way this first reading assignment is used will set the tone for much of your course. Because this text develops from assignment to assignment, if your students do not master this one, they will be handicapped in attempting many of the later assignments. It will be important throughout this book not to move on until you are assured that your students comprehend the major features of the material presented. It will never be more important than during the first assignment. Therefore, we begin with two suggestions.

First, we suggest that you really master this material yourself. That is, read it over more than once, trying to anticipate questions that may come from your students. You amy also wish to consult the full text in Pratt's book and Chapter 9 in Labov's Language in the Inner City, which has been issued in paperback by the University of Pennsylvania Press. In your preparation you should work out your own answers to the questions we have placed at the end of the reading.

Second, we suggest that you begin your discussion by asking your class if there are things in Pratt's discussion that they do not understand clearly. Try to conduct this discussion in such a way as to elicit whatever problems your students are having, however minor or trivial, without implying that they shouldn't have such problems. Your ability to encourage questions without making the questioner seem dumb will be crucial to getting your course off on the right foot. When you have talked over all the difficulties you can elicit, then it is time to go to the specific questions formulated in the book. In the course of your discussion, you should remind students that they are going to be asked to write an anecdote of their own that conforms to the structure discussed by Lavov and Pratt--so if they have questions about that six-part structure, now is the time to ask them.

Discussion and Writing

1. In eliciting answers to these questions, it will be important to get more than one, to allow people to express some disagreement over just where the action turns. The resolution of the discussion should not be an exact determination of the moment of climax, for instance, but a clear sense of how an action rises and turns toward resolution. There may well be more than one good answer to these questions. The important thing is to help students understand why any answers that are really far away from the point should be discarded. You want to work for a consensus that locates climax or resolution within a couple of lines. Your students should be able to point to a reasonable place for dénouement and to argue reasonably for their choice.
2. Because it asks for evaluation, this question will obviously tolerate some range of responses. In conducting discussion of it, the key will be to keep discussion focused on particular passages in the two texts, such as the closing lines of Larry's narrative. You might ask what would be lost if they were missing.
3. This can either be a homework assignment or something done in class. You might break into small groups, for instance, and let each group prepare a narrative; then, compare them in discussion. Or you might have the whole class collaborate,

with you leading discussion and a couple of recorders working on a written version. The point of the exercise lies in what we learn about narrative from trying to construct one.

4. The point of this exercise is to help students realize that written narrative must compensate in some way for the absence of the teller of the tale. Without the tones of voice and the gestures of a speaker, written narrative must try harder to convey tone and expressive quality.

5. This is a writing assignment that looks like "creative" writing in a way, but that really has another purpose. The purpose is to demonstrate that the writer has indeed learned to use the analytic structure of Labov and can turn that analysis upon his or her own writing to make sure all the elements are there. Your students should have fun writing these anecdotes, but they should also use them to demonstrate mastery of the concepts concerned. In making your own written responses to the assignment you should praise what is interesting, but also check each one to see that all the parts are there. You may even wish to have your students label the parts on their written essays.

Four "Literary" Anecdotes (p. 13) These anecdotes are here to show how persistent the anecdote form actually is. They are not here to show how superior a literary anecdote is to a natural narrative.

Discussion and Writing

1. Walter Benjamin, "Ordnance": discussed in the text.

Patricia J. Williams, "The Imagination": This anecdote is headed by an epigraph, which might be considered as an abstract, in that it does summarize what the anecdote is about. There is a brief orientation, and the complicating action consists of the story cousin Marjorie would tell--an allegory in place of a "real life" story--and of Williams's response, her demand for "the truth." The resolution is that nothing is resolved for the listener, who, in a coda, closes off the anecdote by a fall into emptiness that, through its metaphors, may be considered evaluative.

Storm Jameson, "Departures": There's no abstract, and just a brief orientation in the first sentence. This anecdote, like Benjamin's, is about the writer's feelings (in this case, on journeys), and such action as there is--the shift to the memory of the child waiting in the train, anxious for her mother's return--is abruptly shut off by the evaluative comment, "Not true. . . ."

Richard Huelsenbeck, "L.": Read as the story of a marriage, this anecdote covers a longer period of time than a natural narrative. (That one can present one's marriage as anecdote attests to its brevity, however.) This excerpt might also be read as two anecdotes: the wedding night, and the end of the marriage. In the first anecdote, the action--what actually happened--is implied. The result is presented first ("The outcome was total chaos"), followed by commentary that serves to distance actual events. Unlike the natural narrative, where events are given and repetition is used for emphasis, the reader is left to conjecture about the events--or non-events--of the wedding night. The second part is as much--or more--concerned with working out the comparison of rioting moviegoers to stampeding cattle as it is in telling how the marriage ended. The loss seems incidental to the stampede, and it is the writer's concern with language--the development of an appropriate metaphor--that makes his anecdote literary.

2. Cousin Marjorie, we assume, has her reasons for not telling "the truth," her actual experiences as Williams wants to hear them. Instead, she allegorizes, and the literariness of the anecdote lies in Williams's response to the allegories, itself expressed metaphorically ("full of emptiness").

In Jameson, memories of departures are compared to adders; literariness lies in this unusual, unexpected comparison. Note too the use of cold as it moves from weather report to state of being ("barrier of ice"), and to the mother's character traits ("coldly blue eyes"; "cold voice"). Jameson's conscious manipulation of her comparisons is a literary trait. With the use of cold, she goes far beyond the simple repetition of a word as one would find it in a natural narrative.

In Huelsenbeck, we have noted the use of metaphor in the discussion of Question 1.

3. This question opens the door for class discussion of--or written responses to--the question of what it means to "tell a tale properly," or, what features combine to make a "good" story?

4. As far as general experience is concerned, in the anecdotes of Williams and Huelsenbeck there is more overt striving for larger meaning. In Williams this can be seen in her use of the epigraph from Benjamin, and in Huelsenbeck in his remark on "a man's potency" as a general truth, and with his explanation of the appropriateness of "stampede" with respect to people.

William Carlos Williams, "The Use of Force" (p. 19) This is a strong text that should generate plenty of interest in its own right, but you should be aware that it will also figure in later assignments. In short, this is probably not one to skip. You should remind your students to read it with the anecdote structure in mind.

Discussion and Writing

1. This is meant to be a discussion question, though it could be used for a written assignment. You might begin a class with students writing short answers to this question that can be collected and used as the basis for discussion. The point is to note how little the text evaluates or interprets itself and how much it seems to invite interpretation. Surely, the title itself is mainly an invitation to interpretation. To stimulate discussion, you might ask whether the story should be interpreted as a kind of rape. The analogies are actually very close and sustained. You will want to keep reminding your students to anchor their interpretations in the text. Try to suppress any impulses you have to close down discussion by providing the "right" interpretation, while at the same time guiding the class away from readings that cannot be justified by citation of the text or its appropriate context.

2. There is no right answer to the last question posed here. The major point of this discussion should be to note how Williams's text has the structure of action and resolution of natural narratives but requires the reader to provide more of the interpretation. Williams also provides much more descriptive detail than would appear in a natural narrative, and some of that detail conceals or suggests evaluation. Discussion can be focused on this aspect of the text by asking questions about the function of particular descriptive details, in the form of, "What would be lost if this sentence [or phrase] were missing?"

Kate Chopin, "The Kiss" (p. 22) This story will be used for later assignments as well. Its function here is to help students retain and refine their concept of the six-part structure of narrative texts. Perhaps we should say here that we do not feel that "six" is a magic number or that some other system with five or seven divisions would not work in the analysis of narrative. The point is that analysis goes better with a system than without, and this is as good as any other. When your students become very sophisticated, they may be ready to discard this, but for now, learning how to use this system will be a stage on their journey toward literary sophistication. You should feel free to admit this. The system is provisional but learning how to use it is important for now.

Discussion and Writing

1. In this story there is little orientation--or rather, description takes the place of orientation, and of evaluation, too. In particular, the scene before the wedding cries out for evaluation, but none is provided. Chopin wants her readers to perform that act. But the story definitely has a coda. The discussion of this question should take place after the written assignments (Question 1 or 2) have been made. Students who are going to produce their own versions of this text should take a special interest in refining their understanding of its structure.

2. This is an assignment designed to produce a written text. The student who undertakes to produce this anecdote will discover how what is left to subtle innuendo in the literary text needs to be spelled out in a personal anecdote. This exercise will amount to both a reading of the Chopin story and a demonstration of mastery over the Labovian analytic method. It should be both a creative and critical exercise.

3. This written assignment takes the form of an expository or explanatory essay. It can be an extension or development of ideas the student has already considered if the writing assignments for Pound and Williams have been used. We would hope your serious students will be able to make some clear distinctions between the more explicit methods of the natural narrative and the more subtle, implicit methods of literature. This should help them to understand why so much literary criticism takes the form of interpretation: Literary texts demand interpretation; they are structured so as to be incomplete without it. This does not mean, however, that one should like only the literary. There are perfectly valid reasons for admiring the raw vitality and energy of the natural narrative--once one has realized what it is and why it is that way.

Character and Confrontation (p. 26)

One of the purposes of this part of Chapter 1 is to enable students to appreciate clearly the difference between narration and dramatization--and to see how both of them connect to ordinary life and ordinary uses of language. Though acting out dramatic scenes takes time and may seem to be too much like play and not enough like learning, our experience is that time spent on helping students get a feel of what stage action is like is seldom wasted. It is a form of reading and not a trivial one.

Frank Wedekind (a scene from the play) Spring Awakening (p. 26)

Discussion and Writing

1. Do stage the reading. You won't regret it.

2. This is a straightforward question. Obviously, drama puts the emphasis on action and result (with or without a coda). It has no obvious place for orientation (except in stage directions), abstracts, or evaluations. Sometimes, however, dramatists will work in evaluations by putting them in the mouths of characters--but this is a special problem. The form itself is not so adapted to evaluation as is the narrative form. In discussing this question, you may wish to bring out the way that the literary narratives you have been examining move toward the dramatic by suppressing a certain amount of evaluative commentary. The strength of drama lies in its immediacy and in the way that it forces audiences to participate in evaluating the action it presents. It is not surprising that literary narrators should try to capture some dramatic power by imitating drama in this respect. Nor is it surprising that sometimes playwrights work in evaluative commentary. Artists tend to move toward exceeding the limits of their medium. This is an important point.

We assume that you will have some students who prefer the dramatic and some who prefer narration. Obviously there is no right answer, but it is important for the reasons behind the preferences to get as clear an expression as possible. Don't be afraid to state your own preferences and reasons, but don't foreclose their options, either.

3. The point of this assignment is to learn something about dramatic form--its power and limits--but also to think about how certain cultural practices change over time. You should encourage students to deal with contemporary mores as they understand them. We recommend that you also tell them that they must decide whether the presentation should be serious or light. We would not discourage a bit of exaggeration or caricature in an assignment like this. You may well wish to stage or read some of the most successful results.

4. The point of this assignment is that the anecdotal form will allow the evaluation and orientation that is not there in the dramatic scene to be made explicit. It is, in a way, a measure of comprehension of Wedekind as well as of the mastery of dramatic idiom. Such assignments call upon both creative and critical skills.

Kate Chopin (dialogue from the story) "The Kiss" (p. 29) This text has only one question, but, as Kurt Vonnegut might say, it is a doozy. It asks for the transformation of the dialogue from Chopin's story into a playlet that conveys all the action and evaluation conveyed by the original story. This means, just for openers, that your students must understand the story very well. If they want to talk it over again before going to work, that's fine. Give them all the help you can.

You may feel that this kind of writing is beyond the reach of your students. To some extent, it should be, but a perfect response is not the goal here. Whatever they achieve should be of some satisfaction to them. You may well wish to have this assignment begun in class. You might, for instance, begin by working out the scenic structure in a general discussion, and then divide into several small groups, each group working on a different scene. After some input from you, then each individual could take the project home and try to finish it off. Various combinations of group and individual work ought to be possible here. The main thing is that the problems of drama will be brought home to those who struggle with the form. You are also likely to get some results that surprise you.

Things will go best if you talk over at some length the four options mentioned in the question, making sure that everybody knows what a "confidante," for instance, is. We would discourage any use of a commentator who is not also a character, since that solution does not solve the problem but eliminates it by turning the drama into a narrative. All this should be discussed, either before your class starts writing, or after they have begun and before they have finished. The point is to use the creative struggle as a way of bringing out critical questions.

Erving Goffman, Character Contests (p. 31) This is a serious piece of writing by a major sociologist. Encourage your students to read it carefully and note any questions they have as they read. Begin your discussion by asking them to raise those questions with you. This means that you must have read the selection very carefully yourself.

Discussion and Writing

1. This question is designed mainly to give you a chance to make sure that Goffman's ideas and terminology have been understood. Be patient, and elicit as many incomprehensions or objections as you can. This will pay off later.
2. If your class needs a chance to personalize the Goffman, this question is designed to allow just that. If you think they are ready to move ahead without bringing the matter home to their own experience, you can skip this one. But pausing here may save time in the long run.
3. The scene from Spring Awakening is certainly a character contest of a sort familiar to all of us who have lived in families. It is not easy to say who wins that contest, so perhaps no one does, but you should see what your students think about it--and ultimately you should tell them what you think about it, too. We are divided in our own opinions on this one.
4. Here again, you should let a hundred flowers bloom. We are inclined to consider Harvy the winner of this one. What do you think?
5. You may not feel the need for this return to Williams, but the question, even if considered briefly, should help convince students that the character contest is a very frequent form in fiction--and that the concept of character contest can be a help in evaluating or interpreting the events in a narrative text.
6. Larry's anecdote is the clearest example of run-in we have studied. Another assignment could involve the rewriting of this in dramatic form. If you wish, you might offer that as an alternative to rewriting one of their own anecdotes, but most students are likely to prefer their own. The point of the exercise is for the student to learn how to compensate in dramatic form for the orientation and evaluation that was there in the anecdote.
7. Pretty important--a tiny bandit and a towering barmaid would complicate the flow of simple emotions that the present journalistic account clearly wants to generate. One suspects that myth has already intervened in this "objective" account.
8. This is a more complicated question. You may wish to focus on whether the bloodshed would damage the gamelike quality of the character contest.
9. The best way to approach this question is probably to invent some other forms

of words, ranging from simple insults to high-flown speeches. What is so good about the words we have is that they underline the fact that this is indeed a character contest. It is a game and now it's the bandit's move.

10. In making this writing assignment, emphasize the need for the three scenes. The before and after are essential for the orientation and evaluation to emerge. The best solutions will no doubt indicate some change in the relationship between the two bandits after the fiasco. This is a chance for your students with a sense of humor to excel.

<u>August Strindberg, The Stronger (p. 35)</u> Remind your students that this is a complete play. Everything they need to know to understand this scene is presented here--but they will have to do a lot of orientation and evaluation on their own. They will even have to fill in a lot of past action on their own. Suggest that they read Question 1 before they read the play itself.

<u>Discussion and Writing</u>

1. This is <u>the</u> question. Probably you should work out the plot in class, getting suggestions from all sides. Your students will need to understand the full situation in order to answer the other questions--which means you had better work out your own written list of events in the lives of these characters as you glean them from the text.
2. This is an assignment for a rather sophisticated written essay. If you feel your students are not up to it, you may wish to skip this assignment--but don't underestimate them. What most belongs to art in this play is the silence of one character and the way the other's remarks reveal the whole romantic entanglement of three characters. The way the wife maneuvers the slippers in such a way as to make the former mistress laugh at a too-familiar gesture of rubbing one foot against the other is typical of the artfulness of the play. No ordinary confrontation would manage to get quite so much of the past into the play so quickly.
3. This is a fairly sophisticated assignment, in that it requires the student to take over the story of this triangle as a story but change all the orientation and evaluation that the present version generates. You might suggest that one way to solve these problems is to take over as much as possible of Strindberg's outline--to discuss the same events and topics in the same order, but to put a different evaluation on all of them. One is at liberty, of course, to imagine a different future than the one implied by the dialogue (or monologue) we have.
4. This might be an alternate assignment to 3 or a companion piece, if both are to be relatively short. The interest of the piece will depend upon the development of the character of the waitress through her speech or writing. Advise your students to give some thought to what kind of person she is going to be before they try to write about her. Is she, for instance, sweet and sensitive, or brutal and stupid? Is she an innocent bystander or is she implicated in these activities? It might be worthwhile to discuss some possibilities in class before anyone undertakes to write this.

Martin Esslin, "Aristotle and the Advertisers: The Television Commercial as Drama" (passages from the essay) (p. 40) In our introduction we have tried to provide the terminology from Aristotle that the student will need to follow Esslin. It might not hurt to go over it before the students read the passages from Esslin.

Discussion and Writing

1. This question is designed at the occasion for a review of the whole chapter. Kate Chopin's story is an excellent example of Aristotelian principles at work. Your students may have provided some in dramatizing the bakery robbery, too. Try to cover as many things as possible in the discussion, so as to refresh everyone's memory and to establish the Aristotelian critical principles in the minds of your students.

2. If you have access to video equipment yourself, you may wish to select an appropriate commercial and make it available for your students to transcribe. If not, some appointed group of students who do have such access may be able to provide a transcript for the others to work on.

The point of this assignment is to allow for the application of Aristotelian principles and for the development of a parody by means of some distortion of these principles. That is, after transcribing a commercial that works according to the Aristotelian structure, change the structure and destroy the commercial functioning of the commercial. Acting out some of these should be fun. Afterward, you can try in discussion to elicit the common principles to the versions that were acted out. That is, you can ask which alterations in the Aristotelian structure proved most effective in betraying the purpose of the commercial dramatizations.

Chapter 2: TEXTS, THOUGHTS, AND THINGS

The Linguistic Basis of Metaphor

Roger Brown, "What Words Are: Reference and Categories" (p. 46) This description of Dr. Itard's efforts to teach the "Wild Child" can serve as an extended metaphor or allegory of the composition classroom. We should never underestimate the extent to which our students tend to ignore or forget the material nature of language. The warning in this exemplary tale is that without language we might all be hunting squirrels in the woods. The more explicit lesson of the essay concerns the specific or material way in which language functions. Students rarely think about language as a technology that works in a particular, often quite odd, way. Metaphor is one of the most common, useful, elementary, yet bizarre features of this technology. If you have access to François Truffaut's film, The Wild Child, we recommend its use as a means of further stimulating discussion.

Discussion and Writing

1. Before dealing with metaphor, which is a certain kind of relationship between names, we need to understand something about names themselves. In this chapter, we treat the common noun and its metaphorical possibilities. One of the

experiments in Chapter 4--the "signature"--explores the metaphorical potential of proper names.

Brown makes good use of Victor's story to illustrate "concept formation," something that many of our students understand no better than Victor, even if they use concepts correctly in everyday speech. The main point to stress in the example is the power of the name as a generalization covering all the individual items of a given sort. Itard is teaching Victor to generalize: In playing "fetch the referent" Itard and Victor demonstrate what is meant by "semantics." Itard's lesson, while appropriate for Victor, is obviously too simple for the class. If you asked your students to fetch a "book" they would be quite scornful. Similarly, if you asked them to write or recite the alphabet, they would balk at the ease of the task. For this very reason, it is sometimes useful to offer such exercises, to raise the students' awareness of how much they take for granted, and how much they already know of the material quality of language.

Brown goes beyond demonstrating the meaning of the word "semantics" by introducing a few complications into the discussion of concepts. It is useful to note the synonymity of the terms "concept," "category," and "class," all used to refer to or name the way multiple entities are unified and sorted into kinds for ease of recognition or identification. Brown now shifts from "vocabulary" to what some students might think of as "jargon"--the specialized vocabulary of a field of knowledge--linguistics. "Identity category" is a special kind or category of "category." The distinction is worth discussing to clarify the fact that we do not have direct, unmediated knowledge of objects such as books, but come into awareness of them by means of our sense perceptions. The physical properties of a particular book combine to identify it as the same one each time we encounter it or think of it; these properties function, that is, as a proper name. We may define a concept as a "set" of properties collected according to a given criterion of selection. The definition of the criterion of selection turns out to be far more flexible than the students expect.

To establish the status of the general and the particular, and the way they relate in language, by means of such a simple example will be useful later on when we start working with relationships between concepts combined in complex arguments.

2. The purpose of these two questions is simply to familiarize the students with some of the most basic terms used to describe the relationship between thinking and language. To define the more precise distinctions between "identity category" and "category of forms" provides some practice in charting the formal limits of a term in a specialized discourse. This process of setting the parameters of a concept in specialized discourses may serve as a model for a similar delimitation of terms also at work in the discourse of everyday life. The term "category of forms" refers to language itself, reflexively, to point out that it is just as important to be able to recognize the shapes of certain letters, or the sound of a given word as the same each time, and thus to identify its status as a meaningful unit, as it is to recognize that a given book is the same one, or that an item is a "book" (to stay with Itard's example).

The key term in this discussion is "recurrence" or "repetition." People with different accents from different regions of the country can still understand each other in a conversation by ignoring the variables and attending to the significant features that identify a set of sounds as a category of form. Again, the students find a point such as this one quite obvious, scarcely worth mentioning, even if they haven't thought about it specifically. Later, in our discussion of poetry, however, they will be pleased to realize that this simple and obvious phenomenon of recurrence of significant features to establish a set or category is the same material aspect of language exploited by poets to build new, unique, but unstable aesthetic categories of signification. The idea here, as elsewhere in our approach, is to help the students realize how much they already know about language, and that the acquisition of a vocabulary of categories will enable them to extend their cultural skills as native speakers to the understanding and practice of high literacy.

Roger Brown, "What Words Are: Metaphor" (p. 51) The logic of our selections from Brown, as we noted, is to establish first the nature of names of categories (concepts), so that we could better appreciate metaphors as relationships between concepts.

Discussion and Writing

1. One way to help students notice the material reality of language is to inventory the various practices of assigning names to things, official and unofficial, authorized and unauthorized, in society. Brown gives a number of examples that illustrate some of the ways in which language actually grows and evolves over time. Students often find it liberating to learn that language is not permanently set, fixed, defined absolutely once and for all, as it seemed to them to be in their previous schooling. This realization will be helpful later when they are asked to manipulate a conceptual category, which for some will feel like breaking a law.

One of the principle ways language evolves is by means of metaphor--extending the features of a given category to name something that previously was excluded from the set. To make the point that language is essentially and fundamentally metaphorical in nature, Brown uses a figure of "catachresis" for his example of a dead metaphor: "The foot of a mountain." His point in part is that our very vocabulary itself is metaphorical in a way that we fail to notice. He also wants to emphasize that this metaphorical quality is irreducible. Catachresis is the best figure with which to make this point, since it refers to figurative uses that lack any literal substitute. There is no other literal name for which the "leg" is a metaphor, although we could describe the referent in other terms.

The special attitude mentioned, then, involves paying attention to language itself, listening for so-called dead metaphors; this requires the student to suspend the habits of daily life. Brown does not encourage us to extend our attention to puns or homophones, but we could while we are at it, to get into the more playful mood or attitude with which the poet approaches language, especially when we remember that homophones have also played a major role in the growth of language (many words, few sounds). In any case, the "bored of directors" does produce a kind of meaningful joke, in that it is not hard to imagine the accuracy of this descriptive term applied to the serious, responsible directors. Moreover, by suspending the context temporarily (the context of the statement "of directors" would eliminate the meaning "bored" as the category appropriate for those sounds), the student is prepared to appreciate the next step in the production of poetry--the assignment of a term to a new context from which it had been excluded. At the very least the students will be more sensitive to the problem of mixed metaphors, avoiding going where the hand of man has never set foot.

Again, the circulation of words manifested in the passage from living to dead metaphors and back illustrates at a basic level the cycle of exchange between popular and high culture, everyday speech and literacy. Part of our goal is to help the students realize the vitality and practicality of this linguistic cycle for their own needs and purposes. The attitude of suspending one's habits in order to notice figurative usages is the same sort of openness required for learning anything new.

2. Once the students become aware of metaphorical usage they will notice that almost every essayist they read uses metaphors, living and dead--an insight that should improve their ability to read expository and argumentative writing as well as poetry. If they can understand what it means for a rhetorical figure to be either living or dead, they should also be able to understand similar uses of figures in poetry. The strategy is to call their attention to the fact that they already understand and use metaphors themselves, in order to give them confidence in the value of their native knowledge of the language.

Brown, in paragraph 7, talks about metaphors blazing, evoking the category of fire and its attributes to communicate the sense of the death of a metaphor in terms of the dying out of a fire. A comparison with Herrick's poem reveals first that the fire image is present in both cases, but that the poem develops the image more intensely, with greater complexity. The reason students tend to overlook the metaphor in the poem (and hence to have no idea what the poet is saying) is that the metaphor is introduced with great economy--in the term "kindles," which simply goes by them too quickly. They know poems contain metaphors, or the more dreaded "symbols," but the concentrated quality such usage gives to the language leaves them at a loss unless they have already developed the strategies needed to read such language. They overlook metaphors in essays for similar reasons, not only because the figures may be dead or commonplace, but because the reader, not expecting to find a metaphor, fails to exercise the strategy needed to grasp the meaning of the figure (the comparison of the two sets or concepts evoked by the metaphor). Language is a material process, we keep saying, and our students need to be reminded that the usage of language requires effort--reading is as active a process as writing. You can't hit a tennis ball without swinging at it; you can't read (understand) a metaphor without "unpacking" it.

3. For this question a little dictionary work will be in order. You might advise your students to look up these words in a good dictionary, or even make available some material on these words from the Oxford English Dictionary, a resource they should be introduced to. The question of difference in our understanding of a word and Herrick's may be discussed with reference to a word's meaning in the context of a poem versus a dictionary meaning.

"Wild civility" introduces paradox, a statement that, like metaphor, depends upon two apparently contradictory terms.

4. We have been insisting on some very basic, obvious points, but our experience with teaching some of the more difficult texts included in this book indicates that many writing problems may be reduced to the fact that the students lack any start-up strategies or problem-solving tactics. Part of learning to use models involves learning some of the strategies needed to extract information from written text and from classroom instructors. They know, for example, that on a multiple-choice

exam one of the answers for a given question is correct. A similar confidence in the prepared setup of a textbook would improve their ability to use the materials provided for their use. Almost everything needed to answer any of the questions posed for discussion or undertake any of the writing assignments is provided in the readings. Hence, a student need not try to guess or remember the definition of a metaphor, only refer to that part of the readings in which the figure is defined. A question such as this one, then, which lends itself as much to class discussion as to writing, simply checks the students' basic reading habits, forcing them to review the selections for the information they will need to manage the next sections illustrating metaphorical practice in various kinds of writing. The best strategy for reading Text Book, or any textbook for that matter, turns out to be similar to the strategy needed to read poetry--to look actively for the unifying principle of each section, asking why a given selection has been provided, what function it serves specifically in furthering an understanding of the theme and assignment. Read in this way, even the academic prose of a textbook may blaze with a certain figurative life, as we have already seen in the pedagogical parable of the "Wild Child," and as may be noted again in the theme of "disorder" in Herrick's poem, alluding to the disorder that the poetic attitude of play may introduce into prosaic usage.

Metaphor in Three Poems (p. 57)

Before looking at the poems, you might ask your class how many of them noticed the plant metaphor in the first paragraph of the introduction to this section. This will give you some idea of how well or badly they are doing as students of metaphor. If many of them missed it, you had better stop right there and discuss it.

W. S. Merwin, "Separation" (p. 57) You can find a discussion of this poem in Chapter 3 of Semiotics and Interpretation by Robert Scholes (New Haven: Yale University Press, 1982). For classroom study of this and all other poems, we recommend that you begin with a couple of readings aloud of the text--by students or yourself.

1. The obvious expectation here is a sharp object, like a knife or needle. What makes Merwin's metaphor poetic is that it uses the blunt end of the needle: unexpected but appropriate.

2. Merwin's metaphor signifies the speaker's inability to escape from awareness of separation. The thread of memory is everywhere for him.

W. H. Auden, "Let us honor . . ." (p. 57) This poem and its suggested rewriting should lead to a useful discussion of metaphor and literary interpretation. You can ask students to put some rewritings on the board as a way of starting things. One useful version to discuss looks like this:

Let us praise if we can
The living man
Though we admire none
But the dead one

All the questions posed in the last paragraph of the text are important. Try to find time for each one to be discussed.

Sylvia Plath, "Metaphors" (p. 58) 1. For those students who have always found poetry to be a complete enigma, Plath's poem sometimes has the effect of those gestalt-shift perceptual effects--the "rabbit-duck" for example: When the image is suddenly perceived as a duck rather than as the rabbit it first appeared to be there is genuine surprise and pleasure. Similarly, when the reader realizes that all the lines of the poem inventory ways of saying "I'm pregnant," thus supplying the missing meaning, there is a shift in understanding. The reader now has at least a rough and ready strategy for discerning the outlines of a referent in poetic language. The poem shows in addition the way in which clichés and commonplaces may be revived in a poetic context to express, through accumulation and its effect of insistence if nothing else, the feeling of gestation as well as the social attitude toward pregnant women.

In class discussion, it will be useful to go through the poem line by line and metaphor by metaphor, considering how the images are connected to different aspects of the verbal category or abstraction: pregnancy.

2. It will take a little time for students to accomplish this. You might start them working on their lists in class and have them complete their riddle poems at home. This can also be done as a group effort, with the poem taking shape on the board. The purpose of the exercise is to get them thinking about metaphor from the writer's point of view.

Metaphor and Dream (p. 60)

This Freudian material will function best if used with the surrealist poems that follow it in the text. We have tried to present Freud's concept of dream-work in the briefest possible span. If you wish to do more with it, you can supplement this material with examples from either the relevant chapters of the Introductory Lectures or from the chapter on the dream-work in The Interpretation of Dreams. The major point to be made is that poems resemble dreams in their use of images and figures of speech both to express and conceal meaning. The act of interpretation is the raising of the latent content of a text to the manifest level. As a reminder, here are some capsule definitions:

latent--hidden
manifest--apparent
dream-work--encoding
interpretation--decoding
condensation--part for whole
displacement--one thing for another
imagery--a sensory image for an abstraction

Surrealist Metaphor (p. 64)

This examination of extreme cases of figuration should help students understand one limit of metaphor, which is madness or nonsense. The other limit is banality or cliché.

Discussion

You can no doubt find your own illustrations, but here are some chosen from the material in the text.

1. apparent contradiction--"sparkling sewer grill"
2. hidden term--"clown of the eclipse" (moon)
   --"sparkling sewer grill" (stars)
3. concrete for abstract--any image; Freud's example is a picture of someone sitting on an object to indicate possession of it.
4. abstract for concrete--think of Auden's abstractions, "vertical" and "horizontal."

André Breton, "Broken Line" (p. 66) You may discover that the strangeness of Breton's poetry arouses your students' interest in the man. if you want to give them more information, you will find a useful guide in Mary Ann Caws, André Breton (Twayne, 1973). There is also a useful introduction in the Cauvin and Caws edition of The Poems of André Breton, from which our selection was taken.

Discussion and Writing

1. What is asked for here, in a somewhat cryptic way, is some consideration of the relationship between poetic charm or pleasure and the fragmented nature of some poetic language. The peculiar charm of certain kinds of poetry, like the charm of certain dreams, is based on these texts' need for interpretation. They are charming because they invite us to play a role in their games of meaning.

2. This is meant as a writing assignment. If you use it, you may wish to point out that many of these lines might occur in contemporary popular music. A whole song might be developed starting with any one of these lines. Encourage your students to produce such a song.

   In class you might select just one of these lines and have the group free-associate on it. See what ideas turn up. You might also try to understand the line by translating it into a prose statement or paraphrase. Then begin to shape the results of these processes into a meditation or a song.

   For the writing assignment, remind your class that they are not interpreting; they are not seeking some meaning already in the line; they are using their own thoughts. It's what it means to them that counts. (You might remind them also that interpretation is something different.)

3. This is a fairly sophisticated writing assignment. Even if you choose not to use it, you may find it worthwhile to go over the four lines that have been turned into normal prose by changing a single word. Understanding how this was done should enable your students to understand also how the lines were surrealized in the first place.

4. Before turning your class loose on this one, you should discuss the examples in Question 3.

5. This question is meant to serve as the occasion for a review of the material on

surrealist metaphor. In leading discussion, you should begin sometimes by directing attention to a specific line and sometimes by asking about a specific device.

Wallace Stevens, "Domination of Black" (p. 68) One of the points to stress in the discussion of both Breton and Stevens concerns the particular way poems are organized. Students are often more familiar with the other two principal ways to organize a body of thought, narration and exposition. They readily follow a story line or plot, and an argument (somewhat less readily, not through lack of understanding the process so much as through failure of attention). Many students, however, are not aware that poetry has an ordering principle that in essence is as straightforward as the other two arrangements. That principle, as we noted earlier, is repetition, the recurrence of items to compose a pattern. Breton's poem is more chaotic than Steven's, but the process of signification is similar--the effect of meaning is produced by means of a concatenation of items. His poem does not cohere at the level of individual sentences, but only as a whole, as a collection of features into a set, exactly in the manner of concept formation, except that the resultant signification in the poem is not a generalization but a particularization at the opposite end of the scale of meaning from the concept. Or, we could say that Breton has used the process of concept formation to form a unique concept (a contradiction in terms, logically). Every poet uses this process of collection of terms into a set by means of repetition and juxtaposition. The set is more apparent in Stevens because the "beat" of repetition is more pronounced and regular. What does the pattern add up to? What does it mean? Both poems seem to be about the same thing--about a feeling of depression that we learn about as an inference based on the collection of items in the set. We answer the riddle according to the associations we have with peacocks or spiders. Of course there is a level of aesthetic power communicated in the poems, but students often find that dimension to be inaccessible until they have mastered the trick of reference--what does the poem "name"? One goal of this chapter is to help the students see that whether or not they are ready to accept the pleasure of poetic language, they can still learn to use the poetic strategy of arrangement to build arguments for which they will have plenty of use, even if they never write a poem.

Poetic Uses of Metaphor (p. 70)

A substantial paper on metaphor should come out of this material. Your job is to help your students prepare for the paper and even to help them get started on it. You should be willing to discuss the poems in class. You might even invite students to submit a draft of a sample paragraph to make sure they are on the right track. One danger of discussing the poems in class, of course, is that too much will be repeated on the papers. You can try to avoid this by concentrating in class on simply understanding the poems and just pointing out directions for the student to investigate. It will be useful, though, to identify the major metaphors in the various poems, and to help students see how every metaphor involves some kind of comparison, in which both sides must be identified. If X and Y are being compared, the reader needs a good idea of what X and Y are in order to follow the metaphoric process. You should avoid following the process all the way through in too many cases, but help identify the directions in which further study should go.

In their papers, they will need to identify some interesting metaphors, to explain what things are brought together in the metaphor, and to consider how such features as strangeness and appropriateness function--sometimes simultaneously--to make certain metaphors especially effective or interesting. One process they may find useful will be to think of each poem in terms of Breton's list of poetic strategies. This will help them begin to talk about metaphoric process. The text makes a start on discussing Francis's poem, "Pitcher." You might continue discussing the images in that poem, showing how the effect depends upon the metaphor functioning well in both its contexts: baseball and poetry.

Here are some thoughts about the poems that may help you generate discussion while the students are getting familiar enough with the poems to write their papers.

Ono no Komachi, "Doesn't he realize . . ." (p. 71) Ask the class to rewrite the poem with a new metaphor: Doesn't he (she) realize/that I am not/ like . . .

Stephen Spender, "Word" (p. 71) Note the rhyme scheme. The rhyme for fish is saved until the last line, where it does "rhyme upon a dish." The poem may be said to exist because fish and dish do rhyme. Ask your students what it means for a word to be "free." This is a useful poem to consider early because the metaphor is so obvious. Every student should see that fish and words are being compared here. What they should also see is the way that the comparison (or metaphor) leads to some interesting thoughts about the way words exist and function in poems. What does it mean to "rhyme upon a dish?"

Robert Francis, "Pitcher" (p. 71) Some students will resist the notion that the poem is about anything but baseball. Our response to this line of resistance would begin by saying, Suppose it is, but what is the metaphor for baseball here? To what is baseball being compared? In terms of what is baseball being discussed? This question must be answered in terms of such expressions as "comprehended," "misunderstood," "communicate," and "understand." If the poem is about baseball (and it is), it discusses baseball through a metaphor of communication, and it emphasizes a type of communication with certain peculiarities that correspond closely, for instance, to what Breton and Stevens identified as the special features of poetry: in particular, the delaying of the process of comprehension. Try suggesting that "The others" are the other fielders on a team--who are not pitchers --or the writers of prose--who are not poets. And note the second word of the poem.

X. J. Kennedy, "Ars Poetica" (p. 72) Note the pun on the Latin word for art and British slang for backside. Ask students to interpret the last line of the poem--that is, to extend the meaning beyond golden geese. What, in particular, does the word "lay" signify here?

Louise Glück, "Cottonmouth Country" (p. 72) This will go best if perceived as based on a single episode: a couple ("us") swimming in North Carolina ("Hatteras"), finding some fish bones floating in the water, seeing a poisonous snake when they come to shore. The last two lines turn the images into metaphor.

These lines do not destroy the literal level of what has gone before, but they cannot be read literally themselves. Like a dream, they must be interpreted. Let different interpretations be proposed. In every case, you must ask what is being compared to what.

George Barker, "Sonnet to My Mother" (p. 72) It might be helpful to tell your students this poem was written during World War II, when the Germans were bombing Britain. Also, you may have to gloss Rabelais: a sixteenth-century French satirist (and physician) noted for the earthy humor of his work. The figurative language of the poem emphasizes the oversized qualities of this mother, her largeness of size and of spirit. Though the first line of the poem proclaims the mother as "most loved," students sometimes have an initial difficulty of perceiving the positive nature of this woman's bigness.

Margaret Atwood, "You fit into me" (p. 73) In its quick move from simile to pun, this poem offers a sharp surprise. In order for students to understand the shift from utilitarian image to the painful image, you may have to show those who've grown up with zippers and velcro what the hook and eye of higher couture looks like.

Emily Dickinson, "A narrow Fellow in the Grass" (p. 73) Though not quite a riddle poem like Plath's "Metaphors," we do have here a poem of metaphors replacing the word "snake." The grim chumminess of the term "Fellow" is somewhat undercut by the adjective "narrow." The reader is politely questioned in the third line, which is followed by the Fellow's not-so-polite behavior ("His notice sudden is--"). The movements that surprise, the fact that the Fellow never allows one to see him in a static position, force the use of metaphor: one never sees a snake, one sees a "spotted shaft," "a Whip lash," whose moves unnerve, frighten, and as the metaphor in the last line indicates, chill one.

Marge Piercy, "You don't understand me" (p. 74) The Other in this poem is subjected to a series of metaphors. What do they add up to? What do they tell us about "you" and what does their deployment tell us about this relationship?

Adrienne Rich, "Moving in Winter" (p. 74) Ideas in things, as Williams says. These are not metaphors or similes but associations or metonymies between things and events. The moving of furniture through the snow seems to unleash ideas of the life that has been lived in and around these objects. You might ask how the poet makes the objects convey an attitude toward the marriage: looking at the word "grey" in line 9, for instance.

W. S. Merwin, "Inscription Facing Western Sea" (p. 75) This poem simply describes one thing--waves breaking on a shore--in terms of an elaborate metaphor or deep image of another thing--an ancient war. Discussion should focus on the appropriateness of the different parts of the image to the object that it--metaphorically--describes.

Wallace Stevens, "The Motive for Metaphor" (p. 75) This poem is about metaphor, and metaphors are employed to make its point. For Stevens, change is exhilarating (l.13), and in the play of imagination that enlivens our perception, we create metaphors. We find them in autumn in the pathos of change that attends the dying of the year, and in spring, in the tentative new growth and pale changing sky. We find the undesirable qualities of absolute reality ("The weight of primary noon") are assessed in the last six lines. How direct is perception anyway? Isn't it always mediated? Your students may wish to thrash these questions about.

Metaphor as a Basis for Thought (p. 76)

George Lakoff and Mark Johnson, from Metaphors We Live By (p. 76) That our "ordinary conceptual system is metaphorical in nature" (paragraph 4), and that metaphors control our thinking and actions, is a revelation to students. In discussing the "argument is war" metaphor, you might point out, in reference to "the culture where arguments are not viewed in terms of war" (paragraph 7), that the Chinese and Japanese are such cultures. A Japanese garden, with its graceful placement of stones and shrubs, invites, indeed requires, the spectator to view it from various perspectives. So it is with a subject or an issue; it is to be contemplated from various points of view. ESL teachers can tell you how difficult it is to teach the American forms of argumentative essays to their Asian composition students.

Discussion and Writing

1. Practical-minded American students will find in this section the payoff for careful attention to the functioning of metaphor in the previous section. The boundaries separating poetic language from other dimensions of discourse turn out to be much less rigid than they had been led to believe. We learned from Brown that metaphor is a relationship between categories (or concepts) in which the attributes or members of one set are applied to the name of the other set. Lakoff and Johnson understand metaphor in a similar way. Their discussion shows that the term "metaphorical concept" is essentially redundant. Indeed, when they insist that the phrase "argument is war" is to be taken literally--meaning that the concept of argument is structured precisely by means of this metaphor and has no status apart from the metaphor--they indicate the extent to which the opposition between "literal" and "figurative" has lost its meaning. This distinction in a more empirically positivistic attitude toward language was used to suggest that metaphor was at once removed from "truth," serving to help express a signification that could stand on its own, denotatively.

The term "metaphorical concept" is still useful to extend our understanding of concept formation. We noted earlier that metaphor is a relationship between concepts (one way among others of bringing concepts into relationship). Now we learn that concepts themselves are structured internally as metaphors--that the set of attributes constituting a category is itself a certain kind of relationship, and that relationship is metaphorical in nature. The redundancy is necessary also because while the juxtaposition of categories in poems tends to be innovative, producing living metaphors, the metaphors in everyday usage or in expository prose tend to be dead, assimilated into popular usage--hence they pass unnoticed. The most successful metaphors, that is, are those that have become concepts--those that have passed from the unique status of a surprising juxtaposition to the socially approved and adopted status of a generalization.

A review of the examples is interesting because many students realize for the first time that they have been using figurative terms literally. They had not noticed the continuous circulation between the realms of the concrete and the abstract. You may even want to remind them of the two functions of the verb "to be"--one copulative and the other ontological. When we say that "argument is war," the "is" functions to link the two semantic domains without asserting the actual reality of the connection.

2. Both discussions of "foot of a mountain" stress the conventional nature of the attribution, and both identify it as a "dead" metaphor, but without noting its status as a "catachresis." Brown suggests that the geological "foot" and the anatomical one are homophones, implying that the "foot" of the mountain has a historical derivation unrelated to the human "foot," or at least that in practice a speaker uses the geological foot without ever thinking of anatomy. Lakoff and Johnson make a similar point in a different way, by saying that although the "foot of the mountain" is a metaphor, it is unsystematic, meaning that the transfer of the word from anatomy to geology does not involve a juxtaposition of the two sets, with all their features, but is a singular borrowing without resonance. The mark of a dead metaphor is precisely the transfer of a term without its associated set.

There seems to be some conflict between the two discussions, in that Brown suggests that we will notice metaphor better if we suspend the context of a term, whereas Lakoff and Johnson note that metaphor is living only when we relate two contexts in which the term is used. There is finally no real disagreement here, since Brown's point in suspending the habitual context of usage is to take note of all the possible referents of a term (we haven't taken into account "foot" as a unit of measurement, for example); that is, the term enters into a living usage when the full extension of its possible meanings--the sets of attributes it controls as a name--are brought into play.

The value of sorting out these differing approaches to living and dead metaphor has to do with the practice it provides in close reading of expository prose and the variations possible in the definition of a concept--the concept of "metaphor" in this case.

3. This question offers another way to talk about the enlivening of metaphor, or the exchange between ordinary and literary discourses. Students are often warned to avoid clichés in their writing. The discussions here indicate that the strategy is not so much to avoid them as to remotivate or refunction them. Plath's poem shows that the sheer act of collection, of accumulation of clichés into a set renews their meaning, enlivens them through a display of variety. The poem is useful for our purposes because it calls attention to the existence of metaphor in everyday discourse. Her demonstration supplements the insight into the inventive, literary nature of everyday discourse encountered in the section of anecdotes.

One of the most valuable lessons to be learned from Lakoff and Johnson involves their discussion of "the partial nature of metaphorical structuring." The transfer of attributes across sets tends to be quite selective, with catachresis representing one end of the scale, exemplifying minimum transfer, and surrealism representing the other end, maximum transfer. While it may be reasonable to think of the prop holding up a table as a "leg," we would not expect this transfer to include a concern for clothing the leg. The power of metaphor to revive, however, amy be seen in the fact that the prudish Victorians are said to have considered exposure of table legs to be as indecent as exposure of human legs. But the scientist who discovered that he could figure the dispersion of gas molecules by treating them as if they were billiard balls bouncing off one another did not also imagine that gas molecules are wooden and painted (nor did this lack of resemblance weaken the power of the comparison).

One of the most fundamental procedures of invention in any field, scientific and literary alike, is the discovery of a new context in which to consider a term and its referent. That metaphorical juxtaposition brings together whole sets or semantic fields suggests that the procedure of invention may be simulated or generated "artificially," by comparing systematically the full range of meanings available in a metaphor. What begins as a surrealistic exercise may lead to a strategy of thought applicable to other disciplines and practices. It also has considerable value in making and refuting arguments, as we shall see.

4. Remind students that an editorial that uses metaphor poorly will be as useful for their essay as one that uses metaphor well.

5. In this exercise the students begin to put into practice the systematic exploration of the exchanges of meaning that are possible in the juxtaposition of two categories in a metaphorical concept. Several lessons may be learned here. First there is the strategy of invention available in the notion of systematic extension of one category to the other. To write a brief essay on the topic "love is madness" is a matter of setting up the category "madness" as a model, as a reservoir of information constituting potential analogies for "love." One of the most basic problems the student faces when assigned the conventional theme paper--the location of the raw materials for discussion--is at least partly solved by this approach. Some research into the various kinds of madness may be necessary in order to fully explore the concept beyond its partial activation by the culture.

The second lesson has to do with how much one can learn about our cultural attitudes and ideologies by observing what parts of the metaphor are activated and what parts are left out of account. That a murder might be treated more leniently in the court system if it were a "crime of passion," relating love to the "diminished capacity" defense used in "insanity" pleas, tells us something about our common understanding of love. The metaphor legitimated in metaphorical concepts, that is, reflects a general attitude of the culture. What do we mean when we say we are "crazy" about someone? What parts of the cultural attitude toward madness actually carry over to love? The sense of compulsion or obsession is there, but not the stigmas that go with these behaviors--depending, of course, on the context. In general we might observe that reason and rational behavior has a higher status in our culture than does irrationality. At the same time, we expect and approve of certain qualities in given areas of life: someone who approaches love as if it were a science is acting against the grain of our cultural expectation (approved and standardized commonplaces).

The third lesson of this exercise is the introduction to the possibility of going beyond the accepted organization of a concept, either to activate some unused portion of the metaphor, or to substitute a new category to replace the conventional one. The point for now, however, is to experience the inventive capacity of metaphor to generate the materials needed for an essay. To say that "ideas are fashions" is more than just the assertion of a link between two terms: every facet of the category of "fashion" becomes available for our understanding of "idea." The next step will be to learn how to extrapolate from this possibility to the construction of arguments.

Metaphorical Concepts (p. 88)

Robert W. Keidel, "A New Game for Managers to Play" (p. 88)

Discussion and Writing

1. Keidel's article provides an illustration of some of the points made in the preceding theoretical explanations of metaphor. His use of "structure" here is the same point made by Lakoff and Johnson regarding the systematic way in which a category is organized by metaphor. The claim in both cases is that the way we talk about something is not merely incidental, but actually directs our thinking about a given activity or situation. Students do not always accept this possibility readily, despite the strong medicine of Lakoff and Johnson's evidence. They are not in the habit of giving that much credit to language. Nor have they always given much thought to the possibility of modeling behavior in one area of life on behavior in another area. They are familiar with the notion of "role model," but they have not thought about the systematic transfer of role behavior from one area to another.

2. We encounter here the figurative-literal distinction. There is often expressed at this point a curiosity about why people talk in this way, by means of metaphors, analogies, and comparisons. This is a question about the material nature of language. Metaphor is one of the properties of discourse. What sort of discussion would be possible that dealt with business only as business, or argument only in terms of argument, and so forth? As we noted earlier, there are other ways to relate concepts besides metaphor, although that still leaves us with the internal metaphorical structuring of categories themselves. The implication of this fact is that concepts themselves--the concept of "business" for example--may be altered.

Lewis Thomas, for example, suggested in Lives of a Cell that we should recognize the socially constructed nature of our concepts, and their metaphorical quality, as the first step toward the invention of a new mythology or ideology more beneficial to our outlook on the world. He points out that the common view of social relationships is Darwinian--a model of competition and struggle the outcome of which must be the survival of the fittest. Thomas suggested that we find some alternative description of nature--one more morally beneficial--to serve as the "vehicle" for the metaphorical concept of society. He suggests, for example, the entities revealed by microbiology, whose symbiotic or cooperative and mutually beneficial way of living offers an alternative version of nature to serve as a model for social relationships. Whether or not Thomas's account of nature will be incorporated in our culture's view of society, whether it will become a metaphorical concept, remains to be seen. Indeed, the relationship between ideas may itself be figured as a struggle for survival that is either competitive or cooperative.

3. One way to approach this discussion is to think of the way a coach bases a managing strategy on an implied theory of human motivation. This model of human behavior must be inferred by observing the coach's treatment of the players. One

proof that the managing style is based on a model is that the coach tends to apply the motivating formula to all players uniformly, regardless of the individual differences in personality.

4. This essay helps the student get a feel for the systematic exploitation of a category. Most important is the experience of working through what will later prove to be a prewriting stage of preparation--the inventory of the features or attributes of a category to see what it provides to think with, what it makes available informationally as the "vehicle" for the "tenor" or theme of the comparison. The set as a reservoir for invention will generate materials ranging from commonplace expressions to (apparently) absurd nonsense. How far can one extend the comparison of marriage to tennis? What is the equivalent in marriage of the double fault in tennis? When does the literal quality of metaphorical concepts pass over into reality? If a couple actually hit each other, is this like boxing, or is it boxing itself? The important lesson of this selection, then is to grasp what is meant by the systematic structuring of metaphorical concepts. The writer's strategy is to attempt to identify the equivalent of a given item in the parallel set. This matching (or imposition) may not be readily predicted in advance, intuitively, but requires a kind of calculation, as if filling in the blanks of a formula. Indeed, you will recognize in this strategy Aristotle's proportional formula, in which three of the four terms are known, the fourth term being a product of the logic of the relationship set up by the three familiar terms: A is to B as C is to ---.

Susan Sontag, from AIDS and Its Metaphors (p. 91)

Discussion and Writing

1., 2., and 3. In her earlier book, Illness as Metaphor, Sontag announced her intention in writing it: "For it was my doleful observation, repeated again and again, that the metaphoric trappings that deform the experience of having cancer have very real consequences: they inhibit people from seeking treatment early enough, or from making a greater effort to get competent treatment. The metaphors and myths, I was convinced, kill" (14). In the past few years, AIDS has replaced cancer as the most feared disease: "It seems that societies need to have one illness which becomes identified with evil, and attaches blame to its 'victims,' but it is hard to be obsessed with more than one" (16). Sontag's concern in AIDS and Its Metaphors, as in the earlier book, is to show how the way we talk about disease reflects dominant cultural attitudes. She goes on to show how long-standing some of these attitudes are.

Sontag first points out that AIDS is really the name of a condition with multiple illnesses, rather than a single disease. Yet it is perceived as such because "it is thought to have a single cause." Metaphorically, like cancer, AIDS has been described as an "invasion." Unlike cancer, whose causes are unclear, and whose action in the body is seen as "domestic subversion," AIDS is seen as caused by an enemy coming from outside, an "invader." Her example of such paranoid "Star Wars" metaphorizing is taken from Time magazine. We might say the paranoia is the result of the viral assault being perceived as permanent: "the viral enemy would be forever within." Reference to Lakoff and Johnson's discussion of the use of the "argument is war" metaphor will be useful here. The war mentality, as Sontag notes at the end of her book, "overmobilizes . . . overdescribes and . . .

powerfully contributes to the excommunicating and stigmatizing of the ill" (94). Thus, "'Plague' is the principal metaphor by which the AIDS epidemic is understood," now that AIDS has replaced cancer as an "epidemic." Sontag goes on to discuss the qualities that enable a disease to be "promoted" to plague status. Leprosy and syphilis made it because they were "consistently described as repulsive." Usually epidemics are thought of as plagues, and mass illness as an affliction, a punishment. In this, AIDS, like syphilis before it, is considered as a punishment for sexual transgressions. Thus it is understood in a "premodern" way, the use of the term "risk group" reviving "the archaic idea of a tainted community that illness has judged."

Another feature of plague is that it is perceived as a disease that comes from somewhere else, and here Sontag emphasizes the link "between imagining disease and imagining foreignness" (the alien aspect again). Once plague acquires this category, which confers exoticism on the disease, "the illness itself [becomes] phantasmagorical, symbolic." AIDS is thought to have originated in Africa (the "dark continent"), and this Developing World connection brings with it racist stereotypes. On the other hand, the Developing World, beset with a rapidly growing AIDS population, accused the United States (the CIA in particular) of perpetrating "an act of bacteriological warfare" by sending AIDS to Africa. The plague metaphor brings with it a story of "inexorability, inescapability." Plagues "are invariably regarded as judgments on society," and AIDS is described as a punishment on both individuals and groups, as are other sexually transmitted diseases. Until the end of the nineteenth century, society could moralize about epidemics, but in the twentieth, it did not, with respect to influenza and polio: both lacked certain attributes (e.g., polio was largely a disease of children). The exception: sexually transmitted diseases. Sontag's point is that the plague metaphor has become "indispensable . . . in bringing summary judgments about social crisis." When AIDS was identified with the homosexual population, moralizers were quick to shout, "serves 'em right!" (The concomitant movement for gay rights also contributed to the moralizers' zeal for punishment.)

<u>Arguing with Metaphor: Analogy and Parable</u> (p. 104)

<u>Judith Jarvis Thomson, "Abortion and Ethics" (p. 104)</u> 1. A parable, of course, is an anecdote that presents a plain tale used to signify something else. It is an extended metaphor, a deliberate dream, with a latent and manifest level of content. Jesus speaks in parables as a way of illustrating certain principles of faith--for those who know how to interpret them. The plugged-in violinist is not quite a parable, since it is presented as a provisional way of thinking about a problem rather than as the illustration of a truth already known. But both analogy and parable are based upon the metaphorical dimension of language.

2. Thomson's essay--a classic frequently assigned in university courses on ethics--is useful for our purposes for several reasons. The controversial topic, for one thing, makes explicit, as did the Sontag piece, the symbolic, metaphorical dimension of cultural issues. Like cancer, abortion has a scientific, biological, medical dimension as well as a moral dimension. The terms needed to account for these two dimensions are quite different and equally real and valid. This existence at two levels of discourse is typical of most cultural phenomena, and is something a

citizen must be aware of in order to communicate effectively within society. Indeed, in the issue of abortion the ideologies or mythologies of science and religion come into direct conflict, as they did with the issue of evolution in the previous century (a debate that has been revived in the name of "creationism"). A controversial topic so obviously weighted with a symbolic dimension reveals a lesson relevant to all interpretive disagreements, including those that occur in literary criticism. The resolution of the disagreement can not always be achieved by an appeal to the text or phenomenon itself, because the basis of the disagreement has its origins in the different assumptions--the different conceptual categories--operating for the parties to the debate. A creationist and a humanist, for example, have different concepts of "man" or "human being." Their sets are organized differently, structured by different metaphors, containing different if overlapping attributes. This is why one of the strategies of argument is to get an opponent to accept one's metaphor, and never, if possible, to engage the opponent on his or her own ground.

Thomson's article is also useful because her principal analogy is so obvious, so extreme, so lacking in subtlety that the reader can't miss it. In addition to the violinist analogy, the article blazes with living metaphors. Your students should have little trouble going through the article and identifying the various figures: the expanding child in the tiny house, the house-body comparison, the Henry Fonda hypothesis, the brother's candy, and so forth. They could not be expected to notice the way the essay as a whole relates metaphorically to the theme of the chapter, unless they have begun to read for the unity of Text Book as if it were a poem (the strategy we suggested as a learning skill or heuristic device for problem solving)--the metaphorical concept for thinking as conceiving a child, fertility and the gestation of ideas. However low this pun on conception might be, it has been used in discussions of knowing going back to Plato and to the Bible, with the term "abortion" having an active life in other areas of reference in contemporary discourse besides the medical one.

Students may at first find the most exaggerated images to be the least effective in terms of persuasion, but the most effective for understanding how this style of argument works.

3. While it is true that we are not foregrounding argumentative writing in this section, it is also true that we want to note the interpenetration of literary language with other discourses. Our pedagogy involves the close examination of a piece of writing taken as a model in order not only to discern its form but to extrapolate from that form a formula for the generation or invention of our own "original" writing. Therefore it is valuable to discuss with the class not only Thomson's analogies and metaphors, but also the way she combines these figures into arguments.

Argument, as we noted earlier, is one way to bring concepts into relationship. There is more than one way to draw these relationships, of course. The most common form of argument (keeping things at the basic level appropriate for our needs) relates categories by means of cause and effect. The concept of "love," for example, might be used to explain the cause of someone's "crazy" behavior.

Another way to relate categories, a way with which the students are also quite familiar, is comparison and contrast. It is worth discussing the difference between comparison and contrast and metaphor. Metaphor is a figure of comparison, with sets being formed on the basis of resemblance of attributes among the members. To make the distinction we must fall back on the difference between the literal and figurative dimensions of meaning, keeping in mind the unstable character of this opposition. Comparisons are usually expected to be literal--that two terms brought into relation are actually similar at the level of the referents, whereas metaphorical comparisons are figurative, with the vehicle providing an image or representation of the tenor. Comparison and contrast is juxtaposition in the interest of analysis, rather than representation, while argument by metaphor attempts to communicate those aspects of the issue that don't lend themselves to analysis--the experience or feeling of the issue. We might relate the Soviet and American systems, for example, by comparing the two forms of government or the two economic theories; we might also use images to convey what we take to be the freedom of one and the oppression of the other. The metaphor as image would tell what the item in question is like.

The representation of the body as a house is a good one with which to explore the unused part of the metaphor. Thomson herself does this when she passes from the initial situation of the expanding baby already inside the house (womb) to the question how an alien might enter the house (a window left open through which a burglar might enter). This analogy makes available the full range of things we can say about houses, including, for example, the contractual and legal status of property rights and ownership. In fact, the recent New Jersey court case of the surrogate mother (Mary Beth Whitehead) was decided against the biological mother and for the biological father (William Stern) on the basis of the contract signed by both parties promising the delivery of a baby for ten thousand dollars. The law, too, works by analogy, transferring the precedents set by one case to the circumstances of another one. In the case of surrogacy the familiar area--property and contracts--was extended to cover an unfamiliar and "unprecedented" situation. To continue Thomson's line of thought, then, we might propose that the baby is a squatter who has occupied premises without making payment and who may hence be evicted. We could then point out the absurdity of this extension as reason to invalidate the metaphor. Or we might argue that the body constitutes an attractive nuisance (like a swimming pool) for which the owner may be held liable. The woman's kidneys attracted the violinist the way a kidney-shaped pool might attract a small child. If the child drowns in the pool the owner may be sued; if the violinist is unplugged the owner of the kidneys may be sued as well.

Our concern is not that arguments constructed in this way be completely convincing, only that the students begin to experience the literary of fictive, poetic play of the production of such analogies. There will be time enough later to make the analogies as convincing or persuasive as possible. For now it will suffice to have the students find images and figures with which to represent the values they find relevant to this topic. They should also discover that the category they choose to work with (property, for example) will actively guide them in deciding what to say about the issue in question.

4. Preparation for this assignment might include an attempt in class to derive from Thomson's essay a formula for the production of analogical argument. To treat a piece of writing as a model is to generalize its features into the steps of a method. The steps manifested here begin with the selection of the controversial topic. A list

of possible topics might be established by means of suggestions from the students. A typical list includes gun control, nuclear disarmament, women's rights, the Palestinian question, terrorism, drunk driving, apartheid, drugs in sports, and so on.

The essay is argumentative, meaning that the writer should take sides and not try to do a report covering all positions fairly. The strategy will be to link the categories of the topic together in a way that supports one's preference, taking advantage of the flexible nature of concepts as sets.

The formula requires next a review of the opponent's point of view. An important part of redrawing the configuration of the concept is an account of the rival position. The terms of the argument are considerably clearer if we know the main features of both sides. To avoid taking anything for granted, you could also review the most basic features of an argument--a premise from which certain consequences logically follow. In this case, the premise of an absolute "right to life" entails moral and legal obligations restricting the rights of women. An argument is always "dialogical," anticipating and manifesting in its arrangement the assumptions of the other position. Thomson's essay makes little sense unless the reader realizes that she is constructing arguments to refute this logic.

The third step in the formula, then, is to break the connections among categories drawn by the opponent and reconnect them in ways more favorable to the writer's position. This can be done either between categories or within the category. At this point, following Thomson's model, our assignment asks the student to argue by means of metaphor, analogy, parable. We can see here also the strategy of demythicizing the opponent's metaphors as a negative step, taken before the positive act of offering one's own metaphors. The technique of arguing from metaphor includes not only the representation of one's position in a scene or image, but also a brief commentary following the figure that explains the consequences, the logic or reasons that follow from the figure. Poets sometimes do this too, explaining the conclusions of their image, as may be seen in X. J. Kennedy's "Ars Poetica" when he adds, after the image of the goose who died trying to look up its sphincter, "Would you lay well? Don't watch." Of course he still leaves the application of the lesson open (we applied it to a theory of writing). In short, reasoning from metaphors, by analogy, is itself a kind of modeling. One lays out the features of a vehicle, and shows how these features guide the understanding of the tenor in question.

In generalizing Thomson's essay into a model, then, the students may look for two kinds of language marking the two discourses cooperating in the essay: the discourse of logic, indicated by talk about premises, stronger and weaker versions of a case, errors and strict interpretations; the discourse of literature, embodied in the examples, hypothetical scenes, analogies, images, and parables. This formula may be generated in class discussion, thus providing the students with the genre they are to practice in this final substantial paper. (Indeed, it would make sense to use the earlier assignments as in-class exercises and topics for group discussion, all undertaken with this final paper in mind.)

The generic formula:

1. Establish a position on a controversial issue.
2. Review the opposing arguments and metaphors.
3. Demythicize opposing metaphors (if any).

4. Offer alternative metaphors.
5. Reason from these metaphors to their consequences, explaining and justifying the initial position.

It would be possible to write a shorter version of the assignment, eliminating the acknowledgment of the opponent and focusing only on the production of one's own metaphor, thus skipping steps 2 and 3 of the formula. Some students find it easier to develop their own position, however, by reasoning negatively from the position of a real or imagined adversary. You can delimit the lessons of Thomson's model in any way that suits your goals for this section. If the students are not to be confused by the model in doing the shorter version, however, they need to work through the two levels of discourse in class, in order to be sure they understand which part of the model they are following.

The final lesson of such a project, unifying the chapter as a whole, is an insight into the unstable, contestable nature of the categories classifying our experience and organizing our thinking. In Thomson's case, the concept at issue is "human rights." The question is not limited to "abortion," but necessarily extends to the concept of a "right," given the position taken by those who oppose abortion on the basis of a right to life. The prochoice and the right-to-life advocates don't agree on this specific concept, nor on any of the concepts that name the question (what is "life"?--the answer depends on the category one chooses as the vehicle of the explanation). As we noted earlier, this insight into the openness of concepts comes to many students as a revelation. To approach argument from the side of literary discourse exposes this fictional or constructed quality of belief systems and formal disciplines alike, and helps the students appreciate the fluid border joining high literacy with everyday life.

<u>Metaphor and Metonymy: Advertising</u> (p. 120)

<u>"Light My Lucky," "Finally, Life Insurance as Individual as You Are," "Vista" (pp. 121-125)</u> We have tried to keep terminology to a minimum here: metaphor, metonymy, and synecdoche (described here as a kind of metonymy). In class, you should probably talk over these figures, coming up with additional examples, until everyone feels comfortable using the terms--which will be important in doing analyses of texts.

Our discussion of the three ads should be assigned and talked over in class. You might ask students to find some version of the "Light My Lucky" ad and bring it to class. We were surprised when Lucky Strike refused us permission to use the ad, because our discussion mainly pointed out how clever the ad was--but cigarette manufacturers seem to be running scared these days.

It is worth pointing out to your students that the advertisers are indeed concerned about critical scrutiny of ads. In order to get permission to use the Prudential ad, we had to revise our discussion to eliminate certain remarks critical of the ad's effectiveness. This puts a greater burden on you and your students to supply the missing critical thought. The Vista ad is especially useful for demonstrating how advertising texts are often put together using many of the same processes of thought and language that go into the composition of poetry.

Discussion and Writing

1. Advise your students that for best results they should put some real thought into selecting their ads. To end up with two that work well, they should select several and do preliminary analyses of them. It will be easier to write a good paper if they select ads that use clearly different methods and generate different effects. This may or may not mean that one ad will be successful and one not--they may simply be different--but a clear, discussable difference will make the writing much easier to accomplish.

2. This problem can be solved by merely describing the changes that would be required or by actually remaking the ad, using letters and pictures cut out from somewhere else and pasted into the ad that is the basis of the project. Actually making the changes is probably the best way to go on this, though it involves more work. With something as visual as advertising, you almost have to see it to be certain that the effect you anticipate will actually be generated by the changes your make. The least possible change with the most disastrous effect will be the best response to this assignment.

You may wish to ask your students to submit a few paragraphs along with their redone ad, explaining why they made the changes they did and what they believe to be the effect of those changes. These altered ads should be displayed and discussed in class. This section on advertising closes the chapter on metaphor, but is also anticipates the following chapter on intertextuality.

Chapter 3: TEXTS AND OTHER TEXTS

Intertextuality (p. 130)

Students should be reminded that they have been working intertextually all along. In this section, the process of intertextuality is highlighted. Discussion of the introductory material might start with the epigraph from T. S. Eliot. In stealing, one makes something one's own, takes it over and transforms it. Imitations, however, are lesser forms of the original. (For a truly awful example of imitation, compare the poetry of Thomas Holly Chivers to that of Edgar Allan Poe. Another would be the comparison of Dürer's praying hands to all those ghastly ones painted on velvet.) The discussion of bumper stickers can be used to illustrate the difference between imitating and stealing. Ask students to provide other examples. (At this writing, the yellow caution sign proclaiming "Baby on Board" has spawned many poor imitations, such as Golfer, Dentist, Surfer, etc., on Board. Can we consider "Mother-in-Law in Trunk" an effective transformation?)

For further reading on intertextuality, see the American Journal of Semiotics. Vol. 3, No. 4 (1985), a special issue on intertextuality. The critical introduction by Thaïs Morgan is especially useful and has an extensive bibliography.

Three Texts: Judges 16, "Samson"; John Milton, Samson Agonistes; Nike advertisement (pp. 132-135)

Discussion and Writing

1. Judges 16 presents a chronicle of events. Milton has taken these and

elaborated on them. He has used a messenger as an eyewitness, one who is "sorrowed at [Samson's] captive state," but who is eager to see the sport Samson is to provide. Milton imparts spectacle to the scene through description of the theatre, the parade escorting Samson, the types of sport Samson provided. Milton only hints at Samson's prayer to the Lord for strength, and his wish to die. Rather, he emphasizes the way Samson tricked the Philistines, and thus Samson's final speech is rich with irony. Certainly one of the messages of the biblical text is that the Lord God of Israel is stronger than the (false) god, Dagon. This message can be read as implicit in Milton's text--if the reader is familiar with the biblical pre-text (and Milton could assume that his readers were).

2. Part of the discussion might concern the different ways words and pictures carry information. The ad assumes our familiarity with the story, counting on instant recognition of the scene. As E. D. Hirsch pointed out in his book on cultural literacy, these inferences work by means of stereotypes and clichés, meaning that only part of the story--its typical features--will be recalled, while much of the detail will not be activated. The process resembles the partial activation of metaphors discussed in the previous chapter. The designers of the ad place considerable stakes on being able to predict the response of the targeted audience. The experts on cultural literacy, that is, are the ad agencies who sponsor research into the "values and life styles" of consumers. The tone of the ad, for example, is witty, humorous, light--obviously not intended for seriously religious people. It is not clear whether or not the "Rake" alludes to the love interest of the story. For many students "Samson" goes with "Delilah" the way "bacon" goes with "eggs," and some discussion could be directed to the sales appeal of this unrepresented part of the inference. Also, the ad seems to joke with the notion of "ultimate," since this is Samson's last event. Do you suppose it also means to suggest that the ultimate Ultimate also wears Nikes?

<u>Transforming Texts</u> (1) (p. 137)

<u>Raymond Queneau, Transformations (p. 137)</u> This exercise provides a pleasurable introduction to the workings of intertextuality: adaptation, to be specific. As we note in the next section, where adaptation is distinguished from parody, adaptation requires that the writer make significant changes in the original text. This is what Queneau does to his original text ("Notation").

1. and 2. Students enjoy doing this exercise and sharing the results in class. They are fascinated with the diversity of responses, and find this a useful introduction to style as well. Queneau's means of transformation are fairly obvious, but be sure to spend some time going over each transformation before students try their own. For example, "Narrative" should be compared with "Notation" for differences and similarities (as in the use of the first person), because the style of "Narrative" is usually the most difficult for students to analyze. From "Passive," the rules for generating the passive voice should be discussed. Though students frequently overuse the passive voice in writing for academic purposes, they find it the most difficult to produce for this assignment, perhaps because they've been trained to haul it out only for serious academic occasions.

3. This discussion will allow students to share (sometimes gleefully) the rules they've absorbed in their academic careers. We have found this to be both

enlightening and depressing. Here are some of the rules we learned in the dim past:

"Notation": Be concise.

"Double Entry": Use descriptive language; make your subject clear to your reader.

"Precision": Be precise.

"Narrative": Stories should have a beginning, middle, and end. (Is "Narrative" a story? This might be a good place to remind everyone of Labov's six-part structure of a well-formed anecdote. It could be quite useful to consider how "Narrative" fails to be an anecdote.)

"Passive": Be objective, not subjective; always use the passive voice in formal writing.

"Haiku" doesn't conform to the rules--it doesn't present a single image--but it does have the feel of a haiku.

"Zoological": Use figurative language to enliven your prose; use a metaphor to organize your thoughts.

Transforming Texts (2) (p. 142)

Jacob and Wilhelm Grimm, "Hansel and Gretel" (p. 142)

Transformation (1) Coover, "The Gingerbread House" (p. 147)

1. The students' recollection of this story is a good occasion for testing the "decay" of memory, or the selective process by which parts of a unit of signification (which come in all sizes) are retained and other parts suppressed. Many students are surprised by the cruelty perceived in the action of the parents in the Grimms' story. Some students may notice at this point a connection with the story of the "Wild Child," suggesting that he was left in the woods by his evil stepmother. Zipes (see the end of this chapter) makes this possibility explicit in his discussion of the historical context of the Grimms' tales.

As in the relationship between the Bible and Milton's version of "Samson," there is a shift from an emphasis on plot line in the earlier telling to a more psychological emphasis on character and point of view in Coover. We get a different idea of the children in Coover, who reduces the Grimms' emphasis on the trickery, replacing it with a more emotional and sensual representation.

The most striking difference between the two tales is the style in which each is told, taken up in the next question.

2. In looking for comparisons with which to characterize the differences in style, students might be encouraged to draw on earlier sections of the book to express their observations. The Grimms' version is closer to the arrangement of an anecdote, reflecting its oral origins, while Coover's version is closer to poetry, reflecting the complex temporality of high literacy. In Coover the story line is available but subordinated to the patterns set up by the repetition of images. It is also sometimes deliberately "jammed" or led into self-contradiction.

Precisely because Coover's arrangement is poetic, some students (who, as we have noted in Chapter 2, have much less experience with this ordering principle) will not be able to follow it. They may claim the story makes no sense. Discussion in class, by focusing on the visual nature of Coover's descriptions, and the relationships set up between and among the numbered fragments, helps the students see that the story has an ordering principle. Asked to think of where else this style might be used, or other media in which the style might appear, a few of the students may notice the resemblance of Coover's telling to the style of television drama. As soon as this analogy is offered, whether by a student or the instructor, most of the difficulty of the piece disappears, and the technique begins to seem straightforward. Coover's fragments may then be read as if they constituted a shot list for a video translation of the story (we offer this possibility as an assignment in the last part of this chapter). Most of the students are quite familiar, at least tacitly, with the editing styles of television, and can recognize in Coover's imagery the effects of close-ups and cutting back and forth (parallel editing, montage).

It may also help if they conceive of Coover's fragments as shots that have not yet been assembled into a coherent, chronological narrative. In this and other stories by Coover (like "The Baby-Sitter") the reader is often given several versions of the same episode, some of which contradict each other. Final assemblage, including the discarding of irrelevant material, is left to the reader. This responsibility makes some readers uneasy. This would be a good place to discuss why freedom makes us uneasy, and whether art should allow the reader any freedom or should dominate readers completely.

3. Paragraph 5's description of the gingerbread house could be taken for a cartoon version--an innocuous, sweet picture it is, with those lollipops in "neat little rows." The house contrasts vividly with the witch, its dark occupant, yet her description is that of a typical Disney evil witch. It is the contrast between these Disneyfied elements and the violence of the witch's seizure of the dove, and the boy's, and his struggle with his sister--these actions indicative of intense desires--that pervert the cartoon elements.

Disney classics may be counted on to compose part of the cultural literacy of most of the students. Coover's representation of the witch will remind them of Disney's Snow White. Specialists in children's literature object to the way Disney classics sanitize or censor the negative elements out of the old tales, just as naturalists object to the Disney nature films for their anthropomorphic treatment of the animals, presenting the struggle for survival as a comedy in which the weaker animal escapes from the predator. This section on transformations and intertextuality provides an occasion to discuss the uses our culture makes of such material.

Coover's retelling of the Grimms' tale exemplifies a technique common among proponents of "metafiction"--literature generated self-consciously as a commentary on or interpretation of other literature. A number of authors have retold folk tales (Angela Carter and Anne Sexton, for example), tales which, like myths, serve as a reservoir of cultural information. Paragraph 18, with its explicit sexual connotations, is obviously not Disneyfied, and manifests the extent to which this story, like all the transformations in Coover's Pricksongs and Descants, is a work of high literature addressed to adult readers.

Students should not be expected to pin down an interpretation of each event or action in discussing this text, but they should not avoid the sexual implications in the struggles that are narrated. As for the question of desire, we might say that the old man can do nothing more than remember desire; the boy and girl now know desire, and experience the death of innocence. The witch seems to be the seat of desire; her house is the place where the connection between life and death cannot

be escaped, where the fruit of the tree of knowledge is eaten and found bitter.
4. One way to approach the metafictional quality of "The Gingerbread House" is to discuss the manner in which Coover's story functions not simply as another piece of fiction, but as a work of literary criticism, in that it offers an interpretation of the Grimms' version. In general, Coover uses the tale to express a view of the role such stories play in our culture. If the students are asked to analyze Coover's story by means of the structure of the anecdote, they may notice that he foregrounds the evaluative aspect, especially in contrast with the Grimms. Folk tales often end with a moral, similar to the coda of the anecdote, to make sure that the audience grasps the point of the story. (The Grimms offer a proverbial riddle--"my tale is done, see the mouse run"--which may be read as an invitation to interpretation: catch the meaning if you can.) Coover offers a significantly greater quantity of interpretive commentary along the way, as in paragraphs 24 and 26, for example. Indeed, the character of the father is expanded, with interpolations of a good fairy from the generic category of options, to act as a center of consciousness reflecting or mediating within the story on the implications of the world presented there.

One approach to this assignment, then, is to open the question of the "moral" of the stories: both what they are and how they are conveyed. Does Coover's moral--the moral of the tale as a whole--agree with the observations of the father? To the extent that Coover's metafiction is read by adults, while the Grimms' story is read to children, Coover's moral may be seen as an adult's more pessimistic or demythicized view of life--a reading of a children's story from a mature perspective in which one realizes that evil is real and things don't always work out for the best nor people live happily after. In this context we can see that Coover has evoked the Disney images precisely to reintroduce into this story the "teeth" it possessed in its earliest versions. The ordering permitted by the poetic technique of patterns and repetitions allows Coover to end his tale with the imagistic lesson of the unity or interdependence of the life and death principles.

Transformation (2) Jacob and Wilhelm Grimm: "The Little Brother and the Little Sister" (p. 156)

Discussion and Writing

1. In "Hansel and Gretel," dialogue is added, as are details such as the branch tied to the tree to simulate the sound of an ax; the "mother" becomes the "stepmother" in "Hansel and Gretel" (presumably this change would explain her insistence on getting rid of the children--or make it more palatable to the reader); the snow-white bird that leads the children to the gingerbread house is added, as is the duck that ferries them across the river; there is more description of the eating of the house, and of the meal inside; the "old woman" of the manuscript becomes a "wicked witch," with appropriate characteristics (nearsighted red eyes, keen sense of smell); a bolt is added to the oven door, as are the horrible screeches of the burning witch; the father is made more repentant, and the children run to his arms as all is presumably forgiven. The transformed ending of "pure happiness" and playfulness contrasts markedly with the manuscript ending: "but the mother was dead." In the transformed version, the stepmother's death is presented almost as an afterthought. Many of these changes may be discussed as a softening or Disneyfication of the earlier test--a Disneyfication before Disney, of course.
2. The manuscript version is a highly condensed narrative that concentrates on

events and employs little descriptive language. The transformation makes these events into a story, with its addition of details, dialogue, and attention to motivation and plotting. Some might say that the folk material has been gussied up to make a more popular story.

The lure of the fairy tale lies in what is unexplained: the witch, her house, the mother's meanness. In other words, the symbolic nature of the fairy-tale images invites interpretation and reinterpretation. A return to Freud and the dream image might be useful here.

3. The following is a student transformation of a fairy tale.

THE GOOD FAIRY MEETS GODZILLA

The girl laying curled in bed slowly stretches out her arms, flexing the fingers and easing the sleep out of her muscles. As the morning sun warms her cheek, she smiles and thinks about the Saturday (her favorite day) that lies before her. She swings her feet from under the warmth of her quilt ("This was given to me by my mother when I was twelve. Now I give it to you for the day you have children," she remembers her mother saying) and onto the cool wooden floor. Even on this fresh day, the morning routine takes over and she heads for the bathroom.

A fluffy white rabbit hops hurriedly across the path thinking of his boss waiting for him at the club. He stops to check his watch then rushes on.

Somewhere else, a bear roars.

The girl brushes her teeth, humming to a song on the radio. Her new stereo was the envy of all her friends, bested only by the phone she had by her bed. Her wardrobe, too, was nothing modest and she stood before it now, imitating the gestures of her older sister in deciding what to wear. Blue looked good on her, she decided, and picked out her blue dress. Turning up the stereo, she does a striptease with her nightgown and then collapses, giggling onto the floor.

The rabbit looks around and realizes he's lost. Nervously checking his watch, he hurries on.

Somewhere else, a bear roars.

The girl's parents lay awake in bed downstairs. They talk the optimistic talk of a suburban family. Their children are everything they wanted and they playfully remark on their success at child rearing. Upstairs, their youngest stands before her mirror (an antique five-foot oval on wooden legs) and brushes her hair, complimenting her image on its choice of clothing. The brush flows smoothly through her hair, never snagging or knotting.

The rabbit sees a section of the forest that looks familiar now. Hopping quickly for the path, he sees a human girl. A pretty girl, too. One he's never seen before but there's not time to stop now. Being the gentleman he is, he doesn't want to rush by without saying anything, so he pauses briefly. Breathless, he explains, "I'm late, I'm late," and hops onto the path, now a familiar road to him.

The girl is standing open-mouthed, staring at the reflection in the mirror, unsure how to explain to herself that a white rabbit just hopped through her mirror. With the trusting innocence and naiveté that only a twelve year old would possess she thrusts her hand at her mirror and shakes it, as if disturbing the reflective surface of a lake. Dropping her brush, Goldilox steps through the looking glass.

The fluffy white rabbit hops quickly down the path, thinking of ways to explain his tardiness to his boss. He twitches his little pink nose and stops suddenly, smelling danger. A wolf steps onto the path and smiles slyly.

"Where are you going?" he asks, coating his voice with sickening false sincerity.

The rabbit swallows audibly, twitches his nose, and replies, "I'm on my way to my grandmother's," hoping desperately that the wolf will see fit to pity him. The wolf smiles, showing all his teeth, and grabs the rabbit, tearing into its neck. Blood spills over the rabbit's white fur, covering it with a red coat. The wolf carries its prey far into the woods to devour it.

Goldilox inspected her new surroundings and giggled nervously. Goosebumps prickled along her arms and she looked first at her hands, then at the forest around her, as if trying to impose one reality onto another. Normally tears would have come by now, but she was determined to find out what was going on behind her mirror. She felt she at least had a right to know; she began walking through the forest.

Papa Bear roared again as he stretched and awoke. Unconsciously rubbing his hand on his chin, feeling his beard, he thought to himself that it would be a good day for a walk through the woods. He swung his big hairy legs from under the quilt onto the cool wooden floor and walked out to the kitchen. Mama Bear and Baby were already up and Mama had just baked an apple pie to eat for dessert that night. To the disappointment of Baby Bear, she placed the pie on the windowsill to cool. Baby Bear's stomach growled its angry protest.

The forest was a fun adventure for suburban Goldilox and, she reasoned, "Saturdays are made for adventures." She wandered off the path and began picking her way through the brush, stepping on small animals and destroying several budding plants. As she traveled further the forest thickened. Her blue dress caught on twigs, and her hair became tangled and torn. Vainly she kept running her fingers along her scalp trying to straighten her hair. Mosquitoes buzzed around her, biting her arms while gnats flew into her face. She began running, waving her arms frantically around her and kicking at the dense underbrush. By the time she got to the clearing she was tired, scared, and hungry. She also smelled apple pie.

The Bear family finished packing their picnic basket, gathered together fishing poles and a blanket, and set out for a day at their favorite spot by the stream. Baby Bear gave the pie one last longing look and followed his family out.

The apple pie lay cooling on the windowsill. Light breezes whistled down through the nearby pines and drifted across the top of the lightly browned, flaky crust. The smell of cinnamon wafted throughout the house. Apples, flour, and sugar began to meld together into filling as the pie cooled and settled.

Goldilox smelled what seemed to be one of her mother's apple pies as she entered the clearing. She approached a cabin in the middle of the small meadow where the smell was coming from.

All the furniture in the Bear cabin was homemade by Papa Bear himself. Each bed was designed to individual specifications. Mama and Papa Bear's bed was large and very firm to support their weight. Baby's bed was smaller and much softer because of his shorter, more sensitive fur. The dinner table was just big enough for the Bears to eat at comfortably. Each chair was for a designated family member. Papa's chair was large and high and had thick arms on the side; Mama's chair was smaller with a very straight back and no arms; Baby's chair was smaller still, and had small arms and a cushioned back. Papa Bear was a simple and loving father and made all these things on the Bear's first Christmas in the cabin.

On finding the door open, Goldilox went inside. She thought nothing of whom the pie came from. Instead, she grabbed it from the windowsill and took it to the table. She sat in Papa's big oak chair and began to eat the pie right from the pan, but the chair was too large. She tried Mama's chair but it was too uncomfortable. She found Baby's small cushioned chair to be just right and sat down and devoured the pie. Apples dripped down her chin as she transferred handfuls of material from pan to mouth.

In a den on the other side of the forest, a wolf was devouring a blood-soaked rabbit. It tore at the innards, ripping all the meat off the animal's bones and gorging itself. Blood dripped down the wolf's chin.

Papa was just drifting off to sleep when his line tugged. Grabbing the pole from between his knees, he jerked it, sinking the hook into the mouth of the fish. Baby Bear squealed with delight as his shiny, squirming dinner broke the surface.

As Goldilox was getting up (after finishing the pie) the snap on her dress caught the cushion on the chair, ripping a hole in it. Indifferent to the situation she went to the kitchen to get something to drink. After taking a drink of a soda, she left the can on Papa's chair and went exploring the cabin.

Papa rubbed his stomach contentedly and stood up to signal the rest that it was time to go. Mama obediently folded up the blanket and called for Baby Bear. Together, they started back for the cabin.

Having finished his meal, the wolf crawled further into the den and slept.

Mama and Papa Bear's bed was too hard for Goldilox. She was looking for a place to take a nap before going home. Seeing Baby's bed, she crawled in and found it was just like her bed at home. Her stomach was full with the pie and she was tired from walking, and very soon Goldilox was asleep.

Baby Bear could almost taste the apple pie that was waiting for him just beyond the door. As soon as he got inside and put his fishing pole away, he ran to the kitchen to slice the pie, only to find it missing. Mama Bear was the first to notice the table with the pie tray on it. Papa Bear saw the soda can on his chair and knew someone had been in his house. Outraged at the intrusion he began searching each room, seeing if anything was missing or if the intruder was still there. On entering Baby's room, he saw Goldilox and stopped short. It had been a long time since he'd seen an unarmed human and the novelty of a defenseless human girl excited him in a strange way. He watched the girl's young body as her chest raised and lowered with each breath. As he was approaching the girl, Baby Bear came in the door and, startled, screamed. Goldilox awoke and saw the bears around her. Terrified, she jumped out of the bed and out the bedroom window (it was open). Papa ran to get his shotgun to shoot the varmint but by the time he got back with it, the girl was gone. Baby Bear was promised another pie and chair cushion and, after the sheets were changed, Mama read to him to help him sleep after his harrowing experience.

The wolf was awakened from its sleep by the incessant chattering of squirrels. He crept quietly to the mouth of his den, found the noisemaker, and pounced on it. Being full from the rabbit, he only played with the carcass half-heartedly then went back to sleep.

The branches slapped Goldilox in the face as she ran back to the path home. Thorns tore at her dress and her breath rasped in her throat. She felt as if her knees would collapse when she finally saw the mirror in the middle of the path. She thrust her hand at it to disturb the reflective surface, then stepped through into her bedroom. Her hair was matted and full of brambles, her face was smudged with dirt and tears, and her dress was torn nearly beyond repair. Goldilox collapsed on her bed, thankful her Saturday adventure was over. She was quickly asleep and didn't even notice when an ivory chess queen summoned playing card warriors from behind the mirror. Somewhere a cat was smiling.

Completing Texts: The Reader's Work (p. 160)

In this section, we place the activity of the reader in the foreground by asking students to actualize that activity by writing. At this point in Text Book we would expect students to know that reading is not a passive act of consumption, and that a text can elicit different readings. The material here is designed to bring that issue up for discussion. We reject the aesthetic notion that a reader completes a text by "discovering" a particular meaning intended by the author (see Wolfgang Iser, The Implied Reader, Baltimore: Johns Hopkins University Press, 1974). On the other hand, we seriously question the notion of "interpretive community" set forth by Stanley Fish in Is There a Text in This Class? (Cambridge: Harvard University Press, 1983), which comes very close to allowing readers to make whatever they will of a literary text. We have cited Umberto Eco because his The Role of the Reader (Bloomington: Indiana University Press, 1979) strikes the best balance between the activity of the reader in creating a new reading of a text and the text's authority in directing the course of that reading. Eco's word for this process is "collaboration," a term that should be discussed with your students in relation to the reader's engagement with the text. You might ask your students if the term can be applied to the activity of class discussion. Your students may wish to discuss the problems of the reader's work in this section. They might, for example, want to reflect on the kinds of collaboration called for by a surrealistic or a poetic text.

James Joyce, "The Boarding House" (p. 163)

Discussion and Writing

1. The student is invited here to examine the narrative machinery of which the opening paragraphs are composed:

"no open complicity": Paragraph 4 shows us that Mrs. Mooney is in charge of Polly's career as typist and as flirt. The phrase of course suggests its opposite, the hidden complicity that can be inferred from "her mother's persistent silence could not be misunderstood."

"the affair": The connotations of the unmodified noun are generally negative, in relation to politics or to sex. The information we are given concerning Polly's character and actions in paragraphs 3 and 4 would seem to validate the use of the term "affair": her little song, "I'm a . . . naughty girl"; her look: "a little perverse madonna"; her actions: she is described as being "very lively" and she flirts with the young men. And they call her mother "The Madam."

"a little strange": This description of Polly's state, coupled with that of Mr. Doran's ("the young man was evidently perturbed") calls for inference from the reader, as does "the right moment." We know there's an affair, and it's taking an odd (or can we say predictable) turn. And we know we're dealing with a moral problem. When we read that Mrs. Mooney deals with such problems "as a cleaver deals with meat," we should recall the opening of the story, "Mrs. Mooney was a butcher's daughter," and the fact that her husband, also a butcher, had gone after her with a cleaver. Here the text guides our interpretation by setting up what might be called a cleaver code. At the end of paragraph 5, the reader is left to forecast the nature of the moral problem and the nature of Mrs. Mooney's intervention, now that "she has made up her mind."
2. Close attention to details is necessary to construct this scene, which can be written as dialogue, monologue, or narrative. Class discussion of the text should emphasize the sense of entrapment felt by Mr. Doran and the reasons for it. How much information does the story provide to allow the reader to infer the cultural codes of Catholic Dubliners of the middle or lower middle class at the turn of the century? The ghost chapter will address the issue of reparation and why it is an issue. Students should consider the nature of the character contest they are to write.

Dorothy Parker, "You Were Perfectly Fine" (p. 168)

<u>Discussion and Writing</u>
1. The girl presents a somewhat rose-colored version of events. Her understatements come to be seen as such when contrasted with the young man's terse summaries of and questions about his behavior. As a story of entrapment, this text can be compared with Joyce's.
2. Students may want to concentrate on two or three events rather than trying to retell each one.
3. Short narratives by these observers or participants can be written in class and read aloud. Students should have some idea of how difficult it is, if not impossible, to report just the facts of a given event.

<u>Interpreting Texts</u> (p. 172)

Jack Zipes, "The Politics of Fairy Tales" (p. 175)
Bruno Bettelheim, "Hansel and Gretel" (p. 178)

In this section the difference between <u>Text Book</u> and conventional approaches to "writing about literature" may be clearly observed. As in traditional approaches, we ask the students to look closely at the formal organization of literary texts, but instead of expecting them to write interpretive essays describing a close reading we treat the original as a model whose effects and strategies the students attempt to imitate or use as the basis for an extrapolation to a related exercise. There is no reason that the technique of modeling could not be used to learn how to write interpretive essays of the kind written by professionals in our field to communicate with other specialists. Indeed, the formula for an interpretive essay closely resembles the structure of metaphorical concepts, juxtaposing two sets of information--the literary text and the explanatory system. Such interpretive essays perform the work of concept formation in the specialized discipline. Once the students understand the process of classification operating in concepts, they have the methodology they need to undertake interpretive writing. All they lack is "all" that information needed to carry out a "living" cross-referencing of the two sets. Hermeneutics, in short, is best reserved for a more advanced course.

It is still quite useful to introduce the students at this introductory level to critical interpretations, which in this context may be understood not as authoritative statements of truth closing down the possibilities of meaning opened by the texts, but as further transformations and translations of extant materials. Since they have less experience with critical writing, the students are unlikely to have the confidence needed to recognize the typicality of these two essays by Zipes and Bettelheim. That is, they are not yet ready, for the most part, to recognize the generic predictability (or to judge the reliability) of the things each critic finds to say about the story.

Discussion and Writing

1. One way to treat interpretive writing is as a system of invention, providing a reader with something to say in response to art. The process of foregrounding certain elements of a text and suppressing others, with which the students are familiar from earlier sections, may be seen here at the level of critical generalization, for the interpretive system excludes some issues from consideration while guiding the interpreter's perception of possible topics of interest. Zipes's Marxist reading will necessarily look at the social and historical context of the story, ignoring the elements of individual psychology noted in Bettelheim's Freudian reading, or offering collective causes to account for those elements.

Students tend to find the Marxist reading more reasonable or recognizable. They now readily note the parallel between Victor (the wild child discussed by Roger Brown--p. 46) and Hansel and Gretel, given the fact that the two "stories" share the same historical period. They follow the extended metaphor that Zipes elaborates between the witch and the aristocrats of the period. From the earlier discussion of concept formation, the students even accept the necessity of the employment of specialized vocabulary, identifying as Marxist, but not always being able to define, such terms as "class conflict" or "capitalism."

The students accept the witch/aristocrat/parasite analogy because it is confirmed by their general opinion about the relationship between aristocrats, who are seen as exploitive, and everyone else. They are not ready to grant that capitalists exploit workers, however, although the possibility that the First World exploits the Developing World seems more reasonable to them.

2. The comparison of a Freudian and a Marxist reading of "Hansel and Gretel" in the "casebook" form may produce some valuable discussion and insights into the operations and strategies of critical interpretation. Seeing two readings side by side enables students to see how critics actually work.

Bettelheim's reading is more controversial than Zipes's, and some of the class will simply not accept the Freudian interpretation as having any validity whatsoever.

Our assignments do not require belief in the system. The point is to see how interpretation works, which means that it may even be helpful if the interpretation does not seem "natural." But Bettelheim offers the further difficulty that his writing is more abstruse, depending, as it does, upon a detailed allusion to psychoanalytic theory--specifically to the developmental process of personality formation through the oral, anal, and phallic stages. The more obvious (and caricatured) story of Oedipus is not as directly involved, although it is included in a less familiar form (the good and bad mother). Most of the students possess in their cultural repertoires an awareness of Freud's use of the Oedipus story, however, and are able to identify the basic dynamics of Bettelheim's application of it in this case. Thus, the encounter with the witch may be read as a figurative working through of the emotions raised by the hostility of the mother at the beginning of the story. The students may notice that the house-body analogy also appeared in Thomson's essay on abortion.

It is helpful to spend some time in discussion, not trying to convert anyone to psychoanalysis but creating at least some sympathy for the act of interpretation and the pleasures of explanation. Bettelheim, for example, accounts for the insistence of the rejected children on returning home. By pointing out that psychoanalysis addresses real problems, such as the authentic dilemmas of the maturation process and the difficulties of leaving home to face the world on one's own, you can help students attend more carefully to Bettelheim's argument. His general point is that such stories offer a way of symbolically working through the conditions of life, which the reader must experience. This is, of course, a major reason why stories are important and worthy of the kind of attention we give them in courses like this one.

In any case, the purpose of studying critics like Zipes and Bettelheim is not to attain a competency in Marxist or Freudian criticism but to recognize the strategies of all critical interpretation--to note the various ways that critics translate point A of the story into point X of the interpretive system. This would be a useful place for a brief return to Freud's interpretive terms in Chapter 2. There they were related to Breton and surrealist poetry. Here, they can be reconsidered to compare the way that literature constructs images with the way criticism converts them into exposition.

3. If you did not have time to thoroughly discuss "The Kiss" or "The Use of Force" earlier, here is an opportunity to do so--after students have written their interpretations. The introduction, "Interpreting Texts," gives suggestions to help students move from concrete details to the abstract concepts that are characteristic of interpretation.

4. This assignment is another version of the one included in an earlier section of this chapter. The idea now, however, is to translate a folk or fairy tale into a video script, making explicit the videolike quality of Coover's writing (noted in our earlier discussion of "The Gingerbread House"). The writers should imitate Coover's fragmented paragraph, but having in mind that their text will be used as the basis for a shooting script of a film. What will the camera show? What will people say?

The added interest of this exercise is the interpolation of the critic's voice into the script, as if the paper were a translation of one of Siskel and Ebert's television film review programs. Having noted the kinds of things Zipes and Bettelheim say about "Hansel and Gretel," the students should interrupt their tale periodically to insert the critic's observations whenever a similar sort of thing occurs in their story. This interpolation is possible because of the formulaic character of folk tales, which tend to be organized around a highly consistent, repetitive structure. Thus, the sorts of things the Marxist and/or the Freudian say about food, witches, kings, peasants, and so forth in "Hansel and Gretel" may be said about similar items in other tales. This way of reading the tales offers some basic practice in critical interpretation, along with the experience of the similarity between critical writing and other forms of intertextual transformations of extant writing. In this way the stories may be understood as nonconceptual modes of reference, and criticism may be understood as the supplying of the names or categories of referents addressed by the stories. (This would be one line to take in discussing the relationship of this chapter to earlier topics.) The interpretation, that is, accepts the invitation of the tale to find its moral or lesson and make it explicit.

This exercise also lends itself to parody, although it does not require it. Indeed, consideration of the visualization, montage, close-ups, and other devices of editing involved in video or cinematic translation can lead to some powerful, inventive papers. There is no need to follow a highly technical version of a formal script--we would provide a model if that were the kind of writing we expected. Rather, the idea is to perceive that Coover has imitated the film treatment (or informal script) in the style of "The Gingerbread House." It is easier to notice exactly what Coover is doing if one has in mind this analogy with an audiovisual script.

The following is a student response to question 4.

ZIPES AND BETTELHEIM
"AT THE MOVIES"

Siskel: Hello, I'm Siskel Zipes.

Ebert: And I'm Ebert Bettelheim. We're your weekly movie critics at large.

Siskel: Today we're watching and reviewing the familiar children's movie "Jack and the Beanstalk." We will be discussing the Marxist and Freudian views hidden within the context of the movie.

Ebert: So let's turn on the projector and watch a few scenes.

1

A large meadow in the spring afternoon. A small weather-beaten cottage isolated in the meadow. One cow, slowly grazing on bare patches of grass. A small child in the distance approaching the house. Skipping. Merrily. Whistling, to himself perhaps. The child's hair is blond, disheveled. His face dirty, but cheeks bright red. His pants are too short, a dirty brown with patches on top of patches sewn in the knees. His jerkin a faded yellow with worn out stitching. He is barefoot. His whistling tells of the innocence and insignificance of life.

2

Birds and squirrels scatter out of his way as he approaches the cottage. He stops by the cow he has named Milky-White. The thin, bony cow lifts its head for a moment uncaring, then resumes its grazing. He looks in the well covered with brown moss. He picks up a pebble and drops it into darkness waiting for a reply. The one received is not pleasant. The dull sound of rock hitting rock far below. The overused door to the cottage is on its last hinges. Paint peeled off long ago leaving bare, rotting wood. He skips up the front steps throwing open the old door to the cottage anxiously searching for the familiar face of his dear mother. The cottage is sparingly furnished. The wood is rotting and the table bare. Sunlight enters through small holes in the straw roof.

3

Poverty weighs on the old lady. Her dress is simple and almost in rags, its color faded. Her face is full of grief and wrinkles brought about by resignation rather than age. Her apron is in tatters and is covered in grease and loose pieces of straw. Gray hair. She seems sad and tired. She greets the boy with a scolding and concerned gestures. Deep in her sad, blue eyes there is love, but no hope.

4

Jack walks along the cobblestone path, shuffling his feet. His head hung low. He is no longer whistling. His feet have formed hard calluses and are lined with dry mud. The cow follows behind on leash. He holds the halter loosely kicking pebbles in his path. It is almost dusk. The sky is grey with sunset. He is hungry. His stomach empty. Nothing he is not used to. His final destination keeps forcing his shuffle to falter. He would care not if an eternity passed before his destination was reached.

Siskel: The elements of class struggle and the entire feudal system is most apparent in the first few scenes of the movie. The social and political signs are unmistakable. It is obvious at first glance that this tale treats a social problem of utmost concern to the lower classes. It depicts a struggle against poverty and hardships of life that the lower classes are forced to maintain. The boy's clothes as well as his mother's clearly depict the condition of life they are living. The old cottage is their only sanctuary and it is a poor one indeed. The dry well and bare tables show that they are constantly starving. Now the cow, their only source of revenue, is useless. Jack and his mother accept their way of life only because they have lost all hope and they know no other.

Ebert: I disagree Siskel. I believe it is the usual story of poverty, but what is actually being depicted is the boy's deep love for his mother. The boy has an Oedipus complex toward his mother. She has raised him from birth and cared for him. It is important to note that no mention of a father is said anywhere in the story. This is because he is being viewed as totally insignificant in the child's eyes. We do not know if the father is dead or alive, nor do we care because the child does not care. The mother is all-important and he wishes only to please her. The house symbolizes the mother's body. He dwells within the house during his childhood as a mother nurses the infant from her body.

5

The short man stands on the side of the path. He too wears rags. His boots are worn, his back arched. The cloak over his shoulders has seen many days and nights, survived in the scorching sun and pouring rain. His thick grey beard is tangled in knots. His hands and face are parched. He is a loner. The gnarled oak cane bends under his weight worn smooth through the years. Yet there is wise light in the eyes below the thick, busy eyebrows. He smiles. His teeth are rotten and yellow. He presents a few small beans to the boy next to him. The beans are white and dry. Inedible, yet magical. The man is poor, clever, experienced in the ways of the world. Jack's eyes are bright, there is a total innocence behind the caked mug on his face and a little hope. The man ignores the boy's innocence. The cow now walks behind him on leash, uncaring. Jack's face is full of new hope. There is spring in his step, song in his voice and hunger in his stomach. He juggles the beans in one hand. He skips back toward the cottage he calls home. It is almost dark.

6

The ground shakes. The giant is wrapped in huge pelts of fur. He is hugely muscled. Power surges through his body. His legs are as high and wide as the largest tree trunk. His body as big as a house. His head is covered with thick, red, coarse hair as is his chin. His eyes are deep and burn like cinders. His face fat and livid. His snarl conceals the huge man-eating teeth. The rich furs drag behind him as he reaches into the roasting hearth. The powerful hands crack the bones of a roasting pig like a bed of toothpicks. He laughs to himself silently gloating in his power. He bellows to his wife. The pig's bones crush in his jaws. A golden egg lies alone in a nest of twigs.

7

The old woman's face is full of sorrow and anguish more than anger. Her pale blue eyes float deeply in their sockets shrouded by heavy lids and a few tears. She gazes into space. Her mouth is taut. The damage is irrevocable. All at once she throws the tiny beans in her wrinkled little hands out the window. They are forgotten quickly as is any indication of hope. Jack goes to bed hungry. His heart is bruised. His innocence broken. A moist patch of soil. Deeper. Darkness. There is movement, life struggling upwards to breathe for the first time. Pale morning light.

Siskel: We are shown two things in the previous scenes. The lower class, common people are now forced to turn on one another in order to survive. The man is not evil and is considered to be wise by tricking a young boy because this will enable him to survive a little longer. The wars of this period often brought famine and poverty which led to the breakdown of the feudal system. Consequently, peasants were often likely to shift on their own and forced to go to extremes to survive.

We are also vividly introduced to the giant. The struggles depicted in the movie are against poverty and against giants who have food and hidden treasures. Here again the imaginative and magic elements of this movie had specific meanings for a peasant and lower-class audience at the end of the eighteenth century. The man-eating giant could be interpreted here to symbolize the entire feudal system or the greed and brutality of the aristocracy, responsible for the difficult conditions faced by Jack and his mother.

Ebert: The giant here does not represent a feudal system, but a threatening father figure. A boy while going through the Oedipus complex hates and distrusts his father. He is the only thing intervening between himself and his mother. We are introduced to this giant whom the boy sees as a giant father figure and must eventually destroy.

The beans represent the seeds of life. Jack sees them as magical beans. They are fertile eggs which can bring forth more children. Therefore he brings them to his mother wishing her to implant them within herself. They are his "life-line." But the mother cannot afford to bear more children and she tosses them out.

<u>8</u>

Jack's heart jumps with a new hope. He must avenge his mother. His fists clench. He starts to climb. The stalk is huge. Dark green. Tangled and gnarled roots branching in all directions, yet ever upward. His body tires, but his mind does not. Jack climbs onwards through the clouds. Far below are cottages. They are small, insignificant. Perhaps this is his destiny. His mother calls for him. He is gone. She sees the beanstalk. Her face twists in agony. Now she has nothing.

<u>9</u>

The giant is huddled over his food. A mountain of rich furs on muscle. His huge fingers point at a small hen in a little nest. His bellow shakes the castle. A pure golden egg falls into the nest. The huge shoulders of the giant shake with delight, with greed, with lust. He smells gold, he smells power, he smells a boy.

<u>10</u>

The castle looms overhead on a bed of pillowy clouds. The sun radiates above. Jack is amazed. He feels warm, good inside. He is above the clouds, his small hands raised toward the magnificent structure. Its towers disappearing in the sun. He approaches with hunger and caution in every footstep.

<u>11</u>

The giant woman takes pity on the poor starving boy. She will feed him now. He will be the food later. Jack nibbles at the immense amount of food. He feels as small as a mouse. Perhaps he is. The walls are covered with tapestries. The floor with thick rugs. The ground shakes. The walls quiver. Jack hides himself in the oven. The giant roars about smelling a boy. The giant woman points. Jack bolts for the door. Bricks start flying. He grabs the hen or all will be in vain. Jack slips through the giant's legs and under the door. The ground shakes beneath him. He dares not look back. He shimmies down the stalk, panting. The cottage looms closer. He is free.

Siskel: The magic and fantasy elements are closely tied to the real possibilities for the peasantry to change conditions. The emphasis is on hope and action. Jack takes action, he always has hope. Jack climbs to heaven. He feels magnificent, yet he is cautious. The peasantry would view this place as unreal or magical. It exists only in their minds. Jack is prepared to steal from God himself. The giant (God) represents the aristocracy, the extremely powerful and wealthy. The peasantry were forced to risk even death in order to obtain a little wealth. For poverty and famine were waiting below.

Ebert: The giant beanstalk now represents Jack's "life-line" grown toward the sky. A child must face a moment in his life when he says "this is the last day of my childhood." Jack tries to climb this long "life-line" and face the father who stands between him and his mother. The child sees he is not ready to kill the giant father-figure yet and makes the wise decision, bringing some wealth (to please his mother), he barely escapes. Jack is still a child and has escaped the grip of maturity.

<u>12</u>

The giant's rage will not cease. His roars crash like thunder. He knows no fear. He swears vengeance. He bellows for his golden harp. The harp of pure gold shines like the sun. Strings of pure silk. It sings. Songs of lullabies and poverty in lands far away. It soothes the giant beast. He sleeps for now. The sun shines brightly over the castle.

<u>13</u>

For the first time there is a glitter in the old woman's eyes. A glitter not of weariness, but of resistance, perhaps almost hope. Her son has returned. A hen lays a golden egg in a small nest of twigs. The grass has returned. The sun refracts off the water in the well. The boy and his mother live peacefully, almost content. Jack is light-hearted. His innocence returns and his curiosity as well. Early morning. He climbs again.

<u>14</u>

The giant sits on his throne. Gold coins piled next to him. Deep in his glowing eyes there is lust, there is greed, there is ignorance. Jack approaches the castle. He will not be fooled twice. He hides in a box of copper. The giant eats. The harp sings. Songs of battles won and lost long ago. His huge head falls, he snores. Jack runs, harp in hand. The golden harp cries to its master. The walls shake, the castle shutters. Smoke billows from the giant's flaring nostrils. His roar echoes through Jack's ears drowning the harp's song. Jack runs through the clouds. He can feel the giant's breath on his back. He shivers, the giant blocks the sun with his body. The beanstalk sways and croaks under the immense weight. Yet it holds both boy and giant. Jack reaches the ground calling for his mother. She runs, axe in hand, quickly and lightly toward her son. Jack swings the axe with new found strength. The sharp metal glints in the sun, its bite is true. The stalk falls and with it the giant. The ground shutters, it splits open, swallows the giant. The clouds disperse overhead. He is gone.

15

The cottage shines in the sunlight. A hen lays a golden egg. A harp sings sweet melodies. A boy and his mother, perhaps for the first time, smile together. One cow grazes on new, green grass. A small cottage isolated in the meadow. A large meadow in the spring afternoon.

Siskel: The peasantry and lower-class could not be content even if there was food and water on the table. Their hatred toward the upper-class drove Jack towards heaven once again. This time more clever. Jack, a common boy, shows himself to be the equal of a giant if not better. His miraculous escape might represent the collective energies of the small people, the power they actually possess. When these powers are used to attain justice and compensation the people are invincible. The killing of the giant is symbolically the realization of the hatred which the peasantry felt for the aristocracy as hoarders and oppressors. It shows the people as fair and just. Once the aristocracy has been destroyed they are wealthy and content with life. Yet their overall lifestyles do not change as Jack and his mother remain in the old cottage.

Ebert: Jack needs to learn to trust that someday he will master the dangers of the world even in the exaggerated form in which he depicts them. Jack, still a child, realizes this and therefore returns to destroy the giant father-figure. When he finally does he returns home and now finds happiness there. This is psychologically correct, because a young child driven into adventure by Oedipal problems cannot find happiness outside the home. Only through good relations with his mother can a boy truly mature into adolescence. Having overcome his Oedipal difficulties and learned that wishful thinking has to be replaced by intelligent action, Jack is ready to live happily again with his mother.

Siskel: Thus we conclude our film "Jack and the Beanstalk." I have given it a thumbs up.

Ebert: And I have as well. We highly recommend the whole family to see such an enriching tale that was actually not made by Steven Speilberg.

Siskel: May the good movies be yours and remember to save us the aisle seats.

Identifying with Texts (p. 186)

This section, and also the new chapter (Chapter 5), have been added to Text Book in response to the desire expressed by many users to include discussions of ideological questions from the point of view of textuality. Ideology as a concept concerns the social and psychological processes involved in the formation of individual and collective identities. The intertextual approach to this identity formation assumes that individuals actively participate in the construction of their sense of unity, coherence, and continuity (the formation of a self-image) by borrowing and internalizing schemas and icons made available within the culture.

An intertextual approach to teaching the functioning of ideology in experience begins with the recognition that the students are not "experts" in their culture in a disciplinary sense, but that they are its "native speakers." The anthropological metaphor is that of the field worker (the teacher) and the informant (the native). In terms of critical theory, the students have already been "interpellated" into the culture: by the time they get to a college classroom they are fully gendered, sexed, nationalized, ethnicized, and so forth. Like a native speaker, however, they often have no meta- or self-conscious knowledge about the nature of their interpellation. They know what they want or like, but they are less aware of why and how they want or think those things. The Socratic version of this situation relates to the pedagogy of anamnesis. The educator's purpose is to remind the students of what they already know (in Plato's metaphysics, the soul forgot what it had known from the spiritual world when it entered a body; the Socratic pedagogy aimed at reminding or awakening the soul to this previous knowledge).

In practice this memory pedagogy takes as its point of departure the fact that the students already understand the works of entertainment that they consume. This understanding is partly "semantic" (that part of meaning that resides in the language itself--English, narrative form, and the like), and partly "inferential" (derived from a familiarity with the commonplaces of popular culture.) The "intertextual" context of any given text is accessed by inference, a reasoning that depends upon familiarity with the accepted codes and schemas of a culture.

All the readings and questions offered in this section of Text Book are designed to help students become aware of this inferential process and to use it for mapping their own reservoir or repertoire of collective memory. In one way or another all the assignments require the students to make explicit for themselves the connections that bring into contact three levels of signification. The three levels are: the specific work itself (a film such as Bambi or Casablanca); the "myths" or general schemas or codes that organize the particulars of a potentially infinite number of individual works into a much reduced set of stories (the myths of love, hard work, individual rights, and so forth); an even more reduced set of values classified according to the ideological categories of identity (nation, gender, race, etc). Students have little trouble recognizing that their responses to the relationship among specific characters in a film (the triangle among Rick, Ilsa, and Laszlo in Casablanca) are guided if not determined by the assumptions about love and marriage common in their culture. They have much greater difficulty making the next link--between the myth and the ideological category that motivates it.

A strategy for teaching this section, therefore, would be to show Casablanca and Play It Again, Sam in class (or ask students to rent them at a video outlet), and to use general discussion about them to give guidance for individual student papers dealing with other films of their choice. Although the women's movement has made some progress here, one may not assume very much self-awareness about the implications for personal behavior of the categories of American ideology. The first discussion to have, then, might involve an inventory of these categories. Everyone knows the WASP list, and that may serve as a point of departure. The first step is to establish the list of categories: race, ethnicity, religion (to keep with the WASP list) gender, sex, class, age, nationality (to name most of the important ones). The next step is to ask the class to fill in the "preferred" choice of mainstream American culture in each one of the categories: race = white; ethnicity = Northern European; religion = Protestant Christian; gender = masculine; sex = heterosexual; class = middle class (capitalism); age = young;

nationality = American. There may be some disagreements in that these preferences are undergoing modification today. Also, agreement about the above selections within all the possibilities for each category does not mean that the individual necessarily identifies with what each preference represents. At issue are the ideals of the majority.

Once the list of preferences is established, the next step is to figure out what behaviors are motivated by the beliefs represented in the list. This question is by far the most difficult to come to any agreement about at first. The strategy is to ask students to examine their own assumptions in each area to find what is expected of them, and what they expect of themselves (even if they don't always act on these expectations). What needs to be identified in each category is what it values. The middle class, for example, values competition, the work ethic, self-reliance. Why? Because capitalism as a specific form of economic organization requires such values (admittedly this begs the question). To locate the behaviors that follow from such values, look into the nature of capitalism (and perhaps one may have to do a bit of lecturing or assign some outside research). For capitalism to work the citizens of a capitalist society must aggressively pursue their self-interest. A society that does not prepare its citizens to be competitive, aggressive, fairly self-absorbed individualists will not do very well with the profit and free enterprize aspects of the economics of capitalism.

How do these values and their associated behaviors manifest themselves at the level of particular films? For one thing, they may be observed in the aggressive actions of independent heroes. The tactic for making this link apparent is to ask about the purpose of action-adventure films such as those starring Arnold Schwarzenegger, for example. What do such films communicate to a population? The films are not meant to be taken literally; their purpose is not to encourage citizens to become commando killers (even if on the side of justice). Rather, the lesson to be drawn from the combat is the aggressiveness and self-reliance of the hero. The emotional satisfaction derived from the victory of the protagonist serves to reinforce the general commitment of the society to aggression (understood in the best sense, of course). The high value placed on sports, and on "winning" in general, is similarly functional.

The method for these discussions does not in fact require very much expert knowledge about ideology. Rather, the class may reason its way to the insights linking beliefs to actions simply by first discussing what each ideological category values; then by asking what behaviors follow form such values; then by comparing this list with the behaviors manifested in mainstream entertainment works. Finally, it is interesting to discuss how the different categories are synthesized into a general type of national character (and how easily the values associated with this character are reduced to stereotypes). Actually, the coordination of the lists may be dialectical, or proceed in reverse order from the one noted above, in that one may start with the behaviors observable in the films (such as the aggressiveness of the protagonists); then rule out the literal and commonsensically unacceptable inference (e.g., that learning to kill is desirable); and then ask what in our society requires the imaginary reenactment of this behavior.

Russell Banks, "Bambi: A Boy's Story" (p. 187) Russell Banks's choice of films to discuss is useful because it anticipates a common student objection to interpretation, which is that works of entertainment do not really "mean" anything--they are just for fun. The other advantage of beginning with this "children's" story is that it is easier to observe the links from actions to ideology in such works. Another virtue of Bambi is that it is immediately recognizable intertextually (it is included in the cultural competence of most people).

Banks approaches the ideological dimension of Bambi less in terms of semantics (based on some objective or referential quality within the film) and more in terms of "pragmatics" (the impact of the film on him). Nonetheless he is quite certain about the ultimate significance of Bambi and we will want to extend the kinds of things he says about it and about The Little Mermaid to all popular entertainments. Banks's classification of the film as agitprop (agitational propaganda) is not quite accurate, although his point is valid. "Agitprop" is the term used to describe the productions of the Bolshevik avant-garde movements during and after the Russian revolution, which used the arts to help the illiterate masses of Russia learn about the new ideals of Marxism that were to replace the values of czarist tradition. Commentators have pointed out that there are at least two kind of propaganda: the agitational variety aimed at changing the status quo, and also a kind designed to maintain the status quo. Bambi and Mermaid are of this pacifying and reconciling sort, supporting the gender behaviors approved of by the dominant culture.

Banks's essay has some valuable formal lessons for how to write about ideology in this intertextual way. His method of reading the films does not require specialized knowledge of critical theory. Rather, his strategy is to compose an allegorical parallel between the story and the ideological categories of gender in America. The preferred values associated with gender at least seem to be undergoing significant change just now, which makes the dated gender behaviors easier to spot. Mermaid is reactionary in its effort to shore up the traditional values of women as dependent for their identity on their beauty, which in turn makes them eligible for marriage with successful men (whose children they will bear). Bambi, made in an earlier period, espouses the norms of masculinity that are the corollary of the feminine norms in Mermaid.

The reading method compares what the films show about proper male/female heterosexual family relationships to what the society prefers in its ideals. These ideals may be quite far from the actual experience of the majority of the people in the society, of course, as is the case now with "family values." Indeed, the function of mythology in a culture is to reconcile the disparity between the ideals promoted by the ideology and the reality of immediate experience. Banks suggests that not every film "takes" with every viewer, but that in the mass of films viewers are likely to come upon one in which they recognize themselves (with which the identification is profound). Critics agree that to enjoy or even understand most entertainment works requires some degree of identification with the characters or situation. The ideological method links this superficial level of identification (based on sympathy) to the deeper problematic of a person's identity as such.

The second feature of Banks's essay concerns his explicit use of memory as a method for evaluating the film. He does not claim his reading is objective. Rather, when he examines his memory, he finds that Bambi and Gene Autry movies stayed with him. To find a film to discuss, the students too should reflect for a time to discover what story or film or television program is quite simply present or recoverable in memory. Banks has two versions of the film: the one he remembers from when he first saw it at age four, and whose importance is verified by his recollection of all the pictures he drew of stags outlined against the sky; and the fresh viewing of the film with his granddaughter in the present.

An interesting point made along the way is that the viewer will not necessarily identify with, recognize, or accept the position offered by the film. The son with the feminist father, for example, walks out of Bambi. Theory of ideology, in any case, notes that while the point of view of a film might favor the dominant ideology of the culture, the viewer may take a negotiated position (accepting only part of the values, making exceptions for oneself, etc.), or even an oppositional position (feminists simply rejecting the value dramatized in Mermaid). A common response to such films is to find that while one intellectually knows the values offered are wanting in some way, one nonetheless might emotionally agree and identify with the scene (as Banks does with Bambi).

Woody Allen, from Play it Again, Sam (p. 194) An intertextual approach to ideology assumes that an individual's self-image is negotiated through a complex process of mixing and matching of schemas available within the culture and internalized through learning. Upon examination from this point of view, the great variety of stories circulating within popular culture turn out to be making the same ideological points. Most American films, for example, offer protagonists for audience identification that show the preferred scene of American national identity. Indeed, much of the drama of each story arises out of the fact that the protagonists start in some position at variance with the national ideals. Usually the story ends when the protagonists have come into line with the national ideal. The American national ideal might be summarized briefly as requiring for both men and women a balance of individual achievement and collective nurturing, with men approaching this balance from the side of achievement and women from the side of nurturing. Rick in Casablanca, for example, starts out in a position that seems to neglect the side of nurturing. Rick comes around soon enough; there are numerous indications of his generous nature prior to the conclusion of the film.

At the same time, popular entertainments change to reflect evolving ideals, which is what causes films to date. Not only evolving technology, but also this changing "cultural code" as Roland Barthes calls it (referring to the set of stereotypes and clichés constituting the common sense of a culture), account for the dating of a given film. A good point of departure for discussion of ideology in Sam is the scene represented in our selection, since its lighthearted treatment of rape is now unacceptable. That people still laugh at the sexist jokes and gender stereotypes in this film indicates that humor functions as a mark for the anxieties and unresolved tensions operating within a culture. The critical aspect of humor depends on this power of comedy to allow people to admit into consciousness feelings that otherwise might be repressed. Viewing a tape of a stand-up comedy routine is a useful point of departure for discussing this relationship among form, feeling, and ideology. Lenny Bruce based his now classic but then controversial routines on direct representations of the stereotypes of the cultural code. In the same way that the anecdote functioned as a simple form in our first chapter, the joke works here as the simple form that may be elaborated in other media (writing or film) into more complex forms. Class discussion could be organized around the basic joke form that Woody Allen uses to structure this scene. Such an analysis might reveal how jokes depend on violating the taboos or exposing the clichés established by the norms of ideology.

The point to make about ideology is that it exists in experience not in the form of abstractions but within specific behaviors. The ideals of gender and sexuality may be observed in representations of courtship, such as the scene between Allan and Linda which reflects a dated etiquette of seduction. This scene could be compared with student knowledge of the etiquette in force today, an etiquette complicated by the phenomenon of "political correctness." One university has enacted a code of conduct that requires mutual and express consent from the parties involved for each step of "foreplay" (the term "seduction" hardly applies to such a situation). It would not be too hard to imagine how a comedic version of this practice might go (in fact a film parodying political correctness, entitled PCU, written by two recent college graduates, was released in 1994). In any case, Sam makes the sexual codes explicit by making fun of them. Many films of earlier periods often seem unintentionally funny to students, and their laughter at outdated etiquette marks a recognition of the ideology in a film.

The brilliant part of Sam is the way it makes explicit and dramatizes the scene of instruction that, according to critical theory, operates implicitly in every entertainment. Critical theory argues that when the audience identifies with a protagonist they are creating a relationship of consultation like the one shown between the Bogart persona and Allan in Sam. The actions of the characters played by Bogart (Rick in Casablanca or Sam Spade in The Maltese Falcon) are, at the ideological level, instructions for how a man should act to be manly (to have an approved identity). What Allan believes he can learn from "Bogart" is "how to be cool." Discussion of the impersonation of certain popular icons is a useful entry into the formation of stereotypes in general. And fans of cult films or cult figures perform openly and self-consciously the act of identification upon which are founded the behavioral norms of an ideology.

Discussion then might focus on what the Bogart persona represents by beginning with the physical features of "Bogartness." A book on "How to Impersonate Famous People," by Christopher Fowler, lists the following features of Bogie as the hard-boiled characters Spade or Marlow: "Turn collar of raincoat half up. Pull hat down over eyes. Thrust hands deep into pockets. Remove one hand from pocket and push up hat to the back of the head. Pronounce 'sweetheart' with a lisp, 'schweetheart.' A good practice sentence is the following Bogie phrase: 'I never met a dame that ditten unnerstand a schmack in the mouth.' This phrase is not recommended for use in public." It is clear from this incomplete list of mannerisms that the Bogie-man in Allan's head is the hard-boiled one, although the figure of Rick has much in common with this type.

The point of this discussion is to move to the level of values, and to evaluate the persona in ideological terms. The reading by Robert Ray included here goes into this aspect of Rick in detail, but at this point a general discussion of the tough-guy type is possible. In fact the seduction scene displays two male gender types--the tough guy and what now might be called the nerd or (in the tradition of Yiddish humor upon which Woody Allen draws) the schlemiel. The female functions here as comic foil, as if her own (invisible) consultant is the "Doris Day" of 1950s films, in which a woman had to be drunk before she could cooperate with a seduction. The humor depends on the contrast, on the ridiculousness of the schlemiel trying to be the touch guy. The critical point of the humor might be that we all are put in an absurd position when we try to carry out the stereotyped instructions of the cultural code. In any case, fandom (Allan as a Bogart fan) models the process of identity formation: In the same way that a Bogart fan can answer all the questions in a trivia quiz (What doesn't happen in Tokyo Joe? Which statement about Chain Lightning is true?), so can the natives of a culture tell us all about the details of behaviors in that culture. The knowledge students have of fandom, cult film, midnight movies and the like may serve as useful points of departure for understanding the political aspects of identification in ideology.

Robert Ray, from The Culmination of Classic Hollywood: Casablanca (p. 200)
Robert Ray shows us how to make connections among the three levels linking the particulars of a specific film (Casablanca) with the myths and ideologies of American public culture. His scholarly account supports and expands upon the more popular or journalistic reading by Russell Banks. Ray's argumentative strategy is not complicated in itself, consisting of comparison and contrast, juxtaposing the characters of Rick and Laszlo through an inventory of attitudes and attributes. Because Ray's point is that Casablanca has exemplary status--that it is a prototype of the classic Hollywood cinema--his method of analysis and his account of the norms of American mythology may be transferred to a reading of any entertainment work.

Ray's reading is explicitly intertextual in that he makes sense of Casablanca by relating it to other cultural types and works. Casablanca is a "disguised Western," for one thing, with Rick as a kind of Shane figure (the outlaw hero on the side of good). The pattern is found also in Mark Twain's Huckleberry Finn, with a variety of other allusions (to George Washington's appearance; to Hemingway's Jake Barnes, and so forth) serving to place the Curtiz film in an American intertext. Again this strategy is generalizable for use by students, since the premise of ideological critique is that the dominant mythologies are distributed everywhere. Hence, any works already familiar to the students could serve as allusions for placing the film they are reading into an intertext that would show the pattern Ray describes. This claim need not be taken on faith but could be tested in class discussion or written exercises.

Discussion and Writing
All the questions in this section address the general issue of the "pragmatics" of intertextuality: of how in the inferential operation of consuming works readers/viewers confirm and construct their individual senses of identity and in so doing participate in a political (ideological) process. The basic definition of "text," it should be remembered, is "the work plus the reader." A good point of departure for discussing this general phenomenon is to consider the experience of identification as it applies to other areas such as sports teams, rock bands, commercial products, or even one's school. The kinds of loyalty felt for such entities are symptoms of identification. The next step is to examine the nature of exactly what one has identified with (what images are projected by the team, band,

product). Then the ideological necessities met by such identifications may be examined. The idea is that all these phenomena are interconnected and function each in their own realm to maintain national identity.

Another aspect of considering fandom is to contrast it with the kind of reading usually promoted in school. Fandom is the kind of reading appropriate to the institution of entertainment, in which the fans identify openly with the object of taste and project their fantasies onto these figures. In school, however, these projective readings traditionally have been discouraged, and a more objective, critical style of reading promoted. In Chapter 5 we will see how this projective style of identification might also be applied as a research strategy for doing scholarship. It might be worth discussing whether or not this distinction between projective and objective readings is really so clear-cut, or how the two styles might be coordinated for purposes of raising one's self-consciousness.

One value of ideological reading, that is, is to help students discover in themselves the emotional level at which ideology functions. Critique sometimes creates the impression that ideology (the guiding beliefs of the society) circulates in the form of clearly defined ideas when in practice it tends to be that which is taken for granted and hence is transparent, unexamined, learned through the formation of habits in the repeated behaviors of everyday life (playing basketball, doing household chores, going to the mall). The formation, evolution, and transformation of a society's values may be observed in its popular entertainments. Intertextual analysis intends to expose the propaganda operating within tastes and judgments, in order to help students recognize how and why they believe what they do and how these beliefs guide their actions. Whether their premises would be something other than they are is not the question for now. At the same time it might be worth discussing one of the myths of liberal education, which is that school does not tell people what to think but teaches them how to think: In short, the claim is that school does not engage in propaganda. The view of critique, however, is that all the institutions of society are equally propagandistic in that they all serve to interpellate the individual into the dominant beliefs of the society, against the best interests of those individuals who fall outside the preferred groups of the ideological categories. A good discussion might arise from a comparison of the practices of entertainment and of school with respect to their propaganda value.

The challenge of a project based on the Banks reading of Bambi is how deceptively simple it seems. Banks is able to read off the surface of the story the ideological categories it carries (gender roles in the American family). Students will have a bit more trouble with this movement from the particulars of a story to the abstractions of analysis. Using the strategies noted in the introduction to this section, however, students acting as informants of their culture can reason their way from one level to the other. Take the myth of love informing the Bogart stories. What expectation does the culture establish for heterosexual relationships? The expected sequence is love, romance, marriage (with the latter state being of little interest). Each partner is looking for Mr./Ms. Right, leading to a monogamous commitment. According to the theory of mythology, the dramatization of this myth will take the form of the circulation of the woman between or among several men, with the outcome constituting a lesson in the proper roles and positions for each sex. In Casablanca Ilsa is idealized: She stays loyal to her husband; her affair with Rick occurred in the first place only because she thought Laszlo was dead, and was renewed (although this is ambiguous) in order to help her husband escape from Casablanca. In Sam Linda is also idealized, and her circulation between Allan and her husband has the same outcome as the schema upon which it is modeled (and which it parodies). To appreciate the moral lesson of the woman remaining loyal to and dependent upon her husband, one need only review what happens to women in hard-boiled films such as The Maltese Falcon, in which the woman's independence is punished severely. As for the lesson of Bogart's "coolness," he models an attitude toward women that now may seem quite dated but which in fact persists--the idea that a man should not be in thrall to his girlfriend; that he should "love 'em and leave 'em." The persistence or change in these attitudes may be explored in discussion.

In practice, to write one's own version of the scene of instruction modeled in Sam requires some analysis of the kind demonstrated by Banks and Ray. The principle is to use the samples included here as models to be imitated. The two styles of working--dramatic and analytical--are mutually supportive. The major assignment here is just this one of portraying a situation that the students consider problematic in some way (like the problems of romance in Sam--the blind dates Allan undertakes, or the evening with his best friend's wife), and then to select a star or celebrity whose persona or image is relevant to the situation. The brilliance of Sam, as we said, is that it makes explicit the scene of ideological indoctrination that critical theory tells us is the subtext of every work of entertainment. To compose such a scene the students may select any problem situation (not only one concerning romance, but any difficult situation such as job interviews, dealing with family members, and the like), and then, mimicking the formal devices of comedy, work out the details of how ideas or values lead to actions.

Alternatively, or in addition, the Banks assignment is an analytical version of the performative approach in Sam. The title of the volume in which Banks's essay appeared--The Movie that Changed My Life--is an excellent premise for an assignment. Most students will not in fact already have in mind some film or program that has affected them in some profound way. Rather, in response to the exercise, the students discover or invent retrospectively this perhaps mythical event--the moment when they "chose" to be Americans (or chose to be whatever their nationality is). The value of comparing the icons of earlier decades or periods with those current today (as in the comparison of Bambi to Mermaid) is to evaluate what persists and what is changing in our national identity. Composite photographic analysis of the film stars of the 1940s compared with the stars of the 1980s shows a significant change in the ideals of beauty and handsomeness from one period to the other. A similar shift in the values from one period to the other is likely, but needs to be tested. At the same time, the very notion of "national identity" assumes a persistence across the generations that allows people to continue to identify themselves as "American." The institution of entertainment is only one factor in this complex process, with the home, school, the learned disciplines, business, religion, ethnic groups, subcultures of all types contributing to the intertextual mix within which individuals establish a sense of who they are and what they want to become. This theme of identity formation is traditional in the humanities, dating back at least to the Greeks and the commandment inscribed at Delphi: "Know thyself."

Chapter 4: EXPERIMENTS WITH TEXTS: FRAGMENTS AND SIGNATURES

Textuality (p. 209)

Roland Barthes was born in 1915 and studied French literature and Classics at the University of Paris. After teaching French at universities in Romania and Egypt, he joined the Centre national de recherche scientifique, where he devoted himself to research in sociology and lexicology. He was a professor at the College de France until his death in 1980.

Such is the information offered about Barthes on the jackets of his many books, most of which have been translated into English, including his first one, Writing Degree Zero, and his last, Camera Lucida. These jackets include blurbs by the likes of Peter Brooks, who describes Barthes as "the most characteristic and important French intellectual of the structuralist generation." Barthes, he adds, "detested all forms of authority, worried about the power wielded by the teacher, and described his main subject, literature, as 'a grand imposture which allows us to understand speech outside the bounds of power, in the splendor of a permanent revolution of language.'"

Susan Sontag observed that Barthes "compared teaching to play, reading to eros, writing to seduction. His voice became more and more personal more full of grain, as he called it. All of Barthes's work is an exploration of the histrionic or lucid; in many ingenious modes, a plea for savor for a festive (rather than dogmatic or credulous) relation to ideas. For Barthes, as for Nietzsche, the point is not to teach us something in particular. The point is to make us bold, agile, subtle, intelligent, detached. And to give pleasure."

We come now to the most challenging chapter of Text Book. Indeed, some of the reviewers of this manuscript wondered if the writing by such theorists as Barthes and Jacques Derrida (considered in the next section), however important it might be for understanding the debates animating the contemporary critical scene, wasn't simply too difficult, too obscure, for introductory work. It is a good idea to apply the best insights of current critical theory to the problems of composition, and to design a textbook with these insights in mind, they said. But was it necessary to take the pun available in the word "textbook" so seriously as to base a whole pedagogy on the theory of text developed by the French? Or, if it was, did that imply that one had to include texts by the French theorists themselves?

This concern is well taken, requiring a few words of justification in response. The first thing to keep in mind in teaching this section is that it is an experiment. The experiment is to test the claim made by these theorists that textuality offers the means to break the barrier separating experts from amateurs in the field of literature. This claim does not deny the difficulty of theoretical discourse for the uninitiated reader. Rather, it suggests that the best way to understand the textualist insight into literature may be not by struggling to master their concepts, but by practicing for oneself the form of writing in which textualists have represented their thinking.

This advice seems to be worth taking for several reasons. First of all, Barthes, at least, believed that "text" was not definable as a concept in the conventional sense. He invoked the figure of "catachresis" as the one needed to name what was meant by "text"--"there is no possibility of saying the thing in terms other than the metaphor." The common example of catachresis is "the leg of a table." There is no substitute for the word "leg" here. Barthes never ceased looking for the catachrestic metaphor capable of denoting "text"--it is the field of the haruspex, it is a banquette, a faceted cube, an excipient, a Japanese stew, a din of decors, a braid, some Valenciennes lace, a Moroccan wadi, a broken television screen, a layered pastry, an onion, and so on. He once wrote that the best model (understood as a simplified familiar system that provides a map for a more complex unknown) for "text" was the Marx Brothers film, A Night at the Opera. If we try to comprehend what Barthes was naming with these metaphors, we might identify it as "the pleasure" of writing, and we might conclude that, however difficult it is to understand the concept of "text" theoretically, understanding is not in itself necessary for performing textually.

The second reason, then, that we think this experiment is worthwhile is that, in our experience, Barthes's various projects--his experiments with genres and styles of writing carried out in his numerous books and articles--translate readily into assignments that are in fact quite pleasurable to perform, and even more pleasurable to read. But that experience too is part of the claim our experiment is designed to test--that the effect of textualist writing is to stimulate in the reader the desire to write in turn. And this test could not be conducted with any writing other than that offered by the theorists themselves.

The essence of the two projects attempted or essayed in this chapter--the fragment and the signature--is in both cases the use of literary devices and strategies (metaphor, characterization, narration, image, and so forth) for the purposes of critical analysis. Textuality is in the vanguard of those movements that claim to have merged the genres of creative and critical writing, producing out of this merger a hybrid discourse that for lack of a better term is called "theory." In this last chapter, then, we explicitly encounter the anomaly that textuality poses to conventional notions of "writing about literature." When working in the mode of the "text," the student is not writing criticism about literature, but is producing a text at once critical and literary, that is as aesthetic as it is intelligent.

Let us turn now to a more specific discussion of some possible ways to approach one of Barthes's projects--the fragment.

The Fragment (p. 211)

Students tend to be more willing to undertake a new kind of writing if they understand the rationale motivating the experiment. Why does Barthes want to work with this particular dimension of discourse; why does he decide to write about love in this particular way? At one level it is easy to respond to this curiosity, given the topic itself. Everyone understands the interest of "love" as a theme. Indeed, students often accept the value of the topic at once and are ready to move on to the formal question. Nonetheless, it is interesting to discuss the value of the topic at another level as well, so that students may enter more fully into the stakes of the experiment.

One way to open this discussion is to note Barthes's motives for writing about love. He explained that in the highly sophisticated world of Parisian intellectuals, sentimental love had become an object of scorn not to be taken seriously. Given Barthes's temperament, which was always to avoid being on the side of the obvious, of "that which goes without saying"--which he identified with ideology--he wanted to scandalize his peers by writing sentimentally.

At the same time, Barthes's scientific interest was piqued by the peculiar linguistic status of the communication between lovers. From a certain point of view what lovers say to one another is so trivial, so full of clichés, as to be linguistically invisible--to be a kind of limit-case marking the outer reaches of language. Yet this trivial discourse, at least as practiced in everyday life, marks the conduct of a profound mode of knowledge. In the history of thought, essentially two kinds of knowledge have developed--calculation (best represented in science), and conjecture (best represented, it is said, in love). By expressing his interest in love as a kind of knowledge, Barthes acknowledged the association between love and knowledge that goes back at least to Plato, whose dialectic began with a lover's desire for a specific beautiful person, and ended with the love of truth or wisdom (philosophy).

What kind of knowledge does the lover have? How does the lover know that the beloved is the right one, the perfect one? Barthes offers two analogies for the truth possessed by a lover. One is from a zen story about the monk who held his pupil's head under water until he nearly drowned, then told him that he should desire truth as much as he wanted air; the other is that of a baby calling for its mother. Love is a model for a kind of knowledge that does not work according to the logic of calculation, but according to the association of intuition. The beloved, the object of love, the other, is the great unknown, intractable, about whom the lover experiences, Barthes says, an exalted feeling of knowing what he or she does not know. Barthes's idea is that "love" is not so much a psychological as a social experience--the amorous situation consists of certain positions and schemes that recur across the divisions separating everyday life from literature and science. Thus it is possible to orient oneself to love by means of a kind of triangulation superimposing these three discourses one upon the other.

The point of the previous discussion is to establish the possibility that love is itself a kind of knowledge, one our culture has not fully defined or understood. Since students may be expected to be naturally curious about love, they may the more willingly agree to undertake an experiment in a new way to write based on a lover's experience. Which brings us to a discussion of the formal properties of the experiment. This subsection of the chapter provides in outline form a summary of Barthes's description in the opening pages of <u>Fragments</u> of "how this book is constructed." He provides, that is, the principle of invention for a genre of the fragment. One purpose of our experiment is to test the extendability of this genre to other discourses--to the student discourse, for example. To this extent, when the students write their fragments they will be conducting a true experiment in the full sense of the term, and not just reproducing a familiar, established form.

A discussion of the selection and writing of the figures is best conducted in relation to the excerpts by Barthes.

Roland Barthes, from <u>A Lover's Discourse</u> (p. 212)

"So it is a Lover who Speaks and who Says" (p. 213)

1. Selecting the figure.

"Dis-cursis," Barthes reminds us, originally meant "the action of running here and there, comings and goings, measures taken." The fragments reproduce at once the outbursts of the distracted lover, and a stop-action or freeze-frame fixing of the typical or stereotyped gestures of the scene of love. He has in mind something like the "gest" featured by Brecht, whose stagecraft included the technique of the "freeze," all the actors holding a pose while one of the characters analyzed the situation in an aside. This aside is the lover's true discourse.

Everyone can recognize the scene of waiting. Even if we have not all been "stood up," we all know the situation and how we would feel if it did happen. The first step in generating this discourse, then, is to identify the conventional, repeated moments or positions of being in love. Among the figures listed in Barthes's table of contents are: to be engulfed, absence, adorable, anxiety, annulment, to hide, fulfillment, connivance, declaration, demons, flayed, to write, exile, mad, jealousy, I-love-you, letter, magic, silence, crying, gossip, ravishment, scene, remembrance, suicide, union, will-to-possess.

2. Writing the figures.

a. Title, heading, and argument.

The title functions in the usual way, to identify the organizing theme of the fragment. The heading may or may not be the same as the title, the difference being that the heading is a subtitle, naming the argument. The argument does not state directly what lovers say, but refers to it, as a paraphrase. Each fragment, then, represents the unfolding of a banal phrase, such as the one the lover utters when the beloved finally shows up: "Where were you?" The class might want to discuss the phrase referred to by each of the arguments. Part of the test of the validity of the figure is the extent to which the class could agree, at least approximately, on the wording of these general phrases. Barthes suggests, incidentally, that these discourses of everyday life, found on the margins of language, exist at the level of the phrase, and not the word. Their basic units are these idiomatic phrases. The argument of "the Heart" could refer to the phrase, "don't break my heart." "Images" could refer to the phrase, "but I <u>saw</u> you," and so on.

The fragments are presented in alphabetical order, following the order of the headings. The class may be curious why Barthes wanted to avoid telling a story. In fact, when one reads <u>A Lover's Discourse</u> in its entirety, a story of unrequited love does emerge--a story with a definite unity and coherence of feeling. This story is never directly told, but is inferred by the reader. Barthes's intention may be appreciated in the context of contemporary discussions critical of narrative, which has become associated historically with the biases of patriarchal ideology. Barthes wants to liberate the emotions and gestures of love from the standardization positioning imposed on them by narrative form. He offers the reader instead a thesaurus of possible positions, which the reader is free to recombine according to the dictates of his or her own story. The unity will be provided by the reader, not the author--an aesthetic reflecting Peter Brooks's point about Barthes's dislike for "authority." To appreciate the peculiar effects thus achieved, the class may compare and contrast the fragment with other approaches to narrative and story encountered in earlier chapters.

b. The body (numbered paragraphs).

The titling of the fragments is formulaic enough that students have little difficulty with it. Still, a few continue to wonder if their headings have to be in

French, which they don't, or if they have to be in alphabetical order, which they do. Sometimes, on their own, students will translate the headings into whatever language they know (Latin, Hebrew, Spanish), which works fine if they want to capture some of the same flavor of "system." But the "body" is a different story.

At this point we begin to see the value of unfamiliar or even of "difficult" texts for learning to use models. When encountering a text by Barthes or Derrida, the students are unlikely to assume they already know how it works. Now they must apply the motto of our pedagogy: "When in doubt, ask the model." This advice is easily followed in simple cases such as wondering if the figures have to be in alphabetical order. But to learn how the body works requires careful anatomical study. Since Barthes himself introduced the analogy between the human "body" and the "body" of the text--comparing the figures to the poses of dancers; writing the figures is a "choreography"--we may use the analogy to guide discussion. Indeed, the class will be practicing, in its investigation of these experimental forms, the strategy learned in the chapter on metaphor.

We may use the anatomical analogy in two senses: the analytical sense, connoting dissection and classification; and the aesthetic sense, connoting the athletic prowess of the dancer. The body of the fragment both classifies the discourse in question and performs it. The scientist tells us about the parts of the body, and the dancer shows us what the body can do. As Barthes said, this approach to an object of study is not descriptive but "dramatic," a simulation. We could say the same for the pedagogy of Text Book. Part of the interest of this pedagogy is to explore the benefits of teaching literature in a literary way--to use in classroom discussion the methodological powers (long exploited by inventors in all fields) of figurative thinking and speaking. The textualist does not read a work primarily at the level of meaning, then, but rather considers the work as a set of instructions for making another one.

To learn how to get from Barthes's *inventio* to the actual fragments, the student will have to look closely at the examples. We will point out the kinds of things to note in linking the generic principles with the particulars of the sample.

"Waiting" (p. 213) 1. The lover writes in the first person, although at times he/she may shift to the third person, referring to oneself as he/she. The relationship of the writer to the speaker is "novelesque," to use Barthes's term. The phrase that links the generic instructions to the figures--"So it is a lover who speaks and says:"--distances the writer from the statement. What the student writes, then, will not be a "confessional" at the level of content--we learn very little biographically in these passages. We know the situation--the lover waits for the beloved to telephone, as arranged. What matters, however, is the feeling, the experience of this waiting.

The category of "experience" is very much in question in the Age of Science. Feminism has created a renewed interest in the value of experience as knowledge. The cognitive value of experience has been questioned because it did not seem to permit valid generalizations. The fragments bring together the general (the category "waiting") with the particular (the peculiar experience of the writer with that category). This structure suggests that the specific nature of an individual's specific emotions and behaviors associated with a given category constitute valid representations of conceptual categories. How does the writer know what to select for inclusion? The criterion of selection, Barthes explained, is the "sting" of punctum. Having identified the general category of the figure as that which is "so true"--something recognized at once as "the way it is"--the writer then examines her memory in relation to the category for details--the traces marking one's encounter with this situation, for something that affected one sufficiently to have left a mark.

At this point we recognize Barthes's innovation in the dualistic approach to the relationship between the general and the particular, between knowledge and experience--he does not distinguish between firsthand and secondhand knowledge. Rather, he shows that these two ways of gaining information and insight are interdependent. In the generic instructions Barthes indicated that the body consisted of three areas of "reference," including, besides one's immediate life experience, one's "experience" of literature (or the arts), of popular culture, and of disciplinary knowledge. He is waiting for a phone call, and this waiting reminds him of a piece by Schönberg (acknowledged in the margin), Erwartung. The circumstances are not the same (a woman waiting for her lover in a forest), but the anxiety, the feeling of waiting, is similar. And Barthes comments, "I have of sense of proportions."

We may recognize that in comparing his experience to events described in literature (his principal comparison throughout is with Goethe's Sorrows of Young Werther) Barthes, as he acknowledged, is deliberately practicing the "lowest" form of reading--projection. He explained that his intent was to attempt a reading that was at once popular and specialized: to observe himself in the act of identification. He believed that the genres of high and popular culture shaped behavior as much as they reflected it. His approach, in any case, formulates at the level of theory the assumption that has guided Text Book--the inescapable interaction, linguistically and rhetorically, of daily life and high culture.

Barthes's strategy allows us to discuss not only how people should read but how they do read. Literature has a cultural function outside the confines of the school. The choice of Werther as the primary reference, for example, is not casual. It was a best-seller in its day, and many young men of the period so identified with it (so projected their own feelings into it, so derived their own feelings from it) that they imitated Werther's decision to commit suicide. Here lies a dilemma or problem worth discussing. The men who committed suicide after reading Werther badly misunderstood the book, according to Goethe. Or perhaps Goethe misunderstood the nature of literary experience. In any case, Goethe explained that he wrote the book to overcome his own impulse to commit suicide over an unhappy love affair, or that the writing of the book was so therapeutic he lost the inclination to self-destruction. He published it thinking that the story would have a similar effect upon its readers. He ignored, we might say, the difference between writing and reading a work. If his readers had been textualists, they might have understood that the one to identify with was not Werther but Goethe.

The point to discuss might be the distinction between reading for pleasure and reading for school. The first issue to arise is likely to be the fact that few if any students are familiar with Goethe, let alone Schönberg. No matter, since they need only understand what Barthes is doing. When it comes to their own writing, they will imitate not Barthes's content, but his procedure. In the category of waiting perhaps no work from high culture comes to mind for them. Barthes's version of the "references" filling the body is just one among a potentially infinite number of versions, of which our students may produce a few more. The troubling aspect of the problem of projective reading is that, as Kenneth Burke once said, the humanities are supposed to provide "equipment for living." The response to Werther suggests that this equipment, like any other machinery, can be dangerous if not used properly.

2. The "scenography of waiting" recalls the relationship between life and theater noted by Goffman in Chapter 1. Rhetorically this segment expands upon the "anxiety" noted in #1 above. It may correspond to the saying "Don't make a scene," which the beloved might utter if he/she shows up. Our emotional experience follows a recognizable pattern, to such an extent that actors can duplicate it in a theater, which is to say as well that the signs of feeling may be faked or posed.

Students may wonder how Barthes "invents" or finds these things to say: "I have just shifted in a second from absence to death; the other is as if dead." The marginal note refers to "Winnicott," a psychologist. A reference of this sort comes from Barthes's specialized culture. Students may similarly draw upon their specialized readings, undertaken in their present classes or recalled from previous schooling. Someone taking "Introduction to Psychology" might think of relevant information from the textbook as a reference. In principle, the content of any disciplinary subject should provide a collection of potential analogies that the writer may introduce at an appropriate place.

3. It is worth noting the reality, the accuracy, of the feeling, in question. The obsessive focus, the lover's evasion of all distraction, may be assessed for its validity. Barthes outlines in detail the specific quality of the situation.

4. Why is the lover's behavior so peculiar? There is more to it than meets the eye --it is "overdetermined," as the psychologists say. The active or constructed quality of experience is evident in love: The lover's expectation is so high that he momentarily recognizes the voice or face of the anticipated other in the voices and faces of strangers. The technique includes reference to a psychologist, to personal experience, and the introduction of a metaphor: "I am an amputee who still feels pain in his missing leg."

5. The individual experience is placed explicitly in the context of all manner of waiting--is located in the general. "Transference" is the term used in psychoanalysis to name the neurotic behavior in which, in the therapeutic process, the patient projects onto his relationship with the analyst his childhood relationship with the parents. The source of the anxiety which is the theme of this figure is identified as owing to the powerlessness of the lover's position. The initials in the margin refer to the name of a friend who is the source of the observation about power.

6. A proverbial story, an anecdote conveying the experience of the culture, serves to suggest one possible response to the situation, to the anxiety of waiting for someone who is not going to show up. Barthes's lover is in a specific situation, which happens to be an unhappy one. But even in the middle of a happy relationship the structure of the situation is present to the imagination of the participant--"things could go wrong." What other proverbs might pertain to this situation?

"The Heart" (p. 215) All that has been said about the strategy of the figures with respect to "Waiting" applies equally to the other fragments. We will make a few additional comments about the remaining selections.

1. You might not be able to get your students to suspend their natural prejudice, as citizens of American culture, against a rhetorically elaborate style. They may not want to write phrases about a heart "held, enchanted, within the domain of the Image-repertoire." The first step is to recognize that Barthes is saying something comprehensible and useful. The "image-repertoire" (a term borrowed from the psychoanalyst Jacques Lacan) refers to that set or collection of ready-made icons possessed by every member of a given culture: Each of us has a repertoire we share with the collective, and a more private repertoire, a kind of personal mythology, derived from our specific circumstances. The heart as an image exists for most of us in the shape of a valentine. It might be interesting to inventory this repertoire of images and to identify the stock associations that go with it.

The "anxiety" explored in "Waiting" reappears here, suggesting in this repetition a pattern or unity of feeling linking the fragments.

2. The first reference, in our sample, to Werther: the "primary" reference. It consists of both a direct citation and a paraphrase of Werther's belief that one's emotions, not one's ideas, are unique or individualizing. Barthes, however, is suggesting that emotions are as socialized as concepts. A topic for discussion might be the current received understanding of the "romantic."

3. Why is the heart "heavy"? There is something about the quality of emotion associated with sadness, sorrow, loss, the disappointed lover, unrequited love. Perhaps the story Barthes wishes to avoid is the "good" love story, in that a happy affair in which everything goes smoothly is hardly worth telling about, however desirable it might be to live. Werther, as a representative work of Romanticism, expresses the mood of "world weariness," of Weltschmerz, that Goethe identified as the spirit of his age. Barthes tells an anecdote about a situation in which it would be appropriate to use the phrase "my heart is heavy within me." The guiding principle of invention in this experiment, it is worth reminding ourselves, is the lover's discourse--what is said, the linguistic existence of love. The writer wants to itemize the specific circumstances in which one has encountered the typical features of the system. This project, incidentally, makes A Lover's Discourse a prototype for the poststructuralist project in general: Coming after the structuralists, who described the systems of culture, the poststructuralists asked after the status of the individual subject practicing within these systems.

"Images" (p. 216) 1. The organization or arrangement of the "body" should be clearer by now. Each one follows a certain development, and is not simply a random collection of paragraphs. This one begins with an example of a "scene" that, for a jealous lover, has the coherence of a message--the beloved engaged in intimate conversation with another, a rival. Barthes typically uses an analogy to convey exactly the nature of the process by which this scene acquires the configuration of an image--the example of the puzzle drawings. Here is one important device of his inventio, of how he unfolds the saying to produce a series of paragraphs out of a brief exclamation. When he says that the image is without riddle, he indicates that, despite the fact that he does not know what the conversation was about, the lover already interprets the scene in a way consistent with the love situation--as a flirtation with a rival.

2. The <u>inventio</u> continues to clarify itself through repetition: another reference to <u>Werther</u>. Barthes finds an example of the "scene" as image, an example of the lover's way of seeing and of feeling, in his primary reference. The examples from life and from literature converge to suggest precisely the character of a lover's thoughts, in which reason and emotion fail to coincide: What the lover says is, "I know perfectly, but all the same."

3. A variation on the theme: The lover may strike a pose, act a scene, as well as see one, as it would be seen by the beloved. Here Barthes shows himself as "sad." In another fragment, "to hide," Barthes provides a good instance of the "image" used as a message in a discourse. "I want you to know that I am hiding something from you, that is the active paradox I must resolve: at one and the same time it must be known and not known: I want you to know that I don't want to show my feelings: that is the message I address to the other." The example he offers of this principle is the wearing of dark glasses to hide the fact that one has been weeping, hoping that the unaccustomed glasses will provoke the question, "But what's the matter?"

The reference to Caspar David Friedrich again signals the quality of an intellectual's participation in high culture. The technique, however, may be adapted to any repertoire--analogies for the figure may be drawn from anywhere, from any dimension of the cultural encyclopedia. Even if we do not know the painting, the allusion to a polar scene offers a powerful sense of the feeling of exclusion being analyzed in this aside. The quotidian phrase operating here might be "the cold shoulder." We are familiar with this coldness; the trick is not to be satisfied with the cliché, but to extend it, to find a way to make that "cold" more specific.

4. Barthes makes this point several times--that the lover is an artist. What would it be like if life and art were fully merged? The lover, according to Barthes, knows. Sometimes he suggests that the lover inhabits a hermeneutic universe--one in which everything signifies. For the lover, everything the beloved does constitutes a sign, has meaning. Beyond that, a lover not only interprets, but performs life as if it had formal coherence. We like to think that we can tell the difference between the form and the substance of an experience. In education, for example, we talk about the value of getting an education and not just a degree. But we also know that in fact the pursuit of the form may replace the desire for the substance, for learning. In love, we know that the desire to make an image may direct one's choice of a date, or even of a mate.

<u>"How blue the sky was" (p. 217)</u> However different the American student's encyclopedia might be from that of a French intellectual, the experiment still stands or falls on the commonality of the poses. We have to be able to say of the pose, "That's so true!" In #3 here, for example, Barthes calls attention to the "narrative bliss" experienced at the beginning of an affair, before the couple knows one another, so that each must tell the other all his or her anecdotes. Part of the bliss is the discovery that the identity ("This is what I am") is shared by the other. What all those stories add up to is confirmed in this exchange in a way that is fundamentally satisfying. What is the nature of this bliss? The effectiveness of the text rests upon the possibility not that the experience described here will be news to us, but that we will recognize it as our own and call to mind our own

participation in this form. At the same time, we are meant not only to identify with the text, but to become aware of this identification in a critical sense, to understand that all our reading experience relies upon the cultural encyclopedia and our powers of inference in order to produce in us the feeling of understanding.

Discussion and Writing

1. The purpose of this question is to initiate a discussion of Barthes's strategy of invention, to see the sources he drew upon for the composition of the asides. Our comments on the figures indicate the direction this discussion might take. An inventory of Barthes's cultural repertoire, including both his high and low dimensions, demonstrates a useful prewriting operation that the students will want to perform for their own repertoires. The exercise calls for them to begin making explicit at least one aspect of their cognitive map, tracing the conceptual registers organizing their thoughts and feelings about love. Part of the interest of this exercise is that it allows students to examine their own cultural resources. Barthes's example is there to indicate the sort of thing that is possible, but the real purpose of the study is to discover the equivalent in one's own reserve. In the beginning the search is relatively passive--what comes to mind while thinking about the given category. The idea, however, is to recognize the collective, social, shared basis at least of the materials that turn up in this search, and then to realize that the process may become active. The writer is not limited to what happens to come to mind. He or she is free to ransack the cultural encyclopedia and take whatever is needed.

The written exercise could be done in class, or as a one-page take-home assignment. By staying within Barthes's own figure the student may more easily imitate the peculiarities of the written aside.

2. This exercise is more ambitious than the previous one. Its execution draws on the technique of the "ghost chapter" encountered in Chapter 3. Class discussion of Barthes's text may be more animated if students are asked form the outset to find their own equivalents for Barthes's examples, rather than attempting to understand fully what Barthes is saying. Indeed, the parallel between Barthes's case and their own clarifies the reading better than an explanation of Barthes's background. It is worth noting how much of the information about the lover's discourse is secondhand, available from models distributed through the several levels of the culture. Even if an individual has not lived through an entire affair, he or she knows at least the form of the story. We know that generic expectations guide our response to works of literature. To what extent is our response to life experience guided by these same generic expectations?

3. We come now to the central experiment of this section--an extrapolation from a lover's discourse to a student's discourse. It would be possible, in principle, to take the extrapolation in other directions, to other discourses, or subdiscourses, identifiable in daily life, popular or high culture. The wording of the assignment implies that the concept of "style" provides a connection linking the various registers of culture--that the patterns of a student's lifestyle may be organized and understood in terms of the rhetorical features organizing a written composition. The overlapping of this terminology offers another opportunity to discuss the interdependence of language in life and in literature.

"Are any of the figures used in the lover's discourse also relevant to the student's discourse?" Extrapolation involves primarily reasoning by analogy from the model to a new area of application. Discussion of the parallels between the two situations reveals some significant areas of overlap. Foremost among these possibilities is the fact that the love relationship is a prominent feature of the student's experience. Similarly, one of the lover's fragments, entitled "Inexpressible Love," deals with the lover as a writer. The lover's difficulty with "invention," with finding a way to express amorous feeling, overlaps with the student's or any writer's difficulties in overcoming the anxiety of the blank page. Perhaps writer's block could serve as a metaphor for the anxiety of love. The solution to this boundary question is to orient the figure to the specific peculiarities of the discourse in question. In this case, the whole of the lover's discourse may become one pose within the student's text. What are the attributes or references of love as it is encountered in the student's situation? The special relationship between love and knowledge in our culture manifests itself in the student's tendency to use the library the way Barthes's speaker used the cafe--as the place of encounter.

"If the 'heart' is the organ of love sentiment, would the brain be the equivalent for the student's discourse?" It would, obviously, and so the figure of "the heart" is a good one to use as the sample for class discussion, for working through together the extrapolation process. This figure reveals the focus of the fragments--the anxiety of the lover's emotions focused on the beloved. A similar unity might be identifiable in the student's experience by asking if there were an emotion associated with learning, or indeed if the "object of study" in school has a status similar to that of the "object of desire" in love. What are the myths and stereotypes associated with the "brain" in our culture? The current series of films dealing with the conflict between nerds and frat boys offers some references for the relevant stereotypes and their transformation. Is it possible to identify a single emotion at the core of one's relationship to learning? Anxiety, clearly, is not necessarily the dominant feeling in love or in learning. At the same time, it is often the case that some one emotion does tend to dominate an individual's position in the discourse.

The assignment should consist of three to five fragments, depending on the number of paragraphs included in the body of each one. Some of the headings we have received are "registration," "greeks," "money," "party," "jocks," "library," "profs," "independence," "sanity," "misfit," "cheat," "first day," "the paper," "sleep," "lost," "question," "scamming." The following excerpt is typical of the sort of thing to expect.

GETTING UP FOR CLASSES

Awakening

Even when prearranged, awakening (the act of waking from sleep) is a disturbance, subject to postponement.

1. Awakening is an interruption: The alarm rings. I'm not willing to accept the interruption. Regardless of how much sleep I had during

J.C. the night, I always need about ten more minutes to recuperate from the shock of interruption. I can't simply "put my feet on the floor."

Horace Milton 2. Awakening too soon causes anger. "Anger is a short madness." To study for a test I will sleep only from 2 a.m. to 7 a.m. The few tense hours are not at all restful or peaceful. At daybreak I awake--an hour too soon. I'm irritated, annoyed by the chirping of the birds. I cannot appreciate their songs about the "sweet breath of morn."

3. My priorities change during awakening. Last-minute cancellations: in a second I decide to skip breakfast in order to have ten more minutes of sleep. I will take a shower after class; I gain another fifteen minutes. If I wear a sweatshirt instead of the blouse that needs ironing I can sleep another five. With this series of cancellations I acquire a useful thirty minutes.

The following is a student composition utilizing Barthes's strategy.

<u>In the Beginning</u>

begin

The new student enters a foreign world.
He is at first alien to its operation, to
its customs, and to its inhabitants.

1. "The known is finite, the unknown infinite; intellectually, we stand on an islet of an illimitable ocean of inexplicability."

--T. H. Huxley

"By space, the universe encompasses and swallows me up like an atom; by thought I comprehend the world."

--Blaise Pascal

Parents, friends, and all sources of familiar guidance have been stripped. I've been placed in the middle of a new world, lost (Left to die? To make or break?). How sterile! How cold! What once was a guiding hand is now a lifeless map and a few names with telephone numbers. I am expected to share my thoughts, needs, and deepest concerns with an image at the end of a receiver. Perhaps I'll keep to myself.

2. Freedom is another word for lost. I am not a creature of choice ("the choice is your own."), the master of my destiny, fully responsible for my actions and their consequences. Responsibility has been dumped onto my lap like a ton of stone -- alien stone of another world. ("There was a sadness about them, as if this old world was not their home and they were bound for higher ground.") S.M.F. Angelou

Plume

esteem

Acceptance into an institution of selective admittance sparks pride. The student is at first dazzled and seldom sees the ground he treads.

1. ("The statues of the Parthenon's east pediment from left to right: . . . Persephone, Demeter, Hephaestus,
myself . . . ")

The new student projects himself into all that is acclaimed wonderful. He sees himself pedastaled, surrounded by a cheering audience, as though he has accomplished some great task. ("During that period I looked at the arch of heaven so religiously my neck kept a steady ache.") Angelou

2. I see myself as a creature of consequence, of importance, of gravity. The fact that I have been accepted into an institution of higher learning, I see that as the world's acknowledgement--its recognition--of my abilities, of my promise. ("These were the days when my heart was volcanic.") And why should I not strut? Why not preen a few feathers? After all, these are the best years of my life. Poe

3. With my nose in the air I walk about. I see a whole new world. For a while I forget the dirt that lies on the streets and see only sky. Ultimately, I trip and I am reminded of the ground.

The Leech

harrow

Experience has taught the student that nothing is without price. His money's worth is demanded and he has learned to bleed his environment of its fruit. In school, he becomes the farmer, his harvest always knowledge, and the professor, his soil.

1. The student feels the pangs of a hunger (the starving student). He is a vampire, ready to dry wells of information; the instructor, his prey. He is a monster but always dependent, parasitic. ("Behave well to the priest. And take the ransom."). Homer

2. I find myself the pest. I understand the deception but depend upon the spoils. So I play the game. I listen to Dickinson ("Tell all the truth but tell it slant--Success in circuit lies.") and to Machiavelli ("Occasionally words must serve to veil the truth."), but Barthes's body

speaks ("What I hide by my language, my body utters."). The deception escapes.

3. "He who will be proved right in the end appears to be wrong and harmful before it." A comforting idea: the professors understand and often encourage the motives: some because they understand, others out of pity. Ultimately, the leech bleeds and the host receives his check. Koestler

"'Tis so appalling, it exhilarates!"
--Emily Dickinson

Bag-eyed

languish

The student is subject to a bombardment of mental stimulations that often result in a decreased capacity to learn; frustration sets in, fatigue breeds, more frustration; ultimately, an exam is sacrificed for an hour's sleep.

1. Fabric is the limitation. Too often, time and pressure necessitate an approach towards the asymptotic--towards the physical barrier (the proverbial midnight oil must burn). Why do I push myself so? There can be no future in such an obvious neglect of health.

2. And there can be no future (rhetoric: an unsuccessful future) in neglected studies. My time here is an investment, and time is precious; so I join the rat race. "Their future rode heavily on their shoulders . . ." And the world is shadowed by this compulsion. I begin to lost all sense of time, of the world about me, and of needs. "And so the new term advanced rapidly and one day the fields about the town were all brown, cleared of even the few thin patches of snow which had lingered so long." --a wild pursuit. Angelou Trilling

3. But I could not be so driven by a future, so again the question: Why do I push myself? Only a love or passion can be responsible. Plato explains that "Love and the lover desire what they do not possess." A passion for wisdom? As a student it seems likely. "Who are those who love wisdom if not the wise or the ignorant? . . ." she replied, "that they are those who are in a state between desire and wisdom." Diotina

4. So I am driven. But ultimately, the fabric is loosened and the mind must allow it rest; time to repair. I find this, however, rarely to happen before the bags under the eyes find their mark, rarely before the mind, in its compulsion, has time to test the body, to tear at it with its constraints.

A White Flag

Surrender

The student is frequently needled with a desire for the simple life of ignorance.

1. With knowledge comes an awareness (more appropriate term: complications). Simplicity is lost to the rational, creativity becomes the subject of experience, and all that is grand, falls to the known ("What once was heaven, is zenith now"). I often wish for the innocence of youth. What is expected of a child? To be naive can be such a powerful tool of escape. "I was grateful to be Twain able to answer promptly, and I did. I said I didn't know." — Dickinson; Twain

2. Time is irreversible, but what of exposure? Suppose I chose to lock myself inside my head, simply ignore what is reality (Trilling's "classic case"), allow the demise of my importance, my value as an individual; then might I be free? Or suppose I were to simply end it all, wane the tick of the clock? As Dr. Howe: ". . . permit the metamorphosis of Tertan from person to fact." But something always keeps me going. I am driven. — Trilling

"'Dissolve,' says Death. The Spirit, 'Sir, I have another trust.'"

--Emily Dickinson

References for "Fragments of a Student's Discourse (p. 220)

The readings by Angelou and Trilling are provided as materials for the category of primary reference, to serve for the student's discourse the function of literary example for which Barthes used Werther in his fragments. You may wish to assign something else, such as John Updike's "The Christian Roommates," or any work in the genre of "academic fiction" that you prefer. The pieces are worth reading and discussing in their own right, but their specific purpose is to help students identify the poses organizing their situation.

The questions raised during discussion of the lover's discourse may recur in this context--the question of the narrative, for example. Barthes mentions that society expects a certain story from the rejected lover: It expects an account of grievances and lessons learned, mistakes not to be repeated. Similarly, the student finds that a certain story is required by society. In response to the question "How are things at school?" the student may feel obliged to produce the conventional answers, depending on who asks the question. This story need not be told in the fragments, which would allow another level of unity to emerge. There is no need to require this unity. On the contrary, the insight gained from the experiment may be weakened if one attempts to impose a unity of event or affect on the series of poses. Nonetheless, such a unity often emerges in the papers, expressing the author's particular style of thought about the student's discourse. Some of these stories concern the party animal, the druggie or drunk, the grade-conscious achiever, the hopelessly unmotivated.

Discussion and Writing

1. Maya Angelou's autobiographical story suggests the relevance of earlier schooling to the student's discourse. "Graduation" is a figure still fresh in the memories of most students in a writing course. Indeed, one dimension of the asides could be a comparison of the experience of the university or college situation with earlier periods of schooling. A saying that often appears in figures dealing with the teacher is something like "You won't get away with this when you get to college!"

Angelou's piece calls to mind several important areas of reference for the student--the family context, for example, including the expectations and hopes of parents and siblings who constitute part of the audience for the student's performance. One of the most useful features of "Graduation" as a reference is the theme of racism represented in the speech by Mr. Donleavy. The story makes explicit the cultural tendency to treat individuals in terms of a stereotype expressing a reductive image authorized by the dominant ideology. It is not necessary to turn to something like Leslie Fiedler's essay, "The Student as Nigger," expressive of the difficulties of the Vietnam era, for the class to identify with Angelou's protagonist. Outside the immediate confines of the campus, someone bearing all the signifiers of the "student" may find herself or himself treated as a type rather than as an individual.

There are a number of typical features of this specific figure--graduation--presented in the story (the speech for example), but in a way that is specific to Angelou's circumstances as a black. Angelou's emotions and responses to the graduation day address are distinctive enough, different enough from the common scene, to offer an example of how a typical form may be filled in an individualized way. The assignment does not call for a complete story, of course--"Graduation" is not a model for the fragments, but a resource as a reference.

At the conclusion of "Graduation" Angelou states part of her motivation for writing: "We [the black people] survive in exact relationship to the dedication of our poets (include preachers, musicians and blues singers)." This statement offers an opportunity to discuss the question in more general terms of why people write. She is saying that the values of her people are embodied and perpetuated in the literature produced by black writers. The same is true obviously of all writing. The "projective" mode of reading used with the references relevant to the fragments of a discourse is the one appropriate to identifying this level of a work.

Lionel Trilling's story is a bit too long to include in full, for our purposes. You may prefer to assign the complete version (the class may become quite curious about what will happen to Tertan). English classes do not seem to have changed much since the 1940s, in that our students have little trouble identifying the poses contained in this story: "the first day of class," "the office visit," and so forth. This ready recognition permitted by the "student's discourse" facilitates a comparison of the use of types and poses in the narrative ordering of a story with the alphabetical listing of the fragments.

It may or may not be necessary to clarify Trilling's intentions with respect to

Blackburn in the latter's visit to Howe's office to complain about his grade on the exam. Many students will not catch the fact that what Blackburn has written about Coleridge's "The Ancient Mariner" applies rather to "Kubla Khan." Hence they fall quickly into agreement with the saying evoked in this pose: "One opinion is as good as another, unless it is the teacher's opinion." Indeed, the reception of the story, especially in this excerpted form, tends to be unsympathetic to Howe. For the purposes of projective reading, this reception is appropriate, although it may also occasion some discussion of the pedagogical exchange, and of the role of power in the learning experience.

2. This final exercise is provided for those who might wish to spend more time on this section. It also suggests a way to let the students share the results of their experiment. In this case the pieces provided as references become models for a story to be composed out of the thesaurus of fragments. Discussions preparing for this narrative ordering would provide an opportunity for reviewing most of what had been learned during the term about story telling and comprehension, beginning with the anecdote and carrying through to the inferential ghost walks and intertextual transformations. If this exercise is used only as the basis for discussion, it might be interesting to see what extent the class could agree on the choices that would have to be made in establishing the character of the "typical" or representative student emerging out of the collection of poses.

<u>The Signature</u> (p. 240)

Textualist practice deemphasizes the interpretive approach to literature, asking what the meaning of a work, in favor of a generative approach, concerned with the production of meaning effects. Music is a good analogy for the structuralist assumption underlying this approach--like the signifiers in a system of language (phonemes, for example), musical notes have a "value," but not a meaning. People listening to a musical composition, however, understand or are affected by the significance of the piece. Both Barthes and Derrida allude to this musical metaphor for the production of effects of understanding: Barthes with the comparison of the fragments to choreography, and Derrida with the pun on "signature," alluding to the key or time of a musical composition. The signature experiment takes a musical approach to the production of meaning in language.

<u>What's in a Name</u> (p. 241)

<u>Discussion and Writing</u>

1. To begin with one of the most familiar scenes in all of literature, and with one of the most familiar phrases ("a rose by any other name . . ."), allows us to ease into a most unfamiliar way of thinking about writing. In fact, most of the readings in the opening sections are included in part to establish the legitimacy of the experiment. Again, the principle is our belief that students are more willing to undertake an experiment if they understand the motivation that accounts for the project.

The discussion of common and proper names may be used to remind the class of their earlier encounter with this topic at the beginning of Chapter 2, in Roger Brown's description of Itard trying to teach the Wild Child the concept of "concept"--that words are names for categories of things. The word "book," then, applies to all items of that sort, regardless of their physical differences. The possibility of a confusion between the functions of common and proper names is the source of the following scene in Lewis Carroll's Through the Looking Glass in which the White Knight asks Alice if she would like to hear a song (a musical context, conveniently for us):

> "The name of the song is called 'Haddocks' Eyes.'"
>
> "Oh, that's the name of the song, is it?" Alice said, trying to feel interested.
>
> "No, you don't understand," the Knight said, looking a little vexed. "That's what the name is called. The name really *is* 'The Aged Aged Man.'"
>
> "Then I ought to have said 'That's what the *song* is called'?" Alice corrected herself.
>
> "No, you oughtn't: that's quite another thing! The *song* is called 'Ways and Means': but that's only what it's *called*, you know!"
>
> "Well, what *is* the song, then?" said Alice, who was by this time completely bewildered.
>
> "I was coming to that," the Knight said. "The song really *is* 'A-sitting On a Gate': and the tune's my own invention."

Like Lewis Carroll, Derrida's experiment investigates the possibility of exchanges between common and proper names. The signature concerns itself with what someone's name "is called."

2. The two most common theories of how names or words mean were first articulated in Plato's dialogue, Cratylus. One view is that names are purely social conventions, with one community agreeing on "tree," another agreeing on "arbre," and so on. The other view is that there is a "motivation" underlying the name--that there is something "tree-like" in the sounds or letters composing the word.

Languages change over time, through historical evolution. One aspect of this development is the regular exchanges between the categories of common and proper names. Most students are familiar with the fact that proper names in our civilization originated in many cases from common nouns, the names for one's occupation or a description of where one lived. As Charles Berlitz reminds us, the most common family name in the languages of Europe is "Smith," referring to the occupation of blacksmith. He provides this list of the names that mean "Smith":

French: Le Fèvre, La Farge, La Forge, Fernand.
Italian: Ferrari, Fabbri, Fabroni, Ferraio.
Spanish: Herrera, Herrero, Hernández, Fernández.
German: Schmidt, Schmied.
Swedish: Smed.
Russian: Kuznetsov.
Hungarian: Kovács.
Polish: Kowak, Kowalski.
Lebanese and Syrian Arabic: Haddad.
Irish: Magoon.

At the same time, the proper names of inventors serve as the nouns for objects, ideas, techniques, and the like. Indeed, "Romeo" itself names any man who is courting. Other examples of common nouns derived from proper names, according to Berlitz (in Native Tongues, New York: Grosset & Dunlap, 1982) are: bloomer, bowdlerize, boycott, cardigan, raglan, chauvinist, chesterfield, guillotine, hooligan, lynch, macadam, martinet, sadist, masochism, mesmerize, sandwich, silhouette.

The History of Names (p. 242)

Discussion and Writing

1. Part of the value of this topic is the access it gives to the peculiar nature of language, to the material reality of language. Our students for the most part are understandably oblivious to the extraordinarily odd quality of this "technology." As was the case with the fragments of a student's discourse, this experiment addresses the linguistic and rhetorical materials in terms of something about which the students have a natural curiosity--their own names. The motivation for doing much of the prewriting work necessary for the final project comes from the fact that the "research" involves an extrapolation from the examples of one's own situation.

The class may be able to think of some examples of "well-named" individuals in the public sphere--former White House spokesman "Larry Speakes" is a case in point, as is the former quarterback for the Chicago Bears, since "McMahon" means "son of the bear." Journalists often take note of these coincidences (one suggested that Robin Leach, host of Lifestyles of the Rich and Famous, was appropriately named, thinking no doubt of the pun with "leech").

This exercise may be done in class, putting the form of the anecdote to use once again. The purpose of writing rather than telling the anecdote might be the embarrassment that some students still feel about their names. The advantage of the topic--that everyone has experienced the cultural materiality of names--is also at times a disadvantage, in that the topic might become uncomfortably personal. One way around this potential difficulty is to note that a person will be teased through the name regardless of what the name is (although some names are more vulnerable than others). The lesson is worth making, to remove any doubts about the act of identification with language.

2. The students' information about their family names varies considerably from one individual to the next. Some have access to a complete family tree, while others don't know the nationality of their name, and assume that if their name has no meaning in English, it is meaningless. This exercise assists with the tasks of prewriting, collecting information for the main experiment. It may serve also as a library assignment, revealing the amount of materials available on onomastics and its related histories. In some cases it also may lead to some work in oral history, with the collection of anecdotes from the memory of family members.

The Power of Names (p. 244)

Discussion and Writing

1. The selections by Ellison and Spender provide the same sort of perspective on names that Angelou and Rapoport provided on student life. They call our attention

to the political and economic aspects of the history of names. Their experiences and opinions speak to those students who might be inclined to resist the importance of the issue "What's in a name?" Both blacks and women have promoted the practice of changing one's name as a political gesture, marking their protest against one form or another of slavery. The flower children of the late 1960s communes often invented names for their offspring not found in the standard dictionary lists of "common" proper names. Frank Zappa's daughter, Moon Unit, is one example of that trend. Hollywood entertainers frequently changed their names in order to make them more interesting and evocative, and to remove the possibility of evoking ethnic biases in the mind of the public. Students sometimes learn that their family name was altered at the time of immigration in order to make it more pronounceable or less recognizable ethnically. Such shifts or explicit baptisms signal the existence of a dimension of coding to which the names appeal as a standard of signification. As with the figures of the fragments, the signature renders manifest the invisible powers of the symbolic level of existence.

2. Spender and Ellison both pick up on the theme of slavery and bondage identifiable in the history of naming, as noted in Cassirer's allusion to the Roman legal system. To juxtapose the issues of race and sex in naming opens the way for a better understanding of what is at stake in the debate surrounding unusual naming practices. The uninformed instinctive response by outsiders to alterations in the community's dominant conventions of naming tends to be derision or dismissal. A reminder of what it feels like to be teased about one's name puts the issue into perspective. And most students readily acknowledge the slurs communicated in the various epithets applied to "foreign groups" (gringo, honky, pollack, wop, etc.). There is less ready agreement, perhaps because the consciousness-raising work done by the women's movement is more recent, about the gender bias of naming practices.

A comparison of information among the class with respect to the relative amounts of information for the family name as opposed to the mother's maiden name is a good way to make explicit the reality of selection that such practices effect in our awareness and memory. The issue also calls attention to gender differences in this awareness, in that the women students are likely to know more about the mother's name than will the men.

3. Ralph Ellison's struggle with the namesake Ralph Waldo Emerson indicates perhaps something about how the quality of "destiny" enters into a name, in that he is first made aware that there is something significant, a meaning or expectation, attached to his name, and then attempts to live up to the name. Jean-Paul Sartre's massive biography of Jean Genet interprets Genet's life as a project to become the thief that he was accused of being in a childhood incident. He worked to turn the common noun into his proper name, in other words. Jacques Derrida responded to Sartre's study with an alternative reading in _Glas_, showing that it was the common noun available in Genet's proper name (_genêt_ is the word in French for "broomflower") that accounts for his identity in life and in letters.

Ellison also proves the point that a person may be teased even for a name that on the face of it might not seem objectionable. He adds that in black culture wordplay in the form of nicknaming is a prominent custom. We shall have more to say about nicknames later. For now it is useful to discuss in this context our general theme concerning the relationship between the life of language in everyday culture and high culture. The signature experiment, like most experiments, consists of a systematic and extended investigation of a material feature of linguistic culture.

Class discussion may turn to childhood games, to recall a time in life when most people experience the power and pleasure of taking on a desirable name. What names were preferred, and what ones avoided? One student mentioned that in playing "cowboys" as a child the boys did not want to be "Jesse James" because they thought "Jesse" was a girl's name. This point raised the gender issue again, leading to the compilation of a list of names used for either sex.

Writing from Signatures (p. 251)

The discussion of heraldry is provided because of its importance for Derrida's formulation of the signature experiment. Given the textualist principle of the merger of critical and creative writing, it is not surprising to find Derrida extrapolating for critical or theoretical writing a device from contemporary literature. The heraldic form of the "abyss" (the center of the shield) has long been the image of the reflexive strategy of modernist authors who include at the "heart" of their texts a representation of the text itself--a version of the "play within the play," except that now the inner play comments not on the themes of the frame story, but on its form. As Peter Hutchinson explains in Games Authors Play (Methuen, 1983), "This concept of the 'interior duplication' derives from André Gide, who himself proved a major exponent of it in his novel The Counterfeiters (where a character is himself writing a novel entitled The Counterfeiters). Gide claimed to see a parallel in heraldry, in which he felt that the 'outer' design was reflected in the 'inner' one of the shield." He offers as another example of this "construction en abyme" the game of ombre in The Rape of the Lock. In extending the abyss construction into criticism, Derrida applies the representation of the family name in heraldry literally to literature, looking for the way in which the author's names might represent the organizing or generative principle of the work.

Although some of the students might know something about coats of arms from family crests, a more likely source of awareness would be members of Greek organizations or business majors who know something about the logos of certain corporations. In any case, when we come to the passage from Derrida's Glas the students should have in mind this heraldic usage. The way in which the family name determines the decoration of the shield provides a model for the signature experiment, in which the writer's name provides the inventio for the text.

James Joyce, "Shem the Penman" from Finnegans Wake (p. 252)

Discussion and Writing

1. This topic opens the minds of the more skeptical students to the relevance of heraldry to the contemporary world. The discussion might be preceded by some outside preparation, with volunteers contributing information about the significance of a given crest or logo. The symbolic organization of such designs could be compared to the uses of figures in other systems of meaning.

2. and 3. Joyce's Wake provides one model to be used as a resource in the signature experiment. Discussion might focus on the way in which Joyce's prose style extends the linguistic processes of nicknaming--modifying the proper name by

the means listed in the article (mutation, pun/irony, analogy, allusion, and so forth)--to alter not only his own name (moving from "James" to "Sham" in the same way "Joanne," for example, became "Dozy"), but any and all words in the language. His style, that is, represents another one of Derrida's literary sources for the signature theory of invention (promoting the systematic exchange between proper and common nouns).

Several important elements of the social practices of language treated in the discussion of Barthes's fragments, as well as in the selection from Goffman in Chapter 1, recur here in the linguistic register (the link between nicknaming and various aspects of prejudice and stereotyping). The inclusion of several drafts of the passage allow the students to review the compositional process, to identify exactly what Joyce is doing and the invention technique involved. The passage, that is, is a portrait--a self-portrait of the author--written with a mocking, ironic intent. In it the author (but there is the same distance between the real Joyce and the speaker of the text that Barthes created when he wrote "and so it is a lover who speaks") expresses through the description and the nicknames a feeling about himself--a feeling of being a sham or a fraud. Psychologists report that successful people not uncommonly feel that they are fakes. Their success is not necessarily part of their normal, authentic sense of themselves, established in childhood, and so they never quite feel right in this new social position. Whether or not Joyce actually experienced that condition, the portrait offers an account that may serve the students as a model for nicknaming themselves and for drawing a portrait of themselves through the lens of a particular, predominant feeling they may have about their present situation.

The stylistic pressure Joyce applies to the language may be readily imitated by the students when they understand the motivation and the linguistic principle underlying the text (the nicknaming process, now harnessed as a literary technique). The self-portrait in the nicknaming style makes a good exercise on its own. A one-page composition may be produced as an in-class project, to be revised perhaps and included later in the final essay.

<u>Signing (The Proper Name)</u> p. 256)

<u>Jacques Derrida, from Glas (p. 258)</u> Derrida exemplifies in this project the textualist approach to criticism, which, rather than imposing on literature a set of concepts derived from the social sciences, reads literature as itself a source of concepts capable not only of producing knowledge of literature (an immanent critique), but knowledge in general. It is not hard to understand why language departments rather than philosophy or social science departments have been the sponsors of Derrida's importation into the American university. Against the dominant tradition in philosophy, which attempted to master the tools of language by reducing its ambiguity to the ideal point of univocality, with symbolic logic being the most recent representative of that tendency, Derrida bases his theory of language on James Joyce--specifically, on <u>Finnegans Wake</u>--and attempts to develop a model of knowledge and representation that exploits the maximum potential of ambiguity. If his experiment is successful--if he can demonstrate the productive benefits of his position--literature as a discipline stands to gain

considerably in the hierarchy of knowledge, passing from a "debtor" to a "creditor" discourse.

Derrida's reading of Genet, then, may be appreciated as part of this project to find in literary productions a new science of language. In the case of the signature, the experiment is an investigation of the relationship of words to things, a study of referentiality, in which an alternative to the classic theories of reference (motivation versus convention) is proposed. What Derrida discovers in Genet is the model for a self-conscious exploitation of the aleatory or chance associations joining together the different dimensions of discourse with the real. Barthes explored at the level of rhetoric the overlapping of the discourses of everyday life, popular culture, and high culture (including specialized disciplines). Now Derrida, as we will see, carries the study of such convergences into a new dimension. We get a glimpse here of one of the organizing metaphors of "text" as a concept--the textile. A text is made by weaving together the codes of a culture in an idiomatic way, guided by the peculiarities of style and signature.

Jacques Derrida, to quote another blurb (which we accept as representing the norm of an author's identity), is known for correcting a postulate of linguistics that subordinates all language to its spoken form and ties speech to the person, to the will to possess and the passion to assign a unitary structure, a profound meaning to the contradictory play of human appearances. He is widely studied for his researches into the density and complexity of signifying substance--its irreducibility to simple meaning. Derrida is professeur d'art at the École des hautes études en sciences sociales in Paris, and cofounder of the Collège international de philosophie (an experimental university designed to supplement the established, traditional institutions of higher education in France). His best-known work is Of Grammatology (Baltimore: Johns Hopkins University Press, 1974).

Although Derrida is a philosopher whose European reputation rests on his rereadings of the German tradition of phenomenology and other philosophies of consciousness (Hegel, Husserl, Heidegger), his work has been disseminated in this country principally through language departments, English and comparative literature especially. He enjoyed a close working relationship with the Yale School critics (Paul de Man, Geoffrey Hartman, J. Hillis Miller, and Harold Bloom) for a number of years, including a teaching appointment at Yale. This group became associated with the critical position known as "deconstruction" about which there has been so much controversy. Derrida continues to teach and lecture regularly in the United States, having formal association with Cornell and the University of California at Irvine. Recently, some of his writings have appeared in English translation before they were published in France.

The signature experiment included in Text Book is not representative of American deconstructive criticism, which so far is based not on Derrida's own methodology for writing or with literature, but on some of his theories of language articulated in commentaries on philosophical works. The signature project, however, reflects Derrida's own practice as a literary critic, as reflected in Glas and as applied in essays on such authors as Ponge, Blanchot, and Sollers.

Discussion and Writing

1. It is not necessary for the students to follow Derrida's exposition in detail, only that they grasp the essence of his argument--the reading of Genet's corpus as an

extrapolation generated by the name "Jean Genet."

Once the common noun available within the proper name is discovered the next step in the generation of a signature text, followed both by Genet and Derrida (the latter repeated the former's strategy, applying the principle of textualist criticism, which is to mime the object of study), is to elaborate a discourse out of the object thus named. The antonomasia or transfer from the proper to the common noun is clear and explicit in Genet, although the drawback of this explicitness (the fact that *genêt* literally means "broomflower") is that the signature as "science" can only be developed superficially. Derrida makes it clear that the signature is by no means confined to cases in which the proper name directly translates into a common noun. The "key" of a persons's cognitive and compositional style, rather, may operate even more profoundly at the level of "rhythm" (musically). We are not concerned in this experiment with this more complex notion of the signature. It is sufficient for now to initiate the experiment in terms of the more literal registers of signing. The point, in any case, is not to take too seriously any "truth" claims for the procedure, but to stress the experimental value of the name as a guide for invention.

Having found the flowers or the horse in "Genet," or the sponge in "Ponge" (another poet he studies), Derrida describes the nature of these things in detail, constructing his text out of information gleaned from reference books. Indeed, he seems to be using the pun on "reference" to develop an alternative theory of referentiality. Words do not "refer" to the real living things but to other words, whose meanings may be found in dictionaries, glossaries, and encyclopedias. We may recognize the strategy as being similar to the models made from metaphors discussed in Chapter 2, except that here the initial juxtaposition of sets or categories is based on the pun, including the "macaronic" pun across languages (the organizing device of *Finnegans Wake*). The strategy, in short, is to use as a guide for what to say or write both the linguistic or poetic techniques of pun, rhyme, and the like, and a narrative account of the qualities or attributes of the items or things thus produced. In discussion students may want to find examples of both moves.

Having generated the "thing" as name and as referent or meaning, the next step--the move to the level of the third modality of the signature--is to declare that the "thing" is a model or analogy for all metaphor, that is, for poetic or figurative writing as such. Thus the proper name, the most particular register of language there is, designating one individual in the world, is generalized into a generic formula. The process is similar to the construction of an argument by metaphor, studied in Chapter 2. It is also a common practice in theoretical speculation, which textuality adopts as a basic strategy of writing about literature (the use of literary devices for the production of a writing to represent knowledge of literature). Textuality, in other words, tests the proposition that literary language is as capable of representing an understanding of literature as is the language of social science.

It is worth noting that Derrida attends to "Jean" as well as to "Genet," although in this selection very little if any of that production appears.

2. This exercise is quite ambitious, and may be more appropriate for an advanced class. It would be most usefully assigned if you decided to spend more time on this section than might normally be possible. To carry it out effectively could require considerable outside reading, in order to have a large enough sample of an author's

works available to test adequately whether or in what way a particular signature manifests itself. The other problem is that the signature does not always function at the most obvious level--it may be, Derrida suggests, a movement or rhythm in the temporality of the text, such as the coming and going of the eternal return in Nietzsche (rather than the more obvious "nothingness" of the name in Slavic). Unfortunately, the approach is so recent and so unconventional that few if any essays exist, outside of Derrida's corpus, applying the method. The exercise is here in part to stimulate thinking about the relation of authors to works, or of people to life. Is there anything "hawthorne-like" about the works of Hawthorne? Perhaps this question is as much for the instructors as for the students, appealing to you to test the experiment.
3. Much of the interest of the signature experiment arises because one does not stop the lesson at the point of understanding or appreciating the poem and its genre. Rather, the student is expected to replicate the experiment, extrapolating from the models a formula for discovering the poetics latent in one's own name. Again, it is useful to stress the experimental nature of the project. As in the early stages of any "science," or any project within a field of knowledge, the practical value of a given idea will not always be evident. There is no need to accept as truth the results produced by the aleatory or chance operations of this _inventio_ in order to carry out the investigation into the generalizability of one's proper name. At the very least, students will generate prose that bears many of the features of modernist or poetic literary style--replete with enigmas and obscurities--that have tended to baffle them as readers. In short, the piece will be a text with value for them as a heraldic representation of their identities, and of others as an aesthetic composition. It sometimes happens that someone does not identify with the "fate" or destiny prescribed by the name. Ponge, for example, put no special stock in the "sponge"--did not identify with it, did not see himself as a "sponge" or "parasite," to use one of the meanings of the term available in English (alluding, potentially, to the attitude toward poets as unproductive members of society). As one student wrote:

> My last name has always been a depressing subject. I would give my right eye to have my surname teased the way it was when I was a child rather than the way it is now. All through elementary school my classmates and friends turned "Hicks" into "hick-ups." The jest never bothered me, unless it was said with malice. "Hickey" was the nickname I got as an adolescent, although I didn't get the thing it names until college. My last name, in the singular form, also appears in the dictionary. "A gullible, provincial person; a yokel." I will admit only to gullibility (and not much of that) or to provincial (in the most prestigious sense). As for yokel, I completely and entirely refuse to see myself as a "country bumpkin." I do not like country music, I never wear western clothing, and I refuse to ride in a pickup truck or associate with anyone who owns one.

We have here the principal project, the major experiment in its full form. Jarrett's text is the last, and the most complete, model provided demonstrating the strategy of writing. The students should be reminded, of course, that Joyce's

Wake and Derrida's Glas offer examples of the kind of writing and thinking involved.

James (Mike) Jarrett, besides writing for Jazziz, wrote this text while finishing his doctorate at the University of Florida. His dissertation topic deals with jazz as a compositional principle and social point of view in modern literary and theoretical writing. In other words, Jarrett is far enough along in his career to have committed himself to a theme--jazz in his case--that shows up in or is imposed on, his proper name. Many of our students, if not all of them, will not have any such objectification of their style of thought, although they may have declared a major or they may pursue avocations whose attributes might show up in the signature. Of course the signature might be used predictively, to suggest areas that the individual might seek out or avoid. In general, however, Roback's question about the destiny of the name is only of secondary interest, to add a little spice of mystery to the experiment. Still, it is not unusual for a student to be quite surprised by the suitability of the name. One thing that becomes clear about this "destiny" in Jarrett's example is that it is in part if not entirely a "construction" of the genre. Since Jarrett happens to be interested in Menippean satire, which informs one aspect of his dissertation (his "corpus"), he turns to a review of a certain "menippea" to see if he can find any connections with his poetic formula. His discussion of these satires sometimes confuses his readers, who need to realize that in miming this model they need not reproduce the same things Jarrett talks about, but the same procedure or method. The strategy is the same one used in filling in the poses of the fragments. There had to be references, but they did not have to be the ones used by Barthes. The students may substitute for the satires any area of particular interest to them.

The real heart of the experiment is the invention of the third modality--the transformation of the name into a generic principle for the student's own style of thinking and writing. If Barthes's fragments explored the style of life of the student, the signature may be said to explore the style of cognition (in a symbolic way) of the student. The fun of the experiment is the idea that even if an individual does not recognize the text generated in this way as "proper," he or she should be encouraged to save it for future reference, to see if it might not become a self-fulfilling prophecy (this possibility, of course, is presented in a playful way). We mentioned earlier the steps of the method, but we will review them again now as a way to appreciate the value of Jarrett's example.

1. The proper names and nicknames serve as the key for the invention of the text.
2. These names are elaborated into as extensive a list as possible of common names (verbs, adjectives, and the like, as well as nouns),
3. This key list of common names is elaborated into a narrative, part of which is devoted to a description or "showing" of the objects, things, or actions named in the list, and part of which is devoted to a commentary explaining the relevance of these items as metaphors for one's life experience.
4. The commentary mounts an argument by analogy, showing how the named items function as a model for making a text.

Jarrett in fact offers two models for invention--the process of canning jam, and the musical style of jazz. The recipe as a form is a lucky find, derived from the "jar." Notice, too, the introduction of anecdotal material as a means to fill out the term (his grandmother's mason jars). The other model of the third modality, jazz, is introduced through the pun on "cooking." This material is developed more for its biographical interest--the fact that the author really is writing about jazz, and has in his signature terms that refer to musical performance. He does not develop the methods of improvisations as a model for writing as much as he could have, but he alludes to it enough to evoke the idea. This partial development is appropriate for a text attempting to be as aesthetic as it is critical. The point is not to say everything--to generate the descriptions and leave some of the explanations to the inferences of the reader, thus preserving some of the enigmatic strangeness of the models.

It would be useful to do an inventory of all the strategies Jarrett uses to build his discourse; to relate his procedures to the previous readings, to see which devices he privileged, and which ones he ignored. He does very little, for example, with Joyce's style, or with the nicknaming self-portrait. He is also selective within the possible range of materials. He does not activate every term, and the term he chooses to develop as his model is not the only one available. This selectivity indicates the constructed dimension of the experiment. He makes special use of the "macaronic" pun--the pun across languages--moving between English and French. The obvious move is to translate one's name from its original language into its English meaning (from "Kovacs" into "Smith"). Jarrett extends this technique to find a French pun for "Jarrett"--j'arrête"--although again he only chooses to discuss part of the meaning available for this word. Students need not do all of these things, nor is their text likely to be as long as Jarrett's.

One dimension of this model that deserves special emphasis is its use of visual illustrations. One of the elements that enhances the aesthetic effect of the piece, not to mention its heraldic qualities, is its use of visuals. The pleasure of producing a collage of this sort is considerable, and it further enhances one lesson of the experiment--the link between names and things. Perhaps the appeal of such compositions to our students has something to do with their immersion in a video culture.

Two student papers follow that demonstrate the "signature" assignment. The first paper, by Amy Lynn Greenblatt, was originally accompanied by photographs which highlighted the visual quality of her signature. The second paper, by Brian J. Noe, was originally produced on a Macintosh with various type faces and line art.

AMY LYNN GREENBLATT

Greenblatt--green leaf

green	1.	the color of most plant leaves and growing grass
	2.	not ripe; immature; inexperienced
leaf	1.	a usually green, flattened plant structure attached to a stem & functioning as a principal organ of photosynthesis

So my name is a little redundant. Composed of so few elements it must repeat itself. It means forever young, never ripe, always growing. The color of living things, a living thing. Maybe I can absorb energy to create something like food, like the leaf does. I may get eaten by insects. I may turn orange and brown when the winter sets in. The leaf keeps the tree alive. It has a large surface area within a small volume so that it gets the most exposure to light. Perhaps I'll never be ready for anything, if I stay green. Maybe I'll be naive a lot. Like my middle name, this one is found in nature. It could be that I am like the outdoors, or that I like the outdoors. Maybe I am part of a salad, a very vital ingredient in one. This name goes well with my middle name because leaves and waterfalls often go together. In fact, near every waterfall there must be leaves. One nourishes the other, then grows abundantly by its banks.

My interesting initials are ALG, or algae. This is a perfect complement to the rest of my name. It is green, it floats on rivers, and it is of the plant kingdom.

THE WATERFALL

The waterfall, a dynamic liquid flow, is my middle name. The moving water that keeps rivers clean is the meaning of "Lynn." It is like kinetic energy, rushing toward an infinite and unseen goal, always confident that the sea refuses no river. It sweeps the banks, taking dirt along with it. It is beauty, a source of pleasure to those who seek it. But it is not easily accessible. (How many do you find per week?) The paradox is that they are so blatantly displayed. The waterfall is sometimes dangerous to boatmen who don't know how to ride it, though they really should stay near the bottom because the drop is designed for a flexible (liquid) medium. The waterfall is a secret place of downfall, seldom seen as such, hidden by nature--yet so loudly announced. Pure splendor--very majestic. Allowing breeze to spray cool droplets from the mainstream, it has infinite subsets, like a beach. I once saw a diminished waterfall in a test tube. I shook it and the little salt particles swirled around frenetically. The large waterfall must be chaotic, although its motion is directed by gravity. I see one every time I pour a drink and take a shower. There is a great one between New York and Canada that I have never seen. It is a link between two heights that never runs dry. It will be in motion forever.

Amy means beloved. I'm sure my parents thought so. Amy can be rearranged to form yam, a sweet potato. Perhaps this fits in with my physique. I am often consumed at Thanksgiving meals because people love my taste. I grow on vines that have leaves, so this fits my last name. I am found outdoors, as most of my name is.

I seem to be Nature's daughter.

A dearly loved sweet potato with green leaves. Perhaps I'll marry a man named Underwood and then I'll be a Dearly Loved Waterfall Underwood. Amy, beloved, be loved.

MY NAME
by
BRIAN J. NOE
sec. #1309

What is in a name? Some say it is a label that we attach to ourselves. Then there are those that believe that the name bears the passage to the soul. Still there persist critics that are not even worth mentioning here so I will not. I feel that the best way to start an examination of names is by reciting this verse that I heard somewhere:

"to know thy name is to know thyself"

which I then revise as;

"to know thy name is to Noe thyself"

It is truly here that we must begin to investigate the true meanings of names. And what better name to start with than my own, Brian Joseph Richard Noe. One may think not a totally profound name on the surface, but we must look beyond that into its meanings. From the first time a person asked, "Tell me your name," and I replied with some harsh rebuttal, "NOe," I realized that this was a name that I could have fun with.

My next experience in life that led me to believe that my name contained some hint of my destiny was when I saw my first James Bond movie. From that point on in my life I came to the rationalization that I had to get my doctorate. Here my name gave me the clue to what I was to become, a great scientist.

It is now time to see what my name holds and the best place to begin is with the beginning and that is Brian. Brian from the Celtic word briar--a craftsman who carves wooden pipes, and with the suffix meaning an occupation of, and after combination and deletion, we come up with Brian--a craftsman who carves pipes.

I find it not a coincidence that I have in fact carved quite a few wooden pipes. Could this be subliminal destiny, let us proceed further.

Joseph is my baptismal name. It is derived from Joseph, Jacob's son who was given a coat of many colors. And it is from this Joseph that the English word joseph, a multicolored coat worn in the eighteenth century while horseback riding, came from. But do not forget that colors can stand for many things; such as dimensions.

Richard is my confirmation name. Derived from rich and meaning, one who is rich. But there are many things that one can be rich in, there is material wealth, richness in intelligence and intellect, and richness in health to name just a few. And it is from Richard the Lion-Hearted, King of England, a brave and fierce warrior.

And then there is Noe. Not just no, but ______________? The utmost opposite to positive. Noe is not a very common name but indeed one which holds deep and hidden meanings. If traced back in time Noe can be derived from deleting the I in noel. Noel is the French word for the birth of Christ. From its earlier Latin meanings natalis--relating to one's birth, and nasci--to be born.

It is the practice of many languages to put the last name first, and I feel here it is a good idea to do so. So now shall I say that I was born a great and crafty warrior with many dimensions. Here is a prophecy that is very likely to show up in antiquity or in the middle ages about the birth of a son.

We can now come up with some variations upon the name. Let's start by taking Brian and rearrange the i and the a, and get brain. The brain is the core of all thought, and so being it is there that all intellect is perceived and generated. Then it was not just calling me brain in jest that my childhood companions called me, but a prophecy to the future and a homaging praise they employed to me, one of proven superior intellect.

Let's be creative and see what else can be generated. From my brain will be born great and rich ideas about the theory of dimensional travel. Will I indeed find a way to time travel? I certainly hope so, that has been my greatest dream since childhood. But that's enough of that shit. My great grandmother on my father's side was a Cherokee Indian and from my childhood I have been a master at the bow and arrow along with swordsmanship and other warrior attributes, I have progressed along the line to being a great warrior.

How interesting this has become. Where else can we go now? Let's say that we taken the b off brain then we get <u>rain</u>. Here this may lead to an understanding of my personal being dark and gloomy which many have called me. Or if we may wish to reduce it to <u>in</u>. This could lead to the meaning of absorption. Here again we find a comparison with my photographic memory.

Let's now try rewriting my name Bria[neon]. Here we have generated a new word <u>neon</u>. Neon as in neon lights, being bright and luminous. Once again we have struck upon another dimension of my personality, bright and shining.

<u>Noe</u> one is here.
<u>Noe</u> is not a word with
which you can die!!

Predetermination of your nature via your name. This seems an absurd idea but there may be something in it.

<u>No(e)t signed:</u>

BRIAN J. NOE

Chapter 5: EXPERIMENTS WITH TEXTS: TEXT AND RESEARCH

This chapter continues the experimental approach to writing foregrounded in Chapter 4. The students enjoy experimentation once they get into it, but they enter into it more willingly if they understand the context and the motivation of the experiment. It is helpful, for example, to note that the kind of writing tested in this chapter reflects a new tendency in critical writing that has emerged within the cultural studies disciplines during the past decade or so. The specific nature of the experiment may be quickly located by posing it as an alternative to the familiar distinction between objective research and impressionistic response papers. As a hybrid that blurs this object/subject dichotomy, the textual mode of research brings together autobiography and scholarship.

It sometimes makes the students feel better if they know that some authoritative figures have already worked in this textual way. Some of the studies usually associated with personalized research include Kwame Anthony Appiah, In My Father's House, Norma Field, In the Realm of a Dying Emperor, Patricia J. Williams, The Alchemy of Race and Rights, Jane Tompkins, West of Everything, and Gregory Ulmer, Heuretics. Adam Begley wrote an article for Lingua Franca (April 1994) on the critics at Duke University, including Jane Tompkins, who is part of a four-member writing group along with Alice Kaplan, Mariana Torgovnick, and Cathy Davidson, who have turned to personalized research. Other Duke professors writing confessional criticism are Frank Lentricchia and Eve Kosofsky Sedgwick. This turn to autobiographical and confessional scholarship may be accounted for in part by the assimilation into the academy of the values of feminism, with its slogan "the personal is political," along with the emphasis on difference promoted by representatives of all the minority positions in the categories of ideology (see Chapter 3). The Duke School, in other words, is part of a larger movement growing out of the identity politics associated with cultural studies.

The divisions of knowledge outside the humanities have recognized the personal basis of knowledge, at least in principle, as in the theory of relativity in physics, associated with the idea that the presence of an observer modifies an observation. The social sciences developed their own version of this insight in the methods of participant observers, who began to take into account their presence as an intervention in the culture they were studying. Textuality may be understood as an investigation of the possibilities opened up by this new crossing of the private and the public, the self and the other, within academic writing that results from these relativistic points of view.

One of the practices common to many courses in writing about literature or literature survey is the assignment of a research paper. Such a paper brings into one operation all the parts of rhetoric guiding the lessons of the conventional course: gathering information in the library, organizing the information into arguments, and expressing the arguments in a style that supposedly transforms the accumulated knowledge into the personal understanding of the student. The various movements in critical theory noted above have posed serious challenges to the premises of scientific research in general and the academic research paper in particular--especially to the assumption about the objectivity of the researcher. Conventional argumentation always admitted that research had a point of view, but the recommended strategy of presentation was that of a neutral if interested party weighing the pros and cons of an issue, and then exercising fair-minded judgments in favor of the stronger case, based on a rational assessment of the reasoning involved. This stance was based on the humanistic ideal of the individual as an autonomous individual, fully self-conscious, capable of discerning the difference between a true and a false argument.

The textual approach to knowledge could be understood as a variation on the insight that the presence of an observer modifies the nature of the observation. Text is a kind of hybrid of reader response and critique stances, in that the interests of the individual openly guide the research, but these responses are not taken as true or natural but are themselves seen as symptoms of the ideological positioning of the researcher in a specific culture. The textual method of research produces a map locating one's "self" in an intertextual network of cultural references. The learning effect in a textual research paper is dialectical in that the writers learn as much about their own life story as they do about the literary or artistic artifact. The map shows students that identity is constituted by a circulation of the inside with the outside of "selfhood."

That individual judgments turn out to be based on ideologically constructed positions does not lead necessarily to a kind of determinism. One purpose of textuality, in fact, is to learn how to become aware of and begin to acquire some control over this circulation linking the personal to the collective culture. Research is a way to gain access to the collective archives of cultures (a way to remember, to think with the accumulated resources of civilization). Textual writing mediates then between several memories: personal remembrance, popular entertainments, and the specialized disciplines. It is not a turn away from conventional academic practice, but a way to integrate academic practices with the other discourses the students experience as part of their daily lives.

Mystory (p. 277)

One way to approach this chapter is to present it as a review, designed to synthesize into one coherent practice all the strategies and exercises encountered in the previous chapters. In this frame the students already know how to write mystorically. The elements learned separately--personal anecdotes in Chapter 1, reasoning with metaphors in Chapter 2, intertextual encounters with pop icons in Chapter 3, and the generative use of the signature in Chapter 4--all play a role in the mystory. Although Gregory Ulmer wrote a theory of mystory in Teletheory (including an experimental demonstration entitled "Derrida at the Little Bighorn"), this new genre of writing has not yet been widely recognized as the textualist counterpart to the research paper. The challenge of Chapter 5 is to invent or design a set of rules that apply the devices learned in the first four chapters to the practice of scholarship in the students' field of disciplinary interest.

The readings included here, called "relays" rather than "examples" ("relay" in this sense is borrowed from Gilles Deleuze and Felix Guattari) demonstrate how to bring one or the other of the basic devices to bear on research, but no one of them is a complete or finished example of the form we seek. Because of these relays it is possible to grasp the principles of this new genre and to practice it explicitly. In any case, and unlike the traditional argumentative paper, textualist rules are ad hoc, heuristic rules of thumb, not reducible to one universal prescription that fits all cases. Indeed, what might be invented here is a way to do research that generates its rules from the particulars of each case--the particulars of the researcher and the particulars of the object of study. The implications of such a view are that, in contrast with the conventional research paper in which the students attempt to meet the demands of the disciplinary authorities of the profession, in the mystory the students are making up the "laws" that they will then test.

The laws of the essay were made up in this way at one time (the most prominent names associated with the invention of the essay are Montaigne and Bacon), and the purpose of this experiment is to learn about the essay from the side of its invention, rather than from the side of its verification. Ulmer calls this inventive attitude to studies "heuretics" (a term related to "eureka" and "heuristics," and distinguished as the logic of invention form "hermeneutics," which is the logic of interpretation). The pedagogy that works well with this experiment (and with most of the book, for that matter) is to organize the class meetings as think tanks for brainstorming, to engage the group in the cooperative project of locating, naming, and formulating the instructions for the paper they have to write--the textualist research paper known as mystory.

The goal is to produce a "recipe" (poetics, method, genre) for conducting academic research using the sample readings as relays for focusing the lessons of Text Book as a whole. In effect the primary assignment guiding the discussions will be the collective invention of a discourse on method for mystory. The means for carrying out this task are the same ones repeatedly promoted in books on the creative process (any one of which might be consulted for ideas). The point of the experiment has as much to do with the experience of collaborative learning, free-wheeling brainstorming, and thinking out loud as it does with the final production of the writing. As most books on creativity point out, the more impossible the task seems, the easier it is to break the old habits and to try new approaches. "Me? Invent a new method for research? Not!" is a common response from students when they are first put in this situation. They soon discover, however, that the steps they have gone through in the earlier chapters have fully prepared them for this last challenge, and when they do actually produce the method, the learning effect is all the stronger. They may also put on their résumés that they have had training in collaborative learning, group problem solving, and synectic brainstorming.

In fact, the mystory may not be itself the new genre of research, but the method for finding that new genre (in the manner of avant-garde manifestos which preceded the actual works of art, or in the manner of scientific experiments which must first be carefully defined and theorized before the work may be carried out). The mystory is a manifesto for an avant-garde academy (if that description is not a contradiction in terms). In any case, the relays (by Leiris et al.) illustrate one of the basic qualities of discourses on method: They tell or explain what the method of poetics is, and they show it in action--the discourse on method uses the very rules it is in the process of inventing. Michel Leiris, for example, not only states that metaphor may be used to produce instructions for how to write a certain genre (the confession in his case), he actively uses a specific metaphor (the bullfight) to speculate about the details of how to confess.

Discourses on method, in other words, from the first one ever written (Plato's Phaedrus) to the mystory, possess this self-reflexive quality such that they are simultaneously about something else and about themselves (about bullfighting and about how to write a confession, in Leiris's relay). The piece that the students write for this chapter might be a poetics of mystory that would be in part a demonstration of their own performance of the genre and an explanation of how others might compose a mystory of their own. As we will see, the relays show how to achieve this effect (they are all "searches for a method" rather than reports after the fact). Alternatively (or in addition), the process of defining the method could be confined to the class sessions, and the actual writing could be the performance of the poetics or method, without explanation or apology (just as the conventional research paper demonstrates but does not explain the rules of argumentative writing).

Discussion and Writing

1. This exercise may be written or simply serve as the basis for discussion. If the class is organized into subgroups or panels (taking turns leading the brainstorming), one such panel might bring in several examples of textbook guides to the research paper. If a handbook has been assigned it might well include a section on "writing the research paper." The prescriptions itemized in these handbooks could be used to generate alternatives. This negative step of pushing away from an existing practice is a key feature of innovation. Generating positive features of a new method by contrast with existing rules is a principal feature of discourses on method. Plato in Phaedrus uses the Sophist Lysias as the negative example. This strategy of invention by contrast is most clearly exemplified in avant-garde manifestos such as the ones André Breton wrote for surrealism, the point of departure of which is a contrast with the aesthetics of realism.

Unlike the manifesto, the mystory need not adopt an aggressive tone of opposition, however. Mystory is not against the analytical methods of expository writing. Rather it takes advantage of the strong learning effect that occurs whenever anything different is introduced to disturb the habits of convention. The students are so used to the drills of exposition that a further review produces little awareness about the nature of research. However, a review of the practices of argumentative research conducted as a search for antonymic rules has a galvanizing effect on attention. It is not that common suggestions to "explore your library," "follow a search strategy," "evaluate sources for relevance and reliability" are bad advice, only that the way the advice will be used in a mystory will be different. In a way the exercise is an exploration of the adage "you have to know the rules in order to [before you can] break them." The fact is that writing a mystory sharpens students' ability to write conventional research papers as well, so that the adage should read, "you have to break the rules in order to know them."

At the same time, the pleasure derived from breaking the rules (for example, to write without focus on a thesis statement) should not be underestimated. A variation on this exercise based on those sections of conventional textbooks having to do with mechanics is a good way to have fun learning. The instruction is to review all the rules and then to generate a rule that is the opposite or contrary in some way tot the original rule. If this procedure is extended to include the rules of grammar and syntax (rules against dangling modifiers and the like) the result is a formula for comedy. Exaggeration and parody are excellent devices for focusing attention on the relationship between the abstractions of the rules and actual effects created in language by specific arrangements and usages. The very act of laughing at such parodies is already a recognition of the "proper" form. Deliberate parodies are the best way to eliminate unintentional ones.

2. Considered at a formal level, there are really only three ways to organize the release of information through the space/time of a composition: exposition, narrative, poetic pattern. Although every composition contains elements of all three modes, one or the other is more or less dominant in a given work. Through the era of print literacy exposition (argumentation) became the mode associated with the effect of truth. Narrative was the mode approved for fiction (as art and entertainment), and pattern was reduced to "verse" practiced by elite poets. In our electronic era the dominance of pattern in advertising and television amounts to a "return of the repressed." Indeed, so many of the communication practices of

everyday life involve patterning that one of the most important tasks of rhetoric today is to add this mode to the traditional set of competencies taught in school. Academic writing has been strictly expository for some time. Mystory is a way to introduce into this restrictive order the compositional resources of narrative and especially of patterning.

Within expository writing many textbooks offer a choice between two strategies of arrangement. In one the conclusion is posed first--to orient the reader from the beginning to the desired idea or opinion--and then to provide the proof that persuades the reader of the correctness of the stance. A second, more narrative approach is to begin with the problem rather than the solution, to pose the problem as an enigma, followed by the logical or even chronological steps leading to the discovery of the solution. This investigative frame in a way is the one we are adopting for mystory: The students do not already know what a mystory is. The difference is that mystory is not something to be found, but something to be made (invented).

An extreme example of using pattern to arrange a composition is John Cage's pedagogical device of selecting the research materials randomly in what may be recognized in the context of Chapter 2 as a surrealistic style of research. No matter how diverse of unfamiliar the materials were that were brought together in this way, it was always possible to bring them into coherence by means of details that repeated from one sample to the other. Meanwhile, the learning effect of looking at disparate materials in a search for a pattern was reportedly very strong. It is worth noting that the materials themselves, of course, consisted of books composed in the conventional style of exposition. The point--and this is what needs to be tested--is that experimental practices can fulfill the purposes of the research paper as well or better than the conventional practices of argumentative writing.

Archive for a Mystorical Method

Michel Leiris, "Manhood" (p. 279) Part of the purpose of the final project (to write a discourse on method for mystory, or to write the mystory itself) is to gain some experience with the frustrations that arise from the processual nature of invention. The students must begin the design before all the materials are covered. The brainstorming sessions dealing with Leiris, for example, must already be speculating on how to use his ideas knowing that the subsequent readings will modify the understanding of his work. The question then is how to select the features of the reading that will be most helpful as instructions for the final design? Two rules of selection guide the process: 1) Internal evidence--look for the author's meta-comments: when the author says something is important, take notes, even if it is not immediately clear why or how the point might be used. A digression on note-taking might not be a waste of time at this point. The best way to read for a pattern is to take notes on all the relays, then compare the notes to see what aspects repeat. The pattern appears in the collation of the notes. 2) External evidence--context--the previous chapters of Text Book, such as the part on arguing with metaphor in Chapter 2, supply a set of markers (an intertext) that signal--when encountered again in Leiris--the presence of a possibly useful device. These two principles of relevance, in short, are quite conventional: the same reading skills required for the inventio stage of the conventional research paper are also needed for mystory.

The reading included here is not from Leiris's autobiography proper, but from the discussion of method in the afterward. This choice has to do with the emphasis of our assignment on the "how-to" aspect of a discourse on method. Manhood itself nonetheless is a good example of a basic feature of mystory--the exploration of identity formation as an interactive interplay between the personal and the collective, the private and the public registers of culture. Some students become curious about the wholes from which these parts are sampled, and a good exercise or extra-credit project can be to find the original work or something elwe by the same author and to write a short report on it (which may be delivered to the class as part of a panel presentation).

What we said about the "dated" quality of Play It Again, Sam applies even more to Manhood, in the sense of its sexual views being out of line with those of the 1990s. But the special interest of Leiris for mystory (keeping in mind that what the students borrow from any of these authors is not their opinions but their method in order to find their own positions) is his relation to everything in the cultural world by means of identification: "When I go to a bullfight, I tend to identify myself with either the bull at the moment the sword is plunged into its body, or with the matador who risks being killed (perhaps emasculated?) by a thrust of the horn at the very moment when he most clearly affirms his virility. Leiris tells about his emotional understanding of his sexuality by investigating how certain works of the fine arts (paintings, plays, operas) affect him. His account features representations of sex and violence ("I have often more or less identified myself with this cowardly and cruel Tetrarch rolling drunk at Salome's feet," he notes, referring to Richard Strauss's Salome). Our students could write similar accounts, no doubt, but with reference not to the high arts of Leiris's European education, but to the popular arts of America. Leiris is important as an authority for mystory because he exemplifies a style of reading that is not approved of in academic conventions; his reading style has more in common with fandom that with the impersonalized connoiseurship of art appreciation.

Leiris's case indicates some of the difficulties of the textualist approach to ideological criticism. One purpose of the mystory, that is, is to include within the research the researcher's own identity, understood in terms of the categories of ideology that function as filters that constrain learning. Sexuality is just one of these categories that make people uncomfortable. It is much easier (and less effective) to discuss sex, gender, race, and the like in the abstract than to confront them autobiographically. The relays included in this section, nonetheless, indicate how this difficulty may be negotiated. The frame of the "search for a method" is one way to create the personal encounter with the norms of a category without needing to "expose" oneself.

Discussion and Writing

1. This question addresses the heuristics for designing a new method. We saw previously that working by "contrast" with existing rules may produce a new set of features for writing that is different from the expected norm. Another generative heuristic is to work by analogy (figuratively, metaphorically, allegorically). Creators of methodologies tend to find some other practice that gives a feeling for what they

want, and use it to suggest indirectly the practice they are trying to invent. Plato, for example, borrowed his analogy from medicine, saying that he wanted to do for the spirit what doctors did for the body (to create the condition of health).

The analogy works in at least two ways, as may be seen in Leiris's use of the corrida: 1) The mood evoked by the vehicle orients the users to the feeling required for the new practice (to write a confessional autobiography is to take risks). The mystory involves this problematic of "authenticity" in that the personal memory must be engaged for the learning effect to occur. 2) The form guiding the writing comes from the vehicle: the details of the literal organization and arrangement of the contents--putting the information into words, forming relationships among the parts, and the like--come from the analogy. "Lured from cape to pike, from pike to the man who turns into a cape, from man to banderilla, from banderilla to sword, and from sword to dagger, the huge beast is soon no more than a mountain of steaming flesh," Leiris writes. In the analogy, of course, this steaming flesh is Leiris's own sexual passions that have to be mastered by his spirit. The fight is a ritual performance--recognizing and celebrating the power of the beast--of the conquest of nature by culture, the rule of mind over body. (A good description of a bullfight may be found in James Michener's Mexico, pp. 237-268.)

The suggestion of "moving from one house to another" as a vehicle is meant to get at the commonplace view of communicating as the sender putting a content into a package (language) and shipping it to the receiver who unpacks it and gets exactly what was sent. Jacques Derrida alluded to the actual workings of the postal service and the existence of the dead letters office to make the theoretical point that communication must include the possibility of messages not arriving. As for the form/content formulation of communicating, anyone who has gone through the experience of changing residences knows about how much stuff is thrown away, lost, broken, stolen, and the like during the process. To generate a metaphor for method out of this process one creates a corollary in rhetoric of all the features of the move. The result could be viewed in several different ways: as a critique of the form/content view of communication; as a case for celebrating the expertise of the professional writer, who, like the professional mover, is able to get the content where it is going. This celebration has a way of turning back into a critique, however, considering the expense involved in relying on the expert.

2. Proverbs are of course one of the simple or basic forms of oral culture. Barthes observed that the cultural code of the forms of literacy (the code organizing the stereotypes, clichés, and commonplaces of a society into interconnected sets) could be located by identifying the proverb embedded in the work. This cultural code is the one that becomes dated, as in the dating of attitudes towards rape in Play It Again, Sam. The objects common to a culture when represented in a discourse become a set of props whose meanings are governed by the cultural code. The corrida at this level is associated with the stereotypes of Spanish culture, which is not to say that images of the bullfight therefore fail to communicate. On the contrary, the bullfight is to the Spanish what baseball is to Americans: American knowledge of the game of baseball makes it available as a vehicle for an analogy. A difficulty in reading Leiris for Americans might be the lack of familiarity with the details of the corrida, or, just as debilitating, familiarity only with the stereotype. Michener digresses in his description of a bullfight, for

example, to observe that, "whenever I'm talking to people who know nothing of bullfighting, or writing for them, I remind myself. They probably think the big, heavy capes that are so important in three quarters of the fight are red. That's completely wrong." In a work of popular entertainment the evocation of the stereotype often suffices to make the desired point. But in a research use of analogy, for the analogy to be generative, the writer must look into the detailed workings of the vehicle domain.

This exercise proposes the testing of other proverbs or sayings reflecting current common wisdom as a way to generate the larger context of an analogy. An ideological analysis of an existing narrative or exposition would seek out the proverb governing the assumptions of the drama or argument; the mystory inverts this process by beginning with a proverb and then testing what implications it holds for action or behavior. How would it affect Leiris's point if we added another "bull" proverb--"the bull in the china shop"--to the two he already is using? A library exercise might include finding a dictionary of clichés, which could be used in class to brainstorm their implications as models for a practice. The baseball vehicle, for example, would include the proverb stating "that's the way the ball bounces." What would a confession be that was motivated by this saying?

3. It is apparent that these exercises involve some research using basic reference books. The difference with conventional assignments, that also suggest use of reference resources, is the motive, which in the case of mystory is generative: Mystory adds to the acquisition of information the second step of extrapolation--to turn the signified content of the information into the signifier design of a form. When the search through a reference book is motivated in this way--looking for ideas for how to turn practices in the vehicle domain into instructions for writing--the reference book is embraced as a tool rather than resented as a task.

This question suggests that the search may be conducted from the side of the tenor domain as well (from the side of rhetoric). A dictionary such as the one by Bernard Dupriez, A Dictionary of Literary Devices, trans. Albert W. Halsall (Toronto, 1991), might be scanned for terms that resonate with terms from other unrelated fields; a term such as "amphibology" for example--"ambiguity deriving from grammar, morphology, or syntax"--brings to mind the domain of amphibians. The next step is to do some research on amphibians to find qualities that lend themselves to the transfer into writing. The first thing that comes to mind might be a practice capable of functioning fully in two different realms. Mystory is amphibological in this way, since it must operate equally within the domains of personal quotidian experience and the specialized body of knowledge of a school discipline.

A related strategy, adapting to the fact that so many rhetorical terms come from the classical languages, is to select a figure that then could be enlarged to do the work of an entire method--as Jacques Derrida amplified "antonomasia" (the substitution of a proper name of a common noun or vice versa) in his signature method. The goal is not to find direct equivalents in existing rhetoric for the moves or poses of the bullfighter (in Leiris's case), but to attain a sense of the possibility of doing things with words, to help the designers learn to extrapolate from the analogy to the practice. Part of the desired effect is simply to break the habits of exposition along with the habits of ideology in order to get a better sense of how culture works. Creative writers have conducted generative experiments for centuries (from the classics to the present). A book such as Peter Hutchinson's Games Authors Play, Methuen, 1983, offers a good survey of ways to use the resources of language to design generative forms.

Eunice Lipton, from Alias Olympia (p. 282) The subtitle of Lipton's book echoes the "erotic" register of mystory: "A Woman's Search for Manet's Notorious Model & Her Own Desire." In telling the narrative of her research (less about what she found and more about the process of looking for it), Lipton discusses her personal history as a woman within the patriarchal order of her profession, including her various erotic entanglements (close friendships, marriage, unwelcome propositions). As for the "risk" Leiris mentioned, Lipton quit her job as a tenured professor to become an independent writer, an act that marks the authenticity of her critique of the ideology of her discipline.

The passage included here again is devoted more to the statement of Lipton's project than to the demonstration of how to carry it out. Still, Lipton not only tells what she is doing but also gives some hints about method. Her insights into the correspondences of her signature with the model (the red hair, the name) echo the uncanny linkages explored in Chapter 4. The story she tells about the life of an artist's model lends itself to the allegory effect, since the artist's model is often associated with the figure of the muse (the beauty of the body expresses the spiritual power of creativity). The concrete details of the story of the search for the historical person are easily assimilated into the mythical realm of archetypes, so that the external research becomes indirectly the saga of self-examination.

Lipton favors a narrative style, motivating coherence by posing enigmas, asking questions about what happened to Victorine, what did the pictures look like that she painted, what happened to them. Lipton goes so far as to include fictional passages told from Victorine's point of view: "I remember well the day Manet and I decided to work on the Déjeuner sur l'herbe. Julie and I were seated on the terrace of the Café Geurbois on the boulevard de Clichy; it was late afternoon in the fall of 1862. . . ." Lipton's characterization of her project as the history of an encounter could serve as a definition for mystory; every mystory constructs an encounter between the researcher and the object of study. Lipton's identification with Meurent is explicit and is one of the chief lessons for mystory.

The events of the women's movement--especially the consciousness-raising method--are one of the lessons her story grants to a mystorical education. The lesson concerns the context within which the autobiography is composed: An intertextual autobiography is as much about the collective register as about the individual--about the group with which the individual identifies. The image of the individual, the self-portrait, must be caught indirectly in the reflection of what is going on around her: her attitude toward the events in which she is caught up. The expression of emotion is as important to a mystory as the expression of an idea (to get at the emotional experience of having ideas). Each of the relays directly or indirectly includes this emotional register, which in Lipton's case involves "rage." For centuries intellectual work was associated with melancholy (as in Richard Burton's Anatomy of Melancholy). The dominant emotion motivating much critical research today, rather, is anger. This anger again is a symptom of authenticity or of the identification of the critic with the object of study. The combination of identity politics with the tools of ideological analysis is a powerful combination, serving to raise consciousness about how identity is constructed rather than being a natural expression of a unique essence.

Lipton's relay demonstrates an intellectual style that, as Leiris suggested, writes as much with obsessions as with rational ideas. The value of "contrast" for justifying a shift in style is apparent in Lipton's comments on the norms of art history prior to the women's movement--the pretense to objectivity; the formalism; the denial of institutional politics. Why did Lipton delay her project? We glimpse here something of the difficulties of working from the side of invention, for it wasn't obvious exactly how she should act upon her intuitions about "Olympia." At the end of this selection Lipton hints at a link between her disciplinary position and the formation of identities in entertainment culture. Her allusion to Doris Day as a type expressing how women were raised in 1950s America recalls the scene of instruction like the one Woody Allen dramatized between his character and Humphrey Bogart. Lipton had internalized "Doris Day" as her identity consultant, a figure she now wants to replace with Victorine Meurent. The practical lesson is that the ideological forces of a culture are accessible through these icons; abstract analysis is most effective when the personifications of the normative ideals are located in specific figures in the experience of the mystorian. Although Lipton does not elaborate on the Doris Day connection, a mystorian would give much more attention to this struggle between the two icons. To watch a Doris Day/Rock Hudson movie now could have a strong commentary effect on the social conditions that Lipton had to overcome before she felt free to pursue her research in her own way.

Discussion and Writing

1. The issue is the "culture wars," as reflected in the collection with that title edited by Richard Bolton, subtitled, "Documents from the Recent Controversies in the Arts" (New York: New Press, 1992). Students sometimes cannot understand why an audience would get so upset over a painting such as "Olympia." The history of the avant-garde (especially in Europe) is filled with incidents when those attending a concert, exhibition, or reading rioted in protest over what had been offered to them as "art." In recent years, however, debates about the arts have become news when conservative congressmen complained about supporting "pornography, obscenity, and smut" with government funds.

It is worth noting that the kinds of things Lipton says about the expression of the face in "Olympia" (described as being capable of saying no or yes, reflecting her control over her own sexuality) have also been said by cultural critics about Madonna, whose frank construction of her own persona functions for teenage women, the argument goes, the way Lipton experienced Meurent's pose (the rhetorical figure) as "Olympia." It might be interesting to study the expression on the faces of models in advertising; to look at different kinds of magazines to consider the sexual politics implied by the layouts. Compare the expressions of the men and the women. Juxtapose layouts from Vogue, Interview, and Ladies Home Journal and note the similarities or difference of attitude toward the ideological categories. What are the rules about "display" of the body in our culture? How do these rules differ between mainstream culture and the subcultures (at least as represented in the special-interest magazines that target them).

2. The artwork described in the question provides a context for Lipton's project.

The installation by Glenn Ligon illustrates two features important to mystory: 1) The research into an historical or artistic example is motivated by identification with a specific case representing one or more of the ideological categories that apply to the researcher. A note of caution must be sounded here because, as various editorial writers have noted, it is dangerous to start treating individuals only in terms of the groups to which they may seem to belong, since this grouping of individuals into collectivities is also the basis for stereotypes. Moreover, each individual belongs to multiple groups, some of whose interests conflict with one another. 2) The photomontage form is nicely illustrated in the Ligon example. The rules of conventional argumentation called for consistency and warned against too much citation. The collage style of mystory, in contrast, allows considerable borrowing from sources and the appropriation of divergent forms and ideas.

As in the Jarrett signature paper in Chapter 4, the mystory lends itself to the inclusion of images and graphics by means of photocopy, photography, or drawing. Ligon's tactic of introducing friends' descriptions of him into the wanted posters for runaway slaves is a good example of "putting oneself into the picture" which is the attitude of research as identification. Although Ligon created an installation, his method may be readily adapted to collage/montage (using pictures and descriptions of the objects). Nor is it that the students already feel the identification with an historical or cultural figure as natural, but that, based on the research into one's ideological categories, the researcher discovers the reality of the abstract categories: the concreteness of the more dramatic and poetic writing helps the researchers to experience emotionally what they know intellectually.

In "Derrida at the Little Bighorn," for example, Gregory Ulmer decided to explore the pattern linking George Armstrong Custer with Jacques Derrida not because he admired Custer, but because Ulmer was raised in a county and graduated from a high school named after Custer. A little research into the history of his hometown showed the extent to which the name, which everyone took for granted, did in fact mark correctly the ideology of the community whose tastes and judgments Ulmer internalized as his own through his childhood. The juxtaposition of Custer and Derrida does not indicate any similarity in the two icons, but simply shows Ulmer the configuration--the premises--of his judgments. The mystory, that is, maps the pattern of the maker's imagination. The mystory is a way of taking a "core sample" of the layers of one's identity (using the image of psychological development as the laying down of one stratum upon the other, with all the strata present and active in the present, from the most primitive to the most recent). Ulmer had forgotten about his childhood identification with the Seventh Cavalry. Even if he had never consciously identified with the cavalry as a spectator of countless Westerns, his community had done it for him: The individual thinks at least in part by means of the memory of the group.

Susan Howe, from Incloser (p. 288) Howe's project resembles Lipton's in that in the same way that Lipton took up the case and the cause of the artist's model rather than of the artist or the painting, so does Howe identify with the first voice of English women speaking in New England. The germ of the idea came from research--from a study by a woman revisionist historian, Patricia Caldwell, whose book The Puritan Conversion Narrative deals with testimonies given by women to Thomas Shepherd, minister of the First Church of England. Shepherd recorded the testimonies in his private notebook. Becoming aware of these suppressed or subordinated voices changed Howe's understanding of "the New England pattern and its influence on American literary experience" (see Howe's comments on "Incloser" in The Politics of Poetic Form, ed. Charles Bernstein, New York: Roof Books, 1990, 189-195). Reading books of academic scholarship revealed to Howe that for a brief time in the earliest days of the colonies women told their stories of their conversion experience to the assembled congregation. "Public narration represented a democratic expression and allowed a kind of open-endedness of discussion among a mixed group of people. This was something new." Howe stated that the poet is "a receptor of many voices." The political dimension of her work is to find those voices or truths that have been edited out of history and to let them be heard again. Motivated by her view of history, which is that the earlier periods are still present to us now, Howe described her experience of research as that of "being pulled in by the people in Shepherd's church." "I didn't mean to find them; they somehow found me."

As for her collage or photomontage style, Howe suggests that this form best represents the political force of her formal experiment, invoking "a breaking of boundaries of all sorts." "This brokenness interests me," she reported. A good project for the class discussions is to make an inventory of all the devices and issues Howe uses in her montage: an epigraph, dictionary citations, citations from primary and secondary sources, historical information, genre studies (the conversion narratives), critical theory (cites Jakobson, Girard, et al.), personal comments. The piece as a whole has the effect of a "discourse on method"--the effect desired for the mystory--in that Howe's personal comments constitute a running commentary on her own search for a voice and for a way to write--a poetics. Her identification with the Puritan women resembles Lipton's identification with Victorine Meurent.

The special dual nature of a discourse on method demonstrated in "Incloser" is the way that it both shows how to write in a certain way and tells about it too. The difference that this duality makes that distinguishes a poetics from conventional scholarship is the aesthetic impact that comes form the showing (Howe unites the creative and the scholarly styles of writing). The way Howe achieves this aesthetic effect is typical of the postmodern turn to allegory: The allegorical effect (the realization that what is being talked about also means something else in addition) results from the repeated allusion to the concrete details of "enclosure" as a word and as a thing, as a practice, as a concept. Through repetition and accumulation the several multiple meanings of "enclosure" and "incloser" begin to evoke a commentary effect, suggesting to the reader a metaphor or analogy for an emotion--perhaps for the feeling of constraint experienced by the author; her ambivalence regarding herself as an encloser, her appropriation of the earlier narratives for her own purposes (similar to Lipton's guilt over identifying with Meurent's victimhood while herself being a privileged tenured professor). In using all the meanings of "incloser" Howe acts upon her ethics: "I love words. I hope they are allowed to suggest all meanings possible. I hope that language will always be an undiscovered country. All poetry that sets words free is political."

Discussion and Writing

1. This question addresses the theme raised in the preceding comments to stimulate discussion about the dialogue that arises in a mystory between the writers and the object of study. The basic strategy of mystory is to create a hybrid out of the seemingly opposed genres of the autobiography and the scholarly treatise. The point here is to clarify the writer's role--Howe's search for a relationship with the past. The contrast in her method is with the pose of objectivity in scholarship. She retains the scholar's devotion to the accurate representation of the object but replaces the impersonal and transparent voice with the emotion of solidarity linking generations of women across the centuries. The autobiographical element of "Incloser" is found not in the confession of details from her daily life but in this more basic sense of her identity as a woman.

2. The goal of the mystorical assignment is to reproduce Howe's project but with different materials. The effect of "Incloser" does not depend on the specific materials. In principle, in any case, any individual work may give rise to a genre. The method for generalizing the operations of a given work is to take an inventory of the parts and their relationship. The slots to be filled in this case derive from the three levels Howe juxtaposes: 1) historical--the enclosure laws; the conversion narratives; 2) literary--Howe imitates the "cutting out" of "incloser" in her fragmented collage form; 3) personal--Howe's feelings of being herself enclosed by her condition, and at the same time (ambivalently) herself as performing an act of appropriation of public property.

Students could replicate Howe's research by finding an anthology in the library that represented a period of history of some interest to them. The anthology should be one of those interdisciplinary kinds that includes a variety of documents (historical, scientific, quotidian, as well as literary and artistic). The anthology provides a "treasure house" like the storage places of the _topoi_ in the old rhetoric. The anthology would be used in a nonconventional way--not for the sake of the information itself, but as a resource for making oneself an "encounter" or a crossing between one's own moment and the one represented in the book. A shorthand way to characterize the formal task of such an experiment is as the making of a "poem" out of the discourse of the scholar.

3. The students are likely to be able to identify the "purple passages" easily enough by recognizing when the language shifts into strained or nonvernacular syntax and vocabulary ("Coming home though bent and bias for the sake of why so. Awkward as I am"). Howe is a poet as well as a scholar, of course, and she wants to map her lineage from these early New England voices through Emily Dickinson to herself. This participation in a tradition does not happen by itself: Howe makes it happen. The mystory can learn from Howe's project to extend this tradition of poets to any tradition: to tap into the resources of a tradition by mapping the series of transfers joining the past to the present. The signature experiment in Chapter 4 made these links through the family name. Now the idea is to find a pattern that creates a place for the individual within the public history of the cultural record (the history of the specialized discipline in which the student has some interest--the field in which the student plans to major, perhaps, or in which a parent is already a professional). In any case, "Howe" is well-named in terms of the signature, in that her own writing shows us "howe" to make something ourselves.

Salvador Dali, "How to Become Paranoia-Critical" (p. 298) Everything said about surrealism in Chapter 2 supplies a context for Dali's paranoia-critical method. In a word, the method amounts to a decision to make art by lucidly and deliberately (but also selectively) imitating the hallucinatory mannerisms of the psychotic mind. The "analogy" for surrealism as a method, in other words, comes from psychoanalysis. Several of the themes raised in earlier relays are obsession, writing with desire, and the erotic (which Dali expresses in a literal sort of way, although his reference to an erection is his version of what Americans mean when they say that they "get off" on something they like). He demonstrates in his own way how to use autobiography and how to use and to explain a method at the same time (how to relate research into an object of study to his concerns about making art).

Dali adds to the mix of qualities important to mystory a clarification of the "logic" guiding the arrangement of the research materials into a pattern. This logic has both a formal and a political dimension: What is the relation of particulars to the general whole; what is the relationship of the individual to the collective group? Susan Howe was concerned about the individual voices that were not being heard within the group. "The individual voice tends to get erased. Singularities are surrounded and erased by factions. This is also true in the editing of a text. What gradually gets edited out in a narrative is singularity." She goes on to refer to Rene Thom's catastrophe theory and to chaos theory, which suggest how singularities or strange attractors make thinkable another kind of order. Dali shows how the ordering rules of measurement of the mystory might come not from the universal concepts common to disciplinary knowledge nor even from the shared commonplaces of the writer's culture. Rather, the standard of measure might be found within the details peculiar to the writer's experience. The artist famous for inventing the ready-made, Marcel Duchamp, had already mocked the arbitrariness of the meter stick in his collage painting called "Standard Stoppages," in which he uses chance techniques to set his own personal unit of measure. Dali achieves something similar by adopting the train station at Perpignan as his measure of truth. The proof that supports his decision is his discovery that this place that had always been important to him--with which intuitively he identified--turned out to be associated historically with the establishment of the length of the standard meter.

The lesson is that researchers may set their own unit of organization. Dali's method recalls the memory practices of the orators of the manuscript era, who memorized great quantities of information by distributing it through scenes of familiar places (such as their home town or family residence) and associating it with unusual or violent images. How does the researcher decide which place, thing, or event in their personal setting should be selected to fulfill this organizing function? Dali's example shows that the decision is made based on a combination of intuition and analysis: He intuitively identified with the railway station, based on the circumstances of its familiarity. Upon studying the form and history of the place he discovers several associations that link the station with important events and people--not only with the history of measurement but also with a drawing by Freud. The latter's impact is due to Freud's status as the theorist most important to surrealism. In "Derrida at the Little Bighorn" Ulmer made a similar connection between his local place (his father's sand and gravel plant) and the theorist most important to him (Jacques Derrida). Ulmer's mix of research and autobiography turned up a correspondence between an architectural design made by Derrida and the machinery for washing and sorting gravel. The effect of encountering such patterns linking the different areas of one's experience is "uncanny," and produces the excitement of an inventive insight. The emotion of joy reported by Dali may be experienced by any mystorian who constructs or discovers such convergences. Mystory, that is, simulates the experience of "eureka!" that arises from the sudden appearance of a previously unrecognized relationship. It is the experience of invention.

The logic that holds together a mystory, then, is quite different from the logic of conceptual argument. The surrealists refer to "objective chance" to account for these unexpected relationships, but for our purposes we can say that what holds the photomontage fragments of the research together is a pattern rather than a chain of reasoned arguments. The pattern is formed out of links that may have nothing in common at the level of content or meaning (signified) but that repeat at the material level of form (signifier). When Ulmer juxtaposed anecdotes from his personal life (stories about working with his father at the sand and gravel plant), historical information about the public figure associated with his community (General Custer), and readings from his disciplinary specialization (Derrida's philosophical theories), he found two word/things that recurred at all three levels: an "H" shape, and the word "gall." To take the latter instance, for example, his father died of gallbladder cancer; one of the battlefield chiefs at the Little Bighorn was named Gall; and Derrida is a Gallic (French, ancient Gaul) philosopher. The links, that is, often take the form of verbal or visual puns.

Discussion and Writing

1. Freud actually feared that his method or science of interpretation might be mistaken for that which it studied--the obsessive behavior of paranoia, for example --since in both cases (of research and of psychosis) everything means something. The best known symptom of paranoia is the delusion of persecution, but delusional jealousy and delusions of grandeur are also kinds of paranoia. A specialized dictionary could be consulted for detailed information about paranoia as well as other symptomologies. A good one is The Language of Psychoanalysis by J. Laplanche and J.-B. Pontalis, which gives this description of "projection" (one of the behaviors associated with paranoia): "operation whereby qualities, feelings, wishes or even 'objects,' which the subject refuses to recognize or rejects in himself, are expelled from the self and located in another person or thing." The interest for mystory in such symptoms has to do with what they reveal about the circulation of meaning between the inside and the outside of the boundaries of the self. One of the things mystory explores (and this is the textual approach to the question of ideology) is the shifting, unstable, permeable nature of the borders constituting one's identity. Mystory is "paranoia-critical" in that the mystorian, like the paranoid, takes things personally. One way to distinguish the mystory from the conventional research paper would be to note the different views of the individual subject they adopt. The argumentative paper assumes a rational subject of the sort idealized by the eighteenth-century enlightenment (the humanist subject, fully self-conscious and capable of reasoning correctly to reach the most rational conclusion), while the mystory adopts, at least provisionally, a twentieth-century posthumanist view of the subject that admits the existence of an "unconscious." The mystorical assumption is that the ordinary person tends to have considerable difficulty

reasoning according to the rules of formal logic, and that the greater part of what motivates judgments and feelings is a mystery. The class might discuss how the mystorical method could be designed to work with and to compensate for these characteristics of thought.

2. This question continues the process of reasoning with metaphor introduced in Chapter 2. The choice of the vehicle to generate the procedures for research and writing could come in principle from any domain. Anything in the Laplanche and Pontalis dictionary could be used as instructions for selecting and combining information--behaviors such as "parapraxis" (slips of the tongue and other such errors or lapses in speech or memory) might be imitated. Theorists in search of models or analogies to help them invent new ways to link information (alternatives to the strictly reduced linkages permitted by conventional logic) have turned to other sciences as well, to descriptions of processes in physics or biology as analogies for rhetorical practices. Deleuze and Guattari are famous for their adaptation of the "rhizome" (multibranched tuber systems or swarming insect or animal colonies) as an alternative to the treelike dichotomies of literate analysis.

The surrealist adaptation of Freudian dream-logic to poetics could be seen as a continuation of the medical analogy used by Plato, who thought of the orator or dialectician as the "doctor" of the spirit. The interest of this medical analogy for mystory concerns the migration of the methods of diagnosis from medicine to other areas of investigation. Semiotics in general traces its origins to the reading of symptoms, and an association between Sherlock Holmes and Sigmund Freud has emerged in popular culture (as in the film <u>The Seven Percent Solution</u> in which Freud and Holmes team up to solve a crime). One of the most common analogies for disciplinary research is the comparison with detective work. The point to make about paranoia-critical activity is that the analogy is not with the doctor but with the patient: What interests Dali is not the interpretation of the symptoms but the symptoms themselves. The implication for us is that the mystory is not an interpretation of the object of study, but is the construction of a set of symptoms that remain to be deciphered by the writer.

What might need some clarification is the learning effect expected from this approach to research. The argumentative paper and the mystory have in common the library work of scholarship: Both are ways to motivate students to look through the accumulated knowledge of the civilization stored in books. Argumentation tried to motivate this search by attaching it to debates surrounding some controversial point presumably of interest to the student (see the various anthologies available on the market that collect debates about the environment, free speech, pornography, abortion, and the rest). Mystory replaces or adds to this argumentative motivation the autobiographical motivation: The "paranoid" premise is that what one finds in the collective culture constitutes a self-portrait of the individual (you are what you read or view in the same way that you are what you eat).

3. The reason for selecting Dali's obsession with Perpignan station from among his many other obsessions as the most relevant to mystory has to do with its emphasis on the importance of a specific local place. The settings of a life story are one important key to the researchers' ideological positioning. Ulmer for example grew up in a town founded as a direct response to Custer's Last Stand (it began as a cavalry fort). The historical associations of this place with the ideology of

colonialism and the frontier myths in general showed Ulmer one of the sources of his intuitions of judgments. Again, the methodological instruction is to shift the organizing structure of the research from the universal categories of concepts to the particular or singular materials coincidentally present in the life circumstances of the individual writer. Unlike argumentation, for which one set of rules fits every object of study, in the mystory the organizing structure itself, and not only the opinion, will differ from case to case and from writer to writer. In practice this singularity of form means that part of what goes into the mystory will be descriptions of images of a place or places important to the writer. The research paper will include not only the opinions of the writer, but the diegesis (imaginary space and time) of the writer's world. The pattern organizing the mystory will come in part from the object of study and in part from the circumstantial details of the subject doing the study.

N. Scott Momaday, from The Way to Rainy Mountain (p. 302) As the introduction to a collection of Native American autobiographies points out, "that form of writing generally known to the West as autobiography had no equivalent among the oral cultures of the indigenous inhabitants of the Americas" (I Tell You Now, eds. Brian Swann and Arnold Krupat, Lincoln: Nebraska, 1987). The hybrid quality of the genre of Rainy Mountain echoes the mixed-blood, mixed ideology of Momaday. The first autobiography by a Native American, in fact, was a conversion narrative by a Christianized Indian (recalling the conversion narratives that interested Susan Howe). Momaday's hybrid of the collective nature of tribal identity with the individualism of European autobiography constitutes a useful relay for mystory, whose purpose is to explore this inmixing of the collective in the personal experience. Momaday introduces into this genre of individualism, that is, the non-Western values of traditional culture. The instructions to be derived from this relay suggest that what the Kiowa traditions are for Momaday, the disciplinary knowledge is for the mystorian. Further, the mystorian is learning how to combine the experience of oral and literate memories, for oral culture persists within the domestic institutions of everyday life.

Rainy Mountain has been elevated to canonical status; at least a volume has been devoted to it in the Modern Language Association's "Approaches to Teaching" series, edited by Kenneth M. Roemer (1988). This volume may be consulted for background and details relating to the teaching of Momaday for his own sake. The function of his relay here is as instruction for the form of the mystory. One value of this relay is its clear delineation of Momaday's profound sense of identification with his Native American heritage. The mystorians must extrapolate from Momaday's case to their own, of course. The reason that so many of the relays come from minority authors is that the rules of objectivity and universality in scientific and academic research appear now as mythologies legitimating the self-interested point of view of the dominant ideology. The point is not for everyone to abandon their own perspective in order to adopt a Native American point of view, for example, but to learn how to take into account the resources of one's own heritage in the learning process. Not that one's heritage determines forever what one values or how one behaves; rather, the unconscious operations of this heritage must be acknowledged and mapped and not denied or suppressed before one can begin to educate the emotions and judgments as well as the intellect. The relays so far have shown us that the scene of research includes a hierarchy--a biased expectation about what is important and worth studying in the scene. The dominant expectation in art history, for example, was that Manet and not Meurent was the appropriate object of study. The expectation in American literature was that Shepherd and not Goodwife Cutter or Hannah Brewer was the proper focus of attention. Lipton and Howe shift attention so as not to exclude Manet or Shepherd but so as to reframe the research to give equal attention to the subordinated material. Ulmer similarly found Chief Gall as well as the expected Custer in his scene of identification.

That the framing story of Rainy Mountain concerns Momaday's visit to the grave site of his grandmother, Aho, is emblematic of the "monumental" dimension of the mystory. The mystory is a work of "mourning" in the sense that its purpose is to discover and honor the continuities and links that join individuals to their collective settings. The psychology of mourning and the social act of establishing monuments correspond to one another, each having to do in its own realm with the maintenance of identity. In psychoanalytic terms the mystory is a device for bringing into appearance the writer's superego (the figures of authority with whom one has identified, internalized within the unconscious and integrated into thought in the form of intuitions and judgment). Freud compared the superego to an "internalized monument," and an analogy for what the mystory reveals is that of a personalized Mount Rushmore (containing representatives of the founding figures of personal identity the way Rushmore displays the founding fathers of American national identity).

Rainy Mountain offers instructions for the three levels of memory used in the mystory: myth, history, and personal experience. In segment 1 we learn about the name (signature) of the tribe--"coming out." Myths are always about origins. To be able to write about the myths and history of the group requires research. The information is represented in the composition as a series of units, each unit consisting of three fragments (one for each level of memory) linked by at least one stylistic feature in common. Discussion may be devoted to close analysis of this relay to discern its parts and how they function--to see how it was made. Segment 1, for example, tells the story of how the Kiowas "came out." Next comes the historical fragment. Note that Momaday does not retain the style of the academic historian recounting the factual genealogy of the group, but rather he selects one or two details of the events, having to do in this case with the theme of the unit--the name. The historical information concerns the identifying marks of the tribe--their hair, the sign-language gesture of the name. The aesthetic effect of pattern making is clearest in the link to the personal memory, as when Momaday repeats the name antonomasically in its common noun version, using the meaning of "Kiowa" to describe his own "coming out" upon the Great Plains.

Segment 3 shows the metonymic strategy of evoking wholes by means of closely observed details. The theme of the dog holds this segment together, with one story, one historical instance, and one memory combining through repetition and accumulation to create a distinctive image of the Kiowa.

In segment 21 the real grandfather, Mammedaty, is in the position of myth. The segment is a portrait of the grandfather, so that the mythical slot is filled with an anecdote about his spiritual power, his visionary experience exemplifying a non-Western way of knowing. The links within each unit are weak, but not unmotivated. The form itself creates a comment on how Momaday feels about his grandparents. By placing stories about Mammedaty or Aho in the first paragraph of the segment--where we have come to expect a mythical story--Momaday honors and celebrates these beloved figures.

The sacred place of Aho's grave, lost in the landscape of the Plains, establishes a specific location in the landscape as a "standard of measure" similar to the way Dali selected Perpignan station as the center of his personal geography. The difference between traditional and modern culture is evident, of course, in the different sites selected as the grounds of the respective writers' imaginations. At the same time, what they share is the need to locate a place and scene as part of their identity.

Discussion and Writing

1. In locating the instructions to be extracted from Momaday, the class may be guided by the expectations of what to look for set up by the previous relays. Not that every relay has all the features useful for mystory, nor that every feature of the relays has to be included in the final design. Rather, the design of the method is to be a hybrid, a synthesis constructed out of the pattern of what repeats from one relay to the next.

This question concerns how the writer's ideological status provides an inventory for generating ideas that could be applied to the composition. The inventory of elements in Rainy Mountain include samples from the levels of Kiowa myth, history, and the author's memory. Myth at the level of discourse turns out to be a collection of stories or tales circulated by the group that gives a narrative representation of the origin and beliefs of the group. To use Rainy Mountain as a relay, the students must extrapolate to find the equivalent for themselves of materials for each kind of memory. In modern culture, for example the mythical function has been taken over by entertainment discourse such as Hollywood cinema and network television. As Robert Ray pointed out in his study of Casablanca modern mythology translates social or collective stories into the stories of individuals (reflecting the literate practice of selfhood). As discussed in Chapter 3, students will have little trouble finding details to represent the myths of hard work, individualism, romance, progress, and the like that organize the belief system of their group.

The ideological exercise involves some research based on the categories of one's own position. What distinguishes mystory from the conventional research paper is not the use of library scholarship, but that mystory extends this scholarship outside the boundaries of the academic disciplinary object of study to include research into the other primary discourses that constitute the extended memory of a literate citizen. In the same way that Momaday recognizes that his identity is bound up with the oral traditions of his Native American culture, so must the students recognize that their identities are bound up with the written record of their nation and of the other registers of their complex ideological heritage. Thus Gregory Ulmer, for example, might juxtapose some discussion about or citation from his disciplinary object of study--Jacques Derrida (considered one of the more difficult writers working today)--with some information about his German Protestant ethnic background, gleaned from a history such as The Germans by Gordon Craig, which starts with a quotation from Goethe: "The Germans make everything difficult, both for themselves and for everyone else." To this material Ulmer might add a recollection of his German relatives in North Dakota, perhaps something about their love of accordion music. Watching an act on the Lawrence Welk show on television, one of them would always remark: "They sure can play that thing!"

The portrait exercise could be extended by trying to write one unit of three fragments each for each ideological category--not only ethnicity but also race, gender, class, and so on. The stylistic technique would be the same--to find metonymic pieces or details that evoke how that identity category exists in the students' own discursive memories: entertainment, history, and family experience. A fourth category equally important to mystory, of course, is disciplinary knowledge acquired through the institutional practices of school.

2. This question emphasizes the formal aspect of the relay, much of which has been discussed in the comments in the introduction to Momaday. The point to stress is the aesthetic quality of the form. The class might analyze and discuss the specific style of the units--their concreteness and selection of detail. Momaday rarely generalizes or interprets, but only collects and arranges pieces of specific information the accumulated effect of which is dramatic and moving. The third paragraph in each segment--the personal memory--is especially worth examining since it is the most overtly literary or poetic. Momaday uses the craft of poetry to describe the sensory qualities of places and people with the artist's eye for telling details. The lessons of Chapter 2 may be put to work here in the service of this new kind of scholarship. Students should inventory these qualities of the writing and imitate them in their own compositions.

The aesthetic quality of all the relays is relatively high, compared to conventional scholarship. The short formula for mystory is to use the device of the arts to arrange and put into a style the materials found by means of literate scholarship. The way each of the relays uses literary devices could be noted and interrelated, to produce a synthesis of the possibilities for the discourse on method. The goal is to set up a dialogue between the arts and scholarship, with the personal memory as mediator. Thus not only is scholarship used to learn about the creative object of study, but the devices of the arts and of scholarship are used to learn about the self. Further, the effects of literature are explored not only externally by analysis, but from within by attempting to create similar effects in one's own writing.

3. The role of emotion in argument has always been controversial, since it has been seen as antithetical to rational, objective reasoning. Conventional scholarship has inherited the tradition of dialectics that from Plato to modern scientific reports has suppressed rhetoric in favor of "logic." The premise was that the most persuasive argument was the sheer display of the evidence, the "proof." Within the disciplinary natural sciences this claim may be valid (although recent studies have shown that the institutional practices of science are as ideologically biased as any other practices in the society). In cultural areas of experience, however, emotional appeals cannot be suppressed. As we move into an era of electronic communications, in which sound and image are routinely combined with verbal discourse, the emotional register of discourse has to be made an equal partner with analysis in specialized and general cultural practices alike.

An analogy for how the mystory engages with emotion is method acting of the kind introduced into American theater by the Russian director Konstantin

Stanislavski in the 1920s, which is the dominant style of acting in Hollywood cinema to this day. The part of method acting useful for mystory is its lesson that emotions are not necessarily immediately available, but have to be remembered. Once actors have decided what emotion is appropriate for the role they are to play, they perform exercises in emotional recall that begin not with that emotion but with the concrete details of a scene or incident in their own experience in which that emotion is likely to have occurred. Writers have always known that the way to produce an emotion in a reader is not to name the emotion but to show the sensory details associated with it. Since the mystory is addressed to oneself, however, one purpose of the research is to construct an encounter between the author's intellect and feelings. The strategy is not to assume that one already knows exactly what this link will be, but to let the composition be a way of discovering and exploring the emotions of ideas.

A corollary of the personal approach to research in the relays is that each one expresses, explicitly or implicitly, a strong emotion. The class should discuss this emotional aspect of the readings, and compare the emotions named in each example with the effect created in the reader. Lipton states that she is motivated by "rage." Leiris suggests that writing could be like facing a charging bull. Dali speaks of joy; Howe creates irony; and Momaday seems melancholic. Pattern in any case is a relatively loose way of organizing information, compared with argument and narrative. In general the criterion for deciding what materials to include is set by the emotional tone desired or discovered. For the photomontage style to be intelligible to readers there must be a principle of coherence unifying the whole, and that principle as often as not is the evocation of a single emotion (however complex or ambivalent one's attitude to that emotion might be).

Ulmer's experience with this discovery of emotion in the writing suggests a perplexing aspect of mystory. A little research into the pattern of "gall" that emerged from the juxtaposition of his three levels of memory, for example, showed that gall was associated with one of the four humors of alchemical psychology. Instead of the melancholic emotion of black bile informing the scholar's personality in earlier eras, Ulmer's portrait named a different emotion--"choler" or anger, related to yellow bile and the gall bladder. That this emergent emotion constituted a pattern was clear when it turned out that the first sheriff of Miles City (Ulmer's hometown) was named Hank Wormwood. Gall and wormwood are synonyms for a certain feeling of bitterness. What is less clear is what to make of this bitterness. Ulmer's first response (noted previously) was to conclude that this pattern named the emotion that had come to dominate intellectual work in our time, with so much of critique being motivated by emancipatory politics on behalf of victimized minorities. Ulmer also had to consider the possibility that this bitterness reflected something at work in his personal story. He chose finally to pursue one of the other meanings of "gall"--cheekiness--and he set for himself the goal of trying to design a methodology of cheeky research. Perhaps the cheekiness of gall, but not the bitterness, is an appropriate attitude with which to approach mystory.

The Final Assignment

The most comprehensive assignment of this chapter--and of the book as a whole--is to write a discourse on method for a textualist way to conduct academic research, a way we have called "mystory." The relays have shown how to both tell about a way to write and use it oneself, often using a narrative frame dramatizing the search for the practice that is being explained and demonstrated along the way. The mystory as a discourse on method is about trying to understand the parts of one's discursive experience--the language practices acquired through assimilation into a family, a popular culture, and a school system. The recipe, or instructions, for this composition has to be derived or extracted from the relays, none of which were intended to be mystories (hence their status as "relays" rather than as "examples"). Together they evoke in what they say and the way they say it the possibility of a genre that no one of them alone represents.

It would certainly be reasonable and possible to replace this attempt at a discourse on method with some other use of these relays. Indeed, the student paper appended as a reference at the end of these comments is not a discourse on method, but an example of using a public figure as a metaphor for creating figurative insight into personal experience. Nonetheless, there are real advantages to including explanatory as well as performative dimensions in the experiment. The "evaluation" of the experiment addresses the learning effect of working in this intertextual way, comparing and contrasting it with conventional modes of research. The evaluation could take several forms, from class discussion to literal inclusion within the composition itself. The mystory assignment can work by a complete separation of the stages of its invention, or by their integration into a discourse on method. In other words, the assignment could be for three separate items, modeled on the steps of a scientific experiment: First the description of what the experiment is going to be, with some explanation of procedures and goals; then the performance of the experiment (using the aesthetics of pattern to arrange details selected from the different levels of memory); then the evaluation, assessing the quality of the undertaking. The alternative is to incorporate these aspects into one composition. Given the photomontage or fragmented nature that tends to result from using the logic of patterning, this integrated version does not mean that the form of the mystory would be unified in the manner of expository continuity. One virtue of the latter integrated approach is that it corresponds more closely to the nature of the readings we have used here to communicate the project, all of which tend to be fragmentary to a greater or lesser degree, and all of which tend to promise that they are going to do something while only partially carrying out the promise (with this latter effect being due in part to the limitations of the excerpt).

A final reason for trying this experiment is that it should be more pleasurable than the standard research paper. This pleasure may be traced to at least two properties of the mystory--its aesthetic dimension (it is as fun to play with language, as the figurative and patterned style of mystory requires, as it is to play in other ways); and its personal nature. The mystory is a self-portrait, and for the typical student who tends to be young--and perhaps for anyone at any stage--there is nothing quite as interesting as oneself. Not that the mystory as mirror is necessarily flattering: the ideological map that emerges within the text often functions as a self-critique. This map has a predictive value, but not a deterministic one: Once one has the map, the assumption is that in principle one may go in any direction. The map shows the writers the resources of their imaginations. What they do with it is their business.

The following paper was written by a first-year student in response to an assignment requiring the use of a public figure as a metaphor for the emotion associated with a personal situation.

PRISONERS OF FATE

"Did you ever hear of a man named Terry Waite?" I asked my friend. To my surprise her answer was a definite NO. How could someone not know about the incredible Terry Waite? Since disappearing in Beirut in January 1987 while on a mission to win freedom for Western hostages, Terry Waite, the emissary for the Church of England was held captive for almost five years! To many, his captivity seemed the cruelest of all the injustices of Lebanon's sectarian strife, for he was a man of peace who had gone to Beirut on behalf of others, only to end up as a hostage himself, abducted by the very people with whom he had gone to negotiate.

Goju, an ancient art form begun in 1882 in Okinawa, involves punching and kicking. The usefulness of this sport is unquestionable. Self-defense is stressed in this form of martial art. Everyday items are shown to be deadly weapons. For example, the use of sticks and bows are taught since those can be easily found in the home in the form of broomsticks, etc. The classes are held in large rooms called dojos. The teacher is called sensei. Classes are usually very strict and organized. If one is late to class he or she will have to drop down and do fifty push-ups as a reminder that tardiness is inexcusable. Overall mental and physical health is very important to the final outcome in Goju, without it only harmful result can occur.

Six miles north of Beirut, where the Dog River empties into the Mediterranean and the Lebanon wades in the sea to its ankle, the face of the limestone rock bears nineteen inscriptions in almost as many languages, beginning with ancient Egyptian, Assyrian and Babylonian, continuing through Greek and Latin and ending with English, French and Arabic. History knew Lebanon from the earliest of times and never forgot it. Perhaps no other area of comparable size, about 3,977 square miles (half the size of the state of New Jersey), can match it in the volume of historical events squeezed into it and in their meaningfulness and relevance to world progress. Figuratively microscopic in size, it is literally microcosmic in influence. No such historic achievement could have been possible without certain peculiar physical features. These are the mountainous character of the land, its bordering on the Mediterranean, its strategic location in the cradle of civilization and its central position at the crossroads of the world. The mountain is to Lebanon what the desert is to Arabia and the Nile to Egypt. Lebanon lay next to the great international highway which is linked to three historic continents. Immediately south lay Palestine, birthplace of Judaism and Christianity and closely connected with Islam, the third and last of the great monotheistic religions.

Frank Paul van der Kuyp, was born January 29, 1949, in Surinam. He was born to Opa Paul (Opa is what we call grandpa in Surinam or many Dutch-speaking countries), and Oma Ina (Oma is what we call grandma in Surinam). I often heard stories of how my dad would get in trouble every day and get beatings with the belt. This was because he disobeyed little requests like not being allowed to play soccer until certain things were done. Actually that was the reason he got beatings everyday. Soccer was and still is my dad's life, and being denied the pleasure of playing was a tragic event in his life. Opa Paul's reasonings for not letting my dad play as often as he would like was because he felt that my dad should have been putting that much time and effort into school. "Discipline was the name of the game," as he would often say.

[In the original student paper, maps of Lebanon and the Ancient Near East are inserted here.]

Lebanon's so-called civil war, which broke out in 1958, confronted the United States with an extremely sensitive problem in its Arab relations. What appeared to be only an internal dispute in this tiny Middle Eastern country in fact involved major Arab states and superpowers. A military-political impasse arose in Lebanon. The 1958 crisis was a microcosm of the elements and problems of U.S. relations in general and U.S. relations with small countries--such as Lebanon--in particular. This all came about because Lebanon has had a distinctive position in the Middle East with regard to both its Arab neighbors and Israel. Since way back, Israel and Arabs have been having conflicts over religion and land. The United States became a part of the problem when they made an objective to support the state of Israel. "The continuance of Israel as an independent state certainly represents a basic foreign policy commitment of the United States, partly because it rests upon action by the United Nations and partly because it is a national obligation which we have voluntarily undertaken" (Badeau 1958, 235). This support continued during the Eisenhower administration despite the president's conviction that Israel was the reason for his problem in the Middle East.

The room was big and gray with pictures of Oriental men all over the walls. I walked in the mat area one minute late, when I heard, "Drop down and give me fifty push-ups, Nat!" Obediently, I did what I was told. When I was done, the room full of kids about my age (12 to 14), dressed in huge garments called gis, started doing floor exercises. My father walked in just as we started. I could hear him yell across the room, "Move it! You could do better than that!" While I was deeply out of breath doing jumping jacks, sit-ups, and push-ups, I could feel the sweat pour down my back and face just hoping that the sensei would call time so I could stop. When the time came for some "fake" fighting, my dad was the first to volunteer me; he told me that it would make me a stronger person. There I was trying to fight a girl a lot bigger than I was. I hit her once, and boy was I proud. BANG! right across my face. All I felt was my head spinning around so fast until I fell to the ground. I looked up and saw my dad's disappointed face telling me to get up and try again. So I did, only to get kicked in the stomach. I thought that my guts were going to come flying out. Finally the anguish was over. My dad and I both went home and he gave me a speech on how I should keep on practicing to get better.

The next morning I was awakened by a stern voice, "Get up, its 6:30, time to get to work." So I quickly got on the floor and did fifty push-ups and fifty sit-ups. My dad did them right along with me. My eyes were hardly even open, my body was worn out form yesterday's activities, but still I managed to do those exercises. After every 6:30 morning work-out, I got the lecture that people are nothing without discipline and I would thank him when I was older. Day after day my dad would accompany me to Goju when I saw no other fathers there. Morning after morning I would have to wake up an extra thirty minutes early to learn discipline.

Year after year I would have to compete in competitions and win all because of the "discipline" I got at home. Goju was more important to my dad than to me. I always wanted to play with my friend, but instead I would have to go to the Goju. I would watch my friend outside climbing trees and I would be getting ready to go to the dojo.

Lebanon's conflict with Israel and the United States intervention into these matters only aggravates Lebanon. To lash out Lebanon, every so often, takes a few people hostage from the United States, hoping that the United States will give in to any demands they make. Terry Waite was one of these hostages, however, he has been regarded as a special case among his captives. His only intentions in traveling to Beirut were on behalf of others. While others, like Terry A. Anderson, the chief Middle East correspondent of the Associated Press, have been held longer, none commanded Mr. Waite's high public profile. That fact has made the fifty-two-year-old church envoy especially valuable to his Islamic captors in their effort to force Israel and the West to meet their demands.

> There was only darkness. The blindfold over my eyes completely blocked out the light. I was lying on my back on a low bed. The unforgettable sound of adhesive tape being unwound from its roll filled the room. Strong hands wrapped this wide packing tape around my head, over my forehead, eyes, and mouth, and around my neck. Only a small space over my nostrils was left open. Next, my arms and hands were held close to my sides, and the tape was wound slowly around my whole body. . . . Arms lifted me from the bed and carried me out. My body was pushed into a long narrow container. (Waite 1991, 1)

> [In the original student essay, an AP photo of Waite in Beirut, taken shortly before his kidnapping, is inserted here.]

Years went by and the strict attitude of my father still prevailed. Each morning before I went to school if my bed was not made properly, since I was so commonly known to pull the comforter over, I would get grounded for one week. This would make me so angry, because this meant no free time to myself. Of course the regular Goju schedule was never disturbed even if I didn't make my bed at all or if I put my shoes in the wrong place.

Five years of terrible living conditions and torture, encompassed Mr. Waite, but in the fall of 1991 after intense negotiations by the United Nations, Terry Waite was released by his Shiite Muslim captors in Lebanon. "This afternoon, when we were sitting together in our cell, chained to the wall, as we have been chained to the wall for the last five years . . . one of the captors came in and told us that Tom and myself would be freed this evening. He also said to me: We apologize for having captured you; we recognize that now this was the wrong thing to do, that holding hostages achieves no useful, constructive purpose."

After five years, Terry Waite's ordeal finally ended. When he arrived back in his homeland and was greeted by his family and friends, one could only imagine what was going on in his mind. Free at last!

Finally the time came for me to move on to college. My father sat me down and gave me the longest speech of my life. He expressed to me that through my whole life he has tried to teach me the right morals, values, and DISCIPLINE. When I'm on my own I need to remember these things and carry them around with me, all this according to my father. He also told me that maybe he was a little too strict with me, but it was only because he loved me so much and wanted the best for me. After this talk, I realized a lot. Not only did I learn from him, but I also figured out that life is what you make of it. The next day when I was on a plane to my "new" life, I never felt so happy. One could only imagine what was going on in my mind. Free at last!

[In the original student essay, a photograph of the author and her father is inserted here.]

Bibliography

Gilmour, David. Lebanon: The Fractured Country. Oxford: Martin Robertson and Company Ltd., 1983.

Hitti, Philip K. A Short History of Lebanon. New York: St. Martin's Press, 1965.

Korbani, Agnes G. U.S. Intervention in Lebanon, 1988 and 1982. New York: Greenwood Publishing Group, Inc., 1991.

Rabinovich, Itamar. The War for Lebanon. London: Cornell University Press, 1984.

Weir, Carol. Hostage Bound, Hostage Free. Philadelphia: The Westminster Press, 1987.

The New York Times. Nov. 19, 1991. v141, pA6(N), pA16(L),col 1.

St. Martin's